W9-BNT-488

MAPS

A HISTORY OF
THE BALKANS

From the Earliest Times
to the Present Day

FERDINAND SCHEVILL

Illustrated with Maps

DORSET PRESS
New York

Originally published as
History of the Balkan Peninsula

This edition published by Dorset Press,
a division of Marboro Books Corporation.
All rights reserved.
1991 Dorset Press

ISBN 0-88029-697-6

Printed in the United States of America
M 9 8 7 6

A HISTORY OF THE BALKANS

CHAPTER I

THE EPOCHS OF BALKAN HISTORY

THIS book is concerned with the story of man on the southeastern projection of Europe, known as the Balkan peninsula. For practical purposes the story begins with the Greeks, because the Greeks, though not the original inhabitants of the peninsula, were the first to leave a clear record of themselves and their neighbors. From the Hellenic period, when the mists hiding the land from view begin to lift, to the twentieth century of the Christian era is a span of about three thousand years. During that long stretch of time what migrations, wars, settlements, worships, and civilizations make their appearance in the deep perspective of Balkan history! What peoples march across the soil, fair-haired, strong-limbed warriors clothed in skins, succeeded by dark, bronzed men, curved over the backs of horses and alert for plunder! What empires come and go, one moment mounting resistlessly like a wave of the sea, the next dissolving in a cloud of spray! An epic tale is about to engage our attention calling for infinite patience with the intricacies of a deliberately moving plot and demanding an unswerving attachment to pilgrim man as well as a constantly renewed interest in the riddle of his destiny.

The evolution of historic man on the Balkan peninsula: a story of about three thousand years.

In order to give the reader a swift preliminary view of the material to be brought to his attention, it is proposed to devote this chapter to a recital of the leading phases of the Balkan story. If history, like Time itself, is a continuous stream, it falls, under the scrutiny of the ordering mind, into periods more or less distinct and possessed of well-marked characteristics. The epoch

The domination of the eastern Mediterranean by the Greeks.

3

with which the story of the Balkan peninsula begins is dominated, as already said, by the famous name of the Greeks. Their
mainland home, Greece or Hellas, embraced, it is true, only the
southern extremity of the peninsula, but the political influence
and, above all, the civilization of this small area penetrated so
far northward that it gradually brought into some sort of dependence on itself a not inconsiderable section of the Balkan interior. But Greece, or rather its cities, and chief among them,
immortal Athens, became in the course of a memorable movement of expansion not only Balkan but also Mediterranean
powers, and linked with the peninsula, or at least with its southern
Hellenic tip, the adjacent shores of Asia Minor, Sicily, and southern Italy. True, the political bonds joining these scattered areas
were tenuous, since the Greek cities constituted an almost countless number of free states and were held together principally by
ties of religion, language, customs, and commerce. However, in
spite of incurable political dissension, their brilliant achievements
along all lines of human effort gave them a sense of interdependence sufficient to move them to present a more or less united front
to any alien power inclined to threaten their independence.

The Greeks successfully resist the king of Persia. It was in the sixth century B.C., in the days of King Cyrus
(d. 528), that Persia rose over the eastern horizon of the Greek
world, and it was chiefly under Cyrus's successors, Darius and
Xerxes, that the program was adopted and vigorously pursued
of bringing the whole eastern Mediterranean under Persian control. Such a policy, nursed by an absolute monarch of the orient,
meant conflict, an irrepressible conflict with the Greeks and their
civilization, devoted to free, creative expression in general and
not least to political freedom. Threatened in their dearest possessions, the Hellenes undertook to defend themselves by means
of alliances and leagues which, organized among jealous, independent city-states, never achieved other than a loose character
and inclined on little or no provocation to go to pieces. None-
the-less the loosely knit Greek states met and defeated the invading Persian hosts in successive campaigns radiant with such names
as Marathon, Salamis, and Plataea. Brilliant victories in point
of fact, they signify much more than military triumphs to our
imagination by affirming the superiority of free political institutions over the capricious might of a despotic king.

The Greco-Persian crisis in east-Mediterranean affairs belongs in the main to the fifth century before Christ. When, in the following century, Alexander the Great, supporting himself on the power of the newly risen state of Macedonia, came upon the scene, Greece was already well free of the Persian peril. But, resolved to dispel the danger from the East once and for all, Alexander, commanding the massed power of the Greek city-states which Macedonia had subdued, marched across Asia Minor into the Euphrates valley and with a few shattering blows laid Persia prostrate. The conquests of the Macedonian king for the first time bound together all the regions of the eastern Mediterranean into a genuine political fabric. Unfortunately this rested, in spite of the prevalence of Greek speech and culture, on insufficient political foundations, and on Alexander's death fell into prompt decay. To be sure, a Greco-Macedonian state of purely Balkan dimensions survived to remind men of the great conqueror, but its vigor gradually oozed away and when, in the second century before Christ, it fell before the advance of Rome, the first or Greek phase of Balkan history came to a close.

It was left to Rome to achieve the political fusion of the Mediterranean peoples which the Greeks had attempted in vain. We usually think of the Romans as conquerors, and conquerors they were, but happily they were also magnificent organizers and administrators, or they would never have succeeded in gathering the many diverse Mediterranean peoples under their sway. A new territory was no sooner taken with the sword than it was endowed with an effective civil administration, providing for such essential matters as roads, police, and justice. Steadily pushing its way both eastward and westward along the Mediterranean, the Roman state in the second century B. C. subdued not only Greece, but also Macedonia, properly the northernmost extension of Greece, and fitted them into the Roman system.

With the advent of Rome in the peninsula there came a development which makes the Roman phase peculiarly memorable in Balkan history. The Greeks, a commercial and sea-faring, even largely an island people, had been content to move by boat along the Balkan shores, planting colonies and spreading the light of civilization as they went. To a certain limited extent their merchants had also struck out along the land routes leading northward, and so had carried a faint Hellenic influence into the interior plateau. Never, however, had the Greeks succeeded in reducing the rugged, barbarous people living on the slopes of the Rhodope and Balkan mountains to political dependence. This the Romans undertook to do and with their persistent and regulated daring finally achieved in the reign of the Emperor Augustus. To him belongs the honor of having for the first time brought the whole of the Balkan peninsula as far north as the lower Danube within the scope of Mediterranean civilization.

Under Emperor Constantine, in the fourth century A.D., the main seat of the empire is transferred to the Balkan peninsula.

The Balkan peninsula, once conquered and brought in its full geographical extent into the Roman system, soon acquired a peculiar significance. In fact the time came when it imposed itself on the attention of its Roman masters as the very keystone of the arch, the logical center of their far-flung empire. To understand what happened let the reader, map in hand, follow the Aegean coast of Greece northward until he comes to the narrows which the Greeks called the Hellespont and we name the Dardanelles. After the passage has widened to the Sea of Marmora it contracts again to the famous strait of the Bosporus, gateway to the Black sea, or Euxine according to the nomenclature of the Greeks. At the Dardanelles and Bosporus the shores of Europe and Asia face each other with just a dividing silver thread between, and here very plainly is the ordained seat of an east-Mediterranean empire, planned to link together in a single political system European and Asiatic lands. The natural prestige of the city on the Tiber, from which the Latin conquest had radiated over the world, delayed the recognition of the importance of the straits, and it was not till the fourth century after Christ that a Roman emperor, Constantine by name, had the courage and imagination to break with the western tradition and boldly to enthrone himself along the Bosporus. He chose as the site of his capital the ancient Greek trading-post of Byzantium, which presently reared its head above all the cities of the East under the name of Constantinople.

Constantinople a strategic site of permanent importance.

From the day of its foundation (328 A.D.) Constantinople amply justified its choice as the administrative center of the east-Mediterranean world. It grew in numbers and waxed exceeding prosperous, fed by the commerce of the Black sea and of the great caravan routes from Asia. Occasionally, owing to

some grave political disaster, it was threatened with eclipse, but
no sooner had the disturbed conditions reassumed a normal aspect
than it emerged from obscurity and again shone forth over the
eastern world. From the reign of the Emperor Constantine to
the present day, that is, for a period of almost two thousand
years, Constantinople will be found to be playing a variable
but always eminent rôle in the affairs of the eastern Mediterranean, for a reason as simple as it is abiding: the city occupies,
from the point of view of both commerce and politics, one of
those rare strategic sites which geographers call control-positions.
And because we who are alive today exhibit an amazing energy,
and pursue with an intensity greater than at any time of the
world's history a policy of political and commercial advantages,
it is certain that its location on the Bosporus must secure to
Constantinople in the future as large and perhaps even a larger
importance than it has enjoyed in the past.

Not long after the founding of Constantinople the Roman
epoch of Balkan history came to a close and the medieval or
Byzantine epoch began to take shape. Even before the Emperor Constantine reared his new capital, the vast Roman empire
was threatened by a movement on its borders which, in connection with a slow and fatal process of internal decay, proved its
undoing as a world-power and ushered in a new age. I refer,
of course, to the Great Migrations. Numerous tribes of barbarous peoples, Germans and Slavs, dwelling in the inhospitable
north and east of Europe, set themselves in motion toward the
warm south and began to beat at the gates of the empire for admission. It was then that the importance in Balkan affairs of
a hitherto unnoticed factor, the Danube river, rose into view.
With characteristic military insight the Romans had organized
the Danube as a natural line of defense against the tribal plun-
derers. But while serving as a strategic barrier, the Danube was also the route traced by Nature herself for all prospective invaders hailing from the frozen north. As early
as the third century A.D. the barbarians appeared in numbers
on the Danube, and, though often beaten off, renewed the attack with such persistence that their unrelenting pressure
soon became the one absorbing problem of the Government at
Constantinople.

The decay of
the Roman
empire in-
vited the
attack of the
barbarians.

The Roman empire of the East successfully defends itself and emerges, around 500 A.D., as the Byzantine empire.

Turning for a moment from Constantinople to the Roman west, let us remind ourselves that the barbarians, by pushing resolutely, not only southward over the Danube but also westward over the Rhine, succeeded in the course of many generations in undermining the authority of the empire and in occupying in a casual, unsystematic way all its western provinces, Gaul, Italy, Britain, Spain, and Africa. Considering the small number of the invaders and the immense though disorganized mass of the conquered, the triumph won must always remain unintelligible except on the assumption of an internal disease consuming the Roman vitality. However, in its eastern provinces, undermined by the same disease and attacked by the same forces, the empire succeeded, in spite of occasional defeats and considerable losses of territory, in keeping itself afloat. This is the outstanding fact of the fifth and sixth centuries and proves the superior power of resistance of the Roman East, which will have to be examined in detail in its proper place. Suffice it at this point to indicate that the eastern empire, notably diminished in authority and battling for its very life with enemies crowding in from all sides, gradually underwent a number of fundamental changes in structure and civilization. By the sixth century it already presents to view so different an appearance from the *imperium romanum* of Augustus, and even of the Emperor Constantine, that historians have indicated their sense of its transformation by conferring on it the new name of the Byzantine empire.

The Byzantine epoch a long struggle for existence against invaders, chiefly Slavs and Mongolians.

For many centuries after its transformation, in fact throughout what we familiarly call the Middle Age (500–1500 A.D.), the east Roman or Byzantine empire fought for its existence against its civilized neighbors, the Persians, but, more particularly, against the onset of ever new hordes of barbarian enemies. In the main they belonged to two great racial groups, very different in appearance and character, Slavs and Mongolians, though a third group, the Semitic Arabs, hailing from the deserts of Arabia, for a time dwarfed every other peril suspended over the Byzantine state. None-the-less the Slavs, white men of Caucasian race, having their home-land in the plains and swamps of eastern Europe, and the Mongolians with their many congeners, substantially yellow nomads roaming the plateau of western

Asia, stand forth as the leading and untiring enemies of the empire seated on the Bosporus. Beginning with the fifth and more particularly with the sixth century, successive tribes of Slavs and Mongolians, sometimes compactly organized as fighting armies, sometimes more loosely associated as daring raiders, swept over the peninsula like waves of an inrushing sea and battled with the Byzantine empire for supremacy. Occasionally the harassed state gained a breathing-spell through a group of Slavs turning upon the Mongolians or even upon other Slavs. Another not infrequent feature of the situation was that under the guidance and inspiration of some capable leader a Slav or Mongolian state took shape and ambitiously lifted its head above the political and racial welter of the region. Usually it did not last long and, on breaking to bits, fell back into the simmering Balkan crucible. Over and over again it seemed as if the Byzantine empire, in spite of its magnificent strategic position on the Bosporus, would have *finis* written to its story. Then by a supreme effort it would somehow save itself from the ultimate consequences of defeat. Thus with few interruptions the struggle went on until in the fifteenth century it was brought to a tragic conclusion by the fall of Constantinople before the irresistible advance of the last of the medieval invaders, the Ottoman Turks.

It was in the year 1453 that the Turks, hailing originally, like so many of their predecessors among the Balkan invaders, from the central tablelands of Asia, took the city of Constantinople and therewith overthrew the Byzantine empire, itself the legitimate descendant of the Roman empire of the Caesars. In the course of the next few decades the whole peninsula with its strange assortment of peoples who had succeeded in gaining a Balkan foothold in the long struggle for peninsular supremacy, Greeks, Slavs, Albanians, and Rumanians, was brought under the Turkish yoke. Therewith was inaugurated the Turkish or Ottoman phase of Balkan history. From the time of the conquest to the early nineteenth century the rule of the Turks was strong enough to be substantially undisputed, with the result that the older inhabitants of the peninsula were closely shut in the harsh prison of an alien servitude. An added suffering resulted from the fact that the oppressed nations were passionate and intolerant Christians,

The Ottoman empire in undisputed control from the fifteenth to the nineteenth century.

The Turks were far from intolerant ... as the Jew who escaped the horrors of the moslem of Spain

while the arrogant oppressors were equally intolerant adherents of the teachings of Mohammed. The four centuries during which the Christian natives were subjected to a ruthless exploitation by a band of Asiatic and Mohammedan victors constitute as terrible and grinding an experience as is anywhere recorded in history. Even its material scars are still discoverable today in town and country. But worse, far worse than the material injuries were the spiritual wounds, the traces of which it will require generations of educational effort and moral reconstruction to obliterate.

The nineteenth century inaugurates the liberation of the subject peoples from the Ottoman yoke.

At last, with the coming of the nineteenth century, a new day dawned bringing the newest phase of Balkan history, the phase of the rebirth and liberation of the subject peoples. The Christian nations, Greeks, Slavs, and Rumanians, awakening from an age-long sleep, reasserted themselves, and in a desperate and heroic struggle won their freedom. Slowly the flood of the Ottoman conquest began to recede; slowly it flowed back from the interior of the Bosporus, until, in the second decade of the twentieth century, came that total breakdown of the Ottoman power of which the living generation has been the astonished witness.

The five epochs of Balkan history.

Such is the succession of the main periods of Balkan history: an Hellenic period, a Roman period, a Medieval or Byzantine period, an Ottoman period, and a Liberation period, which has just been brought to a close. In this book the Hellenic and Roman periods will receive only superficial treatment in order that space may be saved for the later epochs. With the Byzantine period our story will grow more detailed, and, proceeding cumulatively, will reach its amplest phase with the nineteenth century, that is, with the age of Liberation.

History ultimately concerned with living problems and issues.

Such a plan, more or less arbitrary, calls for an explanation, which however, since it involves the purely theoretic question of the purpose and scope of history, cannot with propriety be fully developed in this place. In lieu of a reasoned exposition, a simple statement will have to suffice and may throw a not unwelcome light on the author's understanding of his task. To him as to most modern historians history is a division of the social sciences dedicated to the study of certain phases in the evolution of man primarily of a political order, to the end of setting forth man's present status and of helping to provide intelligent norms for his future guidance. In other words, history pursues an intensely practical aim and ultimately is always concerned with living problems and issues, for the elucidation of which it assembles data calculated to promote their solution. The solutions, of course, the historian does not himself formulate, for that is the work of law-makers, administrators, and other specialists concerned with government; but while bringing together invaluable material for the use of rulers and builders of states, he at the same time spreads light and information among the general public in the courageous, though perhaps delusive, hope that society may be decreasingly exposed to the operations of chance and increasingly brought under an intelligent control.

Applied to the Balkan field, this theory lays down as the main purpose of the book the communication to the reader of the leading present-day issues of the Balkan peninsula. These, without pretending to solve, it hopes to clarify by disclosing their historical background. While the whole of this vast background, the product of centuries of development, is embraced within the scope of our inquiry, the more recent phases are manifestly more vital and therefore more significant than the more distant past. It is by reason of this consideration that the author is content merely to summarize the earlier periods of the Balkan story in order to gain space for the Byzantine and Ottoman epochs, and above all, for the recent phase of Liberation. The numerous Balkan problems, with which the living generation of men must reckon, and which are admittedly a weighty factor in the troubled international situation of today, should, when the reader has finished this book, be not indeed " solved " in the sense of a problem in mathematics nor even theoretically formulated like the " laws " of the natural sciences, but they should have become visible in their historical perspective and have been grasped in their successive vital stages. It may seem to some that these problems, representing the goal of our long journey, should be enumerated and defined at the outset, but as it is the purpose of this book not to reduce them to a theoretical form, but to show them, as it were, on the march, in practical historical operation, the writer prefers to follow the established procedure of his pro-

This book plans not to formulate the Balkan problems theoretically, but to exhibit them in their historical development.

fession. That means that he deliberately adheres to the method of the pragmatic and chronological narrative.

It is, then, a record of events, a story of human activities, which is to be here unfolded, and as such a story demands familiarity with the physical environment which obviously at all times must have directed and controlled the human agents, we shall by way of introduction to our tale examine the outstanding geographical features of the Balkan area.

CHAPTER II

THE GEOGRAPHY OF THE BALKAN PENINSULA

THE Balkan peninsula, or, if I am permitted to coin a useful word, Balkania, is the easternmost of the three European peninsulas belonging to the Mediterranean area. But while the other two, Italy and Spain, are shut off from the European continent, Italy by the Alps and Spain by the Pyrenees, Balkania can boast of no such well-defined barrier. On the contrary, if, as is usually done, we accept the Danube river as the northern boundary of the peninsula, we are forced to the conclusion that Balkania, instead of being walled off from its European hinterland, is closely linked up with it, since rivers always present the easiest and most natural avenues of communication.

Relation of the Balkan peninsula to Europe.

But this accessibility from the continent turns out, on close inspection, to be more apparent than real. The Danube is indeed a magnificent highway, but intricate mountains to the south of it, covering pretty much the whole surface of the peninsula, make interior communication so difficult that Balkania is in effect a much less accessible land than either Italy or Spain. A historical consequence of this physical peculiarity deserves to be noted at the outset. Whereas Italy and Spain, protected against invasion from Europe and enjoying more or less easy internal communications, have been urged by the forces of geography toward racial, economic, and political unification, Balkania is split into so many geographic divisions separated from one another by natural barriers, that the different peoples settled on the soil have been greatly aided in an instinctive desire to maintain their separate individualities, and down to this day have successfully resisted all efforts made to bring about their political unification.

Its relative inaccessibility.

The usual practice of geographers, as already said, is to accept the Danube river as the inland boundary of Balkania, that is, the Danube from its mouth upstream to Belgrad. At Belgrad the Save, coming from the southeastern Alps, flows into the Danube,

The inland boundary of Balkania.

and the Save River, continued by a short air-line drawn from its
upland sources to the head of the Adriatic, completes, according
to common agreement, the northern line of demarcation. To the
north of the lower Danube lies the fertile Rumanian plain which,
from a strictly physiographical view-point, can hardly be reckoned
as an integral part of Balkania. But the fact remains that this
plain has been so closely tied up with the human destiny of the
peninsula that for practical reasons the Balkan historian is
obliged to include it in his narrative. On the other hand, the
extreme northwestern section, inhabited chiefly by a Slav people,
called Croats or Croatians, and embracing the districts of Croatia,
Slavonia, and Istria, has politically been so closely associated with
central Europe that, in spite of its physical union with Balkania,
it will receive only cursory treatment in this book.

The mountains of Balkania: The Balkans. Apart from the occasional lowlands marking the course of its
many rivers, Balkania may be said to be uniformly mountainous.
The geographer, drawing on his next-of-kin, the geologist, is able
to recount the interesting story of how the mountains came into
being, but such a tale is outside the range of the historian, who
is privileged to take the physical world as he finds it. Let us
therefore proceed to describe the more important ranges. South
of the Danube river and running parallel to its course is the
Balkan range, from which the peninsula has received its name.[1]
The Balkan mountains fall into three nearly equal sections, of
which the central section reaches the greatest elevation, boasting
peaks of a height of about 8000 feet. The eastern section — often
called the Lesser Balkans — is composed of rounded and richly
wooded peaks which gradually decrease in height until at the
shore of the Black sea they fall away to insignificant hills. It
follows that the eastern section is the region of the easiest north-
and-south communication and has the greatest number of de-
pressions or passes. But, though the contrary view is often
voiced, even the higher central and western sections of the Balkans are provided with not infrequent passes, among which the
Shipka pass, the Baba Konak pass, and the Isker valley pass
are the most important. By falling away rather gradually to the

[1] As Balkan is a Turkish word, meaning mountain, the current name
of the peninsula is of relatively recent origin. In classical times the
Balkans were known as the Haemus range.

north, but often in very steep escarpments toward the south, the Balkan range constitutes a better military barrier against an army coming from the south than from the direction of the Danube.

South of the Balkans and separated from them by the broad valley of the Maritsa lies the Rhodope range. In its eastern section, where it touches the Aegean shore, it is composed of low foot-hills; these become steadily higher, as the range pursues its northwesterly course, until at the junction with the Balkans, in the great knot around Sofia, they reach the considerable elevation of 7500 feet. It is significant of the central location of the Sofia region that four rivers flow thence to every point of the compass: the north river, the Isker, makes for the Danube; the west river, the Nishava, reaches Serbia and the Morava basin, while the east and south rivers, the Maritsa and Struma, carry their waters into the Aegean sea. Sofia is without doubt one of the important points of peninsular control. *The Rhodope range.*

West of the Balkan and Rhodope ranges we come upon the very difficult highlands of Serbia and Macedonia. They constitute a region of transverse valleys which have the effect of heavily handicapping communications. The numerous short ranges with their wooded foldings reach their highest altitude in the Shar Dagh, which therefore to a considerable extent dominates the Macedonian interior. In the Shar Dagh, as in the Sofian knot, four rivers — the Ibar, the Morava, the Drin, and the Vardar — take their rise to carry their waters to such widely separated areas as the Danube, the Adriatic and the Aegean. In spite of great irregularities of direction in the Macedonian chains there is noticeable, none-the-less, a prevailing north-south course which becomes particularly marked in the southern area where the Pindus range projects into northern Greece. Southward extensions of the Pindus practically overspread the whole of ancient Hellas as far as Cape Matapan, the rocky southern promontory of the Peloponnesus. *The Serb-Macedonian Highlands.*

West of the Macedonian plateau are the coastal ranges of Albania and Montenegro. These are limestone chains, whose soft surfaces have been deeply cut by rushing streams and which, in the course of time, have been all but denuded of vegetation. They are continued northward in the Dinaric Alps, *The coastal ranges of the Adriatic.*

which, limestone formations like the mountains to the south of them, have little timber and a very sparse population. They lift their frowning battlements, marked by peaks of the most fantastic shape, along the whole length of the Adriatic coast as far north as the gulf of Triest.

Rivers the natural line of penetration.

To this rugged peninsula, criss-crossed with innumerable mountain barriers, the rivers afford the natural avenues of penetration. They can best be classified by the sea to which they are tributary, and if we will now take note that the Black sea washes the eastern shore of Balkania, the Aegean sea the southeastern, the Ionian sea the southwestern, and the Adriatic sea the western shore, we arrive at four groups of rivers corresponding to these four coastal waters.

The Black sea rivers: The Danube.

Beginning with the Black sea rivers we are informed by a single glance at the map that the one overwhelmingly important stream is the Danube. It rises in southern Germany and carries off the waters of the eastern Alps, but our particular interest in it does not begin till it reaches the city of Belgrad, where it is joined by the Save. From Belgrad the Danube moves in the main due east, receiving, before at the end of a long journey it reaches the Black sea, a vast number of streams from the Carpathians to the north, and from the Serb-Macedonian highlands as well as from the Balkans to the south. Only the southern tributaries concern us here. Some twenty miles east of Belgrad, the Morava pours its waters into the Danube. The Morava is the chief stream of Serbia and therefore the main line of approach from the Danube to the Serb highlands. Proceeding eastward we come upon the Timok, which in its lower course serves as boundary between Serbia and Bulgaria; and in Bulgaria we find a whole series of Danubian tributaries maintaining a parallel direction as they flow northward from their source in the Balkan mountains. The most important among them are the Isker, which connects Sofia with the Danubian basin, the Vid, and the Yantra. By virtue of the Danube and its tributaries the whole northern region of the peninsula may be looked upon as dependent on the Black sea.

The Aegean rivers.

Turning to the Aegean sea to follow inland the Aegean rivers, we discover that the Balkan area which they drain is hardly less extensive than that tributary to the Black sea. The Maritsa, the Mesta, the Struma, and the Vardar are the leading arteries feeding the Aegean. The Maritsa is the great river of Bulgaria. Flowing eastward through the fertile valley between the Balkans and the Rhodope, it receives at Adrianople two other streams, the Tundja and the Arda; here, turning sharply south, it makes for the Aegean sea, gathering on its way the Ergene, which brings to it the waters of the plateau of eastern Thrace. The Mesta and the Struma drain the southern slopes of the Rhodope, while the Vardar is the great outlet of the Macedonian highlands. As the Vardar traces the most favorable line of penetration to the interior and from the interior northward to the Danube, it is an avenue of peculiar importance and Saloniki, the city near its mouth, a natural emporium.

From a hydrographic point of view the Balkan peninsula forms an elevated mass inclined in the main toward the Black and Aegean seas. It follows that the area sloping toward the Ionian and Adriatic seas is small. The Ionian sea bathes the shores of western Hellas, the rivers of which are unimportant, since they are short in length and torrential in character, carrying in the season of the spring rains a raging flood, only to go bone-dry in the parched summer. The Adriatic sea, washing the west and northwest shore of Balkania, does not receive many rivers because the water-shed of the peninsula is nowhere far from the coast and sometimes even approaches to within a few miles of it. However, three rivers deserve mention, the Drin, which is the chief artery of northern Albania, the Boyana, which drains the important lake of Scutari, and the Narenta, which drives downward to the sea among the bleak and caverned lime-stone hills of Herzegovina. *The Ionian and Adriatic rivers unimportant.*

Except the broad and hospitable Danube, navigable all the way to central Europe, none of the Balkan rivers is a practical modern highway for the movement of men and goods. An occasional tributary of the Danube, like the Morava, and also some Aegean streams, like the Maritsa and the Vardar, are accessible to small boats near their mouth, but in the main the rivers of Balkania are not available as carriers either because they dry up in the hot season, or are dotted with dangerous rapids, or have had their channels silted up by the heavy wash of detritus from the uplands. *Only the Danube navigable.*

The roads
follow
the river
valleys.
The Belgrad-
Constanti-
nople road.

However, though the rivers themselves, the noble Danube
always excepted, are poor avenues of intercourse, the river valleys
have from the dawn of time pointed out to man the natural
lines of penetration into the interior. Consequently a few well-
marked highways, making use of the valleys as far as they serve,
have through all the ages played an important rôle in the commercial and political control of the peninsula. The first of
these to consider is what we may call the Europe-Asia route,
running from northwest to southeast, from Belgrad to Constantinople. Starting at Belgrad it strikes up the Morava valley
to Nish; from Nish it crosses the mountains to Sofia, to move
thence by the Maritsa valley to Adrianople; and finally from
Adrianople it passes, in its last stage and in as straight a line as
the topography permits, across the Thracian plateau to
Constantinople.

The Belgrad-
Saloniki
road.

If the Belgrad-Constantinople road is the all-important east–
west communication, hardly inferior to it is the north–south
connection between the Danube and the Aegean sea. This also
takes its departure from Belgrad, marching with the Constantinople road as far as Nish; from Nish it branches southward,
climbs the watershed between the Morava and Vardar, and then
slopes down the Vardar valley reaching its terminus on the
Aegean sea at the city of Saloniki.

The Durazzo-
Saloniki-
Constanti-
nople road.

From very early time the venturesome traders from Greece
and Italy must have maintained a sharp lookout for a line of
approach into the peninsula from the Adriatic. As they anxiously scanned the shore from the decks of their ships, they
saw an almost unbroken line of frowning mountains, which
reared their bulk along the coast and offered no hospitable opening other than the mouth of an occasional torrent with little reach
into the interior. This unfortunate sin of omission on the part of
nature the Romans were the first to correct with an artificial
road which was a considerable engineering feat and serpen-
tined its way up ridge after ridge of difficult mountain chains.
Long since fallen into decay, it was known while it flourished as the *via Egnatia,* and starting at Durazzo on the sea, it
cut eastward across Albania to the city of Monastir, moving thence to Saloniki, and finally, by the Aegean shore, to Constantinople.

All these roads, along which have traveled, faintly seen by us as in a magic mirror, primitive shepherds with their flocks, daring Greek peddlers in pursuit of gain, the clanking legions of Rome bent on the stern business of the empire, and the barbarous invading hosts of Slavs and Mongolians, have retained their full significance to this day, only they have recently been replaced by railways. The Oriental railroad now carries the traveler and his wares in comparatively few hours from Belgrad via Nish, Sofia, and Adrianople to the capital city on the Bosporus, while the Morava-Vardar railway carries him in the same speedy manner from Belgrad to Saloniki. An east-west line, joining Monastir by rail to Durazzo or some other Albanian sea town, has frequently been discussed in the hope of reviving the Roman *via Egnatia*, but so far nothing definite has been accomplished. Certainly the reader will be well inspired if he gives the closest attention to the three indicated lines of penetration, for they will direct his mind to what have been the main points of political and economic control ever since men have lived and struggled on the peninsula.

While tracing the leading lines of communication we cannot afford to neglect the harbors of Balkania. First to draw our attention are, of course, the water terminals of the two great overland routes, Constantinople and Saloniki. As nature, in equipping the metropolis on the Bosporus, apparently resolved to withhold none of her gifts, we need not be surprised to discover that Constantinople, in addition to a surpassing beauty of environment, has one of the finest harbors of the world. Its deep and ample waters offer secure shelter, not only to countless merchantmen, but even to the dreadnaughts and superdreadnaughts of modern naval warfare. The harbor of Saloniki has not the depth of that of Constantinople and the city has the further drawback of being afflicted with malaria due to the swampy lowlands of the near-by Vardar estuary, but it has no rival at the head of the Aegean and is certain to grow in importance in the coming days. In a sense Athens with its port, Piraeus, may be looked on as Saloniki's rival for the trade of the Aegean, but though its harbor facilities are excellent, its hinterland is too poor, and the railroad passage northward too difficult to make it a serious competitor of the city by the Vardar

Athens, however, need not despair. It commands the canal which, cut through the isthmus of Corinth, materially shortens the Aegean-Ionian journey, and it is thus destined to prove an increasingly important link along the Mediterranean east–west route.

Minor harbors. While Constantinople, Saloniki, and Athens stand out as the leading Balkan harbors, there are others which may not be neglected. If the Danube should develop, as is likely, into a great European merchant-carrier, the Danubian ports are sure to grow in importance. Under Ottoman domination the Danube delta, which consists of three mouths, known as the Kilia, the Sulina, and the St. George channels, was so shamefully neglected that it became choked with detritus; but dredgings, conducted by a European commission, appointed at the congress of Paris (1856), have entirely changed the situation. Because the middle or Sulina channel carries the least water and is freest from silt, it received the concentrated attention of the commission and has been made accessible to sea-going vessels of considerable draft. In consequence such Danube ports as Sulina, Galatz, and Braila have rapidly come to the front and have a promising future. South of the Danube delta the coast of the Black sea is rocky and abrupt and lamentably devoid of good shelter for vessels. Constanza, which is connected by rail with Bucharest, the capital of Rumania, and the two Bulgarian ports, Varna and Burgas, have been made serviceable by art but possess few natural advantages. Proceeding along the Aegean and Ionian coast, we shall find, excepting always Saloniki and Athens, few places of anchorage suitable for modern needs. Kavala, at the head of the Aegean to the east of Saloniki, and Patras, on the Ionian sea, at the northwest corner of the Peloponnesus, enjoy a certain eminence due to a fertile though restricted hinterland. From Patras north the coast continues in the main to be mountainous and uninviting. In southern Albania, Avlona, much coveted by the Italians as a naval base, has alluring possibilities, while Durazzo and Antivari are useful roadsteads which it would require a large expenditure of money to develop into modern harbors. On the other hand, Cattaro, lying at the head of a deep and picturesque fiord, which washes the base of the Montenegrin mountains, is the best natural harbor of the whole west

coast. Unfortunately Cattaro's barren and inhospitable hinterland condemns it to an insignificance which its selection as a
naval base by its erstwhile Austrian masters mitigated but did
not cancel. Every examination of the long peninsular coast-line
will only serve to underscore the importance of Saloniki and
Constantinople, which, as sea-terminals of the two leading land
routes, must always enjoy an easy ascendancy over all rival ports.

Inseparable from a country's physical features is the consideration of its climate. Balkania extends approximately from the
thirty-sixth to the forty-fifth degree of north latitude. Between
them is embraced all the land from the southern tip of the Peloponnesus to the city of Belgrad on the junction of the Save
and Danube. The whole peninsula is therefore well within the
temperate zone, but owing to the manner in which its different
sections are affected by such factors as wind, rainfall, and altitude, great variations of climate prevail. In the main two types
stand out: a Mediterranean climate in the extreme southern and
coastal sections and a Continental climate, mid-European in character, in the mountainous interior. Included within the area of
the Mediterranean climate is ancient Hellas, together with a
narrow band of shore-land stretching along the Aegean as far east
as Constantinople and along the Adriatic as far north as Triest.
This area, in immediate touch with the Mediterranean sea and
protected from the wintry blasts of the north by tall mountain
barriers, enjoys the same sunshine as Italy and the Riviera
regions and has mild winters followed by summers which, uniformly hot, tend to become very hot in Greece. As little
or no rain falls in the warm season, the land becomes extremely
parched, and plants, like our common cereals, which depend on
a regular supply of summer rain, do not prosper. In the cooler
seasons, however, rain falls in abundance, promoting a luxurious,
semi-tropical vegetation. Special conditions at given points produce a certain amount of climate variation. At Constantinople,
for instance, there is no mountain screen to the north or at
least an insufficient one, and when, as happens periodically in the
winter months, the wind blows from Russia and the Black sea,
a very chilly spell of weather follows. The mountainous interior,
extending roughly from Saloniki to the Danube, embraces a
much larger section of the peninsula than the Mediterranean

*The two
types of
climate:
Mediter-
ranean and
Continental.*

area. It enjoys a climate which, if by no means uniform throughout, is defined as Continental because its rainfall, both as to quantity and distribution, as well as its summer and winter temperatures, are much the same as throughout central Europe. An exception is furnised by the Black sea coast, chiefly in the section of the Dobrudja and the Thracian plateau, which, owing to a very low rainfall, exhibit the arid characteristics of a typical desert.

The Mediterranean products and their effect on the inhabitants.

As we might be led to expect, the vegetable products of the peninsula fall into the same two broad groups as the climate. Within the Mediterranean belt flourish such sub-tropical fruits as the fig, the grape, and the olive; in less degree, and only in the most sheltered spots, the orange and the lemon. The fig, olive, and grape, especially the small dried grape known as the currant, constitute the most valuable harvests of Greece, which, covered with rocky and denuded mountains, has little pasture for cattle and only one considerable wheat area, in the plains of Thessaly. Meat and bread being scarce, it follows that, from the earliest time, the Greeks have had to trade in order to live, and that they have always been at the mercy of a naval power capable of cutting off their foodstuffs. To keep this in mind is to hold an important clue to Greek history from the days of the Persian invasions to the Great War of our time.

The Continental products.

To this Mediterranean vegetation the products of the Continental belt present a sharp contrast. The tumbled highlands, watered by countless streams, abundantly grow every kind of forest tree, both deciduous and evergreen, characteristic of the central European zone. But the immense stretches of oak, beech, pine, and hemlock are, owing to the economic backwardness of the peninsula, only partially utilized. The oak forests of certain regions, as, for instance, of Serbia, constitute an exception, since their abundant acorn mast forms the basis of a flourishing swine industry. The valleys, beneath the wooded hills and mountains, are in general exceedingly fertile, though often inaccessible, and produce good crops of wheat, rye, oats, maize (Indian corn), and flax. The agricultural methods employed are still very primitive, though improvements have recently been inaugurated which promise a gradual increase of the annual yields. Of course all the orchard fruits of central Europe flourish in abundance, the plum enjoying the particular favor of the natives, especially of Serbia, who distill from its juice a much-vaunted brandy, their national drink.

The inland folk, mostly Slavs, have by reason of their soil, climate, and crops, in a word, by virtue of their relation to the earth on which they live, developed in the course of time a different set of characteristics from the Greeks, the leading people of the coastal region. Owing to the inability of the soil of Greece to nourish its population, a large part of the Greeks has been obliged to turn for a livelihood to trade, both at home and abroad, and Greeks will therefore be found in all the east-Mediterranean countries including the Slav uplands of Balkania. In many a Macedonian market town they have opened their shops and set up a modest hearth of Greek civilization, without, however, becoming particularly rooted in the soil. The soil is the true element of the Slav, who is preëminently the ploughman, the peasant, attached with every fiber of his being and with all the force of age-long custom to his cottage and his farm. Thus climate and occupation have contributed through the ages to differentiate the Greeks and the Slavs not only physically but also mentally and morally.

Slavs and Greeks differentiated by climate and occupation.

In conclusion a word about the Danubian plain north of the Danube river. Although in a strictly physiographical sense it may not be part of the peninsula, we have agreed that the Balkan historian cannot afford to neglect it. Watered by many rivers which flow in parallel courses from the Carpathian mountains into the Danube, the Rumanian lowlands are among the most fertile lands on earth, producing in profusion wheat, maize, oats, in a word, all the food and feed crops of the temperate zone. Just beyond the plain rise the low foothills of the Carpathians, which serve as the grazing ground of numerous herds of sheep and cattle, while beyond the foothills tower the wooded uplands, offering an abundant yield of every variety of lumber. Recently petroleum has been discovered in the valley of the Prahova river, directly north of Bucharest, with the result that a flourishing oil industry has sprung up with the mushroom-like suddenness with which the United States is unpleasantly familiar. The lumber, wheat, hides, oil and other raw products of Rumania are carried by the copious water-routes to the main artery of the

The Rumanian plain.

Danube, whence they reach the Black sea and finally the world-markets. As a system of railroads has been developed recently to serve as an adjunct to the water-carriers, the city of Constanza, the railroad terminal on the Black sea, has been lifted to eminence on a wave of commercial prosperity. In the light of this brief review it must be clear that the life of man on the fertile Rumanian plain has been at all times affected by the relation of this plain to its three physical determinants, the Danube, the Black sea, and the Carpathian mountains.

Since the rôle of the Balkan peninsula in human history was bound to be determined not only by its mountains, rivers, rainfall and climate, but also by its relation to its tangential areas, it becomes necessary, in conclusion, to extend our view and take in a wider physical prospect. Projecting into the Mediterranean sea, Balkania would, of course, have a Mediterranean destiny and be linked up more particularly with all the lands lying in a crescent around the eastern Mediterranean — Egypt, Syria, and Asia Minor. Moreover, with these great areas, homes of early and far-reaching civilizations, Balkania was tied up by a stronger bond than the elusive sea. To all intents it was joined to them by land, since the narrow water-passage, consisting of the Bosporus, the sea of Marmora, and the Dardanelles, was no effective barrier between Europe and Asia. At this channel the two continents come so close they almost touch; and so easy and convenient is the crossing from one shore to another that such communications as orient and occident have historically maintained predominantly passed by this route. The straits, which appear to divide, have therefore largely played a mediatory rôle, and the city on the Bosporus, selected as his capital by the far-seeing Constantine, has experienced the full benefit of its dominating position. We may thus fairly conclude not only that the forces of geography have predestined Balkania to play an important rôle in the history of the Mediterranean sea, but also that they have assigned to the peninsula an even larger part as a land of passage between Europe and the fabled East. Indeed, throughout its history Balkania has been a bridge for peoples and empires moving sometimes in one, sometimes in the opposite direction. It was by the Balkan peninsula that the Persians tried to force their way into Europe and that Macedonian

Balkania must be constantly viewed from two angles: (1) it is an East-Mediterranean peninsula, and (2) its position imposes on it the rôle of a bridge between Europe and Asia.

Alexander penetrated to Persia and beyond. Again, against the Arabs and the Turks, representatives of the westward drift, we may set the Romans and the crusaders of the Middle Age, whose expeditions give evidence of a periodic eastward reaction, obliged to make use of the Balkan peninsula as its avenue of penetration.

In our own time, dedicated to world-wide commerce, the Europe–Asia movement and interchange have of course become immeasurably intensified, and though they have opened new avenues for themselves, such as the sea-route around the Cape of Good Hope and, more recently, the Suez canal, the ancient land-route over Balkania via the straits to Asia Minor still holds a foremost place, as the most recent phase of world history amply proves. For at the very bottom of the Great War lay the question whether one European power should be permitted to control this invaluable passage to the disadvantage of the others. In our own day, therefore, as in the past, and to all appearances through all the years to come, Balkania must continue to play its part as a land of passage, a connecting link between two continents.

Growing importance in our time of Balkania as a link in a Europe–Asia route.

BIBLIOGRAPHY

M. D. Newbigin, Geographical Aspects of Balkan Problems.
L. W. Lyde, The Continent of Europe.
Lyde and Mockler-Ferryman, A Military Geography of the Balkan Peninsula.
J. Partsch, Central Europe.
J. Cvijic, La Péninsule Balkanique. Géographie Humaine. (A fundamental work, with forty maps and sketch-maps.)
W. M. Leake, Travels in the Morea.
W. M. Leake, Travels in Northern Greece.
C. Jirecek, Das Fuerstenthum Bulgarien.
F. Kanitz, Donau – Bulgarien und der Balkan. Reisestudien aus den Jahren 1860–1879.
F. Kanitz, Das Koenigreich Serbien und das Serbenvolk.
E. Banse, Die Türkei.
Many and valuable articles dealing with the Balkan Peninsula and the territories of the former Ottoman Empire will be found in the geographical journals such as Bulletin of the American Geographical Society, continued since 1916 as the Geographical Review (New York); The Geographical Journal (London); La Géographie (Paris); Annales de Géographie (Paris); Petermann's Mitteilungen (Gotha); Geographische Zeitschrift (Leipzig).

CHAPTER III

THE GREEK AND ROMAN EPOCHS OF BALKAN HISTORY

The Greek Epoch, 1500 B.C. to 200 B.C.

THE Greek epoch of Balkan history, with which our story begins, covers roughly the period from 1500 B.C. to 200 B.C. Throughout this time the Greeks, settled or engaged in settling on the islands of the Aegean sea and on the southern tip of the peninsula, within the bounds of ancient Hellas, were, in the experimental manner of a venturesome people, reaching out toward the Rhodope mountains and the difficult land beyond. But their advance in this direction at best was slow and, except sporadically, neither they nor their civilization ever penetrated the interior plateau.

The Greeks conquer Hellas in the course of a movement setting in before 1500 B.C.

It is the relatively small importance of the Greek epoch for the Balkan interior which justifies the plan of limiting ourselves for this period to the recital of a few significant facts, touching the degree of Hellenization of the peninsula which the Greeks effected. First of all, let us take note that the Greeks were a branch of the great Indo-European race, to which the Romans, the Germans, the Slavs, and all the other groups who have successively dominated European history belong. Before moving into the region, with which they are indissolubly associated in our minds, the Greeks had been nomads wandering over the grasslands north of the Danube river. Gradually pushing their way southward, to the southern extremity of Balkania, they succeeded in displacing an older people, concerning whom recent excavations have taught us a great deal calculated to arouse our admiration. We are now certain that these Mediterranean predecessors of the Greeks had developed a high civilization, which, having its center apparently in the island of Crete and radiating thence over the neighboring coasts, has been expressively called the Aegean civilization. On seizing the plains and fertile river bottoms of the coastal region the Hellenic nomads gradually took to agriculture and adopted, together with the political forms de-

26

manded by a fixed abode, the arts and crafts practiced within the radius of the Aegean influence. If we assume, as our evidence suggests, that the nomad occupation began before 1500 B.C. and that it continued, marked by the intermittent arrival of new tribes, for many centuries, we are free to predicate an early phase of Hellenic civilization covering a considerable period and of a distinctly transitional character. Scattered indications would seem to show that the northern invaders long retained the loose tribal organization characteristic of wandering herdsmen, and that only gradually, under the influence of agriculture and commerce and in response to the demands of the urban settlements, which had taken root, they developed that political form under which they reached their highest development, the city-state.

The people beyond the Greeks, in the hills and mountains to the north, were, though not Greeks, members of the same Indo-European family. Sharing none of the stimulating experiences of the Greeks on the Mediterranean shores, they lingered in the familiar ways of barbarism and were soon separated from the progressive Greeks by a wide gulf. They may be classified broadly as Thracians and Illyrians, the Thracians spreading away to the northeast of the peninsula, the Illyrians to the northwest. The people, known as Macedonians and holding the region north of Thessaly, were the particular barbarian group immediately in contact with the Greeks. They were the southernmost tribe of the Thracians and as they were in constant intercourse with Greek settlers, soldiers, and traders, they fell gradually under Greek influence which, in the fourth century B.C., in the reigns of their most famous kings, Philip and his son, Alexander the Great, reached its climax. These two sovereigns knew no higher ambition than to be regarded as full-fledged Greeks. They promoted the adoption of Greek speech, dress, and customs with the result that the Macedonians ended by becoming thoroughly Hellenized.

To the north of the Greeks were located the Thracians and Illyrians.

Macedonia marks the farthest northward limit of the triumphant march of Hellenism. The rude tribes of Thracians and Illyrians beyond the Macedonians, among the difficult valleys of the Rhodope and Balkan mountains, stubbornly persisted in their backward customs. It was the natural policy of the Macedonian

Macedonia misses its chance to Hellenize the Thracians and Illyrians.

state, so long as it retained its vigor, to penetrate the interior and effect the political consolidation of Balkania, but its rapid decline in the period after Alexander frustrated this purpose and assured the sturdy tribesmen a continued independence. When in the first half of the second centry B.C., the Romans in a number of vigorous campaigns put an end to Macedonia (Cynocephalae, 197 B.C., Pydna, 168 B.C.), the northern mountaineers must have greeted the event with open glee, for Macedonia was an ancient enemy close at hand, while Rome was a distant power from across the sea not likely to thrust forward into the Balkan wilds.

But if the Hellenization of the Balkan interior, largely because of its inaccessibility, was limited to Macedonia, Greek influence made itself felt with relative ease and freedom along all the Balkan coast. The Greeks were merchants, and owing to the mountain barriers thrown across the whole of Hellas and making movement by land difficult, chiefly maritime merchants. Trusting themselves to their ships they crept from inlet to inlet along the shore and, when they reached a settlement, alluringly spread out their wares upon the beach. In this way they came among the barbarians to the north offering pottery, weapons, ornaments, and cloth in return for wheat, salt, metals, and other raw products. Prompted to establish a trading-post at some convenient spot, they were proud to have it develop and wax strong as the colony of the enterprising mother-city from which they themselves hailed. Even before the Persian wars occurred, that is, before the sixth century, these trading-posts and colonies stretched in a continuous line along the northern shores of the Aegean, past the Dardanelles and Bosporus into the Black sea. The peninsula of Chalcidice, which thrusts three bold fingers into the waters at the head of the Aegean, was thickly planted with Greek settlements; Sestus and Abydus faced each other on the Dardanelles; a plantation called Byzantium, destined many centuries later to become famous as Constantinople, lay at the southern entrance to the Bosporus; and around the Black sea spread in a ring the colonies, on which the industrial homeland came to depend more and more for the supply of wheat, tunnies, iron, and slaves.

Greek trading-posts, assuming often the scale of flourishing colonies, dotted also the west coast. The island of Corcyra, which we now call Corfu, was an important settlement, and beyond Corfu on the mainland, lay Dyrrachium, from which modern Durazzo claims descent. The inhospitable character of the Balkan west coast explains why only rare and weak settlements were to be found north of Dyrrachium. All these colonies, spreading in a continuous chain from the Black to the Adriatic sea, may be likened to the outposts of an army laying siege to the peninsula in the name of Greek civilization. But though the colonies traded with the inland barbarians and even kept a watchful political eye turned in their direction, they never conquered them.

The Greek colonies of the Ionian and Adriatic seas.

Thus matters stood when the Greek period of Balkan history came to a close around the year 200 B.C. From the submitted facts it must be clear that this first period is properly named Greek, since it concerns itself exclusively with the story of the Greeks, and since the barbarous Thracians and Illyrians, occupying the unexplored interior, play no rôle of which it is profitable or even possible to take more than cursory account. But to follow Greek history and civilization is not part of our plan further than to insist on their enduring consequences for Balkania and the world. The Greeks developed one of the noblest cultures ever attained by man, and in art and literature, in philosophy, science, and government piled up achievements which have been the admiration as the well as the envy of succeeding generations. The stumbling-block, over which they fell, and fell to ruin, was their failure to find a cure for the ruinous competition of the sovereign city-states, Athens, Sparta, Thebes, Corinth, and the rest. An orderly, authoritative federation might have proved a solution of the eternal civil war, which destroyed incalculable values, but it had few or no supporters. Foolishly, tragically, the cities preferred to waste the possessions and lives of their citizens in mutual injury, and having bled themselves white, they fell first, before the military and at least partially Hellenized monarchy of Macedonia, and, after an interval, finally and completely, before the Roman legions. With independence gone, Greek civilization, in spite of its transfusion in the period of conquest with doubtful, hybrid elements, and in spite of its lowered moral tone due to the hard yoke of servility, continued

Summary of Greek failure and success.

to exercise an irresistible attraction. The Romans fell completely under its spell, and we of a later age still continue thankfully to draw on it as on an inexhaustible human treasure.

The Roman Epoch covers the period from 200 B.C. to 500 A.D.

The Roman epoch, following on the heels of the Greek, dates from 200 B.C. (approximately, since even before 200 B.C. the Romans had begun to clash with the Illyrian pirate state along the east coast of the Adriatic), and stretches to 500 A.D. These dates are, of course, no more to be taken literally than the dates of the preceding Greek epoch and, for that matter, any dates whatever which pretend to define historical epochs. Indeed, the very notion of an epoch is challengeable and may even prove hurtful to the student unless he understands that one period of history fades into another imperceptibly and that definite time-limits merely serve the convenience of the historian, who, in order to promote the understanding of his material, subjects it to an orderly but distinctly arbitrary arrangement.

The Romans bring all Balkania under their sway.

About 200 B.C. — or rather, to be exact, in 197 — Rome set her heel on the kingdom of Macedonia and began the exercise of her rule in the peninsula. Her advance was careful and deliberate, as the difficult situation demanded. A half century passed before the Romans attacked the freedom of the Greek cities, but when, in 146 B.C., they acted, they did not halt at half-way measures. The whole of ancient Hellas was degraded to the level of a Roman province. Then the conquerors girded their loins for the task which had steadily foiled the Greeks, the overthrow of the barbarous Thracians and Illyrians. Scattered as shepherds and primitive villagers among impenetrable and pathless mountains, they proved, in spite of their lack of organization (or shall we say because of it?), difficult to seize, crush, and reduce to subordination. Costly campaigns often ended without commensurate reward and it was not till the days of the first emperor, Augustus, that is, till the dawn of the Christian era, that the resistance of the stubborn natives was finally broken and the ascendancy of Rome established beyond dispute. Therewith all Balkania was for the first time brought under a single rule and carried as a geographic unit into the circle of Mediterranean civilization.

To secure the peninsula and incorporate it permanently in their empire the Romans proceeded according to the plan followed in Gaul, Britain, and every other province snatched from the hands of barbarian natives. First of all they constructed a network of paved highways, establishing military garrisons along their course as a guarantee of public order. In this manner the *via Egnatia*,[1] with its starting point at Dyrrachium (Durazzo), came into being. Its importance lay in the circumstance that it designated the logical line of entrance into the peninsula for a master hailing from Italy. But in measure as the Romans, in pursuit of the resisting natives, were obliged to cross the Balkans and penetrate all the way to the Danube, the necessity made itself felt for military roads in every possible direction. The natural lines of travel, discussed in the previous chapter, were of course known to the barbarian natives, but had never acquired any other character than that of rough and haphazard trails through the wilderness. These the Romans converted into broad highways, while military camps, which swiftly expanded into marts of trade, were laid out at such places as Adrianople, Philippopolis, Sardica (Sofia), Naissus (Nish), and Singidunum (Belgrad). These city names of Roman origin conclusively prove that the great east–west route from the Bosporus to the Danube was, under the Romans, made fully available for military, administrative, and commercial purposes. The many remains of Roman camps discovered by archeologists between Nish and Saloniki prove the same for the important north–south route along the Morava and Vardar. To protect the growing civilization of Balkania from the unconquered barbarians on the north bank of the Danube, garrison towns, constituting a continuous chain of river forts, were laid out all the way from Singidunum (Belgrad) to the Black sea. Finally, a war-fleet, moving up and down the river, was kept in readiness to thwart any sudden barbarian offensive.

The Romans build military roads and plant camps which become cities.

The military occupation once accomplished, the benefits of an ordered civil rule followed. Roman justice was administered in Roman courts and gave security to life and property. Peddlers from Italy and other Mediterranean centers with their sumpter-mules and wares streamed to the camps and settled down as local merchants on becoming convinced of the possibility of a permanently lucrative trade with the numerous garrisons. On

The process of Romanization sets in.

<hr>

[1] See Chapter II, p. 18.

retiring from active service the Roman soldiers were rewarded by the state with land-grants, preferably in the vicinity of the towns, and were thus in the hale middle period of their life transformed into farmers cultivating the soil. Through all these influences the backward natives, especially those residing within easy range of the camps, gradually gave up their accustomed ways, adopted Roman dress, speech, and manners, and helped build up the province along Roman lines. At the height of the empire's power, in the two centuries following Augustus, during which the Roman system stood forth in unimpaired power and splendor, the Balkan interior must have presented to a chance visitor a general appearance uniform with that of the rest of the Roman world. Roman soldiers and officials were omnipresent, and the provincials, thoroughly reconciled to their masters, comported themselves as though they had been Romans born.

Balkania boasts the developed Roman civilization of the Third Century A.D. When in the year 212 A.D., the Emperor Caracalla granted Roman citizenship to all freemen throughout the empire (and of course also to the Balkan provincials) he merely set the seal of law on a Romanization already substantially effected. At that time a traveler from the great capital on the Tiber, whether bent on business or pleasure, might have moved through Balkania in perfect security, owing to the excellent administration of justice; he would have been carried with dispatch from point to point because of the goods roads; and he would have been prompted to comment admiringly on the transformation of the rude soldier-settlements of an earlier date into the flourishing cities spread before his eyes. Adorned with forum, baths, temples, and theaters, they were all a more or less close reproduction in miniature form of the imperial city of the Seven Hills. Excavations conducted in recent decades of the sites of vanished Roman towns have uncovered broken columns, marble statuary, mosaic floors, metal and glass ornaments which establish with absolute certainty that Balkania was an important part of the Roman world and in the heyday of the empire boasted all the characteristic features of Roman civilization.

The coming of Christianity. Interesting additional evidence of the complete Romanization of the peninsula is supplied to the observer by the advent of Christianity. It is well known that the Romans, very tolerant, as a rule, in religious matters, developed an aversion for Christianity largely on the ground that its Quietist theory and ethics were subversive of political authority. Because the Christians refused to obey the laws, above all, because they rejected the obligatory emperor-worship, they were subjected to occasional bloody persecutions. None-the-less Christianity grew, and when at last it became too powerful to be successfully opposed, its strength won the recognition which had been denied to its infirmity. In 311 A.D. the Emperor Galerius issued, in favor of Christianity, the first important edict of toleration. His suc-

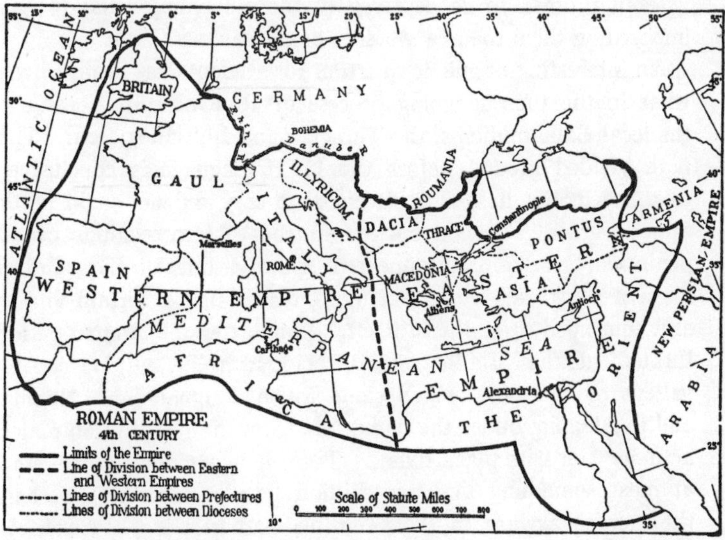

NoT TRue christian only 10% + this nearly in the East

ROMAN EMPIRE
4th CENTURY
—— Limits of the Empire
— — Line of Division between Eastern
        and Western Empires
—·—· Lines of Division between Prefectures
—·····— Lines of Division between Dioceses

Scale of Statute Miles

cessor, Constantine the Great, went further and gave Christianity the active support of the state. It meant the turning of the tide. Slowly the twilight of the ancient gods set in, to end in the complete darkness of night when, in 392 A.D., Emperor Theodosius ordered the closing of the pagan temples. Therewith Christianity became not only the official but also the exclusive religion of the Roman state and, filled with the pride of victory, in its turn began the persecution of its defeated rivals. Incredible as it was and remains, in the course of a single century the Roman world substantially effected its transformation from paganism to Christianity.

The easy
victory of
Christianity
argues the
weakness of
paganism
and the
strength of
the Roman
bureaucracy.

As far as the Balkan peninsula is concerned, the disturbances which elsewhere frequently attended the religious upheaval were conspicuously absent. While this peaceful transition might serve to argue that the pagan religious forms had been long undermined in the hearts of the people, it would also seem to show that the Balkan provincials had been so thoroughly merged with the empire that they retained nothing of their early love of liberty and very little even of their peculiar racial inheritance. Apparently at a word of command from official Rome these servile and overawed subjects of Balkania suffered themselves, without protest, to be deprived of the old temples and to have imposed on them the new worship of the saviour Christ.

Persistence
of the
Illyrian dia-
lect under
its modern
name,
Albanian.

An interesting linguistic question for students has always been: what in the thoroughgoing process of Romanization became of the local Balkan idioms, the Thracian and Illyrian speech? That both yielded ground before the Latin language is conclusively established, but it is also certain that they did not yield in the same degree. Thacian, spoken in the eastern sections of the peninsula, gradually disappeared entirely, but Illyrian, though its area contracted more and more, manifested a certain vitality and continued to maintain itself. Long after the Roman period, throughout the Middle Age, it held sway in the inaccessible valleys of the west, which came to be designated as Albania; and in Albania, under the name Albanian, the old Illyrian dialect actually holds its place today. True, it is a modest place, since at most something like two million people, and these perhaps the most backward in the peninsula and in Europe, speak Albanian, but they have the distinction — such as it is — of being the last remnant of the old Illyrians. A striking evidence of the losing racial struggle, which the Albanian people has maintained through the last two thousand years, is seen in the fact that the Albanian language, as it is used today, possesses many words of Greek and Latin origin, while even Slav and Turk borrowings are relatively common. In other words, the original Albanian tongue is heavily overlaid with deposits indicative of powerful foreign influences.

With the Greek, language, too, the tongue of the victorious Romans came into conflict, though with a different result, since it never succeeded in getting a foothold in the strictly Hellenic area, that is, on the Greek mainland together with the Aegean and Ionian islands. In the matter of so important an instrument of culture as language, the Greeks must not for one moment be confounded with the barbarous Thracians and Illyrians. Boasting one of the greatest literatures of all time, they made it a point of pride to honor and preserve the inheritance of their poets and philosophers. The result was that Greek not only held its own among the Greeks themselves but that when, in the medieval period, through upheavals which remain to be examined, the Latin language lost its grip on the interior, Greek succeeded even in somewhat extending its original Balkan dominion. It is of the greatest importance always to remember that, while Latin in the days of the greatness of Rome became the universal tongue, easily crowding out its rivals almost everywhere, it scored no success against Greek, which not only continued to be used in southern Balkania, but also remained the favored medium of communication of merchants and scholars throughout the east-Mediterranean world. *The Greek language maintains its ascendancy in southern Balkania and throughout the Near-East.*

If we now turn to the causes and conditions which brought about the decline of the Roman empire, we must begin by reminding ourselves that the first two centuries after Augustus, which were also the first two centuries of the Christian era, mark the zenith of the Roman power. Throughout this time Rome was the unchallenged mistress of the Mediterranean world, wars rested, except in certain border areas, and the empire enjoyed a remarkable prosperity. In the main the emperors were capable chiefs, equal to the responsibilities imposed upon them; the administration, whether of justice or the finances, was conducted in accordance with fixed established norms; the army, dedicated to its military duty, did not invade the civil power and oppress the citizens; and travelers, bent on business or pleasure, moved easily and securely from one end of the empire to the other. *The two centuries following Augustus mark the zenith of Roman rule.*

Then a change occurred, at first no more than the shadow of a shade. Was it that incapable sovereigns mounted the throne, that the administrative system broke down, that the processes of production and exchange were paralyzed, that the army became unruly and took the power into its hands? Suffice it, that all these things, constituting a gradual dislocation of the *The breakdown of the third century followed by Diocletian's oriental absolutism.*

machinery of government and a deepening social chaos, occurred, not singly but together, and that they converted the third century into a period of frightful political disturbances. A constantly recurrent happening, alone sufficient to destroy the settled order, was that different sections of the army set up rival emperors, who fought each other without mercy. When the continued chaos had become intolerable, an emperor, Diocletian by name (284–305 A.D.), tried to save the situation by discarding the inherited system of government and setting up in its place an oriental despotism. The emperor now became an absolute monarch, whose power none might limit. But was such a restoration of external order anything more than a superficial makeshift? Even if we admit that Diocletian tinkered the broken administrative machine so that its wheels turned once more, it is certain that neither he nor the emperors after him attacked the gnawing social evils, which had by this time made their appearance, and which were engaged in slowly undermining the public health of the community.

The respective rôle of the Romans and the barbarians in the fall of the Roman empire. Undeniably no thorough social reformation was effected and the Roman empire slowly went to pieces chiefly from dry-rot, although there were many other contributory causes. Among these the most decisive was the ever-renewed attack of the barbarians, chiefly of Germanic race, restlessly moving along the northern frontier and searching for a convenient point of penetration. Although it must always be admitted that the barbarians were the immediate agents, visibly responsible for the wrecking of the Roman state, the fact remains that they were so few in numbers, so poorly armed, so divided among themselves, and so backward in the arts that they would have been impotent against the immense Mediterranean realm if Rome had retained a mere fraction of its early vigor. We may therefore affirm that, deeply considered, it was none other than the Romans themselves who destroyed the Roman empire; but since the barbarians acted as the wrecking crew, and since moreover they became the empire's residuary legatees, it is necessary, however hurriedly, to trace their relation to the Roman state.

As early as the time of Augustus (27 B.C.–14 A.D.) certain tribes of German barbarians on the Rhine gave prolonged and serious trouble to the empire, which was not overcome till a scientific system of defense had been established on a truly imperial scale along the Rhine and upper Danube. A hundred years after Augustus, the Emperor Trajan (98 A.D.–117 A.D.) ran into difficulties farther down the Danube, near its mouth, where a people, called the Dacians, dwelling in what is now known as Rumania, fell into the habit of crossing the river to plunder the Balkan provincials. The Dacians were not Germans and their depredations stood in no apparent relation to the restless barbarian activities along the Rhine. As the Dacians were relatives of the people to the south of them, the Thracians, who after a long and stubborn resistance to the Romans had ended by accepting the conqueror's yoke, it may be presumed that the Dacian attack was largely inspired by the fear that their turn at subjection would come next. In any case Trajan conducted a number of victorious campaigns against the Dacians, pursued them far up the valleys of the Carpathian mountains, and ended by incorporating their territory in the Roman empire (107 A.D.). The new province received the name of Dacia and, in the usual Roman manner, not only was endowed with highways, walled camps, and an orderly adminstration, but was also liberally planted with Roman veterans as colonists. For over a century and a half, from 107 to 274 A.D., Trajan's conquest remained in Roman hands and to all appearances was as thoroughly Romanized as the Balkan lands to the south.

Augustus, Trajan and other emperors protect the Roman border against barbarian inroads.

Augustus, Trajan, and their successors did the work of protecting the Roman border so well that nothing happened, to which we need give attention, till the third century. In this century, as we have already seen, not only did the imperial government break down, but the spreading social-economic cancer produced a general physical debility. Straightway the alert barbarians took advantage of the situation once more to assault the empire's defenses. Very likely, however, the border peoples decided to try conclusions with Rome not only because they found Rome to be weak, but also because they were made restless by wandering tribes pressing on them from the rear, which tribes were spurred on in their turn by agitated groups still farther inland. The ultimate cause of all this linked commotion was not improbably the yellow race, the terrible and war-like Mongolians of central Asia, who in the early Christian centuries

The probable cause of the migrations.

began a westward movement in search of pasturage and spoils. Irrespective of the somewhat uncertain causes, the fact remains that a feverish excitement seized all the peoples of the north and east of Europe, producing the remarkable phenomenon known as the Great Migrations. Of this movement of tribal disloca- tion the initial chapter was written when a powerful German tribe, the Goths, left their seats by the shores of the Baltic sea and moved southward, feeling for some soft spot in the Roman military line. In 274 A.D. they attacked Dacia, the ex- posed Roman province lying north of the Danube. Thereupon the Romans, pusillanimously giving up the struggle, retired to the south bank of the river. Dacia, the last won, was also the first lost of the Roman outposts against the barbarian advance.

The capital of the empire moved to New Rome, called Constanti- nople.   From the time of the Gothic conquest of Dacia the Danubian frontier was imperilled and the emperors were obliged to keep their attention riveted upon it. And since misfortunes never seem to come singly, a danger no less grave now lifted its head along the Asiatic frontier. Shortly before the coming of the Goths the Persian power had experienced a revival under a new, the Sassanian, dynasty and had no sooner gathered impetus than it threatened the whole group of Roman provinces in western Asia. To meet the double peril on the Danube and the Eu- phrates the emperor was compelled to spend much of his time in the East. Diocletian (284–305 A.D.), of whom we already know that he restored the empire administratively, went so far as actually to take up his residence at Nicomedia in Asia Minor; but Constantine, who, after being associated with a colleague, took over the power alone in 323 A.D., with a surer eye for a strategical position, selected as his seat of government (326) the old Greek colony Byzantium, on the European side of the Bosporus. Many a town was stripped of its monuments by Constantine to beautify the new capital, which at the touch of the imperial wand became in a surprisingly short time a magnifi- cent city, worthy to replace Rome as the center of the Mediter- ranean world. With this substitution in mind Constantine went so far even as to call his city New Rome; but the name Con- stantinople, commemorating the founder, gained an early cur- rency and has clung to the city to this day.

The transfer of the capital of the empire to Constantinople had important consequences. For one thing it made the Balkan peninsula what Italy had thus far been, the leading province of the empire; for another it so strengthened the empire in a military sense than the Persians on the eastern and the Goths on the northern frontier might carry off occasional victories, but could not permanently break through the long series of mountain barriers in Balkania and Asia Minor, which the emperors did their best to render impregnable. Besides, a field army, concentrated at or near Constantinople, could be hurriedly dispatched either in the direction of the Euphrates or the Danube to beat the enemies separately before they had arrived at an effective understanding.

Leaving the Persians for later consideration and attending to the more immediate enemy, the Germanic Goths, let us take note that a hundred years after the Goths had seized Dacia, a detached group, known thenceforth as West Goths, crossed the Danube and effected a lodgment in the Balkan peninsula. After conducting destructive marauding expeditions, from which hardly a section of the peninsula was spared, the West Goths were moved, largely by the persuasive argument of gold, to give up Balkania and to turn their faces to the west. It was around the year 400 A.D. that, under their king, Alaric, and carrying with them their women and children, their flocks and their possessions, they crossed the Alps and descended upon unprotected Italy.

At the very time when Alaric resolved to turn his attention to Italy, the Rhine frontier, so long a successful barrier against the barbarians moving in the direction of Gaul, began to give way. The effect of this double breakdown in Italy and Gaul was much as when a strong dyke yields, letting in the sea. Successive waves of Germans flooded the empire with such vehemence that every thought of resistance was given up. Some generations before this time, in the period of Diocletian, the division of the Roman realm into an empire of the East and an empire of the West had been carried through, largely with a view to securing a more prompt and effective defense at every point of the extensive frontier. But in the grave crisis of the fifth century the plan failed to work, especially in the West. Though the emperor of the East showed more vigor than his

Balkania the leading and best defended province of the empire.

The Goths turn westward.

The German barbarians penetrate the Rhine frontier.

western colleague, he was so completely taken up with the problems close at hand that he could send no aid to distant points. Left without support, the western emperor exhibited an amazing impotence. So far had the dissolution of Roman society gone that he had no army on which to rely and no steady flow of revenue. If by some measure of financial wizardry he succeeded in squeezing a little ready money out of an exhausted people, he was obliged to engage, as the only available soldier-material, mercenary barbarians, who of course completely dominated the situation and held him at their mercy. The decline of public spirit, one of the many symptoms of the universal Roman corruption, had, among other things, brought it about that men of Roman birth had long ago ceased to enter the army and, disused to arms, could no longer by even the most frantic appeals be persuaded to sacrifice themselves for their country.

The end of the Roman empire of the West. The details of the great disaster that followed in the West do not concern us here. Alaric, the West Goth, took Rome (410 A.D.), and is memorable in history as the first of its barbarian conquerors. Though he abandoned the city almost immediately after capturing it, the proof had been furnished that the Germans could come and go in the western empire at their pleasure. On Alaric's death his successor led his people into southern Gaul and thence to Spain, where they settled and founded a West Goth kingdom. The fifth century was still young when this event occurred, and in the subsequent decades, in an irresistible rush, the German tribes took over all the other western provinces. Northern Gaul fell victim to the Franks, Britain to the sea-faring and piratical Angles and Saxons, Africa to the adventurous Vandals, and Italy to the East Goths. The East Goths were a branch of the Gothic people who had stayed behind on the Danube and so were separated from the group called West Goths, whom Alaric led across the Alps to Italy. In 476 A.D. the western empire terminated what was left of a craven and dishonorable existence when Odovacer, a barbarian chief, forced the boy-ruler, Romulus Augustulus, to end a shadowy make-believe of sovereignty and retire to private life. Theoretically, it is true, the rule of the empire in the West was not extinguished, and passed with the abdication of the western representative to the Roman emperor of the East, but practically — and facts are, after all, what count in history — the West was appropriated by the German tribes and entered upon that phase of its history which we call the Middle Age and which presents as its leading feature the gradual assimilation of the German conquerors to Roman institutions and ideas, that is, to the remains of Mediterranean civilization.

For the Balkan student the point of peculiar interest in the great catastrophe is that Constantine's timely transfer of the capital to New Rome saved Balkania from the fate of the western provinces. Protected by the peninsula's mountain barriers, the eastern empire developed sufficient strength to beat off the Goths and to deflect them westward together with the massed Germans in their rear. On the dykes giving way in Italy and Gaul, the banked-up German waters discharged themselves in that direction. In doing so, however, they made a vacuum of much of the German homeland between the Danube and the Baltic sea, with weighty consequences for the whole East and particularly for our peninsula of Balkania. *Important results of the westward movement of the German invaders.*

In the great plain, eastward of the Germans, dwelt a people, called Slavs, who, like the Germans, belonged to the Indo-European family. When the Germans abandoned much of their homeland, the Slavs promptly seized the unclaimed territory and in the course of time put in an appearance in the lower Danube area, which, occupied in the third century by the Goths, had, beginning a century later, been by gradual stages again given up. From approximately 500 A.D. certain Slav tribes attempted to cross the Danube and effect a lodgment in Balkania, and although they were repeatedly hurled back by the Roman defenders, they persisted in their purpose, strengthened by a steady flow of reinforcements from the rear. As a result the Slavs became a permanent element in the racial evolution of the peninsula; in fact they came to signify for Balkania very much what the Germans signified for western Europe. Of both peoples we may, in a summary manner, state that, sound in limb and mind though backward in the arts, they served in their respective areas as agents of destruction, only to become in the slow passage of the years notable and invaluable instruments of social and political rebirth. *The coming of the Slavs.*

The coming of the Mongolians: the Huns.

But the Slavs were not the only people who, during the Great Migrations and following in the German wake, harassed the Balkan peninsula. The probable ultimate cause of the German and Slav unrest has already been suggested as likely to be found in predatory Mongolian tribes engaged in resistlessly pushing westward from their grazing grounds on the central Asiatic plateau. The first of these groups of yellow nomads to put in an appearance in Europe were the Huns. They swept triumphantly over Slavs and Germans alike, and toward the middle of the fifth century, under their great khan or ruler, Attila, established their power over the whole European East. Then they crossed the Rhine into Gaul. But here a limit was set to their conquests, for at Châlons (the Catalaunian Fields) the dying empire of the West summoned its last strength and with the aid of some of the German tribes, already firmly established on Roman soil, signally defeated the invaders (451 A.D.). Attila died soon after this disaster. His conquests, which had grown like a snow-ball, melted away like one, and the Huns themselves, the scourge and terror of their age, vanished from history as mysteriously as they had entered it. A faint reminiscence of them may survive in the geographic term, Hungary, the fertile plain of the middle Danube, where in their brief heyday they were wont to take up their winter quarters.[1]

But if the invasion of the Huns, taken by itself, was no more than a passing storm, it proved to be the forerunner of a whole series of invasions of Europe by Asiatic nomads of the yellow race. Capably organized from a military viewpoint and moving swiftly on horseback, they harassed Europe at practically every point, but none-the-less, obliged by their necessities, as herdsmen, to move westward via the grasslands to the north of the Black sea, they were inclined to honor the near-by Balkan peninsula with their particular attention. Here they met with opposition, as might be expected, from the enfeebled, though stubborn, Roman empire. But they encountered also another enemy, for the Slavs, engaged in appropriating the peninsula for themselves, naturally regarded whatever lands they held as their own and

Balkania the theater of a struggle among Slavs, Mongolians, and the Roman empire.

---

[1] It is quite probable that the mid-Danubian plain owes its name, Hungary, not to the Huns but to the later arrivals and present occupants, the Magyars, called Ugri, Ungri, Ungari in early documents.

defended their settlements with all their might and main. The result was a three-cornered politico-ethnological struggle which fills the annals of the Balkan world for many centuries after 500 A.D. In point of fact it constitutes the very kernel of Balkan medieval history.

Our swift review has brought us to the termination of the Roman epoch of Balkan history. Even before 500 A.D., it has been shown, the Roman empire had come to an effective end in the West, inasmuch as its authority had been overthrown and its provinces occupied by the victorious German tribes. However, at the other end of the Mediterranean, in the Constantinopolitan East, the fact stands out that the empire, though attacked by the Persians and sorely beset by the barbarous Slavs and Mongolians, continued to maintain itself. Doubtless this empire of the East, which by withstanding the shock of the Great Migrations had given proof of greater vitality than the empire of the West, is legally and traditionally the authentic *imperium romanum*. And yet how changed in aspect from the empire of the founder, Augustus! To begin with, the absolutism which had triumphed with Diocletian was not only a clear departure from Roman precedent but a conscious and deliberate imitation of the system of the orient, exemplified by all the monarchies from the Egypt of the Pharaohs to the Persia of Darius and Xerxes. Further and still more important, the lopping off of the western provinces meant the loss of the definite and characteristic Latin influences which had directed the growth of the state from infancy to manhood. The empire at Constantinople might continue to call itself Roman but its power rested in reality on Greeks and on the Greek inheritance. To this basic factor must be added the powerful oriental influences, emanating largely from Persia and particularly persistent and dominant throughout the empire's Asiatic provinces of Syria, Mesopotamia, and Asia Minor. Everything considered, it will be impossible to deny that the Roman empire of the East is, after 500 A.D., a state resting less on a Latin than on a Greco-oriental base. Scholars have yielded to this impression to such a degree that they have sanctioned the name Byzantine empire for this altered structure. Of course labels do not greatly matter, though they may be encouraged when they serve a useful purpose. Let us there-

End of the Roman, beginning of the Byzantine epoch of Balkan history.

fore agree that the Byzantine empire is in a legal sense the
Roman empire (or empire of the East), but that besides it is
a transformation so novel and far-reaching that we may date from
its assumption of a Greco-oriental garb the close of the Roman
and the beginning of a new, that is, the Byzantine epoch of
Balkan history.

BIBLIOGRAPHY

J. H. BREASTED, Ancient Times. A History of the Early World. (With
serviceable bibliographies at the end of the volume).

W. L. WESTERMANN, The Story of the Ancient Nations.

J. B. BURY, A History of Greece.

G. W. BOTSFORD, A History of Rome for High Schools and Academies.

A. H. KEANE, Man Past and Present.

BOTSFORD and SIHLER, Hellenic Civilization.

GERCKE und NORDEN, Einleitung in die Altertumswissenschaft.

E. GIBBON, The History of the Decline and Fall of the Roman Empire.
Edited in Seven Volumes by J. B. Bury.

The Cambridge Medieval History. Vol. I. Ch. 1 (Constantine and his City.)
Ch. 12 (The Asiatic Background).

J. JUNG, Roemer und Romanen in den Donaulaendern.

A. D. XÉNOPOL, Histoire des Roumains.

A. REINACH, L'Hellénisation du Monde Antique.

THE BYZANTINE EPOCH OF BALKAN
HISTORY

CHAPTER IV

THE AGE OF JUSTINIAN

ARRIVED at the Byzantine epoch of Balkan history, we shall proceed more deliberately. Our main concern during the period will be to follow the struggle conducted by the Byzantine empire with its Slav and Mongolian enemies in Europe and with the Persians and such other enemies as threatened it in its Asiatic provinces. The outstanding feature of the empire when our period opens may be stated thus: called Roman and legally Roman, it rested on a Greco-oriental civilization and was geographically an East-Mediterranean state, comprising the Balkan peninsula, Asia Minor, Syria, and Egypt. The peculiar Eurasian composition of the empire is pointedly brought out by the situation of the capital, Constantinople, at the gate of two continents. The Byzantine empire is an east-Mediterranean state.

Before going on with our narrative it will be well to look a little further into the reasons why the Roman empire continued in the East in sharp contrast to its complete collapse in the West. It goes without saying that certain forces and factors, absent in the West, must have made themselves felt at Constantinople. Some of these we have already noted. We have observed that the eastern emperor was able, largely by bribery and the resources of a subtle diplomacy, to deflect the West Goths from Balkania to Italy and that immediately afterwards the encouraged Germans penetrated everywhere into the undefended West. We must not ascribe too much merit to the eastern empire in thus diverting the German flood, since the Germans, dwelling largely on the Rhine and North sea, were by the forces of geography urged westward rather than southeastward; but the fact remains that the emperor of the East happily rid himself of the German peril. We are also aware that the mountainous character of the Balkan peninsula contributed to the defensive strength of the empire, while the broad Danube and the impregnable position of Constantinople must have com- Reasons for the continuance of the Byzantine empire: the forces of geography.

47

pleted the dismay of any barbarian chief, taking stock of the
general strategic situation before launching his warriors on an
enterprise directed against the eastern sovereign.

Effect of
Greek speech
and of the
Christian
religion.

But it would be a mistake to hold that the eastern empire
owed its perpetuation solely to accidents of nature. If it continued to live, its success may also be ascribed, and perhaps
preponderantly, to certain social and political factors. Made
up of Greeks, solidly planted throughout Hellas and along the
coast and more or less numerously scattered among the natives of
Syria, Asia Minor, and Egypt, it was unified to a notable extent
by the Hellenic language and culture. Moreover, since the age
of the Emperor Constantine this unity had been strengthened
by the bond of the Christian religion, passionately accepted by
the majority of the people and vigorously enforced by the state.
Speech, culture, and religion, always powerful ties, sufficed to
create a political sentiment, which, akin to patriotism and particularly active against barbarian outsiders, became a conspicuous
spiritual factor in holding the state together.

Reform
of the
army.

Equally important for the perpetuation of the empire was
the reorganization of the army and civil administration carried
through during the last decades of the fifth and the early decades
of the sixth century. The emperors Leo, Zeno, Anastasius, and
Justin, whose combined reigns cover the seventy years between
457 and 527 A.D., are the men who effected it. They were not
all equally capable and some of them possessed no more than
average energy and intelligence, but, considered as a group,
they grasped the point that unless they succeeded in putting
their house in order, it would inevitably be overwhelmed by the
same confusion, already disastrously manifest in the West. The
gravest single factor which confronted them was that the imperial army had become barbarian in head and members. The
cunning barbarian leaders were not slow to grasp the import
of this development, particularly in Italy, where a succession of
German chiefs had usurped control and reduced the emperor
to a puppet long before that famous barbarian, Odovacer, resolved (476 A.D.) to rid himself altogether of the august but
despicable manikin, whom he ostensibly served. In the eastern
half of the empire, barbarian chiefs, commanding barbarian
soldiery, threatened to acquire a similar ascendancy until Leo,

followed by Zeno, had the happy idea of establishing, as a counterweight, a native army. The Romans of the East were by this time as much disaccustomed to military service as their fellow-citizens of the West and had to be omitted from the imperial calculations. But in the Taurus mountains, in southern Asia Minor, there dwelt a hardy race, called Isaurians, untouched by civilization and about as rude and barbarous as the Germans and the Slavs. From them Leo, and Zeno after him, recruited an excellent force, which was not above committing acts of violence, but which, native to the East and incorporated in its system, was essentially loyal to the state. True, the East-Roman armies continued in Leo's day, and for all the centuries to come, to embrace considerable groups of foreigners; none-the-less that first native nucleus brought back an army responsive to the head of the state and made it forever impossible for German and Slav chiefs to play the masterful rôle at Constantinople, which Odovacer and his kind had taken upon themselves in the West.

At the same time the emperors, and particularly it would seem, Anastasius, carried through certain economic and financial reforms. By relaxing the tax on commerce, he stimulated trade and in the end more than made up the deficit, which was the first result of the measure. Besides, he introduced important administrative reforms, based on an improved collection of the taxes and the jealous personal audit of the sovereign. By such intelligent measures Anastasius not only rescued the state from debt but succeeded in leaving behind a treasure of several hundred thousand pounds of gold. A well-equipped army, at least partially native, and sound finances — these are the companion-pillars of a durable government everywhere and always, particularly in an absolutism.

Reform of the administration.

Thus at the beginning of the sixth century the empire at Constantinople had been given a fresh lease of life and seemed prepared to embark on an era of prosperity. It was Justinian, one of the most notable men in the whole long line of Roman emperors, who stepped forward to take advantage of the improved situation. Mounting the throne in succession to his uncle Justin, he ruled from 527 to 565 and planned, and carried through with a high hand, a wide-ranging and ambitious program.

Emperor Justinian, 527-565.

We shall be making excellent preparation for an understanding of the whole Byzantine period if we follow Justinian's policy with greater fullness than we have permitted ourselves so far.

Justinian resolves to reconquer the West.

Commanding a strengthened state and full of the pride of place, Justinian conceived a policy which revolved around the remarkable idea of ousting the German barbarians from the western provinces in order to assume once more the rule of the undivided Roman world. He discovered in Belisarius a general unusually gifted, and in 532 inaugurated his policy by dispatching an army against the Vandals in possession of northern Africa. Having with the greatest ease reconquered Africa, Belisarius crossed the Mediterranean and turned upon the East Goths, who since the end of the fifth century had been masters of Italy. The East Goths, in contrast to the Vandals, proved a hard nut to crack, and Belisarius, whom Justinian, perhaps from jealousy, stinted with insufficient supplies, had to be superseded by Narses, no less capable than the man whom he supplanted, before the last force of the Goths was shattered and Italy once more reduced to the imperial obedience (553). Justinian's military power was strong enough for him to send an expedition also against the West Goths and to seize from them and hold a part of Spain. But therewith the emperor had shot his bolt. Without doubt he appeared in the West in the rôle of conqueror, and after a long interval made the Germans tremble again before the Roman name, but his brilliant project of winning back all of the lost provinces remained a dream unrealizable under the new conditions prevailing in the world.

Justinian's wars with Persia.

Justinian's policy of imperial expansion looked not only westward but also to the East, where the recovered Persian empire, stretching westward beyond the Tigris and Euphrates, planted a troublesome thorn in the emperor's flesh. He engaged in many wars with the Persians, in which Belisarius together with other generals won distinction, but the campaigns were only intermittently successful and a generation of costly warfare brought the Romans no better reward than a restricted boundary and a diminished prestige. The Persians were an oriental people of high civilization, from whom the Romans learned much, both good and evil, but whose strength they broke so little that at a later time, as we shall see, the Roman state almost perished at their hands.

If the stir that Justinian made in his age was mostly due to his victorious warfare East and West, he deserves recognition from us of a later time chiefly because of events and changes which occurred at home. To begin with, he carried the absolutism of the emperors, which had for several generations been steadily gaining strength, to a new level. The occasion for this step was furnished by the famous Nika riots, which owe their name to the rallying-cry, *Nika* (conquer), of the rioters. These domestic commotions had their immediate origin in the passionate rivalry of the two factions of the circus, called the Greens and Blues. These factions served the curious function of backing each its particular color, green or blue, in the great chariot races, which constituted the leading public amusement of the capital. Carried away by the reckless spirit of partizanship, Greens and Blues went to such extraordinary lengths that bloody crowns and even deaths were no unusual termination of an ordinary day of sport. However, the fact was — and we need keep it in mind to account for the prevailing partizan fervor — under cover of sporting organizations the people combined to express themselves on the leading political, ecclesiastical, and economic issues of the day. Without doubt too the sectional rivalry, which prevailed within the walls of Constantinople and which was so marked a feature of all medieval cities, found explosive vent when the hostile local groups faced each other in the vast race-course. While many of the political factors, which entered into the Nika rebellion, remain obscure, it is clear that the riot was more than an accidental clash among the spectators of a chariot-race, and that an attempt was made, under cover of the excitement released by the games, to depose the emperor; and it is no less certain that the emperor, having won the victory, reformed or modified the popular organizations of the Blues and Greens, divesting them, as far as in him lay but certainly without permanent success, of their character of political parties capable of bringing pressure to bear upon the government.

It is impossible to close the Nika incident without at least a passing reference to the Empress Theodora. One of the most

Justinian carries Roman absolutism to its climax.

The Empress Theodora

enigmatical characters of history, she will probably never have her genuine personality disengaged from the mass of legends and calumnies which have thrown an almost impenetrable veil about her. Of low birth and questionable morals but possessed of rare beauty and fascination, she gained such an ascendancy over Justinian that he not only raised her to the purple, but so greatly valued her judgment that, so long as she lived, he sought her opinion in all matters of state. On the occasion of the Nika outburst she showed a brilliant courage and probably saved the state, for she turned Justinian's thoughts from flight and developed the plan of action which resulted in victory.

Justinian claims to be both the administrative and the spiritual head of the church. Having placed his foot on the neck of the people by gaining unquestioned control of civil affairs, Justinian next turned his attention to religion and the church. One of his first acts in this field of activity was to close the philosophical schools of Athens, which still, though in a desiccated, pedantic manner, nursed the dying embers of paganism. Henceforth there was to be in the eastern empire only Christian learning, guided by the Christian church. But what was to be the relation of the emperor to that church? Ever since the days of Constantine the rulers had pursued the plan of making the church subject to the state, that is, to themselves, and in this policy they had been measurably successful. But Justinian went further. He undertook to settle by his imperial word not only matters pertaining to the administration of the church but also all questions of faith and doctrine, exactly as if he were the superior of bishops and councils and the spiritual head of the system. It throws light on his personal prestige that no one dared oppose his presumptions. Clearly, however, this Caesaropapism, as his unlimited control of both church and state has rather lumberingly been called, was not in accordance with Christian tradition, especially in the West, where the pope enjoyed an immense authority and was sure, sooner or later, to register an objection to Justinian's ecclesiastical usurpation.

The prevailing metaphysical state of mind produces theological disputes. It is difficult, perhaps impossible, for a practical-minded modern man to conceive to what an extent in that East-Mediterranean world the religious decrees of the emperor and the debates of bishops, abbots, and learned men over such metaphysical subtleties as the nature of Christ and his relation to God, the Father, engaged public attention. We must remind ourselves that the Greeks from of old were devoted to dialectic and sophistry and that, on becoming Christians, they naturally brought this characteristic to bear on the new faith. Barbers and greengrocers, we are told, stopped haggling with their customers over prices to pursue the more passionate inquiry whether Christ had a single or a double nature, whether he was divine or both human and divine. The emperor and the church councils might, in the interest of unity and orthodoxy, hand down a decision on doctrinal points and declare all contrary opinion to be heresy, but their high authority was far from putting a quietus on discussion. Governmental prohibitions notwithstanding, underground theological opposition flourished vigorously, exploding from time to time in a dangerous outburst of heresy. Such movements more particularly characterized the Asiatic provinces, where Armenians, Syrians, and other non-Hellenic peoples made their home. As these national groups more or less retained their separate racial consciousness, it is highly probable that their departure from strict Constantinopolitan orthodoxy not only was due to the individual character of their Christianity but also was conceived by them as a means of registering a protest against the absolutism and excessive centralization of the imperial government. In other words the numerous Asiatic heresies, which vexed Justinian as well as his successors, were not without a strong taint of politics.

The nimble mental gymnastics of the Byzantine Greeks, though manifestly beyond the powers of the men of our day, do not fill us, with our different and often directly antipodal orientation, either with envy or with admiration. In our practical, pedestrian manner we require of intellectualism that it shall have a definite human purpose and concretely advance the life of man on earth. This the arid dogmatism of the Byzantines did not do and had no idea of doing, as is sufficiently disclosed by the fact that science was utterly neglected, and that literature, though still cultivated, owing to the persistence of the noble tradition of antiquity, became heavy and prolix and lost every trace of spontaneity and freshness. As we feel our way among the learned circles of Constantinople, as disputatious and crabbed as an assemblage of typical, provincial pedagogues, we become aware that the sun of classical inspiration has sunk below the

Rise and spread of the medieval temper.

horizon and that a mental twilight was gaining ground wherein the only source of illumination was the flickering taper of Christian hope and superstition. Here, as in the Latin West, the Middle Age was knocking at the door.

Justinian codifies the Roman Law. And yet in some fields, where it had particularly deep roots, the old pre-Christian tradition continued to manifest its vigor and in none more effectively than in the department of law. In this province the Romans, by virtue of their natural gift for organization, had distinguished themselves for centuries. However, the accumulation in recent generations of new imperial statutes, out of harmony with the ideas and practices of the older pagan period, had gradually produced a serious confusion in the courts and all the administrative bureaus. This growing chaos Justinian resolved to remove by the issue of a collection of the laws, which was to be authoritative and which was called the *Code* (529). This he followed after a few years with a publication called the *Digest*, which reproduced in condensed form and under convenient classifications the opinions of leading jurists for ages back; and finally, he concluded his magnificent reorganization with the *Institutions*, to be used as a handbook in the schools of law, and the *Novellae*, the official register of the statutes of his own reign. Of course the burdensome professional work in connection with these monumental compilations was not done by the emperor but by expert commissions, of which a jurist by the name of Tribonian was the leading light. But the emperor's initiative was undeniable, and as the various labors enumerated were successful in effecting an improved articulation of the government machine, he certainly put the empire in his debt. Moreover, for all succeeding generations of men down to our own day Justinian's codifications have proved an inexhaustible treasure of legal and administrative theory and practice.

Origin and characteristics of Byzantine art. Perhaps along no line of human endeavor was there supplied more conclusive proof than in the arts that the age of Justinian was a transition period, in which, if evidences of decay abounded, promising seeds of a new life, largely of religious inspiration, were not lacking. A distinct Byzantine style took shape which found expression more particularly in architecture and painting, though it was applied also with notable success to such ingenious crafts as ivory, metal, and enamel work. Byzantine art, like all art-forms whatever, is of complicated origin. Without question it must be conceived as the offspring, in the main, of classical art, from which it inherited its technic and the body of its forms. But, in touch with the orient, particularly with Persia, it became imbued with the color-sense and passion of the East for intricate, abundant ornament. Finally, it was both spiritually and materially concerned with the church and Christianity, which, wholly dominating the age, turned the thoughts of men from sin to salvation, from the harsh struggle on earth to the joys of an imagined heaven. These three influences, classicism, orientalism, and Christianity, merged in Byzantine art to give birth to a remarkable product. With the passing of time the classical inheritance, making for fluency, grace, and truth to nature, tended to become weaker, while the dry, didactic spirit of Christian theology, replacing the earlier religious fervor, increasingly gained the upper hand. Between the two influences, orientalism, neither perceptibly waxing nor waning, continued to serve as a connecting link.

The most memorable and impressive work within the field of Byzantine art was done in architecture. Long before Justinian's day the Christians had felt the need of suitable houses of worship, and since the pagan temple with its small cella, hidden within the peristyle, offered an enclosed space wholly inadequate to hold the crowds attending worship, the Christian authorities were obliged to cast about for something different and more spacious. They decided in favor of the basilica, a Roman building used for holding court. This with its rows of parallel columns, falling into a central nave flanked with aisles, was, on the whole, well adapted to the needs of the new service. The first Christian monument of note, this house of worship, called basilica in honor of the source from which it came, flourished throughout the Roman world but chiefly on Italian soil in the period following Constantine's conversion. The architects of Justinian's age took it over, together of course with the rest of the classical inheritance which had come down to them; but though they built houses of worship in the basilican style, they developed also another type of church, which enjoyed particular favor in the East and of which the distinguishing feature was

Early Christian architecture.

its circular design. Sooner or later the thought would come to these architects, borne on a wave of inspiration, to combine the most striking feature of the circular church, the soaring cupola, with the length and spaciousness of the basilica.

Byzantine architecture. The crowning achievement in this new type, representing the fusion of two earlier forms, in fact the crowning monument of the whole Byzantine school, is St. Sophia, the church of Holy Wisdom in Constantinople. Though for the last four centuries it has been made to do service as a Mohammedan mosque, St. Sophia still stands, enjoying an admiration such as is reserved for only a few of the greatest monuments of time. We are told that Justinian laid the foundation-stone, in the year 532, on the site of an earlier church destroyed in the Nika rebellion, and that he chose for architect Anthemius of Tralles (in Asia Minor), a name which the world has not held in the honor it deserves. To one entering the nave, filled with dim, suffused light, the numerous details of the architectural composition may be at first confusing, but presently each element springs to its appointed place and the eye travels upward until it is held spell-bound by the central dome. There are higher cupolas in the world than this, which rises to a height of one hundred and eighty feet from the stone pavement, but there is none which crowns so naturally and nobly a living framework of related parts.

Byzantine mosaics. Painting too, took an original turn in Justinian's day. It is particularly noteworthy that the artists, without exactly abandoning the older technic of wall and panel painting, developed a peculiarly brilliant and durable color-medium in the mosaic. Mosaics are constructed of little cubes of colored glass and stone fitted together into a design, often as elaborate and full of figures as any canvas executed with fluid pigment. Properly classified as painting by virtue of its use of color, form, and composition, the mosaic rose to great popularity among the Byzantines. Something about the vivid color and deep glow which it achieved appealed to the semi-oriental feeling of the people with the result that no church was looked on as complete, the walls of which lacked the subtle enrichment of this form of painting. It is to be regretted that almost all the Byzantine mosaics which have reached us belong to the time after Justinian and do not permit us clearly to estimate the work of his generation. It is established, however, beyond challenge that the mosaic achieved an important development in the sixth century and that, taken in connection with the great creations of contemporary architecture, which needed the mosaic for their full effect, it constitutes one of the most distinguished expressions associated in any place or period with Christianity.

It is certain that a civilization which, in spite of signs of senility, was as creative as this of the age of Justinian, must have rested on at least a relatively solid economic basis. Unfortunately the contemporary records, concerned primarily with politics and religion, communicate very little on this head, but from scattered indices we are permitted to gather that the reputation of Constantinople was firmly established as a hive of industry and a mart of commerce. The city's artisans produced jewelry, pottery, and weapons, but, most of all, apparently their silk-goods enjoyed the favor of contemporaries. It sheds a ray of modern utilitarian light on the old autocrat and theologian to learn that it was Justinian himself who called the silk industry into being by acclimating the silk-worm of China in his dominions, thereby securing to the industrial establishments which had arisen a steady supply of their basic product. *Industry and trade under Justinian.*

The capital's vast population, which may have reached one million souls, was as cosmopolitan then as now. In its streets and squares haughty, silk-clad Greek officials touched elbows with half-Hellenized Syrians and Egyptians, with fire-worshiping Persians, with yellow Mongolians from beyond the Caspian sea, and with rough, bearded Slavs from the Danube area. The presence of so many kinds of foreigners itself suffices to indicate a flourishing trade with all the territories of the known world. In this trade the wheat of Egypt was of vital concern, for from it was baked the bread of the capital, while from the heart of Asia came, by caravan to some Black sea port, to be shipped thence by boat to the Bosporus, the spices, perfumes, and rich embroidered stuffs of India and China. In the days before Justinian the usual westward route of this oriental trade had been across Persia to the great cities on the Syrian coast; but the long Persian wars, by throwing a barrier across this passage, had obliged the merchants to use either the Black sea route to Constantinople, just indicated, or else the Red sea route to Alexandria in Egypt. If *Constantinople the world's metropolis.*

to this eastern trade we add the important trade with the western Mediterranean, in which hundreds of galleys were engaged, we can entertain no doubt that in the sixth century and for many centuries thereafter, Constantinople was not only the most learned and civilized, but also the busiest and richest city of the world. A sight-seeing visitor from foreign parts looking down upon it from a height along the Bosporus and noting, spread beneath his feet, the harbor crowded with merchantmen, the sunlit wharves and markets black with moving throngs, the spacious palaces set in emerald gardens, the numerous monasteries and parish churches, and finally, noble St. Sophia's soaring dome, must have broken into a spontaneous exclamation of pleasure and admiration.

CHAPTER V

THE SLAV AND MONGOLIAN INVASIONS. — NEW PERSIAN WARS AND THE RESCUE OF THE EMPIRE BY HERACLIUS

AMIDST the choric praise sounded by the wars, the legislation, the commerce, the industry, and the arts of Justinian's reign, there rose, ever higher and shriller, a note of despair from the region of the Danube. It issued from his Balkan subjects, exposed not only to injuries inflicted by roving bands of barbarous Slavs but to the worse suffering imposed by the savage nomad hordes, hailing from western Asia and the grasslands of the Black sea. It is a curious circumstance that Justinian was at no particular pains to come to the relief of his suffering people. Were his resources exhausted by the long and costly wars in Italy and Persia? Or — a suspicion that will not be downed — was there a fatal debility beneath the brilliant surface of his reign? Whatever the cause, Justinian failed to make safe his northern boundary, with the result that Slavs and Asiatics alike persisted in their raids and, in the course of the sixth century, gradually changed the racial and social aspect of the peninsula.

The Balkan border harassed by Slavs and Mongolians.

why?

We have already noted that both Slavs and Mongolians shared in the Great Migrations. The Slavs, a white people of Indo-European stock, first pushed toward the Danube after the departure of the last Goths for Italy. Around the year 500 A.D., we hear of their earliest raids into the Balkan peninsula. From then on, year in, year out, with few exceptions, these raids were repeated. Executed by small bands, they were conducted at first for plunder; but when, in the course of time, the Slavs made the discovery that, in consequence of the prolonged disturbances, the whole interior was strikingly underpopulated they took to settling on the waste territories. Thus there occurred a Slav infiltration into the peninsula, which had some of the aspects of a conquest effected by force, and yet was much more decisive than most conquests reported by history, because it gave the soil itself and the fruits thereof to the victors.

Slav infiltration beginning about 500 A.D.

How SlAVS ARRIVED IN the Balkan

But the Slav infiltration had hardly begun when there befell the invasions of an entirely different people: I refer to the yellow Mongolians from Asia. We have already met one of their groups, the Huns, who under their leader Attila were the scourge of Europe during the first half of the fifth century. The Huns were the vanguard of the Mongolian migrations which broke over Europe in successive waves through all the period of the Middle Age. Whether because of the failure of pasturage on the broad steppes of west-central Asia, where these nomads were at home, or because of the need of expansion due to natural increase of numbers, they began a westerly movement into Europe and, with periodic interruptions, persisted in it for centuries. Projected from the time of Justinian as a factor into the peninsula, they invite an examination of their customs and characteristics.

The Mongolians are a very sharply defined branch of the human family. An Indo-European is at once struck by their yellow skin, flat faces, oblique eyes, and short, stocky bodies. The Byzantine chroniclers, who observed them with an interest stimulated by fear and aversion, reported that they wore their shiny, black hair in a fashion unusual in Europe by letting it fall in a braid down their backs. They also remarked with amazement upon the bow-shaped legs of the Asiatics, so weak and bent from constant life on horseback that the dismounted warriors waddled awkwardly like ducks. Their chief weapon was the bow and arrow, and as they fought in cavalry formation on small, shaggy horses extraordinarily swift of movement, they were incalculably more mobile than the Europeans who fought preferably as foot-soldiers. Furthermore, since they had learned in their desert warfare the advantage to be derived from having over them a supreme chief, they possessed an organization and a discipline which made it very difficult to stop them, as with their herds and families, a veritable people on the march, they burst into Europe. The Slavs in particular, who were their nearest Caucasian neighbors and who, organized in small, disconnected tribes, possessed a very inferior power of resistance, went down before them like a wall of lath.

The Mongolian invasions of Balkania, which may be described as an endless succession of swift and terribly destructive raids, set in, in the main, at the same time as those of the Slavs, that is, about 500 A.D. However, in sharp distinction from the Slavs, who came to settle and work the land as peasants, the Mongolians, who had no acquaintance with agriculture, concerned themselves primarily with plunder. In consequence their descents from the Danube were like summer storms, often woefully destructive on the surface, but effecting no very fundamental changes. To this general rule there were of course exceptions. That terrible group, for instance, the Huns under Attila, camped on the middle Danube long enough to found a rudimentary state, which maintained itself for a short time. After the disappearance of the Huns, the next tribe calling for closer scrutiny, because something more than a flash in the pan, is the Avars. This people, worthy successors of the dreaded Huns, arrived in the Danube area about 550 A.D., at a time therefore, when, by the inconspicuous infiltration characteristic of the Slavs, many of their bands had already succeeded in getting a foothold in the peninsula. Thus, issuing respectively from the north and east, Slavs and Avars established contact on the northern rim of the Byzantine empire.

The Mongolians, as nomads, preeminently birds of passage.

It was not till the end of his reign that the Emperor Justinian became actively alarmed at the situation and fitted out an army with the immediate purpose of driving out those Slav groups which had impudently taken up their residence on Balkan soil. But to his disgust his army was defeated, and scattered bands of Slav marauders, crossing the Balkan mountains, were not stopped until they reached the walls of Constantinople. In this unexpected crisis the dismayed Justinian bethought himself of a scheme for getting rid of his enemies which, already employed by an occasional predecessor, remained for centuries to come a favorite device of Byzantine diplomacy, and which, at times successful, at other times proved, like all over-cunning intrigues, a veritable boomerang. He planned to destroy his nearer enemies, the Slavs, through the happy instrumentality of his more distant foe, the Avars. In the roving manner of herdsmen, the Avars had settled along the middle Danube, in the very region where their relatives, the Huns, had entrenched themselves over a hundred years before. With the lure of gold Justinian induced the Avars to attack the Slavs, with the result

Justinian tries to win security by setting the Avars on the Slavs.

that the loosely associated Caucasians were, after a short struggle, overcome and brought as dependents under the yoke of the roving Asiatics. But if the Avars, drawn by the dream of power, were ready to make the most of the Slavs as serfs supplying food throughout the year and as an infantry support in time of war, they were by no means minded to treat the Byzantine empire with superstitious reverence. Justinian had hardly died (565) when sometimes with, sometimes without, their Slav dependents, they thoroughly raided the peninsula as far south as the Aegean sea. Thus the crafty game of setting one foe on the other in the hope of having dog eat dog brought, except for a momentary easement, no relief to the harassed state.

The critical situation after Justinian's death.

It was indeed a perilous situation which confronted Justinian's successors. What made it worse was that the empire showed a sudden and alarming weakness, due in part no doubt to Justinian himself, who had sapped the country's vigor with his numerous and expensive military enterprises. At any rate, on his demise in 565, a crisis followed. The Slav raids were resumed, made worse by the participation of the ruthless Avars; and while the emperors, who followed one another in rapid succession, were still hesitating about the means to adopt to end the Balkan misery, the situation became further complicated by the return of the Persian menace. We have observed that Justinian had curbed but not annihilated his eastern rival. Persia was an absolutism, ably conducted in the main, with a well organized army, ample material resources, and a high civilization of an oriental type. It is proper once more to remind ourselves that the oriental flavor of Byzantine society, the love of color, titles, and display, was largely the result of Persian influence. Persia in its turn borrowed freely from Byzantium, and altogether Persia and East Rome were engaged throughout the centuries of which we are treating in a lively exchange of goods, ideas, and customs.

Renewed war with Persia, 572–91.

Justinian was hardly in his grave when the Persian king resolved on a new attack. A twenty years' war followed (572–91), which absorbed all the energy of the Byzantine state. On the whole the Greeks gave a fairly good account of themselves, though unable at any time to strike the enemy a decisive blow. Finally, on civil war breaking out in Persia, the emperor, Maurice by name, was able to take advantage of the situation by concluding a peace which sacrificed no essential interest of the state.

It was high time, for, engaged to the limit of their power with the Persians, the Byzantines had wholly neglected their northern or Balkan front. In consequence the Slavs and the Avars came and went in the peninsula at pleasure, and to all appearances the Slavs, a peasant folk on the lookout for plow-land, scored a great success by considerably extending their settlements. A Greek chronicler belonging to this time,[1] amidst loud lamentations, unfolds a picture from which we are obliged to conclude that the Byzantine natives, owing to the perpetual forays, have vanished from a wide area, and that the whole interior of Balkania has been practically converted into a land of Slavs.

New raids of the Slavs and Avars.

As soon as the Persian war was off his hands, the Emperor Maurice, fearing the complete loss of the Balkan plateau, made preparations to drive out the enemy. Maurice was a well-meaning man who, by his unusual thrift, had aroused the contempt of the lazy, splendor-loving populace of the capital, and who, by the rigorous economies introduced into the administration of the army, had stirred his mercenary soldiers to suspicion and wrath. In 602, while campaigning on the Danube against Slavs and Avars, the army encountered tremendous hardships; it raised a wild outcry against the superior officers and finally mutinied. Naming as leader a centurion, Phocas by name, it turned its back on the enemy and swept, like an avalanche, on Constantinople. When the light-minded citizens, equally out of sorts with their ruler, received the rebels with joy, Maurice recognized at once that his cause was lost. He tried to flee, was apprehended on the Asiatic shore of the Bosporus, and was forced to view the ruthless slaughter of his four sons before he was himself charitably accorded the boon of death. In his room the mutinous centurion was made emperor amidst the applause of a concourse of soldiers and citizens.

Failure and death of Emperor Maurice, 602 A.D.

The reign of Phocas (602–10) brought nothing less than anarchy and ruin. The emperor, who was only a brutal soldier of low origin, is reported by contemporaries to have been as repulsive in feature as he was weak and depraved in character.

The disastrous reign of Phocas, 602–10.

[1] John of Ephesus. Bury II, 118, note.

Worst of all, from the point of view of the state, he was a totally incapable administrator and when the political dangers, which Maurice had at least courageously confronted, rushed upon him, he showed neither counsel nor resolution. The Persian king renewed the war in the East and had the audacity to ravage Syria and Asia Minor; one of his captains even penetrated to Chalcedon on the Bosporus within sight of Constantinople. Over the Balkan peninsula the Slavs and Avars roamed at will, or if they desisted for a season, it was because the wretched Phocas purchased their inactivity with a bribe of money. Before long all classes, both at the capital and in the provinces, agreed that nothing could save the state but the removal of the " monster." An appeal was made to Heraclius, governor of the province of Africa, and Heraclius, himself too old to act, sent his son, another Heraclius, with a fleet to Constantinople. The mere appearance of this force sufficed to overthrow the sceptred coward. Deserted by all, he was brought in chains before his conqueror and promptly cut to pieces on the ship's deck. To the victor belonged the crown and its responsibilities, and without delay Heraclius was proclaimed emperor.

The essential vitality of the Byzantine empire. Let us pause for a moment to reflect on the curious vicissitudes of the Byzantine state. When the Roman empire failed in the West, it was in the East, as we have seen, rescued in the nick of time by the revival effected under Leo and Zeno and bearing notable fruit indeed in the age of Justinian. Then, after Justinian came another decline, which in the reign of Phocas again threatened extinction. However, under the new emperor, Heraclius, this decline, as we shall see, was checked and followed once more by a renewal. These ups and downs, these successive violent crises, were destined to remain characteristic of the Byzantine empire throughout the centuries of its existence. They argue weakness no doubt, but also vitality, and the vitality deserves to be particularly underscored in view of the contemptuous judgment which all the older historians have pronounced on the empire, and which it is difficult to eradicate or even to modify because it has received the endorsement of the great Gibbon.[1]

---

[1] Gibbon's verdict on the thousand years of Byzantine history as " a uniform tale of weakness and misery " has passed from writer to writer.

However, recent historians have shown conclusively that, owing
to the religious controversies and political clashes of the Middle
Age, we have indulged in a western, Latin bias against the
eastern empire, and that this bias has caused us to concentrate
on what was diseased and despicable in Byzantium to the exclusion of what was sound and admirable. An objective presentation, based on the greatly enlarged information of our day,
may hope in the course of time to popularize a less prejudiced
attitude. Not only shall we then give credit to the eastern
empire for a civilization higher than anything the West knew till
the period subsequent to the crusades, but we shall also freely
acknowledge the invaluable services performed by the empire, in
its own interest indeed, but ultimately for the benefit of the whole
of Europe, in beating off a long succession of Asiatic invaders.
Last, and best of all perhaps, we shall occupy ourselves less
with the details of eastern "weakness and misery" than with
the unexhausted supplies of vigor evidenced by the repeated
rebounds from disaster.

The Heraclian rebound owed its initiative, it is true, to one
man, the emperor, but it was shared by clergy and people and
unquestionably bears the aspect of a general social revival. To
seize its merits we must have clearly before us the main elements
of the situation on Heraclius' accession. Large parts of the
Asiatic provinces of the empire were firmly held by the victorious
Persians, while the Balkan peninsula had become the almost
undisputed possession of the Slavs and Avars; the revenues of
the state had greatly dwindled with disastrous consequences for
both army and navy; finally, the policy of free bread and free
shows, the policy of *panis et circenses*, taken over by New Rome
from the mother-city on the Tiber, had made the population of
the capital idle, turbulent, and inclined to accept as the only desirable end of life the immediate gratification of the senses.

*The revival
under the
Emperor
Heraclius.*

Heraclius' chief title to being considered a great man is his
recognition of the fact that a slow and patient reconstruction of
the institutions and manners of his country was the necessary
preliminary to its rescue. What, stripped of power and resources, could he hope to effect against the Persians, whose
forces, now permanently stationed on the Bosporus, could be
seen from the palace windows, and who paused at the farther

*Political
and moral
factors in
the revival.*

shore for no other reason than that, as a land power, they were incapable of forcing the straits? What could he hope to do against the Slavs and Avars except feebly to set them by the ears in the tricky manner of Justinian? Incisive economies, a total reorganization of the embarrassed treasury, the gradual accumulation of ships, and the enlistment and training of troops would have to be continued for years before he could hope to challenge his numerous enemies with the least chance of success. And since reforms are no more than hollow gestures unless supported by the fire of a great and popular conviction, Heraclius felt that he would, above all, have to alter fundamentally the moral tone of Constantinople. The test came when the Persians, already in possession of Syria, penetrated across the isthmus of Suez to Egypt, from whose fertile soil was wont to come the grain used for feeding, at the expense of the state, the indolent Constantinopolitan masses. Automatically with the loss of Egypt the grain shipments to the Bosporus ceased. Great was the suffering and tremendous the consternation in the capital, but gradually, under the sting of necessity, many habitual metropolitan idlers turned to productive work, while others, in return for bread, consented to join the army and undergo its unwonted discipline. The lamented loss of Egypt had proved a blessing in disguise!

Spread and vigor of the Christian crusading spirit.

Meanwhile the clergy, stirred to the depths of their being by the close-hovering Persian fire-worshipers, spared no effort to arouse the people to a passionate defense of their homes and altars. By this time the spirit of antiquity, long moribund, was dead, and in its place the characteristic medieval spirit reigned from high to low, from emperor and patriarch to simple boatman of the Golden Horn. If men, entangled in the maze of Christian aspiration, were slow to meet their civic duty for its own sake, they might still be made to act, and act enthusiastically, at the bidding of the saints in heaven and for the salvation of their souls. This exalted state of mind gradually gained the upper hand and is significantly illuminated by the rôle played by a piece of wood, a mere religious symbol. In the course of their triumphant march westward the Persians had captured Jerusalem and carried to their own country the Holy Cross, which, miraculously recovered from its hiding-place in the days

of Constantine, the first Christian emperor, was cherished as the
most sacred relic in existence. Its capture by heathen fire-
worshipers was universally felt to be an insufferable disgrace.
By incessant appeals, the patriarch of Constantinople and his
numerous clergy succeeded in inflaming the people to such a
pitch of religious fury that with one voice they asked to be led
against the infidel. Heraclius, who fully shared the common
emotion, was quick to turn it to political advantge. By aid of
it he welded his army into a magnificent machine, moved by the
spirit of blind devotion, and when he was at last ready to take
the field, he initiated a campaign which bore all the characteristic
traits of a crusade.

During the long years of preparation when Heraclius labored
at the regeneration of the state, he suffered with admirable self-
control the many indignities heaped upon him by the Persian
king to the east and the Avar khan to the north. The pride
and contempt, especially of the eastern monarch, Chosroes by
name, who had at last realized the ancient Persian dream of a
Mediterranean empire, and was in apparently secure possession
of about two-thirds of the Roman territory, knew no bounds.
In an epistle in which he summoned Heraclius to surrender without delay, he styled himself "the king and master of the whole
earth" and referred to Heraclius as "his vile and insensate
slave." His hyperbolic language conveys a good idea of the
unreality, amounting, to the western mind, almost to fatuity,
which has habitually distinguished the mentality of oriental monarchs. However much stung in his heart, Heraclius quietly suffered the abuse of the vainglorious Persian until, after twelve
long years of constructive activity, in the year 622 he considered himself ready for the field. Suddenly, and without warning, he assumed the offensive and carried the war into the East.
And then it was seen that, though already proved a statesman,
he was no less a gifted general, for in battle after battle he
routed the Persian foe. But even without their brilliant leader,
by their massed strength alone, his forces were probably invincible, since, animated with tireless crusading fervor, they broke
through every obstacle. In a last desperate effort to save himself from the ultimate consequences of defeat the Persian monarch entered into an alliance with the Avars and elaborated a

Heraclius
attacks and
defeats the
Persian
king.

plan for a simultaneous descent upon Constantinople from the west and east, from Europe and Asia.

The siege of Constantinople, 626. In the year 626 there followed, as the climax of the war, the siege of Constantinople, memorable as the first serious attack ever made on the city. It owed its formidable character to the fact that, while the Persians brought an army to the Asiatic shore of the Bosporus, the Avars crossed the Balkan peninsula and appeared before the walls of the city. Unfortunately for their plan the two allies could not effectively coöperate as they were separated by the wide strait controlled by the Greek fleet. When the Avars, who, we hear, brought with them great masses of subject Slavs to help in the siege, ventured to launch an attack from the Bosporus, their light vessels were annihilated by the Roman galleys and their Slav crews killed or drowned. The Persians, who had no ships at all, were forced to play the part of spectators on their side of the Bosporus and to let their allies bear the brunt of the fighting. After some weeks these had received all the punishment they could stand and gloomily withdrew. The baffled Persians followed suit and the siege was over. On this and every subsequent occasion it was shown that only an assailant possessing the preponderance on both land and sea was dangerous to Constantinople.

The complete triumph of Heraclius, 628. On the heels of this failure the foundations of Persia seemed to give way. The Roman armies, breaking down all resistance, swept on into Mesopotamia; the boastful Chosroes, whose reason, never over-sound, yielded completely under the blows of fate, was seized by his own outraged people and cast — picturesque but ominous name! — into the Castle of Forgetfulness; and the humbled heir to the throne, aware that the end was at hand, threw himself on the mercy of the victor. In 628, on terms which gave back to the empire all the land it had ever possessed in the East, Heraclius signed such a peace with Persia as not even Justinian had been able to wrest from the foe.

Complete restoration of the empire. The victory of Heraclius compassed the ruin of Persia. True, Heraclius himself spared the defeated state, but before a recovery could be effected, the Arab power arose in the East and under its fanatic onset Persia finally crumbled. The restored east-Roman empire, too, was destined, if not to perish, at least to be brought to the brink of extinction by these same Arabs;

but that tale belongs to another chapter. Let us at this point content ourselves with noting that Heraclius' Persian triumph restored to the empire its Asiatic provinces as well as Egypt, and carried the emperor to the crest of the wave. It helps define the new, the medieval spirit which prevailed, to note that an article of the treaty of peace called for the return of the Holy Cross, and that when Heraclius, the heir of pagan Rome and the successor of Caesar and Augustus, entered Constantinople, the *via triumphalis* led to the Christian temple of St. Sophia, where the climax of the celebration for the delivery of the state from a heathen foe was reached when the recovered Cross was uplifted over the kneeling prince and people, in token of their covenant with Christ.

CHAPTER VI

THE SLAVS

The passing of the Avars. THE downfall of Persia under the hammer blows of the Emperor Heraclius synchronizes with the decline of that other power, the Avars, who, during the Persian crisis, had pressed so cruelly upon the Byzantine empire from the west. The unsuccessful siege of Constantinople in 626 practically marks their last appearance in southeastern history. They withdrew to their encampment on the middle Danube, from which, as a center, they continued their plundering expeditions, henceforth, however, directing them chiefly westward against the Germans. Before long many of the tribes of subject Slavs rose against them and threw off their yoke. Like Mongolian folk in general, who, as nomads, move over the earth but drop no roots in it, the Avars developed a temporarily irresistible power but failed in the end for lack of persistence. After being feared for a season as a veritable scourge of God, they followed the precedent set by their kinsmen, the Huns, and on meeting with a final crushing defeat (796) at the hands of the great king of the Franks, Charlemagne, they vanished from history leaving no rack behind.

The policy of Heraclius and his successors toward the Slavs. The passing of the Avars made the Balkan interior the undisputed dominion of the Slavs. We may be sure that with the removal of the Persian peril, Heraclius turned his attention to Balkania, but regarding the details of his policy the contemporary chroniclers supply very few indications. As the Slavs, already widely settled through the peninsula, were continuing to arrive in scattered bands, it was no easy task to drive them out. Besides, although they were bold marauders and appropriated all movable property on which they could lay their hands, their chief purpose was to occupy and cultivate the waste lands, and this was not an injury but an advantage to Heraclius and his state. In these circumstances the emperor was well inspired to enter into negotiations with them, as a result of which many

70

tribes had definite districts assigned to them for residence and cultivation in return for an annual rental or tribute. Of course the agreements were not scrupulously kept. When the occasion prompted, the Slavs spread over more than the stipulated territory or refused to pay their annual dues. On such action being reported at Constantinople the emperor would declare a treaty-breaking tribe to be in a state of rebellion and might or might not, depending on his situation at the time, lead a punitive expedition against it. Weighing carefully the scant data at our disposal, we may safely assert that, while in the days of Heraclius and his immediate successors, that is, throughout the seventh century, the Balkan peninsula continued to be agitated with the coming and going of fresh tribes of Slavs, there was none-the-less effected a very important transformation of the newcomers from marauders to settlers. That so little is known of the details of the process by which a large section of the peninsula, in fact the whole mountainous interior, became the permanent possession of the Slavs, is disappointing. But it is an advantage to know that, beginning with Heraclius, the attempt to drive them out was practically given up and that the emperors resigned themselves to accept the newcomers as subjects, in the thought that thus, at least in theory, the territory of the empire remained intact.

Let us now, from the outlook of the year 700, when the process of Slav infiltration, begun two hundred years before, was about complete, take stock of the racial situation on the peninsula. Though, as just stated, the Balkan interior had become largely Slav, let us be careful not to exaggerate the transformation which had been effected. The older races were numerically reduced and crowded back into the uplands but they were by no means crowded out of the peninsula. The older races were three in number, Illyrians, Greeks, and Latinized provincials. The Illyrians — called Albanians at a later day — occupied the mountains of the west, the Greeks inhabited ancient Hellas as well as the Aegean and Ionian coasts, while the Latinized provincials held practically the whole interior plateau. *The racial situation on the peninsula around 700.*

Now the coming in of the Slavs profoundly affected the status of each of these three groups. Though little that is precise is known of the Illyrians, it may safely be assumed that, already a *The Slavs press upon the Illyrians, still more upon the Greeks.*

diminishing group, they were still further driven into the uplands
along the western coasts. Far more is known of what happened
to the Greeks. Occasional Slav tribes, continuing their southward movement, penetrated into Thessaly, while others even
reached the Peloponnesus and actually took over and settled a
considerable area of this venerable Greek soil. That the Slav
penetration extended so far south used to be heatedly denied by
thoroughgoing Greek partizans. None-the-less the fact has now
been definitely established, and its most reasonable explanation
seems to be that the native Greek population, owing to economic
stagnation and probably also to the long-continued ravages of
malaria, had been so reduced in numbers that the northern
barbarians met little resistance in appropriating considerable interior sections of ancient Hellas. However, to the coasts and to
the cities of the coasts the Slavs did not push their advance.
As a backward, pastoral-peasant folk their interest in the cities
was confined to the hope of plunder, and since the cities had
walls and could not be taken, the invaders regretfully left them
alone. The cities and coasts of Hellas remained Greek, a matter
of tremendous significance, since it alone explains why the traditional Hellenic character of the southern area was not in the
course of time obscured and lost.

The Slavs
largely re-
place the
Latin-
speaking
provincials.

However, the greatest sufferers at the hands of the advancing
Slavs were neither the Albanians nor the Greeks but the Latin-
speaking provincials, for it was chiefly their territory which was
accessible to the Slavs and which the Slavs seized. But even
the Roman provincials did not wholly disappear. It is true
that for some centuries after the Slav conquest no mention of
them occurs in the meager contemporary records. Presently we
hear of bands of them in various sections and around the year
1000 we have evidence of a solid block of this people in the
lowlands north of the Danube. Left to the hazards of conjecture, we may not unreasonably assume that in the age of the
Slav migrations the Roman provincials yielded the valleys to
the invaders and preserved themselves by retiring to the uplands,
where they eked out a meager living as shepherds and peasants.
Exactly how and when they entered into possession of the fertile
Danubian plain is a good deal of a mystery to which we shall
return at a later time. At this point we are content to note

that, reduced to self-governing bands, widely scattered over the upland reaches, they continued to use the Latin idiom, and that this tenacity accounts for the preservation of their individuality and their persistence down to our own time as a separate people called Rumans (Romans) or Rumanians.

Owing to the fact that the Slavs from the time they entered the peninsula began to shape its destinies, it is well to become familiar with their character, customs, and institutions. By way of preliminary let us consider their migrations. According to the best evidence the Slavs may claim as their European home the swamplands of the Pripet river, north of the present city of Kiev, in Russia. This is the probable center of the race from which it gradually radiated in all directions. Our interest attaches exclusively to those groups which first spread southward to the Carpathian mountains and flowed thence in small tribal rivulets into the Balkan peninsula. The organization they brought with them and retained for ages with little change centered about the tribe, and was of a very primitive order. The different tribes were jealous of one another, engaged freely in inter-tribal warfare, and only rarely combined against a common foe. A Greek observer, in fact none other than the Emperor Maurice, who knew them intimately from having spent many years in making war upon them, was peculiarly struck by their lack of organization. His testimony is important: "They have abundance of cattle and grain, chiefly millet and rye, but rulers they cannot bear and they live side by side in disunion."

The tribal system, while securing a rude sort of social equality, inevitably meant political division and military weakness. In consequence the strong attachment of the Slavs to the clan suffices to explain why they did not cut much of a figure in war, and why they fell an easy victim to the Mongolian Avars, and afterwards remained dependent on the Greeks much longer than seems necessary. Not that the individual Slav was not a brave and even an ingenious fighter of the guerrilla type. His ambuscades in forest or mountain were well managed, and when pursued his favorite device seems to have been to disappear under water, where, securely hidden, he breathed so deftly through a reed that he could only with great difficulty be de-

Tribal divisions of the Slavs.

The tribe or clan explains the military weakness of the Slavs.

tected. Not unlikely this amphibian virtuosity was acquired
during the long centuries of primitive existence among the stagnant Pripet waters.

Organization of the clan: zupa, zupan, and grad.

The territory of a clan was known under the name of zupa,
while the clan chief was called zupan. A group of affiliated
clans often acknowledged one of their zupans as grand zupan,
but the title, for a long time at least, carried with it a certain
amount of prestige but very little power. Still as the prophecy
of an ampler organization in the future it deserves attention. In
measure as the tribes became more firmly rooted in the peninsula
and awakened to the necessity of defense, they planted at some
favorable spot, preferably on a hill or by the side of a stream, a
primitive fortress called *grad*, in which they stored their supplies
and to which they retired in time of danger. Naturally the
grads with the development of civilized life became centers of
commerce and the nuclei of towns.

The communistic system of the Slavs.

The democratic equality which was the main asset of this
loose tribal organization deserves an explanatory word. Equality is of course characteristic of clan rule in general, and is no
evidence, as has sometimes been argued, of a peculiar passion for
democracy among the Slavs. Our wisest course will be to
abandon the elastic word " democracy," used in so many different
senses, according to the stage of civilization that is being treated,
and to describe the political and economic system of the Slavs
as a close partnership of goods. In other words, it was an
early type of communism. However, communism is so little
a peculiarity of the Slavs that it may be called the usual form
of association of every people engaged in passing from the
hunting and grazing stages to the stage of agriculture. To meet
the requirements of a primitive economic system the Slav clan
was divided into villages, while the unit of the village was the
family. Each member of the family had assigned to him some
task, such as planting and herding in the case of the men, spin-
ning and weaving in the case of the women, and in return for
this service shared equally with all the rest in the total labor-
product. As the family was the producing and consuming unit,
the title to the property worked, and to the tools employed, inhered in it as a group. This agricultural communism was so
deeply implanted among the Slavs that it has persisted, here

and there, down to our own day.[1] Since among other peoples communism was usually abandoned at an early date in favor of a régime of private property, we may conclude that individual ownership stimulates men to greater personal exertion and rewards them with a larger economic return. But whatever its advantages, private property also has its undeniable drawbacks in that it brings about great differences in wealth, and keeps a considerable element at the bottom of the ladder, sunk in poverty and want. For the communistic system of the early Slavs the boast is made, probably not without justice, that though it produced no affluence, it hindered the spread of a degrading poverty, and that it maintained a substantial economic and political equality among all the members of society.

We have already recorded that the Emperor Maurice credited the Slavs with " an abundance of cattle and grain, chiefly millet and rye." From this testimony it is permitted to conclude that their communistic villages engaged in a combination of herding and farming. But they did more. Since in their early home on the Pripet the Slavs fished and kept bees, they naturally continued these activities in their new home in Balkania. They also conducted certain primitive industries, like pottery and basket-weaving, and in measure as they became cognizant of the higher civilization of the Greeks, they developed a desire to exchange their surplus products for the jewelry, silks, and spices spread temptingly before their eyes by the adventurous merchants of Constantinople or Thessalonica. *The Slavs a pastoral and agricultural people.*

Trade, once engaged in, brought to the villages of the Slavs not only Mediterranean goods but also Mediterranean customs and ideas. Just as the invading Germans in the West gradually fell under the spell of Latin civilization and took it *Slow growth of Greek influence among the Slavs.*

[1] The communistic family is the most characteristic, as it has proved the most tenacious, institution of the Slavs. It was still found in the nineteenth century in various sections of Balkania under the name of zadruga. The zadruga, in the form in which we know it, is now generally considered to be of late medieval or even early modern origin. However, its correspondence in all essential particulars of purpose and organization with the primitive Slav family is so striking that the conclusion that the zadruga is nothing other than a later phase of the traditional Slav communism can hardly be avoided. The literature on the zadruga is voluminous. See Jireček, Geschichte der Serben, p. 138 ff.; Mayer, Die bäuerliche Hauskommunion.

over to the best of their ability, so the Slavs, though with far greater reluctance, yielded to the lure of Greek civilization, in the shadow of which, as official subjects of the Greek empire, they passed their lives. And since Christianity had by the seventh century become the chief ingredient of Greek as well as of Latin civilization, it was certain that, again like the Germans, the Slavs would sooner or later adopt the Christian religion. However, the fact that they accepted baptism only at a relatively late period, in the ninth century, would go to show that, prompted no doubt in the main by the inaccessible character of their country, they remained steeped in an atmosphere of clannish aloofness and looked with suspicion upon the Greeks and their strange ways.

The early religion of the Slavs.

For a long time therefore the Slavs continued to dwell in the new lands as heathen, and this heathenism is an important feature of the picture we are engaged in drawing of them at the time of their coming into the peninsula. Exactly as in the case of their communism, what immediately strikes the observer about their religion is that it closely resembles the religion of all primitive peoples. Its central feature was the belief that nature is filled with invisible spirits, some good and helpful, others studiously malicious. While this is polytheism, essentially like every other primitive worship reported in history, it did not preclude the acknowledgement of a supreme spirit, ruler of all the lesser powers of nature. This supreme spirit the Slavs worshipped under the name of Svarog, meaning Heaven; his favorite children, agents of his will, were the Sun and Fire. The appurtenances for worship probably included idols and temples, though no remains have reached us to support the supposition, possibly because the material employed was perishable wood. There were priests and medicine men whose power was great in exact proportion to the abundant superstitions. However, the priests do not appear to have formed a separate caste. The priestly function apparently inhered in the head of each family, who presided over the religious rites, conducting them in open nature, preferably in shady groves or on lofty hilltops. Some seasonal event, like sowing or reaping, usually furnished the occasion for addressing the gods, and the exercises of a natural and simple order consisted in the sacrifice of animals, together with the offer of flowers and fruits of the field, while the people raised their voice on high in songs of praise and supplication.

Thus the Slavs made their home in the Balkan lands, taking possession of all the territory from the head of the Adriatic clear across the peninsula to the Black sea. Coming in small bands, which held fast to the principle of tribal independence and which had already lost touch with one another generations before, the newcomers gradually developed in constantly increasing measure differences of speech, customs, and political organization. Presently, with advancing culture, attempts were made at new and more comprehensive forms of association which we shall take note of in due time. The point to be made here is that a progressive differentiation among tribes, so numerous and so widely scattered across the broad peninsula, was inevitable, and that it need cause no surprise to discover that after the passing of a few centuries four different groups of Slavs are distinctly recognizable.

The development of differences of dialect and customs among the Slavs.

The practice of ethnologists is to designate all the Slav settlers of Balkania as South or Jugo-Slavs. The four groups into which, through the operation of time and chance, the South Slavs fell are: the Slovenes, the Croats, the Serbs, and the Bulgars. The Slovenes are those South Slavs who occupy the land at the head of the Adriatic including the southern and eastern slopes of the Austrian Alps. Since they are for the most part geographically outside the Balkan peninsula and became politically associated with Austria, they will concern us very little in this book. We must, however, keep them in mind as the westernmost group of the South Slavs. East and southeast of the Slovenes, between the river Drave and the Adriatic sea, we encounter the Croats. They too, through various hazards, became linked with central Europe as represented by Hungary and Austria, and, though physiographically comprehended in the Balkan peninsula, they will pass across our vision only now and then. East and southeast of the Croats we meet the Serbs scattered over a wide area between the Danube and the Adriatic. They occupy the heart of the peninsula and are an out-and-out Balkan people, whose evolution will be one of our most constant interests. East and southeast of the Serbs are the Bulgars. They are bounded by the Danube on the north, the Black sea

The four branches of the Balkan or South Slavs (Jugo-Slavs).

on the east, and in thin rivulets reach as far south as the Aegean sea. Though the Bulgars may be safely reckoned as South Slavs, they are peculiar in so far as they developed from a mixture of Slavs with a Mongolian race of conquerors who came into the peninsula in the seventh century, under circumstances to be examined in a later chapter. This Mongolian race bore the name of Bulgars and, though it vanished from history like the Huns and Avars who preceded it, was successful in giving its name and merging its blood and traditions with the easternmost group of the South Slavs.

Thus the Slavs, who drifted into the peninsula in scores of dissociated tribes, consolidated in the course of time into four distinct and recognizable groups. The consolidation meant a political advance, since what weighs in political affairs is power, and four considerable units are manifestly more powerful than several scores of tiny tribes. However, a single group in place of four would have been more powerful still, and if the Balkan Slavs had fused, or by some conqueror had been forced to fuse, into a union which embraced them all, they would without question have acquired the control of the peninsula, and might possibly, in the progress of the generations, have ousted or absorbed the older Balkan peoples — Illyrians, Greeks, and Latinized provincials (called Rumans in our time). The stubbornly persisting divisions of the Slavs, while of great advantage to their neighbors and rivals, not only cost them the political hegemony of the peninsula but also largely explain the disastrous, internecine character of their history down to our own day.

Disastrous consequences of the failure of the South Slavs to become a single people.

CHAPTER VII

THE COMING OF THE ARABS AND THE RESCUE OF THE EMPIRE BY LEO THE ISAURIAN

In 628, the year in which Heraclius triumphantly concluded his wars with Persia, he received a mysterious letter which apprised him of the birth of a new religion and summoned him under threats to accept it at once. The Christian conqueror must have been greatly amused at the sender, a certain obscure Mohammed, dwelling in the trackless deserts of Arabia. And yet, incredible as it may sound, the epistolary thunder was followed by military action with so little delay that in a few years the luster won by Heraclius in the Euphrates valley had darkened and gone out.

Mohammed was an Arab whose religious genius admits of no dispute. To say as much is not to maintain that the faith which he announced and which is recorded in the book of his sayings, called the Koran, is an entirely original creation. He drew heavily on various sources for his teachings, especially on the inherited lore of the Arab tribes and on the Bible of the Christians, both the Old and the New Testament. His basic teaching, monotheism, was a Hebrew borrowing, which he took over, with the addition that in the long succession of the teachers and prophets of Hebrew history his own name was the last and greatest. In Mecca, his home community, he met with such fierce opposition from unbelievers and scoffers that he was obliged to flee for safety to the neighboring town of Medina. Here, in the midst of grave difficulties, he proved himself a skillful and not always scrupulous politician, who by a judicious mixture of force and persuasion succeeded in extending the range of his influence until it embraced repentant Mecca itself. Before death came, in 632, he had performed what must be ever accounted a politico-religious miracle, for he had welded the divided desert tribesmen into a single mass animated with the

A desert visionary writes to Heraclius

Mohammed and Mohammedanism.

79

desire to carry their faith at the point of the sword and, if necessary, with the sacrifice of life to the ends of the earth.

The successors of Mohammed, called califs, attack Persia and the Roman empire.

Mohammed's mantle fell on his death upon a successor, called *calif*. If Mohammed won Arabia, the early califs undertook to carry the prophet's banner beyond the limits of their native desert. Across the border of the barren peninsula lay two old and famous states, Persia and the Roman empire. On these the Arab hordes, fanaticized by their faith, threw themselves with sudden and irresistible fervor. Persia, already exhausted by the blood-letting effected by Heraclius, succumbed in a very few years, leaving its whole territory in the hands of the victor (641). Compared with Persia, the Roman empire exhibited a far greater strength of resistance, but it was put to a terrible test by the vigor of the Arab assault. In 634 the Romans suffered a crushing defeat in southern Syria and in the following year lost the great stronghold of Damascus, which, because of its advantageous position with regard to their expanding world, the victors presently converted into their capital. Two years after Damascus came the fall of Jerusalem, the Holy, sending a shock to the heart of all Christendom (637). A chronicler has left us a picture, not without pathos, of the venerable patriarch of Jerusalem, Sophronius by name, who, obliged to act as guide of the rude, skin-clad Arab chief, the Calif Omar, among the sacred shrines of the city, paused from time to time in the performance of his cruel errand to give vent to his anguish by calling in broken accents on the Lord. Except for a brief period during the Crusades, Jerusalem has remained in Mohammedan hands down to our own day (1918), astonished witness of the break-down of the Ottoman empire.

Heraclius lives to see the loss of Syria and Egypt.

With southern Syria gone the Emperor Heraclius considered the situation beyond help and gave up the whole province without further resistance. There are those who contend that he was by this time an ill and broken man, the mere shadow of his former self. Undeniably he showed a lack of energy, difficult to understand, for when the Arabs, in possession of Syria, turned next on Egypt, he gave up Egypt too. In the very year of this loss (641) he died, leaving behind a memory divided between admiration and compassion, since, having lifted himself to the pinnacle of success, he lived to see his reputation blasted by a blind, fanatical force, which burst irresistibly into his state and before which his disciplined and laureled army went down like a house of cards.

Like some emperors before him, Heraclius succeeded in establishing a dynasty, of which the one and overwhelming concern came to be the checking of the Arabs. This the Heracliad rulers found to be an immensely difficult matter, for the energy of the desert warriors continued for a long time unabated, as to the cry, " God is God and Mohammed is His prophet," they launched themselves like a whirlwind against every obstacle. It was fortunate for the Byzantines that there broke out occasional civil brawls among the Arabs which naturally paralyzed military action, and that the tribes, as a desert folk, were slow to take to the sea. Through these circumstances, in the years following Heraclius, the Roman sovereigns, his descendants, were able to escape further losses, especially as they contented themselves with the modest but sound policy of defending Asia Minor at the difficult southeastern entrance, the so-called Cilician gates, and of retaining command of the Mediterranean waters with an effective fleet. It is clear, however, that the early califs, fiery men of vaulting ambition, dreamed of nothing less than world conquest. They therefore, in the course of time, comprehended the necessity of building up a sea-power, having its base along the coasts of Syria and Egypt and employing a powerful navy for purposes of offense.

The Byzantine emperors defend Asia Minor and maintain control of the sea.

NOT ARABS BUT SYRIAN et Jelevere

Thirty years after the death of Heraclius the Arabs made their first attempt to capture Constantinople. However, undertaken with insufficient means, the expedition proved a complete fiasco. Thereupon they modified without abandoning their program and by sudden descents on the Byzantine coasts and by piratical raids on merchant vessels made their name a terror throughout the eastern world. Before the end of the century, in 698, they scored a very notable success. They took Carthage, and though it was largely a military victory, gained by the army proceeding westward along the coast from Egypt, it put an end to Roman rule in Africa and made possible the advance of Arab influence along the Mediterranean shore as far west as the Atlantic ocean.

First Arab assault on Constantinople a failure.

The Twenty Years' Anarchy follows the end of the Heracliad dynasty.

Summarizing the half-century following the death of Heraclius, we note that the rulers of his family set themselves the task of conserving their inheritance and that, if not gloriously, at least courageously and doggedly, they kept it (except, as pointed out, in Africa) beyond the covetous grip of the Mohammedans. The last member of the dynasty, Justinian II by name, developed a despotic streak which made him many enemies and in the end cost him his throne. Following his overthrow (695), the succession was seized by one ambitious upstart after another, with the result that the administration, including the army and navy, became grievously disorganized. This confused period, which brought the by no means despicable Heracliad rule to a conclusion, has been expressively labeled the Twenty Years' Anarchy. Such a period must have appealed to the Arabs as an occasion created by Allah himself for disposing once and for all of the one great state still standing between them and world dominion. In the year 717 they resolved on an expedition against Constantinople, on a scale beyond anything they had yet undertaken.

THE MEDITERRANEAN WORLD AT THE HEIGHT OF THE ARAB POWER

SCALE OF MILES
0 100 200 300 400 500 600

▦ EASTERN ROMAN EMPIRE   ▨ MOSLEM REALM.   (Ca. 750 A.D.)

Leo the Isaurian seizes the throne, 717.

The political turmoil at Constantinople so exactly reproduced the crisis associated with the name of Phocas, a century before, that many a citizen, struck by the analogy, must have been moved to prophesy the coming of another Heraclius to save the state from dissolution. And the saviour came, a splendid soldier, Leo the Isaurian, concerning whose origin there is considerable doubt. If the chroniclers, whose reliability is by no means unassailable, are right in designating him as an Isaurian, we must consider him a native of the rugged Taurus mountains in southern Asia Minor. Such an origin would happily conform with his sturdy character. Since the desperate situation called for desperate remedies, Leo, who, when the Arab expedition started, was engaged in active service on the Asia Minor front, marched his men to the capital, seized the crown, too long the plaything of rival factions, and energetically prepared for the expected siege.

That the Mohammedan effort was commensurate with the enormous difficulties of the task is disclosed by the circumstance that the Arab forces closely invested the Roman capital by both land and water. A fleet of many hundred sail cast anchor in the Bosporus, while one army, stationed on the European side of the strait, directly enveloped the city, and a second army on the Asiatic shore cut off supplies and military succor from that quarter. In addition to Leo, their intrepid leader, who enjoyed the full confidence of soldiers and citizens, the besieged found a powerful and apparently magical helper in the mysterious Greek fire. Exactly what it was is still in dispute among scholars. The scanty information vouchsafed by contemporaries makes clear two facts: that it could not be put out with water, and that, squirted from "syphons" — apparently a primitive sort of cannon — on to the decks of the Arab ships, it caused great destruction and even greater consternation. When the winter came, cold, hunger, and disease terribly decimated the ranks of the besiegers, and exactly a year after their arrival they sullenly withdrew the remnant of their shattered forces.

The Arab siege of Constantinople, 717.

Well might Constantinople rejoice at its delivery, and well may all Europe rejoice even at this late date in contemplating the failure of the siege of 717. For, had the forces of Islam broken down the Greek barrier and made their way up the Danube, they would in all probability have brought the whole occident under their yoke. Nay, the probability becomes almost a certainty when we extend our vision to take in the whole Mediterranean world, and observe that the Arabs were at the same time — in 711 to be exact — crossing from Africa to the famous southwestern promontory of Europe, known ever since after the name of their leader as Gibraltar (Gebel-al-Tarik, Hill of Tarik). The western expedition brought about, as its immediate fruit

Significance for Europe of Leo's victory.

the conquest of Spain. Doubtless the general plan of the Arabs was for the western forces to push ahead until they effected a junction somewhere on the Rhine with an eastern army coming up the Danube. Never in its history was Europe exposed to a graver danger from Asiatic foes. But Leo's successful defense of his capital in 717 broke one of the giant nippers of the Arab scheme, and when the western Arabs, undaunted, continued to push on, they were met at Tours and defeated in their turn by the Franks under Charles Martel (732). As a result they fell back toward the Pyrenees. The victory of Tours was the memorable achievement of one of the new Germanic states founded on the ruins of the Roman empire, but it is doubtful if the Franks could have won the struggle, had not their rear been secured by the earlier victory of the eastern emperor. Historians are perhaps too prone to multiply the battles proclaimed decisive of the world's destiny. But to the battles of Constantinople and Tours, representing two intimately connected links in the Moslem policy of conquest, it is impossible not to grant an ecumenical significance.

Conjecture based on desire not fact.

The Arab power begins to decline about 750. Its capital transferred to Bagdad.

Defeated and driven back from Constantinople, the Arabs never quite regained their momentum. The Arab flood began to recede, but so slowly that Leo, while he reigned, hardly experienced a relief. Over and over again the hordes from Syria, breaking through the Cilician gates, terribly ravaged large sections of Asia Minor, while on the highways of the sea the Moslem pirates worked steady havoc among the Byzantine merchantmen. It was only some years after Leo's death that an event occurred which, though it too failed in any effective sense to break the Arab power, robbed it of the unity of its attack and so gave the Christian world a welcome breathing-space. In 750 the struggle among opposed Moslem factions for the possession of the califate led to the rise of a new dynasty, the Abbassids, and caused the defection from the Arab empire of Spain, which set up a separate government under the rule of a fugitive member of the older, the Ommiad dynasty. Shortly after their elevation the Abbassids made the weighty decision to carry the capital from Damascus in Syria eastward to Bagdad on the Tigris. Without doubt this transfer was a serious mistake for a power aspiring to play a Mediterranean rôle. Henceforth the center of gravity of the Arab state was in the Tigris-Euphrates region and, occupied with the numerous problems of Asia, it insensibly relaxed its pressure on Byzantium.

To return to the deliverer from Arab bondage, to Leo the Isaurian, it is important to observe that as soon as the siege of Constantinople was over, he undertook to carry through a sweeping program of reform. This embraced the civil administration and the army, both of which had become corrupt and inefficient, but principally it addressed itself to purifying the church from certain growths of which Leo did not approve. The slow transition from classical antiquity to medievalism, of which we have noted some of the signs in treating of Justinian and Heraclius, was by the eighth century complete, with the result that the views of life and death popularized by Christianity ruled all men in their thoughts and actions. But in being taken over by the numerous and diverse peoples of the East, the religion of the Nazarene had also absorbed many of their practices and customs and had by imperceptible stages been carried far indeed from the teachings of the Founder. Let us briefly consider some of these departures. Most decidedly Jesus had preached unworldliness and had sternly rebuked the rich, but he did not advocate the fierce asceticism which, assuming the proportions of a religious mania, led to the adoption of such extravagant practices as voluntary starvation, prolonged exposure to unendurable heat and cold, and other, often unbelievable forms of self-inflicted torture. The logical outcome of this dark passion was the monastery, to which steadily growing numbers of men retired, convinced that only by withdrawal from the world and a continuous round of penances could they gain that goal of all endeavor, the salvation of their souls. The remains of classical antiquity, though still cherished by a solitary scholar here and there, lost all meaning for a people which willfully shut its eyes on the movement, color, and sensuous charm of life and yielded up its mind to the grossest superstitions. In so restricted a mental atmosphere, however ostentatiously labeled Christian, the spirit of Jesus suffered a profound alteration, and for the immense majority of Christian worshipers religion became a coarse, materialist affair concerned with images, amulets, and wonder-working relics and not much above the fetish-worship of an African savage.

The abasement of religion and the church in Leo's day.

Leo attacks images and incidentally the clergy.

Among the various expressions of religious fervor in evidence in his day, the excessive worship of images, which substituted the symbol for the essence, particularly attracted Leo's attention. Accordingly, he resolved to make it the object of attack. What gave him his more sober and spiritual outlook is hard to say, unless it be that he owed it to his origin among a mountain people of Asia Minor, who are known to have been traditionally hostile to the worship of representative figures. Most likely, too, it counted with the emperor that Christianity, in competition throughout the eastern Mediterranean with Mohammedanism, a faith that strictly eschews the use of images, was commonly held up to contempt by Moslem zealots as no better than idolatry. Some historians are inclined to think that Leo, once launched on a campaign of purifying the Christian worship of images, resolved to attack superstition in all its forms and that, within the modest proportions possible to his age, he planned to play the rôle of an apostle of enlightenment. While this is hardly probable, since Leo was not an eighteenth-century rationalist but, in true medieval manner, a sincerely pious man, it is likely that his attacks were at least partially prompted by the political desire to diminish the excessive power of the clergy, which not only was in possession of a vast property withdrawn from civil taxation but also boasted a moral ascendancy over the citizens calculated to undermine the authority of the state. However, amongst the great body of the clergy it was the monks who were particularly hit by Leo's measures, and characteristically they repaid him, during life, with a deadly hatred and, after his death, with a steady stream of calumny calculated to blacken his memory with posterity.

The decree against images, 726.

In 726 Leo, exercising the ecclesiastical prerogative of his predecessors, began the publication of a series of decrees which aimed at nothing less than the removal of all images from the churches of his dominions. In Asia Minor his religious policy apparently aroused satisfaction, but in Constantinople, and here and there throughout Greece, there were serious riots which had to be suppressed by force. None-the-less throughout the eastern territories of Leo the order was executed, the images being removed from the churches and destroyed. Iconoclasm, the first step in the war on a too predominant clergy, seemed to have scored a victory.

But in a very important part of Leo's dominion the movement failed from the start and failed disastrously. I refer to Italy, which at this juncture projected itself so powerfully into the situation that we must give it our close attention. We treated of Italy last on the occasion of Justinian's reconquest of it from the East Goths (553). However, the great Justinian was hardly dead, when another German tribe, the Lombards, crossed the Alps (568) and in a very short time succeeded in occupying the greater part of the peninsula. Only scattered districts like Rome, Ravenna, and the southern extremity, the foot of the Italic boot, remained in Byzantine hands. From the days of the Lombard conquest to Leo the Isaurian, a period of about one hundred and fifty years, no important changes had occurred in the territorial position of the two antagonists. In spite of frequent wars each had managed just about to hold his own. It was the particular ambition of the emperors not to lose Rome, the ancient capital of the imperium. On the other hand the Roman pope, the leading bishop of the West, was glad enough to be, in strictly civil matters, under the emperor, first, because the emperor had always been his civil head, and second, because the emperor was so far removed in space that, though affording a welcome measure of protection, his more than occasional interference in papal affairs was highly improbable. Under these circumstances the outstanding feature of Italian history in the days after Justinian was the steadily mounting authority of the pope. Not only did he exercise more and more political power in the city and district of Rome, but what was more important, he increased his spiritual control over all the other bishops of the West and was presently in an excellent position to enforce a claim of primacy over them.

When Leo issued his edict against images he naturally forwarded it also to the Byzantine officials of Italy. But the pope no sooner got wind of it than he was up in arms. Image-worship was popular in Italy and the man who broke a lance for it was sure to have the inhabitants solidly behind him. Besides, the pope could maintain with much show of reason that Leo exceeded his rights by taking up a question which, like image-worship, was an internal affair of the church. In any case the pope was bold enough to anathematize the iconoclasts as heretics, and the Italians, encouraged by this act of rebellion on the part of their spiritual leader, by riotous demonstrations hindered the imperial officers from removing the images and successfully set their authority at naught. By quick and tactful concessions Leo succeeded in retaining his hold on the extreme south, but the central and northern districts, with the important exception of Venice, cast off the Byzantine yoke and became substantially independent. The city of Rome, thus far under the at least nominal sovereignty of the eastern emperor, henceforward acknowledged the pope as its sole and rightful ruler.

The pope, obliged to find a protector, turns to the Franks.

Whatever satisfaction the pope may have drawn from his successful resistance to the iconoclastic decree must have been greatly reduced by the circumstance that, in forfeiting the protection of Constantinople, he had exposed himself to conquest on the part of his ever-dangerous neighbor, the king of the Lombards. And truth to tell, his alarm was justified, for the Lombard ruler, already in possession of most of Italy, seized the occasion of the quarrel between emperor and pope to attempt to get a foothold in the venerable capital on the Tiber. His open military preparations obliged the frightened pope to look about for help, and he addressed an urgent appeal to the only remaining power of consequence in the Christian world, the Franks. It was in these circumstances that there began, about the middle of the eighth century, the famous alliance between the papacy and the Frankish state. Its consequences were notable: while saving the pope from the Lombards, it put the temporal power of the papacy on a solid footing and led straight to that famous occurrence of Christmas, 800, when the pope renewed the empire of the West by setting the Roman imperial crown on the head of Charles, king of the Franks.

Leo, in spite of the opposition of the pope, sticks to iconoclasm.

The rebellion of the pope, costing Constantinople the Italian districts which remained to the empire with the exceptions already noted, was a bitter morsel for the Emperor Leo. But retract he would not; the iconoclastic decree remained the law of the land. Fully aware that ecclesiastical opinion, above all, the very powerful opinion of the monks, was against him even in the East, he none-the-less insisted on the firm, though discreet and tactful, execution of his order. It is clear from the records that Leo was not the familiar type of fanatic reformer who takes a special delight in persecuting his opponents. His iconoclasm made no martyrs east or west, and the only revenge he took on the rebellious pope was to withdraw the western part of the Balkan peninsula (Illyricum), which for centuries had been a part of the pope's ecclesiastical dominion, from papal authority and add it to the territory of the patriarch of Constantinople. It should be observed in this connection that the emperor's ecclesiastical policy enjoyed the support of the patriarch of East Rome. But this is not astonishing since the patriarch, as an imperial appointee, had little independence.

The two related acts, Leo's iconoclasm and his new ecclesiastical boundary line between the bishops of Old and New Rome, were destined to produce a division of the Christian world, maintained to this day, into a Latin and a Greek church, a western and an eastern branch of Christianity. The student who cares to look beneath the surface will readily discover that, long before the time of Leo, the schism had been ripening in the womb of time. To go back no farther than the Great Migrations, the Teutonic conquest had effectively separated the East and the West politically. Moreover, ever since the Germanic settlement the civilizations of the two areas, though undoubtedly exhibiting a certain medieval similarity, had followed separate lines and developed a mass of individual features. Finally, the emperor's control of the eastern church, which went to the absurd height of regulating by edict purely internal matters, ran counter to the system of the West, where the successor of St. Peter was looked up to with passionate reverence as the one and only source of ecclesiastical authority.

The Great Schism: The Latin and Greek churches.

By following the history of the iconoclastic movement beyond the days of Leo we are likely to be confirmed in the opinion that the differences between the societies of the East and West were so fundamental that a separation would have come about even without the emperor's provocative act. Leo and the immediate successors of his line — for Leo, too, succeeded in making the crown hereditary in his family — firmly maintained the program of reform. Then, with a change of dynasty, a spirit of compromise gained ground and the monks, who, standing for image-worship, had been under a shadow during the Isaurian régime, powerfully reasserted themselves. The end of the acrimonious

The iconoclastic movement defeated in the long run even in the East.

controversy was that, about one hundred and twenty years after Leo's edict went forth, his work was undone and image-worship was again made lawful throughout the eastern lands. True, eastern images (called *ikons*) henceforth were painted pictures, not sculptures executed in the round, but what of that? For the average man an image is an image whether two or three dimensional, but the distinction drawn by the eastern church is historically interesting, inasmuch as it supplies a striking illustration of the curious, hair-splitting practices of the theologically trained Greek mind. Enough, Leo's reform was writ in water, and painted pictures of the saints have remained and are today as prominent a feature of Christian worship among the Greeks as among the followers of the pope, though the latter make use of sculptured figures also.

The ecclesiastical schism registers the cultural estrangement of East and West. But why, with iconoclasm defeated, did not East and West again become ecclesiastically one? Without doubt attempts to that end were frequently made by well-meaning persons, but they lacked the irresistible impetus which only popular support could give, for the simple reason that the two Mediterranean areas had drifted utterly apart in sympathy and mutual understanding. Besides, and as a final blow, the pope now came forward with a much more sweeping claim to Christian primacy than the Constantinopolitan patriarch, energetically supported by his master, the emperor, was willing to entertain. In the eyes of the proud and powerful bishop of New Rome the bishop of Old Rome held a station hardly, if any, higher than his own. However, the unity of Christendom had been asserted for so many centuries that the idea refused to die and forced the pope and patriarch, almost in each other's despite, to maintain, at least intermittently, diplomatic relations as late as the eleventh century. Then only (about 1050) the estrangement became complete. As every medieval student knows, when, toward the end of the eleventh century, the famous movement of the crusades began, the gulf dividing the Latins and the Greeks had become so wide that each section looked upon the other as hardly better than the Mohammedan unbeliever. Reviewing the whole course of the East-West schism, we may admit that Leo's church policy first brought prominently to light the considerable difference between the two Christian world-groups, but we can hardly fail to see that the schism, when it came, merely registered a Greek-Latin cultural estrangement which by the eighth century was already marked, and which in the following centuries rapidly developed to the point where Greeks and Latins lost every trace of mutual understanding and good-will.

From the day of Leo's iconoclastic decree to his death in 740, and for about one hundred years after his death, the issue between image-breakers and image-worshipers dominated the domestic politics of the Greek empire. In all that time the image-worshipers, who had the monks and the inflamed and ignorant masses on their side, never ceased to agitate against the law with the result, as we have seen, that victory perched at last upon their banners. But other questions, though perhaps less absorbing, were not lacking; for instance, the issue of the imperial succession. Leo, like Heraclius and some of Heraclius' predecessors, succeeded in securing the throne for his family. If the Isaurian line could have become permanently established at Constantinople, it might have made for order and strength, since the periodic succession struggles regularly reduced the state to the verge of dissolution. But every Byzantine dynasty was apparently pursued by a spiteful fate, and Leo's dynasty, which was no exception to the rule, came to an unhappy end less than a hundred years after his accession. The usual uncertainty followed, not to be wholly remedied until Basil I, who, coming to the throne in 867, succeeded in founding a new, the Basilian, dynasty, sometimes known from the province of the founder's origin as the Macedonian line. This family was destined to add a brilliant chapter to the history of the Byzantine state. Without the vigor which the Basilian emperors breathed into the government, it might have suffered total shipwreck in the evil days following the end of the Isaurian dynasty. For a new danger had arisen into which we must now look, a danger precipitated by the coming of a new group of Balkan invaders, the Bulgars.

The Isaurian dynasty followed by the Macedonian or Basilian dynasty.

CHAPTER VIII

THE COMING OF THE BULGARS. — THE CREATION OF THE BULGAR STATE AND ITS GREATNESS UNDER BORIS AND SIMEON

Again the Mongolian invader.

TOWARD the end of the seventh century another of the many migratory peoples who alarmed the contemporary world and kept it in constant turmoil crossed the Danube with intent to harass and plunder Balkania. They were called Bulgars, hailed originally from Asia, and were related to those terrible earlier scourges of the peninsula, the Huns and Avars. They were, at their coming, by no means unknown to the Greeks, since long before the seventh century they had made themselves feared by occasional descents on the empire from their grazing grounds north of the Black sea. This time, however, they came to stay, challenging the resistance both of the Greeks, the titular lords of the land, and of the Slavs, who now for over one hundred years had occupied and tilled the soil. The plan of the Bulgars, who were not numerous but powerfully organized under a military leader or khan, and who, like nomads generally, had no taste for agriculture and a settled life, was to conquer and rule the Slavs and live as lords and masters by the labor of a people of serfs.

The Bulgars make their home south of the Danube.

The first Bulgar detachment crossed the Danube, so Greek chroniclers tell us, in the year 679 A.D., and immediately took possession of the territory between the Danube and the Balkan mountains. Apparently the Greek empire offered no resistance, its attention being absorbed by the Arabs, who were just then at the peak of their power. Such opposition as was offered by the Slavs proved unavailing, since their disorganized tribal system was no match for the effective military machine of the invaders. As a result a Bulgar state was erected which, from the region south of the Danube (called Moesia in Roman days) as a center, gradually reached out ambitious tentacles southward and westward, that is, toward Thrace and Macedonia. Nowhere did the Slavs put up a fight, or if they did, it is not recorded by the chroniclers. The Byzantine empire, on the other hand, proudly claiming all Balkania as its property, was outraged by the intrusion of the yellow invaders, and looked forward with confidence to their expulsion as soon as the occasion served.

For some generations after the coming of the Bulgars the expected favorable moment did not turn up, largely because the Arabs continued to constitute a problem which called for the undivided attention of the Greeks. But when in the days of Leo the Isaurian, the Arab danger began to abate, and he, and more particularly his able son, Constantine V (741–75), felt free to attack the Bulgar power, they found it so well consolidated that they were unable to deal it anything like a decisive blow. Then, naturally enough, when in the reign of the last and weakest ruler of the Isaurian line, Constantine VI (780–97), the scepter was seized by his own mother, Irene, and made the football of intriguing courtiers, the Bulgars were encouraged to make the most of the confusion. They assumed the offensive and dark days followed for the Greek state. In the reign of the Bulgar khan, Krum by name, the energy of the bold Asiatics reached its apex. In 811 Krum caught the Greek army, under the personal command of the Emperor Nicephorus, in so tight a trap in a region of closed valleys, that only a very few Greeks escaped with their lives. Nicephorus himself was among the slain; and when the dead ruler was brought before the savage Krum, the Bulgar issued the command that the head be severed from the body and that the skull be converted into a drinking-cup, in order that thereafter it might make the boisterous round of his captains when he sat down with them to meat.

The failure of the Isaurian line to drive out the Bulgars followed by a Bulgar offensive.

Krum was now free to harry Thrace and attempt the capture of Constantinople itself. In 813 he laid siege to the city, camping before the long land-wall which stretched from the sea of Marmora to the Golden Horn. As the Bulgars had no fleet to interrupt the sea communications and the formidable walls could not be scaled, the Greeks felt reasonably secure and with characteristic curiosity crowded every coign of vantage to stare at their exotic enemy. One of their chroniclers has left us a description of a religious ceremony conducted by the Bulgar

The Bulgars lay siege to Constantinople, 813.

khan, which is so suggestive of the Asiatic origin of himself
and his people that it deserves quotation. ("Krum offered
sacrifices after the custom of his nation by slaughtering men and
cattle before the Golden Gate. He then washed his feet in
the sea and performed his ablutions, after which he besprinkled
the people crowding around to do him honor. Returning to
his camp he passed through the array of his concubines who
worshiped and glorified their lord." In spite of the bloody sacrifices (sacrifices, it should be noted, including human beings), his
gods refused their help, for Krum found his efforts before
Constantinople unavailing and was obliged to retire to Thrace.
While preparing for a new campaign he considerately rid the
Greeks of further danger by falling dead of a stroke (814).

Greeks and
Bulgars
struggle for
Balkan
supremacy.

It is plain that by the early ninth century the question between the Greek and Bulgar states was nothing less than the
question of peninsular supremacy. In the eyes of the Greeks
the Bulgars had impudently taken possession of territory which
had belonged immemorially to the Roman empire, while the
Bulgars, animated by greed and filled with a sense of power, looked
upon the Greeks as a decadent people of a higher civilization, unable in the long run to maintain themselves. And indeed the vigor
of the barbarians, proved by such descents as those of Krum,
might have secured to them an early triumph if the Bulgars,
much like the Greeks themselves, had not suffered occasional
serious setbacks due to quarrels over the succession. Such a
domestic crisis ensued after Krum's death, and since the Greek
empire, as on so many previous occasions, was able to develop
new and unexpected strength, the balance was redressed between
the two rivals. But if this particular Greco-Bulgar crisis passed,
the mischief remained. Whether at war or at peace, Greeks and
Bulgars eyed each other with fear and hate and confidently
looked forward to a day of final reckoning.

Racial
fusion of
Bulgars and
Slavs.

In this period of unstable equilibrium, just before the Bulgars
celebrated the completion of their second century on Balkan
soil, there came to a head a social movement which must have
been long under way and which was of the utmost consequence.
I am referring to the fusion of the Bulgar lords with their
Slav subjects. Fusions among different groups of Indo-Europeans
are common in the history of Europe but here was the rarer and

more difficult case of a merger of the white and yellow races. The issue was probably settled by the fact that the Mongolians were numerically a decided minority, and that besides, they lagged, from the point of view of social and economic development, behind their white dependents. After two hundred years of living side by side the Bulgars gave up their language and customs and, freely intermarrying with the Slavs, became indistinguishable from them. The Bulgar state, though Asiatic in origin and institutions, thus became essentially a Slav state, in fact, the first Slav state of the peninsula, worthy of the name. That the Slavs owed this, their first political creation, to an Asiatic impulse, emphasizes the feeble sense of organization which seems to have been one of their fundamental characteristics. From approximately the middle of the ninth century we must, dismissing the thought of their Mongolian origin, think of the Bulgars as a Slav people with a not unimportant Asiatic strain. Exactly what the social and intellectual significance of the Mongolian contribution to the Bulgar nationality was, there is no means of telling; but doubtless the fact that the Bulgar through the ages and down to our day differs somwhat in physical type and mental endowment from the purer Slav to the west of him, the Serb, may be ascribed to the Asiatic factor in his blood.

To all the Slavs of Balkania, to the composite Bulgars with their strong state centered in the region between the Danube and the Balkan mountains, as well as to the purer tribes scattered over the western highlands, there now came a memorable experience in the form of Christianity. We have noted that the Slavs clung stubbornly to the primitive nature-worship which they had brought with them into the peninsula. But continued contact with Greek traders, missionaries, and captives taken in war was beginning to tell, especially at the border, and here and there a handful of Slavs openly or secretly professed the new religion. Meanwhile the inland Slavs, in touch with the Germans of the upper Danube, were making discoveries of their own about Christianity. The Germans had been won over to the Latin church and, full of zeal for the new faith, began a religious propaganda aimed at the Slavs close at hand. From east and west, from both the Greek and Latin branches of the

The Slavs between the Greek and Latin churches.

church, inroads were thus made into the Slav world, which, presently intensified by rivalry, ended at last in the sweeping conversion of the heathen.

The story of the Slav conversion obscured by interested invention.

The story of the Slav conversion is shrouded in considerable obscurity. Certain details, established beyond cavil, may be set down at the outset. They are that the Latin and Greek churches, equally in touch with the Slavs, engaged in sharp competition to bring the converts under their dominion; that such Slav chiefs and princes as favored the movement were guided not so much by miracles or warning signs from heaven, as by a shrewd hope of political advantage; and finally, that the monastic chroniclers, who are our chief source of information, must be approached sceptically, because they were less interested in giving the facts than in " edifying " their readers, in the familiar medieval manner, with sentimental tales composed *ad majorem gloriam dei*.

Conversion of Boris, Bulger khan or king, in 863.

Instead of attempting to disentangle all the threads of the complicated tale, it will satisfy our purpose to note that there were two separate Greek missionary efforts which became merged in their results. The first effort concerns the Bulgars. Their khan or king, Boris by name, found himself warmly courted by both the eastern and the western church. While he was still hesitating to which side to turn, the Byzantine emperor — it was in the year 863 — descended on him with an armed force and offered him a relatively advantageous treaty on condition that he and his people would agree to accept immediate baptism at the hands of the Greeks. Boris complied, but, filled with suspicion lest his conversion bring him not only ecclesiastically but also politically under Greek domination, he opened parallel negotiations with the Latin church at Rome. An interesting see-saw followed, lasting a few years, when the Greeks, who, near at hand, could act with greater celerity, won the day by a politic concession. They permitted the Bulgars to have their own church, organized under an archbishop and ten bishops, the only limitation imposed on Bulgar ecclesiastical independence being that an honorary recognition should be accorded to the patriarch of Constantinople as supreme head. Boris, on accepting baptism, ordered his subjects to submit to the same rite, and in case of resistance freely employed force against the recalcitrants. By

870 the once heathen kingdom presented itself to view as a Christian state, politically sovereign and ecclesiastically organized in loose dependence on Constantinople.

At the same time the Greeks engaged in a second missionary effort much farther to the west, among a Slav group located in what is now the Czech province of Moravia. As this effort turned out a failure we need not follow it here. But we do need to give attention to its leaders, remarkable men, destined, because of their powerful influence on the whole Slav world, to stamp their names on the pages of history as the Apostles to the Slavs. The two men were the brothers, Method and Constantine, the latter known also as Cyril, the name he adopted on becoming a monk. They were born at Thessalonica in the upper circle of society and illustrate the overwhelming trend of the time in that they renounced the high civil careers, which their birth and training opened to them, in favor of a life of religious study and missionary service. Constantine (Cyril), the younger of the two brothers, enjoyed the particular esteem of his contemporaries. He served as the librarian of the Constantinopolitan patriarch, and at the same time apparently held the chair of philosophy at the great university of the capital.

The Apostles to the Slavs, Method and Constantine (called also Cyril).

The fact that the brothers hailed from Thessalonica accounts for their familiarity with the Slav tongue, for Slav was spoken throughout the country districts surrounding the Aegean metropolis. Occasional Slav historians have, on the strength of no evidence except this gift of tongues, claimed the apostles as of their own blood. It irks their patriotic bias to owe anything to the Greeks, their ancient enemies. None-the-less the brothers were Greeks, Greeks so well established in the favor of the highest circles of Constantinple and so deservedly honored for their religious zeal that when, probably in 863, the very year of the Bulgar conversion, the question arose of sending a mission to the distant Moravian Slavs, the choice fell naturally on them.

The Apostles to the Slavs, Greeks by birth and training.

Not true They were Slavs

Though the mission, as already said, was a failure, the details of which need not be related here, it had highly important consequences by reason of the literary activities in which the brothers, in pursuit of their enterprise, engaged. That these were a necessity of the situation will appear when we recall that the Slavs were as yet on a very low cultural level and did not even possess

The Apostles help create a Slav alphabet, literature, and religious service.

a system of writing. First of all, therefore, the brothers invented an alphabet.[1] Not only were the holy books of Christianity now made available for general use, but schools were organized for the training of native priests in the elements of Christian faith and practice. Following this initial venture a body of Slav literature was gradually built up, which, though at first nothing but a literature of translations from the Greek, effectively opened to a backward people the door to intellectual culture. To these important services of the apostles we must add another which constituted a considerable innovation and did not pass without a challenge. In their eagerness to win the heathen to the true faith the brothers were ready to go to great lengths and gave permission to have the mass chanted in the Slav tongue. This was a serious concession, as the Greek church was committed, for purposes of the service, to Greek and the Latin church to Latin, and the superstitious view was current that these two tongues were so sacred that it was doubtful whether Christ and the saints above would give ear to supplications addressed to them in a less distinguished language. Of course the cry of heresy was raised against the Slav liturgy, especially on the part of the Latin church, but in the long run the brothers carried their point. The Slavs, far more fortunate in this matter than the Germans, succeeded in acquiring a Christian service which was chanted at the altars in the national idiom.

Effect of the literary labors of Method and Constantine felt throughout the Slav world. It admits of no doubt that Method and Constantine rendered the Slavs, not only a religious but also an educational and literary service of the greatest moment. Admitting again that

---

[1] The Slav alphabet is one of the many matters belonging to the episode of the conversion which are in dispute among scholars. Very probably the brothers did not so much invent an alphabet as give currency to one invented before their day. This earliest Slav alphabet is known as the Glagolitic. Its letters were so intricate and difficult that it was replaced, though long after the death of the brothers, by a simpler alphabet borrowed with little change from the Greek. This second alphabet, in order to honor the apostle Cyril, received the name Cyrillic; but it cannot be proved that Cyril invented it or in any way promulgated its use. Let us note that the Cyrillic symbols have persisted in the Slav world of the Greek or Orthodox faith and are employed to this day by Russians, Serbs, and Bulgars.

they failed in Moravia, where the Latin propaganda finally won the day, this was a small matter compared with the Slav alphabet, books, and liturgy which went abroad among the Slavs generally and aroused something akin to a national enthusiasm. In Bulgaria, which, as we saw, hesitated for a long time to choose between the pope and the patriarch, the Slav ritual and literature unquestionably helped to decide the issue in favor of Constantinople. Without more ado the young Bulgar church appropriated the literary labors of the brothers, who, though they never appeared in Bulgaria, may be, and have in fact been, claimed as the spiritual fathers of Bulgar Christianity. In the same way the brothers are to this day regarded as their national and religious champions by the Serb groups of the peninsula, for, on adopting Christianity, as, following the Bulgar conversion, they began increasingly to do, they entered into automatic possession of the Slav alphabet and literature. When finally, though a whole century later, the Russians, planted along the upland courses of the Dnieper, became Christians, they too built up their faith and church on this same foundation. Rarely, if ever, have the labors of holy men spread so far or had such consequences for the cause of religion and civilization as those of Method and Constantine.

We now return with quickened interest to the Bulgars, who by virtue of the disappearance, as a separate racial element, of the Mongolian ruling class, have become a united Slav people, and who by the adoption of Christianity have entered the circle of Mediterranean civilization. Their ruler, Boris, no longer now an Asiatic khan, drew the logical conclusion from his change of faith. He opened his realm to Greek influences, fostered trade with Constantinople, and, as a final sign of his change of heart, sent a younger son, Simeon, to the Golden Horn to receive the advantage of a Greek education. On the approach of old age he resigned his crown and retired to a monastery, but when his legal successor proved a weakling, the vigorous old man left his retreat, deposed his feeble first-born, and put the capable Simeon on the throne.

Boris fosters the commercial and cultural relationship with Constantinople.

In Simeon (893–927), in whom the barbarian strength of his ancestors was interestingly blended with the intellectual culture of the Greeks, we encounter the greatest ruler of the First

The reign of Simeon, 893–927.

Bulgar state. Through a long reign he pursued two conspicuous ends: he wished to help his people forward on the road of civilization; and he held fast to the program inherited from his ancestors of destroying the Greek empire and uniting Balkania under Bulgar sway.

Simeon patronizes learning and reopens the struggle with the Greeks.

To promote the cause of learning Simeon had numerous Greek books translated into Slav; nay, not content with hiring others, he actively participated in these literary labors. Though the multiplication of books doubtless aided knowledge, the particular kind of knowledge cherished by medieval Greeks, it did not necessarily make for originality. On the whole the Bulgars were slow to take to literary expression and never accumulated a literature of outstanding merit. Under the circumstances our chief interest shifts to Simeon's second object, to his political ambitions. He was hardly well established on the throne when he renewed the ancient struggle with the Greeks. One at least of our sources informs us that the Greeks rather than the Bulgars provoked the war which, if true, would go to show that the conflict, as has already been said, was irrepressible. Whether Simeon was or was not the aggressor, he in any case defeated the emperor who, hard pressed, resorted to the familiar Greek device of summoning a savage people from beyond the Danube to attack the foe in the rear. The strangers, won by gold and precious robes, invaded Bulgaria from the north, thereby instantly affording the Greeks the desired relief.

The coming of the Magyars.

The folk thus summoned were the Magyars, another one of the many Asiatic tribes who had long been engaged in driving westward from the wide steppes beyond the Caspian to the rich grazing-ground north of the Black sea. For several years the Magyars raided Bulgaria in force and were a terrible burden to the country. Then an opportunity, which Simeon was quick to seize, rid him of his foe (895). Joining hands with another band of Mongols, enemies of the Magyars, he raided their encampment on the Pruth river with such destructive thoroughness that the Magyars abandoned their Black sea home and, moving west, pitched their tents on the middle Danube in the fertile plain where the Huns and the Avars had successively settled before them. Henceforth they spared Simeon, preferring to carry terror into the more opulent regions of Italy and Germany.

Through imitation of their neighbors and by the gradual assimilation into their stock of surrounding German and Slav elements they became, in the course of some generations, Europeanized, and founded, under the name of Hungary, a mid-Danubian state which has continued to our day.

BULGARIA
AT THE DEATH OF
TSAR SIMEON, 927
▬ LIMITS OF MEDIEVAL BULGARIA
▨ EASTERN EMPIRE
SCALE OF MILES
50   0   50   100

The Magyar or Hungarian state, located just across the northern border of Balkania, was destined henceforth to figure considerably in the political story of the peninsula. While these occasions will be dealt with when they occur, it may be useful, before going on with the Bulgars, to submit two reflections bearing on the historical importance of the Magyars. First, the Magyars have the distinction of being, if we except the case of the Turks to be discussed at a later time, the only tribe of Asiatic nomads, who, settling in Europe, have succeeded in maintaining to our own day an unbroken tradition of speech and political organization. Of course the Magyars with the passing of time

Two historical reflections on the Magyar state.

absorbed numerous Indo-European elements and are at present substantially Indo-European in type and civilization; but the fact remains that they were the absorbers and not, as for instance in the case of the Bulgars, the absorbed. Our second generalization is concerned with the tremendous influence on the general destiny of the Slavs of the coming of the Magyars. By founding a state in the plains of the Danube, they drove a wedge between the Balkan or South Slavs and their northern relatives, the Czechs and Poles, thus keeping them from ever successfully welding their forces into a single Slav mass. Perhaps it is not too much to say that the Magyars, by virtue of their location, have been and remain the chief obstacle in the way of a single Slav *imperium* stretching all the way from the Baltic and the Vistula to the Adriatic and Aegean seas.

Simeon conquers large sections of Macedonia and Thrace.

On the removal to the mid-Danube of the Magyars whom, yielding to long-established custom, we shall henceforth call the Hungarians, Simeon was free to attend again to the Greek empire. By attempting to extend his power over the Serb tribes to the west of him he created fresh alarm on the Bosporus, where the Serbs were looked upon as subjects of Constantinople. Accordingly new wars followed in which Simeon was highly successful. He overran large sections of Macedonia and Thrace and failed to reach the Aegean shore only because, being without a sufficient navy, he could not cut the Greek communications by sea. Full of animosity against an enemy whom he looked upon as both weak and treacherous, he girded his loins to take Constantinople and on four different occasions carried the war to its gates. But the capture of the city by a land power pure and simple, like Bulgaria, was out of the question.

Simeon reduces the Serb tribes to obedience.

However, as a result of these successes the Greek empire was greatly reduced in territory, while the demoralized Greek army hardly dared show itself outside the walled towns. Conscious of his mastery of the situation, Simeon now adventured far into the difficult mountains of the northwest. Since Boris, his father, had for a time forced the submission of some of the Serbs, Simeon could persuade himself that he was only following a blazed trail. When, after stubborn resistance, most of the Serbs had bowed to Bulgar supremacy, Simeon, in the familiar manner of successful soldiers, was moved to push still farther west into the land of the Croats. Defeated in this venture, Simeon died (927) before he could organize a new force and square accounts with the Croat tribesmen. Reviewing his many campaigns, it may be said quite soberly that he all but united Balkania under his sway. The diminished Greek power, cowering behind the impregnable walls of Constantinople, still held out against him but its days were apparently numbered.

Long before his death Simeon had won so dominant a position that he felt urged to remove from the institutions of Bulgaria every trace of inferiority to Byzantium. If Boris had been content to set up a national church which, though enjoying local independence, acknowledged the supremacy of the Constantinopolitan patriarch, this no longer suited the son's pride. In consequence Simeon published a decree making the archbishop, the highest ecclesiastical official of Bulgaria, a patriarch, and proclaiming the national church free and independent. At the same time he abandoned the various titles of his predecessors as lacking in dignity, and styled himself tsar, the Slav equivalent of the Latin Caesar. That he adopted this title [1] is evidence of the almost superstitious respect in which he, like all the barbarian conquerors, held the Roman empire. True, he was engaged in mortal combat with the enfeebled representative of Rome, but in attempting to outshine him before the world Simeon could think of no more effective means than the appropriation of his most famous title. Altogether it is clear that Simeon carried the Bulgar power to a dazzling pinnacle. If a contemporary of a prognosticating turn had declared that Bulgaria and Balkania were destined to be interchangeable terms he would have been looked upon as neither bold nor original.

Simeon frees the Bulgar church from Constantinople and adopts the title tsar.

None-the-less the Bulgar greatness proved to be wholly ephemeral. Doubtless the state was at no time a very solid fabric since it embraced too many conquered and unwilling peoples. An energetic ruler had accumulated the parts of the structure and an energetic ruler was needed to hold them together. But Simeon was succeeded by his son, Peter (927–969),

Rapid decay of Bulgaria after Simeon.

---

[1] The full title adopted was: "Tsar of the Bulgars and Autocrat of the Romans" (Greeks). In the face of this title we cannot but feel confirmed in the opinion that his ultimate design was to crowd out the Greek sovereign altogether and to take over his dignities and lands.

who, in spite of some personal merits, for he was a man of great Christian piety, was totally unfit for the headship of an empire of conquest. Having no fondness for war, he reversed his father's Greek policy and tried to establish good neighborhood relations with Constantinople. To this end he even contracted marriage with a Greek princess. The Bulgar war party, nursing the traditions of Simeon, was offended by this turn of events and prompted the tsar's brother to revolt against him. Though this particular storm was weathered, the domestic troubles, once begun, continued unabated until in the year 963 a nobleman, Sisman by name, led a revolt of the western provinces which ended in independence. The great Simeon was dead only a few decades and already his empire had fallen into two parts! As misfortunes usually do not come singly, the Serbs, taking advantage of Tsar Peter's embarrassments, rose in revolt, while the Hungarians and other powerful neighbors plundered the reduced state at will. In these circumstances it required only one of those periodic revivals, for which the Greek empire was famous, to reduce Simeon's tottering state to ruin absolute.

CHAPTER IX

THE BYZANTINE EMPIRE AT ITS HEIGHT UNDER THE BASILIAN DYNASTY (867-1056)

In the days when Bulgaria was disintegrating under Tsar Peter another revival of the Greek empire took place which was destined to carry it to its medieval apogee. The revival really began before Peter's time, though imperceptibly, and may be largely referred to Basil who, of Macedonian peasant origin, and possibly a Slav by blood, was by a series of romantic accidents carried to the imperial throne. The notable thing about Basil I, who reigned from 867 to 886, was that, a vigorous, capable man, he founded a dynasty — the Basilian or Macedonian dynasty — thereby considerably stabilizing the restless situation on the Golden Horn by eliminating, at least temporarily, the troublesome succession issue. However, Basil's immediate successors proved to be weak and of such little moment that they cut but a sorry figure by the side of the towering Simeon of neighboring Bulgaria. On Simeon's death (927), followed by the accession of the pious Peter, the fallen Greek prestige rose almost automatically. At the same time the Fates, presiding over men and governments, made another and a most notable gift to the Greeks in the relaxation of the pressure so long exerted by the Arab empire on the Asia Minor front.

Stabilization of Greek affairs under the Basilian (Macedonian) dynasty.

The reader will recall that the Arab empire had, about the year 750 and under guidance of a new dynasty, the Abbassids, withdrawn from Damascus in Syria, and established itself at Bagdad on the Tigris river. From that vantage-point it continued to harass Christian Asia Minor for about two hundred years, that is, till the middle of the tenth century. In all that time therefore the Greek empire was held by the Arabs in the east, and the Bulgars in the west as in an iron vise. But toward the middle of the tenth century, the two arms of the vise began simultaneously to give way, in either case because of fatal flaws

Simultaneous failure of the Bulgar and Arab empires about 950.

developed by the mechanism. The immediate result for the
Greeks was to experience an enormous sense of relief. Girding
its loins for a new effort, the empire quickly mounted to the
highest level which it attained in the whole medieval period.

Nicephorus Phocas begins the offensive against the Arabs.

The man, to whom more than to Basil I or to any other single
individual the new forward movement was due, was a general
by the name of Nicephorus Phocas. A noble of Cappadocia,
in eastern Asia Minor, Nicephorus had been brought up in the
constant guerrilla warfare with the marauding Arabs which the
Greeks were obliged to maintain on this border. The great fact
of his day in the East — a fact which must have filled him
with rejoicing — was the disintegration of the Arab califate
into small separate dominions under rival chiefs called
emirs. In the imperial councils at Constantinople, Nicephorus
urged that this situation be promptly and prudently taken advantage of by a general offensive against the weakened Moslems.
His opinion carried the day, and after some preliminary sparring
at several points along the extensive line of Christian-Moslem
contact, the island of Crete was fixed on as the first objective.
Some generations before the Arab corsairs had seized this Aegean
stronghold and from its sheltered bays had since that time pursued the profitable game of waylaying the passing traders and of
descending at pleasure on the neighboring Christian coasts. It
indicates the extraordinary vigor of these Saracen freebooters
as well as the depth to which Greek sea-power had temporarily
fallen, that year in, year out, the Cretan pirates carried on their
nefarious occupation. An ample armada was now with a
sudden access of energy brought together, with Nicephorus, the
champion of the war-program, put in charge. In 960 he set
sail and, shattering the unbelievers with a succession of well-
directed blows, put himself in complete possession of the island.
Shortly after, the emperor under whom Nicephorus served,
Romanus II of the Basilian line, died. Owing to his great
credit among the people and soldiers alike, the heroic Nicephorus
was made guardian of the emperor's little sons and appointed
co-regent with the full imperial title (963).

The success and murder of Niceph-orus.

Nicephorus was now free to pursue his military plan without
let or hindrance, and turned his concentrated energy upon the
Arab emirs along the Asia Minor front. In successive campaigns

he smote them hip and thigh, compelling them entirely to release
their grip upon the Taurus mountains. Then he pursued them
into the Syrian plain, recapturing territory which had not seen
a Roman soldier since the far-off days of Heraclius. But in
spite of his victories Nicephorus gradually lost his hold on the
people of Constantinople, first, because a famine, for which the
superstitious mob blamed the government, made bread scarce,
and second, because his financial straits led him to debase the
currency, a measure responsible for a general advance of prices.
The clergy too ceased to support him when, alarmed by the concentration of estates in the hands of the church, he issued a
decree forbidding further testamentary bequests of land to this
all-powerful organization. Finally, the personal element, subtly
effective as always and everywhere, helped to set the stage against
him. Brought up in camp and accustomed to hardships of all
kinds, Nicephorus exhibited a stern military temper highly re-
pugnant to the easy-going, luxury-loving court and nobles. In
these disgruntled upper circles a conspiracy was formed against
him, headed by his own wife and nephew, and in the year 969,
after only six years of rule, the famous "Hammer of the Arabs"
was foully murdered without a single hand being lifted in his
behalf.

The plotting nephew, John Zimisces by name, now became
guardian of the imperial children and co-regent under the title
John I (969–76); and although he had made his way to the
throne by a shocking crime, it cannot be denied that he proved
a sovereign of exceptional distinction. John Zimisces was a
handsome man of courtly manners, who, in personal appearance
the very antipodes of his crusty predecessor, did not yield to
him one whit in military talent. From the policy so successfully pursued by Nicephorus he saw no reason to depart. What
remained to be done in the East in the way of securing Asia Minor
from Moslem depredations and surrounding it with a broad belt
of fortified territory, he carried out in his short reign, letting the
emirs feel repeatedly the power of his sword-arm. But the
liberation of the East had already gone so far by virtue of the
labors of Nicephorus, that the new emperor was able to direct
a large part of his attention to the Balkan peninsula, that is, to
the Bulgars.

The reign
of John
Zimisces
(969–76).

The Russians, as allies of the Greek empire, attack the Bulgars.

We are aware to what a pass the ephemeral greatness of the Bulgar state had been brought in the later days of Tsar Peter by reason of the revolt of western Bulgaria under its leader Sisman (963). To Nicephorus, just then mounting the throne, the schism in the Bulgar camp must have looked like a lucky stroke, for, busy to the full with the Arab emirs, he would have been greatly hampered had he been obliged to reckon with the possibility of a Bulgar diversion in his rear. However, resolved to make assurance doubly sure, Nicephorus appealed for aid to a heathen and barbarous folk, the Russians. In execution of a characteristic Byzantine intrigue these remote people were now for the first time effectively projected into the destiny of Balkania. In the days of Nicephorus, the Russians made their home on the Dnieper river in the general neighborhood of Kiev. Slavs by race, though ruled at this time by a band of Norse conquerors, they were near relatives of the Bulgars and the Serbs. Mere blood ties, however, spun few threads of friendship in that era. On Nicephorus' inviting them to invade Bulgaria, lured by the prospect of plunder they eagerly responded and crossed the Danube with a large force.

The Russians conquer Bulgaria, 970.

Faced by this grave national crisis, the feeble Tsar Peter in blank despair gave up the ghost (969), and though his son and successor Boris II made what resistance he could, before many months had passed he was defeated and captured and his country taken over by the victors (970). Thus perished Bulgaria, or rather East Bulgaria, since West Bulgaria, owing to the revolt of Sisman, was a separate state not included in the Russian conquest. East Bulgaria fell, as our story has revealed, primarily by reason of its domestic ills, but the fatal blow, it is curious to reflect, was delivered not by the Greeks but by a kindred Slav people from the flats of the Dnieper.

John Zimisces drives out the Russians.

The Russians were now to learn that he who spreads the table does not always sit down to meat. To the Greeks who summoned them they were but a savage horde, good enough to use as a battering-ram against the Bulgars but under no circumstances to be suffered permanently in the peninsula. Although the Emperor Nicephorus, who had called them into Balkania, died too soon to take decisive action against them, his successor, John I, was promptness itself in attacking the unwelcome guest. In the year 971 he conducted a masterly campaign between the Balkans and the Danube, defeated the northern visitors signally and on repeated occasions, and finally sent the decimated remnant flying home to the plains of Kiev whence they came. Bulgaria, wrested from the Russians, became the emperor's prize and was promptly incorporated in the Greek state.

When after a short and, from a military view-point, brilliant reign John Zimisces died (976), he was succeeded by his ward, Basil II (976–1025), the legal representative of the reigning dynasty. At Basil's accession to the empire the stage was visibly set for great achievements. Control of the eastern Mediterranean had been regained by the Greeks, the Arab power had been forced back from Asia Minor into Syria and Mesopotamia, and the Bulgar state, the most dangerous of Constantinople's recent foes, had been trampled in the dust. Basil II, a young man of twenty, might well feel proud and satisfied as he looked about him to take stock of his inheritance. But if he or any minister in his employ imagined that henceforward there would be smooth sailing for the ship of state, they were destined to be quickly disillusioned. For one thing the Arabs, though beaten, by no means ceased from their destructive forays, and for another the constant wars had produced, together with a powerful army, that ominous, concomitant phenomenon, the ambitious general, with an eye directed to the main chance. Basil found himself confronted with civil brawls, hatched by his own unscrupulous captains, which it took years of cautious diplomacy and energetic fighting to suppress. But, out-topping these troubles, grave as they were, was the rapid and alarming development of West Bulgaria.

The situation at the succession of Basil II (976–1025).

In the very year (976) in which Basil mounted the throne at Constantinople, Tsar Samuel, son of the successful rebel chieftain, Sisman, took control over the western section of Bulgaria not included in the recent conquest of John Zimisces. Samuel was a man of extraordinary vigor who, assuming the leadership of the national party, aimed at nothing less than to build anew the great empire of Simeon. So audacious a program could only mean renewed war, in fact war to the knife, between Greek and Bulgar.

Tsar Samuel, ruler of West Bulgaria.

Samuel's
early suc-
cesses.

Samuel's early enterprises were all highly successful. East Bulgaria, after all only superficially subdued by John I, rose against the Emperor Basil and hailed with enthusiasm the Slav liberator from the west. Basil, whose hands were tied by his youth and inexperience as well as by rebellions in his army and by periodic difficulties in the Arab east, was obliged to bide his time. Encouraged by this inaction, Samuel assumed the offensive, repeatedly invaded Thessaly, and even ravaged Greece with vindictive thoroughness as far south as the isthmus of Corinth. When, provoked by these raids, Basil attacked in his turn, he was signally defeated (981) and had meekly to suffer the control of the peninsula to the very borders of Thrace to pass into the hands of the tsar. With the Bulgar star again in the ascendant the first phase of the struggle between Basil and Samuel came to an end.

Samuel's
Bulgar em-
pire has its
center of
gravity in
Macedonia.

Samuel, who, while fanatically hating the Greeks, was no mere plunderer but a statesman and a general of parts, did not make the mistake of thinking the struggle won by his early triumphs. He took up his residence by the Macedonian lakes, Prespa and Ochrida, where he built himself a number of lofty castles as the center of a remarkable system of defense. Around his Macedonian capital, in ring on ring of natural bulwarks, rose the mountains, which he strengthened with castles and forts and every military means at his disposal. Since the mobile forces composing his field army were effectively concealed from the Greeks by a screen of mountains, he was in a position to hurl himself at pleasure either southward into Thessaly or eastward into Thrace. By these cautious yet provocative tactics he suspended a drawn sword over every European province of the empire. Had it not been for the circumstance that a new dynasty occupied the throne and that the government was directed from Macedonia instead of from the Danube area, the Bulgar people might have been led to think that Simeon's glory had never been extinguished.

Basil turns
the tables on
Tsar Samuel.

Certainly Emperor Basil II was not in an enviable position. But he too, like his Bulgar adversary, was an unusual and sturdy ruler, not easily broken by defeat. In the hard school of adversity he manfully conned the principles of politics and war and became a master in both fields. After that one premature venture of 981, when he had been badly punished for his precipitation, he possessed his soul in patience and, while strengthening the state financially, labored with particular zeal to render the army efficient in every department. Not till fifteen years had passed was he ready. Then, reopening the struggle, he completely turned the tables on his foe. In a succession of daring campaigns he not only defeated and drove back the tsar's field armies but reconquered so much territory that only Macedonia, the heart and central stronghold of the Bulgar state, was left in the hands of its ruler. After a breathing-spell of some years he attacked Macedonia too, in spite of its natural difficulties increased by all the resources of military science. In a great battle fought in the Rhodope mountains he destroyed the last great army of the tsar, almost capturing the tsar himself, who only just managed to effect his escape.

Grimly resolved to bring the struggle to a close and animated with the vindictiveness born of a lifelong, deadly feud, Basil was now guilty of an act which filled even his rude contemporaries with horror and won him in history the crimson title of the Bulgar-killer. The recent victory had delivered into his hands some fifteen thousand Bulgar captives. These, incredible as it sounds, he caused to be blinded and divided into hundreds; then, appointing as leader of each hundred a man who, in order to act as guide, had in hideous mockery been deprived of only one eye, he set the blank, staring faces homeward to carry the message of his omnipotence to his beaten adversary. When the ghastly procession approached the tsar's capital the people crowded the walls to see, and the tsar, as though struck with a bolt, sank to the ground in a stupor and died without recovering consciousness (September, 1014). *Basil earns the grim title of Slayer of the Bulgars.*

With blow on blow the implacable Basil followed up his advantage. But four years more passed before he could complete the capture of the inner strongholds around the lake of Ochrida and so force the surrender of the last Bulgar bands. Master of the whole of Bulgaria, he now proclaimed its annexation to the Greek state (1018). What John Zimisces had begun in capturing East Bulgaria only to have undone by the doughty Tsar Samuel, Basil the Bulgar-killer, after forty years of unremitting effort, carried to a victorious conclusion. *Finis Bulgariae, 1018.*

Reasons why
Bulgaria was
sure to rise
again.

Defeated Bulgaria remained a Greek province for almost two hundred years (1018–1186). After his cruel final blows Basil adopted a policy toward his conquest which was neither ungenerous nor unwise. The Bulgar state and church were brought into dependency on Constantinople, but local self-government was not destroyed nor were the burdens of taxation increased. Most probably the emperor entertained the hope of gradually reconciling the Slavs to their lot by means of a studied moderation. Needless to say he did not succeed, and his successors, many of them avaricious, debauched, and unbridled men, succeeded much less than he. The fact was that, though Bulgarian independence was no more, the Bulgar *people* lived and, distributed in large numbers over those Balkan areas which they had made their own, defied assimilation by the numerically inferior Greeks. If the Bulgars had still been the barbarians they were on their first appearance in the peninsula, they might perhaps, on losing their freedom, have vanished from the scene as a separate nationality. But they had become stalwart peasants and were now, as it were, part of the earth itself; they had been Christianized and through Christianity had been introduced to the boon of Mediterranean civilization; and finally, they had built a state of their own and accumulated imposing national memories of which the names of Boris, Simeon, and Samuel were the flaming symbols. For all these reasons the Bulgars, though buried in 1018 under the Greek avalanche, might confidently look forward to a resurrection.

With Basil II
the Byzan-
tine empire
attains its
highest point.

The victorious Basil, however, for his part, was free to hope that the Bulgar overthrow would prove permanent. And indeed as he looked about the peninsula a remarkable situation met his eye, for not only had the Bulgars been incorporated in his empire but the Serbs to the west of them, and even the Croats to the west of the Serbs, freely acknowledged the Greek supremacy. Not since the days before the wanderings of the tribes had the empire enjoyed such an unquestioned ascendancy in Balkania. If we consider further that the disrupted Arabs had been pushed from the confines of Asia Minor and now no longer seriously threatened the eastern border, we may easily convince ourselves that under Basil II, the Roman empire, stretching from the Danube in Europe to the Euphrates in Asia, had reached its medieval summit. On conquering Bulgaria after the effort of a lifetime, Basil, now an old man, could afford to rest on his laurels. We are told, in connection with the glittering rôle which he played, as the central figure in the elaborate pomps of the Byzantine court, that he habitually wore beneath the embroidered and jeweled robes of office the coarse garment of a monk. How characteristic of the Middle Age is that trait! And how peculiarly Byzantine too, in its cheek-by-jowl of luxury and asceticism! Though we moderns are hardly likely to feel a lively admiration for a sovereign belonging so peculiarly to a time grown strange to us, we cannot but yield him a cold respect because in a long life, replete with the severest trials, he bore himself in a manner worthy of a ruler of men. It remained to be seen if there would appear a Greek emperor after him capable of holding together what he and his predecessors had assembled.

Basil's long reign constitutes so manifestly the summit of the Greek empire that we shall be well inspired to pause for a moment in our narrative of events in order to arrive at some estimate of its place among medieval states by taking a brief survey of its government and society as well as of the state of learning and the arts. We have seen that this empire, legal heir of the *imperium romanum,* may be assumed to have taken on its characteristic Byzantine form in the time of Justinian, five hundred years before Basil II. In all that period it was without question the greatest state in the world. Not that other empires did not arise from time to time prepared to challenge comparison with it. Thus the Arab empire had for a while obscured and threatened the Greek state, but the Arab empire, already sunk into a feeble senility, was now slowly tottering to its grave. Of the Bulgar empire, its rise and fall, we have just spoken. Again, the Frank empire of the West, in the days of Charles the Great, had boasted an impressive façade, but as early as the ninth century, the Frankish power, too, fell on evil days. As for the Byzantine state, though on several occasions it had been almost crushed, it had always shown a remarkable resilience and, regularly recovering the lost ground, succeeded, about the year 1000 A.D., in reaching the pinnacle of its career. In such a story there is little to justify the slurs and reproaches with which it is still customary to dismiss this enduring edifice. Surely a more

A survey of Byzantine achievements necessary at this point to determine the empire's place in history.

reasonable procedure is not only to treat it with respect but to inquire into its characteristic institutions and the sources of its strength.

Persistence of the principles of Roman law, administration, and taxation.

It is clear to even cursory inspection that what sustained the Byzantine empire in the long period of its power were its solid Roman foundations. The corner-stone of the structure was the orderly system of Roman law, codified under Justinian and repeatedly revised, particularly under Leo the Isaurian and Basil I, to meet the requirements of an altered age. Under this system persons and property enjoyed that security which is the primary characteristic of a society aspiring to be civilized. Commanding the services of a body of lawyers and judges trained in a great tradition and animated by an invaluable *esprit de corps,* the state boasted also a body of civil servants, who drew their inspiration from the same source. In a period of European history dominated by gross, anarchic feudalism the Byzantine bureaucracy continued to show unusual skill in handling the manifold business of a well-governed state. However, one notable departure from the Roman tradition deserves to be set down. Instead of the military and civil administrations being kept strictly divided, they had since the seventh century been fused, with the result that the emperor was represented in the provincial divisions, called themes,[1] by a single, powerful official, the general or *strategos.* In the days when the empire was fighting for its life against Arabs and Bulgars, this concentration may have been necessary in the interests of an increased efficiency, but undoubtedly it must be construed as a growing militarization of the state. Judged by the finances, however, which everywhere and always furnish an excellent gauge of a government's capacity, the empire did not suffer from the adoption of a militarist régime. It admits of no dispute that the budget of the Greek state represented far and away the most scientific achievement in this kind of the whole Middle Age. Here again the Roman tradition ruled. The taxes were based on a careful census of persons and property periodically revised, and though they were by no means few or light, they tended to remain fixed and were, on the

---

[1] The word theme, originally meaning regiment, came gradually to designate the district in which a given regiment or group of regiments was quartered.

whole, very little perverted by the individual whim of a strategos
or even a minister or emperor.

In the army and navy, supporting pillars of the state coördinate
with justice and administration, the Roman system celebrated
another and not its smallest triumph. The army and navy were
maintained at a remarkable degree of efficiency, with arsenals,
shipyards, professional staffs, and the whole richly diversified
organization and equipment devised by the Roman world-con-
querors. The Byzantines even added to this inheritance by an
occasional invention such as the redoubtable Greek fire. Of
course the establishment had its drawbacks, the most striking
to the modern eye being that the army and navy lacked a national
basis. True, a modest percentage of the rank and file and a considerable section of the officers were recruited from the native-
born population, but unquestionably the bulk of the fighting force
consisted of foreign mercenaries — Armenians, Slavs, Bulgars,
Franks, Scandinavians, and even Asiatic Moslems. Though such
an army, distinctly deficient in what we understand as patriotism,
could with relative ease be seduced by a successful and magnetic
general to raise the banner of rebellion, the fact is undeniable
that, in spite of their mercenary character, a common discipline
knit the armed forces into a remarkably uniform and coherent
whole. If there were times when the war-machine, both army
and navy, was permitted to run down, recovery under an energetic
emperor, like Heraclius or Leo the Isaurian or Nicephorus, was
swift, and the long string of victories won on land and sea
eloquently proclaims the unbroken superiority of the science and
discipline of East Rome, daughter and heir to the war-like city
on the Tiber.

In all the centuries from the sixth to the eleventh there was
little change in these fundamentals of the system, but that little,
subtly cumulative, was destined to be an important factor in
the collapse of the state. The system just described was crowned
by an absolute monarch, conceived as the chief official of the
empire in command of the army and the navy and entrusted with
the execution of the law, of which he was the living voice. However, by slow changes he had become differentiated from the
Roman emperors, his predecessors. Under influences hailing from
the East he had, on the one hand, become immersed in a languid

> Persistence of the Roman tradition in the army and navy.

> The Byzantine absolutism and its gradual impairment by the rise of feudalism.

atmosphere of oriental despotism and, on the other, by his identification with Christianity he had received the sacred character
of an Anointed of the Lord. Of this reputed divinity a striking
evidence was supplied by the Byzantine painters who in their
pictures encircled the emperor's head with a golden aureole, exactly as in the case of authentic saints. Apart from occasional
riots in the circus, the people meekly bowed their necks to an
emperor, proclaimed the plenipotentiary of God, while the church,
in spite of its immense social influence, made equally humble
submission, especially after the termination of the controversy over images. If a shadow gradually appeared which
threatened to obscure this unrivaled splendor, it came
neither from the people nor the church, but from the great
nobles. By amassing vast estates their power steadily grew in
the provinces till they boasted a position like that of the feudal
magnates of the West. Even the popular Macedonian line, including the iron-willed Basil II, was frequently troubled with the
revolt of the great lords, whose status, due in the first place to
their landed wealth, was dangerously enhanced by virtue of their
holding the great positions at court and in the army. As soon as
Basil II's strong hand was removed it became apparent that his
weakling brother, Constantine VIII, was not equal to the occasion,
and a preponderance of the feudal elements made itself felt
which, by making the crown the plaything of noble factions,
largely accounts for the overthrow of the state effected by the
Fourth Crusade.

The unregu-
lated succes-
sion.

The unsettled succession to the throne also figured in the
Byzantine decline, although to what extent is subject to dispute.
Theoretically the Roman monarchy was from of old elective,
each new sovereign representing the choice of the senate and the
people. Since senate and people were not in a position to act
promptly when a ruler died, an ambitious general, commanding
an armed force, was able with comparative ease to impose himself
on the state; or, if the army failed to act, the deft intriguers
of the court could step in and set the stage in a manner favorable
to one of their number. Although the succession, thus left to
the play of chance, precipitated, as we have seen, a periodic
turmoil, some historians have contended, with a good show of
reason, that it gave the state on the whole much more active and

capable sovereigns than are customarily secured under the principle of heredity. Since the monarchy was a prize, awarded to the victor in a struggle, there was, we may admit, an inherent probability that it would be won only by a man of more than average endowments. However, such a strong man, especially if, like Heraclius or Leo, he gained a wide popularity by a great military triumph, would be tempted to establish a dynasty, and the rule, for about a century, of respectively the Heraclians and Isaurians and, for two centuries, of the Basilians, shows that the hereditary principle was constantly tending to supplant election. It was not a confirmed preference for election but the accidental failure of offspring which brought the rule of the above, and of all other dynasties, to a premature end. In sum, a curious alternation of election and heredity continued to characterize the succession to the Constantinopolitan throne to the last. But whether in the long run the state gained more than it lost from this irregular manner of filling the imperial office is very hard to say.

Administration, law, army, and navy, however well organized, are at best only machinery. In final analysis a state is weak or strong, feeble or vital by reason of the men who compose its society, and are or are not materially, mentally, and morally disciplined, energetic, and creative. We have commonly referred to the inhabitants of the eastern empire as Byzantines or Greeks; but Greeks in a strict racial sense they certainly were not. The old and heroic Hellenic strain at home on all the islands and coasts of the Aegean including Asia Minor, was on the whole but feebly represented in the total population of the empire. The outstanding fact is that the subjects of the Byzantine emperors represented an astonishingly large number of different races, some of which lived side by side in all but complete isolation. In Asia Minor alone half a score of separate ethnic elements could be traced, and while some were doubtless disappearing through absorption by the dominating Greeks, others, like the Armenians, showed remarkable vitality and succesfully cultivated their own language, customs, and personality. In Balkania we have become familiar with Greeks, Albanians, Serbs, and Bulgars, who certainly were distinct peoples and often enough drove violently apart.

The Byzantine empire a racially composite state.

Unifying el-
ements in
Byzantine so-
ciety.

If so many diverse elements were none-the-less held together in imperfect fellowship, it was undoubtedly due to the cement supplied by a common government and church, and to the prevalence of the Greek language and culture. Besides, a ruling group of great families and officials exercised a wide authority and were no doubt a unifying factor. Greeks to all appearances, these magnates called themselves not Greeks but Romans, since in their eyes the state they served was the authentic Roman empire. This strange obsession they even carried to the point of calling the language which they spoke, Greek though it was, Romaic, that is, Roman. Not till the crusades produced an active enmity against the West was this make-believe Roman patriotism replaced by a powerful local sentiment, in which we recognize the beginnings of Greek nationalism. As for the common people they boasted few or none of the attitudes and opinions of the upper crust. What stirred them more deeply than aught else was a passionate enthusiasm for the Orthodox church, which had stood like a rock amidst the wild surging of the Moslem sea. Of patriotism, a purely civic sentiment, these lower orders, oppressed and without the smallest share of political responsibility, had hardly an inkling, but for that institution which counted far more than the state, because it dealt not with temporal but with eternal values, they could on occasion be filled with such fervor as to risk their very all.

The classes:
great and
small land-
holders.

A crucible of peoples of European and Asiatic stocks, the Byzantine state, like its Roman model, fell into well-marked social strata. The leading class consisted of the great landholders. They constituted the nobility and furnished the high officials of the civil and military establishments. Largely absentees, consuming their vast revenues at Constantinople, they permitted their estates to be worked by tenants whose legal status was subject to considerable fluctuation and who, enjoying a decent measure of rights in one age, might in another be delivered over as serfs to the mercy of their masters. Interspersed among the great proprietors was to be found a class of small farmers settled in village communities and rated as freemen by the law. A noticeable shrinkage of their ranks took place under the Basilian monarchs, who by means of legislative enactments were at great pains to save this important yeoman group from extinc-

tion. However, the movement toward large estates, owned by
the nobility and church and worked by tenants increasingly degraded to serfdom, and in many instances by gangs of out-and-out
slaves, proved irresistible, and after the reign of Basil II, gave
the empire an agricultural organization suggestive to a certain
extent of the feudal West. That the victory of feudalism, with
its suppression of the small freeholder and its movement toward
the large serf or slave-worked estate, weakened the structure of
society and helped prepare the downfall of the government
admits of no doubt.

A contributory cause to that overthrow was the decline of the
middle class. However, in the five centuries we have under
review, the middle class, far from being in decline, was perhaps
the most vital factor in Byzantine society. From it came the
artisans, shopkeepers, merchants, and shipowners whose activities
not only gave the state its unchallenged ascendancy in the whole
Mediterranean area in the matter of production and exchange,
but also yielded to the government the abundant taxes which
were the very breath of its nostrils. We have noted that as early
as the days of Justinian the industrial activities of the towns
were directed to silk-weaving and the artistic crafts, and that the
Byzantine trade flourished largely by virtue of products properly
classifiable as luxuries. The rude Roman-Germanic West was
supplied with practically all its articles of this kind by the Greek
merchants, who, in addition, profited by that commonest and most
revolting article of early medieval commerce, the slave. But
the largest returns of the Greek merchant firms came undoubtedly
from still another source, that is, from the monopoly enjoyed by
them as the European distributors of the specialties of India and
China consisting of spices, drugs, dyes, and costly stuffs. This
eastern commerce, which still as in the days of Justinian used
the caravan routes of Asia to the Caspian and Black seas and
thence the water passage to the Bosporus, made the Byzantine
capital not only the central market for oriental goods but also
irresistibly drew to it representatives of all the backward and
aspiring peoples contiguous to the empire, such as the Bulgars,
Russians, Arabs, and Italians. For five centuries the prosperity
of Constantinople showed no signs of abating and in the eyes
of friend and foe alike it continued to stand out in point of wealth
and splendor as the leading city of the world.

Prosperity of the middle class.

Decay of the
middle class
and of soci-
ety generally
after the
eleventh cen-
tury.
A combination of many causes, apparent and concealed, was
necessary to deprive the middle class of its lofty position of
wealth and power.   Manifestly the political events and domestic
revolutions (to be traced in the next chapter) are an important
part of the story since they destroyed the security which trade
and industry regularly require if they are to flourish.   But such
a complete and hopeless fall as that which overtook Byzantine
society must after all be chiefly due to inner, moral causes which,
if not easily defined, may at least be broadly indicated.   Undoubtedly the growing feudalism, which treated the offices as rewards to be meted out to partizans, not only clogged the machinery of government but despoiled the people and spread a general habit of corruption.   Again, the hollow formalism of the
orient, not content with confining court and church in the strait-
jacket of an endless round of empty ceremonies, extended like a
slow gangrene to the merchant class until their native energy and
resolution were undermined and ruined.   Finally, we must reckon
with the possibility that the Byzantine Greeks were even at their
best only relatively vigorous and quite naturally went down before
the untiring and resourceful activity of the new urban class developed in the West, above all, in the Italian cities.   From these
and other causes, beginning with the eleventh century, a shadow
darkens Constantinople as well as such provincial towns as
Thessalonica, Athens, Thebes, and Corinth, with the result that
their once crowded shops, wharves, and markets show the effects
of a flagging vigor and a diminished confidence in life.

The Byzan-
tines develop
architecture
but express
themselves
primarily in
the art of
painting.
Turning to the arts for evidence of the peculiar quality of this
society, we need have no hesitation in declaring that the only
architectural creation of the Byzantines commanding our attention was the type of church which we still call Byzantine, and
which has as its leading feature the central cupola or dome.
St. Sophia, built in the days of Justinian, remains the shining
example of this style.   But a broad consideration will disclose
that the Greeks possessed no passion for church building
to compare, for instance, with the European West in Gothic
days.   In view of the relatively small number of churches which
have survived, and these usually of very modest dimensions, the
conclusion would appear to be justified that the appeal of a noble,
costly, and laborious art like architecture was not particularly

strong or persistent. On the whole, the art of painting would
seem to admit of expression far more consonant with the superficial and ceremonial quality of the Byzantine spirit. In any
case, among the arts, it was painting which particularly flourished,
and altar panels of the Virgin-Mother and the saints, as well
as mosaics illustrating popular religious episodes and intended
to invest the bare walls of churches and monasteries with a rich
and suffused glow, issued in large numbers from the Constantinopolitan studios. For these embellishments of the house of God
a great demand arose in every part of Christendom, and as the
Byzantines were for a considerable time the only Christians far
enough advanced in civilization to possess an art of painting,
they enjoyed a practical monopoly as ecclesiastical decorators.
When in the thirteenth century the Latin West began at last to
develop its own art of Christian painting, its practitioners went to
school, as it were, and took their first timid steps at the hand of
the Byzantine masters. But till the West was sufficiently advanced to meet its own demand for altar-pieces and mosaics, its
entire supply in this kind came from Greek artists.

With regard to the character and the constituent elements of
Byzantine painting we have noted in a previous chapter that it
was a child of classical art modified by oriental influences and
Christian feeling and ideas. In the course of time the classical
tradition, which implied a more or less joyful pagan attitude toward life, very largely disappeared, leaving behind a curious
mixture of oriental attachment to colorful designs and of fanatic
Christian hatred of the innumerable pleasant forms of things
noted by the senses. Under these circumstances painting tended
to be drawn into the bleak prison-house of ecclesiastical and of
even narrower monastic concepts and to become stiff, hieratic,
grave, and, in the ultimate phase of its development, repulsive
and morose. Arrived at this stage, it was so completely out of
touch with ordinary human experience that there was nothing
left for it to do but to fade out and perish. However, that un-
lamented end came only after the period we are here considering.
During the five hundred years when Byzantine civilization
counted in the world, painting with its subsidiary technics, such
as enamelling and parchment miniatures, was the art which, of
all arts, flourished most extensively and which, everything con-

The spirit of
Byzantine
painting.

decline of Byz. art

sidered, was best suited to this semi-oriental society. The genius of that society was never, not even in its heyday, marked by a fiery, youthful pulse-beat urging toward adventure and large creativeness. At its best, however, it displayed a fine and even exquisite feeling for formal decoration, to sink, at its worst, to a level of pompous futility and senile feebleness unique in the annals of mankind.

Byzantine learning.

Byzantine learning repeats the impression of something valuable and yet not wholly and consistently vital communicated by Byzantine painting. In every generation from Justinian to Basil II, a larger or smaller group of scholars continued to blow upon the dying embers of classical culture in order to warm themselves at the thin, ensuing flame. As it is to this traditional love of literature that we owe the preservation of the works of the ancient poets and philosophers, who without their medieval parasites would in the course of time have become mere names, let us across the chasm of the years, not without gratitude, salute these bat-eyed scholars as authentic, though somewhat ludicrous bearers of the torch of knowledge. For scholars they were, or rather pedants, since they clung grimly to the dead letter of the text and remained wholly untouched by its inner spirit. Occupied with the worthy work of copying manuscripts, they filled the margins of their pages with quotations from other authors or with their own leaden comments. In short, they made a perpetual parade of learning and were in a way really learned; but they had not the least inkling how to render scholarship tributary to the dimly discerned, creative ends of life. Though browsing over and weakly imitating the classics, they of course also browsed over and imitated the Christian Fathers, whom they looked on as intellectual authorities on much the same level as the poets and philosophers of Athens, though of a distinctly higher inspiration. That the classics and the Fathers represented two hopelessly irreconcilable worlds hardly dawned on the dull consciousness of the average Byzantine pedagogue, who in many cases was further hampered mentally by being, as a monk, limited to the narrow experience of his cell. Since both groups of works had been handed down in precious manuscripts from a remote past, they were necessarily coördinate in the sight of these sapient book-worms, who asked for nothing better than to be permitted to act according to their nature and to live and die munching parchment. Originality, therefore, is a quality that shines by absence, and since what we call literature results without exception from a fresh, responsive attitude toward life, the Byzantines did not produce a literature which need arrest our attention. Of course under the spur of classical imitation men wrote books, some of them, as for instance, the chronicles and histories, of great value for the present-day scholar, but of literature of a vital sort there is as good as nothing.

Summarizing these impressions, we are moved to declare that Byzantine government, society, and civilization have the same dominant characteristics and are conspicuously of one piece. The vitalizing element is the stream of inheritance, consisting of the Roman tradition in the state and the Hellenic tradition in commerce, literature, and the arts. But no inheritance, however rich, is able of itself to keep a people alive, and such achievements as the Byzantines have to their credit and as still have weight with us of today, they owe, after all, to something more than to ancestor and fetish worship. Probably their best title to fame is that they effected an interesting and not wholly uncreative combination of the various influences, Greek, Roman, Hebrew, and Persian, centering in the eastern Mediterranean. None-the-less, owing to the absence of a strong well-spring of native energy, Byzantine civilization, considered as a whole, cannot remotely rank with the great civilizations of which history bears record, and which at the slightest touch and at the remove of centuries quicken our spirit and excite our admiration. It is by reason of this meager harvest that we yield the Byzantine empire at best a distant homage and remain unmoved before the storms which gathered round it in its old age and swept it, an enfeebled despotism content to eke out a bare existence and incapable of a single generous thought, into outer darkness and oblivion.

Relatively low rank of Byzantine civilization.

CHAPTER X

THE DECLINE OF THE BYZANTINE EMPIRE AND ITS OVERTHROW BY THE FOURTH CRUSADE

The end, amidst confusion, of the Basilian line, 1056. HAVING reached the summit under Basil II, the Byzantine empire entered upon a decline which in less than two hundred years, but not without intermittent recoveries bearing witness to the solid fabric of the state, ended in destruction. Basil's successor was his brother, Constantine VIII, an effeminate courtier, who was succeeded after a short reign (1025–28) by his daughters, Zoe and Theodora. Lawless women, particularly Zoe, who shared the control of the empire with an amazing succession of husbands and lovers, they systematically promoted disorganization. However, not long after the middle of the century their rule came to an end. In the brief generation which elapsed between the death of Basil II and the last heir of his house, the administration had by the most offensive favoritism become so unsettled that the Roman system with its proved and established principles was no longer recognizable. When, on the death of Theodora (1056), the succession was as usual thrown open to intrigue and violence, the chaos deepened still farther, producing a situation so ominous that the end of the empire would have come before the century's close had it not been for the accession to the throne in 1081 of Alexius Comnenus. The herculean labors of this statesman and general gave the imperilled empire a new lease of life.

New dangers West and East. But before the dynasty of the Comneni was established, enabling a revival to take place, a number of things happened to which we must give close attention. It goes without saying that the renewed weakness of the empire was promptly taken advantage of by enemies, old and new. In the Balkan interior, subjected afresh to the Greeks by Basil II, lived the Bulgars and to the west of them, the Serbs, restless peoples both and unwilling bearers of the imperial yoke. Prompted by the un-

warranted exactions which were imposed by Constantinople owing
to its financial embarrassments, the Bulgars started a movement
of rebellion, and though they were put down, certain Adriatic
tribes of Serbs followed their example, defeated the Byzantine
army, and made good their independence. Though far from
harmless, this successful insubordination in the outskirts of
Balkania was as nothing compared with the appearance of the
vanguards of the two peoples who were destined between them to
push the empire into the abyss. I refer to the Normans of
southern Italy, harbingers of the bold crusaders of the Latin
West, and to the savage nomad Turks hailing from the tablelands of central Asia.

In the first half of the eleventh century small bands of Normans
from northern France, bent in the spirited fashion of their race
upon adventure, began to arrive in southern Italy to take part in
the chronic struggles of that region. The southern tip of the
peninsula was still a part of the Byzantine empire and represented the last and greatly diminished territory left over from the
reconquest of Italy effected by Justinian in the sixth century.
The Normans, powerful men-at-arms and wily diplomats withal,
soon made themselves so important a factor in the confused
affairs of the Byzantine province that they were moved to form
the bold design of seizing it for themselves. They pushed out
foot by foot the Byzantine officials, defeated the forces sent
against them, and shortly after the middle of the eleventh century
found themselves masters of the land. It was an achievement
as resolutely conceived and executed by these buccaneers as that
of their kinsman, that still more famous buccaneer, Duke William
of Normandy, who in these same years crossed the channel and
conquered England. Once established in southern Italy, the Normans crossed the straits to Sicily, held since the ninth century by
the Saracens, and soon wrested this important island from its
Moslem lords. As in their rise to power they had gained ample
evidence of the weakness of the Byzantine state, it was only
too likely, considering their love of war and booty, that they
would turn their attention next to the Balkan peninsula.

While this storm was slowly gathering in the West, across the
Adriatic sea, another even more threatening tempest not only
gathered but actually broke in the East. It is associated with

The Normans conquer the remaining Byzantine territory in southern Italy.

The rise of the Seljuk Turks.

the coming of the Turks, a people of terrible significance in the years to come for the Byzantine empire as well as for all Balkania. Mongolian nomads from central Asia, related to the Huns, Avars, Bulgars and a score of other tribes who had harassed Europe since the fifth century, the Turks became a factor in the history of the Near East when, in the course of the ninth century, their outposts established contact with the Arab empire. Gradually converted to Mohammedanism, they took military service under the calif and by virtue of their war-like character assumed a rôle of constantly increasing importance in the affairs of the Arab state. In the tenth century a Turk leader by the name of Seljuk brought together an immense band of followers who, unified by successful plundering expeditions, perpetuated themselves under his descendants as the Seljuk Turks. From their first foothold in Persia the Seljuks triumphantly spread over a large part of western Asia. In 1055 they seized the city of Bagdad and put an end to the Arab power by appropriating all the political functions of the califate and making the calif himself a mere religious figure-head. Thus, just as the Basilian line was dying out at Constantinople, thereby reviving the periodic and perilous struggle over the succession, the Arab state, long moribund and negligible, was replaced by the fresh and highly enterprising power of a Turkish warrior-band.

The disastrous battle of Manzikert, 1071.

Since the Turks lived by raids, that is, by theft organized on a military scale, it was not long before they began to harass the eastern borders of the Greek empire. The Byzantine rulers however, beginning with the last Basilians, were so much taken up with party politics at home that they did little or nothing to put an end to the incursions. Consequently for many years bands of swift Turkish horsemen harried eastern Asia Minor with impunity. When at last an emperor was found who gave ear to the cry of distress mounting with ever-increasing vehemence from his people, the Seljuk problem had grown to grave proportions. It was Emperor Romanus IV (1067–71), a courageous but headlong soldier, who undertook to deal with the marauders. Ardently pursuing their scattered bands for several years without ever defeating more than a fleeing detachment, he at last, at Manzikert, in distant Armenia, came upon the whole force of the Turks drawn up in battle array (1071). His warrior exultation rose in a cry of triumph at the sight, but the day ended in wailing and sorrow, for at Manzikert was fought the most disastrous battle in Byzantine annals. When night closed on that bloody scene the wounded emperor was himself a captive and his men were either dead or scattered to the winds. Constantinople, as if paralyzed by fear, did nothing in the face of this calamity, and during the years following Manzikert, the Seljuks overran without resistance the whole interior plateau of Asia Minor. In 1081 they took the city of Nicaea, not far from the sea of Marmora. Only the coast districts of Asia Minor, capable of being succored from the sea, continued to hold out against the enemy.

Beginning with characteristic nomad raids, the Turks had ended with a conquest. But conquests are by no means all of one type, and many are recorded which, like a spring flood, are exceedingly disastrous while they last but not very durable in their effects. Though Asiatic conquests have usually been of the transient kind, the Seljuk conquest of Asia Minor is an exception to the rule, for its significance lies in the very fact that it was permanent. Before the disaster at Manzikert, Asia Minor was essentially a European country, largely Greek in culture and wholly Christian in religion. It boasted many flourishing cities, chiefly on the coast, while the interior plateau, together with the mountains lying about it in a circle, was occupied by peasant peoples of various stocks, who paid ample taxes to the government and supplied numerous and valiant recruits to the imperial army. Not only did the invading Turks now systematically oppress and exterminate the native Christian population, but behind the victorious army poured in a steady stream of nomad tribes of Turkish stock who repeopled the inner tableland, and in shallow rivulets filtered as far as the Aegean coast. It was this race movement which, by replacing white with yellow people, Christians with Mohammedans, makes Manzikert so memorable in the annals of the Near East. From this transformation two consequences stand out in somber relief and should be carefully noted: Asia Minor was delivered over to a primitive Asiatic folk, which, ever strengthened by succeeding waves of immigrants, has continued to form the bulk of its population to our own day, and the Greek empire was robbed of its largest and richest province and threatened with final ruin.

Asia Minor permanently lost to the Greek empir and to European civilization.

Alexius Com-
nenus (1081-
1118) drives
back the
Normans.

For the moment, however, final ruin was warded off. In the year 1081 an intelligent and enterprising general, Alexius Comnenus, succeeded in winning the Byzantine throne and immediately set about reducing the political chaos at Constantinople to some sort of order. Like Heraclius, Leo the Isaurian, Basil I, and other energetic rulers, he even founded a dynasty, the dynasty of the Comneni, which ruled the empire from 1081 to 1185, and which, as already stated, effected a revival of the state, the last of any real consequence in Byzantine history. Already reduced on his accession, so far as Asia Minor was concerned, to a narrow strip of shoreland, Alexius, when his reign opened, was forced to face west in order to meet a sharp threat addressed to his European provinces. The threat came from the Normans under the famous leader, Robert Guiscard. Having consolidated his south Italian conquests, he now crossed (1081) the Adriatic to appropriate the remaining lands of the apparently dissolving empire. In a sudden rush, Guiscard and his intrepid, grasping son, Boemund, captured the seaport of Durazzo and established themselves in Epirus. The Emperor Alexius, however, though defeated repeatedly in open battle, managed in the long run to beat off these hardiest warriors of the age (1085). It was an undeniable triumph, once more giving the lie to the opinion that the Greek state was at its last gasp. Though the disappointed Normans were obliged to steer their pirate-ships back to Italy, their invasion presently disclosed itself as the mere rehearsal for a vast movement of conquest directed eastward by the whole European West.

Did Alexius
summon the
crusaders?

Therewith we touch that period, the most magnificent and at the same time the most sordid of the whole Middle Age, the period of the crusades. Of course our concern with the crusades is strictly limited, for we desire to know only how, for better or for worse, they affected the lot of the Greek empire. It has often been affirmed on the strength of questionable evidence that Emperor Alexius himself helped create the crusading movement by repeatedly petitioning the Christian West for aid against the infidel enemies engaged in steadily crowding him out of Asia Minor. Though whether he issued such an invitation is uncertain, it is clear that the hard-pressed Alexius would welcome an auxiliary force, bent on crossing swords with the Turks, provided it agreed beforehand to transfer whatever conquests it might make to him as rightful owner. But even if the western warriors signed such an agreement, would they live up to it if, as a result of victory, they were once in possession of the land?

To glance at the crusaders supplies an answer to the question. They were largely ambitious adventurers, who did not care a fillip for the empire and its affairs. Like typical feudal barons they were land-hungry and risked their lives in a dangerous enterprise for the purpose of carving liberal duchies and lordships out of the provinces which they hoped to take from the Turks. But as these provinces were the very regions on which Alexius had his eye for himself, he and the crusaders were predestined and implacable opponents. If the rivalry was not clear from the first, it flared up in an indubitable manner the moment the successive bands of crusading knights arrived on the Bosporus. Though some sort of an agreement between them and their imperial host was eventually patched up, distrust had by no means been dispelled when, in the spring of the year 1097, the western warriors, constituting the famous First Crusade, set out from Constantinople on their way through Asia Minor to the Holy Land of Palestine. The world has ever since rung with the unique story of the hardships which they bore and the battles which they won against overwhelming odds. At last, in July, 1099, by scaling the walls of Jerusalem they accomplished their amazing purpose. The ancient dream of the West had come true: the Holy Sepulcher was again in Christian hands.

For the Byzantine historian the center of gravity of the First Crusade lies not in Palestine but in Asia Minor. There, by the defeats administered to the Seljuk Turks by the brave warriors of the West, the alien Asiatics were, if not destroyed, at least greatly weakened. A spendid opportunity now beckoned to Alexius which he straightway seized. By following in the wake of the victors and falling on the Turks while they were still dazed by the blows of the crusaders, he succeeded in tearing from their clutches considerable western and southern sections of the peninsula. Enabled in this wise partly to rebuild the Greek power in Asia Minor, what cared he if the mailed knights of the occident sneeringly referred to him as the jackal hunting on the trail of the lion? An objective observer will hardly be inclined

The First Crusade. 1097–99.

Emperor Alexius wins back parts of western and southern Asia Minor.

On a whole the crusaders adventure banditti. They more than took what they took! (handwritten margin note)

to find fault with the emperor for making the most of a happy turn of the wheel of chance; but, on the other hand, he will not be surprised to learn that the crusaders developed an unmeasured contempt for a ruler so cunningly eager to reap a field which others had plowed and fertilized with their blood.

Alexius pays the Venetians for political aid with economic privileges.

With the relations between the East and West, between Greeks and Latins, thus unhappily and permanently strained, a new danger arose, originating also in the West but in a quarter sharply distinct from the feudal, Christian knighthood, largely responsible for the crusading movement. In meeting that first Balkan invasion of the Normans of the year 1081, Alexius, who had obtained the scepter of an utterly demoralized state, was obliged to look about for help. He appealed to Venice. The city of the lagoons at the head of the Adriatic had been and still technically was a subject-city of the Greek empire. It had profited from its connection with Constantinople by assuming the distribution of the Asiatic wares arriving at the Bosporus among the rising peoples of the European West, and it had waxed both opulent and powerful by virtue of this trade. Naturally, as the empire decayed, Venice pursued the plan not only of making itself wholly independent in a political sense but also of gathering within its ambitious embrace more and more of the Byzantine commerce. By the time Alexius mounted the throne these policies had been already partially realized, and when the emperor, in sore need because of the Norman debarkation on the Albanian coast, appealed to Venice for aid, the calculating merchants who controlled the city coolly named their price. They would put a fleet at the disposal of Alexius in return for a charter of privileges by which they acquired a quarter in Constantinople, together with wharves and warehouses under their own officials, and by which, in addition, they received the right to buy and sell throughout the empire free from all imperial dues.

The tightening grip of Venice on the Byzantine empire.

It was only because Alexius was fighting with his back to the wall that he accepted (1082) these hard conditions, by which he virtually handed over a part of his sovereignty to the Adriatic republic. The ancient commercial dominance of Byzantium, already on the wane like all else connected with the aging state, now went disastrously to pieces in the face of the youthful energy of the Venetians who, relieved of imperial taxes, could undersell all rivals, including the Greek merchants themselves, in every market in the world. To somewhat reduce the swagger and tyranny of the western traders, politely miscalled guests, Alexius and his successors gradually permitted the trading Pisans and Genoese to enter the empire on similar, though not equally favorable terms. While such a policy might bring a certain mean satisfaction by sowing rancorous divisions among the competing Italian cities, it certainly failed to achieve the main desideratum, which was the reconquest by the Greeks of the Mediterranean trade and its attendant profits. Occasional successors of Alexius went so far as to declare war against the Venetians in the hope, since all other means had failed, of shaking off by force the leeches who were sucking the very life-blood of the nation. Unfortunately the effort had no further effect than to plant deep in the heart of the occidentals an impassioned hatred and contempt for their feeble victims. The whole course of medieval history furnishes no more instructive example than this supplied by Byzantium of how a nation, on being brought into economic subjection, gradually lapses into hopeless political dependence on the unscrupulous exploiter.

Alexius I, very properly reckoned among the restorers of the empire, ruled with a strong and, on the whole, a happy hand to the end of his days (1081–1118). Of his son, John II (1118–1143), and his grandson, Manuel (1143–1180), it may also be said without fear of contradiction that they conducted the government with considerable distinction. But all three of these really notable sovereigns showed a marked preference for issues of land-power and fatally neglected that element of at least equal importance for the empire, the sea. In consequence the war and merchant fleets of rival Venice grew steadily more preponderant, and when, with the final extinction (1185) of the dynasty of the Comneni amidst the usual horrible excesses, the crown again became the shuttlecock of factious nobles, a situation was created which the western merchant-republic could dominate at pleasure. Quietly awaiting its opportunity to bring matters to a head, it seized, at the beginning of the thirteenth century, on a new crusade as a means admirably calculated to promote its purpose. This crusade, known, or rather notorious, as the Fourth, reveals itself, when stripped of its religious label, as a simple war of

Venice and the Fourth Crusade, 1202–4.

conquest conducted by the republic of St. Mark against the Byzantine state. Of course Venice did not act alone, for she had as allies large companies of western knights and barons, who had taken the solemn crusading vows and who, like their predecessors of the famous First Crusade, were animated by strangely mixed motives of honest Christian zeal, repulsive greed, and high romantic adventure. In fact the Fourth Crusade, promoted zealously by that most ambitious of popes, Innocent III, and supported by the feudal nobility of large sections of Europe, had in its earliest stage little or nothing to do with either Venice or Constantinople. But when, in 1202, the knights, hailing chiefly from France, Flanders, and Lombardy, began to arrive in the Adriatic city, whence they planned to have themselves carried to the East in Venetian galleys, negotiations of a business nature necessarily ensued between them and the heads of the republic. Though a sum to cover the cost of transportation had been agreed on in the first place, owing to the addition of entertainment charges, it soon reached a height beyond the exiguous purse of the crusaders. Obliged to default, they fell, like any other company of debtors, completely into the power of their creditors. Venice could do with them what she pleased.

Enrico Dandolo, doge of Venice, the leader of the Fourth Crusade.

At this point there enters on the scene, in the double capacity of spokesman of the merchants and head of the Venetian state, the famous doge, Enrico Dandolo. A greybeard of ninety years, who combined with the prudence matured by a far-ranging experience the flaming enthusiasm of unreflecting youth, he stands out as one of the most original and forceful characters of the age. The complex political and economic factors, entering into a crusading expedition of world scope, were masterfully utilized by him for the selfish ends of Venice; but as that story of imperialist diplomacy is beyond our ken, we must content ourselves with noting that, as the upshot of much argument and deft manipulation, he embarked the crusading hosts on Venetian galleys and loosed them, not on the infidel camped in the Holy Land of Palestine, but on the Christian state which for many centuries and through many moving vicissitudes had safeguarded Europe against the Moslem. The slight pretext needed to lend a face of respectability to what was a buccaneering enterprise, plain and simple, was supplied by the fact that the crusaders carried in their midst a fugitive Greek prince, Alexius Angelus by name, whose father, the Emperor Isaac Angelus, had been driven from the throne and for whom, they hypocritically declared, they intended to win the dominion whereof he had been wrongfully deprived.

In the person of this Byzantine princeling we are once more confronted with the eternal Constantinopolitan succession question. When, in 1185, the line of Alexius Comnenus had come to a bloody end, a new house was, amidst severe disturbances, promoted to the throne in the person of the feeble Isaac Angelus. The reign of Emperor Isaac (1185–1195), and for that matter of the whole Angelus dynasty, constitutes a story of unrelieved disgrace. Hardly was Isaac seated on the throne when his financial exactions in Balkania caused both Bulgars and Serbs to rise against him in sustained movements which he was unable to suppress. On publicly proving his incapacity by letting most of the Slav interior escape from his grasp, he was dethroned and blinded by his own brother, who seized the succession as Alexius III (1195–1203). The new Angelus, as feeble as Isaac in government, successfully outdid him in debauchery by acting as master of the revels in wild and repulsive orgies which served as a fitting prelude to the catastrophe of the state. Very probably it was the report of the waxing chaos on the Bosporus which prompted the Venetians to convert the Fourth Crusade to an attack upon the Greeks. In any case the doge's resolution to utilize the crusaders against the empire synchronizes perfectly with Constantinople's new access of debility. In 1203 the western armada actually set forth from the Adriatic city and still the deluded Angelus took no measure to strengthen the defenses of his capital. If a generous human spirit, contemplating the two adversaries about to come to grips, is chilled by the callous commercialism of the Venetians, he is not likely to be moved to shed a single tear for the degenerate people on the Bosporus engaged in pulling down on their own head the pillars of civilization. In the eternal flux we call existence the Venetians at least enjoyed the advantage of representing youth.

Senility and vigor, orient and occident, the Greek and Latin churches — such are some of the contrasts involved in the memorable conflict, which, with the coming of the year 1203, began

The weak reigns of Isaac and Alexius Angelus prepare the way for the attack by Venice.

The crusaders arrive before Constantinople, June, 1203.

flowery!! Not rhetorical writing!

to loom above the horizon. As the galleys of the crusaders swept along the Adriatic and ran over the blue waters of the Mediterranean a great elation fluttered the hearts of Dandolo, the bold mariners of Venice, and of all the sturdy barons of the West. Though for the most part they were undoubtedly revolving ambitious thoughts of personal gain, still they were sailing under an opal sky by day, a purple sky by night, into the mysterious East. Without meeting the least opposition from the helpless Byzantine government, they entered the Dardanelles, crossed the sea of Marmora, and on June 23, 1203, reached the goal of their desire, the great metropolis on the Bosporus.

Alexius, having won the throne, loses it attempting to find the money to pay his allies.

Throwing themselves promptly and eagerly upon the city, the Latin hosts were making excellent progress toward its capture when information reached them that the cowardly usurper, Alexius III, had fled, and that the blinded and imprisoned Isaac together with his son, Alexius, the young prince in their midst, had been proclaimed joint sovereigns by a triumphant faction. With the avowed object of the expedition gained, the restoration of the line of Isaac, the order was given to desist from the assault. Barons and merchants alike, however, could hardly conceal their irritation at being deprived of the prize — and what a prize! — already in their grasp. They resolved to solace their disappointment by insisting that their ward, Alexius, now emperor, should hand over to them without delay the huge sum solemnly promised by him in the event of his restoration. When, in order to meet this engagement, the young man attempted to squeeze the very last farthing out of the distressed and starving people, such indignation flamed up against him in the city that, after a few feverish months of rule, he and his wretched father were again deposed. Immediately the patriotic party, electing a new emperor, closed the gates in the face of the crusaders and the war broke out afresh.

Capture and sack of Constantinople, April, 1204.

It was the second assault on Constantinople of April, 1204, some nine months after the first, which brought about the real capture and devastation of the city. It does not belittle the remarkable military feat of the crusaders to declare that they could never have succeeded if the degenerate Greeks of the capital had still been animated by a spark of civic virtue. They lamented, they prayed, but as they were wholly disaccustomed to war, they left the defense of the walls to a handful of foreign mercenaries. For their part the besiegers, men of another mettle, followed the bold plan of throwing bridges from the decks of their ships to the sea-wall, close by which they lay anchored, and in a comparatively short time, by a mixture of skill and the most amazing daring, they overwhelmed the defenders and forced an entrance. Then followed such a sack as is rare even in the brutal annals of medieval conquest. Every church was stripped of its treasures, every house plundered from cellar to garret, and when everything portable had been seized, the victors, shaking off the last human restraint, indulged their lusts and perpetrated every outrage forbidden by the religion whose chosen instruments they professed to be. In the face of these living horrors the aesthetic plaints of the lovers of beauty, who record the wanton destruction of many masterpieces of ancient art set up by the founder Constantine to adorn the squares and palaces of his brilliant capital, sound a thin note hardly heard above the tumult. Very characteristically the Doge Dandolo, the fiery but level-headed Venetian business man, managed to save out of the general wreck four horses of gilded bronze which he dispatched to his Adriatic home and ordered set up over the portico of the great church dedicated to Saint Mark. There they prance and curvet to this day, reminding the beholder of how victorious Venice broke and despoiled the Christian metropolis on the Golden Horn.

After four days conceded to the wildest license the baronial leaders once more got their men in hand and sat down to decide what to do with their victory. Since young Alexius, as well as his blind father, had perished in the recent upheaval, the view was championed and adopted that the Byzantine state belonged to the crusaders by right of conquest. They therefore eagerly set about its distribution. First they satisfied the claims of Venice which, as the purseholder of the expedition, had a lien on everybody and everything. The Adriatic city received the islands of the Aegean and Ionian seas together with such trading posts along the mainland shore as she considered necessary for her program of commercial hegemony in the Levantine waters. These concessions totalled about three-eighths of the whole empire and enabled the doge to add to his dignities the curious title: *lord of a quarter and the half of a quarter of the whole*

Venice becomes the successor of the Byzantine empire.

empire of Romania. Romania was what the Latin West called the Byzantine empire, in the place of which, broken apparently beyond recovery, queenly Venice now indisputably assumed the scepter of the Mediterranean. When all is said, the sea-rule of Venice is the leading political result of the Fourth Crusade and with this primacy we shall for several succeeding centuries have to reckon when dealing with any issue affecting the Near East.

The western barons set up the Latin empire.

The appetite of domineering Venice placated, her baronial allies proceeded to satisfy their own famished cravings. It was natural that men of their type should follow a course in harmony with the feudal and ecclesiastical conceptions which at that time ruled all Europe and were born and bred in the western bone. After electing one of their number, Baldwin of Flanders, Latin emperor of Romania, they proclaimed the union of the Greek church with Rome and raised a Venetian churchman to the dignity of patriarch of Constantinople. Then they proceeded to distribute all available territory as fiefs among themselves. Of course every lord and knight desired as vast an estate and as large a revenue as possible and to hold it as independently of his suzerain, the Emperor Baldwin, as he dared. In consequence of this attitude of outspoken greed, quarrels and even armed conflicts promptly broke out among the victors, sufficient by themselves to lay a mortal curse upon their new-hatched state.

The Latin empire, 1204–61.

A dwarfed, misshapen thing from birth, the Latin empire need not detain us long. True, it lasted over half a century, from 1204 to 1261, but in all that stretch of time it never boasted a single day of health. The western barons, who alone sustained it, were after all a mere handful compared with their conquered subjects; they never agreed among themselves; and they refused to turn a hand to conciliate the people whose peculiarities and customs they visited with open scorn. The resolution, formed and carried through without delay, to bring the Greeks ecclesiastically within the Latin fold was of itself enough to dig a yawning gulf between the rulers and the ruled. It helps bring home the weakness of the Latins that even at the height of their triumph and in full possession of the capital, they never laid their hand on more than a part of the Byzantine empire. Under the guidance of spirited Greek leaders, several provincial districts took matters into their own hands, set up independent states, and balked every effort of the Latin emperor and his barons to reduce them to obedience. Especially vigorous was the resistance offered across the straits at Nicaea in Asia Minor, where a great Byzantine dignitary, Theodore Lascaris by name, assumed the style of emperor and declared himself the protector of the persecuted Greek church. Not so many moons after the ringing proclamation of the Latin empire, its sovereign knew that his claim to the Greek state was hollow and that he actually controlled but little more than the immediate vicinity of Constantinople. Had it not been for the strategic strength of his capital and the jealousies and suspicions which kept his many enemies from combining against him, he must have promptly lost Constantinople too.

Utterly helpless in the face of difficulties which grew more perplexing every year, the Latin sovereigns came to see that nothing could save them except the continued support of western Europe. In pursuit of this will o' the wisp, they wrote countless begging letters and made many vain journeys to the occident, knocking as suppliants at every door. But what possible interest could the West have to help the foresworn soldiers of the Lord retain their stolen goods? With exemplary prudence the western powers refused to raise a finger for the phantom emperor and his phantom throne. One western state indeed, commercial Genoa, from hatred of its Venetian rival, even went the length of allying itself with the Greek enemies of the Latin sovereign; and it remains an interesting fact that when, in 1261, the Greeks recaptured Constantinople, they owed their success in large part to the aid given by the Genoese fleet. Of course the restored Greek state, thenceforth heavily in the debt of Genoa, had to satisfy its importunate creditor by the concession of a permanent commercial quarter on the Golden Horn as well as the monopoly of the lucrative Black sea trade. As the gain of Genoa was the loss of Venice, the two Italian merchant republics were from now on more deeply embroiled than ever over the control of the Mediterranean commerce. But we are anticipating. At this point we are alone concerned with the passing, in 1261, of what the Greeks called the Latin shame. Making his way to the West, where he belonged, the last Latin emperor became one of those

The Greeks recapture Constantinople with the aid of Genoa.

shadowy figures of knight-errantry for whom sentimental singers long continued to twang their plaintive harps.

Thedore Lascaris creates a center of Greek resistance at Nicaea.

Of the various Greek states formed on the morrow of the fall of Constantinople the one called the empire of Nicaea is the most important. Under its ruler, Theodore Lascaris (1204–22), it became solidly established in northwestern Asia Minor, while under Theodore's successors its power spread westward beyond the straits until it embraced important sections of Thrace and Macedonia. Undoubtedly its chief strength was its championship of the Greek race and church against the Latin oppressors. By this course it rallied around it the sanest and most independent elements of the population. As is not uncommon in similar misfortunes, the terrible affliction visited upon the Greeks even produced among them something like a moral rebirth, which unfortunately proved ephemeral. However, it lasted long enough to give valiant support to Theodore Lascaris and his immediate heirs, who, without exception, exhibited governing talents of a high order. A Lascarid dynasty could it have been permanently established, might have added an important element of strength to the, at best hazardous, venture of a revived Greek state. Unfortunately the succession question among the Greeks was destined to remain the stone of stumbling which it had always been. An ambitious nobleman, Michael Paleologus, took advantage of the minority of the great-grandson of Theodore Lascaris and in 1259, on the eve of the recapture by the Greeks of the coveted Constantinople, put the crown on his own head.

The empire of Constantinople under the Paleologi.

In this way the empire of Nicaea, created by the prowess of the Lascarids, became the empire of Constantinople, ruled by Michael Paleologus (1259–1282). Himself a usurper, Michael found the attempt to establish a dynasty, which he now made in his turn, challenged by the heads of the rival noble houses. Long before this, it will be remembered, the empire, becoming feudalized, was exploited for their own ends by the great magnates. From the days of Michael to the last gasp of the restored Greek state, two hundred years later, the nobles continued their purely selfish game of intrigue for the possession of the crown. None-the-less the capture of Constantinople, though effected by Michael largely with the aid of the Genoese, achieved the result of throwing a glamour about him which went far toward setting his family above its rivals. It is a Paleologus dynasty with which we shall have chiefly to reckon in this last or sick-room phase of the dying state.

The empire over which Michael held the scepter may repay a rapid inspection in a summary attempt to define its character. Of course it pretended to be the same Roman or Byzantine empire which, after lording it over the East through centuries, had ended ignominiously in 1204. Though technically there is something to be said in favor of this claim, it fails in the light of every essential historical criterion. The Byzantine empire was the heir of Rome, holding together many diverse peoples of the east-Mediterranean area by virtue of administrative and judicial services of a high order, higher in any case than those of any rival state. Finally however, after a long period of decay, the Roman institutions perished and perished utterly in the catastrophe of the Fourth Crusade. With them sank into oblivion the last remnant of Roman tradition and of Roman pride. The restored empire, originally called the empire of Nicaea, was a state exclusively of Greeks nursed to life by Theodore Lascaris on Greek national and Greek ecclesiastical sentiments, and its successor, the empire of Constantinople, closely resembled it in all these distinguishing particulars. Built on the narrow foundations of Greek language, faith, and culture and pursuing a program which all non-Greeks instinctively rejected, it made itself incapable of resuming the unifying rôle of the Roman empire and therewith of serving as the rallying-point of all the Christian peoples of the East.

The empire of Constantinople built on narrow Greek foundations.

new Byzantium

Even apart from its narrow nationalism and its vicious public spirit, the latter largely due to the contentious nobles, the territorial and economic conditions of the revamped empire were such as to condemn it with absolute certainty to a mean and insignificant rôle. The territory controlled by Michael Paleologus never amounted to more than the northwest corner of Asia Minor together with scattered bits of Thrace, Macedonia, and ancient Hellas. Small as this dominion was, instead of growing it began, even before Michael closed his eyes, to contract through persistent pressure applied to it both in Europe and in Asia. An empire of such straitened boundaries, visibly engaged in shrinkage,

The empire of Constantinople lacks the territorial and economic basis required to figure as a power in the East.

could not be an empire in anything but name. When we consider further that the population had been greatly reduced by the wars and disorders of the Latin period and that it lived in the meanest circumstances without industry and commerce, it will be understood that the economic misery was so general and complete as utterly to preclude any manifestation of military strength. Almost the only thing about the state enabling it to figure at all in the politics of the Near East was the possession of Constantinople together with what that implied of commercial and strategical advantage.

Necessary distinction between the empire of Constantinople and the Byzantine empire.

By every serviceable standard then, this state is properly designated as the empire of Constantinople, the wholly despicable posthumous offspring of the Byzantine empire, which the episode of 1204 had effectively laid in its grave. Owing to circumstances to be treated in the chapters that follow, this weakling state dragged out a malingering existence for two hundred years, that is, till 1453. Among the many contemptible political creations of men it would be difficult to find one more contemptible than this. For once we may harden our hearts and agree that the jeers which it has invited from every quarter are deserved. But again, and for the last time, let us insist that its predecessor, the Byzantine empire, with which it has not unnaturally been confounded, does not deserve to be treated in the same cavalier fashion. As our story has clearly shown, the Byzantine empire was for five hundred years the bulwark of European civilization and, as such, calls for both serious and respectful consideration. With that empire we are now done. As for its successor, the puny empire of Constantinople, we have traced the circumstances of its birth and set down convincing reasons for its puniness. That is enough. In the coming chapters we shall hear of it only now and then, for we shall give our main attention to other and more vital creations of the Balkan area.

CHAPTER XI

THE SERB EMPIRE OF THE FOURTEENTH CENTURY

EVER since the time in the sixth century when the Serb tribes crossed the Danube, they necessarily played a part in the history of the Balkan peninsula. The reader will recall that they settled in small separate organizations or clans, that they were rude barbarians living by hunting and herding but also, in growing measure, by agriculture, and that they were drawn into the circle of Greek civilization when, in the ninth century, they accepted the form of Christianity represented by Constantinople. We have thus far had chiefly to do with the Slavs of the lower Danube who, conquered by the Mongolian Bulgars, fused with their masters and created the Bulgar state. The history of the first Slav state of Balkania, its greatness under the Tsars Simeon and Samuel, and its final overthrow (1018) by Emperor Basil, the Bulgar-Killer, has received our close attention.

The Slavs to the west of the Bulgars for a long time founded no state and, continuing to live in scattered groups, were dangerous neither to the Bulgars nor the Greeks. Starting with a passionate and natural preference for their ancient tribal organization with its local independence, they were confirmed in their conservatism by the mountainous character of the country, which made communication difficult and tended to confine each tribe within a closely circumscribed district. When, in the ninth century, under the auspices of the missionary movement associated with the names of the Apostles Method and Cyril, Christianity with its close-spun and far-reaching ecclesiastical ties penetrated the mountains, it helped to develop a growing sense of nearness and kinship, of which irrefutable evidence was presently supplied in the adoption by the upland clans of a common name, the name of Serbs. A similar movement toward association among the tribes still farther west, at the head of the Adriatic, led to the adoption by them of the designation Croats. Essentially the

The Bulgars the first Slavs to form a state.

The author (proud of the Serbs) [handwritten marginal note]

The Slavs to the west of the Bulgars fall into two groups: Serbs and Croats.

like Switzerland [handwritten marginal note]

same peoples racially, that is, South Slavs, Serbs and Croats have been divided down to our own day. The chief reason is to be found in the circumstance that the Croats took their Christianity and civilization not, like the Serbs, from Constantinople but, like the German tribes, from the great western hearth of faith, from Rome. Not only did the Catholic Croats thereby become separated in fundamental ways of thought from the Orthodox Serbs, but, geographically close to Central Europe and in active, cultural exchange with it, they fell into gradual political dependence on their nearest neighbor, Hungary. By virtue of these associations the fate of the Croats became tied up with the peoples to the west and north of them and has been relatively little affected by developments in Balkania. The Croats will therefore only occasionally engage our attention, while the Serbs, holding the very heart of the mountainous interior, will be found to supply one of the main strands of Balkan history.

The Serb tribes long enjoy substantial independence.

For four hundred years, from Heraclius in the seventh century to Basil II in the eleventh, the Serb tribes lived in fairly amicable relations with their powerful neighbor, the Greek empire. Their heads, called zupans, as a rule acknowledged the suzerainty of the Greek rulers and even paid them an occasional tribute. As the conduct of local affairs, involving justice and taxes, remained in the hands of the tribes, they looked upon themselves as substantially independent and were fully justified in so doing. This happy condition of primitive liberty was first threatened not by the Greeks but by the Bulgars. Under the rulers, Boris and Simeon, the rising Bulgar state attempted to extend its boundaries westward and for a time brought much of the Serb area under Bulgar control. To meet this unwelcome pressure the Serb chiefs sought the alliance of the Greeks, who, equally exposed with the Serbs to the movement of Bulgar conquest, readily joined hands with the threatened Slavs. We have followed the turns in this struggle for hegemony to the final victory of the Greek empire, which in 1018 destroyed its Bulgar rival and absorbed its territory.[1]

Most likely the end of Bulgaria filled the Serb tribes with delight. But with the Bulgar threat removed, a new danger loomed above the horizon in the strengthened Byzantine state

[1] Chapter VIII.

now exercising an unchallenged ascendancy in the peninsula. The Greek
And in point of fact the Basilian sovereigns, full of a haughty empire, after
sense of power, were no longer minded to be content with the the Bulgar
old meaningless vassalage of the Serbs. Thinking to give it a state, at-
more substantial character, they began to bring pressure to bear bring the
which, by deeply irritating the native tribes, gradually terminated Serb tribes
the era of cordiality and precipitated a struggle on the part of the dependence.
Serbs for full independence. The Serb movement started when,
shortly after the death of Basil II in 1025, the signs of disorganization in the Greek state began to multiply. Successes of the
Serbs who, familiar with the pathless mountains and narrow
gorges of their home, inflicted severe losses on the Greek troops,
are reported by the chroniclers as early as 1040. On the strength
of these victories a Serb zupan of the coast region went the bold
length of assuming the title king and the style of an independent
sovereign; but throughout the eleventh century and even during
the twelfth the military resources of the Byzantine empire proved
on the whole to be such that the Greeks in the long run always
succeeded in forcing the Serbs to admit their inferior status.

It should be understood that the information which has come Beginnings of
down to us regarding the Serb people during the early medieval Serb political
centuries is very fragmentary and unsatisfactory. We know, concentra-
however, for certain that, by the eleventh century, not only the tion.
movement of resistance to the Greek empire was well under way
but also that the necessities of the struggle for existence against
the Greeks as well as against the neighbors to the north, the
Magyars, were beginning to consolidate the scattered tribes into
larger units. More particularly in two areas, the one located on
the Adriatic coast between the lake of Scutari and the bay of
Cattaro, the other in the mountainous interior along the Ibar river,
definite steps were taken toward improved political organization.
In the coastal region a state arose called Zeta, while in the
interior another raised its head, which from its central stronghold
received the name of Rascia; and as the sponsor and chief of
each of these creations appeared a new official with the title
grand zupan. Undoubtedly this dignitary represented a logical
development from the ancient tribal chief, the zupan, and was set
above the other zupans as their overlord, at first only for the
limited period of some special emergency like war. Having

proved his worth against the enemy, he was enabled to capitalize
his renown by making his office more or less permanent. Grand
zupans of both the Zeta and Rascia districts come and go amidst
a confusion which the scanty records refuse to clear up until we
reach the second half of the twelfth century. Then, with apparent
suddenness, a grand zupan of Rascia began a startlingly successful
activity forever memorable in Serb annals because it joined together for the first time nearly all the Serb tribes. I am referring
to Stephen Nemania in whom the Serbs honor the founder of their
political greatness.

*the unifier
of Serbia*

**Serb union
effected by
Stephen Ne-
mania (1165–
1196).**

Over Stephen Nemania too, in spite of his importance, the
documents throw but a grudging light. Though descended from
ancient Serb chieftains, he apparently did not inherit but usurped
the power in the Ibar region, where lay the zupanate of Rascia.
In any case the rôle of usurper comports well with the audacious
energy which marked the man. If we assume, as is usually
done, that he became grand zupan of Rascia around 1165, we
may credit him with a reign, marked by dogged purpose, of more
than a quarter of a century, for he resigned the throne — of this
date we are certain — in 1196. In those thirty years of power
he either drove all the other zupans and grand zupans from
office or made them bow down before his might, thus for the
first time merging the coast and mountain districts into a political
whole. The unification, largely the result of one man's enterprise
and vision, admits of no dispute, but touching the steps of the
interesting process we are left very much in the dark.

**Stephen Ne-
mania fails to
shake off
the Greek
yoke.**

In organizing the Serbs as a nation, Stephen had primarily in
mind the freeing of them from the ancient and easy but, latterly,
galling Greek yoke. This was no new idea for, as we have seen,
the struggle for Serb independence had been intermittently going
on since the days of the last Basilians, that is, for a hundred
years before Stephen's time. Stephen in a restless, ambitious
way engaged in many wars with the Byzantine empire, and on
these wars, reported by Greek chroniclers, we are much better
informed than on the purely domestic concerns of the Serbs. A
bold warrior, the Serb chief at times won important victories
over his enemies, but, viewing his campaigns in the long perspective of his reign, we become aware that, for all his being head
of a united Serbia, he was not yet a match for the heir of the

Roman strength. On more than one occasion he was obliged to make peace with the Byzantine ruler by the most abject surrender. Doubtless he looked toward independence as toward the Promised Land, but he did not live to enter it and he closed his reign as he began, the vassal of the Greek state. After a lifetime of intense activity he made up his mind to bid farewell to strife and, resigning his power into the hands of his son, he withdrew — a characteristic medieval ending — to a monastery on Mt. Athos in order to prepare himself for death by prayer and contemplation.

The solid achievements of Stephan Nemania, coupled with the reputation for holiness to which his monastic retirement gave birth, accumulated such prestige around his name that he was enabled to found a dynasty. It lasted for two hundred years and carried the Serb state to its medieval apogee. Stephen's successor, also called Stephen (1196-1228), was a prudent diplomat and warrior who realized his father's dream of Serb independence without the necessity of striking a blow. His reign befell in the time when the Latin West through the agency of the Fourth Crusade put an end to the Greek empire (1204), thereby accommodatingly, though quite unintentionally, promoting the interests of Serbia. Automatically, on the fall of Constantinople, the struggling Slav state became free and Stephen was enabled to concentrate his attention on making that freedom as secure as possible by means of a general recognition by his neighbors. As we have seen, his father, as a Greek vassal, was never anything but a grand zupan; the son aspired to the title king. As in his eyes and in those of his contemporaries only the church had authority to grant this highest dignity, he opened negotiations with the pope at Rome, which in 1217 led to his being crowned by a papal legate king of Serbia. However, the Serbs were Ortho-dox, not Catholic Christians, and Stephen shrewdly argued that if the western blessing was good, the eastern was still better. He consequently appealed to the patriarch of Constantinople, who, in dire straits just then, in fact, owing to the Latin conquest of Byzantium, in painful exile in Asia Minor, made concessions which he would not have entertained for a moment in his more prosperous days. Without wholly severing the Serb church from the Greek patriarchate, he nevertheless gave it a national char-

The son of Stephen Nemania wins freedom for Serbia and is twice crowned king.

acter and unity by putting it under the king's younger brother, Sava, as archbishop. Then, in 1222, he authorized a second coronation, conducted by Sava in strict accordance with the rites of the Orthodox church.

Elements contributory to the strength of the Nemania dynasty.

Sava, considered a very holy man in his time, became after his death St. Sava, a cloudy, legendary figure working countless miracles and worshiped as one of the leading patrons and heavenly intercessors of his people. In a superstitious age the reputation for holiness of this scion of the ruling house added to the security of the Nemania dynasty in hardly less degree than the double coronation of Stephen I and the adoption of the mystic and authoritative title king. It should be observed that the royal successors of Stephen Nemania all bear the name Stephen, though often, for purposes of distinction, with another name attached. They clung to the name, partly because by means of it they emphasized their descent from the founder of the state, and partly because they desired to gain the protection of St. Stephen, the proto-martyr of the Christian faith, whom the Serb people worshiped as their patron-saint. Taking stock of the long reign of Stephen I, we cannot refuse him our regard as an energetic promoter of his people's fortunes, for he left a state and a church free, or as good as free, from Greek control.

Leading political forces in Balkania in the thirteenth century.

In the days of the first king and of his immediate successors the affairs of the Balkan peninsula remained inextricably ensnarled. While the Latin emperor, as we have seen, was never anything more than a phantom, the Latin barons established in many parts, especially in the Hellenic south, were a very substantial fact, and the leading beneficiary of the Fourth Crusade, sea-faring Venice, assumed not only a prominent, but the leading rôle along the Adriatic and Aegean coasts. Moreover, the various centers of the revived Greek resistance, especially the empire of Nicaea, proved far from negligible, and when, in 1261, the Nicaean Greeks recaptured Constantinople, no intelligently manipulated Serb foreign policy could afford to neglect to reckon with their renewed power. But more important for Serbia, at least for the moment, than all these governments was Bulgaria, which, rising like a phoenix from the ashes, resolutely set about to rebuild its ancient fortunes.

Only monarchs of the prudent yet venturesome type of the founder could have steered the Serb ship of state safely among the rocks and shoals of so many Balkan rivalries. Unfortunately such capable pilots were the exception rather than the rule and, to make matters worse, perpetual divisions among the members of the reigning house, often involving prolonged civil war, delayed the consolidation of the royal authority. The loss of the king was the gain of the tribal chiefs and the nobility in general, with the result that that bane of Serbia, the spirit of tribal particularism, retained an alarming vigor. Under these circumstances the young state did not, in the century following Stephen Nemania and his son, move forward at the fast pace set by them. Throughout this period we may perhaps best think of Serbia as preparing for a new advance by a gradual improvement of its social and economic organization. When in the fourteenth century the advance occurred, it took a form which to understand requires us to take note of the contemporary development of the Slav neighbor to the east, Bulgaria. Slow growth of Serbia after the sudden rise under the early Nemanias.

For many generations after the crushing of Bulgaria (1018) by Emperor Basil II, the Byzantines exercised a more or less effective rule in the Bulgar lands without, however, arriving at their purpose of extinguishing the national memories cherished by the people. Then, toward the close of the twelfth century and after the passing of the vigorous dynasty of the Comneni, the long threatened disorganization of the Greek state became an indubitable fact. In these circumstances a single misstep sufficed to raise a storm. When a new and sadly necessitous emperor, Isaac Angelus, tried to levy an exorbitant tax on the Bulgarian provinces, for which moreover there was no warrant in tradition, he met with a resistance that almost overnight assumed the proportions of a revolution. The general rising befell in 1186. One hundred and sixty-eight years after the end of the First Bulgaria a second Bulgarian state made its appearance in the peninsula. The Bulgar revolt of 1186.

Champions and creators of the new state were two brothers, John Asen and Peter, of the city of Tirnovo, lying on the northern Balkan slope. It is likely that they were not Bulgars at all but Vlachs. In the twelfth century groups of a people called Vlachs were turning up mysteriously in many widely separated parts of Balkania. A noticeable feature about them was that they The two brothers, John Asen and Peter, leaders of the revolt and first tsars of the renewed Bulgaria.

made their homes always in the mountains, never in the plains. Vlachs is the name given them by their Slav neighbors; but they called themselves by various designations and we now call them Rumans or Rumanians, recognizing in them the descendants of the Roman colonists and Latinized natives, who at the coming of the Slavs, back in the sixth century, had sought safety from the invaders by withdrawing to the uplands. As an important factor in the Balkan population we shall have to deal intimately with them at a later time. For the present we are content to note that many Vlachs, making a living as shepherds and peasants, dwelt on the slopes of the Balkan mountains and that, joined with the Bulgars of the plains, they rose in 1186 against the Greek empire. Though the question whether the brothers, John Asen and Peter, were of Vlach origin must be left open, we may confidently affirm that the Second Bulgaria was transfused, at least in its inception, with a strong Vlach element. In view of the general enthusiasm elicited by the revolution which they started, the two brothers courageously burned their bridges behind them, crowned themselves tsars of Bulgaria, and set up their residence at Tirnovo.

The tsars, John Asen and Peter, succeeded by their younger brother, Kaloian (1197–1207).

The Greek empire, though tottering to its fall, could still offer resistance and the cause of the new tsars was not immediately won. In the renewed grim struggle between Greek and Bulgar we meet the familiar ruthless devastation by each of the other's lands, coupled with the usual domestic acts of perfidy and treason. In spite of defeats inflicted on the Greeks, John Asen and Peter were none too secure. Then, a sign of fierce divisions at home, they were in rapid succession murdered by some of their own followers. But, instead of collapsing with this loss of its champions, the Bulgar rebellion actually gained increased strength by virtue of the accession of a third brother known variously as John, Johannitsa, and Kaloian (handsome John). The new tsar, who reigned for the decade from 1197 to 1207, combined great gifts of mind with the remorseless cruelty of a beast of the jungle. His hatred of the Greeks, the ancient enemies of his race, was an appetite that grew with feeding and led to a harrying of Thrace and Macedonia and to a slaughter of their inhabitants that must have gone far toward reducing these regions to a desert. As an example of his methods we may note the case of the city of Varna, where, after crushing a brave resistance, he had the whole population driven into the moats and buried alive. Let it in justice be observed that this report comes to us from an enemy source and may be an " atrocity " manufactured by the Greeks in order to bring their enemies into ill-repute. Such propaganda methods, familiar enough in these days of the newspaper, were already known and vigorously practiced in the thirteenth century. When all deductions are made, Kaloian still seems amply to merit the title, Slayer of the Greeks, to which apparently he ardently aspired in order to win the same immortal luster as the Greek sovereign of an earlier century, admiringly hailed by his countrymen as the Bulgar-killer. After some years of Tsar Kaloian's murderous activity the Greek empire, at the end of its resources, was constrained to open negotiations. In 1201 a peace was signed, by virtue of which Kaloian became undisputed master of the whole territory between the Danube to the north and the Rhodope mountains to the south. Bulgaria was again a Balkan power.

The heavy hammer-blows of the three brothers largely help explain why the Greek empire went down so unresistingly before the Fourth Crusade, which in the period 1203–04 stepped in to finish what the Bulgar revolution had begun. With the capture of Constantinople the ancient Byzantine state disappeared, at least for a while, to make room for a Latin empire set up on the ruins. Tsar Kaloian, who, as may be readily believed, shed no tears over the demise of his hated foe, prepared to extend the hand of friendship to the new emperor, Baldwin of Flanders. But the Latins, treating him as a half-savage usurper, peremptorily demanded his submission. Blind with rage, the tsar mobilized his forces and, in the spring of 1205, won a battle near Adrianople, in which he not only administered a stinging defeat to the crusaders but also captured Baldwin himself. It was this disaster more than any other one thing which at its very birth threw the Latin empire on a sick-bed. The victorious tsar did not long survive his triumph. The wild license of his warrior chiefs, to which his two older brothers had already fallen victim, brought about his own end also. In 1207, with the connivance of his faithless wife, he was murdered by one of his captains.

Tsar Kaloian and the Latin empire.

Kaloian seeks
and accepts
the papal
sanction for
his sover-
eignty.

Very Important
see Kings & sons
of Bulgaria
Died 1241

An interesting episode of Kaloian's reign of politico-ecclesiasti-
cal nature deserves to be mentioned. Indubitably he owed his
throne primarily to his own and his brothers' prowess but, like
many another conqueror, he felt that he needed a higher sanction than mere force in order to perpetuate his rule. We have
recounted the similar case of the ruler of Serbia, Stephen I, who,
in spite of his actual exercise of the sovereignty, did not feel
secure till he had won the blessing of the pope. On seizing
the throne Kaloian appealed to the Roman pontiff, and in 1204,
only a few months after the capture of Constantinople, was
crowned at Tirnovo in the presence of a papal legate, though the
actual ceremony was conducted by the newly appointed head of
the Bulgar church. The pope apparently received pledges to
the effect that, as a return for the papal favor, the Bulgar church
should be brought into the Roman fold. But once in possession
of the pope's blessing, Kaloian with characteristic perfidy forgot
his commitments to St. Peter's chair. The Bulgars were Orthodox, the Bulgar clergy fanatically so, and the cunning Kaloian
in all likelihood never had the least intention of affronting the
religious prejudices of his people in order to swell still further the
already excessive authority of the church of Rome.

Bulgaria con-
tinues to
flourish un-
der John
Asen II
(1218-41).

The difficulties of a state like Bulgaria, brought together by
conquest, were fully illustrated after Kaloian's death. Its composite racial elements, Bulgars, Greeks, and Vlachs, refused to
blend, and the turbulent members of the nobility, who had risen
to influence and power on the tide of war, seized every opportunity to make themselves independent of the central authority.
The death of the terrible tsar caused a general bursting of bounds
with resulting anarchy which lasted until the son of John Asen
and nephew of Kaloian managed to win recognition under the
name of John Asen II (1218-41). If not the most energetic,
John Asen II proved to be the most talented and cultured
member of his line, the so-called Asenid dynasty. Without concerning ourselves with the labyrinthine policies of his day, than
which it is difficult to imagine anything less profitable, let us
be content to note that John Asen ruled a Bulgaria which, territorially, was easily the leading state of the peninsula. Doubtless,
too, it was for the time being the most flourishing of the Balkan
states, for the tsar, very different in this respect from most of

his royal contemporaries, had at least an inkling that life is properly concerned with the productive occupations and the arts, and that, in order to practice them to any advantage, a people needs to have peace and the blessings of a regulated administration.

However, in the eternal human welter called Balkan history, a relatively prosperous period like that of John Asen II has never been anything more than an interlude. He was scarcely dead when the old anarchy broke loose which his descendants proved incapable of mastering. By 1258 the Asenid dynasty had gone out in dishonor. As always and everywhere, political feebleness seemed almost magically to create enemies on every hand. For one item a new Mongolian horde, the Tartars, establishing itself in the south-Russian plain, adopted the habit of almost annually overrunning Bulgaria with fire and sword. Quick to profit by every opportunity, the Hungarians, planted on the middle Danube, renewed their ambitious attempts to extend their control to the lower course of the Danube. Of course the Greek empire, weak though it might be, was prompt to seize an opportunity to wrest territory from a still weaker neighbor. And finally the Serbs, elated by the achievement of political unity, undertook to push into Macedonia, even then a doubtful borderland between Bulgaria and themselves. The successive adventurers upon the Bulgar throne following the end of the Asenids, their plots against local rivals and their rivals' plots against them, the endless wearisome chain of treason, violence, and murder, have no historical significance beyond confirming that the Second Bulgaria, like the First, was essentially an unsound fabric gnawed by every kind of social and political disease. Let us grant, as in justice we must, that the Balkan peninsula, more than any other part of Europe, was thrown into recurrent turmoil by overwhelming invasions from without, which will have to be set down by the judicious inquirer as historical accidents, utterly beyond human control. We have recounted many such invasions, among which the Tartar invasion of the thirteenth century figures as no light affliction. In fact the repeated invasions of the swift-moving Tartar horsemen wrought a terrible havoc and must be adduced as a leading cause of the gradual disintegration of the Second Bulgaria. But with every allowance made

The Second Bulgaria overwhelmed by invasion coupled with domestic disturbances.

for contributory factors, we are yet driven to the conclusion that the Bulgar people of the close of the thirteenth century had failed to develop that minimum of moral stamina and institutional stability which history proves to be essential to the maintenance of a commonwealth, tolerably ordered and measurably civilized.

The battle of Küstendil (1330) decides the fate of Bulgaria.

Confronted with unsolvable outer and inner difficulties, Bulgaria inevitably dropped to its setting. In the fourteenth century one of her tsars, alarmed by the forward movement which had carried the Serbs far into Macedonia, resolved to drive them out again. The Serb monarch of the time was Stephen, called Deshanski, from a famous church built by him at Deshani in western Serbia. On July 28, 1330, he met the Bulgar host at Küstendil (Velbuzd), in the upper Struma valley, and won a complete victory. The tsar himself was slain and the Bulgar army scattered to the winds. It is true that the Serbs did not now assume the government of Bulgaria; they even recognized a new Bulgar sovereign and left him undisturbed in the exercise of all authority of a purely local character. However, it was substantially as a vassal state of victorious Serbia that Bulgaria lived on for another half century, when she was extinguished wholly by a more terrible enemy than the Serb, the Ottoman Turk. From every essential point of view the Second Bulgaria sank into the grave at Küstendil, while over the whole Balkan interior shone the unchallenged might of Serbia.

Stephen Dushan, 1331–55.

We have now reached the period of the greatest bloom of the Serb state, a period which modern Serbs still look upon with passionate pride. The victory over Bulgaria marks its beginning. However, King Stephen Deshanski, who won the battle of Küstendil, did not live long to enjoy his triumph. The Nemania line, like all the royal lines of the peninsula, was torn by bloody family feuds and presents a story repeating in cold fact all the mythical horrors of the ancient house of Atreus. Stephen Deshanski, who had in his youth been blinded by a revengeful father, was in his old age overthrown and murdered by his son, the twenty-two-year-old Stephen Dushan. It is Stephen Dushan (1331–55) who gave the Serb state its greatest extent and luster.

Looking about in the peninsula in the days of Stephen Dushan, we may easily convince ourselves that the moment was favorable for the achievement of Serb primacy. Hungary, the mid-Danubian power, whose ambitious designs frequently threatened Serbia, was just then absorbed in its struggle with Venice for the possession of the Adriatic coast; Bulgaria, already reduced to vassalage, was completely helpless; and the remaining Balkan power of any dignity, the Byzantine empire, was plagued with every disease of a dying state.

The moment
favorable for
Serb
ascendancy.

BALKANIA AND ASIA MINOR AT THE DEATH OF THE SERB TSAR
STEPHEN DUSHAN (1355)

|||||||| BYZANTINE EMPIRE   //// BULGARIA   \\\\ SERBIA
===== OTTOMAN TURKS   ■ VENETIAN POSESSIONS   ∷∷∷ LATIN STATES OF GREECE

As if the narrow boundaries, the economic misery, and the diminished productive energy of the Greek empire were not unhappiness enough, there broke out in Stephen Dushan's time a civil war between rival emperors of the two houses of Paleologus and Cantacuzenus, which lasted with little interruption for fifteen years and which, with a minimum of expense and effort to the Serbs, delivered all the western districts of the empire into their hands. By leisurely occupying Macedonia, Albania, Epirus, and Thessaly while the ambitious imbeciles from Constantinople and their selfish adherents chased each other in a circle around Thrace, Stephen Dushan doubled the area of his state.

Stephen Dushan occupies
all the western provinces
of the Greek empire.

He could now look forward with considerable confidence to the time when, having picked up the poor remainder of the Greek empire, he would send out his commands from the marble palace of the emperors on the Golden Horn. Undeniably, in respect of the Greek provinces which he added to the Serb mass, Stephen Dushan appears less as a conqueror than as a lucky bystander. The suspicion that his power was rather showy than solid cannot be suppressed and draws further nourishment from its astonishingly swift collapse after his death.

The titles emperor and tsar symbolize Balkanian unity.

However, the mighty spell still exercised over his countrymen by Stephen Dushan's name is only partially due to his enlargement of Serb territory at the expense of Byzantium. With a natural turn for pomp and grandeur he divined that nothing impressed the average man like high-sounding titles and gorgeous ceremonies. As heir of his Nemanian predecessors and by the operations of fortune, coupled, it is true, with great personal initiative and a prudent diplomacy, he had risen to the top of the heap in the peninsula. According to the historic concepts which ruled the consciousness of all the inhabitants of Balkania and which were inherited from the days of the *imperium romanum,* political overlordship expressed itself in the title of emperor, of which the Slav equivalent was tsar. As long as the Byzantine state was the dominating power in the peninsula, it seemed natural and proper that the Byzantine chief should wield the imperial scepter with its implications of universal Balkan rule; when, as under Simeon, the Bulgar state exercised the widest sway, the Bulgar sovereign felt justified in arrogating the imperial title to himself; and when, as now, a Serb king was in possession of almost all the Balkan land, it seemed no more than right to him and to his followers that his title should be brought into exact correspondence with the facts.

Stephen Dushan creates a Serb patriarchate and has himself crowned tsar (1346).

Moved by these considerations, Stephan Dushan carefully laid his plans. As we have repeatedly seen, in the minds of medieval men the church was as important or even more important for the control of human affairs than the state, with which it was on terms of intimate association. Taking in hand the church, Stephen conferred upon the archbishop of the Serb establishment, autonomous since the days of St. Sava and the first king, the title patriarch. By this act the Serb church was for the first time completely severed from the Greek church with the result that the new patriarchate, with its seat at Ipek, looked upon itself as fully equal in authority, if not in the dignity conferred by years, to the older patriarchates of Constantinople and Ochrida. This measure accomplished, the king in 1346 ordered the patriarch, who by virtue of his title was supposed to have gathered round his person something of the glamour attaching for ages to the great titulary of Constantinople, to crown him tsar at Skoplje (Uskub). This town in central Macedonia became Tsar Stephen's capital in correct recognition of the fact that a Serb hegemony over Balkania, in order to be effective, would have to establish itself on the Vardar line in Macedonia, the great north–south thoroughfare. The full title he chose for himself was Tsar of the Serbs and Greeks, by which composite form he clearly served notice that he did not think of himself as a narrow national sovereign but as the heir of Constantinople. Without question the city on the Bosporus was his final goal. But weak as the Byzantines were, their great stronghold could not be taken without the coöperation of a fleet. Fully aware of the fact, Stephen was willing to bide his time but, biding, death overtook him at the early age of forty-six (1355). Apparently he died in his own realm after a brief illness. It is not improbable that he was collecting an army at the time in prep-aration for a final and exterminative expedition against the Greeks, but no document exists throwing the faintest light on either his last designs or the manner of his death. In view of these uncertainties the social psychologist will be deeply interested in the popular Serb legend, which came to envelop the personality of Stephen Dushan like a brilliant halo and which represented him as finding his death mysteriously, most likely from Greek poison, while leading a victorious army against the imperial city on the Golden Horn. It is a striking instance of national romanticism, which, taking the will for the deed, corrects an imperfect reality by piecing it out with *maia*, with illusion.

The Serb tsar, who undoubtedly possessed great administrative and organizing gifts, left a monument behind for which historians owe him sincere thanks. He had the laws and customs of his country assembled in a code, which unrolls a very detailed picture of the state of Serb society in the fourteenth century. Since

The state of Serb society in Stephen Dushan's time revealed by the *Zakonik*, his famous code of laws (1349).

the time in the sixth century when the Slav barbarians, organized in tribes and practicing a primitive form of communism, had burst into the peninsula, important changes had taken place. Undoubtedly the greatest single advance was represented by Christianity. Since its coming the nearby Byzantine empire, hearth of the new religion, had exercised an irresistible attraction, and when the Nemania kings undertook to build a state, they naturally took the highly organized government on the Bosporus as a model. The great changes in the political and social structure effected by the direct and indirect influence of Byzantium are accurately recorded in the code of Stephen Dushan. It assigns to the sovereign a dominant position, for he is regarded as the owner of the land and its inhabitants, and the fountain-head of law. Such is the theory of the code, plainly of Byzantine origin and miles removed from the tribal conceptions of primitive Serb society. In practice, however, exactly as among the Greeks in post-Basilian days, instead of being absolute, the sovereign power was seriously limited by the great dignitaries of the church and state. The Serb dignitaries, moreover, resembling in this respect the feudal magnates of the West, met from time to time in a national assembly or parliament, by virtue of which they exercised a considerable check on the sovereign. It is further certain that their pretensions to rule were powerfully strengthened by their hereditary possession of large landed estates. These ample properties were worked by tenants, of whom some were free and others serf, and who, a peasant mass, constituted the overwhelming majority of the Serb population. Under cover of the centralized and feudal forms, both of relatively recent origin, the native Serb institutions, embracing the family and village, stubbornly continued to flourish. This is a most important circumstance to keep in mind, for when, owing to the Ottoman conquest, of which we are presently to hear, the central government was wiped out, family and village government, the really vital elements of Serb institutional life, unobtrusively persisted, thereby enabling the people to preserve their racial integrity in the teeth of a crushing subjection to a body of Asiatic conquerors.

Medieval Serbia essentially feudal and agrarian.

On turning to consider the towns, we are at once struck by a startling difference between Serbia and the Byzantine empire. Large, numerous, and important among the sea-faring Greeks, they were both rare and small among the inland Serbs, and the handful of merchants and artisans who inhabited them were largely foreigners and an unimportant though, it must be admitted, a steadily increasing factor in the life of the nation. Taking in the whole of Serb society as revealed by the code, one gets the impression that, in obedience to general forces operative on the Bosporus and throughout the peninsula, it had begun to assume forms curiously like those of western feudalism. However, in the Latin West feudalism was, in the fourteenth century, already disintegrating under the mighty impulse of the rising cities, while no urban movement of any consequence as yet made itself felt in the inaccessible Serb hills, where foresters, trappers, and plowmen, a manifestly backward society, maintained an almost uninterrupted sway. A final resemblance to the feudal West, deserving of mention, was furnished by Stephen Dushan's army. A part of it was made up of the great lords, who brought into the field with them the required contingent of their followers, but, in addition to this feudal body, the tsar commanded a mercenary army, composed of foreigners and brought to as many companies as his fluctuating means permitted. On these mercenaries, who constituted a heavy cavalry and who were excellently trained, fell the brunt of the fighting. They supply an interesting clue to Dushan's success as an empire-builder.

When Tsar Stephen was succeeded by his young son, Urosh, mild-mannered and without any of the talents of mind and character essential to a ruler of men, the lofty Serb structure almost at once showed signs of going to pieces. With the strong hand removed, the many non-Serb elements, Greeks, Bulgars, and Albanians, held together by no other bond than force, drove violently apart. Among the Serbs themselves the ancient tribal spirit was still powerful, and though it had recently been somewhat curbed by means of a super-imposed royal administration, it had without question received fresh nourishment by the general drift toward feudalism. With little difficulty the great dignitaries of the state, noblemen more or less identical with the old tribal chiefs, the zupans, could set up virtually independent sovereignties the moment the central power showed signs of losing its grip.

Serbia falls apart under the tsar's successor.

The coming of the Turks inaugurates a new epoch of Balkan history.

As chance would have it, at the very time when feudal anarchy was making ready to apply its deadly acid to Tsar Stephen's too personal creation the peninsula was confronted with the gravest crisis of the whole medieval period. The Turk peril, threatening since the days of Manzikert (1071) but relieved by the victories of the emperors of the Comnenus line, was once more becoming acute. At the precise time at which Stephen Dushan, enthroned in the Macedonian uplands, was cogitating how to seize what was left of the Roman heritage, a new tribe of Turks, the Ottomans, having brought northwestern Asia Minor under their control, were moved to entertain an exactly identical plan. Shortly before the death of the great tsar they succeeded in gaining (1354) a foothold on the European side of the Dardanelles. The Turks were in Europe! They were at the gates of Constantinople! And at this breathless moment the only Christian state which seemed to have the strength to defend the peninsula dissipated its energies by falling into feudal confusion. Therefore the Turk invasion met only scattered and weak resistance and inaugurated a new epoch of Balkan history.

Backward glance over the eight hundred years constituting the Byzantine epoch.

On coming to the end of the Byzantine epoch we may, as from a height, look back over the long road which we have traveled. It covers a period of eight hundred years. In all that time the Byzantine empire with its good and bad fortune, with its constructive labors and destructive passions, is the natural focus of interest. Unable in the first place to keep the Slavs from settling in the peninsula, it was equally unable to hinder them from gradually forming two political centers of resistance, Bulgaria and Serbia. A three-cornered struggle followed, and while on the whole the Byzantine empire was oftenest in the ascendancy, Bulgaria, twice, and Serbia, once, had their triumphant, though brief innings. And yet throughout that long time of conflict and, for the most part, passionately embittered conflict, the three political groups had in many important respects been drawing together. The ancient and highly developed Byzantine state had gradually transferred a large part of its religion, its literature, its arts, its legal and administrative institutions, in short, its civilization, to the younger Slav societies. It is no exaggeration to say that in matters constituting the essential basis of significant human intercourse the Balkan peoples, almost against their will and certainly without particularly perceiving it, had, in the course of the Middle Age, been brought to something like a common cultural denominator. And yet the remaining differences, involving race and language and the ineradicable human instinct for political self-expression, sufficed to produce the unceasing struggle of which we have been the astonished spectators.

And now, a little past the middle of the fourteenth century, there was introduced into the human welter another element certain to intensify the strife. The Turks, Asiatic and Mohammedan, entered the peninsula and made themselves its masters. By breaking all resistance they could, for a time at least, produce a superficial appearance of peace and unity, but since they neither could nor did destroy the Balkan peoples, they were sure to be confronted with open or latent warfare during all the centuries of their Balkan occupation. Moreover the Turks, as Moslems and non-Europeans, would probably resist that measure of assimilation to a common type which Time had imperceptibly effected among the Greeks, Serbs, and Bulgars. They would remain obstinately alien and therefore the struggle among the Balkan peoples, cruel enough in the medieval period, was sure to wax more cruel and more irreconcilable in the years to come. Add that other races, like the Rumans (Vlachs) and Albanians, submerged and quiescent in the Middle Age, were rousing themselves from slumber and making ready to claim their just place in the sun, and the troubles ahead were certain to present an embroilment unique in the annals of Europe.

Intensification of Balkan strife in the Turkish epoch.

Surely the history of Balkania must be the despair of a philosopher bent on reducing the world to an intelligible order, for in Balkania throughout its long agony it is difficult to discover so much as a trace of any evidence that human affairs work out to the ends of reason or morality. Luckily for the historian he is not concerned, like the philosopher, with final things nor is it his business to explain why men fail to realize an ethical society. His is the practical task of dealing with the organization of a relatively definite body of facts of a social and political order, and though he is pushed to assume that men are free agents on the human stage, responsible alike for the good and the evil which be-

The historical viewpoint.

fall them, he wisely refrains from pressing the point and meting out praise and blame according to an abstract moral scheme. What laughable presumption it would be if, to go no farther than Balkan history, he would categorically assert that the Greeks, Serbs, and Bulgars deserve their sufferings and that one or all of them are, wholly or in some determinable ratio, responsible for the seething chaos of the peninsula! Let us therefore abandon every pretense to explain the Balkan imbroglio in ultimate moral or philosophical terms, and let us rather, like a good cobbler, stick to our last and be content with a strictly historical viewpoint. From this outlook we may, on bringing the Byzantine epoch to a close, look backward and forward for a moment over the peninsula and dispassionately note that the Balkan peoples, engaged throughout the Middle Age in a bitter struggle for political supremacy, have without respite or relief trod the mill of that same struggle, as terrible as it is unsolvable, down to our own day.

APPENDIX

A. *Mt. Athos*

HOWEVER much the Balkan peoples struggled with one another for political power, they had, as we have seen, in more than one respect developed common interests and a common mentality, that is, through proximity and intercourse they had achieved something like a common civilization. Easily the strongest tie uniting them was the Christian religion in the form represented by the Orthodox or Greek church. When the political ambition of Bulgaria and Serbia led to the creation of nationally independent churches under Bulgar and Serb primates, the moral union of the various Christian peoples continued to be expressed in an interesting as well as vigorous manner by the monastic communities established on the slopes of Mt. Athos. These communities constitute so characteristic an expression of Christianity in its eastern medieval phase that the student of Balkan society cannot afford to pass them by.

The Athos peninsula, commonly called among the Greeks the Holy Mountain, is the easternmost of the three tongues of land which project from the Macedonian shore into the northern Aegean and which are embraced collectively under the name of the Chalcidean peninsula. The Athos tongue, about twenty-five miles long and varying from three to five miles in width, is, especially at its southern end, a region of precipitate steeps and romantic gorges which find their natural culmination in the Athos summit, towering like a giant sentinel over the Aegean waters.

It was not till the ninth century that Mt. Athos acquired any special significance in the religious life of the East. By that time attention began to be drawn to it by reason of the stream of holy men who directed their footsteps thither in search of that solitude and release from worldly cares enthusiastically proclaimed as the the highest goal of Christianity. Always eager to appear as protectors of the faith, the Byzantine emperors did not delay to endow these seekers of the Lord with copious privileges. The earliest authentic charter was issued in the tenth century by Emperor Nicephorus Phocas. His successors outdid one another in multiplying favors to the monks and hermits by new charters until the Holy Mountain was a unique religious polity, a veritable self-governing monastic republic under imperial protection. By virtue of their privileges the religious residents were freed from the payment of taxes and dues, be it to the state or to the church; they were exempted from the ecclesiastical authority of the neighboring bishop and, finally, of the patriarch himself; and while each community was authorized to govern itself in internal matters in full independence, the common affairs were entrusted to the management of a federal council which met at Karyas, in the heart of the peninsula, and which conducted its business under the presidency of a protos or supreme abbot.

The earliest seekers of Mt. Athos lived apart as hermits but, exactly as in the west, they were gradually drawn together into monastic communities which, constantly enriched by the gifts of the pious, were enabled to erect churches and dormitories often on so impressive a scale that a monastery settlement, surrounded by its wall, rose among the cliffs like a veritable fortress of the Lord. The rapid material development is indicated by a statement of the year 1045 to the effect that there were then scattered over the peninsula twenty monasteries giving shelter to over seven hundred monks. What particularly strikes the modern observer is that these strange seekers of the Lord carried to the point of fanaticism the beliefs, superstitions, and prejudices, which, in their sum, constitute the peculiar medieval view-point. The world from which, in order to win salvation, they were fleeing was symbolized by woman; the sin of sins was sex. The extravagant consequences of similar views entertained among the Latin monks are well known, but we may doubt if the more balanced temper of the western nations ever indulged in such orgies of oriental unreason as the Athos monks. It goes of course without saying that Athos was a grave male community and that the frivolous daughters of Eve were forbidden so much as to set foot on the Mountain's holy soil. But the tormented imagination of these strange zealots did not stop there. Females of every variety and species, including the harmless, necessary cat and such docile purveyors to our fleshly comfort as the cow and the hen, shared the rigorous taboo designed to keep Mt. Athos clean, godly, and — masculine.

Originally the creation of the Greeks, Mt. Athos gradually attracted the attention of all followers of the Orthodox church. From an early time, Serbs, Bulgars, and even Russians found their way to a region dedicated so exclusively to the highest ends of Christianity. We learn, for example, that Stephen Nemania's son, Sava, while still a youth, sought the sacred slopes, and that he owed to this retirement the reputation which led to his being appointed in his later years as the first archbishop of Serbia: · Then again, Stephen Nemania himself, when old age knocked at the door, sought the Athos solitudes where, assuming the cowl, he founded (1198) and richly endowed for his Serb countrymen the famous monastery of Kilandar. Moved by the Serb example, the Bulgars and, in the course of time, the Russians endowed prosperous establishments for men of their own blood. Probably every Orthodox people of the East would be able to establish the claim that from an early time down to the twentieth century it never failed to be represented among the large, peaceful, and prosperous population of the Mountain.

Neither scholarship and literature nor the education of the young nor good works ever played other than a subsidiary rôle among the Athos monks. They have therefore but small resemblance to such learned western orders as the Benedictines or to such foundations dedicated to active human service as the begging friars. In their own eyes, however, they represented the very flower of medieval religious purpose in that they sought as their unique end release from life's concerns and tribulations amidst an incessant round of prayer and worship.

The coming of the Turks, which revolutionized and obliterated so much in the peninsula, did not effect any considerable change on the Holy Mountain. Before the middle of the fifteenth century the monks, foreseeing the end of the Greek empire which had given them such distinguished protection for so many centuries, quietly submitted to the Turks and accepted the infidel sultan as their patron in place of the Orthodox emperor. Under Mohammedan protection, which, it is only fair to state, was exercised with astonishing tolerance since it left the venerable monastic republic wholly intact, the communities remained from the middle of the fifteenth century until the Balkan war of 1912, when the whole Chalcidean peninsula was absorbed into the young and triumphant kingdom of Greece. During the long overlordship of the Turks the Mountain with a conservatism suggesting petrefaction, kept unchanged all its peculiar medieval features with the result that the Mt. Athos of today, with its numerous hermitages, dormitories, and churches, boasting a population of over seven thousand monks, appears as a living or — may we not say? — an embalmed section of the Middle Age, projected into an era dedicated to science and industrial competition and in all its main manifestations diametrically opposed to the ascetic ideal.

B. The Bogumil Heresy

We have had occasion to remark that throughout the Middle Age the Christian East was troubled with heresies, which the Orthodox church fought bitterly and which the state, the ally of the church, attempted to suppress by force. The most important departure from the true faith which took root in the Balkan peninsula was the Bogumil heresy. Owing to its wide distribution and remarkable persistence a brief account is not without value for the student of Balkan affairs.

Both origin and tenets of the Christian heretics called Bogumils are subject to dispute. Doubtless the heresy is lineally descended from one or another of the earlier heresies of the Mediterranean world, possibly from the sect of the Paulicians, who were at home in Asia Minor where they long defied the efforts of the watchdogs of orthodoxy to put them to rout. Some scholars hold that, in point of doctrine, the Bogumils were of the Manichaean or dualist type, that is, that they believed that God and Satan were coördinate powers, the authors respectively of good and evil, of the spirit and the flesh. Another view, warmly defended, is that they were primarily Adoptionists, that is, they held that Jesus was a man like other men to his thirtieth year, when he was *adopted* by God and was entered into by the Holy Spirit through the act of baptism performed by John. It is difficult to come to definite conclusions about the teachings of the Bogumils, because our information comes to us exclusively from their enemies. However, offensive as their heretical opinions were, it is likely that the fierce wrath visited upon them was due to other causes and, more particularly, to their opposition to the hierarchy with its wealth, power, and passion for theatrical display. This critical attitude toward the governing powers of the church made them in effect an ecclesiastico-political opposition party, sounding a puritanical note and drawing its strength chiefly from the downtrodden masses. Not improbably something like a democratic protest against the ruling classes may be attributed to the Bogumil movement. However, not to squeeze the few documents which have come down to us for more than they will yield, it is best to think of the Bogumils as more concerned with religion than with politics, and to see them preëminently as haters of the too elaborate ceremonies and sacraments of the church and as single-minded preachers of a return to a more simple faith with an immediate appeal to God by the avenue of prayer. An extreme, minority group apparently advocated pacifism, socialism, vegetarianism, and free love, that is, they cultivated a dangerous and fanatic radicalism, but the rank and file, filled with a more compromising temper, may more properly be characterized as evangelical puritans seeking a return to the simpler worship of the Apostolic Age.

The heresy first made its appearance in Balkania in the tenth century under the auspices of a Bulgar priest, Bogumil, from whom it derives its name. Though persecuted, it was not suppressed and for generations dangerously divided the country. The overthrow of both the First and the Second Bulgaria was unquestionably facilitated by this religious schism, which created two irreconcilable factions in the land and dangerously weakened the government. From Bulgaria the heresy spread westward into Serbia, where it invited the denunciation of the hierarchy and was finally suppressed by the strictly orthodox sovereigns of the Nemania line. Next, it turned up in Bosnia where it won a signal and exceptional victory, for it became so strong that the attempt to suppress it, though often renewed, had to be given up. In the fifteenth century a king of Bosnia went so far as openly to avow himself a Bogumil, apparently because he wished to secure his throne by taking his stand with the majority of his people. When, shortly after the middle of that same century, the Turks conquered Bosnia, the Bosnian Bogumils in large numbers and apparently without the need of much persuasion went over to Mohammedanism, the simple practices of which were more congenial to them than the elaborate ritual of the Orthodox church. As is well known the Bosnian Moslems, erstwhile Bogumils and of Serb race and speech, became one of the chief supports of Turk rule in the peninsula. In this way Bogumilism has remained an element in Balkan affairs down to the present time.

Beyond Bosnia the student of Balkan history does not feel called on to follow the course of the Bogumil heresy. It may, however, be remarked that it is, in point of doctrine, more or less identical with the heresy which under the name of various sects, such as the Cathari, Patarenes, and Albigenses, during many centuries disquieted the Latin West. In sum, Bogumilism not only traveled beyond Balkania but became the most general of all medieval heresies and registered, wherever and under whatever name it raised its head, a protest, democratic and evangelical in character, against the ritualistic forms and aristocratic organization of the Christian Church.

C. *The Latin States on Hellenic Soil*

When the crusaders took Constantinople in 1204 and set up a Latin empire with an emperor at the head, they considered this but a preliminary measure to taking over and exploiting for their benefit as victors the whole Byzantine state. More easily thought than done. In Asia Minor, in Epirus, and at several other centers Greek magnates met the Latin challenge by setting up local governments, which it proved impossible to overthrow; in fact, as noted in the text, the Greek resistance, in spite of its scattered character, was maintained with such energy that it succeeded in the course of little more than half a century in putting the feeble Latin creation to complete rout.

However, on the morrow of the capture of the metropolis on the Bosporus, the elated conquerors sat down to carve up the defeated state, and after commercial Venice, which insisted on being served first, had preëmpted the islands and coastal stations conceived to be advantageous to her trade, the western knights, mostly Frenchmen, though there was a notable sprinkling of Flemings, Lombards, and Germans among them, had their turn and divided the remainder of the fair Greek lands among themselves. The next step was to take possession and, except for certain areas, chiefly in Asia Minor and in Epirus, where the Greeks offered successful resistance, the seizure was in so far carried out that large territories, especially in ancient Hellas and among the Aegean islands, came into the hands of the Frankish knights. Accordingly, they set up a group of states of a western, feudal type, which, nominally under the new emperor at Constantinople, were really independent and which together make up a not inconsiderable part of the history of the Near East for the following two hundred years. In some instances the Latin lordships outlived the cheap glories of the Latin empire and several of them, against all expectations, even proved themselves of hardier growth than the revived empire of the Greeks.

The problem of all these predatory foundations was essentially identical with that of the imperial Frankish state at Constantinople. Representing, like it, conquest pure and simple, naked and unashamed, they were likely to survive in measure as they developed skill to conciliate the conquered by politic concessions. In taking cognizance of the situation let us not forget that, however degenerate in comparison with their classical ancestors the medieval Greeks might appear to be, they boasted a powerful church, an honored language, and an established system of legal relations, in short, a developed civilization, which the western knights, after all a mere handful in proportion to the conquered mass, could not by any chance hope to scatter and uproot. The knights, for their part, brought along with them into the East a civilization of their own, of which the feudal system and the Catholic religion were the most substantial features. While it is true that, after surveying the local scene, they prudently gave up the idea of imposing their cultural forms by force on their new subjects, none-the-less they persisted in living after their familiar ways, with the net result that they effectively maintained the chasm between themselves and the Greeks. Consciously and purposely isolated from their subjects, they were in the long run doomed to political failure.

Stubbornly alien, the Frankish rule never lost, while it endured, its military character and occidental quality. Although this circumstance has served to impart to it a certain romantic color and render it extremely popular with poets and novelists, such favor must be admitted to be out of proportion to its historical significance. Amazing warriors like Othon de la Roche, William de Champlitte, Geoffrey de Villehardouin and some scores of others, who with a horse, a lance, and a goodly suit of armor ventured to face a world more remote and strange to them than China is to us, exhibit a spirit of daring which the artist in each of us cannot but hail with delight, even though we agree that what they accomplished does not weigh heavily in the scales of fate. Constantly joined by new adventurers, lured to the magic East by the astounding tale of the rewards awaiting a nimble wit or a sword that sat loose in its scabbard, the various feudal courts set up by these stalwart conquistadores became hotbeds, where new and exciting forays were perpetually hatched, where perilous amours relieved the tedium of periodic peace, and where palace dramas were enacted which in the play of unrestrained passion surpass the imagined instances bodied forth in Boccaccio's *Decameron* or in the plays of the Elizabethan age.

Apart from the empire at Constantinople, the outstanding Latin states were three in number, the duchy of Athens, the principality of Achaia, and the duchy of the Archipelago. The two former owed their existence to enterprising bodies of French knights, the duchy of Athens more particularly to the boldness of Othon de la Roche, and the principality of Achaia to William de Champlitte supported by Geoffrey de Villehardouin, nephew of the famous soldier who, himself a leader of the Fourth Crusade, added the clerk's renown to his warrior reputation by inditing the story of the expedition with simple and magnificent sincerity. The duchy of Athens embraced, besides Attica with its famous capital, Thebes and its countryside, and proved itself uncommonly vigorous for some generations. Overwhelmed at the beginning of the fourteenth century by a band of Catalan freebooters, it passed, in curious anticipation of the developments of the modern world, into the hands of a family of Florentine financial magnates possessed of the will and cunning to make money count for more than crude military power. Once established, chiefly through the machinations of the adroit Nerio Acciajuoli, this family of Tuscan tradesmen lost no time in adopting the airs of barons to the manner born. Nerio succeeded in founding an Acciajuoli dynasty in Athens, which, amidst checkered fortunes, sat on the ancient rock of the Acropolis till a little past the middle of the fifteenth century, when the advancing Turk, to whom a Latin state was as desirable a meal as one of Greek origin, put an end to the Frankish duchy.

The principality of Achaia, territorially identical with the ancient Peloponnesus, played undoubtedly the leading rôle among the Latin states set up on Hellenic soil. Owing more particularly to the prowess of Geoffrey de Villehardouin, who founded a dynasty destined to rule for several generations, the Achaian state acquired fame both for its arms and commerce. However, as early as the second half of the thirteenth century, a decline set in and new rulers winning the throne succeeded one another with such startling rapidity that the revived Byzantine empire, taking advantage of the confusion, managed once more to get a foothold on the southern shore. In the course of the fourteenth century the Greek eperors steadily enlarged their territory, until in the year 1432 they rais d their banner over the last remaining Frankish castles. After over two hundred years the peninsula was again under Byzantine sway! But little good did the Morean subjects get from this return of their legitimate princes. In the course of another generation the irresistible Turk broke through the defenses of the isthmus of Corinth, not to rest until he had triumphantly raised the Crescent over the whole Peloponnesus.

As a sheer product of human daring the duchy of the Archipelago yields place to none of the Latin creations. The Aegean islands were largely claimed by Venice, but as the republic lacked the means of effecting occupation, it encouraged its citizens to take over the islands on their own initiative. To Marco Sanudo, nephew of the great Enrico Dandolo and as undaunted as the doge himself, this lure did not sound in vain. Fitting out an expedition, he conquered the centrally located Naxos and soon afterwards brought most of the neighbor islands under his rule. Once established, however, he showed no inclination to hand over his conquest to the august republic and preferred, acting on his feudal instincts, to attach himself to the Latin emperor, who accorded him the title of duke of the Archipelago and made him the immediate vassal of the prince of Achaia. The Sanudo dynasty, possessed of a healthy appetite and a vigorous grip, held on to its duchy among the sunny isles of Greece for several generations. Then their possessions passed to another house, which in the growing political confusion of the East was soon caught in the general decline of the Latin fortunes. In the fourteenth century, with the advent of the Turk corsair, troubles rained down upon the islands thick and fast, and when, in the following century, the Asiatic Moslems set

their foot on the Greek mainland the fate of the duchy was as good as
sealed. In this declining phase Venice at last succeeded in making good
her claim to sovereignty, which, dating from the conquest of 1204, she
had withheld but never quite renounced. The protection of the great
naval power explains why the islands fell only slowly under the rule of
the sultan, and why some of them retained a precarious independence
under a Latin princeling for some generations after the Turks had seized
Constantinople and the near-by Morea. However, in the course of the
sixteenth century the Ottoman avalanche descended also on the weak and
already greatly diminished duchy of the Archipelago, thereby burying from
sight the last relic, as well of the Byzantine empire as of the Latin upstart which had made the audacious but vain attempt to replace it in the
Levantine waters.

D. *The Republic of Ragusa*

Whoever sailing northward through the straits of Corfu into the
Adriatic neglects to disembark at the port of Ragusa misses an opportunity to enrich his spirit with a rare combination of artistic and historical
impressions. Ragusa lies by the smiling sea at the foot of a bare, sun-
scorched mountain raising a nigh impassable barrier between it and the
peninsula, of which the city is a port. Still enclosed by its medieval wall,
which rises and dips over the uneven ground with the rhythmic movement
of a bird, it is a compact town of narrow, winding streets occasionally opening into an imposing square, where church and public building stand
shoulder to shoulder in ancient unbroken fellowship. The architecture,
sounding with its frequent porticos and arcades a decided note of gaiety, be-
trays a north-Italian and, more particularly, a Venetian influence and
quickly rouses the suspicion in the traveler that Ragusa is blood-kin to the
city of the doges. The deep blue sky, the penetrating light, the transparent
Mediterranean atmosphere confirm the impression that this is Italy.
And yet, hard though it be to believe, Ragusa is not and never was
Italian. It is a Serb city and Serb speech beats everywhere upon the
visitor's ear. For the site it occupies is part of that section of the Adriatic
coast which the Serbs have held since the migrations. To its Slav inhabitants it is not known as Ragusa, the name given it by its Italian
neighbors, but as Dubrovnik.

Ragusa, though still a lively town, is now hardly more than the
shadow of its former self. These squares, these public buildings,
these marble churches and palaces flushing pink and white under
the summer sun, speak confidently of the power and importance
which Ragusa enjoyed all through the Middle Age as an emporium of
commerce and the center of distribution for the Serb back-country. The
city's story is essentially an economic story, a story of trade. The Serb
communities entrenched behind their mountain bastions were most easily
accessible from Ragusa. From the shore the old trade route wound

painfully up the mountain, at the foot of which Ragusa lay, and then divided, one branch taking the merchant and his wares northward toward the Danube, the other eastward toward the Vardar and Macedonia. It was not till the Turkish régime laid its paralyzing hand on the Balkan interior, reducing both its productive and its purchasing power, that the wealth of Ragusa began to decline. Slowly the medieval stir and energy were replaced by a stagnant provincialism. However, in the course of time the economic expansion, characteristic of the nineteenth century, reached Balkania and made itself felt also at Ragusa, but, owing to the fundamentally changed conditions of the modern world, it has, thus far at least, failed to draw the hinterland in any effective way within the city's radius of action. For one thing the hinterland is in our day more easily and cheaply supplied by the rail routes from central Europe and, for another, the narrow harbor of Ragusa is not suited for modern trading vessels of heavy tonnage and corresponding draught. Not improbably the future may see these difficulties obviated with Ragusa again coming to the front as the chief outlet of Serbia to the sea.[1]

The political history of Ragusa recounts the story of a lively community of traders, who were ever desirous of maintaining their freedom but who were usually obliged to accept the protection of a powerful neighbor. The town was founded in the seventh century by Latin colonists, who fled from ancient Epidaurum when that city was taken and destroyed by the invading Slavs. Acknowledging of course the sovereignty of the East Roman empire, it exercised from the first the extensive municipal rights of Roman origin guaranteed to all the Adriatic towns. Since the country round about was settled by Slavs the population gradually lost its original Latin character and became Slav like its environment. That ethnic transformation, completed before the close of the Middle Age, did not, however, alter its political relation to the Byzantine empire, of which, while proudly exercising a traditional autonomy, it remained a part till the catastrophe of the Fourth Crusade (1204). Thereupon Ragusa fell under the rule of Venice and for a century and a half a representative of the doge dwelt within the walls without particularly encroaching on the cherished municipal self-government. Far more incisive in its consequences, however, than the vague overlordship conceded to Venice was the cultural primacy which the queen of the Adriatic exercised over her Slav dependency and which, continuing even after the doge's banner ceased to wave over the townhall, accounts for the atmosphere, peculiarly mixed of Venetian charm and vigor, which envelops the city to this day. As soon as the Venetian political control was broken (about 1350), fresh claims to exercise political protection were put forth

[1] The English language supplies interesting evidence of the former importance of Ragusa in the word *argosy*. It is a corruption of the name of the Serb city and signifies the Ragusan vessel which before the establishment of a native English trade carried Levantine goods to the English markets.

by aspiring neighbors like Hungary and Serbia, but the city, though prudently yielding when the pressure became strong and agreeing to pay a tribute, substantially kept its destiny in its own hands. It is worthy of note that never, not even under the mighty Tsar Stephen Dushan, was Ragusa incorporated in Serbia.

never incorporated into Serbia, although inhabited by Serbs

When the Turks, superseding one after another of the older Balkan powers, loomed up over the eastern mountains, the Ragusan merchants met the new political situation in their usual elastic way. In return for an annual contribution they were left unmolested, and during the many centuries of the harsh Turkish rule in the peninsula they presided over a commonwealth which, if declining in prosperity, was to all purposes a free state, howbeit of an oligarchic type. The republic of Ragusa, governed by princely merchants, and the peasant state of neighboring Montenegro enjoy the proud distinction of being the only Slav communities of Balkania on which the Turks did not plant their foot. In consequence in all the centuries between the fall of Serbia and its revival in the nineteenth century, whatever was left of Serb learning and culture foregathered in Ragusa as in a haven of refuge. A mild literary activity, inspired by Italian examples, kept alive the flame of national life and won for the town the proud title of the South Slavonic Athens.

NB

With the coming of the new age heralded by the French revolution, the end of the aristocratic republic, grown a bit grotesque and rococo with the passing of time, was at hand. Napoeon Bonaparte, nursing the dream of Mediterranean power, in the year 1805 (Peace of Pressburg) seized the Dalmatian coast. Intolerant of the little mock-republic in the midst of his Adriatic dominion, he autocratically bade it begone and brought the city under French administration. When Napoleon fell, Ragusa, together with the rest of the Dalmatian coast, was handed over to Austria (1814); and with Austria it remained to the catastrophe of that state following the Great War (1918). Incorporated at present in Serbia, with which it is nationally one, it may with reasonable confidence look forward to a commercial revival due to the resumption of its natural rôle as outlet for a rich and productive hinterland.

BIBLIOGRAPHY

Bibliographical Aids. The great bibliographical treasure-house for the whole Byzantine period is *Karl Krumbacher,* Geschichte der Byzantinischen Literatur von Justinian bis zum Ende des Ostroemischen Reiches (527–1453). Published as Vol. IX, 1, in Handbuch der klassischen Altertumswissenschaft. *Byzantinische Zeitschrift.* 1892 + (ed. K. Krumbacher) is an important bibliographical aid since, besides original articles, it lists and discusses current publications. *E. Stein,* Die Byzantinische Geschichtswissenchaft im letzten halben Jahrhundert (In Neue Jahrbuecher fuer das klassische Altertum, Vol. XLIII, 1919). A useful summary of the present state of knowledge in this field.

On the Slavs two excellent bibliographical works owe their origin to R. J. *Kerner*, (1) The Foundations of Slavic Bibliography; (2) Slavic Europe: A Selected Bibliography in the Western European Languages, comprising History, Languages, and Literature. The latter indispensable work lists all publications up to 1914.

Manuals. *C. Diehl*, Histoire de l'Empire Byzantin (an English translation of this excellent sketch is reported to be in preparation). *H. Gelzer*, Abriss der Byzantinischen Kaisergeschichte (published as a section of Krumbacher's Byzantinische Literaturgeschichte). *E. Foord*, The Byzantine Empire: the Rearguard of European Civilization. *C. W. Oman*, The Byzantine Empire. *D. G. Hogarth* (and others), The Balkans. *W. Miller*, The Balkans.

General Works. *E. Gibbon*, The Decline and Fall of the Roman Empire (ed. in 7 volumes by J. B. Bury with Introduction, Notes, and Appendices). *G. Finlay*, A History of Greece from its Conquest by the Romans to the Present Time (ed. by Tozer). *K. Hopf*, Geschichte Griechenlands vom Beginn des Mittelalters bis auf unsere Zeit (395–1821). *G. F. Hertzberg*, Geschichte der Byzantiner und des Osmanischen Reiches bis gegen Ende des 16ten Jahrhunderts. *Lavisse et Rambaud*, Histoire Générale, Vols. I, II, III. *Cambridge Medieval History*, Vols. I, II, *H. F. Helmolt*, History of the World, Vol. V. Southeastern and Eastern Europe.

Special Works (*dealing with periods, individuals, special topics*). *J. B. Bury*, A History of the Later Roman Empire from Arcadius to Irene (395 A.D.–800 A.D.). *J. B. Bury*, A History of the Eastern Empire from the Fall of Irene to the Accession of Basil I (802–867). *C. Diehl*, Byzance, Grandeur et Décadence. *C. Diehl*, Théodora. *G. Schlumberger*, Un empereur byzantin au Xe siècle, Nicéphore Phocas. *G. Schlumberger*, L'epopée Byzantine à la fin du Xe siècle (969–1057). *Vogt*, Basile I et la civilisation byzantine. *K. Dieterich*, Hofleben in Byzanz. Zum ersten Male aus den Quellen uebersetzt, eingeleitet, und erlaeutert. Mit einem Plan des alten Kaiserpalastes von Konstantinopel. *J. Ebersolt*, Le Grand Palais de Constantinople et le Livre des Cérémonies. *G. Schlumberger*, Sigillographie de l'empire Byzantin. *J. B. Bury*, The Constitution of the Later Roman Empire. *E. Pears*, The Fall of Constantinople, being the Story of the Fourth Crusade. *G. de Villehardouin*, The Conquest of Constantinople. *W. Norden*, Der Vierte Kreuzzug. *A. Gardner*, The Lascarids of Nicaea. *J. B. Pappadopoulos*, Theodore II Lascaris, Empereur de Nicée. *J. K. Fotheringham*, Marco Sanudo, Conqueror of the Archipelago. *F. Gregorovius*, Geschichte der Stadt Athen im Mittelalter. *W. Miller*, The Latins in the Levant: a History of Frankish Greece (1204–1566). *A. Harnack*, Monasticism: its ideals and history. *W. F. Adeney*, The Greek and Eastern Churches. *L. Bréhier*, La Querelle des images. *L. Bréhier*, Le schisme oriental du XIe siècle. *W. Norden*, Das Papstthum und Byzanz. *K. Lake*, The Early Days of Monasticism on Mt. Athos. *H. Gelzer*, Vom Heiligen Berg und aus Mazedonien. *P. Meyer*, Die Haupturkunden für die Geschichte der Athosklöster. *H. F. Brown*, Venice. *W. C. Hazlitt*, The Venetian Republic. *A. Rambaud*, History of Russia, Vol. I.

The Bulgars, Serbs, Rumanians. *G. Krek*, Einleitung in die Slavische Literaturgeschichte. *P. J. Safarik*, Geschichte der suedslavischen Literatur. *L. Niederle*, La race slave (trans. by L. Leger). *L. Leger*, Cyrille et Methode. Etudes historiques sur la conversion des Slaves au Christianisme. *J. A. Ginzel,* Zur Geschichte der Slavenapostel Cyrill und Method. *C. Jirecek,* Geschichte der Bulgaren. *W. N. Slatarski,* Geschichte der Bulgaren. *C. Jirecek,* Das Fuerstenthum Bulgarien. Seine Bodengestaltung, Natur, Bevoelkerung, etc. *P. F. Kanitz,* Donau-Bulgarien und der Balkan. Historisch-geog-ethnogr. Reise-studien aus den Jahren 1860–79. *L. Leger,* La Bulgarie. *J. Samuelson,* Bulgaria past and present. *C. Jirecek,* Geschichte der Serben. *C. Jirecek,* Staat und gesellschaft im mittelalterlichen Serbien (Denkschriften d. kais. Akademie d. Wissenschaften. Phil.-Hist. Cl. Band 56, 58). *F. P. Kanitz,* Das Koenigreich Serbien und das Serbenvolk. Von der Roemerzeit bis zur Gegenwart. *B. Kallay,* Geschichte der Serben von den aeltesten Zeiten bis 1815. *H. W. Temperley,* History of Serbia. *L. Ranke,* The History of Servia. *Lazarovic-Hrebelianovic,* The Servian People, their past glory and their destiny. *Wlainatz,* Agrarrechtliche Verhaeltnisse des mittelalterlichen Serbiens. *N. Iorga,* Geschichte des rumaenischen Volkes. *A. D. Xénopol,* Histoire des Roumains.

Ethnology, Travel, Topography, Commerce. *W. Z. Ripley,* The races of Europe. *L. Diefenbach,* Voelkerkunde Osteuropas (insbesondere der Haemushalbinsel und der unteren Donaugebiete). *J. Cvijic,* La Péninsule Balkanique. *J. Jung,* Römer und Romanen in den Donaulaendern. *P. Fallmerayer,* Geschichte der Halbinsel Morea. *Zur Kunde der Balkanhalbinsel* (A score of special studies of geographical, topographical, and historical import published by the Landesmuseum at Sarajevo). *H. G. Dwight,* Constantinople old and new. *A. Van Millingen,* Byzantine Constantinople: the walls of the city and adjoining historical sites. *H. W. Hutton,* Constantinople. *H. Barth,* Konstantinopel (Beruehmte Kunststaetten). *Beazeley,* The Dawn of Modern Geography. *W. Heyd,* Histoire du commerce du Levant au moyen âge (trans. from the German, revised and enlarged by the author).

Civilization, Literature, the Arts. *K. Krumbacher,* Geschichte der Byzantinischen Literatur. *C. Diehl,* Justinien et la civilization byzantine au VIe siècle. *C. Diehl,* L'art byzantin est son influence sur les arts en Occident. *O. M. Dalton,* Byzantine art and archaeology. *A. Van Millingen,* Byzantine Churches in Constantinople: their history and architecture. *G. Schlumberger,* Sigillographie de l'empire byzantin. *A. Rambaud,* Psellos. *N. Turchi,* La civiltà byzantina. *H. Gelzer,* Byzantinische Kulturgeschichte.

THE OTTOMAN EPOCH

CHAPTER XII

THE COMING OF THE OTTOMAN TURKS

In making acquaintance, in a former chapter, with the Seljuk Turks, we noted that, organized as bands of marauding Mongolian horsemen, they began to appear on the borders of Asia Minor toward the middle of the eleventh century; that in 1071, at Manzikert in Armenia, they disastrously defeated the Byzantine emperor; and that in the years following Manzikert, they and the nomad kinsmen who traveled in their wake largely repeopled the interior plateau of Asia Minor. For about two centuries the Seljuks maintained a state, the sultanate of Rum (Rome) with its capital at Konia (Iconium). It was a typically Asiatic state, created by conquest and threatened with disruption whenever a sultan died, because his heirs, abetted by ambitious local chiefs, quarreled over the heritage. In addition to such inner difficulties, the familiar concomitants of military conquest, the Seljuk dominion had to defend itself against assaults from formidable enemies outside its borders. Very early in its history, the reader will recall, it was obliged to face the fearless warriors of the First Crusade, who with Palestine and the Holy Sepulcher as the goal of their desire not only plunged undauntedly through the Seljuk barrier but incidentally opened a path for their Christian ally, the Emperor Alexius, thereby enabling that shrewd diplomat to reincorporate parts of western and southern Asia Minor in the Byzantine state. In the years after Alexius the boundary in Asia Minor between Seljuks and Byzantines shifted frequently according to the fortunes of war, but on the whole the Seljuks may be said to have held their place, due less to their own vigor than to that painful sapping of the Byzantine strength which culminated in 1204 in the capture of Constantinople.

The fateful overthrow of the Greek empire by the adventurers of the Fourth Crusade did not, as might be expected, redound to the advantage of the rival state in Asia Minor. It failed

The Seljuk Turks in Asia Minor

Asia Minor falls into a confusion of petty emirates.

175

to do so because, by the beginning of the thirteenth century, the Seljuk power itself had split into a number of jealous emirates and was in so critical a condition that before the year 1250 it was as good as extinguished by a new wave of Mongolian conquest associated with that name of terror, Jenghis Khan. When the swollen empire of Jenghis Khan, a purely personal creation, in its turn collapsed, the sultanate of Rum revived in name but not in fact, and Asia Minor, more divided than ever, fell into scores of little lordships, presenting a picture of complete political chaos. Under the circumstances any energetic leader commanding a firm nucleus of troops would inevitably rise into a position of prominence. Such a leader was found in Osman, forever memorable as the founder of a power destined not only to dominate Seljuk Asia Minor but to destroy the remnant of the Byzantine state and to create a new Mediterranean empire.

Osman, village chief at Sugut.

The origin of Osman and the beginnings of his power are wrapped in an obscurity which the early Ottoman historians have done their best to render impenetrable by means of a thick though colorful veil of legend. As these inventive writers did not put in an appearance till the descendants of Osman were powerful princes, they were both consciously and unconsciously moved by the desire to curry favor at court and, giving free rein to their oriental fancy, they invented for the remote founder a history in respectful conformity with the grandeur of his offspring. Let us, resolutely setting aside the nursery tales which these polite flatterers concocted, assure ourselves that Osman began his career as a very unimportant person: he was the chieftain of a small tribe of Turks located at Sugut in northwestern Asia Minor. There were several dozens of such chiefs as he, some of them heirs of the rapidly dissolving units of the great Seljuk band, others late comers who with their warriors, their women, and their flocks had but recently sifted into the peninsula from their home in Turkestan. It was not Osman himself but probably his father, Ertogrul, who in characteristic desert fashion had led a small company of a few hundred fighters with their families across the mountains of Armenia and who, around 1240, had settled at Sugut. There is a tale told of Ertogrul in all the history books to the effect that, while roaming over the Anatolian plateau with his small band, he stumbled accidentally upon a battle, won it with an impetuous charge, and was rewarded by the general, whom he had saved from defeat and who turned out to be none other than the Seljuk sultan himself, with a grant of land. It is a picturesque myth incapable of substantiation, but not without interest, since it serves to demonstrate how chaotic and fluid the political and social conditions of Asia Minor were in the thirteenth century and how nomad tribes of Turkish stock were engaged in periodically making their way into the country.

The outstanding feature of Osman's village chieftainship was that it was located on the border of the Byzantine empire, which when Osman succeeded his father Ertogrul in 1289 was in irresistible decay. All about Osman to the west and north were petty Christian lordships in size much like his own and, now that the dissolving Byzantine empire had relaxed its hold on them, obliged to shift more or less for themselves. Sometimes by force, sometimes by persuasion, Osman brought many of these districts under his control. He was a tolerant Mohammedan as the Turkish tribesmen, in distinction from the fanatic Arabs, originally were, and apparently without much difficulty he persuaded many of his Christian dependents to adopt his faith. The Greek church, like the Greek state, had sunk to so despicable a condition that the residents of the old province of Bithynia had lost their Christian enthusiasm and may not unreasonably have persuaded themselves that they were better off under a vigorous and kindly Mohammedan prince than under a feeble Constantinopolitan sovereign, who refused to concern himself about their safety. Before many years Osman's good sense and energy had carried him far toward creating a state and a people. His prosperous followers gathered around him as their leader and sage and gratefully called themselves Osmanli, the sons of Osman, which term, in the course of time, the maladroit English tongue has converted into Ottomans.

In the light of this origin it is somewhat unfortunate to refer, as is our established habit, to the sons of Osman as Turks and to their state as Turkey. Far preferable are the terms Ottomans and Ottoman empire. The Ottomans have indeed a Turkish strain, for not only Osman and his original village nucleus were Turks, but other Turkish tribes of Asia Minor merged gradually with the Ottoman mass. However from the first, natives of Asia Minor

Osman creates a state and a people.

The Ottomans, only partially Turk in blood, preserve a Turkish mentality.

other than Turks, more especially Greeks, were incorporated with the Ottomans, who in consequence, after only a few generations, began to show distinct Caucasian characteristics in such physical matters as color, hair, stature, and facial feature. From the time, let us say, when Osman's grandson wielded the scepter it was probably impossible to detect in the rising nation any very striking ocular evidence of a yellow origin. All recent scholars agree that the people, started on their historic journey by Osman, had become by the time they played a leading rôle in the East, as mixed and cosmopolitan a group as has ever come to the front anywhere in the world. However, these same scholars also insist that, though only slightly Turk in blood, the Osmanli throughout the ages and with an amazing consistency have exhibited a characteristic Turkish mentality. Let the riddle be solved as it will, the Ottomans, who entered history as recognizable Asiatic nomads of a war-like disposition, have, in spite of many transfusions of blood and a physical approximation to the European or Caucasian type, clung to a characteristically nomad and Asiatic outlook through all the centuries of their historical importance down to our own day. Can it be that it is, after all, not so much blood and race that count in determining a people's character as habits and ideas? If this is so the Ottomans, whom we have just taken such pedantic satisfaction in proving to be hardly Turks at all, are as completely Turks as it is possible to be, since they are Turks in the only respect that really matters, in their minds!

The Ottoman mentality shows a Caucasian tinge gained by contact with the Byzantines.

And yet, however Asiatic in heart and soul the Ottomans strike us, who have the occidental, the European outlook, the fact is that, when we compare them with other Tartar peoples, a certain Caucasian quality in them and in their political handiwork immediately stands out to view. Consider for a moment the vast empires brought together by such Tartar and Mongolian conquerors as Attila, Jenghis Khan, and Timur. All lasted but a day, while the state founded by the Ottomans triumphantly weathered all storms from the fourteenth to the twentieth century. Only the Caucasian blood and the politico-social experience which that blood implies will serve to explain the difference. For, fundamental to every consideration to Osman's success is the fact that, founding his state on the border of a decrepit but civilized

European empire, he not only absorbed the racial groups planted on the conquered soil but modeled his creation to a considerable extent on the legal, administrative, and military institutions before his eyes. Whether conscious or unconscious imitators, the Ottomans built up their polity largely with the aid of Byzantine borrowings. True, the governmental machinery of East Rome had long before Osman's time lost its effectiveness, but, taken over and operated with the fresh vigor of a people fiercely martial and admirably disciplined, its excellencies proved sufficient not only to consolidate the first Ottoman conquests around Sugut but in the long run to bring about the union of all the lands around the eastern Mediterranean. Deeply and historically considered, the Ottoman empire represents a renewal of the age-old effort to gather the Mediterranean territories into a single political unit, and in this sense it may fairly be defined as the taking over by a vigorous new folk from Asia of the burden laid down by the exhausted Byzantine state.

To return to Osman — his political program, directed to the absorption of the petty Christian lordships around Sugut, received a serious check when he found himself confronted with the nearest Greek city of the neighborhood, with Brusa. His mobile, light-armed troops, chiefly cavalry, were incapable of conducting siege operations and Brusa proved impregnable for years. In 1326, however, it was taken. Although the circumstances of its fall are unknown, we are fairly safe in assuming that it was not taken by storm but that its inhabitants, basely abandoned by their Byzantine overlord and deprived of the use of their trade routes by Osman's swift-moving cavalry, at last made up their minds to come to terms with their tormentors. When the news of Brusa's surrender reached Osman he was lying on his death-bed. During his last hour on earth he had the satisfaction of knowing that the consistent effort of a lifetime had been crowned with success.

Orkhan, Osman's son and successor (1326–59), set up his seat at Brusa and continued his father's policy of eating leaf by leaf, as if it were an artichoke, the Christian province of Bithynia. Two other towns of great importance as commercial and industrial centers, Nicaea and Nicomedia, remained between him and the sea. Nicaea, the second city of the Greek empire and famous

Osman
crowns his
life by taking
Brusa, 1326.

Orkhan,
1326–59.

throughout Christendom because of that ancient council of the Fathers which formulated the Nicaean creed, yielded (1329) to Orkhan, but only after every hope of succor from the Byzantine emperor had vanished.   A decade later (1338) Nicomedia submitted to the same hard fate.   Thereupon Orkhan, clearing from his path the few remaining castles of the Greeks, penetrated to the coast, opposite which rose Constantinople, a purple sea of houses wearing like a crown the far-seen dome of noble St. Sophia.   For the remainder of his life his leading purpose was to span the narrow chasm of the straits and carry his banner into Europe.

Orkhan couples toleration of the Christians with special military favors to the Moslems.

For a policy of conquest ranging so far afield Orkhan needed the firm support which only a substantial state can give.   If our information did not flow so meagerly, nothing would be more profitable than to examine the elements of his statecraft and the political means at his disposal.   In lieu of indisputable facts we must rest content with indices.   And, first of all, let it be said again that the Ottoman people in process of formation was already in Orkhan's time to no small extent, perhaps even preponderantly, Greek.   How could it have been otherwise in view of the circumstance that the Ottoman territory was coextensive with Bithynia, one of the oldest Hellenic regions of the peninsula?   In the new state Moslem and ·Christian lived side by side on the basis of an unusual toleration.   But Orkhan, much like Osman before him, was, if a generous, by no means a lax Mohammedan.   Assuming that he perceived that without toleration he could hardly hope to build up a state among a Christian population, we may still be sure that his innate prejudice would prompt him to make adherence to Islam more advantageous than a stubborn persistence in Christian error.   He therefore reserved the use of arms and a share in the spoils after a successful campaign to the followers of Mohammed, and at the same time he ordered that the Christians, exempted from military service, should pay increased taxes to the government, commonly in the form of a special head-tax.   In theory this impost affirmed no more than that, if the Moslems served their ruler with their swords, it behooved the Christians to do so with their money. Under these circumstances the adventurous, as well as the propertied, Christian elements gradually experienced a change of heart

and, by avowing themselves Mohammedan, sought escape from
an inferior position. To such conversion they would be further
prompted by the desiccated and priest-ridden Orthodox church,
which had lost the power to enlist the deep devotion that makes
men suffer martyrdom rather than betray a cause. Without
fanatic violence on the part of the Mohammedans, without wholesale spectacular desertions on the part of the Christians, but
rather, to all appearances, by easy, imperceptible stages the native
Bithynian population turned its back upon the Cross to bow down
before the Crescent.

However wisely tolerant, Orkhan was then a faithful Moslem;
far more to the point, he was a Moslem conqueror. Obviously
his chief business in life was to push out his boundaries, to win
new lands and subjects; and to this end his need would be,
above all, an army. We may even go farther. Since the army
was so preponderant a factor in his plans, the army would also
be his means of government, and army and government be
practically indistinguishable. Although the historians of the
Ottoman empire have probably been guided by a true instinct
in referring back to Orkhan the formation of the characteristic
Ottoman system, which identifies the military and civil agencies
of the state, they have doubtless gone too far when they have
ascribed to him not only the inception but also the completion of
the work. Like everything else in the world the Ottoman institutions represented a gradual growth, and Orkhan's genius, in
all likelihood, did no more than make a beginning. However,
since it was an important beginning, having the army as its
kernel, we should become acquainted with the army in his day.
The later phases of a significant institutional development will
then be easier to follow.

Orkhan develops as his chief tool the army.

Orkhan's army, though composed of many racial elements, was
held together by the common bond of Moslem sentiment. It fell
into two main sections. First, there was the cavalry made up of
Moslem landholders who, possessing their land somewhat in the
western feudal fashion, owed Orkhan military service. When the
order came they gathered at the appointed place and formed a
mobile force of horsemen, which grew with every victory since
each new victory was attended by a fresh distribution of land
among the conquerors. Not satisfied with this force, which was

Orkhan's army falls into two sections, a feudal and a standing army.

not instantly ready and which, composed of men of means, might develop a show of independence, Orkhan formed also a permanent, a standing army. This was the innovation destined to become famous. He recruited his permanent force from captives in war and purchased slaves, mostly Christians, and supported it from his private means. Since his landholders supplied him with a cavalry, he very wisely developed his hired troops as a body of infantry. Very likely even in Orkhan's day they were called New Troops, that is, *Yeni Cheri*, transformed by English usage into Janissaries. That, as is sometimes said, they were the first professional troops developed in the medieval period is of course absurd, although we may admit they soon rose above all others in fame. Professional beginnings may be noted all over Europe at this time and, without roaming far and wide for analogies suggestive of the Janissaries, we may point to the Byzantine empire, which throughout the Middle Age continuously maintained permanent, paid, and highly skilled troops. In all likelihood Orkhan first got the idea of a standing army from his decadent but more civilized neighbor to the west of him. In any event the equipment of his new infantry as well as many features of their tactics represented borrowings from the Christian state which still preserved, however imperfectly, the military tradition of imperial Rome.

Orkhan directs his thought to Europe.
Toward the middle of his long reign Orkhan felt strong enough to let his thoughts soar across the straits to Europe. It illustrates the single-minded and compact energy of the man that he made no effort to expand eastward into Asia Minor, over which a score and more of Moslem emirs, some far more powerful than himself, held rule. He had fastened himself on the flanks of the Byzantine emperor: this was his quarry while life lasted. As for the situation within the feeble state, which Orkhan had deprived of its last possessions in Asia Minor, it must be admitted that everything augured its approaching end. Agriculture and commerce were dying, the revenues had contracted to the vanishing point, the sturdy Roman inheritance in army and administration had been squandered. In the capital a senility tantamount to political dementia held carnival. The great nobles quarreled with one another for the offices of state while the emperors, almost without exception, proved themselves sorry manikins, whom the

clown's motley would have suited better than the royal purple. Orkhan was not alone in remarking the opportunity offered by the dissolution on the Bosporus. From the Macedonian uplands the Serb king, Stephen Dushan, closely scanned the Byzantine chaos, firmly resolved to make the most of it for his own state and people. Even before Orkhan had cleared the decks in Asia Minor, preparatory to crossing the Dardanelles and driving upon Europe, Dushan had seized lower Macedonia and penetrated far into Thessaly and Epirus. Thus, toward the middle of the fourteenth century, at precisely the same time, two young and vigorous powers pressed, from the east and west respectively, on the aging Greek state, which with insane frivolity chose this very moment to fall apart in civil war. An ambitious nobleman, John Cantacuzenus by name, undertook to crowd from the throne his imperial ward, the youthful John Paleologus. The struggle which followed is a wholly unprofitable tale, of which we have already heard enough in connection with the southward push of Stephen Dushan and to which we refer here solely in order to recount the circumstances surrounding the advent of the Ottomans in Europe.

It was John Cantacuzenus who in his ferocious struggle with the Paleologus faction for the possession of the power at Constantinople issued the first appeal for help (1345) to the Ottoman emir; and it was as allies of a Christian sovereign, not as conquerors, that the first Moslem troops trod European soil. After conducting several campaigns in the service of John Cantacuzenus, Orkhan politely presented a bill of expenses. It called, among other items, for the surrender to him of a Greek stronghold on the European side of the Dardanelles. Like many another foolish and ambitious schemer, the Greek nobleman discovered too late that it was easier to summon the devil than to get rid of him. After vain expostulations he was obliged to make over the small castle of Tzympe to his Ottoman ally. In this manner, by unholy but peaceful barter, the Osmanli acquired their first possession in Europe. The event occurred, probably, in 1354 — a memorable date in world annals. Immediately after, the Turks spread over the whole peninsula of Gallipoli, converting it into a military base against the Byzantine empire. The people of Constantinople, shocked suddenly into a sense of danger, rose indignantly against the traitor sovereign, John Cantacuzenus, and

Orkhan acquires a foothold on the Dardanelles, 1354.

deposed him; but as they raised in his place John V. Paleologus
to the throne, who was no whit better than his feeble predecessor,
they gained nothing but a scant measure of moral satisfaction
from the change. Instead of trying by a courageous rush to
tumble the Ottomans out of Europe, the new weakling docilely
accepted the accomplished fact. To keep what was left of Thrace,
he even signed an agreement by which he became, in effect,
Orkhan's vassal. Therewith the great emir had accomplished
his life's aim. Before death overtook him (1359), he could see
in his mind's eye an endless procession of Moslem warriors pass
into the lands of the Cross over the bridge which he had built.

Murad I
(1359–89)
conquers
Thrace and
turns to the
interior of
Balkania.

His son, Murad I (1359–89), was a chip of the old block.
Energetic and resourceful, he clung to the simple shepherd ways
of his fathers and was honest and straight-dealing far beyond
his various Christian adversaries, who in their weakness clutched,
like drowning men, at every straw. He began his reign by invading Thrace, which he conquered in short order. By 1361,
Adrianople, the great emporium and fortress which commanded
the road up the Maritsa valley into the Balkan interior, had
fallen into his hands. Henceforth the Byzantine empire, shut
off from its hinterland, was reduced to the compass of a single
city, whose inhabitants, as a contemporary movingly complained,
lived like wild beasts in a cage. If Murad did not at once lay
siege to Constantinople, it was solely because of his lack of
sea-power, without which he knew full well the great stronghold
could not be taken. Contenting himself with forcing the Emperor
John V. to acknowledge his possession of Thrace, he turned his
back on Constantinople and set his face to the interior. Here,
he was aware, was the only organized power which he need
fear, the state of Serbia. True, Serbia was rapidly falling apart,
owing to the selfish policy of its feudal magnates, whom the great
Dushan's irresolute successor did not know how to curb, but
Murad needed evidence of Serb dissolution which nothing save
a test of strength could give. In 1363 Ottomans and Serbs had
their first serious clash on the Maritsa river and Murad learned

from his victory that Serb vigor, though still a fact, was patently
ebbing. Encouraged to stake everything on his European venture,
he presently (1366) transferred his capital from Brusa in Asia
Minor, where his father had planted it, to Adrianople in European
Thrace.

With Murad once settled in Europe, the gravest problem before him was how, with a mere handful of Mohammedans, he could exercise rule over a vast Christian population. It was useless to hope that the Christians of Thrace and Macedonia could be forced or bribed to renounce their religion except in scattered instances. The policy which he finally adopted and which was natural enough in view of the success already achieved with it in Asia Minor was to incorporate the conquered Christians in the Ottoman state on terms, by virtue of which they were granted the free exercise of their religion in return for the surrender of their weapons and the payment of a head-tax. These terms, be it observed, were extended only to those Christians who freely submitted to the conqueror. Such others as resisted and were taken with arms in hand became by Mohammedan practice chattels of the victors and might be sold as slaves. While the sale of captives was remunerative and, from the contemporary viewpoint, morally unobjectionable, it by no means solved Murad's problem, for the emir needed, in order to conduct his government, the active coöperation of the Christians, intellectually far superior to his Asiatic Moslems. By slow degrees he worked out a plan by which the Balkan Christians would prove a main pillar of the state, and as a first step toward its execution he provided for a regular supply of youths by means of an ordinance (the famous *devchurne*), requiring the subject population to deliver to him at stated periods a certain number of boys, sound in mind and body. Separated from their homes at an early age, they were to be gradually converted to Mohammedanism, given careful training in special schools conducted at the ruler's expense, and, on reaching maturity, to be drafted into the civil or military service according to their talents. We shall hear more of this favored slave-mass, which with the Ottoman victories grew steadily in numbers and became, as a specialized governing class, the outstanding feature of the Ottoman political structure; for the present we shall content ourselves with noting that it was from these Christian youths, regularly recruited by legal process, that Murad chiefly filled the ranks of his standing infantry, the famous Janissaries.

The Janissaries, dating back to Orkhan's reign, but first put on a solid basis by Murad's legislation, for a long time numbered

Policy of
Murad to-
ward the
Christians
of Balkania.

The Jan-
issaries.

only a few thousand men. They were attached to the sovereign as his special guard and proved themselves strong and terrible in battle. But, being only a handful, they cannot be credited, or at least solely credited, with the imposing victories won in ¯Murad's day. In the fifteenth and sixteenth centuries, that is, in the triumphant period following Murad, they experienced a remarkable development and grew in numbers as well as in importance. When that day came, like the Praetorian guard of Rome, they overshadowed the state and held the destiny of the empire in their hands. However, in the period we are treating, they were still in process of formation and interest us chiefly as throwing light on the cunning Ottoman plan of building up a Moslem state with Christian brain and muscle.

Murad conquers parts of Bulgaria and Macedonia and reaches out toward the heart of Serbia.

Having drawn the teeth of the Byzantine empire, Murad could afford to treat it as a negligible quantity. His immediate goal was the Maritsa valley, a possession of Bulgaria. This ailing state put up no better fight against him than Constantinople had done, with the result that before long the fertile territory between the Rhodope and Balkan ranges was in Murad's hands. Like his Byzantine contemporary the Bulgar ruler was glad to purchase a precarious peace by becoming Murad's vassal. Next, the Ottoman emir turned to Macedonia, a Serb province since Stephen Dushan's day. That tsar's great empire was by now a hopeless wreck. The southern sections had definitely detached themselves from obedience to his son, Stephen Urosh, and everywhere feudal lords, aspiring to independence, raised a disloyal head. Pressing boldly forward, Murad seized area after area until by a second victory won on the Maritsa, some twenty miles west of Adrianople, he completely broke the resistance of the southern Serb lords (1371). A few months after this disaster the wretched Serb tsar died and with him the house of Nemania came to an inglorious end. Following up their Maritsa victory, the Moslems swept westward over the Macedonian plateau, occupied its cities, and did not pause till they had watered their horses in the Vardar. Shortly after, elements of their raiding cavalry penetrated into Albania and threatened the very heart of Serbia. At the same time the conquerors followed another route by pushing up the Maritsa valley into the highlands of the northwest. Certainly by 1386, perhaps before, they were firmly planted at Nish and thus held Serbia from two sides as in a vise. In the light of all that had happened since Murad's arrival in Europe, it looked as if Serbia would go down before Ottoman prowess as weakly and disgracefully as the Byzantine empire and Bulgaria.

It is medieval Serbia's title to distinction that she refused to perish without a blow struck in her own defense. Murad, master by this time of perhaps two-thirds of the peninsula, had been immensely helped in his victorious advance by the irreconcilable divisions among the Christian princes. Each stood aloof from the other or even looked on with malicious glee as his neighbor drained the cup of defeat. But now the alarm, spread by the startling Ottoman successes, was such that for the first time something akin to Balkan unity was brought about. It was Serbia, after all the soundest of the decaying Balkan states, that found a heart and sent its word of cheer and friendship to the other peoples. The most powerful and martial of the great Serb lords, Lazar by name, made himself the spokesman of his nation. With something of the crusader's uplifted spirit he rallied his people about him, while the princes of Bosnia and Wallachia and some of the tribal chiefs of Albania sent contingents to swell the numbers of his army. It was indeed a general host of Balkan Christians, but not even now, in the hour of the supreme struggle, a united Balkania which confronted the invader. Murad, making ready to meet the storm gathering in the west, found helpers among the lesser Serb and Bulgar lords, mostly, it is true, constrained to this service by a cruel master who held them at his mercy. In the great interior plain of Kossovo, set like an amphitheater among the Macedonian mountains, on June 28, 1389, the hosts of Cross and Crescent met to decide the fate of the peninsula.

Lazar of Serbia rallies the Balkan Christians around his banner.

The facts in regard to the battle of Kossovo have been so obscured by the legend-loving spirit of the South Slavs that the actual course of the struggle will probably never be made clear. A hundred songs sprang up in later years, each new singer taking pride in contributing a fresh detail to the already rich embellishments of his predecessors. We hear of heroisms, treasons, murders, making a national epic of magnificent proportions on which, as on spiritual manna, Serb patriotism has for centuries kept itself alive, but which, to say the least, is historically

The tragic day of Kossovo, June 28, 1389.

dubious. And yet, whatever happened on that memorable field, the final upshot is like an open book: Lazar, the Serb champion,[1] perished, the rout of the Christians was complete, and Serbia was stretched prostrate at the feet of the conqueror. That Murad, too, died on that fateful day was hailed with satisfaction by the Serbs but proved no mitigation of their lot. True, Bayezid, Murad's son and successor, did not at once destroy the Serb state, root and branch. He was content with the formal submission of the country under a native ruler whom he put in office, but the Serbs themselves, undeceived by this act of grace, mournfully hailed Kossovo as the grave of their liberty.

The Ottoman succession. Bayezid I, who ruled from 1389 to 1402, is he whom men called Ilderim or the Thunderbolt. He inaugurated his rule, which began on the battlefield, with an ominous act. He had his brother Yakub murdered. Appearances notwithstanding, the succession in the reigning house was far from being regulated by the western rule of primogeniture. That was not a process familiar to the Turkish tribes. Among them the succession regularly went to the strongest male relative of the deceased ruler, the one who understood how most effectively to assert himself. On this account the death of an Ottoman sovereign was always, potentially at least, the occasion of a struggle among the next of kin. Bayezid's fierce preventive measure showed his keen sense of the necessity of keeping a military power like that of his father in a single hand, and of not subjecting it to division, amicable or otherwise, among numerous heirs. That his view was shared by his successors is proved by the fact that in the following century it was formulated as a law of the state by Mohammed II. By virtue of this enactment the murder of his brothers was declared to be the solemn obligation of the new ruler who succeeded in seizing the throne.

Bayezid defeats the king of Hungary at Nicopolis, 1396. There was much work for Bayezid to do both in consolidating the Balkan conquest and in meeting threats from a new quarter. For now Hungary, the nearest Catholic neighbor of Balkania, became alarmed by the Ottoman successes, while a

---

[1] The legend, aiming at grandeur, concedes to Lazar the title tsar. In fact he was only knez (lord), the modest possessor of the northern rim of Stephen Dushan's tsarate. This rim constituted, however, the ancient heart of Serbia.

faint sense that even the more distant West was threatened began to spread through Europe. The pope, traditional head of Latin Christendom, raised a warning voice and did his best to blow into a flame the dying embers of the old crusading spirit. Nor, in spite of the changed age, was he wholly without success. In 1396 King Sigismund of Hungary led a Hungarian host, sped by the blessings of the church and strengthened by compact contingents of western knights, chiefly French and German, against the feared and hated infidel. At Nicopolis on the Danube Moslem and Christian clashed in fierce combat only to prove once more the superiority of the Ottoman troops in discipline and tactics. Though the hapless Hungarian king escaped with his life, hundreds of western knights were killed, while other hundreds, captured, languished for years in eastern prisons before their ransom was effected. Following this heavy disaster, Hungary and the West were obliged for a while to keep their hands off Balkan affairs.

Bayezid, relieved of all danger on the side of Europe, was now free to turn his attention in a direction which seems to have exercised a peculiar fascination over him from the first. His ancestors, as we have seen, had pressed with a consistency enforcing our respect, first into Caucasian Bithynia and then onward into Caucasian Europe. By cautious, cumulative labors they had built up a solid state, a trick no mere Turk or Tartar had ever turned before or could turn. An integral part of this program was to avoid entanglements in Asia Minor, with the affairs of which they accordingly meddled but little. Perhaps they felt dimly that, once successful in their European plans, the relatively disorganized Turk emirates of Asia Minor would fall like ripe fruit into their lap. Not that Orkhan and Murad had not had occasional brushes with their nearest Moslem neighbors. Generally successful too, they had not inconsiderably extended the area of Ottoman control around Sugat and Brusa. But a lively sense of the gravity of their position on the straits kept them from becoming too heavily involved with the emirs of the East. Bayezid, a less politic and far more passionate man, now broke impulsively with the inherited tradition. Immediately on assuming rule he divided his attention between Europe and Asia and before long was inspired to make the conquest of Asia Minor

Bayezid conquers Asia Minor.

the leading object of his policy. His success was startling. Blow on blow fell on the chiefs to the south and east of him, with the result that in the course of a few campaigns the whole of the peninsula to the mountains of Armenia was added to his empire.

The
catastrophe
of Bayezid
at Angora,
1402.

His dramatic conquest of oriental states gave Bayezid something of the aspect of a typical oriental conqueror, an aspect which his more prudent forbears had carefully avoided. Inevitably his headlong plunge eastward projected him into Asiatic politics and presently involved him in one of those amazing catastrophes sufficiently common to Mongolian soil to be termed normal. Moralizing historians have been inclined to charge his disaster to his defects of character. Doubtless his overbearing, heedless temper was a considerable factor in his overthrow; but it was certainly not so much his fault as it was his fate, his kismet, that in his time the fertile loins of Asia should have given birth to another of its many irresistible conquerors, to Timur the Tartar. From a physical defect called also Timur the Lame, he is famous in English annals as Tamurlane, under which designation he was immortalized by Marlowe in a magnificent drama. Having overrun Persia and Syria even to the gates of Egypt, Timur next turned to Asia Minor, thereby precipitating a struggle with its Osmanli rulers. Bayezid, blinded by pride, made the mistake of underrating his opponent, who to him, heir of European traditions, was a mere Mongolian raider. When, in 1402, at Angora in central Asia Minor, the two conquerors clashed, the Ottoman army was crushed and Bayezid himself, by being captured, met with the most cruel fate conceivable for such a man. In a litter set round with bars like a menagerie cage he was carried along by the victorious Tartar chief, as though he were a jungle beast, until, his haughty spirit broken, death effected his release. Timur, making the most of his victory at Angora, poured over Asia Minor like a spring-time flood. Whether through the folly of Bayezid or by a decree of the gods, the state built by Osman, Orkhan, and Murad seemed to have reached its earthly term and all its enemies rejoiced.

CHAPTER XIII

THE SECOND CENTURY OF THE OTTOMANS: THE CONQUEST OF CONSTANTINOPLE AND THE CONSOLIDATION OF THE OTTOMAN EMPIRE IN EUROPE

IF the Ottoman empire had been a casual creation of Mongolian raiders, it is certain that it would never have been heard of again after Angora. But, in spite of that huge disaster, it not only refused to disappear but on the morrow of Bayezid's overthrow spontaneously developed a number of compact centers of resistance. Without doubt it owed this resilience primarily to the solid statesmanship of the early emirs, who had been at pains to give their state an at least partially European character by rearing it with Caucasian help among Caucasian lands. Across the straits in Europe, to which Timur's long arm did not reach, the government rocked ominously but did not crumble. Never since the first appearance of the Ottomans did the Christian states — the Greek empire, Bulgaria, and Serbia — have a better opportunity to shake off the foreign yoke. That they remained quiescent, permitting the great occasion afforded by Angora to pass unused, is the best proof that they were exhausted organisms and that the scepter of Balkania had slipped definitely and irretrievably from their hands. *The Ottoman state survives the battle of Angora.*

As if the overthrow at Angora were not calamity enough for the hard-hit Ottoman state, at the disappearance of Bayezid from the scene his four sons simultaneously stepped forth to seize what was left of the inheritance. Since by Ottoman custom each had as good a claim to power as any other, there was nothing to do but to bring the issue to the decision of the sword. For about a decade civil war raged among the Moslems, while the dispirited and inactive Christians hovered round like frightened birds. A first improvement of the situation from the Ottoman standpoint occurred not many months after Angora, when Timur, in the manner typical of the restless Mongolian conqueror, permitted his atten- *Civil war among the sons of Bayezid.*

tion to be drawn elsewhither and wandered off to Asia. There, in 1405, he died and the crude rule set up by him in Asia Minor promptly collapsed. Without delay the Anatolian home-lands of the Ottomans hurried to reaffirm their allegiance to the house of Osman. In the years following Timur's death, the war of the four brothers brought to light that the youngest, Mohammed by name, possessed by far the best gifts among them both as man and ruler. Eliminating from the contest one fraternal rival after another, he entered at last into sole and undisputed command of the Ottoman lands. By 1413 Balkania, and Europe generally, knew that their rejoicing over Angora had been premature.

Mohammed I (1413-21).   Mohammed I (1413-21), worthy to be ranked with the leading members of his house, pursued a moderate and cautious program. Content to rebuild slowly, he sought to avoid war and granted his neighbors and dependents peace on relatively easy terms. More original even than his moderate policy was his character. Resembling the shepherd-kings, his forbears, in his prudence and understanding of men, he marked a departure from their rude and primitive type by his devotion to poetry and learning. His contemporaries gave him a title which may be rendered as " the gentleman," and if we complete his portrait by remarking his high standard of personal honor as well as his kindliness and benevolence, we may agree that in his time he had few rivals among rulers either East or West.

Murad II (1421-51) resumes the subjection of the Balkan states and principalities.   Murad II (1421-51) was not unlike his father, since he combined love of justice and an active patronage of the arts with pronounced fondness for a life of contemplative retirement. However, the die once cast for war, he exhibited the same indomitable energy in the field as his most virile ancestors. And, first and last, there was a good deal of war in Murad's day. At the uncertain, fluctuating boundaries an inevitable friction made itself felt, while within the loosely jointed state there were numerous hearths of dissatisfaction and unrest. Though uncursed by the proud and choleric temper characteristic of sovereigns overfond of war, Murad was distinguished by an impressive firmness of purpose. In consequence he became engaged in a long succession of wars with the Greek empire, Serbia, Albania, Wallachia, and Hungary, not to mention the Moslem emirs of Asia Minor. We need note but a few of these clashes. In 1430 he took the city of Thessalonica (Saloniki) which, near the mouth of the Vardar, commands the sea-approach to Macedonia. A Byzantine city, second in importance only to Constantinople, Thessalonica had lately been surrendered by the feeble Greeks to the Venetians, who, fearing its capture by the Ottomans, hoped to circumvent the Moslem purpose by planting themselves within the walls. The defeat in this matter of the " queen of the Adriatic " was a plain indication that her star was not likely to ride the sky much longer than that of the unhappy empire on the ruins of which she had built her throne. With Thessalonica in his hands, Murad felt that he could venture to penetrate southward into Hellas, and, entering the Morea, he reduced to subjection the Greek princes, members of the reigning house of Paleologus, who had been governing this outlying province of the Greek empire in practical independence. In Albania alone he encountered spirited resistance in the form of guerrilla warfare, so ably organized by a native chief, the famous Scanderbeg, that he was unable to master it. Of this we shall hear more later on.

However, far and away the most critical struggle of Murad's time was with the Hungarians. Their kingdom on the middle Danube had long given evidence of being peculiarly sensitive to Balkan weather conditions. Immediately after Kossovo, for instance, King Sigismund of Hungary, taking alarm at the Ottoman advance, had led a force, in fact, a crusading army, against Bayezid, only to have it go down in utter defeat at Nicopolis (1396). From that encounter the issue rested until the Ottoman recovery renewed the anxieties of the Hungarians. Even had they been willing not to take a hand in Balkan affairs, they would have been obliged to reckon with their Ottoman neighbor because his light cavalry, maintained for outpost service, lived by more or less systematic raiding and in many a plundering expedition carried the terror of the Turk name far beyond the Danube barrier. Against these Ottoman incursions there arose in Murad's day a native champion in the person of John Hunyadi, a magnate of Transylvania. Though partly Rumanian by race, he has become so identified with Hungarian history that, in the light of his warrior activity

The struggle with Hungary. Rise of John Hunyadi.

he can hardly be conceived of other than as the embodiment of the Magyar nation. Hunyadi was a valiant and magnetic soldier, of headlong courage indeed, but of small prudence and still smaller statesmanship. He proved himself a splendid partizan, who by lightning-like descents repeatedly delivered the Hungarian marches from their plundering tormentors. His border victories inspired the pope to renew the plan of driving the Moslems out of Europe by a general attack endowed with the solemn character of a Christian crusade. The Hungarian king Ladislaus, hardly more than a boy, was named captain of the movement, and once again, as in the days of King Sigismund, enough of the old religious fervor was stirred up to lure a large body of German and French knights to the Hungarian camp. Though nominally led by the king, the Christian host was actually under the command of the renowned Hunyadi. In 1443 he took the offensive, repeatedly defeated Murad's generals, and penetrated far into Balkania, returning thence with an immense booty. Murad, deeply impressed with the strength of the enemy, resolved to forestall a second invasion by offering peace on the basis of a renunciation of his claims to Serbia and Wallachia and of a truce which was to last ten years. On the advice of Hunyadi the offer, extremely favorable to Hungary, was accepted, and Murad and Ladislaus sealed the arrangement by solemnly exchanging oaths on Bible and Koran.

Perjury of
the
Hungarians
followed by
their defeat
at Varna,
1444.

This, the first notable success of Europe against the Ottomans, must, like strong wine, have gone to the head of the crusaders, producing nothing short of a moral vertigo. As soon as the pope's personal representative, a cardinal of the church, heard of the peace, he adjured the Hungarians to resume the offensive; and when they declared their inability to do so, owing to their oath, he asserted his readiness and power to free them from its consequences. Christians, he pretended, need not keep vows made to infidels. His specious arguments carried the day and the ink of the treaty was hardly dry before Ladislaus and Hunyadi again invaded Murad's territory. They advanced unopposed as far as Varna on the Black sea. There Murad, who, placing an undeserved faith in the sworn word of Christians, had stripped the Balkan boundary of troops and had himself crossed over to Asia Minor, came up with the Hungarians and beat them as Bayezid had beat their fathers, a half a century before, at Nicopolis. King Ladislaus himself, less fortunate than Sigismund, perished in the fierce mêlée, while Hunyadi was only saved by precipitate and ignominious flight. As long as this redoubtable champion of Hungary and Christendom lived, the Magyars, far from despairing, repeatedly renewed the attack, but though they succeeded in checking the Ottoman advance, they always failed to deliver their adversary a really crushing blow.

Among the reigning houses which have taken a leading part in the history of Europe the house of Osman is probably unique in its long succession of capable representatives. Men like Osman, Orkhan, the first and second Murad, stand high above the average ruler in the particular qualities making for political success. Moreover, to an unusual extent they remained true to a high ideal of personal integrity and public service, and although they offered evidence at times of falling victim to that self-indulgence and lordly insolence which are the besetting sins of monarchs, they managed to keep themselves relatively free from vice and to retain much of the character of frugal, active, and straight dealing tribal chiefs, at home in the open air and satisfied with the simple comfort of a blanket and a tent. But with their improved fortunes a change gradually announced itself. Bayezid I, coupling with vast ambition a passionate attachment to the pleasures of the table and the harem, flashed a first warning touching the dangers of his station. Contemporary accounts picture him as a typical oriental despot. Great was the likelihood that his successors, commanding the resources of a vast empire, would follow his example and develop the evil qualities inseparable from the exercise of irresponsible power.

Mohammed II, who succeeded his father Murad in 1451, is a striking illustration of an apparently inevitable dynastic decadence. He was secretive, cruel, and passionately ambitious. He broke with the custom of his predecessors, who had lived with their viziers and generals in the close intimacy born of military life, and kept himself sedulously apart as if to emphasize the divinity that hedges in a king. Terror preceded him when he appeared, due to his fits of anger, which, likely enough, were as often simulated as real, since his policy in its main features

High standing of the house of Osman.

Character of Mohammed II (1451-81).

was directed by the cold calculation suggestive of a typical
tyrant of the Renaissance. In fact, the Renaissance movement,
sweeping over the whole Mediterranean area in his day, exercised a decided fascination over him, prompting him to surround
himself with oriental poets and philosophers as well as with
the craftsmen and artists of the occident, chiefly, of course, of
Italy. Yet, with these moral and mental traits, ominous of
change, were joined the political energy and military talent of
his ancestors. If he rises before our eyes, a suspicious despot
surrounded with luxury and responsive to the appeal of art
and literature, he was yet an active and able ruler, perhaps the
ablest of his time and place. To such a figure the insignificant
title emir, with which his predecessors, as late as Murad I, the
victor of Kossovo, had been well pleased, was no longer suited.
Mohammed II proudly called himself sultan, a designation
roughly equivalent to king, with which the victorious Arabs had
long ago familiarized the orient.[1]

Mohammed
resolves to
capture
Constanti-
nople.

When Mohammed II (1451–81) mounted the throne, he was
a youth of twenty-one but already so mature that he had a
program of his own which he at once set out to carry through
with iron resolution. To his mind it was no longer possible to
conduct the affars of his great empire without the possession of
its logical capital, Constantinople. That single city had long
been about all that was left of the Greek state, which, slowly
stripped of its outlying territories, had been reduced, as early
as the days of Murad I, to Mohammedan dependence. Only
the stragetic position of the old imperial stronghold, coupled
with the naval weakness of the Ottomans, explains why it had
been spared so long. Ever since the Asiatics had got a footing
on the Dardanelles, its capture was an inevitable aim of Ottoman
policy and on more than one occasion an attack upon the city had
actually been made. The siege, to give an instance, which Bayezid
undertook would almost certainly have doomed the Greek cap-

---

[1] Bayezid I (1389–1402) seems to have been the first member of the
house of Osman to employ, though only intermittently, the title sultan.
On this subject of titles it may be noted here that in the period
after Mohammed II sultan was replaced by a still more magniloquent title
of Persian origin, padishah (king of kings). It is under the latter designation rather than as sultan that the Ottoman sovereign has been known to
his own people down to our day.

ital, had not Timur the Lame diverted the sultan's attention
to Asia Minor and himself. When Mohammed II resolved on
the Constantinopolitan campaign, he was at pains to assemble
and employ every means of pressure at his disposal. His first
step was to build (1452) a fortress on the European side of the
Bosporus just above the city. With the aid of another fortress
already in existence on the opposite Asiatic shore and with
the Dardanelles, the bottle-neck below the city, in his control,
Mohammed now held his prey in tight embrace. Then, having
gathered a fleet of four hundred sail and an army of one hundred
and fifty thousand men, among them twelve thousand Janissaries,
than whom there were no better storming troops in all the world,
in April, 1453, he began what men have always regarded as one
of the memorable sieges of history.

The man called upon to defend Constantinople was Constan- Constantine
tine XI, Paleologus. He had mounted the throne in succession XI, the last
to his brother in 1449, and proved himself quite the most notable Roman
and stalwart member of an otherwise feeble and disgraceful line. emperor.
He renewed the old appeal to the Christian West and again, as
some of his predecessors had already done under stress of similar circumstances, proclaimed the union of the eastern and
western churches under the headship of the pope. The concession, too plainly a move prompted by political considerations
only, aroused no enthusiasm among the Latins and brought no
crusaders to his aid. In fact it probably did him more harm
than good, because it alienated the stiff-necked Greek clergy and
their equally stiff-necked popular following. The emperor's stirring appeal to his subjects to defend their lives and honor brought
together an army of less than five thousand defenders, a figure
that tells volumes touching the depopulation of the city and
the enfeeblement and degeneracy of its inhabitants. A few
thousand Genoese and Venetian volunteers, who, having trade
interests to defend at Constantinople, put themselves at Constantine's disposal, proved a welcome addition, but the home governments of the two great Italian cities, although conscious of
the significance of the occasion, lamentably failed to rise to it.
An army, which, when all its elements were counted totalled no
more than eight thousand men, undertook to defend a city of so
great a circumference that several times eight thousand could

not effectively have manned the walls. Constantine XI nursed no illusions about the situation. The task mapped out for him by fate was to play the man and perish in the breach.

The defenses of Constantinople.

Constantinople is built, roughly, in the shape of a triangle surrounded on two sides by water, on the north by the Golden Horn, on the south by the sea of Marmora. Only by the third or western side is it joined to the land and there, in the fifth century, Emperor Theodosius II had built the great wall which ran north and south to the length of about four miles. The wall was really three walls, built in successive tiers and defended by a broad ditch or moat. No more solid fortification existed in the medieval world, for while the first wall was no more than a breastwork surmounting the moat, the second wall was twenty-five feet high, and the third, set at intervals with towers capable of sheltering large detachments of soldiers, soared to the impressive height of forty feet. Under medieval conditions of warfare and with an adequate supply of troops this mighty ring of masonary was impregnable. The whole history of Constantinople, even the capture of the city by the crusaders in 1204, goes to confirm the statement. In 1453, two general factors fell heavily into the scales against the defenders; first, the emperor, as already noted, had so few soldiers that the line of defenders along the wall was dangerously thin; second, the recent invention of gunpowder had put a valuable new weapon in the hands of the attacking party. Mohammed possessed an equipment of perhaps sixty guns of various sizes, crude engines in our eyes, but capable of shooting breaches into the walls so fast that the undermanned Greek army could not adequately repair them.

The stratagem of the ships.

The siege had been proceeding without success for some weeks when the sultan perceived the necessity of supplementing the attack on the land-wall by an attack from the sea. For this purpose he would have to bring his fleet into the Golden Horn. The move was difficult, if not impossible, because the Byzantines had closed the entrance to the Golden Horn by stretching an immense iron chain from shore to shore. The most famous single incident of the siege was the stratagem by which the Ottomans got into the Golden Horn without forcing the iron boom. It is a tribute to Mohammed's mental alertness that he had surrounded himself with what was probably the best engineering corps then to be found in the world. There were Christians in it too, for the sultan had no desire to cripple his military establishment for the pleasure of indulging his religious prejudices. His engineers now developed a bold plan. They constructed an inclined plane of greased planks over the promontory which lies between the Bosporus and the Golden Horn, and one night, when all was ready, with the aid of pulleys and oxen dragged some seventy small vessels over this improvised viaduct, letting them slip quickly and stealthily into the waters above the city.

Portage of Mohammed's fleet

To meet the new threat the Greeks had to divert some of their troops from the land defenses to the sea-wall, and, cheered by this further thinning of the defenders opposite his main army, the sultan, after a prolonged and furious bombardment, ordered a final assault with all his forces. The day set for the attempt was May 29, 1453; the siege had been going on for seven weeks. Line on line of Moslems threw itself on the walls only to be hurled back by the besieged. In their tragic hour the emperor and his faithful handful of defenders did much to wipe out the memory of that pretentious senility and stubborn conceit which has unloaded the world's scorn on the feeble empire of the Greeks. Constantine himself set a high example by electing, rather than desert the wall, to be buried under the heap of his foes. In a manner worthy of the great tradition personified in him, he brought the long line of Roman emperors to a close. But the walls were breached and scaled at last, and while the victorious Ottoman soldiers scattered in all directions to loot and murder, Mohammed, picking his way on horseback over the corpses blocking the streets, proceeded to St. Sophia to offer thanks to Allah. This famous edifice, one of the marvels of the eastern world, was straightway converted into a mosque.

The capture of Constantinople, May 29, 1453.

what happened to greek fire?

During several days unimaginable license reigned, for the inhabitants and their possessions had been conceded to the soldiers as their legitimate booty. When at length from very weariness the orgy ended, there stood the ancient city, an empty shell of houses, palaces, and churches. Then only Mohammed bethought himself that without the inhabitants Constantinople was of little or no use to him and took measures to repeople the city. He permitted as many prisoners as possible to ransom themselves

Mohammed repeoples Constantinople and proclaims toleration of Christian worship.

and return to their homes, and he settled, sometimes forcibly, people from the country round about, mostly Greeks, in the deserted quarters of the town. Plainly he took this course because, having no desire to forfeit the revenues of Constantinople, he recognized that, in so far as the city was an emporium of trade, its affairs would have to continue to be conducted by Christians, since his Moslems had neither the capacity nor the will for commercial pursuits. To conciliate the Greeks he went the length of proclaiming toleration of Christian worship. Moreover, he ordered the clergy to elect a patriarch, whom he ceremoniously installed in office with the grant of very nearly the same rights of ecclesiastical control as those enjoyed under the Christian emperors. Thus did the Greek church, taken under the protection of the sultan, survive the Greek state.

Mohammed decides on a policy of Balkan consolidation.

Having established himself on the Golden Horn in the city designated by nature herself as the capital of an east-Mediterranean empire, Mohammed, hailed by his people as the Conqueror, looked about him. As far as the Danube on the north and the Ionian sea on the west he claimed suzerainty over all the Balkan peoples and their rulers. But these rulers, permitted by Mohammed's predecessors to continue in the exercise of local autonomy, were visibly restive under the foreign scepter. Not only might they, under favorable circumstances, come together to effect his overthrow, but they would always be tempted to cast furtive glances toward Hungary and the West in the hope of rescue from that quarter. Feeling none too secure, Mohammed resolved, as soon as the Constantinopolitan campaign was over, to bring Balkania completely under his sway. He was enamored of the story of Alexander the Great, whose spectacular career it would be wonderful to duplicate in a reverse sense by setting out from Asia to conquer Europe. Such a plan was of course a dream for idle hours, to be realized, if at all, in the dim and distant future. The immediate, practical task was to consolidate the loosely strung provinces of the Balkan peninsula.

The final extinction of Bulgaria in 1393.

Within the confused Balkan mass Bulgaria alone in Mohammed's time was no longer a problem. More than half a century before, in fact immediately after Kossovo, Bayezid I had resolved to end the many conspiracies of the Bulgar tsar against him by a final act of surgery. In 1393 he took by assault the old

Bulgar capital, (Tirnovo) leveled it with the ground, carried off the patriarch, and killed or scattered the reigning family. Therewith Bulgaria, incorporated in the Ottoman empire, had ceased to give further trouble. In Mohammed II's view a similar fate meted out to his other unreliable dependencies would go far toward giving him the security he coveted. He began his oper ations with Serbia.

Since the disaster at Kossovo, Serbia, under a vassal sovereign set up by the Ottomans, had continued to enjoy a limited self- government. Deliberately Mohammed precipitated a final strug- gle with this unhappy state. But no sooner had he involved himself with his army in the difficult Serb mountains than the Hungarians, alarmed for their own safety, came to the aid of the Serbs. Once more John Hunyadi, the ancient and valorous foe of the Moslem, appeared upon the scene and using Belgrad, at that time a Hungarian outpost, as a base, he exposed Moham- med to such dangers that the sultan resolved to launch his whole strength at this Danubian key-fortress in a systematic effort to get it into his possession.

The importance of Belgrad.

It was in 1456 that Mohammed undertook the siege of Bel- grad, prosecuting it with such large forces and so much vigor that the fortress would have been taken, had not the energy and fa- natic courage of the Christians for once outrun that of the Mo- hammedans. John Hunyadi performed miracles of bravery, ably seconded by a volunteer crusading host brought from the West by an eloquent Franciscan friar, John of Capistrano. A bold sortie, made at the moment when the Ottomans had exhausted themselves by a vain assault on the walls, broke the sultan's ranks and sent him reeling home with the decimated remnant of his troops. By a sad fatality the two Christian paladins, Hunyadi and Capistrano, died of the plague a few weeks after their triumph, with the result that the Hungarian as well as the general western effort to follow up the success at Belgrad came to a sudden stop. Hungary for the moment was safe, but since Hungary, torn by civil war, now withdrew her hand from Serbia, Mohammed was free to resume his Serb policy and to bring it, with the aid of the familiar, fatal divisions among the Serbs themselves, to a successful issue. By 1459 the last Serb rulers and their kin had either been killed or scattered, and Serbia,

Hunyadi's last victory at Belgrad, followed by the reduction of Serbia, 1459

merged in the Ottoman empire, had disappeared beneath the
Moslem flood.

The fall of
Bosnia, 1462.

To the west of Serbia lay Bosnia, which next attracted the
attention of Mohammed. Bosnia, a mountain region, like Serbia,
and racially homogeneous with it, had never, except for certain
border sections, been united with Serbia even in the heyday of
Nemania rule. Exposed equally to attack from the Serb sovereigns and the kings of Hungary, it had somehow managed to
lead a more or less independent existence under rulers of its own.
Its princes, who finally took the ambitious title of king, were, like
the sovereigns of Serbia, involved in constant quarrels with a
powerful nobility. Consequently in both domestic and foreign
affairs they had exhibited the shiftiness and irresolution which are
the usual concomitants of political weakness. Only on one occasion so far had the state identified itself with the general Balkan
cause: it had sent a contingent to take part in the struggle at
Kossovo. Plentifully occupied nearer home, the Ottoman sovereigns were regretfully obliged to postpone their revenge for this
show of hostility. But, with Serbia conquered, the road into
Bosnia was open, and Mohammed's hosts were soon pushing
into the valleys and attacking the Bosnian strongholds. Bosnia,
even more than Serbia, was a house divided against itself, though
not merely because of its cantankerous feudal nobility. For
centuries it had been a battle-ground of the Latin and Greek
churches. Bewildered by the quarrel of the two irreconcilable
Christian groups, the inhabitants had in large numbers turned
their backs on both faiths to attach themselves to the beliefs
and practices stigmatized by the Orthodox as the Bogumil heresy.[1]
The cruel persecutions to which the Bogumils were subjected,
sometimes in the name of eastern, sometimes in the name of
western orthodoxy, had alienated popular affection from the
established churches so completely that whole sections of the
Bosnians did not scruple to see in Islam a deliverer. Numerous castles treacherously opened their gates to the enemy,
and when the wretched Bosnian king, despairing of his cause,
surrendered, he was, in spite of a solemn promise made in writing,
cruelly decapitated under the eyes of the sultan (1462). Like

[1] See Appendix B, p. 163.

his Christian contemporaries Mohammed held the convenient doctrine that a pledge made to a dog of an infidel possessed no binding character.

Thus Bosnia, sharp on the heel of Serbia, perished, and throughout Balkania the land of the Serbs with the single exception of the Zeta, passed under the heel of the oppressor. The historic Zeta comprised the shoreland together with the bare and barren mountain ranges between the lake of Scutari and the city of Cattaro. Only into the more accessible parts of it did the Ottoman cohorts succeed in penetrating, pushing forward slowly and under immense difficulties. Ancient Zeta's wild and rocky core, called Crna Gora by the Serbs and Montenegro (Black Mountain) by the rest of Europe, was never conquered by Mohammed or more than intermittently occupied by any one of his successors. A tiny commonwealth of hardy mountaineers, it alone in all Balkania successfully defied the Moslem host and, perched among the eagles, heroically preserved an eagle freedom.

Montenegro, the land of freedom.

never conquered by Turks

South of Montenegro and commanding the approaches to the Adriatic sea lay the lands of the Albanians, which in his policy of taming the peninsula Mohammed could not overlook. He was the more urged to subdue this people as they had but recently awakened from their medieval slumber and given evidence of a desire to take their national affairs into their own hands. Some years before Mohammed's accession, in the days of his father Murad, there had occurred an uprising, to which we have already referred and which constitutes so important an episode in Albanian history that we must now develop it at greater length. In fact the episode is the one brilliant and outstanding chapter in Albanian national history until we reach the nineteenth century. Its hero was a tribal chief, George Castriotes by name, but better known under the Turk designation, honorable withal in its intention, of Scanderbeg (beg or prince Alexander). Young George, carried off by the Moslems as a hostage while still a boy, had, on arriving at man's estate, made his escape from Turkish bondage and boldly struck for his native hills. There he had been joyously acclaimed by his tribe as its hereditary leader. The warrior deeds which he immediately performed had electrified his own and all the neighbor clans to such a point that perhaps for the first time in their

Scanderbeg, the national hero of Albania.

history they had forgotten their ancient animosities and joined in a truly national effort to maintain the sacred freedom of their hills. Scanderbeg had adopted against the Ottoman army guerrilla tactics, excellently suited to the cramped valleys and steep declivities of his native land, and Murad, defeated again and again, had been obliged in the end to desist from further attack.

Mohammed subjugates Albania after Scanderbeg's death, 1467. Mohammed II was not the man to accept a situation so injurious to Ottoman pride. He renewed the attempts at Albanian subjugation until, balked, like his father, at every point, he was forced to enter into negotiations with the despised rebel. The fame of Scanderbeg, the guerrilla fighter, who with inferior forces consistently beat the irresistible Ottoman armies, went like wild-fire throughout Balkania and the West. Great states like Hungary and Venice sought his alliance; the pope hailed him in quaint and picturesque phrase as " the athlete of Christendom." But, of course, Mohammed had no idea of putting up forever with an independent and defiant Albania. On recovering his breath after defeat, he reopened the struggle, and though he made little headway so long as Scanderbeg lived, the heroic leader had no sooner died (1467) than the hill tribes lost their coherence and yielded one by one to the overwhelming forces dispatched against them. Albania now became a part of the Ottoman empire. However, neither then nor afterwards was it ever much more than nominally incorporated in the sultan's dominion, because the Albanian tribes, especially of the north, where the mountains are as inaccessible as in neighboring Montenegro, possessed in their warrior habits and hard, flint-like tempers an incorruptible guarantee against enslavement.

The Rumans create two north-Danubian states, Wallachia and Moldavia. In taking inventory of the Balkan situation, Sultan Mohammed was obliged, if he would win the full control at which he aimed, to reckon also with two states in the lowlands north of the Danube, inhabited by a people speaking a Latin dialect and calling themselves Rumans (Romans). Although the Rumans, in the main, are probably descendants of the ancient Dacians, they owe their speech to the Roman colonization of Dacia carried out by the Emperor Trajan.[1] Their boast that they are sons of ancient Rome has therefore only a qualified justification. The total disappearance from history of the Dacians as

[1] See pp. 37, 38, 72, 73.

well as of the other Romanized provincials for five hundred years following the Slav and Mongol invasions deepens the mystery which envelops them. Most probably when the imperial defenses of Balkania gave way they sought refuge in the Balkan and Carpathian uplands, whence, on the subsiding, around the year 1000, of the Mongol floods, they slowly made their way once more into the Danubian lowlands. By degrees these reappearing Ruman groups, prevailingly of a pastoral type, absorbed the Slav and Mongol remnants round about them, and after having been repeatedly strengthened by fresh accessions from the large Ruman center in the Carpathians, they founded at last two considerable states, Wallachia and Moldavia. The outlines of these two political creations are distinctly discernible before the end of the thirteenth century. Wallachia lay compactly between the Carpathians and the Danube; Moldavia extended eastward from the Carpathians toward the Dniester river. The infant states were obliged to engage in severe and often disastrous struggles with their ambitious and stronger neighbors, Hungary and Poland, and they were still deeply entangled with these powers when a fresh peril arose to their south in the form of the Ottoman advance.

Wallachia and Moldavia were governed by princes (*voivodes,* *hospodars*) of great power but dependent in some respects on a landed nobility (*boyars*), who enjoyed the right of choosing the sovereign. That this privilege generally meant a disputed succession goes without saying. Alive to the threat extended by the conquering Murad I, the prince of Wallachia, Mirtchéa by name, had sent a detachment of Rumans to fight for the freedom of the peninsula at Kossovo (1389) and, following the Christian rout, had discreetly agreed to pay the Ottoman sovereign tribute. Thenceforth Mirtchéa and his successors found themselves hitched more or less helplessly to the Ottoman chariot. The prince of Mohammed's day, Vlad IV (1456–62), roused himself to a last vigorous effort at resistance. Though Vlad was a man of undoubted military gifts, he is even better remembered as a leading figure in the long succession of perverse, bloody-minded monsters, whose peculiar distinction lies in having given to Balkan history a deep tinge of crimson. Master and past-master in every method of slaughter, he yet had a diseased preference for dis-

Mohammed breaks the resistance of Wallachia.

posing of his victims by pinning them to the ground, often in companies of hundreds, with pointed pales on which they slowly writhed to death. Even his contemporaries, of whom no one will aver that they were burdened with a fastidious spirit, professed to be horrified by Vlad's ingenuity in torture and called him Vlad the Impaler. Nevertheless the Impaler could fight like a fiend and repeatedly defeated both the lieutenants of Mohammed and the redoubtable Mohammed himself. But he fell victim in 1462 to domestic strife and on his flight from his country the sultan was able to appoint a successor who declared his willingness to give up the struggle and acknowledge Mohammed as suzerain by paying him tribute.

Moldavia becomes a vassal state after Mohammed's time, 1512.   In Vlad's time and for many years after, the other Rumanian province, Moldavia, was ruled by the most capable prince in its history, Stephen IV, called the Great (1457-1504). Partly by his skill as a general, partly by his cunning as a diplomat, he turned Mohammed back from Moldavia again and again, and after Mohammed's death (1481) gloried in complete independence to the end of his days (1504). On his death-bed, despairing of the ability of his people to hold out longer, he advised his son and successor to make voluntary submission to the sultan. The submission was accordingly made in 1512. It is worthy of note that the policy of Mohammed as well as that of his successors was not directed upon complete incorporation of the two Rumanian provinces in the Ottoman empire. Perhaps because they lay beyond the Danube and hence on the border rather than in Balkania, the sultans were content to make them tributary, permitting them to retain their own princes, religion, laws, and institutions.

Dispersion of the petty rulers of Hellas, 1460.   It remains to speak of the Conqueror's relation to Greece. As a result of the Fourth Crusade the ancient land of Hellas had been largely distributed in the form of fiefs among the Latin barons. These western chiefs had set up several states of the familiar feudal type, the most important being the duchy of Athens and the principality of Achaia (Morea).[1] There followed an age of feudal strife attended by every kind of petty family intrigue — a dark chaos into which a ray of light was thrown by the

[1] For the story of the Latin states on Hellenic soil see Appendix C, p. 165.

gradual recovery of most of the Peloponnesus by the original owner, the Byzantine empire. However, the feeble emperors of the Paleologus line had found no better use to make of their Morean acquisition than to apportion it, in the form of appanages, among their male relatives. Already Murad II had acted on the plan of extending his influence to ancient Hellas, but it was not till Mohammed the Conqueror's day that the policy was adopted, entirely consistent with measures taken by him elsewhere in the peninsula, to put an end, once and for all, to the breed of petty Latin and Greek dynasts lording it over the land. In a number of campaigns Mohammed broke their resistance, ruthlessly executed them or drove them to flight, and by 1460 had brought the whole area, with the exception of a few shore positions retained by the Venetians, under his direct administration.

While pursuing his policy of Balkan consolidation, Mohammed everywhere ran into a power which he never doubted he would, sooner or later, have to call to account if he wished to be master in his own house. I refer to Venice. We are aware that Venice, following the Fourth Crusade, in the course of which its wildest imperialist dreams gloriously came true, had entered into control of the Mediterranean sea and markets. The immense commercial profits accruing to the city of St. Mark, while enabling it to wax powerful, had had, however, the less agreeable effect of bringing rivals into the field, the most notable among them being Genoa. By shrewdly playing off the Byzantine against the Latin empire the Ligurian city had succeeded gradually in cutting deep into the Venetian trade monopoly in Levantine waters. Especially had this been the case after 1261 in which year the Byzantine emperor, with important aid from the Genoese fleet, had once more taken possession of Constantinople. Genoa and not Venice was henceforth the pampered favorite of the Greek state, with the result that the two city-republics had become involved in rivalry so bitter that each frankly sought the other's extermination. Gradually, however, the scales of combat had inclined in favor of Venice, although Genoa always retained many points of vantage in the East, chiefly in the form of trading posts on the Black sea. As late as 1453, when Mohammed II took Constantinople, the Genoese had held a small fortified town, called Galata, on the

Mohammed obliged to reckon with Venice and Genoa.

opposite or northern shore of the Golden Horn. One of the Conqueror's first acts had been to renew the commercial privileges of the Genoese at Galata in exchange for the obligation of razing its walls. When this had been done, the Genoese were no longer in the position to threaten the sultan as they had threatened and bullied the feeble Paleologi, and with an entirely correct estimation of political values Mohammed turned his attention to the Venetians as to the leading representatives in the contemporary world of the riches created by trade and the might represented by an all-powerful navy.

Mohammed not adverse to trade and industry.

The Balkan policy of Mohammed, which we have been engaged in describing, was guided by the wholly intelligible and statesmanlike concept of bringing the peninsula under his rule. Together with the Byzantine empire he had inherited the Byzantine policy, which from Justinian to Basil II pursued this identical purpose. In spite of the turban on his head and the sayings of the Prophet on his lips, Mohammed's thoughts ran along lines devoid of anything peculiarly Asiatic. Therefore, contrary to the erroneous statements still too often encountered in western books, Mohammed had an excellent appreciation of the value of trade as a basis both of private wealth and public revenue. The trade of Galata, for instance, he had no more notion of paralyzing than that of Constantinople, which city, as we have seen, he was at pains to repeople, preferably with Greeks, in order to foster its economic life. And he meted out the same measure to the Venetians. In 1454, on the morrow of the capture of Constantinople, he signed a treaty with Venice whereby he confirmed to her the bulk of the vast trading privileges enjoyed under the Byzantine emperors.

Political necessity of the war with Venice, 1463-79.

It was his imperial, not his commercial policy that pushed Mohammed into an inevitable conflict with the Adriatic republic. The sultan possessed a certain limited amount of sea-power. Without it he could never have undertaken to capture Constantinople. But as his Balkan policy unfolded, he began to see that, in order to secure his dominion, he would have to control the Balkan shore and all the circumambient seas. Actually these were controlled by Venice, whose dominion rested on her fleets manned by skilled mariners, and on the numerous islands and coast settlements strung in a vast garland across the Adriatic,

Ionian, and Aegean seas. To hold Balkania in secure subjection the existing Ottoman military power would have to be
supplemented by the maritime might which Venice had long
ago wrested from the Byzantine empire and which Mohammed,
the heir of Byzantium, determined to reclaim. The irrepressible
conflict over this issue between land and sea power began in
1463 and lasted for sixteen years. From post after post along
the eastern sea routes, from Albanian strongholds, from Morean
fortresses, and finally, from the great island of Negroponte
(Euboea) the famous banner with the Winged Lion fell in disgrace to be replaced by the triumphant Star and Crescent.
When, in 1479, Venice, thoroughly beaten, sued for peace in
order to save the remnant of her empire, she was, in return for
an annual payment — really a tribute — permitted to resume
her eastern trade. Although she was still powerful enough
to cut an impressive figure in the Mediterranean world, it was
none the less clear that her fortunes were declining and that the
future in this historic area belonged to the Ottomans.

Having broached the question of sea-power, Mohammed
followed up the Venetian war with an attack on Rhodes. This
island, near the entrance to the Aegean sea, was held by a
Christian fighting brotherhood, the famous Knights of St. John,
who could, from their coign of vantage, fall at pleasure across
the flank of the Ottoman sea-power. In 1480, Mohammed
sent an expedition against Rhodes which failed in the face of
the dauntless courage of the Knights. He was preparing to
follow it up with a more formidable attack when he died at the
comparatively early age of fifty-one (1481). Harassed Europe
breathed a sigh of relief.

In a career of thirty years filled with the clash of arms
Mohammed had done notable work. Viewing himself, after
his capture of Constantinople, as the successor of the Byzantine
emperors, he had not only broken the manifold resistances
within the Balkan peninsula but had largely given that province
a central administration dependent on himself. Further, he had
renewed the sea-power of Constantinople and taken at least
partial revenge on Venice, usurper of the eastern waters. On
the other hand, he had left many questions unsolved. Belgrad
remained in the hands of the Hungarians and might at any

Failure of
the
expedition
against
Rhodes,
1480.

Solved and
unsolved
problems of
Moham-
med's reign.

moment be used as a gate of sortie against Mohammedan rule. Further, as the failure at Rhodes had shown, the Ottoman sea-power was still so frail that it was unable to assume full command of even the limited Aegean waters. Clearly the sultans would have to develop more naval strength or give up their dream of empire. Finally, eastward beyond the Dardanelles lay the vast, unsolved mystery of Asia. On what Mohammed's successors would make of these pressing issues depended the future of the state.

CHAPTER XIV

THE OTTOMAN EMPIRE AT ITS HEIGHT

BAYEZID II (1481–1512), Mohammed's older son, succeeded to the throne only after a sharp struggle with his brother Jem. He owed his victory to the Janissaries whom he bribed with a large donative. Plainly this professional corps was developing an inordinate sense of power and becoming the decisive factor in the succession. If this movement grew, producing the dragon-brood of an irresponsible militarism, the Ottoman empire was certain before long to face a situation fraught with ominous possibilities.

Prince Jem, after his defeat, managed to escape to the Knights of St. John at Rhodes and with that step inaugurated a career marked by so many sudden and romantic changes as to engage the rapt attention of the west. How he was carried from Rhodes to France, and how, in the teeth of a solemn engagement to the contrary, he was held a prisoner on French soil to be ultimately transferred to Rome in order to be directly under the kindly eye of the Christian shepherd of Europe cannot be told here. Suffice it to point out that his fortunes have a certain historic interest in that they serve to illumine the political morality of the Latin West, for the shameful fact is that Jem was held in captivity by his various Christian masters solely for the purpose of squeezing money out of his brother, the reigning sultan, Bayezid. There is even some ground for the suspicion that Pope Alexander VI finally went the length of having Jem poisoned in order to collect the large lump sum offered by Bayezid to whoever would do him this friendly service.

By historians generally Bayezid has been listed among the slothful sultans, which ranking can be accepted only with reservations. A devoted Moslem, fond of philosophy and poetry, himself not without literary talent, he was, it is true, out of love with the energetic tradition of his house and sought to avoid unnecessary wars. Not only did he break with his father's forward policy but he tried to avoid, as far as possible, the burning issues which had been left upon his hands. He may have thought and, if he did, the thought could be defended, that a period of rest after the tempestuous movement of the last fifty years would serve to promote an interior adjustment and, in the end, make for greater security. Certainly he was not indolent in the evil, physical sense of vicious self-indulgence, and he was alert enough to protect his inheritance wherever it was threatened. Without question, however, he marks a pause in the expansion movement, and in the light of the last act of his reign raises a legitimate doubt as to whether that movement was sufficiently in the hands of the sultan to be stopped by a personal decision. Owing to the long peace coupled with military inaction, the Janissaries, the chief agents of expansion as well as its chief beneficiaries, grew restless and irritable. At last they rose in rebellion saying: " Our padishah is old and sickly; we demand that Selim shall be sultan." And the over-peaceful, philosophic Bayezid, tumbled from the throne, died a few days later not without the suspicion of foul play at the hands of his successful son and heir.

Selim I called the Grim (1512-20).

Selim I (1512–20) began his reign with the customary struggle with his brothers for control and was not safe in the saddle till, in accordance with the practice elevated to law by the Conqueror, he had, by the avenue of the bowstring, promoted them to a better world together with all the nephews, sons of his unhappy brothers, on whom he could lay his ferocious hands. With the unity of the realm assured by these abominable means, he began what proved to be one of the most eventful careers of any member of his house. Extraordinarily vigorous in mind and body and coupling with entire indifference to the pleasures and amenities of existence a fierce passion for war and its blood-lusts, he fully deserved the epithet " The Grim," by which he is known to history.

The Ottomans in Anatolia.

The feature setting its special mark on Selim's reign was his concentration on the questions raised on his eastern front, in Asia. Of course his turning to Asia was no unheralded innovation on his part, for his people had come from Asia, and Anatolia had always been to them an object of interest though, especially since Murad I, decidedly second to Europe. The many Seljuk emirates, which once divided the lands of Asia Minor among them, had not in their totality become subjected to the Osmanli till the time of Bayezid I (the Thunderbolt). Following his collapse at Angora (1402), they had regained their independence and had been brought a second time within the Ottoman fold in so gradual a manner that the largest Turk state, Caramania, with its capital at Konia, was not finally reduced to obedience till the time of Mohammed the Conqueror (1473). From the reign of the Conqueror the whole of Asia Minor was a secure possession of the Ottomans.

During the long reign of Selim's father, Bayezid II, a number of things had happened in the East which drew that languid sovereign's attention, without, however, moving him to abandon in any essential way his policy of inactivity. Nevertheless, regardless of Bayezid's personal preferences, the simple fact of neighborhood would oblige any Ottoman sultan to reckon with two states beyond his Anatolian province, both of them Moslem like his own. There was, however, a religious difference to be noted between them. The empire of the Mamelukes, founded in Egypt, had gradually spread to Syria and was, in matters of faith, like the Ottomans themselves, Sunnite, that is, orthodox. Beyond the Euphrates and Tigris the old state of Persia had lately experienced one of its periodic revivals, but since the Persians belonged to a sect called Shiites, they were classed by orthodox Mohammedans as heretics. Although the fanatic aversion with which Sunnites and Shiites regarded each other inevitably created an atmosphere of bitterness between sultan and shah, this circumstance can hardly be set down as the fundamental reason for the struggle which, after much preliminary bickering, broke out uncontrollably in Selim's day. That struggle was political rather than religious and was precipitated, so far as Selim was concerned, to the end of obtaining a secure and scientific frontier for his Asiatic possessions. As he was guided by similar territorial motives in his dealings with the Mameluke sultan of Egypt, who, as we have seen, was orthodox (Sunnite), he precipitated a war with Egypt also. Conformer and heretic looked alike to Selim when it came to an issue of power, and the common orthodoxy of Ottomans and Mamelukes was impotent to maintain

The two Moslem empires of Persia and Egypt.

peace from the moment the Mamelukes reached out from Syria, as they had lately done, to grasp Cilicia, the southeastern corner of Asia Minor.

Selim defeats Persia and annihilates the Mamelukes.

Selim's campaigns in Asia were attended by amazingly swift successes. In an invasion involving an heroic march of over a thousand miles across mountain and desert Persia was defeated and the territory of upper Mesopotamia, at the head-waters of the Tigris and Euphrates, added to the Ottoman state (1516). However, the Shiite power showed abundant vigor and, far from being crushed, was merely pushed back from the immediate proximity of Anatolia. An entirely different fate was meted out to the Mamelukes, who were completely annihilated. Defeated first in Syria (1516), they were with relentless vigor pursued southward into the desert and across the isthmus of Suez to their home in Egypt, where, near Cairo, they suffered a final, crushing blow (1517). The Mameluke sultan, captured after the battle, was executed, and Selim by right of conquest entered into the Mameluke heritage. This included, besides Syria and Egypt, Arabia, which in the person of its most important ruler, the sherif of Mecca, made submission to Selim by accepting him as protector of the Holy Places, Mecca and Medina.

Selim assumes the califate.

The conquest of Egypt brought to the sultan not only an increase of territory but also a valuable though somewhat threadbare dignity. Ever since the extinction of the Arab power at Bagdad, the sultans of Egypt, in order to enhance their own importance, had maintained a descendant of the Abbassid califs in shadowy state at Cairo. While refusing to permit the incumbent of the califate, a mere puppet, to exercise control, they nevertheless presented him to the Moslem world as the successor of the Prophet Mohammed. They even permitted him to maintain the semblance of a court. This purely titular head of Islam now resigned (1517) the califate into Selim's hands with the result that since Selim's day the Ottoman sultans have claimed to be the supreme religious chiefs of all right-thinking Mohammedans. There is, however, a flaw in their claim, since it is a fundamental principle of the faith that the calif must be of the Koreish, the Arab tribe of the Prophet. Of the blood of the Koreish there was not a single authentic drop either in the veins of Selim or in any of his successors. On this account many Moslems, even among Sunnites, have refused to take the Ottoman califate seriously. On the other hand, the fact that after his conquest of Egypt the Ottoman sultan was indisputably the greatest ruler in the Moslem world, coupled with his actual possession of the Holy Places of Mecca and Medina, has sufficed to give his somewhat dubious dignity a basis of reality.

Though Selim, judged by a crude territorial scale, was as much and more of a conqueror than Mohammed II, his conquests befell in Asia and Africa, not in Europe. From this circumstance have followed consequences of enormous import for the Ottoman state and society. We may admit without discussion that the provinces conquered by "the Grim" naturally and logically rounded off that Levantine empire which, since their first encroachment on the Byzantine state, the Osmanli had been engaged, though often unconsciously, in establishing. In view of the movement toward east-Mediterranean unity which has repeatedly made itself felt from the distant days of the Egyptian pharaohs down to the Arabs and Byzantines, we are obliged to reckon with a certain physical interdependence of these linked shorelands. Seen in this light, Selim's conquests take on the character of an intelligible historical recurrence, although that is not saying that they are not also an expression of his personal passion for adventure. But leaving undecided the mooted question of the relative importance of environment and ambition in a conqueror's career, it is certain that the sultans following Selim would have to give an alert, unflagging attention to the complicated concerns of the three continents of Europe, Asia, and Africa. They would have to develop a truly ecumenical vision and exhibit from day to day a superhuman vigor if they were as much as to keep abreast of their monumental daily task. Would the sultan-autocrats be able to meet this criterion, not in an isolated instance but steadily from generation to generation? Though the house of Osman had thus far supplied a perhaps uniquely capable crop of rulers, was there any reason to think that the supply would continue indefinitely? Here loomed a peril which sooner or later would certainly prove the undoing of the Ottoman state as it has been the ruin of every absolute monarchy in history.

Conse-
quences of
Selim's
conquest: (1)
administra-
tive difficul-
ties too
great for
any but a
ruler of
genius.

Conse-
quences of
Selim's
conquest:
(2) growth
of an irre-
sponsible
militarism.

A second consequence of Selim's exploits was the necessary increase of the army and incidentally of its standing branch, the Janissaries. Occasionally unruly under Selim, under a feeble sultan they would with absolute certainty get completely out of hand. From the first, Ottoman rule was of course military, but it was under authoritative leadership and was linked to a definite political purpose. If ever the Janissaries resolutely took the bit between their teeth, order would immediately give way to anarchy, the anarchy of rampant militarism which no state or society can long endure.

Conse-
quences of
Selim's
conquest:
(3) growth
of the
Moslem
element and
of religious
fanaticism.

Finally, the conquests in Asia and Africa added an enormous Moslem population to an empire which, built up largely in Europe on a conquered Christian society, had found it both necessary and profitable to practice religious toleration. Counting henceforth far more than before, the Moslems would tend gradually to dominate the state and to infect it with their religious fanaticism. We have seen that the Osmanli, possessed of a Turk and pagan background, were originally not greatly given to persecution. This reasonable disposition through increasing Asiatic, and particularly Arab, influences now began to yield to a more rigorous mood. Undoubtedly too the change was stimulated by the sultan's exercise of the califate. Identified with Islam, a faith that believed in the use of the sword in order to spread its rule, he found himself launched by the sacred obligation of his office on a policy of unlimited conquest. Under these circumstances, the Ottoman state, originally an end in itself, might very easily degenerate to the mere tool of an insatiable religion and renounce those sober dictates of policy constituting the rock on which it was founded.

Solyman the
Law-giver,
called also
Solyman the
Magnificent,
1520–66.

While all these tendencies and dangers were illustrated by the reign of Selim's successor, they were effectively held in check by him and failed to precipitate a crisis owing to his remarkable personality. Sultan Solyman (1520–66) possessed in ample measure the military talents of his line. He was tireless in improving his army and even in old age kept in intimate, personal touch with his soldiers by putting himself at their head whenever they took the field. He was also a capable administrator, who loved order and even-handed justice, and who endowed his people with a body of legislation so equitable and well considered that he won from them the grateful title of the Law-giver. Finally, though he was, like all autocrats, not free from caprice and sudden assaults of wrath, he combined with a loyal, upright nature, a discriminating patronage of literature and art. Since he manifestly approximated to the ideal which Europe in the age of the Renaissance entertained of a ruler of men, the occident, in spite of his alien faith, admiringly called him Solyman the Magnificent. Under the Magnificent the empire of the Osmanli now reached its zenith.

Solyman's first move was to stop the hole at Belgrad through which the Hungarians never ceased to pour in order to threaten and harass Balkania. In 1521 he conducted a leaguer which no new Hunyadi rose to interrupt and which ended in complete success. Henceforth Solyman not only possessed the key to his own house but commanded the gate by which he might go forth at will to sweep on into Hungary. In the very next year (1522) the sultan attacked and took the island of Rhodes. Lying directly across the line of communication between Syria and Constantinople, it could not possibly be suffered to remain longer in the hands of the Knights of St. John, whose pirate ships preyed freely upon Moslem commerce. By the terms of the capitulation the Knights were permitted to withdraw and, establishing themselves to the westward on the island of Malta, from this new point of vantage continued for generations to be a thorn in the flesh of the unbelievers.

Solyman captures Belgrad and Rhodes.

These victories put into Solyman's hands two prizes which his great-grandfather, Mohammed II, had tried in vain to seize. Won at the very outset of his reign, they gained for the sultan a prestige and for his empire a security which might have suggested to an older and more cautious man to rest upon his laurels. But not only was he flushed with youth and pride, he was also the head of a system, to which war was the very breath of life; moreover, he found himself in contact with disturbed conditions on at least three fronts which in all probability could not have been cured by amicable means, even had he tried. First, on the Danube front Hungary was utterly unable to rest content with the existing situation. So long as the Ottoman power hung over her like a cloud, she would be stirred with an alarm which would pass in agitated waves to the

Inevitable conflicts on three fronts.

westward-lying states of Austria and Germany. His second front, along the eastern Mediterranean, brought him into touch with Venice. True, Venice had been shown her place in the course of the long war conducted against her (1463-79) by Mohammed II. When, twenty years later, she had been audacious enough to forget her proved inferiority, she was punished in a second war (1499-1503) which caused her to sustain fresh losses, chiefly in the Morea. Though manifestly unable by her strength alone to resist the Ottoman arms, the aging queen of the Adriatic was none-the-less far from negligible, and apart from her firm possession of the long and important Dalmatian coast, sounded a perpetual challenge to Ottoman sea-power merely by virtue of her hold, in addition to scattered points of support in the Aegean, of the great islands of Cyprus and Crete. It would therefore have been premature to consider the struggle with Venice over, especially as behind Venice, and likely to give her support, loomed another power, Spain. The Castilian monarchy had lately extended its influence over southern Italy and therefore now dominated in both the western and the middle areas of the Mediterranean. Finally, we must take note that along Solyman's third, his eastern front, in Asia, hovered Persia on revengeful lookout for any opening in the Ottoman armor. Defeated though the great Shiite kingdom had been by Selim, it was on both religious and political grounds bound to return to the conflict as soon as it had recovered its breath.

Solyman again successful over Persia.

It is not my purpose to follow in detailed, chronological order Solyman's activity along these three fighting fronts. Let it suffice to present a summary view of the sultan's many political entanglements. And first as to Persia, with which we are least concerned. Solyman conducted three difficult wars with the shah from which he issued with such success that the city of Bagdad together with the wide plain of the great Tigris-Euphrates system (Lower Mesopotamia) was added to his empire. But therewith the question of supremacy between the two Moslem states was by no means settled. Their rivalry continued to smoulder, especially over the control of the mountain area of Armenia and Kurdistan, and long after Solyman's time, in fact down to our own day, sultan and shah have proved implacable enemies.

Of enormous importance for the future of the empire were the events along the Danube front. Some years after taking Belgrad, Solyman decided to proceed against Hungary, which, in the face of a situation calling with a thousand voices for strong, concerted action, presented the melancholy spectacle of a weak king and a divided people. In a battle fought (1526) at Mohacs in the great Hungarian plain, the Christian forces went down in complete defeat. While fleeing from the field of carnage the youthful King Louis of Hungary, last of his line, met with death by drowning. What Kossovo had been to Serbia, such Mohacs was to Hungary, which now lay humbled and broken at the feet of the victor. But Solyman, though triumphant, was not permitted to rest upon his sword, for Ferdinand of Austria, brother of Emperor Charles V, now came forward to claim the Hungarian crown on the strength of an agreement with the deceased King Louis, designating the Hapsburg prince as heir to Hungary in the event of Louis' dying without children. In conquering Hungary, Solyman thus precipitated a new war, which in his usual bold manner he resolved to end with an attack aimed straight at the heart of his foe. He determined to march on Vienna and break the power of Austria.

Solyman's memorable siege of Vienna befell in the year 1529. It meant another acute crisis in the fortunes of Christendom. But the small Austrian garrison, valorously supported by the undaunted burghers, beat off the Moslem host and obliged Solyman to raise the siege. Great was the rejoicing throughout Germany and Europe, for the victory had set a term to the westward march of Islam. And in very truth Vienna proved a landmark, for, though returning frequently in thought to the project of a new siege, Solyman never again invested the walls of the Austrian capital. In so far as he had time and energy for the Danubian front he was obliged to devote them to the completion of his conquest of Hungary. For Ferdinand, archduke of Austria, calling himself also by virtue of the above-mentioned treaty king of Hungary, was not minded to renounce his claims.

For a while the sultan, exercising a wise caution in the face of a complicated situation, put a Hungarian nobleman, John Zapolya, on the Hungarian throne as his agent and vassal. On the death of this dependent, he flung discretion to the winds and, setting up a pasha at Buda, boldly incorporated Hungary in the Ottoman empire (1541). However, be it observed, not all of Hungary. Ferdinand managed to cling to the western rim, from which he was never ousted and which girdled Vienna in a wide defensive belt. Occasionally Solyman and Ferdinand, exhausted by prolonged strife or called elsewhither by other interests, came to terms on the basis of *uti possidetis*. But such an arrangement was never made without Ferdinand, as the manifestly weaker party, acknowledging his inferiority by agreeing to pay tribute for the section of Hungary in his hands. The various Austro-Ottoman peace treaties were ill observed and an irregular raiding warfare, from which neither side was willing to desist, kept the border in perpetual turmoil. Never throughout his days did Solyman find peace and content in his Hungarian acquisition; and although formal warfare, to which he repeatedly resorted, usually brought him a sheaf of victories, he did not ever quite succeed in breaking down the resistance of Ferdinand and of that section of the Magyar nobility which rallied to the Hapsburg banner. The situation, envisaged from the viewpoint of Europe, continued to be highly precarious; but it was also not without hope inasmuch as it presented to view a Christian sovereign possessed of the necessary means to stem at Vienna on the middle Danube the westward-rolling Ottoman tide.

Solyman's chief Mediterranean enemy is Spain.

On the Mediterranean front Solyman no longer faced, like his predecessors, only Venice, but also and predominantly a state of much greater might, Spain, which had recently become the greatest power of Europe. Through various accidents Spain had acquired Sicily and Naples, that is, the southern half of the Italian peninsula, while its Hapsburg sovereign, Charles, by being elected (1519) to the throne of Germany as Emperor Charles V, exercised a directive influence throughout central Europe. In this manner Spain laid her grasping tentacles about a large part of the continent. Even distant Austria became in a sense a Spanish outpost since it was ruled by Ferdinand, Charles's younger brother. In a word Emperor Charles V was in his day the leading sovereign of Europe and, as such, the life-long antagonist of Solyman. For the most part the struggle between them was fought out in the Mediterranean.

This struggle was, in essence, the conflict of two irreconcilable civilizations. Of the irrepressible sort, it was conducted regardless of treaties and usually without the formality of a declaration of war. The common weapon of both Christians and Moslems was the pirate-ship, which pounced upon the slow-sailing merchantman or raided the unguarded coast, plundering and carrying off to slavery the miserable inhabitants. In this evil game the Moslems enjoyed a distinct advantage over the Christians by their possession of the long and indented coast of Algiers and Tunis, which they used as a naval base. It also profited them greatly that they found in Chaireddin, called Barbarossa, an ideal pirate chief. Sultan Solyman, little scrupulous about his means, was quick to recognize in Chaireddin a powerful tool for the realization of his Mediterranean plans and supported the fierce, red-bearded pirate with all the resources at his disposal. As a final act of grace he raised Barbarossa to the command of his regular battle-fleet. In return Chaireddin acknowledged himself the sultan's vassal and by this act added a large part of the north African coast to the Ottoman empire. Owing to Chaireddin's powerful intervention Solyman was able, often for prolonged periods, to assert his mastery over the whole Mediterranean sea. Again and again Emperor Charles V, reduced to dire straits, was obliged to divert all his energy to the task of clearing the Algerine pests from the waters of Spain and Italy; and although not wholly without success, although on one occasion he even besieged and took Tunis (1535), Barbarossa's central stronghold, the corsair evil was always recrudescent and constituted a heavy drain on the finances of Charles, besides proving a nameless curse for the all but helpless population of the Christian coasts.

However, neither the skill of Chaireddin great though it was, nor the naval resources of Solyman, considerable as they proved to be, would have sufficed to press the Spanish sea-power so hard if the Moslems had not found support in the Christian camp. With the Hapsburg power, represented by Charles V, established in Spain, Italy, the Netherlands, and Germany, the emperor fairly overshadowed Europe. But this ascendancy was irksome to the Valois dynasty, which ruled in France and which by resolutely going its own way precipitated a tremendous struggle be-

Mediterranean warfare largely pirate warfare.

France becomes the ally of the Ottomans.

tween the two houses. Between 1521 and 1544, Charles V and
his French rival, Francis I (1515–47), engaged in four devastating
wars. The relations between them were at all times so strained
that, even when they were not involved in actual fighting, they
were doing their best to balk each other by political intrigue.
Success, however, almost uniformly attended Charles, with the
result that Francis, in order to save himself, was reduced to
pluck at every straw. The only power that seemed capable of

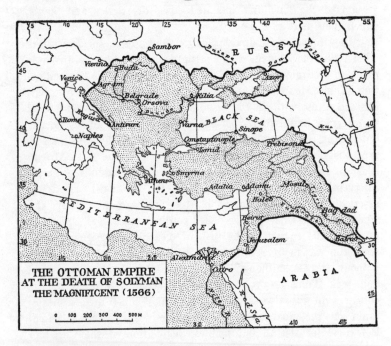

THE OTTOMAN EMPIRE
AT THE DEATH OF SOLYMAN
THE MAGNIFICENT (1566)

0   100 200 300 400 500 M

imposing due respect upon the greatest figure of the West was the
greatest figure of the East and Francis accordingly appealed to
Solyman. Treaties of alliance were concluded, by virtue of which
Solyman gave aid to Francis by joining his fleet to that of the
French and by urging Chaireddin to still more destructive efforts
against Spanish commerce. The French for their part opened
their Mediterranean ports to Chaireddin, enabling him, as it
were, to throw a bridge from Africa to Europe and thus to hold
the Spanish-Italian coasts completely at his mercy.

The unscrupulous association of Francis, whose medieval ancestors had been the chief support of the crusading movement, with the hated infidels produced a vehement outcry from Christian public opinion throughout Europe. This must have caused Francis some embarrassment, for, while continuing as secretly as possible to profit politically by the Turk, he never wearied in his clamorous denial of any intimacy with him. The tortuous and distasteful hypocrisy of the French king is interesting because, far from proving an isolated instance, it became the rule in the dealings of one and all of the European powers with the Ottoman empire down to our own day.

The moral predicament of France and, later, of all Europe.

That Francis was fully resolved to squeeze the situation for every ounce it would yield is proved by the fact that he did not let the opportunity slip of turning his political association with the sultan to commercial account. A Franco-Ottoman agreement was signed in 1535, by virtue of which France was granted freedom of trade throughout the Ottoman empire, so-called consular jurisdiction, that is, immunity of French subjects from the operation of Ottoman laws, and, in the field of religion, the right of acting as the protector of Catholics on Ottoman soil as well as of the Christian Holy Places of Palestine. In general tenor, especially on the commercial side, these privileges were similar to those which it had been usual to grant to foreigners in the defunct Byzantine empire. They find, to cite an express instance, a close parallel in the rights enjoyed by such Italian cities as Venice and Genoa in the period when they controlled the eastern trade. The Ottoman empire, as the successor of the Byzantine empire, followed the same and, as the event proved, disastrous legal maxims in regulating its dealings with the foreigners within its gates. Historically considered the Capitulations of 1535 were therefore no innovation, except in so far as they put France in the position of assuming, both in matters of commerce and religion, the place of the most favored European nation. Not only was the decline of Venice, endowed with privileges distinctly inferior to those of France, accelerated from this date, but the other western peoples, like the Genoese, the English, and the proud Spaniards themselves, in order to trade with any advantage, or even in order to trade at all, were constrained to ask for the protection of the French

France acquires a privileged position in the Ottoman empire by the Capitulations of 1535.

flag.[1] Thus the alliance of Francis and Solyman inaugurated a period of French commercial ascendancy in the Mediterranean. Would it be followed by political ascendancy, as had been the case with Venice? That question only the future could answer.

In his difficult and burdensome naval struggle with Solyman Charles V naturally tried to win the Venetians to his side. Their reputation was above their power, but even their power, as expressed in merchantmen, war-vessels, and colonies, was by no means contemptible. On the other hand they had been heavily chastised in the two wars which they had already ventured to wage against the sultan, and with the pusillanimity characteristic of a people with declining fortunes, they had evolved the perilous maxim that it was advisable to maintain peace with the Ottomans at any cost. Therefore Charles V, sounding his most dulcet notes, long encountered only deaf ears among the merchants of the lagoons. Occasionally, to vary the monotony of his song, the pope joined him with a passionate diatribe against the infidels which, couched in the language of a religious age, now dead and buried, sounded curiously hollow in the period of the French-Spanish rivalry and of — Macchiavelli! However, in a sudden access of courage or perhaps only in a fatal moment of absent-mindedness, Venice fell away from her political maxims long enough to permit herself to become Charles's ally and to begin (1537) her third war against the Ottomans. Immediately Solyman unloaded his wrath on the Venetian colonies directly under his hand. From the first Venice got little and, by and by, no help from the Spaniards until, disillusioned, she determined to make peace by pocketing her losses (1540). These consisted in the surrender of her remaining positions in the Morea and of scattered islands in the Aegean sea. She signed the treaty of peace under French mediation, another clear sign pointing to the western power which was preparing to assume the mantle of Enrico Dandolo.

Looking backward over the reign of Solyman, we see him waging war in Persia, along the middle Danube, and in the Mediterranean, besides making his might felt in other less signifi-

Sidenote (left margin, paragraph 2): Venice, at the invitation of Spain, once more tries conclusions with the Ottomans and once more is defeated, 1537–40.

Sidenote (left margin, last paragraph): Credit and debit of the reign of Solyman.

---

[1] Of course this was irksome to the other peoples, and they tried to obtain the concession of trading under their own flag. The English acquired this right under Elizabeth; the others later or not at all.

cant directions. His influence was a world influence and made the Asiatic Shiites, as well as Germany, Italy, and Spain, tremble at the thought of him. But a conqueror, engaged all his days in building up an empire of conquest, he brought nothing to completion. The very last year of his life, when he was already seventy-one and undermined in health, he spent in a new effort to solve the unsolvable Hungarian problem, and characteristically enough he died in his tent (1566) during the siege of the town of Szigeth. To his successors he left the problem of the maintenance of an empire which had no natural boundaries, which was surrounded by powerful enemies, and which, in order to be administered successfully, required an executive of almost superhuman vigor and intelligence. Destiny thus far had undoubtedly smiled upon the projects of the Osmanli. But in its challenging way it had also piled up a situation which called for personal talents and a political ability to effect changes and adjustments such as most states, and particularly most military states, on being put to the test, have failed to exhibit. An intelligent European observer, reasoning, on the death of Solyman, about the future of the Ottoman empire, would have noted few signs from which he might have felt justified to conclude that its apex had been reached. Yet it was so, and, though at first imperceptibly, before long with multiplied evidence, gross and palpable, the decline set in.

CHAPTER XV

THE OTTOMAN INSTITUTIONS AND SOCIETY

The Ottoman spirit and institutions a confluence of many streams.

FOR some time we have been looking at the Ottoman empire from the outside, as it were, watching it rise slowly story after story, until it stood an impressive edifice, dominating the eastern Mediterranean and threatening to overshadow all Europe. We shall now undertake to scrutinize it more in detail to the end of defining its institutions and society and of getting into more intimate touch with its underlying spirit. It goes without saying that innumerable streams of influence helped shape the Ottoman state and people, some of them reaching far back to the Mongolian deserts of Asia, others recognizable as of Persian, Arab, Seljuk, and Byzantine origin and ascribable to the physical and mental contacts incorporated in Ottoman experience during the long upward struggle from obscurity to fame. Obliged to take the slow, formative processes more or less for granted, we shall content ourselves with sketching the broad prospect which Ottoman society presented to view in the days when the empire reached its apogee under Solyman the Magnificent.

The sultan as autocrat and preserver of the Sacred Law, the sheri.

The government of the Ottoman empire rested in the hands of the sultan as autocrat. Historically, he owed his absolutism to the fact that he was head of the army and that the army not only served as his tool of conquest but was utilized at the same time as his instrument of government. However, if a conqueror, the sultan was a Moslem conqueror and, like every other Moslem, owed obedience to the Moslem Sacred Law. The Sacred Law, called the *sheri,* had as its sources the Koran, certain sayings and decisions attributed to the Prophet Mohammed called *sunna's,* and a body of commentaries and interpretations emanating from the early califs; in other words, the Sacred Law was based on the Holy Book of the Mohammedans reënforced by a mass of venerable tradition. Since, theoretically, the sheri was a complete and finished system fully capable of holding together

226

the Moslem universe, the sultan was but an executive agent charged with the duty of taking measures to the end that the Sacred Law be upheld.

Plainly the implication of this theory was a fixed and changeless society under a divinely appointed administrator. In practice however, Ottoman society, though relatively static, was, like every other society founded by man, subject to change and encountered, as its conquests spread, new circumstances and conditions imperatively calling for new legislation. Accordingly, from time to time, the sultans were forced to issue laws of their own called *kanuns*, while especially active sultans, such as Mohammed II (the Conqueror) and Solyman the Magnificent, brought out systematic collections of kanuns in order to smooth out such legal relations as had become tangled and uncertain and to serve the convenience of judges and administrators. The kanuns, though regarded as inferior in authority to the sheri, constituted an important supplementary factor in the Ottoman legal system.

The mobility of Ottoman society secured by the kanuns.

Finally, as bringing a great but indeterminate weight to bear upon the Ottoman legal structure, ancient and unwritten custom must not be neglected. So important a matter as the succession to the throne may serve to illustrate the point. By force of custom the scepter had passed for generations from father to son until, in the fifteenth century, Mohammed II resolved to strengthen custom by the issuance of a kanun. But his much-cited kanun on the succession contained no innovation, for it declared in substance that the throne belonged to that one of the sons of the deceased sultan who succeeded in seizing it, and that the successful candidate was justified to execute his brothers in order to preserve the realm from civil war. In this way was the succession regulated by law after Mohammed's time, but it is certain that before Mohammed it devolved in much the same manner by force of a custom, reaching back no doubt to a remote desert stage of Osmanli evolution.

Custom as a basis of law illustrated by the Ottoman succession.

As with the expansion of the empire the sultan-autocrat could not possibly manage all the affairs of state, an elaborate administration had been gradually created around his person. Its chief official was the *grand vizier* who, with a number of councillors, usually three in number, called *viziers*, constituted a supreme advisory body. Since the word vizier means burden-bearer, it is

The government, called the Porte, concentrated at the sultan's palace, known as the serai.

clear that the function of the viziers was to lighten the weight of office for the harassed padishah. Other important officials were two *defterdars* or treasurers and two *kaziaskers* or supreme judges. A conference of the high dignitaries called to consider the affairs of state and army was called a *divan*. Since the divan served the convenience of the sultan it met within the precincts of the imperial palace, known as the *serai*. Of all the striking physical features of Stambul, as the Ottomans called their capital familiar to the rest of the world as Constantinople, none was so picturesque and charged with the specific atmosphere of the orient as the sultan's residence. Not so much a palace as a vast compound, the serai was surrounded by a wall three miles in circumference and included, grouped around four great courts, a bewildering number of offices, council-chambers, kitchens, storehouses, kiosks, pavilions, fountains, and gardens. To this town within a town, dedicated to the sultan's sacred majesty, there was admission by a single ornamental gate, the famous *Sublime Porte*, which as the public portal to the ruler's house gradually acquired the figurative significance of the Ottoman government. An immense population of officers of state, soldiers, grooms, gardeners, valets, pastry-cooks and other useless, if ornamental, menials crowded in gay eastern costumes appropriate to their rank the two outer courts and the many buildings which surrounded them; the third court, in which a more distinguished air prevailed, was reserved to the sultan and his sons, while the innermost court, the fourth, to the charmed secrets of which none but the sultan had admission, harbored the imperial harem with its numerous female population of wives, concubines, and servants, all under the watchful government of a debased company of eunuchs.

The system of administration.

The grand vizier and the other officials constituting the divan must be thought of, if their position is to be fully understood, not only as civil chiefs but also as heads of the army, for the army was the administration. This was particularly apparent in the provinces, which were divided into two main groups, one of Europe and the other of Asia. At the head of each stood a *beglerbeg* (beg of begs), whose duty it was to administer the army of his section and to assemble and lead it to war. The territory of the beglerbegs was divided into *sandjaks* commanded by *sandjakbegs*. Occasionally a number of sandjaks were thrown together into a larger unit under an official who might, in order to distinguish him from an ordinary beg, receive the designation *pasha*. Pasha was at first an honorific rather than an administrative title and, at least in the early period, was used sparingly, being conceded only to dignitaries of the highest station.

From all this it is clear that a student desirous of comprehending the Ottoman system must give particular attention to the army, for the army, let it be said again, was the government. With the army we already have some familiarity, for we have been obliged to take account of its two component elements, the feudal and the professional section. A third element, which, as relatively unimportant, we have neglected thus far, deserves at least passing notice. When a sultan took the field, he mobilized not only his professional and feudal troops but also invited the aid of volunteers who, usually responding in large numbers, were organized as an irregular infantry and cavalry, called respectively *azabs* and *akindjis*. As azabs and akindjis received no pay, they joined an expedition solely for the purpose of enriching themselves with plunder. Though possessed of some slight fighting value as scouts and advance guards, and though indubitably a pest worse than locusts to a country which they overran, they cannot be accounted a decisive factor in the Ottoman military machine. All has been said that is worth saying if it has been conveyed that they were a wholly barbarous as well as a relatively worthless implement of war.

The Ottoman army: the irregular troops.

The feudal army was closely associated with the Ottoman land system. We are aware that the sultans on the morrow of each new military success rewarded their followers with gifts of land carrying with them the obligation of military service. Large estates were called *ziamets*, smaller ones *timars*, and holders of timars and ziamets were obliged to take the field on horseback attended by a number of mounted soldiers proportionate to the size of the holding. The landlords, turned warriors, were called *spahis* and constituted a cavalry which rode to war under the command of the sandjakbegs, who in their turn fought under the orders of the beglerbegs respectively of Europe and of Asia. The total number of the spahis has been calculated at about 80,000. They were brave and even ardent warriors, but naturally lacked the

The feudal army of spahis.

Like the Pomyesta of Russia

training and coherence which characterized the regular troops. The analogy between them and the feudataries of a king of medieval Europe will strike every student of comparative institutions. However, a distinction favorable to the spahis was that, unlike their western brethren, they were not in perpetual revolt against their liege lord.

The standing army: (a) the Janissaries, (b) Spahis of the Porte.

The regular troops, regular in that they were a permanent body maintained at the sultan's expense, were divided into infantry and cavalry. With the infantry, the famous *Janissaries*, we are already familiar. In Solyman's time they numbered from twelve to fourteen thousand men and were at the height of their reputation. Of their fighting spirit, of the marvelous order which they kept in camp and on the march, of their instant response to the command of their superiors, contemporary European observers could not say enough. True, in great public crises, such as a succession, they were inclined to get out of hand and had to be placated with gifts of money, but, the occasion removed, they again returned to their posts without suffering any impairment of their military efficiency. In order to enable them to concentrate their whole energy on the service of the sultan, they were forbidden to marry and lived in barracks in a sort of monastic seclusion. Though the rule of celibacy was increasingly violated with the passing of time, as late as the seventeenth century the majority were still unwived. The regular cavalry, called *Spahis of the Porte* in distinction from the feudal spahis, numbered from ten to twelve thousand men. On going to war their ranks were greatly increased by the fact that each spahi was obliged to bring an average of four horsemen along with him. The whole standing army of infantry and cavalry, on war-footing, may thus have reached from sixty to seventy thousand men, a figure incomparably larger than that of any professional army of the West. If we add to it the feudal spahis, we get a field-force of almost one hundred and fifty thousand men. The irregulars — the azabs and akindjis — may have amounted to another fifty thousand. When Solyman went on a campaign, when, for instance, he invaded Hungary or marched against Vienna, he must have commanded an army of close to two hundred thousand effectives. This estimate is considerably lower than that of most contemporary western writers, but when we remember that armies of this size were unknown in sixteenth century Europe and that the Christians, unwilling to admit inferiority, were inclined to explain their repeated defeats on the score of numbers, we are prepared for a certain exaggeration in the statements which have come down to us.

The whole body of regular troops, Janissaries as well as Spahis of the Porte, was recruited either by capture or later, more often, by the somewhat less violent method of a levy upon the children of the Christian population. Captures were usually effected on the border by means of war or raids, while the levy was an inland measure resorted to in order to secure a steady and dependable supply of recruits. It is this organized seizure of Christian boys which has traditionally roused the indignation of western Europe against the Ottoman military system. Once every four years officials visited the Christian villages and selected a certain number of the most promising youths between the ages of fourteen and eighteen for the service of the padishah. It was Murad I who made this toll of boys one of the solemn obligations of his Christian subjects.[1] The inhumanity involved in violently severing family ties, which to the Caucasian mind are sacred, makes it impossible to condone the measure. It stands hopelessly condemned in occidental eyes. However, the issue of morality apart, the system, considered on its purely practical side, was not without alleviating features. In the first place the sultan saw to it that the Christian boys entering his service were treated kindly and given an introduction to Islam calculated to bring about their conversion to the ruling faith by gradual stages. At the same time they were entrusted to a school system dedicated to the praiseworthy program of developing the bodies of the pupils together with their minds. Those who impressed the instructors with their natural gifts were drafted into special institutions, the colleges of pages, of which there were three in Constantinople and vicinity with a total enrollment of twelve hundred students. In these three well-appointed institutions the training was on a relatively advanced level, being conducted with an eye to preparing the boys for the highest administrative offices of the realm. In short, the erstwhile Christians were treated like the spoiled children of fortune, were provided for

[1] See p. 185.

Special training of the tribute boys for the service of the army and the state.

physically and mentally at the sultan's expense, and were rewarded, according to the degree of merit they disclosed, with positions of dignity and power. From all this it must be clear that not only the whole regular army, both Janissaries and Spahis of the Porte, were made up of former Christian boys, but that from the ranks of these boys, become men, the sultan appointed all the important administrative officials of his realm beginning with the grand vizier.

The empire ruled by the sultan and his slave family.

From the moment the tribute boys were handed over to the sultan they became in legal status the sultan's slaves, and slaves they remained to the end of their days. But — another difficulty for the western student wrestling with a world so strange as to be almost fabulous — there was nothing dishonorable about the slave status. Under the sultan, their master, and with his consent, his slaves, constituting an immense family of tens of thousands of members, ruled the realm and shone in his reflected light. They sat in the seats of the mighty and were the observed of all observers. None-the-less all their vaunted glory hung by a thread. Should the sultan's favor be withdrawn from the slave whom he had exalted, there was nothing to hinder him from seizing the property he had bestowed and from taking the life which was legally at his mercy. These capricious rights and privileges did not, however, extend to the children of the slaves. Born into the Moslem faith, they were accounted free in accordance with a saying of the Koran which reserved slavery for the infidels. For this reason if a member of the Janissaries married and had children, as, in spite of the regulations, was not unusual, these children, having the status of free Moslems, were denied admission to the Janissary corps. Later, in the period of decline, the prohibition against the marriage of the Janissaries, as well as the ordinance against the admission of their children into the corps, became a dead letter, but we are here concerned with the reign of Solyman when these regulations were still generally observed. Our amazement at this uncanny system reaches a climax on discovering that in this empire of Moslems there was, with the exception of the sultan himself, hardly a born Moslem among the men entrusted with the affairs of government. The sword and the scepter were wielded by ex-Christians, who, though accounted slaves dependent for weal and woe on the sultan's nod, constituted a specially trained and highly favored ruling caste. Doubtless the system had many weaknesses, some of which we shall presently view. In the end it fell because of them. Yet the fact stands out and should be carefully noted that for several generations the sultan's slave family gave the Ottoman state a government, which in point of efficiency far surpassed anything familiar to contemporary Europe.

Since the Ottoman empire was a Moslem state, purporting to exist for the sole benefit of Moslems, what place was reserved for them, the free-born subjects of the sultan? Were they prepared meekly to submit to being systematically excluded from all the honors and emoluments of government? An apparently successful means of placating their discontent was found in the reservation to them as their particular domain of all the learned professions. Than this there was nothing more natural, since the service of the mosque, the school, and the law-court imperatively called for born and convinced Moslems. In this connection we must keep in mind that the Sacred Law, the sheri, was not only a revealed religion but constituted besides a theology, a code of morals, and a system of social and economic relations. The whole life of a Mohammedan, in its civil as well as in its religious aspects, was regulated by the Sacred Law. Complex and many-sided, it was therefore the common field of study for all who aspired to enter the profession.

The free-born Moslems monopolize the professions.

Under these circumstances it is clear that the educational system of the Mohammedans possesses a deep significance, and that, essentially religious, its subject-matter embraced the manifold materials of the Sacred Law. In principle and, usually, in practice a boys' school was attached to every mosque. A poor mosque might boast no more than a common school or *mekteb*, content to teach the children to mumble in Arabic, the sacred language, a few verses of the Holy Book, but every large and wealthy mosque aspired to the dignity of a *medresseh* or college, where a curriculum obtained much like the Seven Arts of the Middle Age with particular emphasis on the Koran and such studies as rhetoric, logic, and geometry. Mosques and schools alike were supported by the revenue from landed estates donated in perpetuity by the sultan and other pious Moslems. They

The educational system of the Moslems

constituted the Moslem religious property and, a sign that
Moslem religious zeal matched that of the Christian West in the
days of faith, were said to amount to one-third of the total lands
of the empire. This vast religious endowment, known as *vakuf*,
was of course inalienable. While the income served for the
physical upkeep of the mosques and schools, together with the
hospitals and soup-kitchens which clustered round them, it was
also used for the support of the administrators, that is, of those
who, under the broadest definition of the term, may be designated as the clergy. This numerous body fell into many groups,
among whom we may note the *imam*, or leader of daily prayers,
the *hodja* or teacher, and the *muezzin* who issued the call to
prayer from the lofty minaret; but neither individually nor as
a body did the clergy enjoy anything like the authority exercised by the clergy of the two great Christian churches of the
Latins and the Greeks. Without question this was due to the
relatively insignificant rôle reserved to the clergy by Mohammedan theory and practice. In spite of many features open to
criticism, Mohammedanism was after all a very spiritual faith,
which by means of prayer and contemplation sought to bring
the individual face to face with God, thereby dispensing with
the priest as mediator and leaving in his hands none but the
purely secondary function of leadership in public worship.

Judges and
jurists.

A more exacting course than that laid down for the common
clergy and the teachers in the lower schools awaited those who
desired to win distinction as judges and jurists. They were
obliged to attend one of a group of higher medressehs, which
were in effect law schools of university grade. When after years
of study students had succeeded in satisfying the severe requirements of the law schools, they could, according to their talents
and the measure of their learning, choose one of several callings.
They might become professors of law in their turn; if they had
a preference for public service, they might enter the Ottoman
judicial system in the capacity of *cadis* or judges and begin
the tedious ascent of the ladder of preferment; or, finally, they
might join the select and very distinguished class of jurists.
It is in harmony with the respect which this society felt for
the Sacred Law that it treated this last group, the jurists, with
peculiar veneration. Called *muftis*, they must not be considered

as attorneys or barristers in our sense. The usual practice was to attach them to the higher courts in an advisory function to the judge, though private individuals too were privileged to apply to them for an opinion. This, handed down in writing, was called a *fetva*, and was regarded with as much awe as an authentic sibylline leaf.

Naturally the mufti of Constantinople, whom the sultan himself consulted in grave matters of public interest, enjoyed a peculiar prestige and came to be looked upon as *the* mufti, head of all those charged with interpreting the law. Gradually, perhaps in order clearly to distinguish him from other lesser muftis, he came to be known under the title of *sheik ul-Islam.* Such was the veneration with which he was regarded, and such was his following among the people, that, although a mere appointee of the sultan, he could in many instances offer successful opposition to his lord and master. Contemporary western writers, not without a certain exaggeration, compared him with the pope. The figure in the eastern world bearing the closest resemblance to the pope was without doubt the sultan himself in his capacity of *calif.* Since Selim's day, it will be remembered, the sultans claimed that the mantle of the prophet had descended on their shoulders. However, the sultan's califate was largely theoretical, while the sheik ul-Islam, as practiced in the law, was prepared to say authoritatively what the law permitted and what it forbade.

The whole body of learned men, graduates of the colleges and occupied with reading prayers, teaching school, judging their fellows, and interpreting the law, formed a clearly defined class within the body of Ottoman society. They constituted the *ulema,* a word meaning learned men, and they acknowledged as their head the leading jurist of the realm, the sheik ul-Islam. In a country where the religious and the civil law were one and the same, the influence of such a body as the ulema, made extraordinarily compact by a common philosophy of life and an identical training, was bound to be tremendous. Moreover, that influence was certain to be exercised in a conservative direction, to be stiffly set against change. Since in the Koran the Mohammedan world possessed an absolute criterion of truth, which it was blasphemy to challenge, the function of the ulema had necessarily to be the inculcation of the statements of Holy Writ and the condemnation of every

The sheik ul-Islam.

The ulema: its enormous prestige together with the strength and weakness of its position.

innovation, however slight, as a whisper emanating from Satan. On the other hand, the ulema's ethical purpose was to hold the Moslem world to those standards and ideals, without which it must have collapsed in very short order. Most of what in the story of the Ottomans appeals to us, who admittedly dwell in a different moral and spiritual world, as having a certain quality of distinction and nobility, may be traced to the learned class and to that unalterable Sacred Law of theirs which they undertook in the spirit of humility to study, interpret, and uphold. None-the-less it is plain that if ever a new day should dawn and a truth be proclaimed at variance with the Koran and irreconcilable with it, the conservatism of the ulema would prove a serious peril to the state. For, in that case, an unchanging society, persisting in its traditional course and rendered obtuse by its enslavement to ancient custom, would find itself confronted with neighbor-groups vitalized with new thought and courageous experiment and armed in consequence with irresistible power. Though in the days of Solyman a development of this revolutionary kind did not seem to threaten from any quarter, it is clear that if it ever befell, it would prove disastrous to the Moslem world dominated by an intellectual group which confidently taught that there was nothing worth learning except what was already known.

The two leading institutions, the slave family and the ulema, in inevitable rivalry.

To summarize, we have been engaged in sketching two institutions: (1) the sultan's slave family, which was utilized by him as an army and an administration, and (2) the ulema, which in various professional capacities occupied itself with the Sacred Law. One of the leading Ottoman scholars has called them respectively the Ruling Institution and the Moslem Institution. They might also, with rough justice, be called the state and the church. The names we may invent for them is of course of small concern, but the substance of the two master-institutions must decidedly be grasped if the Ottoman empire is to assume an intelligible character. Between them they embraced very nearly everything of institutional importance in Ottoman public life. And observe that, while in some respects they very impressively supplemented each other, they were also in inevitable rivalry over the question to which of the two belonged the superior influence in the state. In the time of Solyman, as well as during the reigns of his predecessors as far back as the founder of the line, the Ruling Institution was undoubtedly of greater importance owing to the almost uninterrupted warfare in which the Ottomans were engaged. As long as the spirit of conquest held undisputed sway, the sword and the scepter were sure to count for more than the Sacred Law. But when, shortly after the demise of Solyman, the Ottoman decline set in, the situation was gradually reversed, for the decline undermined the authority of the slave family, entrusted with the government, while the ulema with its unimpaired prestige waxed ever larger until it fairly overshadowed the army.

The most important private institution of any society is the family, and Ottoman society is no exception to the rule. The Ottoman family is so different from ours and plays so important a part in the life of the East that we are obliged to scan it closely. Its outstanding feature is the seclusion of women. We can be in no doubt that this practice has the effect of impairing the development of Moslem women and of making them inferior, as human beings, to the Moslem men. The main instrument of seclusion is the *harem* (more properly *haremlik*), the name applied to the section of the Moslem house reserved to its female inmates. Within the harem the woman, wife of the master, is closely confined, together with her servants and children. Her daughters the wife retains with her in the harem until they marry, but her sons she keeps only until they reach the age of ten to twelve, when they abandon the mother's quarter and pass under the care of the father in the wing of the dwelling, called *selamlik*, reserved to him. In eastern eyes the harem is a sacred precinct and may not be entered by any man except the lord of the house. When the wife leaves the harem, as she is permitted to do on stated occasions, she makes herself as nearly as possible unrecognizable by concealing her face under a veil called *yashmak* and by swathing her figure in a black circular mantle (*feridje*), shrewdly calculated to obliterate every trace of feminine charm by giving the wearer the appearance of a repulsive giant beetle, playfully walking upright. While the legal status of the Moslem woman is not without a measure of dignity, for she can inherit property and retains a claim to her dowry in the event of divorce, it is unquestionable that her mental and moral status is distressingly low. This could not be otherwise since she is

The Ottoman family: the harem.

treated all her days like a child, nay, like a prisoner, and, as a result of her limited experience, exhibits perforce a starved mind and a dwarfed soul. Lamentable as this is for her own sake, it is even more regrettable from the point of view of the family served by a wife and mother incapable of exercising the authority to which she must none-the-less lay claim.

The harem co-exists with slavery. The harem is closely intertwined with the institution of slavery, which has existed immemorially in the East. The menials of the Ottoman house have usually been slaves and very frequently the wife herself comes into the household by the easy, though somewhat dark and devious, avenue of slavery. True, the institution of slavery has many alleviations among the Ottomans, since slaves are treated kindly and manumission is both easy and common; but the fact that men are willing to choose their wives among bondwomen offered for sale in the slave market, on the despicable ground that they will prove submissive, is further proof of the low esteem in which marriage is held and of the injury suffered by every member of the family group through the degradation of its natural head, the wife and mother, whom all the noble peoples of history have without exception held in special honor.

Polygamy. While the harem, associated with and supported by domestic slavery, sufficiently defines the quality of the Ottoman family, there remains for consideration a final family feature, polygamy. This, as particularly revolting in our eyes, has not only received undue attention from western writers but has often been positively misrepresented. The average occidental thinks of the Ottoman home as crowded with dark, almond-eyed houris, alluring priestesses of forbidden pleasures, and with such sensuous pictures in his mind he concludes that polygamy is the universal and hateful basis of the oriental family. The actual fact is that polygamy is rare and that perhaps as high as ninety per cent of the Ottoman families are at the very least, to put it mildly in view of the sexual gregariousness of western men, as severely monogamous as our own. On the other hand, polygamy is a permissible practice expressly sanctioned by the Koran. There exists therefore no moral sentiment against it and its practice is a matter that each man is free to decide for himself. However, the vast majority of heads of families for reasons first, of economy, and second, of family peace, reasons quite as imperative in the East as in the West, prefer to stake their matrimonial fortunes on the possession of a single spouse. Polygamy is the rule among the great dignitaries and, whenever adopted, no doubt still further enfeebles the family already none too strong. But the abolition of polygamy alone would not prove much of a benefit, since it is not the sporadically practiced polygamy, but the universal system of the harem with its hard sentence on women of perpetual minority, that depresses the moral and mental atmosphere of the Ottoman home far below the western level.

The institutions which we have been engaged in describing belonged to the Ottomans or, in common parlance, to the Turks, who, so far as the Balkan peninsula was concerned, made up no more than a thin upper crust of the population. We are aware that the Moslem conquest did not displace the Christian peoples, Greeks, Serbs, Rumans, and Albanians, who in the course of the ages had settled and made their homes there. On being defeated in the field they were given the option of joining the ruling group by a voluntary surrender of their faith. This, except in sporadic instances, they refused to do with the result that they were treated as subject and inferior peoples under the name of rayahs. A rayah was therefore a non-Moslem, usually either a Christian or a Jew. Men of these conquered faiths, who became subjects of the sultan, were granted religious toleration together with security of person and property. Their inferiority, their rayah status, expressed itself in a series of disabilities of which the most important were the following: (1) they were not allowed to carry or possess arms; (2) they were more heavily taxed than the Moslems, particularly by means of a head-tax from which the Moslems were exempt; (3) they were subjected to the cruel periodic tribute of children in order to replenish the sultan's slave family.

The status of the Christians, called rayahs.

In the light of these oppressive burdens the rights enjoyed by the rayahs in the way of religious toleration and security of life and property seem insignificant. However, they sufficed for self-perpetuation and by the addition of a measure of self-government even enabled the Christians to maintain a certain social coherence. The grant to the vanquished of self-government was due to the circumstance that the Ottomans, as Moslems, had

The rayahs enjoy certain advantages of self-government.

a personal and not a territorial conception of law. Let us again remind ourselves that the Sacred Law laid down for the individual Mohammedan exact rules for all the concerns of life, and that it constituted both a civil and a religious code. Wherever the Moslem went this code went with him, regulating his existence to the last detail. Naturally, therefore, the Moslem looked upon the Christians and the Jews as people living by their own sacred law, which, though false, hateful, and accursed, was none-the-less the only law they knew. Since the sultans had not insisted on conversion and even went so far as officially to proclaim religious toleration, they were logically forced, in agreement with their view of the personality of law, to suffer the alien communities under their scepter to live according to their own code. Mohammed the Conqueror on taking Constantinople had set an example 'in this matter which is typical. He himself invited the Christian clergy of the capital to elect a new patriarch, whom he expressly acknowledged as head of the whole body of the orthodox within the empire. The internal affairs of the Christians were put in the hands of the patriarch and his clergy in close analogy to the power over Moslems conceded to the Moslem Institution. Not only was the Christian clergy given a free hand in the control of the church and its revenues, but it was also authorized to exercise jurisdiction over Christians in such civil cases as touched Christians alone. Only in the case of litigation between Christians and Moslems were the Christians amenable to Moslem courts. In view of these extensive privileges the orthodox Christians must be looked on as constituting, within certain limits, a self-governing unit of the Ottoman fold. And the same may be said of the Jews, who because they lived by their own Hebrew law, were organized as a separate community amenable to the Moslem courts only in case of conflict with a Moslem fellow-citizen.

The social and economic condition of the Christians. As to the general social and economic condition of the rayahs under this system, so strange to us with our territorial conception of law, very insufficient data have come down to us for the time of the Magnificent Solyman. Since there was frequent war coupled with an occasional outburst of fanaticism, it may be safely assumed that there were numerous instances of the oppression and murder of those who ventured to defy the conquerors.

But the record of the greatest of the sultans is probably no worse in the matter of religious persecution than that of his Christian contemporaries of the West, of sovereigns like Charles V, Francis I, and Henry VIII. Everything considered, Solyman must be accorded a high place as a ruler devoted to justice for Moslem and Christian alike and desirous of extending to his subjects of whatever faith or race that measure of security without which life is not worth living. Apart from the ever-present sense of subjection to an alien people, which must have spread an unbroken pall of darkness over their lives, the Christians lived much as they had always done, for they courted, married, worshiped, and went stolidly about their affairs in field and shop. In so far as the strong Ottoman empire put an end to Balkan strife and established a more perfect public peace than had been known in centuries, the conquest must even have produced a material improvement as compared with the last phase of the Byzantine state. Apparently, too, the early sultans succeeded in clearing the provinces of robbers and in maintaining a more efficient system of communications. It is not improbable that the peninsula, taken as a whole, experienced a slight economic revival; but to conclude that this even remotely compensated the Christians for the loss of their liberty would be rash and unwarranted indeed.

Our final judgment on the Ottoman system in its sixteenth century form must be that, in the light of the victories which it consistently won over its enemies and of the relatively high degree of order which it maintained at home, it cannot be refused a modicum of sincere, if cold, respect. Certainly it constitutes an important link in the long chain of eastern imperial experiments. But if it represents the latest phase of the age-old effort, successively made by Egyptians, Greeks, Romans, and Arabs, to bring under a common government the east-Mediterranean lands which by the verdict of nature would seem to constitute an indivisible whole, it signifies more particularly for us students of Balkania an attempted cure of the distressing peninsular divisions by the method of armed force. But even if, persuaded by the general desirability of peace in human affairs, we should regard the sultan's militarist régime with a certain leniency, we shall still find ourselves assailed by doubts as to its feasibility

Credit and debit of the Ottoman system with its essential basis of military force.

and permanence by reason of its purely coercive character. The extraordinarily troubled life of the states which in the preceding centuries the Byzantines, Bulgars, and Serbs had set up on exactly the same sort of a foundation cannot but serve to confirm our scepticism. In establishing itself in Balkania the Ottoman empire took as little thought of the people and of the political and moral value of their consent as the most recklessly despotic government of which history preserves the record. That circumstance alone suffices to deprive it of the sympathy of all men who regard the growth of human liberty as the central theme of history.

Small likelihood of the Ottomans solving the age-old Balkan problem.

However, as between Balkania, on the one hand, and the Asiatic and African provinces, on the other, there is a difference to be noted in the attitude adopted by them toward the central government. While all alike had been taken with the sword, the subject-regions of Asia and Africa were in overwhelming preponderance inhabited by Mohammedans and might, in the long run, find it convenient to make their peace with a Mohammedan overlord. Balkania, however, a wholly Christian area, could not under any conceivable circumstances ever look upon the sultan as other than an alien tyrant. From the outset therefore there was as good as no prospect that the Ottoman conquest would solve the secular feuds of the peninsula. Moreover the sultans, even the most intelligent of their number, never showed the slightest comprehension of the factors involved in a political unity worthy of the name. Solyman, for instance, considered that the demands of unity were satisfied if he maintained peace, security, and open roads for trade by means of an irresistible army. A union of a voluntary type, eliciting the spontaneous mental, moral, and cultural coöperation of all the inhabitants of the peninsula, conceived as free human agents, never as much as entered his mind. Furthermore, the Ottoman system of separate religious communities, each living under its own law as in a hermetically sealed compartment, was as if purposely devised for the perpetuation of the historical divisions of the peninsula. Add that the Moslem invaders were a numerically inferior element in Balkania, that they possessed the arrogant mentality of conquerors with complete faith in the sword which they never sheathed, and it will be granted that the Ottoman rule, by every test known to history, must be pronounced precarious. Doubtless it might survive for many generations, owing to the effectiveness of its organization and to the factional divisions of the conquered; but, lacking the consent of the conquered and failing from shortsightedness or immobility to evolve a policy of domestic fusion, it was bound before long to present the appearance of a tree which, though still impressive to the eye, has been effectively hollowed out within by an insidious dry-rot.

CHAPTER XVI

THE BEGINNING OF OTTOMAN DECAY

Selim the Sot, 1566–74. THE brilliant Solyman was followed by a son who failed to inherit a single one of his father's merits. Selim II (1566–74) was incapable, indolent, pleasure-loving, and as foreign to the field and council-chamber as he was at home in the soft atmosphere of the imperial harem. Because he was addicted to the use of wine, forbidden to Moslems by their Sacred Law, he won from his disgusted subjects the title of the Sot or Drunkard. It was his good fortune to take over from his father a body of trained administrators, among whom the grand vizier, Mohammed Sokolli, a statesman of rare vision, was the outstanding figure, and owing to this circumstance the ship of state continued for a time to sail proudly on its course with its acquired momentum.

Selim makes war on Venice and captures Cyprus, 1571. The war in Hungary, in the course of which Solyman had met his death, Selim, averse to the exertions of a distant campaign, brought to an abrupt close. Gradually he rivetted, as if hypnotized, his attention on the island of Cyprus, which, together with the slightly smaller island of Crete, represented all that was left to declining Venice of her possessions in the eastern Mediterranean. From the standpoint of the empire-builder it would be possible to defend a policy looking forward to the capture of these two strongholds by the Ottomans. Cyprus, more particularly, lay in the very center of the Ottoman political sphere. In so low a personal regard, however, was Selim held that, instead of being credited with a statesman-like project, the rumor went the rounds in the capital that his real reason for the descent on Cyprus was his hankering after the sweet wine for which the island was famous. When the Venetians indignantly refused to hand over their possession on demand, an expedition was prepared, which in 1570 forced a landing and in the next year obliged Famagusta, the great Venetian fortress on the island, to surrender.

The moving appeal for help which the doge and signiory made to the Christian world, did not on this occasion, as on so many others, pass unheard. The pope, bethinking himself of his medieval role of Christian champion, took up the Venetian cause with such energy that he succeeded in creating a Holy Alliance pledged to resist with united strength the further extension of Turkish power in the Mediterranean. The leading members were the pope himself, Venice, and Spain. An immense fleet, under the supreme command of Don John of Austria, half-brother of King Philip II of Spain, was assembled, but with the usual Christian dilatoriness, too late to hinder the capture of Cyprus and the slaughter under revolting circumstances of the heroic garrison of Famagusta. Scouring the western waters of Greece with two hundred galleys, Don John at length came upon the Ottoman fleet of even greater size near the entrance to the gulf of Lepanto. On October 7, 1571, the two armadas engaged in a battle on a scale such as the Mediterranean had not witnessed since the time of the Romans. And not since Octavius defeated Antony near the same spot was a greater victory won than that gained by the Christians on that day. Except for some forty vessels, which made a bold dash for safety, the whole Turk fleet was either captured or destroyed. Immense was the rejoicing throughout Christendom. Bells were rung, masses chanted, and sanguine men meeting on the streets of Mediterranean towns spoke confidently of the passing of the Turk and of the impending capture of Constantinople. But instead of hoisting sail for the Dardanelles the prudent Don John put back to Italy to refit, for his fleet, though victorious, had suffered heavily in the fight; and before many moons had come and gone, the disillusioned Christians knew that all the good that would ever come to them from their glorious victory was the elation due to the knowledge that the Ottomans were not invincible.

Only in case Lepanto had been followed by victorious blow on blow could the Ottoman empire have received permanent damage from the lost battle. But for so united and persistent an offensive the mismated Christian allies were not ready. On the very morrow of their victory they fell to such bitter quarreling over the rich Ottoman booty that the commander of the papal contingent reported home that only by a miracle were they

The Holy Alliance of the pope, Spain, and Venice followed by the battle of Lepanto, 1571.

Christian division versus Ottoman unity.

hindered from leaping at each others' throats. The common enthusiasm which had carried the Christians into battle did not survive the victory. How different was the picture presented by the Moslem enemy! Defeat but prodded the government of the sultan to redouble its energy. By special financial measures it secured the means to extend the shipyards at Constantinople and succeeded, in the course of a single winter, in completing one hundred and sixty new vessels. These, joined to the forty saved from the wreck at Lepanto and supplemented by forty more picked up at scattered points, actually regained for the Ottomans complete naval superiority in the Mediterranean. In the year 1572, the outnumbered Christians carefully avoided battle, and when the mutual recriminations of the allies, becoming more exacerbated every day, put an end to all united counsel, the Venetians, despairing of a successful issue, sued for peace. Signed at Constantinople in 1573, it not only confirmed the sultan in the possession of the coveted Cyprus but also ignominiously saddled Venice with the expense of the island's capture, a sum of three hundred thousand ducats.

The "passive" sultans and the growing domination of the serai.

In the light of this outcome of the Cyprian war the oft-repeated statement that the Ottoman decline dates from Lepanto fails to carry conviction. Not Lepanto so much as Selim the Drunkard and the régime which he inaugurated effected the gradual disorganization which makes his reign a turning-point. He was the heir of ten Ottoman rulers, all, with the single exception of Bayezid II, extraordinarily vigorous as generals and administrators; many of them, besides, had been kindly and humane; a few had been devoted to poetry and philosophy. It is doubtful if any dynasty known to history can boast so unbroken a succession of capable representatives. They and they alone were the architects of the empire, beside whom no grand vizier or pasha or mufti deserves mention. With Selim II came a dramatic break, for with him begin the slothful or "passive" sultans, as they have been called, who, to the number of twenty-five, spin themselves out to the present day, a pitiable roster of degenerates staging a hideous travesty of government. Of course an occasional sovereign shook off or attempted to shake off the fatal lethargy holding him in thrall; in the main they convey the impression of being afflicted with an incurable paralysis. They cease appearing in the field with their troops, they give up attending to the affairs of state, they disappear from public view buried in the luxurious depths of their great palace compound, the serai. Historians have offered various explanations for this change in the virile house of Osman from action to indolence, from courage and enterprise to the basest inertia. We shall not be going far wrong if we ascribe it substantially to the complex of evils growing out of the sultan's residence. This vast enclosure dedicated to intrigue, luxury, and soft indulgence of the senses was bound to undermine the manhood of its occupants. Held by its sensuous spell, the sultans ceased to give attention to the affairs of the realm and, as a consequence, the autocratic state lost its directive will.

If the grand vizier, entrusted with the administration under the sultan, had been invariably endowed with character and ability, the injury done by the sultan's failing initiative might not have proved fatal. We shall hear of an occasional grand vizier who rendered invaluable services in restoring and leading the state. But usually the grand vizier, as well as the other high officials at Constantinople and in the provinces, owed their appointment to harem influences and, elevated through bribery and dark intrigue, they were dismissed the moment influences adverse to them gained the sultan's ear. Nominally, at least, important decisions were still taken by the sovereign, only they no longer emanated from the divan after a thorough discussion with the assembled ministers of state, but were reached behind the silken curtains of the inner serai amidst a conflict of opinions as capricious as they were baleful for the public weal.

> The grand vizier and ministers appointed and removed by invisible harem influences.

In line with this usurpation of power by the imperial harem, composed of a debased crew of illiterate women and eunuchs, was the damage done by the sale of offices. This practice was a gradual growth, having been in evidence as early as the reign of Solyman the Magnificent. It remained for his successors to exact a price for every important post in the administration and the army. Before long the evil infected the judicature and the clergy. That meant that the practice, after undermining the central government, that is, the region reserved to the sultan's slave family, contaminated also the free-born and learned membership of the ulema. But if all these officals — viziers, pashas,

> The sale of offices followed by oppressive taxation and economic decline.

judges, and muftis — were obliged to buy their posts, they were under the necessity, and indeed were expected, to reimburse themselves by every means within their grasp. They therefore sold the offices dependent on themselves to other men, who followed the same plan, and so on down the line to the lowest employee in the service of the state. In final analysis the cost of these boundless irregularities had to be met by the common people, both Moslem and Christian, though the latter, as subjects of an inferior rank, were of course conceded a polite preference in the matter of oppression. As taxes of every kind, which among the early sultans had their origin in custom and were not excessive, arbitrarily multiplied, loud complaints arose on all sides which rarely if ever met with redress. The upshot was desertion of farmsteads, decreased production, beggary, and depopulation. By the year 1600, at the latest, an economic decline had begun in succession to the economic rehabilitation which had attended the Ottoman conquest and which to have achieved constitutes perhaps the most impressive apology of the Ottoman empire before the bar of history. By gradual stages the country took on the same desolate appearance as under the last Byzantine emperors, and for much the same reason of a corrupt administration unscrupulously squeezing the last penny from the people.

Increased numbers and changed constitution of the Janissaries.   The army was not slow to show the effect of this universal decay. By the simple device of failing to appear when summoned to war, the spahis brought about a gradual shrinkage of the feudal army. On the other hand, the Janissaries and Spahis of the Porte experienced a marked increase. If the Janissaries had numbered twelve thousand under Solyman, they waxed close to fifty thousand by the middle of the seventeenth century, with every prospect of a continued increase. And the enlarged troop failed signally to maintain the discipline and ardor which had made the old Janissaries the most feared foot-soldiers in Europe. For with the growth in numbers went certain inner changes which practically revolutionized the body. For one thing, the rule of celibacy was more and more frequently relaxed with the result that Janissary fathers, anxious to provide for their offspring, discovered means of getting their sons adopted into the ranks once obstinately closed to them. As soon as some Moslems were admitted, there was no reason for excluding any, especially if they came with cash in hand, with backsheesh, the universal lubricant of the Ottoman machine in the days of decline. By the time the Janissaries numbered fifty thousand it is not likely that more than a small percentage were ex-Christians. It is a notable fact that around the year 1640, the levy of Christian boys began to be abandoned and not, as has been suggested by some writers, from reasons of humanity. It fell into desuetude in consequence of the steadily mounting clamor of the sultan's Mohammedan subjects to be admitted to the benefits of the favored corps. Apparently the clamorers, described by a Mohammedan writer as a riff-raff of muleteers, camel-drivers, pastry-cooks, and brigands, saw no reason why all the soft berths in the army should be reserved to the sons of the despised rayahs. Of course when the wastage of war thinned the Janissary ranks faster than they could be conveniently filled by Moslem volunteers, the government might still have recourse to its ancient privilege of drawing on the supply of Christian boys. But these occasions became less and less frequent until, in 1676, the last levy was made of which there is record.

Thus, in the light of their original constitution, the Janissaries in the course of the seventeenth century became Janissaries only in name. They had earned their reputation as a small, compact body recruited from the Christian population and professionally trained for war in the honorable station of slaves of the padishah. Shortly after 1600 they began to be composed liberally, and toward 1650 overwhelmingly, of Mohammedan elements who were the off-scourings of the population, received but a mediocre training, and failed to uphold the reputation of the Ottoman arms. Only in one respect, in the tradition of lawlessness, did they improve on the ancient model. Conscious of their power, the old Janissaries had often taken the bit between their teeth, especially on the occasion of the succession of a new sultan, whom they obliged to pay for their support with a liberal donative out of the imperial treasury. The new, the corrupted Janissaries went farther: they made riot their pastime and on the pretext that their pay was in arrears, or on no pretext at all, plundered the shops of the citizens. At not infrequent intervals they rose in rebellion against the government, murdered a distasteful grand vizier, and even deposed the sultan. It was

The Janissaries, as lawless Praetorians, hold the government and population at their mercy.

the irony of fate that, in measure as they became less terrible to the enemy, they became more terrible to the master who employed them, and who long before the seventeenth century came to a close directed passionate prayers to Allah to rid him of the blessing turned a curse.

The changed succession as a cause of Ottoman decline.

A change in the law of succession undoubtedly deserves a place among the causes which produced the ruin of the empire. Hitherto, as we have seen, the scepter had devolved from father to son, though not according to the rule of primogeniture. In 1617, on the death of Sultan Ahmed I, the divan, unwilling to see his son, a mere child, succeed to the throne, deliberately changed the succession by passing an ordinance to the effect that, on the demise of the sultan, his oldest living male relative should ascend the throne. In the nature of things this was more often a younger brother or a nephew than a son. Although the scramble among brothers, due to break out the moment their imperial father closed his eyes, now ceased, the sleepless suspicion, which constituted the very atmosphere the sultan breathed, created a peculiarly strained and difficult situation. Not daring to leave his younger brother, who was the heir apparent, or for that matter any of his male relatives out of sight, the sovereign retained them in the serai in carefully guarded kiosks, which were no better than gilded cages. Under rigorous surveillance from their birth, meagerly instructed during youth, and systematically excluded at all times from contact with men and affairs, the Ottoman princes became a wretched breed, stunted in mind and body. When such a prince was at last drawn from his seclusion to be set upon the throne, he was almost certain to prove incapable of bearing the heavy burden of autocratic rule. In point of fact he was usually either a voluptuary or an imbecile or both at once. Everything considered, though the old succession arouses a just indignation because it imposed fratricide as a public duty, it was, from the point of view of the good of the state, decidedly preferable to the ordinance of 1617, which has governed the succession for the last three hundred years, and which by further weakening the already weakened fiber of the princes royal has effectively contributed to the ruin of the house of Osman.

Directing our attention, on again resuming our narrative, to the events of the seventy-five years lying between the death of Selim the Sot (1574) and the middle of the seventeenth century, we are at once struck by the fact that the forward movement, consistently maintained since the days of the founder of the Ottoman state, has either slowed down or ceased entirely. Of course the friction with neighbor-states continued as before to be most grave at the fluctuating boundaries in the east and west. In the west the raids along the Austro-Hungarian frontier, which, begun by the Turks, were paid back in kind by the indignant Austrians and Hungarians, meant perpetual border warfare. Only once, however, during the period under consideration did open war follow from this eternal bickering. Its termination in 1606 by the peace of Sitvatorok, which liberated Austria from the obligation of paying tribute for the western or Hapsburg section of Hungary, may be accepted as a clear indication of the decline of Ottoman might, since the sultans of the early days would not have dreamt of dropping their pretensions to the whole of Hungary. In the east, where Persia was the heredi tary foeman of the Turk, the situation was peculiarly troubled and precarious. Never for any considerable span of time did the mountain areas of the Caucasus and the sun-scorched plain of Mesopotamia cease to be in dispute between the two Moslem powers. The decisive factor in the situation was the countless local lords, who changed sides at pleasure and cunningly played off one would-be master against the other. Doubtless the Persians scored occasional gains, but in the end they were always defeated as the result of campaigns which furnished ample proof that the Ottoman military system was a hardy plant, very difficult to uproot.

Of that war only which represents the apex of the struggle in the eastern area need we take note in this summary account. To no small degree does it owe its interest to the circumstance that it was waged by a sultan who is an historic curiosity in asmuch as he marks a reversion to the "active" sultans of an older time. Murad IV (1623–40), who came to the throne as a minor, boasted a temper as fierce and warlike as that of any of his conquering forbears. To the surprise of all he demon strated that a sultan could burst the silken bonds of the harem

The border struggles continue in the east and west during the period of decline following Selim the Drunkard.

Persia + Turkey continued at each other threat.

Murad IV (1623–40) resumes the tradition of conquest in the East and become a leader in the field and council-chamber. After signally defeating the Persians he dictated a very favorable boundary settlement and shortly after, at the zenith of his reputation, died at the early age of twenty-eight. His reign was a nine days' wonder which changed nothing in the decaying Ottoman state. Its chief interest for the reflective student lies in its bringing out the importance in the Ottoman system of a strong, a warrior sultan.

Changes in the European situation: the decline of Spain.

Since the decay of the Ottoman might could not and did not escape the Christian powers of Europe, the question arises why they did not make the most of it and in their turn assume the offensive. A rapid political survey will explain the European inaction. In the time of Solyman the Magnificent the Christian powers constituting the first line of defense against the Mohammedan onset had been, as we have seen, Venice, Austria, and Spain. With the death of Philip II in 1598, Spain entered upon a decline so swift that before long the country dropped completely out of the class of the great powers. Thenceforth the Moslem bucaneers held undisputed sway over the western Mediterranean until the maritime successors of Spain, France and England, began a series of descents upon the Barbary coast for the protection of their growing commercial interests. When the two pirate states, Tunis and Algiers, discovered that the Ottoman empire had become too weak to give them help, they practically terminated their connection with Constantinople. For France and England this had the decided advantage that they could punish the African corsairs without precipitating a war with the sultan, with whom neither power was as yet willing to lock horns. Though the Barbary pirates long remained a terrible pest, in fact down to the early nineteenth century, plainly France and England were, by the middle of the seventeenth century, beginning to assert their control of the Mediterranean sea; and about the same time the once feared and respected flag of Spain as good as disappeared from these inland waters.

Decline of Venice and the precarious situation of Austria.

Hardly less decadent than the Iberian monarchy was Venice, the low ebb of which is indicated by its willingness to swallow every insult rather than face another Ottoman war. That left on the firing-line maintained against the Ottoman empire only Austria, which, if showing more vigor than Spain and Venice, was seriously paralyzed by the domestic troubles due largely to the cantankerous Catholic-Protestant rivalries of the seventeenth century. These culminated at last in the vast struggle familiar to all as the Thirty Years' War (1618–1648), in which Austria and the house of Hapsburg were so badly worsted that, when the peace of Westphalia was signed, dynasty and country looked like broken reeds. If a Solyman had ruled at Constantinople, he would hardly have let pass this wonderful opportunity to renew the attack upon Vienna. But the contemporary Ottoman state, by reason of being quite as seriously disorganized as Austria, failed to reassume the offensive and Austria was given the breathing-space she needed. However, her recovery had no more than started when the Ottoman empire experienced a surprising and far-reaching movement of reform, which inaugurated a new epoch in its history.

The new epoch dates from a little past the middle of the seventeenth century and is associated with a family of grand viziers bearing the name of Kiuprili. The substance of the Kiuprili achievement was to effect a revival of the Ottoman military power considerable enough to enable the Turks to make another and, as it proved, their last assault on Europe. The story of this flashing episode begins with the year 1656, when a certain Mohammed Kiuprili was, at the advanced age of seventy, appointed to be grand vizier. A Moslem by birth, though of Albanian descent, he had in the fabulous manner recalling the Arabian Nights climbed from the service of the imperial kitchen all the way to the topmost rung of the official ladder. Since the sultan's slave family was by this time rapidly breaking up, the army and administration were gradually being taken over by born Mohammedans. Many of these were, like Mohammed Kiuprili, more or less remotely of Christian descent. But born free, though of renegade ancestry, they serve to inform us that the system of tribute boys, which had been so important a factor in the upbuilding of the state, was passing away.

The Kiuprili grand viziers inaugurate a reform of the Ottoman state.

The significant trait of Mohammed Kiuprili was a clean heart and an upright spirit maintained amidst surroundings of the most flagrant corruption. Appointed grand vizier during the minority of the boy-sultan, Mohammed IV, he set himself the Herculean task of cleaning the Augean stables of the government.

Mohammed Kiuprili cures corruption by terror.

As he was endowed with an energy which shrank from no severity, he chose terror to achieve his end. Janissaries who abandoned the field to the enemy or who threatened mutiny at home, brigands who infested the highways, officials of high and low estate guilty of taking bribes were seized and executed without ado. If the report that fifty thousand malefactors met death during the five years (1656–61) that Kiuprili purged the state is an exaggeration, the fact remains that this inflexible old man employed an iron besom in his house-cleaning operations at Constantinople. Of course there was a limit to what could be accomplished by wholesale execution. It could not restore the caliber of the house of Osman nor create securities against the recrudescence of the fatal harem influences. Moreover, no amount of terror could revive the slave family of specialized and efficient servants of the state. But all that one lone man could do the grand vizier put through, for he made men understand that the government was not a feeding-trough for the idle and corrupt and that every functionary must do his duty in his appointed place.

The grand vizier resumes the policy of war.

Instinctively, too, Mohammed Kiuprili understood the peculiar genius of the Ottoman empire. It was not a state dedicated to trade and pursuing ideals of peace and plenty, but a military enterprise concerned primarily with conquest and secondarily, as a justification of conquest, with spreading the one true faith. The Ottoman nation, he rightly divined, was an armed camp, which could be saved from the corruption engendered by indolence only by being kept busy. The lesson to be extracted from the recent period of decay was the need of reverting to the policy of the great or "active" sultans, to the policy of war; and the war certain to arouse the greatest enthusiasm was the war along the Danube against Christian Europe. For this reason the vigorous old man resumed, not without caution in view of the internal disorders which he was engaged in correcting, an aggressive policy in the Hungarian area. There Transylvania was debatable ground, for, though considered by the Ottomans to be a dependency like Wallachia and Moldavia, its princes were perpetually intriguing with Austria in the hope of regaining their freedom. The grand vizier, after permitting matters to take their course for a time, invaded the province and promptly forced it back to obedience. Owing to the help given by Austria to the rebels a breach was now threatened with the Hapsburg power, but before military measures followed the ferocious old reformer was overtaken by death (1661).

His successor in the grand vizierate was his son, Ahmed Kiuprili (1661–76), a young man, who to the firm principles of his rude sire added the advantages of a broad culture and the graces of a humane spirit. Without doubt Ahmed was a distinguished personality even by the more advanced standards of the West. Since his father had introduced order into the administration, he was able not only to remove the pall of terror which had been suspended over the state but also to prosecute the military offensive against Europe on a large scale. Deliberately he resolved on the march up the Danube, that is, on war with Austria, for which the late troubles in Transylvania furnished a sufficient pretext, supposing a pretext were needed to convert the permanently unstable border situation into formal war. In 1663 the Ottomans invaded western or Austrian Hungary from their bases at Belgrad and Buda, and while the regular army undertook to reduce the belt of fortresses protecting Vienna, the savage irregular horsemen raided the country far and near. In the next year's campaign (1664) Ahmed aimed at Vienna itself. But the Austrians, warned by the events of the previous year, had raised a field army strengthened by contingents from Germany and France, and under their general, Montecuculi, a capable exponent of the new, methodical warfare coming into vogue, resolved to offer resistance. On August 1, 1664, a great battle took place at St. Gotthard on the Raab river, in which the Mohammedans, in spite of their numerical superiority, were signally defeated. However, the resources of the victors did not permit them to follow up their success, and when Ahmed, a consummate diplomat, offered to treat, a peace was concluded by virtue of which the grand vizier surrendered far fewer advantages than he retained. Rightly considered, the peace of 1664 was but a truce which, stipulated for twenty years, declared in substance that the Ottomans condescended to adjourn their aggression.

None-the-less we are warranted to assert that in the military history of the Ottoman empire St. Gotthard marks a milestone, for it records the first capital defeat in a pitched battle suffered by the Ottoman arms at the hands of a Christian power. In

Ahmed Kiuprili makes war on Austria and is defeated at St. Gotthard, 1664.

St. Gotthard and Lepanto compared.

this respect it deserves a place by the side of Lepanto, which registered the first great naval defeat of the Turks. St. Gotthard suggests Lepanto too in the meagerness of its immediate results, since the defeated infidels now as then kept a level head and refused to be stampeded into ignominious concessions.

Ahmed Kiuprili attacks and conquers Crete, 1669.

On his return to Constantinople Ahmed resolved to divert his aggression in the direction of Venice. Not only was the westward movement along the Mediterranean as well established in native tradition as the invasion of Europe, but Ahmed, in a sense, had no choice in the matter since he found a war with the Adriatic city on his hands on taking up the reins of government. Almost twenty years before, in 1645, in one of those spasms of energy characteristic of an ancient state in process of decay, the then reigning sultan had ordered an attack on Crete, the only possession retained by the Venetians in the eastern Mediterranean. A successful landing had been effected and a large part of the island occupied, and then, before the powerful fortress of Candia, the Ottoman army had come to a sudden halt. For twenty years it had conducted a feeble siege of the great stronghold, which the Venetians, roused to an unusual effort, had done all in their power to defeat. Convinced that the long-drawn-out Cretan war seriously compromised Ottoman prestige, Ahmed resolved to bring it to an end. Concentrating all his resources on this single object, he persisted in the siege until, in spite of the heroic resistance of the garrison, he forced Candia to capitulate (1669). A hundred years after the naval expansion of the Ottomans had suffered the check of Lepanto, one of the largest islands of the Mediterranean was added to the Ottoman possessions. Once more the fear of the Turk, almost laid to rest by long maritime inaction, ran like wild-fire along all the Christian coasts.

The dispute over the control of the Dnieper borderland, called the Ukraine.

But already a new war began to outline itself on the northern horizon. Beyond the Ottoman dependencies of Transylvania and Moldavia lay the vast, though incoherent, power of Poland. As vitally effected by the Ottoman advance, Poland had not scrupled to take a hand from time to time in various anti-Ottoman combinations. Toward the middle of the seventeenth century a grave issue had arisen for the Polish kingdom in connection with the Ukraine. This territory was a somewhat indeterminate borderland along the Dnieper river inhabited by the warlike Cossacks, who belonged to the great Slav family of nations and were adherents of the Orthodox church. Since the Ukraine lay between Poland and the rising might of Russia, it became an object of dispute between these two powers, which aspired each one to reduce the Cossacks to dependence on itself. In the year 1667 the two Slav rivals came to an agreement, by virtue of which they simply cut the unhappy object of their greed in two. At this outrage those Cossacks who, located on the right bank of the Dnieper, fell to the lot of Poland, did not scruple to turn to Constantinople for help; and Ahmed Kiuprili, after carefully weighing his chances, resolved to accept the proffered hand and open war on Poland.

Feudal disorganization, the ancient bane of Poland, had so far eaten into the vitals of the Slav state that the grand vizier by a sudden invasion succeeded in obliging the Poles to accept a disgraceful peace. However, its publication so deeply wounded the proud spirit of the nation that the nobility was moved to raise a mighty, if belated, clamor against craven submission. Resumed without more ado, the war was sanctified by a great victory under the leadership of a spirited nobleman, John Sobieski by name. To reward his services Sobieski was now elected (1674) king of Poland, but the landed magnates, who were the real rulers of the country and by no means inclined to resign their authority, refused to make the considerable financial and personal sacrifices which alone would have enabled Sobieski to keep a strong army in the field. Though the brilliant king preached and harangued and by straining all his resources won another splendid victory at Lemberg (1675), he was at last through lack of support obliged to make a peace with Ahmed Kiuprili, in which he ceded the province of Podolia to the Ottoman empire (1676). Ahmed died the same year. He had made war on Austria, Venice, and Poland and had improved the boundaries of his state in three directions. Upholder of the traditions of the early sultans, he proved to be an increaser of the realm, the last in the history of his race.

The grand vizier makes war on Poland and acquires the province of Podolia, 1676.

Ahmed's successor as grand vizier was his brother-in-law, Kara Mustafa, a man with neither the blood nor the virtues of the Kiuprili. Brazenly avaricious, he once more spread corruption

The new grand vizier, Kara Mustafa, renews the war with Austria.

through the administration; and, though entirely lacking in military talent, he determined to adhere to his predecessor's policy of conquest. Sweeping the European horizon with his glance, he resolved, in view of the rebellion against their Austrian overlord on which the restless Hungarian nobility had just then embarked, that the time was ripe to renew the struggle with the Hapsburgs. Emperor Leopold I, " a small man in red stockings," did not look like a very formidable opponent. Apart from the Hungarian difficulty, which, if grave, was local, he had to take account of the issue on the Rhine, created by the ambitious eastward thrust of Louis XIV, king of France. Perplexed, in fact paralyzed, by the plots and activities of Louis, Leopold kept his eyes riveted on Paris and inexcusably failed to take note of the clouds gathering in his eastern sky above the Danube valley. As a result Kara Mustafa could hatch his designs without the least interruption until in 1683, his preparations made, he suddenly discharged such a storm on Austria as threatened to bring it down in final ruin.

The failure of the Turks before Vienna, 1683.

Commanding an army of over 200,000 men, the grand vizier resolved to waste no time reducing the ring of border fortresses, and moved straight on to his goal, the city of Vienna. So completely were the Austrians taken by surprise that their small army was obliged to abandon the field and, with the panic-stricken emperor in its midst, to fall back toward Bavaria. A garrison of about ten thousand troops was left in Vienna in the hope that while it held up the advance of the enemy, the Austrian fighting force to the rear might be sufficiently strengthened by contingents from Germany and Poland to enable it to come to the relief of the capital. Passionate eleventh hour appeals had gone forth to the German princes and to John Sobieski, king of Poland, calling on these neighbors, hardly less threatened than Austria, to send immediate succor. Nor did Vienna's cry of distress remain unheard. German and, above all, Polish troops were feverishly assembled and directed to a common point of junction on the Danube above the endangered metropolis. But long before they arrived the situation of Vienna had become critical. On reaching the city on July 17, Kara Mustafa had found the fortifications in a neglected, and partly even in a dilapidated condition. It was said at the time, and has often been repeated since, that had he at once ordered the Janissaries to storm in the reckless fashion of the early Ottoman leaders, he must have captured the city. Be that as it may, Vienna offered a defense valiantly sustained not only by the trained troops but by the citizens themselves, who with conspicuous devotion performed every service demanded by the occasion. However, by early September the outlook was desperate. The walls had been breached at several points and the end was at best but a few days off. Sure of his quarry, Kara Mustafa made the mistake of relaxing his vigilance, and when on September 11, in the very nick of time, the relieving army appeared on the hills to the west of the city, he was in his turn taken unawares. Under the supreme command of the king of Poland, tried veteran of many Turkish wars, the Christian forces, composed of Poles, Austrians, and Germans, came down like an avalanche on the careless and too confident Moslems, and in a mighty battle, in which the exultant garrison, issuing from the city, fell upon the enemy's rear, broke the ranks of the infidels. Worse than a defeat, it was a rout. To the ringing of the bells of all the churches and to the pealing of their organs Johan Sobieski made his way into the town, wildly acclaimed by the citizens as their preserver and deliverer. At the same hour Kara Mustafa's shattered army made its way down the Danube in a mad scramble for safety. Arrived at Belgrad, the grand vizier met the order of the sultan, which, in accordance with the grim fashion of the orient, obliged him to pay the penalty of defeat with death.

Following the failure of the first siege of Vienna conducted by Sultan Solyman a century and a half before, in 1529, the Turk terror continued to stalk the land because the Turk power, if checked, had not been broken. Vienna's second siege of 1683 marks emphatically a turning-point, for the spurt of reform associated with the Kiuprili family came to an end and the decay, dating from Selim the Sot, quietly resumed its sway. Closely scanned as to its scope and method, the brief Kiuprili revival was no more than a whole-hearted return to the traditional policy of aggression against Europe. On the collapse of this policy before the walls of Vienna, all the old evils which had been at work undermining the manhood, organization, and resources of the Ottoman empire once more gained the upper hand.

End of the Kiuprili reform followed by resumption of decay.

So little was decay resisted henceforth and so disastrous were its ravages that the Ottoman empire became definitely and palpably moribund. That does not mean of course that it declined to the level of a helpless antagonist without the spirit and the means of resistance. On the contrary, on many a future occasion a too confident enemy was to learn that it could still deliver a stinging blow. None-the-less the offensive against Europe, which had been going on for three hundred years, came to a close, to be followed by an almost equally long period of defensive and, presently, of losing warfare which has continued to our day. From 1683 on our attention will be directed to the disintegration of the Ottoman empire and to the distribution of its spoils among the Christian powers.

Austria, Poland, and Venice join in an offensive alliance.

The Christian aggression began promptly on the morrow of the victory at Vienna. Austria and Poland would have been blind not to see the collapse of the Ottoman army, and they would have been criminally negligent if they had not taken advantage of it to penetrate, in their turn, into Ottoman territory. But even in the elation following the deliverance of Vienna they realized that, in order to make successful headway, they would have to proceed carefully and methodically. Accordingly, in 1684 they formed an alliance, which they invited the republic of Venice to join and which promised to each member-power the territory it might succeed in capturing. Austria, Poland, and Venice now began a war which marks the first phase in the long story of the Ottoman agony.

CHAPTER XVII

EUROPE ASSUMES THE OFFENSIVE AGAINST THE OTTOMAN EMPIRE

THE war, which Austria, Poland, and Venice began in 1684 lasted till 1698, and revealed to an astonished world a decrepit Ottoman empire almost entirely shorn of the strength with which it had once imposed itself on Europe. Among the three allies Austria played by far the leading rôle, and by virtue of her successes greatly fortified and improved her position among the powers. Considerable as her triumph was, it might have been even greater, if she had not been obliged to meet simultaneously a new attack in the Rhine region on the part of Louis XIV of France. As stated in the previous chapter, throughout the reign of this ambitious monarch, Austria was between two fires, between the Turks and the French, who in a sort of tacit and unofficial alliance played into each other's hands. To illustrate: the war begun by Austria in 1684 against the Turks was progressing auspiciously when the most Christian monarch attacked the emperor on the Rhine (1688). While desirous of embarrassing his Hapsburg rival's altogether too successful campaign against the Moslems, Louis was also actuated in his move by the long-established French policy of eastward expansion. His attack promptly obliged Austria to dispatch a large part of her forces toward the Rhine and therewith to relax her grip upon the enemy on the Danube. The necessity of fighting on two fronts, many hundred miles apart, must be kept in mind if we would understand the rise and fall of the tide of victory in Austria's first offensive war against the sultan.

While supplying evidence of the growing consolidation of the Hapsburg monarchy in finance and administration, the Austrian successes were more immediately due to the recently attained fighting power of the army. Reorganized on French lines by General Montecuculi, the victor of the battle of St. Gotthard, the army boasted a trained corps of officers, a well-drilled infantry, and an increasingly effective artillery. Presently, in succession to Montecuculi, there rose to prominence a number of other leaders, of whom Charles, duke of Lorraine, and Eugene, prince of Savoy, both of them foreigners drawn into the Austrian service by their hatred of France, deserve especial mention. Prince Eugene won his spurs in the long war against the Turks. On being promoted to an independent command, he caused such havoc among the infidels that an irresistible public opinion swept him into command of all the Austrian forces and gradually wove for him that halo as vanquisher of the Turks which he wears to this day.

The Austrians capture Buda, deliver Transylvania, and win the battle of Zenta.

In the course of the war we are considering, in which long-drawn-out siege operations alternated with bloody battles in the field, the Austrians forced their Ottoman enemy foot by foot and fortress by fortress down the Danube. In 1686 Buda, the seat of the pasha of Hungary, was captured; in 1687 the great province of Transylvania was occupied; and in 1688 Belgrad, the key to Balkania, fell before a swift and irresistible attack. At this point the forward march was interrupted while the Austrians turned upon their western enemy, the French. The Ottomans, quick to note the diminished pressure, recovered the offensive, recaptured Belgrad, and once more loosed their wild hordes on delivered Hungary. But their energy was not sufficent to carry them beyond the southern edge of the Danubian plain. To this they clung till the termination of the struggle on the Rhine (Peace of Ryswick, 1697) enabled Austria to transfer the bulk of her forces eastward under the tried command of Prince Eugene. Confidently advancing to find the Ottoman army, Eugene came upon it at Zenta, at the moment when it was attempting the difficult operation of crossing the Theiss river. In a masterful attack he completely overwhelmed the enemy (1697). Since for the moment there was no more help forthcoming from the French, the beaten Turk was obliged to sue for peace.

The military action of Poland unimportant owing to growing anarchy.

Before examining the terms the Austrians granted, it will be necessary to cast a swift glance at the achievements of their allies. Those of Poland, of which state much might reasonably have been expected in view of the merited renown of King

John Sobieski, amounted to very little. Needless to say the fault was not the king's. The military plans he formed were invariably rendered futile by the accumulated domestic ills, which now rapidly assumed calamitous proportions. In wild and exclusive pursuit of their class interests the Polish nobles not only rejected every measure calculated to strengthen the national defense but in their reckless egotism went the length of despoiling the king of the last vestiges of his prerogative. Condemned to inaction, Sobieski's life went out in misery and despair. He was the last sovereign of his country worthy of the name, and with his death (1696) the feudal anarchy, passing completely out of hand, prepared the ground for the destruction which was to overtake the unhappy state in the following century.

Compared with Poland, Venice proved a very creditable member of the Christian alliance, although it is patent that she owed her successes to the circumstance that the Ottoman forces were mainly concentrated in Hungary to meet the vigorous Austrian attack. However, deserved praise must be accorded the Adriatic city for the deeds which, against all expectation, it performed in this war. Decadent like the Ottoman empire, though for different reasons, the ancient republic could, under favorable circumstances, still present a brave front. Under the leadership of Morosini, one of the last great citizens produced by the nobiliary régime, the Venetian forces invaded the Morea and in three campaigns (1685–87) wrested it from the Ottomans. In 1687 the soldiers of the republic even crossed the isthmus of Corinth and took Athens. A memorable and tragic episode of the siege of Athens was the destruction of the Parthenon, the ancient temple on the far-famed Acropolis, which, used by the Moslems as a powder-magazine, was by a stray Venetian shell reduced to its present desolation. But no sooner was Athens won than it had to be again given up, and all subsequent attempts of the Venetians to penetrate beyond the Peloponnesus ended in failure.

At last, in order to end the long war, a congress met in 1698 at Carlowitz in southern Hungary and, early in the following year, agreed to establish peace substantially on the basis of each of the allied powers retaining the territory which it had succeeded in capturing from the Turks. An exception to this rule was made in favor of Poland, which, in spite of its slight participation

Venice captures the Morea.

The Peace of Carlowitz, 1699.

in the struggle, regained the province of Podolia, lost to Ahmed Kiuprili in 1676. Venice received the Morea, which once again made her a Mediterranean and even an Aegean power, while Austria, which had borne the brunt of the fighting, scored also the largest territorial gains, to wit, fertile Transylvania and even larger and more fruitful Hungary with the exception of the small district on the Danube around Temesvar (the Banat).

With the advent of Peter the Great, Russia reaches toward the Black Sea.

But, in addition to Poland, Venice, and Austria, another Christian power made peace with the Turks at Carlowitz. I refer to Russia, which, though only entering the war toward its close, sprang at once into prominence as a claimant to the territory of the declining empire. By gradually spreading over the east-European plain Russia had by the seventeenth century come into contact with the sultan in the region north of the Black sea. In this area ruled, in the uncertain fashion of nomad raiders, a tribe of Moslem Tartars under a khan who in his turn acknowledged the supremacy of the Ottoman empire. In 1689, in the midst of the losing war fought by the Turks against the Christian alliance, a new era had dawned in Russia with the accession of Tsar Peter I, called the Great. A ruler of amazing energy, he evolved no less a plan than to win for his backward country an honored place among the European powers. One of his objects, imposed by the geography of Russia and the direction of its southern rivers, was to gain access to the Black sea. Observing that the Ottomans were in desperate straits through the pressure applied by Austria, Peter concluded that his opportunity had come and pounced suddenly on the port of Azov at the mouth of the Don. Balked in his first attack in 1695, he succeeded in capturing Azov in the following year. In his sanguine way Peter now looked forward to a rapid expansion of his country southward, but, pressed with other affairs, he discreetly made up his mind to bide his time. At Carlowitz he signed a provisional agreement securing him the coveted outlet on the Black sea and after an interval of two years converted it into a formal peace with the sultan.

The effect of the peace of Carlowitz was to establish a belief in the early end of the Ottoman empire and to create a general appetite on the part of its Christian neighbors to share in the plunder. These neighbors, as we have seen, were four in number.

Two of them, however, Poland and Venice, hardly counted, or if they counted temporarily, were unlikely to count in the long run. The only powers commanding the material resources and the military organization required for a prolonged struggle were Austria and Russia, and from the peace of Carlowitz to the French Revolution, that is, throughout the eighteenth century, it was these two powers that pressed upon the sultan, administering blow on blow, till the spacious house in which he dwelt began to fall about his ears. But let no one imagine that the two great monarchies won an unbroken string of victories over their Moslem foe. Often enough, just as they appeared to have the enemy at their mercy, they had to meet a sudden leap which proved beyond a doubt the war-like temper of the Turk. The best judges agree that, in spite of the frightful corruption of the Ottoman administration and the manifest decline of the military machine, the individual Moslem soldier, hardy, frugal in his habits, and deeply devoted to his faith, was as good a fighting man as could be found in Europe. This spirited warrior, constituting the best asset of the dissolving Ottoman empire, was largely responsible for the fact that the advance of Austria and Russia, if in the main unchecked, was on repeated occasions brought to a rude and unexpected halt.

Throughout the eighteenth century Austria and Russia are the leaders of the European aggression against Turkey.

Before many years had passed the fiery Tsar Peter was himself to learn that in dealing with the Ottomans he was not dealing with a corpse. In the year 1711 he let himself be drawn into a new war with the Porte, which he hoped to end by a thrust at the very vitals of the empire. Invading Moldavia with reckless precipitation, he found himself, to his surprise, completely surrounded by the enemy among the marshes of the river Pruth. Never was an army in a more hapless plight; in Peter's own opinion surrender at discretion was inevitable. On dispatching an emissary to open negotiations, he discovered with an amazement that may be left to the imagination, that the grand vizier, who led the Ottoman host, was willing to permit him and his army to escape in return for no more than a treaty ceding back Azov to the sultan. The story has been told and has gained a general credence that the accommodating grand vizier was bribed by Peter's wife, who made him a present of her jewels. Without doubt political intrigue, by now a permanent feature of the

Renewing his aggressions, Peter suffers a complete defeat (1711) and is obliged to surrender Azov.

Ottoman system, played a part in the result; but as the exact nature of the transaction on the Pruth has never been disclosed, we must content ourselves with noting that Peter made a lucky escape from the trap in which he had been caught, though with the loss of his cherished outlet on the Black sea. It was a set-back, which he never made good, and when he died (1725) Russia was still without its window on the southern waters.

In a new war (1715–18) the Turks clear the Morea of the Venetians but are again defeated by Austria.

Filled with confidence by this success against Russia, the Porte resolved to win back the Morea and in 1715 began a war, by which in the course of a few weeks the Venetians were driven from the entire peninsula. The suddenness and completeness of their collapse lends support to the view that their Peloponnesian success some thirty years earlier was in the nature of a spurt favored by a happy combination of circumstances. In its dismay over its defeat the republic raised a loud cry for help, which brought Austria into the field, not so much, it is true, to succor the Venetians as to forestall an eventual attack on itself. In 1716 the Ottomans were obliged to divert their armies northward to the Danube and there abruptly their successes ceased. The Austrian forces were led by Prince Eugene, now at the zenith of his fame and skill, and in two battles, of which one was fought at Peterwardein (1716) and the other before the walls of Belgrad (1717), his troops literally annihilated the opposing Turks. The defeat suffered by the Turks was even more decisive than in the earlier war and was duly registered in the peace that followed at Passarowitz (1718). While the Moslems were permitted to retain the Morea, where they had firmly reëstablished themselves, they were obliged to cede to Austria their last foothold in Hungary, the Banat of Temesvar, and to yield besides the great fortress of Belgrad together with important slices of Serbia and Wallachia. As a glance at the map will show, the peace of Passarowitz carried Austria into the Morava valley, thus opening a lane southeastward to Constantinople. For a brief moment it looked as if the Hapsburgs would come in for the lion's share of the Ottoman empire and that they might ultimately reach the shores of the Bosporus.

The Austrian dream of expansion, if it was ever entertained, met with swift disillusionment. The next move in the Ottoman game was made by Russia, which in the reign of the Tsarina

Anne (1730–40) considered the time ripe for another attempt to win an outlet on the Black sea. It had become the conviction of Anne and her advisers that, as long as the mouths of the Russian rivers were dominated by the Ottoman empire, Russian commercial and political expansion would be effectively stifled. In 1735 Marshall Münnich, a general of more than average capacity, was entrusted with the task of dislodging the Turks together with their dependents, the Tartars of the Crimea, and in a succession of stubbornly contested campaigns he at last reached the coast of the Black sea. When this Russian offensive, which from the first had the secret approval of Austria, was well under way, the Danube power also declared war (1737) in the hope of extending its conquests further into Balkania. This time, however, Austria overreached herself. Be it that on the death of Prince Eugene, which occurred in 1736, the command of the Austrian army fell into incompetent hands, or be it that the Turks made one of their periodic military recoveries, the fact remains that the Austrians were overtaken by an uninterrupted succession of small disasters which precipitated a panic. While still in firm possession of impregnable Belgrad, the dejected generals opened negotiations, in the course of which they offered to cede back to the Porte most of the gains of the previous war, including the Austrian portions of Serbia and Wallachia and the uncaptured city of Belgrad. The precipitate and disgraceful peace, signed (1739) in the Ottoman camp outside Belgrad, brought the third offensive war waged by the Hapsburg monarchy against its Moslem foe to a close. So great was the hurry of the negotiators to come to a settlement that the ally of Austria was not even consulted. Confronted with an accomplished fact, the Russians could do no more than come to terms in their turn or face the concentrated Ottoman fury. They chose the safer course and restored all the lands which they had seized. In addition they submitted to the continued exclusion of their merchant vessels from the Black sea, though, as a tiny concession on the part of the Turks, Azov was neutralized and its fortifications demolished (1739).

Russia and Austria wage (1735–39) a combined war against the Porte in which they are worsted.

The successful defense made by Turkey against her two powerful neighbors somewhat revived her prestige, though the period of peace that followed must be ascribed less to fear of the Turk

Effect on Austria of the rise of Prussia.

than to the preoccupation of Austria and Russia with other matters. These distractions call for a brief elucidation. Shortly after the Peace of Belgrad was signed, the Austrian sovereign, Charles VI, the last male of the line of Hapsburg, died (1740). When the accession of his daughter and heir, Maria Theresa, was challenged by the leagued enemies of Austria, a war was precipitated, called the war of the Austrian Succession (1740–48), in the course of which a north-German state, Prussia, ruled by a monarch famous in history as Frederick the Great, advanced claims that threatened the traditional ascendancy of Austria in Germany and central Europe. Passionately aroused by this unexpected challenge of its ancient German hegemony, the house of Hapsburg forgot for a while its Danubian interests and riveted its gaze on Berlin.

Catherine II of Russia acquires control of Poland.

Meanwhile the attention of Russia was concentrated on Poland. The decay of that state, already patent to all observers in the days of John Sobieski, had in the first half of the eighteenth century made such rapid progress that Russia, the watchful enemy of Poland, resolved to take advantage of her neighbor's weakness. The view of the tsars, long hardened to a dogma, was that Poland hindered Russia's legitimate expansion westward. In 1762 a palace revolution at St. Petersburg put on the throne Catherine II, one of the ablest and most far-seeing, if also one of the most unscrupulous, sovereigns who has ever exercised autocratic power anywhere in the world. What Poland meant for Catherine she put with picturesque compression into the saying that the western kingdom was her door-mat to Europe. As by this time the domestic chaos of Poland had become chronic and incurable, there was no lack of pretexts on Catherine's part to interfere in the name of " order." The pretext she chose was the succession to the throne. When, in 1763, the Polish king, Augustus III, died, the necessity arose of calling together the diet for the purpose of electing a successor. As the tsarina was determined to have a Polish king whom she could control, she had the country quietly occupied with troops. Under these circumstances the diet, overawed, did her bidding and elevated her candidate, Stanislaus Poniatowski, to the throne (1764). But a group of Polish nobles, deeply offended by this open usurpation of power on the part of Russia, organized a revolt,

and, on being scattered by Russian troops, took refuge across
the Polish frontier in the dominions of the sultan. In this way
the Ottoman empire was dragged into the Polish imbroglio. Quite
apart from the moving appeal for help made to him by the Polish
fugitives, the padishah could not fail to see that the imminent
disapperance of Poland in the capacious maw of the Russian bear
compromised his own safety. After a sharp exchange of notes
he declared war (1768).

The war between Russia and the Porte, which lasted from
1768 to 1774, is the first struggle against the Ottomans in which
Russia showed an overwhelming superiority. By 1770 the
Russian armies had irresistibly pushed across Moldavia and
Wallachia and for the first time had planted their feet on the
banks of the Danube. In the same year a Russian fleet swinging
round by the Atlantic entered the Aegean sea, and after destroying the Ottoman fleet at Tchesmé, sailed up to the gates of the
Dardanelles. For a moment a dazzling prospect unfolded itself
before Catherine, for both Poland and Turkey seemed to be at
her mercy. Immediately, however, unrest and jealousy seized
the chancelleries of the other European powers, notably those
of Austria and Prussia, neighbors of Russia and equally or almost
equally interested with her in the destiny of the two declining
states which Russia had by the throat. Strong enough to bring
pressure to bear upon Russia, the two German monarchies obliged
Catherine to submit to a common discussion the question of
Poland, which country she would, of course, have preferred to
regard as exclusively her own preserve. The result of the negotiations was the First Partition of Poland (1772). A slice
of Polish territory was assigned to each of the three high-handed
sovereigns, to the Tsarina Catherine, Frederick of Prussia, and
Maria Theresa of Austria, and with this distribution the immediate hunger of each was appeased. The undistributed remainder, approximately two-thirds of the original kingdom,
continued to rest as before in the hollow of Catherine's hand.
It was plain that, should the occasion arise, the partition process
would be resumed and the doom of Poland sealed.

The negotiations culminating in the First Partition of Poland
somewhat interrupted the war on the lower Danube between
Russia and the Porte. When the struggle was renewed, the

The Russo-
Turkish war
of 1768–
1774 inter-
rupted by
the
Partition of
Poland,
1772.

Russia
dictates
the Peace of
Kutchuk-
Kainardji,
1774.

Russian army won fresh honors, triumphantly carrying its banners across the Danube to the outskirts of the fortresses which defended the approaches to the Balkan mountains. At this point the Moslems admitted they had had enough and humbly sued for peace, which was negotiated and signed at the Bulgar village of Kutchuk-Kainardji (1774). The actual territory gained by Russia was not large, but the implications and ulterior consequences of some of the articles were such that it may unhesitatingly be asserted that probably never in its history has the northern power signed a more favorable treaty. The acquisitions embraced Azov and a number of points along the Black sea coast; also, as it turned out, the Crimean peninsula. As a matter of fact the Mohammedan Tartars, who held the Crimea and the neighboring mainland, were in the treaty declared to be wholly independent of both sultan and tsar, but the cunning Catherine gradually asserted her control over them, and before a decade had passed, had effected their subjugation (1783). But more important than the territorial gains were the following commercial and political advantages secured by the Slav state: (1) Russian merchantmen received the right to trade freely in the Black and Mediterranean seas and to pass without hindrance through the straits; (2) Russia, though retiring from the two Rumanian principalities, Moldavia and Wallachia, which she had occupied during the war, secured a position toward them which made her their acknowledged protector; (3) Russia obliged the Porte to promise to protect the Christian religion. After such a document, with such stipulations indicative of the might and influence of the Slav giant, the oppressed rayahs naturally looked toward him as their active champion and probable deliverer. In sum, with this success of Catherine Russia became the leading factor in Ottoman foreign policy.

Austria, jealous of the Russian successes, obliges the Porte to cede the Bukovina, 1775.

Because of the rapid growth of Russian influence in the Balkan area effected by this war, its progress was followed by Austria, the occasional partner and perpetual rival of the great Slav power, with ill-concealed jealousy. The guiding principle of the two courts of Vienna and St. Petersburg had thus far been that neither must be allowed to improve its territorial position without a corresponding increase on the part of the other. Following the Russian triumph, Austria therefore demanded an Ottoman province by way of compensation. She urged at Constantinople that if Russia had been persuaded at Kutchuk-Kainardji to return Moldavia and Wallachia to the sultan, that concession was solely due to Austria, which had taken up a threatening position on the Russian flank. Since this argument was an entirely normal expression of the moral code which obtained among the sovereign states of Europe, and since the sultan in the days of his might had recognized no other, it was difficult not to admit its cogency. By a mixture of cajolery and threats the Porte was induced to cede to the Hapsburg monarchy the northern district of Moldavia, known as the Bukovina (1775).

For Catherine of Russia the next logical step was to expel the dying Turk from Europe and to appropriate his heritage. It was at this period of her relation to the Ottoman problem that the project of a Russian Constantinople dominating a Russian Bosporus and Dardanelles took shape in her ambitious mind, to be passed on to her successors and to remain down to our own time the lodestone of their policy. But to carry through such far-reaching schemes, involving nothing less than the total destruction of the Ottoman empire, she needed the consent and coöperation of Austria. So long as the Empress Maria Theresa, who much preferred a limited security to boundless but problematical gains, wielded the Hapsburg scepter there was no likelihood of Austria's being won for the tsarina's plans. On the death of the wise empress in 1781 the accession of her son, Joseph II, radically changed the situation. Joseph, though lacking the conspicuous ability of Catherine, was every whit as ambitious and was therefore drawn irresistibly into her net. Following a long preliminary discussion, secret arrangements were concluded, by which Austria and Russia agreed to make common war on the Porte in order to appropriate practically the whole of Turkey-in-Europe. When, in 1787, all was ready, the conflict began which was confidently expected by the two conspirators to put an end to the Ottoman empire. Without doubt it was a perilous moment for the decaying state, since recent developments had made clear that disagreement among its enemies was its best safeguard; however, now as on many a later occasion the danger looked greater than it turned out to be. For not only were Russia and Austria, on the exposure of their plot, threatened by

Catherine plans to oust the Turk from Europe by means of an Austrian alliance.

Failure of
the Austrian
war against
the Porte.

the other European powers, bitterly jealous of the prospective
gains of the two eastern autocracies, but the Ottoman energy
once again proved to be far from spent and negligible.

Though Russia began the war, Austria joined her after a
brief delay, and the year 1788 brought the inauguration of a
coördinated attack in two widely separated areas. The Austrians
were at first singularly unfortunate, perhaps because the Emperor
Joseph, who lacked the gifts of a successful general, exercised
the command in person. When in the following year (1789)
Joseph was by illness constrained to remain at home, the Austrian
army made an almost magical recovery under the command of
Marshal Loudon. Loudon penetrated into Serbia and captured
that old bone of contention, the city of Belgrad. But his triumphs
turned out to be vain by reason of the intervention of unforeseen
forces. Joseph, an enlightened if impatient reformer, had carried
through a series of domestic measures which, well-intentioned
and reasonable in themselves, lacked popular support and stimulated the opposition of the various nationalities making up the
polyglot Hapsburg empire. When in the Austrian Netherlands
(Belgium) and in Hungary the opposition went the length of
raising a rebellion, the state was rent with civil war. At the
same time Prussia, the bitter enemy of Austria, drew close to
the sultan and began the mobilization of her forces as if in preparation for an assault on Austria in order to relieve the hard-pressed
Ottomans. In the midst of these difficult circumstances, which
threatened to ring the knell of the Austrian monarchy, Joseph II
died (February, 1790). He was succeeded by his brother, Leopold
II, who by swift and daring diplomatic action saved the state
from ruin, not, however, without considerable sacrifices. While
quashing the rebellions in Belgium and Hungary by a sweeping
withdrawal of his predecessor's obnoxious reform legislation, he
was able to placate Prussia only by agreeing to make peace with
the Turks on the basis of a restoration to them of all the lands
they had lost. Again the crucial Belgrad, which, if held, would
have meant a door open to the Austrians for a later advance
into Balkania, was handed back to the sultan and locked and
double barred against the Hapsburgs. Concluded on the basis
of the *status quo ante bellum*, the peace of Sistova was formally
signed between Turks and Austrians in 1791.

The Russians, for their part, fared much better than the Austrians in this common war, chiefly perhaps because they were less interfered with by unexpected agencies. They too, however, had to reckon with a flank attack launched against them by Sweden, their ancient Baltic enemy. When this danger had been overcome by means of a peace concluded with the Scandinavian kingdom in 1790, Catherine was free to concentrate her energy once more on Turkey. In the light of previous experience the result might have been accurately forecast. General Suvarov, a rude soldier of great military genius, stormed and bayoneted his way southward, winning his most brilliant success at Ismail, a Turkish fortress on the lower Danube, which he took by an assault of an almost incredible boldness. Presently the disheartened Porte, unable to score any notable success against the Russians, offered to negotiate, and in 1792 concluded the treaty of Jassy, by virtue of which Russia added the territory between the rivers Bug and Dniester to her Black sea dominion. Before Catherine died (1795) she had constructed a naval base at Sebastopol in the Crimea and a commercial port at Odessa. Firmly established in the south, she could close her eyes, sure that the future belonged to her beloved Russia.

Russia wins new territory by the Peace of Jassy, 1792.

The failure of the first war fought by an European combination for the express purpose of ousting the Turk from Europe justifies the opinion that, in spite of the palpable Ottoman decay, many factors, notably the jealousy which ruled the conduct toward each other of the Christian states, would regularly interpose in favor of the Turks. In this particular instance it was Prussia, abetted by Great Britain, that paralyzed the arm of Austria, while it was Sweden that interfered with Russia. France, however, which under ordinary circumstances would have been sure to enter a firm claim for consideration in Ottoman affairs, was on this occasion hindered from coming forward by a tremendous development within its borders. In 1789, at the moment when the Austro-Russian attack on Turkey was at its height, the French Revolution began its amazing career. Gathering headway, it gradually drew the countries bordering on France into its vortex and ended by engaging the whole continent in a vast struggle, which lasted for a quarter of a century and which, in its later phases, is stamped in flaming letters with the name

Partition plans dropped by Russia and Austria as they turn to face the French Revolution.

of Napoleon Bonaparte. The Hapsburg empire, as relatively close to the French border, was almost immediately affected by a movement, the characteristic feature of which was the sowing abroad of democratic ideas of the greatest danger to all autocratic monarchies. Russia, lying so far to the east as to be almost in Asia, was of course less disturbed than Austria, but manifestly not even the remote world of the Slavs could or would remain indifferent to the siren song of the French republicans promising to all who heard a new heaven and a new earth. Anxiously facing westward, the autocrats of Russia and Austria perforce gave up for the time being their plans of partitioning the Ottoman empire. That disease-racked state gained a needed respite from which, however, owing to its constitutional weakness, it was not able to draw a single permanent benefit. In this condition of feebleness it attracted the gaze of Napoleon Bonaparte, who, cast to the surface by the upheavals of the Revolution, revolved vast plans of world dominion. There followed a Napoleonic interlude in Ottoman history to which we must now turn our attention.

CHAPTER XVIII

THE OTTOMAN EMPIRE IN THE ERA OF THE FRENCH REVOLUTION AND NAPOLEON BONAPARTE

In its early stages at least, the movement, called the French Revolution, was essentially a movement of ideas which, summarized in the magical watch-words, Liberty, Equality, Fraternity, proposed nothing less than the destruction of the inherited feudal world of privilege and the fullest possible realization of the program of democracy. Ideas so alluring to the oppressed and downtrodden classes of society were sure to win converts by the thousands in every section of Europe, especially as France did not rest content with words but set a flaming example by putting its faith to the test of practice. However, the conservative forces, opposed to change and content with things as they were, proved strong enough, even in France, and so overwhelmingly strong outside of France as to develop a resistance which, drawing ever wider circles, ended by assuming the staggering proportions of a world-war. Old and New Europe locked horns and for a whole generation, down to the congress of Vienna in 1815, that is, throughout the period concerned with the issues raised by the French Revolution, strained and tugged and bled in mortal combat.

The vast struggle precipitated by the French Revolution.

So universal a movement could not possibly leave unaffected the Ottoman empire, remote though it was from the central scene of action. True, its backward, barbarous peoples, both Moslems and Christians, had hardly arrived at the level of civilization required to make the democratic message intelligible. More particularly the Asiatic-minded Ottomans would find nothing either significant or desirable in the French program. They would meet it simply with a closed mind, and if certain leaders of the rayahs, vaguely quickened by its sounding promises, would feel the flutter of a new hope, the misery of the mass of the Christians was such that it would require the patient educational labor of

The Ottoman society undisturbed at first by the revolutionary ideas.

275

decades to lift these victims of oppression out of their centenary stupor. However, it is certain that the doctrine of popular rights proclaimed by the Revolution began, as the eighteenth century came to a close, to circulate gropingly in the benighted areas of Balkania, throwing stray rays of light into the gloom and starting a social and political ferment which ultimately achieved an enormous importance. To this domestic commotion we shall in due time give our attention. By way of introduction, it will be well first to occupy ourselves with the relation of the government of the Ottoman empire to the Revolution as incarnated in its champion, France.

French policy traditionally favorable to the sultan in return for commercial and religious advantages.

In order fully to understand the form which the relations of France and Turkey assumed in the era of the French Revolution, it will be necessary to review the policy pursued by France toward the Sublime Porte during the preceding centuries. We have taken note of the intimacy struck up between Francis I and Sultan Solyman and commemorated by the famous Capitulations of 1535.[1] Although this agreement gave France commercial and religious privileges in the Ottoman dominion far beyond those of any other European power, it was looked upon by the prudent French government as no more than an entering wedge. To the length of a formal political alliance involving military action against the Christian enemies of the Porte, France, herself an ostensible Christian power in the midst of a Europe still animated with a strong Christian sentiment, could only occasionally go. Even the sentiment of her own people would have been against a too complete identification with the infidels. Besides, the Ottoman empire was still almost fabulously remote from western Europe and its immediately pressing affairs. Therefore, generally speaking, in the period following Francis I the French kings pursued the canny plan of maintaining friendly but unbinding relations with the Osmanli with the intent of rendering an occasional service in strict exchange for an equivalent advantage. It must not, however, be imagined that for generation after generation the successive sovereigns unwaveringly adhered to this line of policy. Not only did individual rulers permit themselves periodically to indulge in the familiar occidental lux-

[1] See Chapter XIV.

ury of despising the Turks, but untoward incidents occurred in Mediterranean commerce, especially in connection with the irrepressible Algerine corsairs, calculated to cool the frank enthusiasm which Paris and Constantinople usually professed for each other. Such brief misunderstandings apart, the French may be said to have clung tenaciously to the policy laid down by Francis I, and to have proved themselves shrewdly alert not only to maintain the privileges conceded in 1535 but to increase them on every favorable occasion.

Repeatedly, therefore, in the course of the sixteenth and seventeenth centuries the Capitulations granted by Solyman were renewed, usually with additions over which France had reason to rejoice. When, in the eighteenth century, Austria and Russia began their offensive, which revealed to an astonished world that the Ottoman titan rested on feet of clay, France, far distant from the scene and engaged, besides, with England in an absorbing colonial struggle for India and America, was unable to give its Moslem friend effective and systematic aid. Unavoidably the court of Versailles had to limit itself to action in the field of diplomacy with, however, the attendant advantage of being able, when the crisis was over, to present a bill for broker's services. In 1739, for instance, when the French ambassador, intervening between Austria and the Porte, negotiated the peace of Belgrad so unfavorable to the emperor and so advantageous to the sultan, he promptly demanded his fee in the form of a new charter for his country. As a result, the Capitulations of 1740 indicate an apex, a high-water mark. Not only did they heap fresh commercial advantages on France but they brought, above all, increased religious rights. The French king was confirmed as the guardian of the Holy Places of Palestine while receiving the most precise recognition as protector of all Catholic establishments such as churches, missions, schools, and monasteries in the Ottoman realm. Since the Catholic missionaries and pilgrims from the West as well as the — it is true — not very numerous Catholic subjects of the sultan were inclined henceforth to look upon the French king as their sword and buckler, the infusion of French influence by this subtle channel may be left to the imagination. Reaffirmed in all agreements with the Porte down to our own day, the prerogatives conceded

France confirms her moral preponderance in the Near East by means of the Capitulations of 1740.

England unable to help Turkey

France intercedes & Austria & won a good deal for Turkey!

in 1740 have served as the solid foundation of the French edifice of power in the Near East.

The French Revolution reaches Egypt in 1798.
When in 1789 the French Revolution broke out with sudden and bewildering fury, the chief feeling of the padishah on the distant Bosporus must have been a sense of pleasant relief because the attention of Europe, including his two relentless enemies, Austria and Russia, was withdrawn from Constantinople to become hypnotically fixed on Paris. As in the case of all decaying organisms, to remain unnoticed, to be left alone was the substance of his hope, and for a time he may have thankfully regarded the Revolution as a shrewd invention of Allah's for bringing confusion to his enemies. If such was the sultan's thought he was, before long, rudely disillusioned, for in 1798 the French tide rushed with a sudden leap up the unprotected shore of his province of Egypt. About a decade after its birth the Revolution, drawing ever wider circles from its center at Paris, found the sultan out in order to serve notice that no monarch was so remote or secure as to escape its devastations.

The French expedition to Egypt a war measure against England.
The event which was directly responsible for drawing the Ottoman empire into the revolutionary whirl was the war between republican France and monarchical Europe. In this struggle France had developed vast armies filled with missionary zeal and patriotic enthusiasm, and had ended by defeating all her continental opponents. In 1797 the last of them to offer resistance, Austria, was forced to her knees by the treaty of Campo Formio. Therewith the hegemony of the young Republic over Europe became an accomplished fact. The general to whom the victory over Austria was due, Napoleon Bonaparte, was hailed by French opinion as the national hero. One thing only remained to be done: to humble the great sea-power, England, which had driven French commerce off the seas and had proved unassailable behind its moat of water and its wall of ships. With the continent subdued it seemed to the elated Republic that the moment had come to square the ancient account with the power across the Channel by winning back the colonial position lost in the long and fateful struggle of the eighteenth century. However, a direct attack on the island-kingdom, now as ever, proved unfeasible, since France, invincible on land, possessed but an inferior navy. In consequence General Bonaparte, in cooperation

with the government of the Republic, worked out a plan whereby England was to be subjected to an indirect attack by means of a blow aimed at her communications. For various reasons Bonaparte hit upon Egypt as his goal, his leading calculation being that with Egypt in French hands the English hold on India and the east would be profoundly shaken. To be sure, the land of the pyramids belonged not to England but to the Ottoman empire, a circumstance that made it probable that the sultan would resent the violent invasion of his house and take up arms in its defense. Of course Bonaparte reckoned with this chance. However, he hoped somehow to persuade the sultan that the French action meant no disrespect to him and that France, at war with Great Britain, was justified in levelling a blow at its enemy even if it went all the way to Egypt to do so. The casuistry of the French argument as well as the extraordinary hazard of the whole enterprise must appeal to every man possessed of a shred of political discernment. From the moment of its inception there was less than a sporting chance that the hare-brained scheme would accomplish its purpose of making England, beaten, sue for peace.

The famous Egyptian expedition of Napoleon Bonaparte need not occupy us long. Prepared in deep secrecy and favored by fortune in its early stages, it scored a few startling but wholly ephemeral successes against the Mamelukes, the armed militia which ruled Egypt under the nominal suzerainty of the sultan. In a series of bloody encounters fought on the march from Alexandria to Cairo the Mamelukes were broken and had to yield their country to the French. But while the French were marching up the Nile, the English fleet under Nelson boldly sailed into Aboukir Bay, where the French fleet lay at anchor, and attacking without delay (August 1, 1798), totally destroyed it. General Bonaparte might go on conquering Egypt, but in the long run it was absolutely certain that, cut off from France and Europe by the disaster of Aboukir, he would be forced to surrender. *Napoleon Bonaparte lands in Egypt.*

To make matters worse, the sultan, encouraged by Nelson's victory, now made an alliance with the English and set about driving the intruders out. For Bonaparte, facing the difficult situation which he had himself created, a severe crisis ensued. *Bonaparte confronted by an Anglo-Turkish alliance.*

Since to him, the born fighter, fighting was both meat and drink, the busy campaigns that followed constituted the least of his troubles. In 1799 he crossed the isthmus of Suez into Syria with the plan of holding this province against a possible Ottoman advance by land. Failing to take the important port of Acre, he was obliged to return to his Egyptian base and immediately after, near Alexandria, found himself confronted with a Turkish army which the cunning English, aiming a blow at the heart of his power, had convoyed across the Mediterranean sea. Though he escaped from the net by means of a brilliant victory over the Turks (August, 1799), he recognized the futility of further military effort and turned his thought to plans of safety.

Bonaparte abandons Egypt and makes himself dictator of France.

Nothing in Bonaparte's whole career is more characteristic than the gambler's chance he took when he embarked in a small sloop and, attended by a handful of devoted followers, ventured to run the English blockade. Almost miraculously successful, he landed in France in October and carried along by the favor of the French people, who refused to lay the fiasco in Egypt at his door, he overthrew the Republic and set himself up as dictator. The army, which, in taking ship with a few friends, he left behind in the shadow of the pyramids, was of course lost and in 1801 surrendered to the English.

Napoleon Bonaparte takes over the French revolutionary inheritance.

Even this ignominious close of the Egyptian venture did not in the least detract from Bonaparte's popularity at home nor prove a stumbling-block to his career. Beginning with his seizure of the government (November, 1799), he steadily strengthened his usurped position until in 1804 he was able to throw aside all restraint and proclaim himself emperor of the French. Strange indeed had been the circle traveled by the French Revolution in fifteen short years! Begun as a movement of human liberation, it had been gradually diverted to the familiar and insidious program of territorial conquest, and in this form had been appropriated by a military genius to serve as the broad foundation of his throne.

Emperor Napoleon's life and death struggle with Great Britain.

Meanwhile the immediate tangle precipitated by the French descent on Egypt had been straightened out. In 1802, by virtue of the treaty of Amiens, the French and English, equally tired of the long war and unable for the moment to do each other further injury, brought their conflict to a close. In accordance with one of the articles England restored Egypt to the sultan, who, despite the buffets sustained by him in the late war, was thus enabled to retire from it without any territorial loss. But as between the main combatants, the peace of Amiens decided nothing, was in fact no better than a truce. Before much more than a year had passed, the struggle broke out again because it was unavoidable so long as Napoleon looked upon the continent of Europe as his domain and would brook no interference with its affairs. From 1803 to 1814 the Corsican battled for European supremacy, first and always with England, and on occasion with such continental powers as ventured to oppose him by throwing in their lot with the great sea-power. In the end, as everybody knows, he lost the game, surrendered to the English, and died a prisoner on the lonely mid-Atlantic island of St. Helena.

Turning now to an examination of the policy toward the Ottoman empire which Napoleon pursued as emperor of the French, we note that it was very different from that represented by his Egyptian expedition. After achieving a resounding failure on the banks of the Nile, he apparently felt no desire to return to that scene of unhappy memories. However, continuing to be obsessed with the thought of defeating the English, he was driven to leave no stone unturned to gain his end. In the circumstances he resolved to reverse his Ottoman policy and do his best to attach the Porte henceforward to himself. Such a program meant substantially a return to the traditional policy of Ottoman friendship pursued by his predecessors in office, the Valois and Bourbon kings. And within certain bounds Napoleon was successful in his plan, since French influence again became predominant both in the deliberations of the divan and within the walls of the serai. Naturally this considerable triumph, due to the adroit employment of diplomatic wiles, induced the English to redouble their own cunning and, above all, to move heaven and earth to draw the Russians, equally alarmed at the prospect of French control at the Bosporus, to their side. The Austrians, who because of their repeated defeats by the soldier on the French throne had been temporarily reduced to a minor power, were during the Napoleonic period a negligible factor in the perennial drama of Ottoman intrigue.

Napoleon, as emperor, reverses himself and plays the rôle of friend of the sultan.

A new
Russian
attack on
the Porte
(1806)
interrupted
by
Napoleon's
victory over
the czar at
Friedland
(1807).

Into the details of the shifty statecraft of Napoleon and his two rivals, Russia and Great Britain, it is not necessary to enter. Let it suffice to single out a few important events, among which none takes higher rank than the new war which broke out between Russia and the Porte in 1806. Needless to say, it was provoked in large measure by the machinations of France, with which Russia was just then at grips, owing to the tsar's joining with England and Austria in one of their many coalitions against the overweening power of the Corsican. In their first rush into Ottoman territory the Russian armies occupied Moldavia and Wallachia, but before they could persuade the sultan to make peace, Napoleon, carring his forces eastward across Germany, first roundly defeated the tsar at Friedland (June, 1807) and then cajoled him into negotiations. The Russian sovereign was Alexander I, a young and very impressionable man, who in the course of an interview, romantically staged on a raft moored in the river Niemen, fell under the great soldier's influence and agreed not only to sign a peace but to turn a complete political summersault by contracting an alliance with his late enemy.

The alliance
of Tilsit
followed by
discussions
over the
partition of
Turkey.

The spectacular arrangements between tsar and emperor were concluded at Tilsit in eastern Prussia in July, 1807. Alexander agreed to join Napoleon in his war on England and in return for this favor Napoleon undertook to begin discussions looking forward to a partition of Turkey. Just twenty years had passed since Russia had entered into a bargain with Austria on this same head. Without the least scruple Emperor Napoleon deserted the sultan, whom he had been largely responsible for pushing into the Russian war, as soon as it seemed more advantageous to join Russia in a common scheme of plunder. However, the partition was a grave business which could not be settled in a twinkling. When the discussion, adjourned at Tilsit and spun out subsequently in elaborate diplomatic notes, reached the question as to how the different Turkish provinces were to be divided, serious differences of opinion arose; and when Alexander broached the issue of Constantinople, which city he boldly claimed for himself, he ran into adamant. The very first time the tsar named this redoubtable prize, Napoleon, we are told, burst into indignant protest: " Constantinople! Never! It is the empire of the world!" This hot response, taken together with remarks of the same tenor which he let fall at other times, has by the credulous and uncritical been interpreted to mean that he was arrogantly reserving Constantinople for himself as his ultimate goal and throne. While we may admit that Napoleon's unbridled imagination was quite capable of playing, in moments of excitement, with the preposterous scheme of a world empire having its seat on the Bosporus, we should be on our guard against taking at face value his every idle word and boast. Not the least evidence of his genius was his power to coin vivid and suggestive phrases opening immense political vistas, but a discriminating student will not be misled to read the emperor's actual program in their light.

The alliance of Tilsit produced a temporary coöperation of tsar and emperor against Great Britain and carried Napoleon to the zenith of his might. But it did not lead to the planned Ottoman partition. The lion's share in such a deal must necessarily have fallen to the Muscovite and the grasping nature of the Corsican was such that he was unwilling to adjudge the lion's share in any enterprise to another than himself. In order that the Franco-Russian negotiations might take place in an atmosphere of tranquillity, it had been agreed that the hostilities between Turks and Russians should be brought to a close with an armistice, during which Russia was to keep a surety in her hand by continuing her occupation of the Danubian principalities. Waiting with considerable patience on Napoleon's constantly adjourned decision on the partition project, Alexander at last, under threat of deserting the alliance, forced the emperor to accord to him at least Wallachia and Moldavia. It now became necessary to persuade the sultan to agree to his own spoliation, and when this proved impossible, war, as might have been expected, again broke out. In 1809 the Russo-Turkish struggle, suspended for two years, was resumed with the now familiar result of an unbroken string of Russian victories. However, though some of the great fortresses on the southern bank of the Danube, such as Silistria and Rustchuk, were captured, the Russians were not able to gain possession of the passes of the Balkan mountains.

None-the-less it might have gone hard with the Turks if the friendship of Napoleon and Alexander, after all but poorly ce-

Napoleon grants Moldavia and Wallachia to the tsar and, on the sultan's refusing assent, the Turco-Russian war is resumed, 1809.

By threatening Russia with invasion Napoleon obliges Alexander to contract the Peace of Bucharest, 1812.

mented at Tilsit, had not at this juncture definitely gone to pieces. In the year 1811 the tsar, increasingly suspicious of the French designs and thoroughly alarmed at their scope, refused further to support the emperor, who, still clinging fanatically to his continental union against England, determined to bring Alexander to his senses by means of an overwhelming invasion. The French preparations were conducted on such a scale as to oblige the Muscovite to look to his safety by withdrawing his forces from the Turkish front. With a heavy heart he opened negotiations with the sultan, resolved to make peace even at the price of an all but complete sacrifice of the Balkan victory just won. In this way Napoleon rendered his puppet and victim at Constantinople a belated and unintentional service by enabling him in the very nick of time to draw his head out of the Russian noose. In May, 1812, the peace of Bucharest brought the first Russo-Turkish war of the nineteenth century to a close. The harassed tsar, anxious to get his army home without delay, renounced his intention to keep the principalities and regretfully handed them back to the Porte with the exception of Bessarabia, constituting the eastern district of Moldavia. By acquiring Bessarabia Russia carried its Black sea boundary a further stage toward Constantinople. Henceforth no longer the Dniester river, but the Pruth and the northern or Kilia arm of the Danube, formed the boundary line between the two states.

The overthrow of Napoleon restores the diplomatic situation of the eighteenth century at Constantinople.

Sharp on the heels of the treaty of Bucharest came Napoleon's invasion of Russia (1812), destined to prove the first act in the dramatic and overwhelming ruin which overtook him. Leipzig, Fontainebleau, Waterloo, Paris, suggest some of the great events that followed, but lie beyond our scope. Let it suffice that by 1815 the great Corsican had been swept, a helpless prisoner, from the European scene, while the victorious allies, England, Russia, Prussia, and Austria, undertook to make peace and, at a great congress held at Vienna, to rearrange the map of Europe on their own terms. As the curtain drops upon the period inscribed with Napoleon's name, the student of the Near East may ask himself what lasting effect, if any, the great soldier's ambitious projects and capriciously fluctuating enmity and friendship had on the Ottoman empire. Search as he may, few durable consequences will be discovered. Decidedly Napoleon's eastern policy, wholly opportunist and changing with every wind that blew, was writ in water. Therefore no sooner had he disappeared than the old, familiar diplomatic conditions were spontaneously restored, the various powers resuming substantially the rôles which they had played at Constantinople throughout the eighteenth century. That means that Austria and, more particularly, Russia, because their geographical proximity and military might enabled them to hold the sultan at their mercy, stood forth as leaders on the Bosporus, while France, fallen from her dizzy Napoleonic eminence, found herself, as formerly, too weak and far-away to pursue a policy other than one of a general good-will shrewdly tendered to the Porte in exchange for material benefits. None-the-less one novelty of vast import is bound to strike the intelligent observer of world-relations. The republic of Venice, which had been an unconscionable time a-dying, was finally thrust into its grave and in its place, as the leading Mediterranean power, appeared the expanding might of England.

The overthrow of the Venetian state may be set down as perhaps the one memorable contribution which Napoleon made to the near eastern question. It was in the year 1797 that, in pursuit of certain plans directed toward the control of Italy, the young French general decreed the end of the ancient republic of St. Mark. All that was left at the time of the once considerable Venetian colonial empire was the long stretch of the Dalmatian coast and the group of the Ionian islands, of which the largest and most valuable was the little paradise of Corfu. The Ionian islands Bonaparte from the first planned to keep for himself as a maritime base against England, but with the weak navy at his disposal he had a problem on his hands which the developments of the following years proved to be beyond his strength. With the shifting vicissitudes of these strategical islands we are concerned no further than to point out that in the long run Great Britain, the omnipotent wielder of Neptune's trident, picked them up one after another as chance served. When in 1815 the congress of Vienna assembled, she presented herself as their actual owner, and as a result was solemnly accorded their possession in the form of a protectorate. The mainland dependency of Venice, the long coast-strip of Dalmatia, Napoleon also treated as a pawn in his vast military game.

The end of Venice and the disposal of its colonial territory.

After giving it first to Austria — in the treaty of Campo Formio, 1797 — he seized it later (1805) for himself and held it as an element in his Continental System till the time when he and all his fantastic projects crashed to the ground. In the auction-sale of the Napoleonic booty conducted at Vienna, Dalmatia was promptly bid in by Austria, which, by means of this Adriatic shore-land, greatly strengthened its position in the Mediterranean.

Great Britain becomes a leading power in the Near East.

Thus, though revolutionary France destroyed Venice, it was Great Britain and Austria which benefited by the Venetian colonies and which by virtue of them greatly improved their position in the Near East. The case of Great Britain is particularly noteworthy since the possession of the Ionian islands effectively made her, and for the first time, a Balkan power. If we add that at the congress of Vienna she gained also the island of Malta, a position of unique value for the control of the middle Mediterranean, we are prepared to see her play not only an important but perhaps the leading rôle in Ottoman affairs in the years ahead.

Probability, in case of continued decay, of the partition of Turkey among Russia, Austria, France, and Great Britain.

Gathering together the elements of the near eastern situation as they present themselves to view at the moment, when, with the congress of Vienna, a new era was inaugurated in European history, we observe that four powers, Russia, Austria, France, and Great Britain, were acutely interested in the Ottoman empire and prepared to insist on some share of its territory in case of its continued decay. Moreover, many ominous signs imposed the deduction that the decay, which the eighteenth century had revealed as the crying scandal of the Near East, would continue without interruption in the new century. In any case it was clear as day that unless some radical reforms were put into effect the four powers on or near the ground would share the inheritance of the Turks among them in proportion to the influence which each would be able to bring to bear upon the situation. A striking instance capable of being adduced in support of such a forecast was the recent fate of Poland. Poland, too, fallen into domestic chaos and unable to find a remedy for her grave ills, had by successive stages been carved up among her neighbors. Despite the violence done to the boasted moral sense of Europe the various agreements wiping Poland off the map had, after all, proceeded in strict obedience to a biologic law, which, far more potent than an ethical code more honored in the breach than the observance, categorically declared that organisms incapable of periodically renewing themselves must go the way of death. If the Ottoman empire had in it the seeds of destruction and could not choke them with the more abundant seeds of life, what valid reason was there for thinking that its case would not fall under the universal rule?

In point of fact the Ottoman empire of the nineteenth century failing, as we shall see, to reform itself, was obliged to suffer the recurrent seizure of enormous areas belonging to it by the pushing European powers. In this steady interplay of decay and encroachment will prove to lie the substance of its recent story. None-the-less the smooth working of the two related processes was considerably modified by the injection into the situation of a third and unexpected factor. This was the rise of the Christian subjects of the sultan, the despised rayahs. First at one point of the Balkan peninsula, then at another, they heard the call to a new life and shook off the numbing sleep which had as by enchantment enveloped them for ages. Rubbing their eyes and looking about them in bewilderment, they at last struggled to their feet and, in flat contradiction to what a close observer of the year 1800 might have felt justified to prophesy, succeeded in becoming a factor, and a leading factor, in the history of Balkania. It is this feature of the new epoch about to engage our attention which will serve to dispense not a little comfort to the student who, depressed by the unedifying spectacle, on the one hand of uninterrupted dry-rot, on the other of the sleepless greed and mutual envy of the strong, must needs rejoice to have his attention diverted to the heroic struggle of the rejuvenated Christian peoples to shake off a degrading yoke and to assert their inalienable right of directing their own destiny.

Inter-play of decay and partition modified by the renaissance of the subject-peoples.

BIBLIOGRAPHY

Bibliographical Aids

A. H. LYBYER, The Government of the Ottoman Empire in the Time of Suleiman the Magnificent. Cambridge. Harvard University Press. 1913. Appendix V (pp. 305–31) presents a valuable discussion of the material available for the study of Ottoman history and institutions in the sixteenth century.

H. A. GIBBONS, The Foundation of the Ottoman Empire. New York. 1916. Bibliography, p. 319 ff.

R. J. KERNER, Slavic Europe: A Selected Bibliography in the Western European Languages. Cambridge. Harvard University Press. 1918.

The Cambridge Modern History. Vol. I, pp. 700–5; Vol. III, pp. 782–85; Vol. V, pp. 840–45.

Manuals

S. LANE-POOLE, Story of Turkey.

LORD EVERSLEY, The Turkish Empire: its Growth and Decay.

D. G. HOGARTH, Section "Turkey" in The Balkans: A History of Bulgaria, Serbia, Greece, Roumania, Turkey.

General Works

Cambridge Modern History, Vol. I, ch. iii (Bury); Vol. III, ch. iv (Brosch); Vol. V, ch. xii (Lodge).

LAVISSE ET RAMBAUD, Histoire Générale, Vol, III, ch. xiii; Vol. IV, ch. xix; Vol. V, ch. xx; Vol. VI, ch. xxii; Vol. VII, ch. ix.

HELMOLT, History of the World. (Trans. from the German.) Vol. V, South-eastern and Eastern Europe.

J. VON HAMMER-PURGSTALL, Geschichte des Osmanischen Reiches. 10 vols.

E. S. CREASY, History of the Ottoman Turks (an abridgment of Hammer).

J. W. ZINKEISEN, Geschichte des Osmanischen Reiches in Europa. 7 vols.

E. GIBBON, The History of the Decline and Fall of the Roman Empire. Ed. by J. B. Bury. 7 vols.

N. JORGA, Geschichte des Osmanischen Reiches. 5 vols.

A. DE LA JONQUIÈRE, Histoire de l'empire Ottoman.

Special Works (presentations of limited periods or lives of individuals or studies of such fields as government, laws, customs, religion, etc.)

H. A. GIBBONS, The Foundation of the Ottoman Empire.

A. H. LYBYER, The Government of the Ottoman Empire in the Time of Suleiman the Magnificent.

R. KNOLLES, Generall Historie of the Turkes (first published 1603).

SIR P. RICAUT, A History of the Present State of the Ottoman Empire (first published 1682; a continuation of Knolles).

G. F. HERTZBERG, Geschichte der Byzantiner und des Osmanischen Reiches bis gegen Ende des 16.ten Jahrdunderts.

J. VON HAMMER-PURGSTALL, Des Osmanischen Reiches Staatsverfassung und Staatsverwaltung (with important documents such as kanuns, fetvas, etc.).

L. RANKE, The Ottoman and Spanish Empires in the sixteenth and seventeenth Centuries.

E. PEARS, The Destruction of the Greek empire and the Story of the Capture of Constantinople by the Turks.

W. MILLER, The Latins in the Levant.

Sir W. Muir, The Caliphate: its Rise, Decline, and Fall.
P. Herre, Europaeische Politik im Cyprischen Krieg, 1570–72.
Sir W. Stirling-Maxwell, Don John of Austria or Passages from the History of the Sixteenth Century.
O. Klopp, Das Jahr 1683 und der folgende grosse Tuerkenkrieg bis zum Frieden von Carlowitz.
A. Arneth, Prinz Eugen von Savoyen.
A. Huber, Geschichte Oesterreichs.
N. G. Mailath, Geschichte der Magyaren.
M. Brosch, Geschichten aus dem Leben dreier Grosswesire.
A. Heidborn, Manuel de droit public et administratif de l'empire Ottoman.
W. Eton, A Survey of the Turkish Empire (first publ. 1798).

For the following works, important for the study of the institutions of the empire, the reader should consult the discussion by Lybyer in Appendix V of his admirable work on Suleiman the Magnificent: J. Schiltberger, The Bondage and Travels of Johann Schiltberger (publ. by the Hakluyt Society). Ricoldus, De vita et moribus Turcarum (publ. 1509). G. A. Menavino, Trattato de Costumi et Vita de Turchi. Marino Sanuto (the Younger), Diarii, 1496–1533 (58 vols). B. Ramberti, The Second Book of the Affairs of the Turks (written in 1534; printed as Appendix I by Lybyer). O. G. Busbecq, Life and Letters (trans. from the Latin). I. M. D'Ohsson, Tableau Général de l'empire Othoman (publ. 1788–1824 in 7 vols.)

The Christian Subject Peoples

G. Finlay, The History of Greece (140 B.C. to 1864 A.D.) Ed. by Tozer. 7 vols.
F. Gregorovius, Geschichte der Stadt Athen im Mittelalter.
K. Hopf, Griechenland im Mittelalter und der Neuzeit (Parts 85 and 86 of Ersch und Gruber's Allgemeine Encyklopaedie).
J. F. Fallmerayer, Geschichte der Halbinsel Morea.
C. Jirecek, Geschichte der Bulgaren.
C. Jirecek, Geschichte der Serben.
L. Ranke, History of Servia.
B. von Kallay, Geschichte der Serben von den aeltesten Zeiten bis 1815.
J. Pisko, Skanderbeg (Historische Studie).
L. Kupelwieser, Die Kaempfe Ungarns mit den Osmanen bis zur Schlacht von Mohacz.
A. D. Xénopol, Histoire des Roumains.

Ethnology, Geography, Topography, Travel, Commerce

A. H. Keane, Man Past and Present.
Cambridge Medieval History. Vol. I. Ch. 12 (Peisker), The Asiatic Background.
E. H. Parker, A Thousand Years of the Tartars.
L. Cahun, Introduction a l'histoire de l'Asie: Turcs et Mongols.
C. Day, A History of Commerce.
W. M. Ramsay, Historical Geography of Asia Minor.

W. M. RAMSAY, The Geographical Conditions determining History and Religion in Asia Minor (Geog. Journal, 1902. Vol. XX).

A. H. LYBYER, The Ottoman Turks, and The Routes of Oriental Trade (Engl. Hist. Review, Vol. XXX, 1915).

Civilization, Literature, Arts

H. VAMBERY, Die primitive Cultur des Turko-tatarischen Volkes.

M. BITTNER, Der Einfluss des Arabischen und Persischen auf das Turkische (Situngsberichte der k. Akadamie der Wissenschaften. Phil-hist. Cl. Vol. 142.)

F. SARRE, Reise in Kleinasien, Sommer 1895. Forschungen zur Seldjukischen Kunst und Geographie des Landes.

H. G. WRIGHT, Constantinople old and new.

The Ottoman Empire and Europe (Diplomatic History)

J. DUMONT, Corps Universel Diplomatique. 8 vols. Amsterdam, 1726–31.

G. F. VON MARTENS, Recueil des principaux traités conclus par les Puissances de l'Europe depuis 1761 jusqu'à présent (with continuations).

A. F. PRIBRAM, Freiherr von Lisola (1613–74) und die Politik seiner Zeit.

A. F. PRIBRAM, Die Berichte des kais. Gesandten Franz von Lisola aus den Jahren 1655–60.

A. BEER, Die orientalische Politik Oesterreichs seit 1774.

A. SOREL, La Question d'Orient au XVIIIme siècle: le partage de la Pologne et le traité de Kainardji.

A. SOREL, L'Europe et la Revolution Française.

E. DRIAULT, La Politique orientale de Napoléon (1806–8).

THE EPOCH OF LIBERATION

CHAPTER XIX

A SURVEY OF THE OTTOMAN EMPIRE AT THE BEGINNING OF THE NINETEENTH CENTURY

HAVING reached the threshold of the nineteenth century, we are confronted by a new epoch of Balkan history, the Epoch of Liberation, during which our interest will be chiefly directed to the awakening to new life of the Christian groups subjected to the sultan. We have permitted them to sink from sight since their conquest, not without justification in view of the torpor which crept over them and which was so complete that for several centuries the political historian finds little or nothing of interest to report concerning them. Still we are legitimately curious as to how these victims of oppression fared during the long centuries the Moslem night endured and, more particularly, we would fain know something of their social status and frame of mind when the first faint flush of a new dawn hung out its banner in their sky. Before engaging, however, in such a review of the ruled, it may be advisable first to examine the rulers in order to gain precise information as to the form which the Ottoman government and administration had assumed at the moment when the rayahs were preparing to become a factor in the situation.

To the purely outward view the Ottoman empire was, in spite of the crushing calamities of the eighteenth century, still one of the greatest powers in the world, for, embracing within its jurisdiction all the lands and islands of the eastern Mediterranean area, it had a foothold in Europe, Asia, and Africa. But it was plainly shrinking at the peripheries, with the process most advanced perhaps in Africa. In the days of unquestioned Ottoman might, the unruly Moslem tribes of Algeria, Tunis, and Tripoli, who, to an alarming extent, lived by preying upon the Christian commerce of the Mediterranean, had found it profitable to acknowledge the suzerainty of the sultan; but when the sultan's sea-power declined to the point where it was no longer able to afford them as much as a shadow of protection, they cut the bond connecting them with Constantinople and became to all intents and purposes independent. Europe in its turn, quick to sense the situation, dealt with the bold corsairs of the Barbary states as free agents and punished them whenever the occasion served. In the eyes of friend and foe alike they had passed from the sultan's fold.

The Ottoman empire and Egypt.

There remained of Turkey-in-Africa only Egypt, by reason of its fertility as well as of its position at the bend of the Mediterranean, one of the rocks on which the empire had been reared. But in Egypt, too, the Ottoman authority had become uncertain and precarious. An organized soldiery, called the Mamelukes, had long ago possessed itself of the power and permitted the sultan's representative to reside in the Nile basin solely on the understanding that, in return for the customary tribute, he would withhold all interference in local affairs. Then in 1798, Napoleon Bonaparte unexpectedly injected himself into the situation, overthrew the Mamelukes, and conquered Egypt for France. When this conquest collapsed in short order, an English occupation followed and was maintained until, by virtue of the treaty of Amiens (1802), the English restored the country of the Nile to its legal owner, the sultan. But only nominally, since a local struggle for control ensued, out of which, the Mamelukes, scotched but not killed by Bonaparte, threatened to issue victorious. Their triumph was hindered, singly and solely, by an Albanian adventurer of the name of Mehemet Ali, who succeeded (1805) in persuading the sultan to grant him the government of Egypt as pasha, and who by making the most of his position and by the ruthless exercise of violence and treachery ended by totally exterminating the Mamelukes. Thereupon Mehemet Ali, an impressive oriental combination of cunning and vigor, undertook to build up an independent power in Egypt and to play a rôle in the eastern world of which we shall presently hear. The upshot of the disturbances precipitated in the Nile basin by Napoleon Bonaparte was that Mehemet Ali became the effective lord of the land with the sultan as much of a figure-head as ever. Measured by every genuine standard of government, Ottoman rule along the whole length of the north African shore had collapsed. Though the reasons for the collapse were many, the most immediate cause lay in the circumstance that the control of Africa could be effected only by means of a powerful fleet and that the Ottoman fleet had become a thing of the past.

The situation in Asia, though less desperate than in Africa, was far from encouraging, for the weak hand of the sultan had permitted the actual power to be seized, on the one hand, by hereditary tribal chiefs and on the other, by governors exercising the local rule in the sultan's name. Under these circumstances it had come about that almost the whole of Asia Minor (Anatolia and Armenia) was in the hands of feudal lords called derebeys (lords of the valleys), while the governors of the great provinces of Syria and Mesopotamia ruled their territories with little or no regard for distant Constantinople. The title which had by this time become usual for a provincial governor was pasha, and such was the weakness and decentralization of the empire that the pashas, around 1800, comported themselves very much like sovereigns. Derebeys and pashas still, as a rule, remitted the customary tribute to the sultan, but they had to be gently entreated or, as had recently happened at Bagdad and Acre, they boldly defied their feeble master.

The decline of Ottoman power in Asia.

If the foundations of Ottoman power in Asia generally seemed undermined, in Arabia they had crumbled entirely. For in that ancient home of the Moslem faith a sect, called Wahabites, had arisen and by means of a sincere and eloquent protest against the corruption of the religion of the Prophet had gathered together the fanatic tribes of the peninsula and cast out the Ottomans, finally, even from the Holy Cities of Mecca and Medina. To the proud Arabs, associates of the inspired Mohammed, the Ottomans had never been other than barbarous, upstart intruders.

Arabia in revolt.

— New Arab sect

In Europe the same picture of dissolution and insubordination everywhere met the eye. Particularly interested in this section of the Ottoman empire, we have already dealt with the provinces which, as a result of the decline of the sultan's power, had been taken over by Austria and Russia. To enumerate them once more: Hungary, Transylvania, and the Bukovina (the northern extremity of Moldavia) had by successive treaties been surrendered to Austria, while the Black sea coast as far as the Dniester,

The decline of Ottoman power in Europe.

and by the year 1812 (treaty of Bucharest) as far as the Pruth and the Kilia arm of the Danube river, had passed under the double-headed eagle of the great white tsar. Furthermore, since the peace of Kutchuk-Kainardji (1774) Russia not only possessed a qualified protectorate over the Rumanian provinces of Moldavia and Wallachia, but threw her shadow over the whole peninsula by virtue of her claim to act as spokesman for the sultan's Orthodox subjects. The surrender of so many territories, relatively removed from the capital, might have been less of a blow if the loss had been accompanied by a firmer grip on the remainder. But such was by no means the case. The pashas of Europe usurped the sultan's authority with the same nonchalance as did their brethren of Asia. They intrigued against his ministers, they carried on secret negotiations with one another, and on the slightest pretext they took the bit between their teeth. Often enough they began their career as mere brigands and were advanced to the dignity of pasha as the only means in the possession of the helpless Porte of bringing them to some sort of terms.

Pasvan Oglu of Vidin and Ali of Janina.

The case of Pasvan Oglu and the even more famous case of Ali of Janina throw a lurid light on the desperate internal situation and especially on the decrepitude of the central government. Pasvan Oglu, indistinguishable from any other highwayman except by a greater measure of luck and impudence, seized the important Danube fortress of Vidin, defeated every effort on the part of the sultan to oust him, and finally condescended to make peace on condition of his being made pasha of Vidin, an honor which carried with it the rule of a large part of Bulgaria. Only his opportune death (1807) freed the sultan from this obedient servant. Ali behaved even more flagrantly. After seizing Janina, in Epirus, he proceeded to extend his power over the adjoining territory until, at the beginning of the nineteenth century, he was engaged in rapidly building up what looked very much like an independent Albanian state. What respect and devotion he chose to show the sultan was entirely a matter of his own pleasure.

Review of the causes of decay.

With such a situation before him wherever he turned his gaze, the padishah could hardly feel that he was still master in his own house. Long before 1800 the sultans and such occasional councillors as had the good of the empire at heart were not only aroused by the terrible decay but often surprisingly well informed as to its causes. We took account of the signs of Ottoman dry-rot as far back as the seventeenth century and, as the situation had not been ameliorated since, we may at this point profitably summarize the analysis of a previous chapter.[1] The leading factor in the decline was the "passive" sultan, recluse of the imperial harem. Then there was the harem itself, inner shrine of the great palace compound known as the serai. The harem had gradually usurped the functions of government, which had thus in simple truth become the prerogative of an intriguing clique of women and eunuchs. With the triumph of these debasing influences at the core of the state, it became customary to sell the offices for money, thereby opening ever wider the flood-gates of bribery and corruption. Obliged to recover their expenses, the great administrative officials of the government, the viziers and pashas, brought pressure to bear on their subordinates, who of course could hardly do otherwise than in their turn apply the thumb-screws to those dependent on themselves. It was an endless chain of oppression, the brunt of which fell finally upon the common people. No whit less corrupt than the administration were the financial and judicial services, for the taxes were farmed out to private individuals bent on making their fortune in the shortest possible time, while the judges (cadis) very generally rendered decisions, eloquent less of their learning in the law than of their shameless venality.

However, since the Ottoman empire was a military state, whose power rested on the sword, the most serious of all the elements collaborating to produce decay was the decline of the standing army, the Janissaries. Their disorganization, already deplorable in the seventeenth century, had by the year 1800 become complete and irremediable. By gradual changes, as the reader will recall, the Janissaries had ceased to be recruited from the Christian subjects; they had become Moslemized and, in measure as their numbers grew — and they grew steadily in consequence of the crowding into service of pastry-cooks, street-vendors, and vagabonds — they had cast off the bonds of discipline and degenerated to an unmilitary rabble. By the end of the eighteenth century

The decaying Janissaries.

[1] Chapter XVI.

very few of their companies were quartered in barracks and subjected to regular training. Many lived as civilians, carried on a trade, and thriftily reduced their connection with the service to an unfailing appearance on pay-day. In fact the striking thing about the degenerate Janissaries was that, instead of being any longer a highly trained professional force, in which capacity they had earned their great reputation, they had become metamorphosed into a shambling militia without a trace of discipline and with no more than a rudimentary knowledge of the simplest military evolutions. Constantly beaten by the specialized forces of Europe, they would in any other state have been buried under a mountain of public ridicule. But in Turkey, conservative to the bone, such public opinion as existed viewed the whole body of national institutions as a sacred inheritance from the past. And as for the Janissaries themselves, privileged praetorians who for centuries had made and unmade sultans, they were not likely to suffer abolition without the fiercest kind of resistance.

None-the-less, their end was for the first time seriously threatened when, in 1789, Selim III mounted the throne. Measured by oriental standards, Selim was exceptionally intelligent and vivacious, and could boast besides an unusual insight into the abuses of the Ottoman system. Somehow, in spite of the impassable walls of the serai, European influences had penetrated to his seclusion, imposing the conviction that a program of reform, in modest imitation of the West, was absolutely necessary if his empire was to be saved from ruin. Accordingly, he planned to reinvigorate the central authority by bringing to heel the insubordinate vassals, especially of his Asiatic provinces, and by reducing the pashas in both Asia and Europe to their former rôle of obedient servants of the crown. He looked forward even to financial reforms by abolishing the wasteful system of farming the taxes, but above all, and with creditable wisdom, he gave his attention to the creation of a new army and navy built on the models furnished by the triumphant and irresistible occident. Some enlightened officials associated themselves with him and notable steps toward rehabilitation were taken by the establishment of special infantry and artillery troops armed, uniformed, and disciplined in the western manner, as well as by a sweeping reorganization, largely

Advent of a reforming sultan, Selim III (1789–1807).

under the direction of French instructors, of the arsenal, the cannon foundry, the officer schools, and the shipyards of Constantinople. In view of the stubborn prejudices of his subjects Selim had perforce to move slowly. Even so, the suspicion and soon the wrath of all those who profited by the old abuses were violently aflame. The Janissaries, when asked to adopt the weapons and learn the manoeuvres of their hated European foes, angrily refused, and the ulema, champions of a religious system fanatically hostile to change, circulated the report that the reforming padishah was secretly that most terrible of curses, an infidel, a giaour. The result might have been foreseen, for it was inevitable. Janissaries and ulema, joining hands, successfully stormed the serai, and though Selim was at first only deposed (1807), he was later murdered as the surest guarantee against his return to power.

With Selim's overthrow the whole frail and laborious structure of reform was scrapped without delay. The first effort of any consequence which had ever been made in the Ottoman state to assimilate it to the ideas and institutions of a changing and advancing Europe had ended in overwhelming failure. And yet salvation by any other than Selim's remedy was out of the question. Therefore it was fortunate for the state that a few men of Selim's circle held fast to his views, though for the time being it was not conducive to health to avow them. Among them was Selim's cousin Mahmud, who in 1808 succeeded to the throne. While adopting a waiting attitude, Mahmud was secretly resolved to return to Selim's program as soon as the occasion served; and in point of fact, as we shall see, in the course of a long reign (1808–39) he carried through, amidst alarming commotions, a notable, if by no means an efficient and complete, transformation of the inherited governing system.

The alert Selim had not failed to see another problem confronting his state due to the recent awakening of the rayahs. Ominous movements of revolt among them were already no longer a rarity. During the wars conducted against the Ottomans by Catherine of Russia, the Greeks of the Morea and the archipelago had listened to her promises of freedom and risen against their masters, and though on being abandoned by the shifty empress, they were once more whipped and massacred into submission,

Mahmud II (1808–39) cautiously takes over the reform program of Selim.

The rayah problem enters on a new phase.

the spark of rebellion was not extinguished in their hearts. In the same way whenever the Austrians threatened the sultan in the region of the Danube, groups of daring Serbs joined them in the hope of arousing the countryside and preparing the independence of their people. Selim gave these novel phenomena serious thought, but it is not reported that he elaborated, much less applied, a remedy. The truth was that a cure, that is, a fundamental and effective cure of the rayah evil was not possible by means of an ordinary reform. The problem was so inextricably interwoven with every deep-rooted conviction of the Moslem mind and with every characteristic Ottoman institution that the mere attempt to solve it was almost certain to drive the state upon the rocks.

The rigid character of the Ottoman state makes revolution inevitable.

Confronted with the issue of the sultan's Christian subjects, which, as already stated, will henceforth be our chief concern, we shall be doing well, by way of a beginning, to recall the analysis in an earlier chapter [1] of the peculiar genius of the Ottoman state. The Ottomans, having come into Europe as alien conquerors, never entertained any other idea with regard to their state than to use it as an instrument to perpetuate the advantages which they had won. If they spared the lives of the Christians and granted them the possession of their property, together with the right to worship as they pleased, it was on the distinct understanding that the conquered would, in return for these concessions, patiently submit to exploitation. On this account the haughty masters applied to them the designation rayah, which means herd or flock, and reveals with brutal frankness the function reserved to these victims of the Moslem sword. The social and religious barrier, raised like an insurmountable wall between conquerors and conquered, between Moslems and Christians, was intended to fix their mutual relations in perpetuity and provide against intermarriage and assimilation. If the Christians humbly accepted the situation which resulted from the hard verdict of war and consented to play the part of hewers of wood and drawers of water, that is, essentially of slaves, their lives would be spared and certain rudimentary benefits would follow. But if they should ever take it into their heads to

[1] Chapter XV.

assault the Ottoman prerogatives on some such theoretic plea as liberty and equality, they would be sure to invite a policy of stern repression and to provoke a war of mutual butchery such as has always marked the struggle of lord and risen serf. Owing to the rigid character of the Ottoman state and to its central principle that government belonged of divine right to Moslems only, a voluntary recognition of the rayahs as civil equals was absolutely out of the question. For these reasons we are justified in declaring that if the rayahs ever undertook to improve their lot, there might, due to the growing weakness of the Ottoman state and the pressure of the European powers, be politic talk of concessions and reform; in the long run the downtrodden Christians would be sure to discover that they could gain nothing except by revolution.

Abundant evidence for this conclusion will be supplied by the story that follows. However, before taking up our narrative, we owe ourselves an account of the Balkan Christians during the long generations when they accepted, however reluctantly, the conditions imposed by their masters, and obediently served them as rayahs. Having concluded to let the Christians live and possess property and enjoy religious toleration, the sultans were obliged to work out for them a system of government. Its peculiar forms were largely settled by the Moslem conception that the precepts and ordinances of religion constituted also a system of civil law. Since Moslems lived, not only on holy days and in the matter of faith and morals, but at all times and in respect of all their actions, under the Koran and the Sacred Law, it was natural to conceive the Christians as living in the same inclusive manner under their own divine dispensation as represented by the Orthodox church. The padishah had, therefore, no hesitation in entrusting the rule of the rayahs to the head of the church, the patriarch of Constantinople. To him and his bishops were conceded such sweeping powers that under the Turks the authority of the church waxed greater in some respects than it had been in the days of the Byzantine empire. For not only was the church (and that substantially means the patriarch as its head) given complete control over the buildings, seminaries, and revenues as well as the appointment of priests and officials, but its influence over the Christian laity

The Christians live as a wholly separate body under the Christian law as represented by the Orthodox church.

was gradually increased by the accumulation of an exclusive prerogative in all matters pertaining to marriage, inheritance, and litigation among members of the fold. Of course the sultan cunningly retained in his hand a check on so great an organization governed by so great a chief. The patriarch was the sultan's appointee, just as in the earlier days he had been the appointee of the Byzantine emperor, and if he indulged in any hostile practices or even as much as fell under suspicion of disloyalty, he could be made to pay with his head. Many were the patriarchs who from Mohammed the Conqueror to the reforming Selim III either were abruptly deposed or perished by violence.

[handwritten margin note: Peter I did away with the Patriarch & became czar ...]

The unwritten alliance between the the patriarch sultan and of Constantinople.

On the whole, however, the sultans had reason to be pleased with the conduct of the patriarchs. To the indolent Asiatic, averse to taking trouble, it seemed that the problem of the rayah had been decidedly simplified by being transferred to the shoulders of a single man, who could be brought to account at a moment's notice and who was, in spite of an apparent grandeur, a miserable slave like the rest of his race. It was from this characteristically oriental consideration that the sultans steadily advanced the powers of the patriarch until all Orthodox Christians without exception were included in his fold. Back in the fifteenth century, when the Ottomans established themselves on the Bosporus, there were, besides the patriarchate of Constantinople, two other patriarchates in existence in the peninsula, relics of the former greatness of Bulgaria and Serbia. They were the patriarchates of Ochrida (Macedonia) and Ipek (Serbia). While their incumbents fell under the suspicion of the Porte because, being remote from the capital, they necessarily enjoyed a certain freedom of action, they were at the same time the objects of the jealousy of the patriarch of Constantinople, who had originally been alone in the field and who looked upon them essentially as interlopers. In consequence of this double animosity they led a precarious existence, their independence was gradually reduced, and in the eighteenth century (1766–67) they were completely suppressed, their authority being merged with the great Constantinopolitan see. Just before the dawn of the movement of liberation all the Orthodox churches of Balkania were in this way united under a single head. Since the coming of

Christianity it would be difficult to name a period when the patriarch of New Rome towered so loftily over the eastern church.

Unhappily this outward splendor of the Greek prelate did not proclaim a corresponding inner dignity and worth of the institution which he governed. Learning and piety, which had long ago reached a low ebb in the East, increasingly in the Ottoman period abandoned the councils of a priesthood whose whole activity came to be directed to the exact performance of the traditional rites and to the inculcation of a fanatically defended body of doctrines. Without doubt the Greek clergy, considered as a body of teachers and leaders of men, fell far below the level maintained in the same period by the Christians of the West, both Protestants and Catholics. But the dark ignorance and furious intolerance of the eastern clerics were not even their worst traits for they were corrupt to the core. This unclean condition, however, they could, at least in part, charge fairly to the Ottoman masters. We have followed the terrible march of corruption through Ottoman public life and noted how the time came when every office of state was, in effect, put up at auction. So great a post as that of patriarch could not escape the general trend, since, with the financial necessities of the sultans growing with every decade, it became incumbent to find rich Greeks and to induce them to offer ever waxing sums for the greatest dignity within their reach. The Christian church soon presented a close counterpart to the abuses afflicting the Moslem state. The patriarch, in order to recover his expenses, was obliged to sell the bishoprics, and the bishops on arriving in their dioceses had to mulct the priests, who of course revenged themselves by outrageous charges on their parishioners. It was a vicious circle, that did much to bring the clergy into contempt and disrepute.

The manifold abuses in church and clergy.

Another charge commonly flung at the clergy concerns the policy of Hellenization. The patriarch and the members of his immediate circle were Greek, passionately Greek, and did not scruple to use their immense power to further the Greek national cause at the expense of their Slav and Rumanian fellow-rayahs. Not only were the prelacies reserved exclusively for Greeks, but systematic warfare was made upon all languages other than

Hellenization policy of the Orthodox church.

Greek in the hope of suppressing their use within the organization. Not content with gradually eliminating the Slav language
from the religious service, the Greek rulers actually persecuted
Slav seminaries and libraries by closing the former and by
scattering and even ruthlessly applying the torch to the latter.
Although the Orthodox church became Greek, in fact as well
as in name, and although the Slav and Rumanian learning,
which, such as they were, had always been essentially ecclesiastical, were now brought to extinction, the national memories
continued to be secretly cherished and might, under more favorable circumstances, arise and bear witness against the oppressor.

Mounting importance in the Ottoman state of the Greeks.

The deeper we penetrate beneath the surface the clearer it
becomes that, though all Christians were rayahs, contemptuously
suffered by their Moslem masters, the Greeks were rayahs with
a difference and enjoyed a privileged position within the empire,
which, if associated with their control of the Christian church,
did not exclusively depend on it. Circumstances of an historical
order contributed to lift them above the regular rayah level: they
were a people mentally alert, the heirs of an ancient tradition
of culture of which they were exceedingly proud; planted along
the Mediterranean coast, they fed the arteries of trade and
were economically indispensable to the whole Near East; and
in view of the mental sluggishness of the Ottomans and their
aversion to the pursuit of commerce and learning, the Hellenes
were freely called on by their masters to help manage the affairs
of the complicated Ottoman realm. It is hardly an exaggeration
to say that it was the Greeks who by their diverse labors of an
economic and administrative nature kept the empire afloat as a
going concern.

The Phana-riotes.

In the eighteenth century the Greek influence in the Ottoman
state reached its height and naturally it was particularly manifested at the capital, at Constantinople. Here, in the quarter
inhabited by the patriarch and known as the *phanar* (lighthouse),
were congregated not only the numerous officials of the patriarch
but also the fiscal and administrative servants who had found
their way into the civil service of the Porte. In consequence
all Greek officials, employed by the sultan, were usually called
Phanariotes. Among them were included some of the most
important men of the empire, for instance the dragoman of the

Porte and the dragoman of the fleet. The former was, in effect, a secretary for foreign affairs, while the latter administered the fleet and at the same time the Greek coasts and islands, on the inhabitants of which the fleet was obliged to draw for its able seamen. Of course the two dragomans were technically under Moslem superiors, but these, yielding to the indolent oriental temper, were usually pleased to transfer the responsibilities of office to the ambitious hirelings, whom, as Christians, they were free to despise. The highest dignities, however, conferred upon the Phanariotes were the governments of the Rumanian princi- palities, Wallachia and Moldavia. If all the Ottoman offices had to be purchased with liberal sums of money, the Rumanian governments, which exalted the incumbents with the princely title of hospodar or voivode, called for a king's ransom. On setting out for the Danube the successful candidate carried with him a retinue of greedy adventurers of his own race, and, arrived at Bucharest or Jassy, he devoted his attention exclu- sively to the uplifting task of collecting money to pay his debts and to enrich a vicious spawn of usurers and sycophants. To the native Rumanians it was the Greek who was the leech and oppressor, and not the Moslem, who never showed his face. What wonder that to the Rumanians, and to their fellow-rayahs generally, the Greeks often appeared as no better than a more cunning variety of Turks! For all these victims of oppression, longing for liberation and the end of misrule, there was a Greek as well as an Ottoman master to be overthrown.[1]

---

[1] The Phanariote rule in the Rumanian principalities was of relatively recent origin, having been introduced in 1711. When, as related on p. 206, Wallachia and Moldavia made submission to the sultan, they were per- mitted to retain a considerable autonomy under princes of their own race. The system never worked very well, since the native hospodars plotted against their suzerain as soon as they stood a good chance to shake off the yoke. With the rise of Russia under Peter the Great they became a direct menace to their overlord on the Bosporus, and when, in the war of 1711, they either helped or tried to give help to Peter, the sultan seized the occasion to terminate native rule. Because he felt reasonably sure of the Greeks as strangers on the Danube, and also because he coveted the money they would pay, he hit upon the device of putting the hospodarships up at auction among the Phanariotes. The Greek rule lasted for about a hundred years (till 1821), when, owing to the Hellenic revolt, the Greeks in their turn fell under suspicion and made room once more for Rumanian appointees.

The dis-
abilities of
the rayahs
and the
question of
their
conversion
to Islam.

Exalted as the Greeks might feel above the Slavs and Rumans, in the eyes of the Moslems they were indistinguishable from the other rayahs and were, like them, subject to certain disabilities. These still were what they had ever been, though the tribute of children had, as we have seen, ceased to be collected in the course of the seventeenth century. Thus the rayahs were forbidden to possess arms and every male, beginning approximately at the age of ten, paid an annual capitation-tax, called *haratch*, from which the Moslems were exempt. In addition an endless string of minor tribulations served to bring home to the Christians every hour a sense of hopeless inferiority. Their clothing had to be of a simple pattern devoid of anything suggesting ornament or pride; if, while riding to market, they encountered a Moslem, they had humbly to dismount and stand to one side; in the court of the cadi their evidence was rejected as unworthy of belief; they were forbidden to ring their church-bells, and even, without special permission, to repair their dilapidated churches. When we remember that all these vexations ended at once for every rayah who went over to Islam, we cannot but marvel at the refusal of the oppressed to terminate their misery by a process of wholesale conversion. True, while sporadic changes of faith took place at all times, now and then a considerable group, moved by the desire to retain their arms or perhaps to acquire an unchallenged control of their property, did go over to the enemy. In Bosnia, for instance, the powerful landholders, called begs, were genuine Serbs who had accepted the Koran; moreover the people in the Rhodope mountains, known as Pomaks, were converted Bulgars, while in the Albanian highlands something more than half the population had, under the leadership of their tribal chiefs, gradually transferred their allegiance from the church to the mosque. Grievous defections these, which broke the solid Christian front and heaped up grave troubles for the coming time; none-the-less the fact remains and strikingly brings out the fidelity of all the Balkan peoples to the great memories of their past, that, generally speaking, omnipotent and triumphant Islam sounded its lure in vain.

If in this result, so creditable to the moral fiber of the rayahs, the Orthodox church with its worship maintained in every village and with its subtle penetration into the daily concerns of all its communicants has doubtless the largest part, another factor is by no means negligible. As our investigation has shown, the Ottoman state was a haphazard contrivance run by sluggish, Asiatically minded individuals to the sole end of maintaining a supremacy substantially assured by means of an army. As the tedious details of civil administration interfered with that dreamy contemplation which for every true Turk is symbolized by the cup of fragrant mocha and the long-stemmed chibuk, the men in power were by no means averse to leaving local government everywhere very much as they had found it on coming into the peninsula. The result was that while the great affairs of state were taken over by the sultan with a brilliant staff of viziers and pashas, the narrow and mean concerns of the villages and towns were in most cases left where they had always been, that is, in the hands of the local authorities. In this way, under cover of a group of ornamental Moslem dignitaries, a great deal of native self-government managed to preserve itself. Though we shall hear of it in more detail later, in connection with the story of the rayah rebellions, some of its leading centers may advantageously be indicated here. In the heart of Serbia every village had its own elected headman and every group of villages its chief or knez, while in the Greek Morea there was a whole hierarchy of local administrators culminating in a general assembly of so-called primates who assessed and collected the taxes. In the lawless mountains of Albania, where the conquerors had never been able to get a firm footing, such government as existed was wholly local; it was of the traditional tribal sort and the sultan's part in it amounted to next to nothing. Indeed, a close inspection of the many provinces of European Turkey brings to light the fact that the greatest diversity of local conditions prevailed and that, due to the quiet persistence everywhere of ancient forms, a certain measure of self-government was the rule rather than the exception. If we now recall that the central authority was rapidly dissolving in the eighteenth century, we shall not be surprised at the discovery that the free spirit behind the native institutions was steadily waxing stronger and bolder.

A striking evidence of the new and courageous spirit among the rayahs was furnished by the growing number of individuals

Failure of the Ottomans to destroy the local government and importance of its persistence.

The new spirit: klefts and heyduks.

who, impatient of the Turkish yoke, possessed themselves of weapons and on their own authority declared war upon the tyrant. They became of course outlaws and highwaymen living in caves and woods in instant peril of death, but they succeeded in doing immense damage to their enemies in life and goods and, although always pursued, were never eradicated. Called klefts among the Greeks and heyduks among the Serbs, they were looked on by the common people as avengers of their wrongs and as a species of national heroes. A popular ballad literature gathered around them and carried to every rayah fireside the stirring tale of the blood paid by the oppressor for his age-old crimes.

The sum of circumstances favors a Christian revolt.

Considering the Christians collectively from the outlook of the year 1800, we may easily persuade ourselves that never since their conquest had there been an equally favorable prospect of liberation. The most important circumstance was of course the dissolution of the Ottoman power which, patent to all, had also proved itself, at least thus far, beyond any reformer's skill to arrest. Inevitably in the face of this decay a new hope visited the conquered, which showed not only in the under-ground rumblings of a general unrest but in the individual action of brave klefts and heyduks. Finally, it augured well for the future of the rayahs that, should they ever rise and attempt to resume the inalienable rights of freemen, they would not be without the notable advantages resulting from organization; for they would find, on the one hand, in their church and, on the other, in their local institutions an invaluable support for their perilous and virile enterprise.

CHAPTER XX

THE SERB REVOLT AND THE FOUNDING OF THE SERB STATE

To the average person of today inclined to identify history with national politics, the outstanding fact in the history of the Serb people must be that they never achieved their political unification. The nearest they ever came to it was under the famous Tsar Stephen Dushan. But from even Dushan's broad empire some groups of Serbs were missing. Thus the important city of Ragusa, which served as Serbia's chief seaport, was, though allied with Stephen, not subject to him; and more important still, mountainous and inaccessible Bosnia, lying to the west of Serbia, stubbornly maintained its independence under its own line of rulers. Then, on Stephen's death (1355), the short-lived glory of Serbia perished and the state fell disastrously apart into separate lordships. These the conquering Ottomans picked up one by one, the last to go being the old Serb nucleus, called Rascia in the difficult mountains between the Lim and the Ibar. *Significant lack of political unity in Serb history.*

During the long Ottoman night the tendency among the Serbs to disintegration grew, if anything, more pronounced, so that, taking inventory of the situation at the beginning of the nineteenth century, we are struck by an unusual picture of weakness and dispersion. Leaving minor nuclei out of consideration, we detect four centers of Serb life which not only were distinct politically but which intellectually and culturally also had become almost completely cut off from one another. If the nationalist enthusiasm characteristic of the new Europe should ever reach Balkania, it would in all probability awaken an irresistible tendency among the scattered fragments of the Serbs to draw together, but as, around the year 1800, nationalism in Balkania was at best a hope, each of the four Serb centers calls for separate consideration. It simplifies the situation, as it also greatly promoted the cause of national unity in the years to come that, of the four centers, one completely overshadowed the rest. That was the *Four distinct centers of Serb life around the year 1800, of which the pashalik of Belgrad is most important.*

Serb nucleus, the old principality of Rascia; only its center of gravity had in recent generations been slightly moved to the north and now rested in the broad angle made by the Morava, Danube, and Save rivers. Called in the Ottoman period the pashalik of Belgrad, this region lighted the first fires of rebellion and registered the first successes against the Moslem overlord. Inevitably its daring and initiative earned for it the leadership of the Serb people, but before following the developments at this decisive point it is advisable to take account of the other three centers.

Bosnia a land of Serbs.

To the west of the pashalik of Belgrad lay Bosnia, the people of which, never drawn into the main current of Serb history, had under the Turks been exposed to influences which threatened still further division. For, following the Ottoman conquest, the Bosnian nobility had gone over to Islam, and, though of the same blood, they were now the oppressors of the Christians, who, as peasants, constituted the majority of the people. These nobles, called begs, still spoke the Serb tongue but were among the most fanatic Mussulmans of the peninsula. As the ruling element in Bosnia they were sure to delay the spread of national sentiment and make Bosnia a very difficult special problem within the general Serb field.

The Serbs of southern Hungary.

Another Serb center lay in southern Hungary. In the Middle Age the Serbs reached hardly at any point as far north as the Save and the Danube rivers. But their peasant-pioneers had been slowly moving northward, and even as early as the fifteenth century they began to pass the rivers constituting the traditional southern boundary of Hungary. The long, devastating border warfare between Hungary and the Ottomans seems to have completely driven the original agricultural population from the river districts and to have created a vacuum which the Serbs filled by gradual infiltration. Then toward the end of the seventeenth century, in the days when Prince Eugene's victories over the Turks aroused the first rebellious stir among the Serbs, a deliberate migration took place which is estimated to have transferred more than thirty thousand industrious peasant families from the heart of Balkania to the fertile plains of southern Hungary. Like their scattered predecessors these later colonists carried with them their Orthodox faith and struggled resolutely to

preserve their national identity, including, as an important item,
their ancient and beloved local self-government. In this political
effort they were unsuccessful, for the Hapsburg government
insisted on fitting them into its absolute and bureaucratic system.
However, in intellectual and educational matters they remained
relatively free and enjoyed besides the advantage of easy access
to western ideas and civilization. The result was that, while
remaining politically unimportant, the young Serb center in
southern Hungary developed a mental activity destined to act
very stimulatingly on the Balkan Serbs, especially during the
earlier phases of their struggle for independence.

There remains the fourth center, which, though small, boasts
so fascinating a history that it calls for development at greater
length. It will be recalled that back in mediaeval times there
was, in addition to Rascia, a second Serb political center, located
along the Adriatic coast and called, from its leading river, the
Zeta. Having been fused with Rascia under the Nemania dynasty, the Zeta disappeared for a time from the political story of
Serbia. But when Dushan's empire dissolved, the Zeta reasserted
its individuality and under a line of its own began a career of
independence. It was around 1360, under the house of Balsha,
that this movement of separation was effected. And no sooner
was the new Serb state founded than it became an object of
Ottoman greed. Although occupied with more pressing matters
than the tiny creation among the difficult mountains overlooking
the lake of Scutari, the sultans never entertained any other
thought than that, when the time was ripe, they would lay a
conquering hand upon it. Beginning with the fifteenth century,
in the days when Scanderbeg won immortal fame by defending
the freedom of Albania, the Ottoman monarchs resolutely proceeded to reduce the Zeta, joining Albania on the north, to
obedience, but neither in the fifteenth nor in any other century
did they ever fully achieve their purpose. To be sure they
exercised an unremitting pressure on the brave mountaineers and,
in the course of time, succeeded in pushing them out of the
fertile valleys, adjoining the lake of Scutari, into the bleak and
unproductive uplands dominating the fiord of Cattaro. This
lofty eyrie, serving as a last refuge from slavery, greatly endeared
itself to the few thousand dauntless warriors with their families,

The gradual
formation of
Monte-
negro as a
mountain
center of
Serb life.

who made their homes among its barren crags and called it Chernagora (Crna Gora) or the Black Mountain. Under the Italian name of Montenegro its frame has circled the world. As a curtain-raiser to the Balkan liberation drama of the nineteenth century no story could be more appropriate or inspiring than that of Montenegro.

Montenegro shut in between the Ottoman empire and Venice.

Aside from the fact that its inhabitants were obliged to exercise eternal vigilance as the price of freedom very little information of a detailed sort touching the early history of the Black Mountain has come down to us. The typical highland organization into clans obtained, each clan being under a chief, with the ideal unity of the group represented by the reigning family, the Balshas. While the Ottomans were engaged in gradually taking over the fertile lowlands around the lake of Scutari, the Venetians, hardly less aggressive, pressed upon the small state from the opposite or northern boundary by occupying the inlet of Cattaro and cutting the highlands off from the sea. From the fifteenth century on Cattaro was an important post in the chain of coastal positions by which the republic of St. Mark defended the Adriatic sea against the infidels. Although Venice came as a conqueror to the Montenegrin coast, it was no sooner established than it became a factor in the Montenegrin defense, since by fortifying Cattaro it not only safeguarded the mountaineers against an attack from the rear, but also provided a door by which a constant supply of food and ammunition could be transmitted to the uplands. Not from any motive of altruism of course, but for the simple reason that it was promoting its own interests against the sultan, the common foe of Venetians and Montenegrins, Venice for several centuries, though very capriciously, extended a helping hand to the highland clansmen.

Truth and poetry in early Montenegrin history.

In the course of the fifteenth century the Balsha dynasty was supplanted by the Chernoievich family, under which, in consequence of the relentless Moslem pressure, the restriction of the ancient Zeta to the bare circumference of the Black Mountain was finally effected. Our only evidences for the period are the ancient ballads (pjesmas), which flourished among the Montenegrins as among the other Serbs and which, by heartening the people with a recital of the deeds of their forefathers, rendered an incalculable service in keeping alight the fires of resistance. One of these ballads permits the inference that around the year 1519 the reigning Chernoievich, despairing of the rude task before him, resigned his power and sailed away to pass the remainder of his life in pleasant Venice. It is possible that, following this desertion, some kind of submission was made to the sultan and a slight tribute (*haratch*) paid in sign thereof. Patriotic Montenegrins refuse to believe it, and the matter remains clouded; but if the situation among the neighboring Albanian tribes may serve as an index, the tribute may have been paid to meet an overwhelming momentary pressure without in the least impairing the essential independence of the wild clans secure in their rocky fastnesses.

If the question of submission to the sultan must remain open, it is certain that on the failure of the second dynasty a new government was gradually formed, which represents a remarkable political experiment and under which the war for independence was vigorously resumed. With the departure of the hereditary ruler for Venice the most distinguished person left on the Black Mountain was the bishop of Cettinje, a small settlement harboring a monastery and perched high over the waters of Cattaro. The bishop, elected in accordance with Orthodox practice from among the monks of the monastery, became the natural leader of the people and gradually added to his ecclesiastical control a number of civil functions. Under the title *vladika*, or prince-bishop he rallied his Christian flock to persist in the struggle with the Turk; and with the true instinct of warriors the Montenegrins so fully recognized the need of leadership that they gave their support to the steady development of the bishop's power. That power signified a theocracy and, what is more, a fighting theocracy, if ever there was one.

The bishop of Cettinje becomes the Montenegrin chief under the title vladika.

For almost two centuries following the establishment of this peculiar government, as good as no light is shed upon the little state, for even the ballads desert us in this period, communicating nothing but a confused tale of combat with the eternally encroaching Moslem. We hear vaguely of armies of twenty and thirty thousand Ottomans invading the uplands, which, some-

More generations of legendary struggle with the Turks.

times crushed by an ambuscade or buried beneath an avalanche of stones, on other occasions advanced victoriously to Cettinje, where they destroyed the monastery and set the Crescent in place of the Cross on the ridge-pole of the vladika's house. Though the details will never be recovered, the heroism of the men who met these attacks is as legible as print and is beyond praise. The Montenegrin was and remained in all his habits a very primitive type of clansman but his spirit acquired the elastic temper of fine steel. For, though he lived in a rude hut among limestone crags so bare of vegetation that he had to depend for his living on a few sheep and goats, together with the yield of an occasional patch of fertile ground, he dedicated himself from boyhood to an idea and, to remain free, engaged in a life-long battle not only with the Turk but also with dire physical want and a terrible, upland climate. In an effort to account for his wild courage as well as for his splendid physique the theory has been advanced that the Montenegrin freemen represented what was left of the old Serb nobility, which, following the destructive battle of Kossovo, is assumed to have made its way into the mountain wilderness as to a citadel of refuge. As not a trace of evidence can be adduced in support of this contention, it is difficult to see how it can be maintained. Warrior qualities, it is true, have generally distinguished the aristocracies of the past, but the warrior qualities of the Montenegrins had time to develop during the constant struggle of centuries, and require, in order to account for them, no assumption of derivation from the fighting chiefs of ancient Serbia. Whoever takes pleasure, in view of their daring and hardihood, in hailing the Montenegrins as noblemen may do so, but they are noblemen by patent of nature and not by reason of a mythical descent.

The reign of the vladika, Danilo (1696–1735).

Around the year 1700 the veil hiding a long-drawn, epic struggle lifts somewhat and events take place which have a definite outline. In the year 1696 Danilo I of the Petrovich family was elected vladika, and during his long reign, which lasted to 1735, there befell a number of events which greatly consolidated the loose community of highland peasants and shepherds. First of all the country was purged of its Christian renegades. Apparently a considerable number of Montenegrins, especially in the valleys at the point of contact with the pashalik of Scutari, had gradually been weaned from their faith and had won consideration for their persons and security for their property by conversion to Islam. Of all such the vladika and his followers resolved to rid themselves by a concerted massacre like the famous St. Bartholomew's Eve of French history, but unlike it in the sweeping character of its success. The ballad, which in the first flush of triumph a native poet fashioned to celebrate this bloody deed, breathes a fierce religious exultation and is tinged with not a shadow of doubt touching the righteousness of the act. To this primitive bishop and his people the massacre meant simply the destruction of the traitors within the citadel and was as natural as breathing.

Destruct of Monts who became muslim [margin annotation, handwritten]

Encouraged by their victory over a rival religion, the Montenegrins next resolved to take advantage of the growing decay manifested by the Ottoman empire. They offered their aid to Austria and Russia in the offensive movements against the sultan which these powers had recently inaugurated. Especially toward Russia, Orthodox in faith and Slav in blood, did the vladika turn his gaze, and inasmuch as the reigning tsar, Peter the Great, was a statesman of large vision, communications passed to and fro which in 1711 led to a formal alliance. It is true that Montenegro paid the price of this adventure by being deserted by the tsar when, on his defeat by the Turks, he was obliged (treaty of the Pruth) to come to terms with the foe, but it is also undeniable that an intimacy was established between big Russia and little Montenegro which, with interruptions, lasted for two centuries and gave the mountaineers a much needed champion among the great powers.

Friendship with Russia.

In the border struggles with the Moslems of Scutari, which continued as usual in Danilo's reign both before and after the Russian friendship was cemented, the vladika won more decisive victories than had ever been won before and was rewarded by liberating from Moslem rule and adding to his realm the wooded district to the east, called Brda. It was the first step in the territorial expansion of the small community.

The border struggle with the Turks.

Such notable achievements gained for Danilo a merited prestige and enabled him to effect a change in the system of government. Hitherto the vladika had been elected from among the monks of the monastery of Cettinje by the coöperative action of clergy

The vladika becomes hereditary as well as more powerful.

and people. The election signified that Montenegro was essentially a republic of freemen Danilo's lofty reputation now made it possible for him to abolish the election and to make the sovereignty hereditary in his family. Since, however, in accordance with the requirements of eastern Christianity, the bishop was obliged to be a celibate and would therefore be without legitimate offspring, it was arranged that the incumbent should choose his successor from among his nephews. On these strange terms the Montenegrin theocracy became hereditary and, supported by public opinion, succeeded in gradually undermining the authority of the rude popular assemblies which had hitherto played a considerable part in Montenegrin political life. Though the vladika, burdened with episcopal duties, found it advantageous to delegate the management of secular affairs to a special agent, who, if capable, might exercise considerable power, it admits of no doubt that, from the time of Danilo I, the vladika, much more thoroughly than ever before, dominated both church and state.

Full independence of Montenegro acknowledged by the Porte in 1799.

Although the eighteenth century, like all the centuries which preceded it, echoes with the resistance offered by the small Christian outpost above Cattaro to the Moslem hosts ever advancing from Scutari, we may content ourselves with taking note of a single event befalling in this period. In 1799, after a series of signal defeats, the reigning sultan, Selim III, signed a treaty with Vladika Peter I, by virtue of which he recognized, without any qualification, the full independence of Montenegro. If the question must remain undecided whether the Ottomans ever at any time exercised an effective sovereignty over the Black Mountain, it is established beyond doubt that, beginning with the founder of the Petrovich line of vladikas, the highlanders presented so stubborn a front to the foe that, in the course of a few generations, the sultan was obliged to put his signature to a document declaring that Montenegro owed him not the slightest semblance of allegiance.

Condition of the Serbs of the pashalik of Belgrad around 1800.

We may now turn from the handful of free and heroic Serbs of Montenegro to their brethren of the pashalik of Belgrad, who, though rayah and unfree, constituted the vital center of the race. It is their particular distinction to have, around the year 1800, inaugurated a movement of Serb independence which swept in an ever-broadening flood down the nineteenth century. We are aware what these Serbs had to suffer in their purse and dignity at the hands of their masters, but we have also seen that the Ottomans conceded religious toleration to the Christian population and largely left in its hands the management of local affairs. The Ottoman mailed fist was represented in the province by a governor or pasha who resided at Belgrad, by a cadi (judge) in every town, and by the landholders or spahis, who, in return for rendering service as a cavalry in time of war, had a claim to a tithe of the product of field, vineyard, and beehive. Though often compared with western feudal landlords, the spahis, whose number in the pashalik did not reach a thousand, had in reality much less power than the occidental nobility, since, instead of having the actual title to their estates, they possessed merely a claim to a percentage of the peasant's product. Moreover, very unlike western noblemen, they did not reside among the fields but congregated with their followers in the few small towns. These therefore had a mixed Moslem and Christian population, whereas the numerous villages of the countryside presented an unbroken Serb aspect. Along the valleys and wooded slopes the Christians could accordingly live out their lives with little regard to their Moslem overlords, whom they rarely, if ever, saw, and could cultivate their national traditions without interference. Of these a very important one was the system of local government. An agent, called *knez* (lord), represented the village, while the *oborknez* (grand knez) ruled a group of villages constituting a district. The knezes assessed and collected the taxes and exercised besides all police and judicial functions of a purely local nature. In the judgment of competent scholars, if the Ottoman rule in Serbia was an alien tyranny, it had its distinct mitigations inasmuch as it did not greatly affect the life of the peasant mass. True to everything that was deeply rooted in their past, to the Christian religion, to their traditional village and district organization, to their ancient beliefs, festivals, and mores, the Serbs of the eighteenth century convey the impression that if they were under an eclipse, they still boasted everything essential to the perpetuation of a national group and to its eventual organization as a separate polity.

That great world movements were conspiring to help the Serbs regain their independence we have already noted. Apart from the decay and weakness of the Porte and the successful aggressions of its immediate neighbors, such as Austria and Russia, we must take account in this connection of the great transformation of European thought, of which the *Aufklaerung* in Germany and the revolution in France, with its battle-cry of liberty and equality were characteristic expressions. All these events and influences reached, if they did not penetrate, the remote pashalik of Belgrad and by communicating a certain mental restlessness prepared the way for change. But it was, after all, a local circumstance that was responsible for the popular agitation leading directly to revolt. In the eighteenth century the heaviest curse of the many curses under which the Ottoman empire groaned and labored was, as we know, the lawless Janissary soldiery. Only recently established in Serbia, which for generations had enjoyed immunity with regard to them, they undertook in their impertinent way and in open defiance of the pasha and the other Ottoman authorities to help themselves to everything in sight. As chance would have it that rare phenomenon, a reforming sultan, mounted the throne in 1789 in the person of Selîm III, and Selim, secretly resolved to rid himself of the Janissary pest, took advantage of a clause in the treaty of Sistova, concluded in 1791 with Austria, to exclude the ever mutinous praetorians from the pashalik of Belgrad. At the same time he sent thither as pasha, an excellent man, Mustapha by name, who made every effort to regain the favor of the rayahs and who so fully succeeded that the grateful Serbs acclaimed him as their " mother." He even went the length of organizing the Serb peasants as an armed militia in order to enable them to fight the Janissaries, should the need arise. If we recall that the disarming of the rayahs was a fundamental principle of Ottoman state-craft, we can appreciate what a startling innovation it was of which the benevolent pasha was the sponsor.

The new and enlightened régime proceeded happily until the sultan's domestic necessities drove him to make concessions to his enemies, the Janissaries, and to grant them permission to reënter the pashalik. In 1799 they swarmed back into their old haunts and, filled with the spirit of vengeance, succeeded in a short time in turning everything topsy-turvy. Not only was the good pasha foully murdered (1801), but the spahis and all other representatives of the sultan were openly flouted, while the despised Christians were subjected to every outrage which a fiendish soldiery could devise. Under four chiefs, called dahis, they held the land at their mercy. The inhabitants, Moslems and Christians alike, appealed to Constantinople for relief, and on a hint from the sultan that their cause was just, they resolved to help themselves. It was a fortunate circumstance that the Serbs still had the arms supplied them by their "mother," and it was equally fortunate that they now found that blessing, a leader, without whom a rebellion, be it never so boldly sustained, is sure to end in failure. The leader was George Petrovich, called Karageorge or Black George from his dark, shaggy locks and piercing eyes. Though in intelligence and energy a man in a thousand, Karageorge was a typical Serb peasant, who understood his people and was instinctively understood by them. In his youthful days he had joined the Austrian army in order to fight against the Turks, and again, in the rôle of heyduk, he had grimly relieved rich, traveling Moslems of their purses or, if it better pleased his errant fancy, of their lives. In recent years he had taken to deal in that most bountiful of Serbia's national products, the pig, and had proved a most successful trader. By his commercial excursions over the Serb countryside he had become widely known, and as there was something magnetic and authoritative about the man, his word came to carry an extraordinary weight. No wonder that when, in the spring of 1804, he declared for the revolution, he straightway became the guiding spirit of his people.

The revolution of 1804 was supported by the Serb peasantry with such entire courage and devotion that it swiftly achieved its purpose. The Janissaries were scattered to the winds and their leaders, the dahis, slain amidst general exultation. What next? Though conducted against the Ottoman soldiery, the insurrection had enjoyed the sultan's tacit approbation, since the Janissaries, as mutineers, were hardly less the enemies of their master than of the Serbs. Now that the Serbs were rid of their oppressors, the sultan expected them to return to the fold and sent a pasha to negotiate with them to this end. Great

The war against the Janissaries becomes a war for independence.

was his surprise to learn that, possessed of weapons and elated by their recent victory, the humble rayahs demanded an extension of their local rights. To Selim this was intolerable impudence and therefore, after a futile exchange of opinions, the war entered its second phase and became a war against the sultan. Begun to gain relief from the Janissaries, the struggle developed into an open war for independence.

The War of Independence, 1804–13. With splendid resolution the spirit of the Serbs rose to meet the new situation. They beat the armies which the Porte sent against them once, twice, and many times, until in the course of a few campaigns they had effectively cleared the whole pashalik of the enemy. In these encounters Karageorge, acting as commander-in-chief, proved himself much more than a guerrilla fighter, for the Ottoman armies sent against him could not have been beaten except by the skill and daring of a born military leader. From 1806 on, however, Karageorge was aided by an extraneous factor. In that year Russia, for reasons, it is true, having little to do with Serbia, engaged in a new war with the Porte and necessarily attracted Ottoman attention to itself. In consequence of tremendous European events culminating in 1807, at Tilsit, in the alliance between Emperor Napoleon and Tsar Alexander, the Turco-Russian war was hardly under way when it was halted by a truce. But as the truce was not followed by a peace the fires of conflict had only been banked down and, in 1809, flared up more lustily than ever. In that year the Russians recommenced their assaults on the Danube line. For the rebel Serbs this Russian war was a veritable godsend, as the sultan, obliged to defend the approaches to Constantinople, could spare but inconsiderable forces for a campaign on the distant Morava and Drina. When, however, in 1812, in the treaty of Bucharest, the Russians at last came to definitive terms with the Porte, the situation of the Serbs grew suddenly alarming. Serbs and Russians had become allies, but that did not hinder the Russians from acting at Bucharest exactly as they pleased. Having got what they wanted from their peasant friends, they practically surrendered them to the mercy of the sultan. Free of the Russian embarrassment, that sovereign resolved to break the resistance of the rebels with an overwhelming attack. In 1813 the Turk armies invaded Serbia simultaneously from three sides.

In the face of this concentrated assault Karageorge soon exhibited signs of distress. He was not the kind of hero one meets in fiction, who always and invariably does the heroic thing, but a man, victim, like other men, of an occasional attack of nerves. Dismayed by a succession of minor defeats he lost his head, gave contradictory orders, and finally deserted his post. With his ignominious flight across the Austrian border the whole movement collapsed and the Moslems triumphantly entered Belgrad. In a war lasting nine years the Serbs had won their independence only to lose it.

The Moslems, however, would not have been Moslems if they had not now taken every measure calculated to bring about a new Serb rising. They celebrated at Belgrad and at the other centers of the unhappy land bloody orgies of revenge, with the result that the peasants came to the conclusion that it was better to die with arms in hand on the field of honor than to be butchered like sheep in a pen. Once more the situation called for a leader and once more he was found, on this occasion in the person of Milosh Obrenovich. Milosh was a well-known knez who had rendered important services in the recent struggle. On Palm Sunday, 1815, Milosh unfolded the banner of revolt and immediately rallied thousands of his people to the cause. By swift movements, which showed that he was not without military talents, he routed the surprised enemy at several points and then shrewdly offered to the Turk commander to open negotiations. This, on orders from Constantinople, the general declared himself ready to do. His action proved that the Porte was aware of certain recent changes on the European checker-board which affected its position unfavorably. It was the year of the Congress of Vienna and the powers, engaged in laying the foundations of a world peace, were inclined to frown on any new struggle. Besides, Russia, full of confidence by reason of her recent defeat of Napoleon, was almost certain to seize any available pretext to interfere in Ottoman affairs. If, however, owing to these various alarms, the sultan agreed to treat with the Serbs, he was also resolved to grant them as little as possible. Luckily for Serbia, Milosh, himself half an oriental from long association with men of the East, was more than a match for the subtleties and chicanery of the Porte. Not without Karageorge's ability to deliver

The second rising of 1815 under Milosh.

a hard blow in the field, he was by preference a diplomat, who put his faith in his ability to weary his adversary and in his skill to out-manoeuvre him.

Milosh
plays the
diplomatic
game.

In this struggle of wits, continued literally for years, Milosh won, though, in the very nature of the case, not by a single capital victory such as overwhelms the imagination of men, but rather by a slow accumulation of small advantages like those of a clever chess-player. While the game lasted and the issue remained undecided the Serbs held fast to their arms and their military organization. On that circumstance, of course, depended the consideration conceded to Milosh as a negotiator. But it is interesting to observe, and a decided tribute to his genius, that throughout this prolonged debate he kept unswervingly before him two great purposes: first, to obtain the greatest possible reduction of Ottoman power by means of a genuine Serb autonomy; and second, to create a native government of which he should be the sole responsible head. His first success of note befell in the year 1817, when the other knezes formally elected him supreme chief and the sultan acknowledged the appointment.

Return and
murder of
Karageorge.

While this measure put the Ottoman negotiations exclusively into his hands, it also fortified him against Karageorge, the hero of the war of independence. That the former leader was by no means forgotten by his people had only just been shown. Secretly making his way back to Serbia (1817), he had set preparations on foot for a new war of liberation. In swift alarm for his position, Milosh — so at least his enemies charge — informed the pasha of the presence of the outlaw, and the pasha promptly took measures to have him apprehended and killed. Though the case against Milosh is by no means clear, it must be granted that neither he nor, for that matter, Karageorge himself was above employing delation, murder, or any other crime as a means for ridding himself of an inconvenient foe. The times were violent and the manners of men were in harmony with them. In any case the many devoted followers of Karageorge did not hesitate to denounce Milosh as Karageorge's assassin, and from this unfortunate conflict sprang a family feud of national proportions which threw a bloody shadow on Serb history for the next one hundred years.

While successful in steadily strengthening his power over his own people, Milosh was long obliged to be content with minor successes in negotiating with the Porte over the issue of autonomy. Cunning, stubborn, and patient, he waited on events, and in 1821 an event occurred very favorable to the Serb leader because it shook the Ottoman empire to its foundations. That was the insurrection of the Greeks, which we shall consider at this point only to note its effect on the interminable Turco-Serb negotiations. From the moment the Greek rising began the sultan was heavily embarrassed not only because of the struggle itself but also because, as usually happened when the sultan was in trouble, the Russian bear began to growl ominously in the north. Not till 1826, however, did the bear proceed actively to intervene, with the result that, in the Convention of Akkerman, the Porte, in order to avoid war, granted all of the Russian demands, among which was a promise to settle the grievances of Serbia. Though this, as a typical Turk promise, was forgotten as soon as it was made, war, in spite of Akkerman, broke out between the Porte and Russia in little more than a year, and in the course of two campaigns the Moslems were so badly beaten that they had to sign the disastrous peace of Adrianople (1829). In this document the Russians once more intervened in Serb behalf and repeated the demand of Akkerman. Reluctantly, under persistent Russian pressure, the sultan at last toed the mark and in the period 1830–34 made the various concessions by virtue of which Serbia became an autonomous state with Milosh as hereditary prince.

Serb autonomy conceded by the Porte with Milosh as hereditary prince.

The autonomy granted to the young state went the length of putting the whole body of domestic affairs, justice, administration, and the taxes, into the hands of the Serbs. An important article ended the Greek or Phanariote domination of the Serb church and provided for a national clergy enjoying the confidence of the people. Another article disposed of the Moslem landholders, the spahis, who were to be withdrawn from Serbia, though not without receiving a compensation for their surrendered property rights. As against these weighty concessions, the sultan's sovereignty over the principality was solemnly affirmed, but it was limited in the main to the payment of an annual tribute and to the right to retain garrisons in certain fortified places. Among these was Belgrad, the capital of the young state. Finally, the bound-

The terms of the settlement of 1834 with the sultan.

aries were fixed to include a perceptibly larger area than the old pashalik of Belgrad since the line was drawn on the east at the Timok river, on the west at the Drina, while on the south it crossed the Morava just beyond Alexinatz.. The boundaries, so traced, remained unchanged till the Congress of Berlin (1878).

The three main factors of Serb politics: the prince, the oligarchy of knezes, and the people.

Relations with the sultan having been at last clarified, it became necessary to consolidate the chaotic domestic situation. Without doubt the internal troubles were grave with three leading forces struggling for ascendancy. First, there was Prince Milosh, for such was now his title, resolved, if possible, to make his power absolute; second, there were the knezes and voivodes, that is, the politicians and generals, who were firmly minded to perpetuate their influence by some form of oligarchy; and third, there was the body of the people, the simple peasants, democratic but incredibly conservative and sure to be suspicious of any innovation, especially of a new-fangled central government demanding novel and heavy taxes for its upkeep. These were the main native elements constituting the successive political crises through which Serbia passed during the next few decades. Add the sultan's interference by right of sovereignty and the perpetual intrigues of Russia and Austria, each desirous of promoting its own interest in the new principality, and it will be conceded that a peaceful, regular, and systematic evolution of Serb political life was out of the question. What the country primarily needed was a constitution providing for the security of life and property and serving as a practical instrument for the spread of European civilization. But this constitution was a long time in getting realized, and though the conflicts which raged over it were complicated and numerous and throw an informing light on this rough community, we must content ourselves with a bare outline of the domestic broils.

Frequent revolutions delay the consolidation of the Serb state.

Probably the chief obstacle to an orderly settlement of the young commonwealth was for a long time Milosh himself, the country's prince. He had the fixed idea of making himself absolute and refused to yield an inch to his opponents. Besides, his vulgar peasant greed, frequently manifested by his seizure of meadows, forests, and houses, ended by creating a positive dislike for him among the people to whom he had rendered such conspicuous services. Occasional storms, which raged around his person, were, however, successfully weathered until in 1838 an untoward combination of circumstances obliged him to accept a constitution dictated by his sovereign, the sultan, but really by an invisible power behind the sultan, by Russia. This constitution was distinctly oligarchic in character and put the power in the hands of a select and limited body called the senate. When Milosh continued to prove himself recalcitrant, the senate, strong by reason of its foreign backing, went the length of forcing him to abdicate. In 1839 he left Belgrad and went into exile. Thereupon the senate raised his son, Michael, to the throne, but the disputes between senate and prince continued and in 1842 Michael was unceremoniously dispatched along the road his father had traveled before him. The next move of the senate was to offer the headship of the state to Alexander Karageorge, grandson of the liberator, and Alexander, a mild-mannered man not given to impose his will, succeeded in holding his uneasy post till 1859. Then the familiar combination of local intrigues and foreign influences proved too much for him and he was deposed to make way for none other than old Milosh. It was a movement not of the knezes but of the people which brought Milosh back to power, and his return proved not only that he still had a strong following among the grateful peasantry, but also that the peasant masses were no longer willing to be kept systematically in the background. Milosh, seventy-nine years old at the time of his restoration, died the following year and was quietly succeeded by his son Michael, who thus, like his father, mounted the throne for the second time.

With the restoration of the Obrenovich dynasty we may for the present drop the tangled skein of Serb political evolution with the reflection that in almost half a hundred years there had been less progress toward domestic consolidation than might reasonably have been expected. A leading cause of the persistent confusion lay in the possibility for intrigue afforded, on the one hand, by the sovereignty of the Porte and, on the other, by the diplomatic struggle between Russia and Austria to draw the little state within their respective spheres of influence. Nevertheless the situation was not without signs of improvement. The points of contact with European life had multiplied; increased economic

A summary of Serb progress.

activity, resulting from order and settled legal relations, had raised the standard of living; and a system of popular education, as general as the scant fiscal resources of the government permitted, had contributed its share toward ending the long reign of eastern obscurantism. Slowly, almost imperceptibly, the young principality was being transformed, morally, socially, and politically, into a modern state.

CHAPTER XXI

THE REVOLT OF THE GREEKS AND THE FOUNDING OF THE GREEK KINGDOM

WE are aware that the Greeks, although they were numerically inferior to the Rumanians and probably to the Serbs and Bulgars, played a larger rôle in the Ottoman empire than any other rayah people. They had a richer past and a more advanced civilization; through the patriarch of Constantinople they controlled the Orthodox church; and through the agency of the officials, called Phanariotes, they operated, though at the price of a demoralizing servility to their masters, important sections of the Ottoman administration.[1] Then, too, their geographical position gave them important economic and strategical advantages, for they were still, as of old, a coast people, holding besides the mainland of ancient Hellas the shores of the Ionian and Aegean seas and all the islands of the archipelago. The forces of geography, which had made them from their earliest appearance on the stage of history an urban people dependent on trade, were uninterruptedly operative and, though trade had declined under Ottoman misrule, and though the meager remainder had largely fallen into the hands of the enterprising western nations, the modern Greeks, much like their forbears, still made their living by the sea. So great indeed was the strategic value of the Greek coastal position that, if an economic revival should ever be effected in the Near East, the Greeks would inevitably be its first and possibly its most permanent beneficiaries.

In order to understand how the Greeks roused themselves from their long winter's sleep it is necessary to glance at their general condition, particularly with the view to noting such novel forces and opinions as made themselves felt among them immediately before and after the year 1800. While a similarity of the Greek

> Reasons for the more important rôle played by the Greeks than by the other rayah people.

> Persistence of self-governing institutions among the Greeks.

[1] See p. 304.

condition to that of the Serbs, already considered, is undeniable, it is also certain that, in accordance with the diversity manifested from province to province and even from district to district in the Ottoman empire, special circumstances obtained which call for consideration. Thus the local self-government, so prevalent in Serbia, existed among the Greeks, but varying in amount and quality with each locality considered. In the islands of the archipelago, for instance, it went to surprising lengths. In this favored region each island, often on the basis of a written charter, conducted its own affairs and practically never saw an Ottoman official except on the occasion of the annual visit made to collect the stipulated tribute. Again, in the mountain regions of Thessaly and Epirus the village communities not only governed themselves but enjoyed the unusual right to carry weapons. Their armed companies, known as *armatoles,* charged themselves with the task of keeping the countryside clear of brigands. In spite of the armatoles, however, bands of highwaymen, called *klefts,* infested the mountains, often with the secret connivance of the Turkish pashas, who adopted this dubious but characteristic means for exercising a check on the armed Christians. As a final instance of self-government among the Greeks let us consider the case of the Peloponnesus, known in modern times more commonly as the Morea. In order to facilitate the collection of taxes the pasha of the Morea had put the responsibility for them on the shoulders of a body of well-to-do Christian landholders, called *primates,* and these in their turn collaborated with the chosen representatives of the districts and villages. While the primates, as Turkish agents, were involuntary, and often, perhaps, voluntary oppressors of their poorer coreligionists, constituting none-the-less a Moreote representative body standing between the government and the people, they might under favorable circumstances assume the character of a genuine parliament.

Brigandage a form of patriotism.

In consequence of the general decline of public security in the dissolving empire, the kleft phenomenon, already noted for Epirus and Thessaly, had put in an appearance in the Morea also. With single-minded regard to their professional honor, the Greek brigands indiscriminately robbed all travelers, whether Christian or Mussulman; none-the-less, like the Serb heyduks, they enjoyed the passionate patriotic approbation of the common people on the ground that they made private war on the existing régime. Without question, if the time for revolt ever came, the Greeks would find not only their rudimentary political institutions but also their growing practice of self-help a useful aid toward a general reconstruction of their national life.

Into the Greek conditions, hopelessly stagnant for generations, the eighteenth century projected a number of new and vivifying forces. First and foremost was a revival of commerce due to the peace of Kutchuk-Kainardji (1774). Among the terms imposed by the victorious Russians was one, by virtue of which the Greek traders found it possible to sail their vessels under the Russian flag and to claim for their goods the privileges and immunities belonging to Russian citizens. To the relief obtained in this way from Ottoman chicanery was presently added the considerable advantage accruing from the wars of the French revolution. The great convulsion, by reason of its taking generally, and certainly so far as the Mediterranean was concerned, the form of a struggle between France and England for maritime ascendancy, had, owing to the British victories, the effect of driving French commerce off the sea. This circumstance enabled the Greeks, already rapidly coming to the front, to rush in and fill the vacuum. During the Napoleonic wars hundreds of vessels under Greek masters, often penetrating beyond the straits of Gibraltar, plied the Mediterranean waters. In addition to diffusing an unaccustomed prosperity among the islands and along the coasts, they provided the Greek people with a potential war-fleet, since, as a defense against the Barbary corsairs, each merchantman carried a small equipment of cannon.

Running parallel to the revival of trade was a significant educational and literary movement. Enterprising Greeks, brought, after a lapse of centuries, into immediate touch with civilized Europe, settled in western cities to attend western schools, and, on return to their home-land, promoted the founding of educational establishments dedicated to the diffusion of modern knowledge. Even in the darkest period of Ottoman tyranny, it is true, schools had continued to exist in Greece, as the tradition of learning was slow to die, but these establishments, weighed down with a petrified orthodox curriculum, showed little vitality and, in order to serve a useful purpose, decidedly needed

New forces: the revival of commerce.

The educational and linguistic revival.

to be renovated. Chiefly representative of the medieval and Christian past of the race, they preserved hardly a trace of the older and nobler traditions of pagan antiquity. What the students returning from Europe brought back was, above all, a reawakened passion for the history and literature of ancient Hellas together with a firm resolve to reconstitute the Greek tongue as a worthy and serviceable medium of expression. Since of the many elements entering into self-conscious nationalism language has proved itself perhaps the most important, it throws much light on the degradation of the Greeks and every other Balkan people that, following the Ottoman conquest, they had permitted their respective national idioms to fall into a condition of revolting and barbarous neglect. In the case of the Greeks the many dialects which prevailed among them had indeed a common Hellenic foundation, but these dialects had been affected by so many and such different foreign influences that the speech of one district was often incomprehensible to a neighboring community only a few miles away. The central problem of linguistic renewal was to agree upon and develop a common literary medium which, while adhering in the main to the familiar spoken forms, inclined sufficiently toward the forgotten classic speech to make its incomparable monuments accessible to the living generation. This difficult problem a learned patriot, Korais by name, who had made a long stay in the West, solved, though not wholly to the satisfaction, it would seem, of the crabbed race of classical philologists. They complained at the time, and their complaints in our own day have by no means ceased, that Korais created a hybrid, an artificial tongue, but the Greeks themselves, whose judgment from every practical viewpoint alone counts, gave, and still continue to give, their countryman's grammar and syntax an enthusiastic endorsement.

Political revival stimulated by the French Revolution and the Philiké Hetairia. But perhaps the most important impulse contributing to the awakening of the Greeks sprang from the French revolution. The echoes of its lively, though often rhetorical, declamations on liberty and equality did not fail to reach the Near East, and presently provoked the Greeks, best prepared of all the rayah peoples to react to western influences, to found, in imitation of their French exemplars, clubs and debating societies to promote political enlightenment. By 1814 the political agitation, which was obliged of course to remain more or less in the dark, had acquired such momentum that a much more ambitious society was formed, the Philiké Hetairia (Friendly Society), which proposed to plant a lodge in every town and village of Greece and, as soon as its plans had matured, to start a national war of liberation. The Philiké Hetairia had its main seat at Odessa, that is, outside the Ottoman empire, and communicated by numerous subterranean channels with its adherents among the subjects of the sultan. Its plans, as is usual with the schemes of idealistic conspirators, were wildly impractical, but it served to provide an organization prepared and willing to conduct a general rising against the Moslem tyrant.

It was in the spring of the year 1821 that the long-awaited signal to rise was given and the moment, it must be admitted, was well chosen, for the Ottoman empire was passing through another and a very desperate inner crisis. We have already heard of the Pasha Ali, called the Lion of Janina and famous as one of the boldest of the many recalcitrant satraps of the sinking state. By 1820 he had, by a mixture of cunning and violence, built up such a personal power in the region of Albania and was so plainly aiming to divest himself of every trace of dependence on the sultan that Mahmud II was obliged to meet the impudent challenge or face complete disaster. Accordingly he ordered an attack, which Ali met with so much resolution that nothing short of a complete concentration of the Ottoman might succeeded, and then only after several campaigns, in breaking the rebel's power. In 1822 an Ottoman general at last tracked the Lion of Janina to his lair and there dispatched him. It was while this struggle, of which the Hetairists wished to take full advantage, was at its height that the long-planned movement of Greek independence was set afoot.

The Hetairists start the movement of revolt in the spring of 1821.

However, an even more important factor than the rebel Ali in the calculations of the Hetairists was the tsar of Russia. They persuaded themselves, and not unreasonably in view of the Russian past, that the tsar would take advantage of a rising of the rayahs to start a new war of conquest against the Porte. But in this they went completely astray because the tsar was Alexander I, who, though originally cherishing generous senti-

Alexander Ypsilanti invades the Danubian provinces.

ments toward the oppressed Christians of Turkey, had recently been converted to the Metternichian principle of immobility and was now filled with a lively horror of revolution in any and every form. Instead, therefore, of supporting the Hetairist action, he openly condemned it, permitting it to run its course without the least support from him. The Hetairist chief was Alexander Ypsilanti, a Greek belonging to a well-known Phanariote family but living on Russian soil and serving as an officer in the Russian army. It was largely because he was supposed to have influence with his namesake, the tsar, that he had been promoted to the presidency of the society. In the month of March, 1821, at the head of an inconsiderable band, he crossed the river Pruth and invaded the Danubian provinces. His immediate purpose was to arouse the Rumanian people and add their strength to that of the Greek insurgents farther south. But in this effort he was as mistaken as in his reliance on the tsar. The Rumanians had no enthusiasm for the Greeks; on the contrary, they had been taught by their experience to regard Phanariotes of the type of Ypsilanti as worse oppressors than the Moslems and accordingly refused to budge. Ypsilanti was left without popular support, and when the Ottoman army encountered his slender forces, it had no difficulty in scattering them to the winds. By June the Hetairist chief was a fugitive on Austrian soil. His rebellion had proved itself a mere flash in the pan.

The rebellion in the Morea. None-the-less Ypsilanti's fiasco did not spell ruin to the Greek cause. For, simultaneously with the action in Rumania, a movement took place among the Greeks of the Morea which, begun among men with a real and not an imaginary Greek patriotism, produced a general popular upheaval passionately dedicated to liberation. Without a concerted plan and without other than local leadership the Moreotes rose spontaneously throughout the peninsula and in wild frenzy fell upon and butchered the Turk officials and residents in their midst. In a war-chant which went from mouth to mouth they sang: "The Turk shall live no more either in the Morea or in the whole world." It was the bloody payment exacted from infidels and tyrants for centuries of oppression, and sounded at once the terrible note which was henceforth to dominate the struggle.

When the news of the uprising reached Sultan Mahmud at Constantinople he was in his turn seized with a passion for revenge. Once more it is proper to point out that the Turk, in ordinary circumstances a kindly and rather phlegmatic individual, is given to uncontrollable outbursts of fanaticism and blood-lust. In such an access Mahmud ordered a massacre of Greeks in the Turk capital and capped the bloody orgy by seizing the patriarch and having him hanged in his pontifical vestments, with a bishop on either side to keep him company, from the gate of his own palace.

A war begun with such unbridled acts proved that Moslems and Christians, masters and slaves, were alike barbarians, and that the struggle between them would be a war to the last gasp, a war of extermination. For the present, owing to the suddenness and magnitude of the upheaval, the advantage lay with the Greeks. In an incredibly short time the insurrection, passing the isthmus of Corinth, had lighted its signal fires in continental Greece as well as in all the islands of the archipelago. In the face of a conflagration of such dimensions the sultan, impatient as he might be to bring the rebels to obedience, was obliged to delay. For one thing, his main forces were occupied with suppressing Ali of Janina, while his fleet, which was chiefly manned by Greek sailors since the Turks had never been seamen, was, by the wholesale desertion of the Greeks, immobilized in port and rendered helpless. In fact, the Greeks by promptly converting their numerous merchantmen into light vessels of war acquired the command of the Aegean, and, as long as this condition lasted, the revolution was secure. The Russian support, which the more intelligent leaders, capable of appreciating the vast resources of the sultan, considered vital to success, could under the circumstances be dispensed with, at least for the present. At the first news of the insurrection not only Russia but all the governments of Europe, held in the bonds of the reaction which followed the Napoleonic wars, unanimously declared in favor of a policy of non-intervention. Completely isolated, the Greeks became aware that they must depend on none but themselves.

Since it is neither possible nor necessary to follow all the twists and turns of the vast struggle known as the Greek War

Spread of the insurrection and early Greek advantages.

The three periods of the struggle.

of Liberation, it will suffice to indicate the three periods into which it falls and to summarize the events of each. In the first period (1821–24) Sultan Mahmud made every effort in his power to crush the rebellion and failed; in the second period (1824–27) he appealed for help to the pasha of Egypt and came within sight of his goal; in the third period (1827–29) the European powers gave up their policy of non-intervention and not only saved Greece from destruction but also procured it its independence.

The efforts of the Greeks in the first phases of the struggle directed at capture of the Turk fortresses.

In the first period the Greeks, while continuing to fight in separate bands under local leaders, largely former brigand chiefs, resolutely pursued the plan of getting complete control of their country. The fortresses alone had been able to resist the sudden rush of the rebel hosts and constituted, so long as they were held by their Ottoman garrisons, the possible basis of a Turk reconquest. Tripolitza, Navarino, and other strategical points of the Morea were accordingly besieged and taken, and similar tactics, pursued in continental Greece, gradually brought Missolonghi, Thebes, and other key-positions into native safekeeping. When the Acropolis, the ancient rock rearing its fair, temple-crowned mass over Athens, capitulated (June, 1822), the elated Greeks may not unreasonably have felt that their cause was secure. An incident attending the surrender of the Acropolis is so characteristic of the temper of the combatants that it deserves to be recorded. As the Moslem survivors, chiefly women and children, descended from the eyrie where they had so long held out, they were, in spite of solemn promises of safety, attacked by the infuriated Christians and with few exceptions massacred in their tracks. Such apology for the act as can be offered is less an apology than a statement, and consists in pointing out that the Turks behaved in the same way or worse, and that they had just perpetrated an act of nameless horror on the island of Chios. Falling on the unsuspecting population, the Moslem tigers in the guise of men raged among their Christian enemies until a little Aegean paradise had been turned into a desert and one hundred thousand men, women, and children had been slaughtered, sold as slaves, or driven into exile.

Through their consistent successes the Greeks had acquired a reasonably secure hold on the Morea, central Greece, and the islands of the Aegean sea before the Porte, having overcome the rebel Ali and remanned its depleted fleet with Algerine pirates and Constantinopolitan riffraff, was ready to take the offensive in its turn. A compact assault upon the Christians followed (1822–23) but yielded no durable result. Great havoc was made among the cumbersome Ottoman war-vessels by the small, swift sailing Greek craft, especially by their daring use of fire ships, while the Ottoman land forces, marching southward from Thessaly and Epirus, were disorganized by incessant attacks on their supplies, defeated piece-meal, and obliged ignominiously to beat a retreat. By the end of the year 1823 the sultan was brought to the humiliating conclusion that unless he succeeded in bringing fresh resources to bear upon the situation his cause was lost.

The Greeks beat off all Ottoman attacks by land and sea, 1822–23.

The capture by the Porte of unexpected means for prolonging the struggle introduces us to the second period of the war. Off in Egypt, one of the richest pashaliks of the empire, a cunning and energetic Albanian, Mehemet Ali by name, had, in the audacious fashion of Ali of Janina, made himself practically independent of his suzerain. In distinction from Ali, however, he had introduced a number of reforms which in the petrified East possessed something of the aspect of a miracle. Following European precedents and with the assistance of European advisers, chiefly Frenchmen, he had improved the cultivation of the ancient soil of the Pharaohs, had promoted the introduction of new plants such as cotton and the mulberry (for silk-raising), and had dedicated the enhanced returns of his treasury to the enlargement and modernization of his army and navy. Secure in the possession of ample power, he had withheld support from the sultan in the Greek crisis on the shrewd calculation that his help would be better appreciated after his master was beaten. It was only when Mahmud, who, naturally suspicious, did not fail to see the snare that was laid for him, was stripped of every means within his immediate reach for fighting the Greeks that he humiliated himself by going to Cairo as a suppliant; and it was only after offering heavy bribes, among which was the promise of the pashalik of the Morea to Mehemet's son, Ibrahim, that he

Sultan Mahmud forced to turn to Mehemet Ali of Egypt for help.

succeeded in winning the Egyptian's assistance. By 1824 the bargain had been closed, and no sooner had the disciplined and well-equipped Egyptian hosts appeared upon the scene under the command of the grim and capable Ibrahim than the fortune of war promptly deserted the Greeks and declared for the sultan.

The Egyptian army crushes the revolt in the Morea.

Using Crete, an Ottoman island and a natural half-way station between Egypt and the Morea, as a base, Ibrahim's first efforts were very properly directed to obtaining command of the sea. Only partially successful, because the light Greek ships, following established tactics, avoided a general engagement, he was yet successful enough measurably to secure his communications with his bases in Crete and Egypt and to begin, in 1825, the invasion of the Peloponnesus. With the instinct of the born commander he fixed upon the deep, protected bay of Navarino, on the southwestern coast, as his military and naval center, and then, when all was ready, undertook the systematic reduction of the country. In indefensible folly the Greeks had recently weakened themselves by conflicts among their headstrong leaders — conflicts which often assumed the proportions of a civil war — and though they now, in the face of the common peril, made up their differences, their brave guerrilla bands were no match for the disciplined troops of the Egyptian. Fortress after fortress, district after district, fell so swiftly into his power that it soon became alarmingly plain that the Morea was doomed.

Turks and Egyptians together conquer central Greece.

In the meantime and in coöperation with Ibrahim's fleet, a Turkish army, proceeding by land, invaded central Greece and appeared before Missolonghi. This west-coast fortress, guarding the entrance to the gulf of Patras, was the heart of the resistance of the continental Greeks and around it, already attacked before, though unsuccessfully, a stubborn and remorseless combat raged for months. The baffled Ottoman general was obliged to appeal to Ibrahim in the Morea to come to his aid with all his available men, but even against the overwhelming numbers of the combined Turco-Egyptian forces the dauntless garrison held out until it was overcome by a stronger enemy than the Turk, by hunger. After a last heroic attempt to break through the enclosing lines had failed, the gates were entered by force and the defenders together with their women and children perished rather than surrender, fighting from street to street, nay, literally from house *like nassador* (handwritten marginalia)

to house, until the city which they had sworn to defend to the last drop of their blood became their grave. When in April, 1826, the victorious Moslems took possession of the smoking ruins of what had once been Missolonghi, they must have thought that the end of Greek resistance was at hand. Only the spirited defense of the remaining strongholds, coupled with the activity of scattered bands in the mountains, delayed the final Ottoman triumph. But when, in 1827, Athens fell after another prolonged siege, the palpitating tale of which flew around the world, the sultan might fairly be satisfied that the revolt was crushed.

But just as the curtain seemed about to descend on the dream of Greek independence a sudden and dramatic change occurred, completely reversing the situation. Although the governments of the great powers maintained, as we have seen, a studied policy of aloofness, the peoples, in sharp distinction from their governments, followed the moving fortunes of the Greeks with lively interest and constantly growing favor. The cultured classes of all the western nations, nurtured on the classics, had a rooted admiration for the heroes of Marathon and Salamis, and when the submerged slaves, who claimed to be their descendants and whose very existence had been forgotten for centuries, arose and duplicated the deeds of their ancestors, the enthusiasm was unbounded. Philhellenic societies sprang up in all the leading city-centers, and not only was money collected for the purchase of arms and supplies but scores of volunteers embarked for the East to fight side by side and give their lives, if necessary, in aid of the brave rebels who were honoring the cause of human liberty. When Lord Byron, the most romantic figure of the age, put his sword at the service of the Greeks, and when, after a few months devoted to a sane and creditable effort to put an end to the dissensions among the leaders, he died of fever (April, 1824), the cause acquired a glamour which no folly of its chiefs could afterwards destroy.

The popular sympathy of Europe enlisted on the side of the Greeks.

No wonder, therefore, if under the pressure of public opinion, which even reactionary monarchs cannot wholly ignore, the governments began gradually to change their tone. The English cabinet was the first to manifest a cautious interest in the Greeks, and though the Russian government, unable to forget that Turkey was its traditional enemy, spoke an occasional word in

The treaty of London and the battle of Navarino, Oct. 20, 1827.

favor of Turkey's rebels, the Russian policy was wholly unreliable so long as the wayward Alexander sat upon the throne. He had no sooner died (1825), however, than the Russian policy perceptibly stiffened. The new tsar was Alexander's brother, Nicholas I, a man as firm in his purposes as his predecessor had been irresolute and wavering. Within a year of his accession Nicholas had arranged with the court of St. James a modest program of intervention, and when, in 1827, France signified her adhesion, a treaty was drawn up at London by virtue of which the three allies committed themselves to a plan of Greek autonomy under the sultan's overlordship, coupled with the demand for an immediate cessation of hostilities. It was very hard for Ibrahim, intent on stamping out the last embers of the Moreote revolt, to believe that the allies meant what they said when they communicated the order to ground arms. An European fleet had to be dispatched to Ibrahim's base at Navarino to supply him with ocular evidence that the allies were ready in the last resort to use force to execute their purpose. On sailing into the stately bay to deliver their message the admirals of the combined fleets faced one of those tense situations in which the careless scratch of a match might suffice to produce an explosion. A chance shot was fired, another followed, and without more ado Moslems and Christians leaped at each other's throats. When after a few hours the combat ceased, over half of Ibrahim's proud fleet had been sunk or shot to driftwood. The famous battle befell on October 20, 1827, and was a far more drastic punishment of the Moslems than the timid home governments had planned. The duke of Wellington, speaking for the English cabinet, practically apologized to the sultan by referring to Navarino as " an untoward event." But done was done, the power of the Mohammedan fleet was broken, and the allies, whether they would or no, were by their act irrevocably bound to the Greek cause. The guns of Navarino were the salute of Europe fired to celebrate the birth of the newest Christian state.

The intervention of Europe leads to another Turco-Russian war.   Sultan Mahmud, deeply chagrined at being constrained to break off hostilities at the very moment of triumph, impotently revolved dark schemes of vengeance. His wrath burned more particularly against Russia, his hereditary foe, and Nicholas, eager to follow in the footsteps of the famous Catherine, quickly flamed up in his turn. Scrutinizing the Ottoman situation, the tsar could not fail to see that never had there been a more favorable moment for striking at the Porte. Not only were England and France bound to him for the time being by an alliance, but in addition the Ottoman state was in confusion and its army in the midst of a far-reaching reorganization. Long persuaded that the Janissaries were the plague-spot of the state, in 1826 Sultan Mahmud had at length taken his courage in his hands and excised the evil growth by a single cruel operation. In the next chapter we shall return to this measure in order to consider it in connection with the sultan's whole reform movement. Here we may content ourselves to note that in the interim between the abolition of the Janissaries and the creation of a new army, built on the European pattern, the padishah was helpless. No one was better aware of the fact than the sovereign of Russia and, sardonically pleased with the acrimonious debate begun by his adversary, he spun it along until the spring of 1828, when, everything being ready, he exultingly declared war.

As soon as the action of mighty Russia began in the north, little Greece was almost automatically freed from further molestation. Egyptian Ibrahim, chilled in his ardor by the blow of Navarino, sullenly agreed to withdraw his soldiers from the Morea, and a French force, acting as the mandatory of Europe, lent its assistance in peacefully clearing the Moslem garrisons out of the peninsula. At the same time the Ottoman soldiers in central Greece, being wanted on the Danube, began to thread their way northward, vigorously prodded whenever they lingered by the impatient Greeks. Not very many months after Navarino the southern and central sections of Greece were free of every trace of Ottoman supremacy.

Greece cleared of Moslem troops.

Meanwhile the war between the Russian and Ottoman empires was proceeding both in the Caucasus and in Balkania, and though the successes of the Russians on the eastern theater were immediate, the first campaign in the west was a distinct failure. However, Nicholas, undaunted, returned to the charge, and under a new commander, Diebitsch by name, the Turk lines were assaulted with such energy that the momentum of the victors carried them for the first time in history clear across the Balkan passes. In August, 1829, the daring Diebitsch, with a mere

The victory of Russia followed by the treaty of Adrianople September, 1829.

advance guard, entered the unresisting city of Adrianople. Panic-
stricken, the sultan opened negotiations, and in a feverish haste,
which utterly failed to take account of Diebitsch's precarious
situation, signed peace with the Russian in the old Turk capital
on the Maritsa. As a masterpiece of subtle policy the treaty of
Adrianople deserves a place at the side of that other monument of
Russian diplomatic skill, the peace of Kutchuk-Kainardji (1774).
On the side of territorial acquisitions it observed a studied
moderation, asking for nothing in Europe and, in Asia, for no more
than enough to secure the final control of the east coast of the
Black sea as well as of the Caucasus range.   More important were
the provisions regarding the increase of Russian influence in
Balkania.   In the Danubian principalities the sovereignty
of the sultan was still further reduced and the Russian
protectorate proportionally enlarged.   Again, in the matter
of Serbia, the sultan, while forced to concede the long delayed autonomy, was obliged to put it under a Russian
safeguard.   On the side of trade Russia gained enormously by a
sharper definition of the privileges already secured.   Incidentally
she conferred a benefit on the whole world by having the Bosporus
and Dardanelles opened freely to the merchantmen of all sea-
faring nations.   Finally, with regard to Greece the Porte agreed
to accept whatever solution the three allied powers might see fit to
adopt.   The true significance of the treaty, to be read between
the lines rather than in its actual words, was that Russia, absorbing bit by bit the authority of the sultan over Balkania, was
brought measurably nearer the time when she might completely
replace his sovereignty with her own.

The three
protecting
powers
declare
Greece an
independent
kingdom
and draw
its bound-
aries.

The Russian triumph at Adrianople almost succeeded in putting
an end to the harmony thus far maintained among the three
powers acting as the sponsors of Greece.   Since the days of
Tsarina Catherine the opinion had been gaining ground in
England that Turkey was an absolutely necessary bulwark of
the British empire and that only by its preservation could expanding Russia be restrained from pushing southward to the
Mediterranean and ultimately to India.   For the British cabinet,
therefore, the treaty of Adrianople with its informal subjection of
the sultan to the tsar created an intolerable condition of affairs
and British diplomacy bestirred itself to assure Mahmud of its

friendship. Incidentally it grew much less enthusiastic- for
the cause of Greece. Only foot by foot did British alarm
and stubbornness yield to the pressure of circumstances
and agree to resume the inter-allied negotiations necessary
to stabilize the uncertain affairs of the modern Hellenes.
Months and even years passed over the drawing up of abor-
tive protocols and the exchange of futile notes before at
last, in 1832, the three protecting powers reached a
working agreement. It attempted to find a solution of the two
most urgent issues, to wit, the government of the new state and
its boundary with the Ottoman empire. In the matter of the
government the decision ultimately reached was that, instead of being autonomous under the sultan, as had been at
first proposed, Greece was to be a wholly independent kingdom under Otto, the youthful second son of the sovereign of
Bavaria. As for the boundary of the new-born state, it was
drawn at the Arta-Volo line, thereby including within the kingdom southern and central Greece together with those islands of
the archipelago which hugged the European shore. These were
exiguous limits indeed, since they excluded from the state
and left under Ottoman sovereignty Thessaly and Epirus to the
north, the numerous Greek islands along the shore of Asia Minor,
and Crete, important because of its size as well as by reason of
its strategic position at the entrance to the Aegean sea. There
was a loud outcry among the Greeks against the harsh territorial
decision, and in point of fact a reasonable doubt might be entertained not only whether the new state, confined within such narrow limits, would be able to develop the political and economic
strength necessary for a sound existence, but also whether the
leaving of so many Greeks under the Ottoman yoke would not
produce a nationalist ferment sure, before long, to lead to new
disturbances. All such doubts were amply justified in the coming
time. In defense of the erring diplomats it may be urged that
the boundary which they drew represented the resultant of the
conflicting hopes, passions, and interests of England, Russia, and
France, the three masterful fates who spun the thread of Hellenic
destiny. When all is said for and against the imperfect Greek
settlement, the fact remains that Greece had been ushered into
existence and, however feeble, had been incorporated in the
system of European states.

When King Otto I set foot on Greek soil in February, 1833, he faced a situation of such confusion that it may without exaggeration be described as chaos. Since 1821 the Greeks, while conducting their valiant struggle against the sultan, had at the same time been engaged in the attempt to give themselves a central civil government adequate to their needs. But no sooner had they attacked this problem than violent and fatal divisions appeared among them. The island Greeks, shipowners living by a mixture of trade and piracy, had no sympathy for the Moreotes, largely peasants and klefts, and neither of these groups would coöperate harmoniously with the mainland Greeks, who passionately pursued provincial interests of their own. Besides, the guerrilla warfare had brought to the front a flock of self-willed local leaders unwilling to yield an inch of the power exercised by them in their respective territories. Twelve years of debate (1821–33) had brought nothing better than intermittent civil brawls and had failed even to sow the seeds of a new and modern social order. The plain truth was that, owing to centuries of Ottoman misrule, the Greek ex-rayahs presented themselves to view as a body of courageous individualists of semi-savage disposition who had slipped back to the Homeric ways of their early ancestors.

Facing this backward, undisciplined people there was an inexperienced prince, but seventeen years of age, entrusted with the task of giving to the Greeks the modern state which they themselves had conspicuously failed to achieve. Not only was young King Otto utterly alien to the situation, but he was obliged, because of his immaturity, to rule through a regency of three men whom he had brought from his native Bavaria and who were as unfamiliar with Greek conditions as himself. The only kind of a government which the imported regents were capable of conceiving was an orderly, patriarchal bureaucracy of the contemporary German type. This they tried, sincerely enough, to set a-going, but the Greeks, who, if wild and barbarous, were also rudely democratic, would have none of it. When in 1835 the regency was abolished and King Otto declared of age, the situation did not improve. A certain measure of progress was without doubt effected. Athens, during the revolution no more than a huddled mass of squalid dwellings at the foot of the

The domestic situation at the advent of King Otto I.

Difficulties and achievements of King Otto I.

far-famed Acropolis, was rebuilt according to a plan which has produced the modern over-regular but airy and sanitary town. Among its earliest and most stately structures was a national university. In 1837 it opened its doors to a public which crowded its classrooms and soon successfully demonstrated that the intellectual fervor of the ancient Greeks still animated their modern progeny. Finally, brigandage, the not unhonored employment of a considerable section of the population, was sedulously fought and at least somewhat curtailed.

Even had these achievements been more considerable than they were, they would have failed to conciliate a public opinion firmly set against the king's autocratic régime and patriotically indignant that the heroes of the war of independence, recalcitrant though they had proved themselves to the demands of law and order, had received but scant honor from the court and been systematically forced into the background. It was only necessary for the many-headed opposition to combine against so weak and unsupported a government and it would fall. In September, 1843, the expected happened and when the conspirators, backed by the inhabitants of Athens, demanded a constitution, Otto was obliged to yield. A national assembly was accordingly summoned which drew up a fundamental law whereby the autocratic régime was replaced by a constitutional and parliamentary system. Otto, as constitutional king, regained some of the popularity which he had lost, but it is certain that he never found his way into the hearts of his people. The autocracy replaced by a constitution, 1843.

Examining the Greek state and society around the middle of the nineteenth century, we are justified in declaring that, in spite of the persistence of evils incidental to a backward community accustomed for ages to every form of official and private violence, a resolute advance in the direction of western ideals of civilization had taken place. Brigandage was being gradually mastered, production and trade were increasing, and a widely diffused system of education was inculcating a new social attitude by creating a preference for the orderly processes of law. The greatest issue agitating, and destined for long to continue to agitate, this vigorous and promising society was without doubt the familiar one of the fellow-Greeks outside its bounds bowed under the yoke of the Porte. The passionate nationalism of the Slow advance of the Greek state and society; the Great Idea.

people caused them to look forward to the time when the unredeemed brothers in Crete, in Thessaly, in Epirus, in Macedonia,
and in the islands along the coast of Asia Minor should be
added to the kingdom, thus at last joining all the scattered
fragments of the race and creating a state which, like the old
Byzantine empire, would dominate the whole Near East. The
fervor and universality of this ideal, referred to with mystic
ardor by the Greeks as the Great Idea, was sure to make it
count heavily among the forces which were agitating the Balkan
and Levantine world in preparation of changes which no one
could foretell but which were sure to be significant and far-
reaching.

CHAPTER XXII

CONTINUED DECAY OF THE OTTOMAN EMPIRE. — FIRST ATTEMPTS AT REFORM. — THE CRIMEAN WAR (1854-56)

WHEN, in the year 1807, Selim III lost his throne, owing to his attempt, the first of any consequence on record, to arrest the decay of his realm by transfusing it with European ideas and institutions, he might have been less filled with despair could he have known that his cousin, Mahmud II (1808-39), would return to his policy and carry it through, at least in part, in the teeth of the same conservative opposition to which he had succumbed. It would be an exaggeration to represent Mahmud as one of the great sultans of the line of Osman, but it may truthfully be urged that, apart from an occasional access of fanatic rage, he was a man of good judgment, and that, scorning the slippered ease of the palace compound, he had the unusual energy to shoulder the heavy burden imposed upon him by his autocratic inheritance. However, the distinguishing feature of his personality and reign was his perception that nothing short of systematic Europeanization could save his tottering state. Unfortunately his knowledge of Europe was meager and indirect, and he had the usual obsession of the autocrat that to give an order to a secretary was enough to secure its execution. Utterly disconcertive of this naïve conception was the circumstance that the viziers, pashas, and other functionaries, on whose coöperation he was obliged to depend, were heart and soul with the traditions handed down from the past. They constituted a body of " Old Turks " and stood in his path like a stone-wall, which by tireless assaults he might succeed in breeching at isolated points, but against which he was bound in the long run to bleed himself to death. If we will now recall that, in addition to this opposition from his immediate servants, he had to meet the dangers created by insurgent pashas, like Ali of Janina, and by rebellious rayahs,

Mahmud II (1808-39) and his program of Europeanization.

345

like the Serbs and Greeks, as well as the problems raised by the sleepless greed of the European powers, we may fairly be surprised that this reforming sovereign, the infidel-sultan, as his outraged subjects called him, should have accomplished anything at all.

Mahmud
destroys the
Janissaries,
1826.

From the moment of his accesssion Mahmud shared the conviction of the unhappy Selim that the most urgent reform was the abolition of the Janissaries. But since they had just shown their power and were in complete control, Mahmud had perforce to dissemble his opinion. He could move only with the utmost caution. At the first auspicious moment, he put new life into Selim's schools established at the capital for the training of officers and engineers in the European manner, and gradually, almost surreptitiously, he assembled an artillery corps equipped with powerful modern batteries. The disgraceful failure of the Janissaries to suppress the rebellious Greeks, together with the demonstration given by Ibrahim's Egyptian troops of the irresistible might of European discipline, convinced Mahmud that he must wait no longer. In June, 1826, the memorable order was published which cancelled the ancient privileges of the Janissaries; and when the turbulent militia answered, as was expected, with revolt, Mahmud, who had prepared himself for every eventuality, ordered out the new artillery corps. With its superior weapons this body ruthlessly exterminated the mutineers, who, to their honor be it said, showed that they were not afraid to die. Wherever in the provincial towns at which they were stationed, the Janissaries imitated the rebellious conduct of their brethren of the capital, they were likewise tamed with a whiff of grape-shot. In a few weeks every trace of the once famous troop had been eradicated throughout the length and breadth of the realm and the long chapter of its history, mixed of fame and infamy, had been brought to a close.

The humili-
ations of
Mahmud.

The tenacity of Mahmud had conquered, but at what a price! To be sure he promptly set about the creation of a modern army, uniformed, armed, and disciplined in the European manner, but, obliged to put the task into the hands of European instructors, who were blocked at every step by the sullen opposition of the official and unofficial Moslem world, he had to be content with snail-like progress. Even before the first confusion attending the disappearance of the Janissaries had subsided, Russia, the wariest and most persistent of the enemies of the Porte, resolved to take advantage of the temporary defenselessness of the sultan by beginning another war. We have already treated of the Turco-Russian conflict of 1828, taking note how it ended in the signal defeat of the Ottomans and in the treaty of Adrianople (1829), which substantially made the tsar co-sovereign with the sultan in the Ottoman empire. Nor was that the end of Mahmud's humiliations. What he needed, above all, was a respite from conflict until he should find himself in command of a new and effective army, but, instead of a respite, he was, while still dazed from the blow administered by Russia, brought face to face with the greatest of all the many crises of his reign. Before treating of this new disaster, which was responsible for Mahmud's death and which came within a hair's breadth of wrecking the state, we must concede a word to the civil phase of the sultan's reform activity.

Mahmud was fully aware that the modernized absolutism, at which he aimed, called not only for an obedient and disciplined standing army but also for an efficient civil service. The prerequisite for such an organization was the abolition of the self-willed pashas as well as of the proud hereditary chiefs to be found in certain parts of Asia and called derebeys. With this struggle his whole reign was taken up and brought him, amidst the almost uninterrupted din of civil war, a no inconsiderable list of successes. Ali of Janina, for instance, as we are aware, was crushed and his head publicly exposed at Constantinople as a solemn warning to traitors. Many of the derebeys, who had established themselves as independent feudatories, chiefly in the mountains of Anatolia and Armenia, were made to bite the dust. It would be too much to say that Mahmud asserted his power throughout the length and breadth of his realm, but he inaugurated a policy of centralization, which, toward the middle of the century, after he had closed his eyes, finally triumphed, largely by reason of the strength conferred on the ruler by an obedient and nationally coherent army. If the Ottoman empire, which at Mahmud's accession lay in utter ruin, was patched up sufficiently to count for something in the move-

Mahmud centralizes the administration.

[handwritten margin note: ruled Selio / Ataturk Kema]

ments of the nineteenth century, it owed its renewed vitality primarily to the reforms of Mahmud, which, though ill conceived and poorly coördinated, had the undeniable effect of making the sultan master once more of what was left of his shrunken dominion.

Abolition of the spahis and the serai; adoption of European dress.

Certain minor acts bear equal witness to his determination to remove abuses and regain for the sovereign a larger liberty of action. Since with the standing army established on a modern European basis the feudal army of spahis had become useless, it was abolished and the military fiefs (timars and ziamets), on which it rested, were added to the public domain. Furthermore, the serai, that intolerable incubus upon the ruler, was reorganized with a view to economy and simplicity by curtailing its ceremonies, abolishing its useless officials, and, finally and most effectively, by the abandonment of the ancient purlieus, haunted by the shadows of so many crimes, in favor of a new palace raised along the radiant shores of the Bosporus. In his aping of Europe Mahmud went the length of exchanging the flowing, many-hued garment of the orient for the tight trousers and ugly, crow-colored frockcoat of western Europe. He even discountenanced the use of the impressive turban, substituting for it the simpler and less distinguished fez. External trivialities, one might be tempted to remark, but, as every sociologist knows, far-reaching in their subtle implications! Undoubtedly they contributed a definite, measurable share toward replacing the empire of Solyman the Magnificent, compounded of Asiatic and Byzantine features, with the "Turkey" of our day, weakened in counsel and diminished in territory, but with a relatively European aspect.

The marvelous rise to power of Mehemet Ali of Egypt.

The crisis which brought Mahmud's life and efforts to a tragic close is associated with the name of Mehemet Ali, pasha of Egypt. In another chapter we have recounted this adventurer's rise to power by a series of steps involving the crushing of the Mamelukes, an intelligent though tyrannical exploitation of the resources of the Nile basin, and, last but not least, the creation of an army and navy on the European pattern. We have now to note the rapid expansion of his territorial might. When a religious sect, the Wahabites, arose among the desert tribes of Arabia and raised the standard of revolt, the sultan,

lacking the means to scatter the rebels, was obliged to entrust
the task to Mehemet Ali. As a reward the pasha claimed and
received for his son Ibrahim the government of the Holy Places
of Mecca and Medina and by implication the control of the
whole Arabian peninsula (1818). Shortly after he undertook
the conquest of the middle Nile (Nubia) and by 1822 had become master of its sun-tanned people. When the Greek insurrection broke out, the cunning Egyptian left his master in
the lurch until, as we have seen, Mahmud was obliged to buy
his vassal's help with a new outlay of concessions. As early
as 1822, in return for suppressing the rebellion of Crete,
Mehemet Ali was rewarded with the governorship of that important island; and two years later he received for his son,
Ibrahim, the promise of the Morea in return for military and
naval help against the mainland Greeks.

Never in the history of the Ottoman state had a provincial
governor built up such a power. Mahmud, who, pressed by
misfortune, had promoted the ambitious schemes of the insatiable lord of Egypt, was fully alive to the threat they extended to himself and his empire. Then, in 1827, with the
battle of Navarino and the accompanying fiat of the allied
powers, addressed alike to Turks and Egyptians, to remove
their clutch from the Greek throat, came the first crisis between master and man. Undeniably Mahmud and Mehemet
had together lost the Greek war; but, instead of sharing the
consequences of defeat in an equitable spirit, Mehemet persistently importuned Mahmud for a concession to take the place
of the lost Moreote pashalik. Bold to the point of impudence,
he at last indicated Syria, the natural boulevard leading from
Egypt to Asia, as the prize that would solace him for his un-
merited loss in Europe. In terrible straits because of the recent destruction of the Janissaries and of his subsequent defeat
at the hands of the tsar, Mahmud still had the courage to
refuse. Scorning further debate, the insolent Mehemet ordered
his son to cross the isthmus of Suez and seize the coveted
province by force of arms (October 1831).

The war between sultan and pasha took from the first a disastrous course for the hapless Mahmud. Again and again his
crude forces were beaten by the trained armies of Egypt led

Mehemet Ali
by seizing
Syria (1831)
provokes
war with
the sultan.

The first
Turco-
Egyptian
war (1831-
33);
triumph of
Mehemet
Ali.

by the masterful Ibrahim. Before a year had passed the victorious vassal was in possession of the whole of Syria. Crossing the Taurus mountains, he encountered the last Ottoman army at Konieh (Iconium), in the heart of Asia Minor, and scattered it to the winds (December, 1832). The road ahead was now clear as far as Constantinople. Beside himself with fear and hate, the sultan at this desperate turn addressed passionate appeals for help to all the European powers, but only Russia was close at hand and only Russia responded to his cry. Tsar Nicholas swiftly brought a fleet and an army to the Bosporus and peremptorily ordered Ibrahim to negotiate a peace under Russian mediation. Having no stomach for a war with Russia, Ibrahim yielded and signed a treaty (May, 1833) with the sultan, by virtue of which he and his father acquired the whole of Syria as well as the control of the district of Adana, the key to Asia Minor.

The treaty
of Hunkiar
Skelessi;
triumph
of Tsar
Nicholas.
Saved from his immediate foe by tossing him a king's ransom, Mahmud was now obliged to square himself with his protector. By a treaty concluded a few months later, at Hunkiar Skelessi on the Bosporus (July, 1833), sultan and tsar formed, a close, defensive union. When in the game of politics a pigmy and a giant hitch up together, their alliance can have but one meaning. As the alarmed cabinets of Europe, caught napping by Russia, perceived too late, the effect of Hunkiar Skelessi was to make the sultan the tsar's vassal. The treaty represented the culmination of the cool and insidious policy of the Russian rulers since the days of the great Catherine, for, by giving the tsar control of the Ottoman foreign policy, it established a strong presumption that Russia would ultimately gather the whole empire within its arms.

The second
Turco-
Egyptian
War, 1839.
Sultan Mahmud, brought under the yoke of Russia by the action of an impudent inferior, lived henceforth only for revenge. He redoubled his activity in behalf of a new army and navy only to be choked by the red tape of a chaotic administration and to run into the endless obstacles raised by corrupt and unwilling servants. As soon as Mahmud, whose crude mind reckoned by quantity rather than quality, observed that his ships and fighting men bulked large on paper, he became hot for a new war against the pasha of Egypt. In vain his advisers implored him to delay. Lying at death's door and unwilling to depart this life without

glutting his vengeance, he sent his strict command to his general at the front to open the attack. But the second Turco-Egyptian war of 1839 was decided even more swiftly than the first. In a single battle fought in June at Nisib, on the upper Euphrates, the invincible Ibrahim ruined the Ottoman army. Mahmud off at Constantinople was providentially spared the grief of the irreparable disaster. Before the news reached his bedside he died, leaving as his successor his son, Abdul Medjid, a frail lad of but sixteen years.

Again, as in 1833, Ibrahim took the road to Constantinople and again the sultan or rather, since he was a minor, his advisers of the divan eagerly scanned the horizon for a favorable sign. But on this occasion all the powers of Europe were on the alert, resolved not to permit Russia to steal a march on them a second time. They interposed themselves between the Moslem foes and by way of preliminary notified the sultan that they would treat with Mehemet Ali in his stead. Then the powers sat down to deliberate together on the fate of the Near East. In view of their known differences it was clear that their diplomatic conferences would not have smooth sailing. As the nub of the whole situation there presently emerged the question whether it was better for Europe to bolster up the feeble Ottoman empire, with which the powers were familiar and which, dominating at present, they might divide some day among themselves, or whether it was preferable to endorse a renovated Moslem state headed by the energetic conqueror from the Nile and embracing the whole eastern Mediterranean. Confronted with these alternatives, the powers with an instinctive grasp of what best comported with their advantage pronounced for the empire of the Osmanli. All the powers arrived at this decision except France. France inclined toward Egypt on the ground that Mehemet Ali had an open predilection for French advisers and that, should he become master of the Near East through French help, he would have to concede to France a paramount position in his realm. Over this conflicting evaluation of the interests involved in the crisis, the concert of Europe went to pieces, with France audaciously confronting the other four powers with a program of her own.

Conceiving that they were strong enough for every eventuality, the four antagonists of France proceeded presently to en-

The European crisis of 1839–40.

Europe confronted by the specter of a general war.

force their conclusions in the teeth of their defaulting colleague. They presented Mehemet Ali with an ultimatum to the effect that he must without delay withdraw his hand from the Ottoman empire and content himself with his original pashalik of Egypt. Openly encouraged by the French, the pasha refused to comply with the order, and throughout the summer of 1840 a nervous expectation of a general war kept Europe breathless. But no sooner did the allies pass from words to action than the crisis vanished through the sudden collapse of the overrated Egyptian power. An Anglo-Austrian fleet was ordered to blockade the Syrian coast and succeeded in inflicting such heavy losses on Ibrahim that he was obliged to abandon all Syria. Then the fleet boldly sailed to Alexandria, and when the expected assistance of Mehemet's French ally did not materialize, the pasha ceased to struggle and announced his willingness to abide by the verdict of the victors. The threatened general war over the Ottoman empire was thus avoided by the quelling of Mehemet Ali and the diplomatic humiliation of his champion, France. Europe heaved a sigh of relief, but the grim specter of a world upheaval, which had been laid with such difficulty and only after a feverish agitation of public opinion, was destined henceforth to make a periodic reappearance on the European scene in connection with each new phase of the ever-changing eastern question.

The settlement of the Egyptian question and the substitution of the informal protectorate of the five powers over the sultan for that of Russia, 1841.

When the smoke, less of battle than of rancorous debate, cleared, the concert of Europe, made harmonious once more by the return to the fold of wayward France, effected two settlements of the greatest consequence for the Near East. The first regarded Mehemet Ali. Cast in the form of a treaty between the sultan and his vassal, it conceded Egypt to the pasha in return for the surrender of Arabia, Crete, and Syria. However, as a balm for his many wounds, Mehemet was permitted to hold the rich Nile basin as an hereditary fief. Though Turkey, dramatically rescued at the point of death, might reasonably congratulate itself on this solution, the fact remains that its grip on Egypt, never particularly strong, was still further weakened and that Egypt, by being settled under a sovereign line of its own, was enabled to enlarge its self-government to the point of practical independence. The second settlement regarded the Ottoman

empire and was laid down in a document of July, 1841, signed
by all the powers and known as the Convention of the Straits. By
virtue of it the treaty of Hunkiar Skelessi was permitted to lapse
and the obligation assumed by the signatories to regard the waters
of the Dardanelles and Bosporus as under the absolute sovereignty of the sultan. He, for his part, undertook to close them,
in time of peace, to the war-ships of all the powers alike, that is,
to give no one of them an advantage over any other. That
Russia by the substitution of the Convention of the Straits for
the treaty of Hunkiar Skelessi lost heavily hardly needs elucidation. Not only was the alliance by which she bound her victim
to herself, and to herself alone, dissolved, but in its room
appeared the collective guarantee by all Europe of the sultan's
sovereignty of the two channels leading from the Black sea to
the Mediterranean. If, as had been the case in 1833, Russia
could also in 1839 have safeguarded the Ottoman empire by her
sole action, her privileged rôle of protector of the empire might
have been perpetuated. But since on the occasion of the second
crisis all the powers had insisted on sharing in Turkey's delivery,
the logical consequence was the informal collective protectorate
registered in the Convention of the Straits.

For the time being Russia failed to give any evidence of
chagrin. Tsar Nicholas was a partisan of the view that the near
eastern question could only be solved by the cooperation of Russia
and Great Britain, and as such an understanding had been conspicuously realized in the diplomatic history of the great crisis
of 1839–41 he testified to his satisfaction with what had been done.
But — and the particle is most important — he desired the cooperation to develop into a regular alliance with specific arrangements as to the ultimate division of the eastern spoils between the
contracting parties. As Great Britain, for her part, entertained
no thought of an alliance, and as she, instead of wishing to partition Turkey desired rather to strengthen it as a bulwark against
none other than Nicholas himself, there lay concealed in the
Anglo-Russian friendship a germ of misunderstanding which,
as we shall see, led ultimately to a rupture and produced the
Crimean war.

The seed
planted of a
future
Anglo-
Russian mis-
understand-
ing.

Even during the crisis attending the death of Sultan Mahmud,
and long before the settlement registered in the Convention of

Continuation of Ottoman reform under British auspices. The *tanzimat* of 1839.

the Straits, Great Britain adopted at Constantinople the policy of encouraging the ruler and his ministers to strengthen their realm by every possible means, especially by the adoption of European reforms. Therewith, without the intervention of a formal treaty, by the stern and unescapable logic of action, Great Britain became the special champion of the Porte. It was a source of deep satisfaction to her that the youthful sultan, Abdul Medjid, and his chief advisers met her views with much more than simple acquiescence. Firmly resolved to continue, expand, and systematize the reforms begun by Mahmud, they issued in November, 1839, from the kiosk of Gulhané, an organic statute for the empire known as the *tanzimat*. Its author was the head of the party of reform, Reshid Pasha, and its articles bespoke Reshid's admiration for the public order and equitable administration of the West. Conceived as a charter of Ottoman liberties, the *tanzimat* promised security of life, property, and honor to all the subjects of the padishah, the imposition of regular and just taxes, equality before the law of Christian and Moslem, in fact it poured out over the sultan's backward realm the whole cornucopia of blessings which we regard as constituting the substance of our occidental civilization. Of course, in view of the distressing social and moral actualities in the Near East, these fatherly promises constituted, if not a cruel hoax, at least a monstrous self-deception and were presently more honored in the breach than the observance. Moreover, before long their leading champion, Reshid, fell from power (1841), owing to the intrigues of the conservatives, who met the good intentions of Abdul Medjid exactly as they had met those of his father, sometimes with open resistance, more often simply with the characteristic *vis inertiae* of the orient. In short, the tanzimat worked no western miracle; the East remained the East.

Actual, as distinct from imaginary, reforms.

None-the-less the reform impulse continued to manifest itself throughout the reign of Abdul Medjid (1839–1861), largely in connection with the periodic restoration to power of Reshid, head of the Europeanizing faction in the state. Certain hesitating advances were therefore made and are decidedly worth recording: the administration was better harmonized and brought more completely under a central head by distributing the excessive powers of the provincial governors, the pashas, among several officials, much less capable of becoming centers of resistance; a system of modernized education was at least sketched on paper and timid steps were taken to realize its measures; and, above all, the reorganization of the army, feebly attacked by Mahmud on the passing of the Janissaries, was at last carried through with professional seriousness. Based like the armies of western Europe on conscription, the reformed Ottoman forces were divided into two sections, the regular troops called *nizam* composed of men who served for five years with the colors, and the reserves called *redif*, embracing the men who, having passed through the ranks, were for seven years following their dismissal liable to service in time of war. Behind the irregular and wavering reform activity of the government the British ambassador at Constantinople, the all-powerful Lord Stratford de Redcliffe, acting on instructions from London, put the whole weight of his influence, while his Russian colleague viewed the vague agitation of the stagnant Ottoman pool with jealous or ironical contempt. A close observer stationed on the spot could entertain no doubt that Russia and Great Britain were pursuing with regard to the Porte diametrically opposed aims.

From the very beginning of his reign Nicholas I had maintained toward the Ottoman empire an attitude of firm but reasoned aggression, as is sufficiently illustrated by the war of 1828–29 and the treaty of Hunkiar Skelessi. Being cautious as well as consistent, he had recently preferred to march with Great Britain, to march, be it understood, not to stand still with her. When after patiently waiting for years he perceived no inclination on the part of the cabinet of London to fall in with his anti-Turkish views, he began to show signs of irritation. Then, just after the middle of the century, an incident occurred which thoroughly roused his autocratic temper. It involved the Holy Places of Palestine, still as in the past the cherished goal of popular pilgrimages from all parts of Christendom. From a period as remote as the days of Solyman the Magnificent, France, in behalf of the Catholic church, had exercised certain rights of protection over the Holy Places. Though the earliest privileges conceded to Christianity, they were not the last, for in the eighteenth century, the Greek church, represented by the patriarch of Constantinople, had from the sultan's favor obtained similar conces-

The issue of the Holy Places between Tsar Nicholas and Emperor Napoleon III.

sions. From then on cantankerous disputes between Latin and Greek monks, acting as agents on the ground of their respective churches, were by no means uncommon, but were regularly settled by mutual concessions. Unfortunately a new dispute, which broke out around the middle of the century, was taken up by France and Russia in their capacity of protecting powers of respectively the Latin and Greek monks and carried into the realm of diplomacy. Sparring for advantage and prestige in the Near East, the two powers not only resorted to liberal abuse of each other but vigorously threatened the overlord of Palestine, the sultan, whose sole fault lay in his attempt to please both sides and win approval as a modern Solomon. As is usual enough in this very human world a dangerous personal factor contributed to the exacerbation of the European disputants. In 1851 the upstart Louis Napoleon seized the power in France and in the very next year reestablished the Napoleonic dynasty by proclaiming himself emperor of the French. To a dyed-in-the-wool legitimist, like Nicholas, this revolutionary behavior was intolerable, and he showed his displeasure by refusing to Napoleon III the title "brother," a trifling amenity imposed by custom on European sovereigns in their epistolary exchanges. Desirous of squaring the account by irritating the haughty Romanoff, the new French emperor, personally a very advanced type of skeptic, became fanatically insistent about the exclusive and sacred character of the Catholic rights in Palestine and the consequent contemptibility of the Orthodox claims. The absurd issue dragged on for months, marked by the publication of contradictory rescripts on the part of the pliant sultan, first in favor of one, then in favor of the other of the two sovereigns obstinately hounding him for concessions, each in behalf of his particular brand of Christianity. In the upshot the tsar, at the end of his patience, resolved to settle the matter once and for all by bringing the sultan under his orders.

Tsar Nicholas proposes to Great Britain the partition of the Ottoman empire and is rebuffed.

True to the policy pursued for more than a decade, Nicholas began with an amicable approach to Great Britain. In January, 1853, he summoned the British ambassador at Petrograd to his presence and spread out before him his inmost thoughts on the subject of his neighbor, the sultan. "We have on our hands," he said, "a sick man, a very sick man; it will be a great misfortune if one of these days he should slip away before the necessary arrangements have been made." He then sketched his idea of appropriate " arrangements," and while definitely indicating Crete and Egypt as the share to be awarded to Great Britain, he was studiously vague about Russia, although it was as clear as day that his thought was fixed on Constantinople and the straits. On receiving these overtures the London cabinet immediately rejected them as destructive of the policy of the preservation of the Ottoman empire, which had been adopted a generation ago and to which Great Britain was as firmly committed as ever. Angry at the sultan, irritated by Napoleon, and rudely rebuffed by his erstwhile English friends, Tsar Nicholas, now thoroughly aroused, resolved on drastic action. In March, 1853, he dispatched a special envoy to Constantinople with a double ultimatum, involving first, the immediate and sweeping acknowledgment of the rights claimed by the Greek church in Palestine, and second, the formal recognition of the tsar as the protector of *all* the Greek Christians resident on Turkish soil.

The ultimatum, presented by Prince Menshikoff, well known for his brusque military manners, threw the divan into a panic, for it meant either immediate surrender or another war with Russia, which the Porte was by no means ready to face. In their terrible and crushing dilemma a *deus ex machina* appeared to the sultan's frightened ministers in the form of the English ambassador, Lord Stratford. Well acquainted through long service at Constantinople with every twist and turn of the eastern question, and a passionate believer in the world mission of the British empire, he regarded the rival Russian empire with deep-seated suspicion and looked on the preservation and rebirth of Turkey as the very keystone of the arch of British policy in the Near East. Putting himself squarely behind the members of the divan he counselled them with great acumen to separate the two Russian demands. The first, touching the Holy Places, was harmless, and with regard to it the English envoy advised the Porte to offer complete satisfaction. This done, there remained the crude second demand, which alone counted, and touching this he encouraged his Turkish friends to be adamant. To him, as to the Ottoman cabinet, it involved nothing less than the question

The two demands of the Russian ultimatum.

of the sultan's sovereignty, for if the tsar became the legally acknowledged protector of the Greek Christians, constituting the majority of the inhabitants of Turkey-in-Europe, the sultan would no longer be master in his own house. It should be observed, however, that in the view of the tsar his demand, far from constituting a novelty, was nothing but the formal restatement of a concession embodied in treaty-form as long ago as Kutchuk-Kainardji (1774). Without doubt some diplomatic jargon had been inserted in that famous document acknowledging the tsar's right to protect the Greek church, but its terms were highly ambiguous and the interpretation given by Nicholas was indignantly rejected by the Porte. Lord Stratford was determined that the Russian interpretation never should be admitted, for it was the crux of the issue between the two powers, between Great Britain, which wished to preserve, and Russia, which wished to protect in order the more securely to destroy the Ottoman empire. It took the Russian ultimatum to bring out the wholly irreconcilable character of the Russian and British policies. Fully assured of British support, the Ottoman ministers plucked up courage and in May, 1853, rejected the Russian claim. The overbearing Prince Menshikoff immediately stamped out of Constantinople as a few weeks before he had stamped in, and diplomatic relations between the sultan and tsar were broken off.

The dove of peace hovers over Europe until the will to war triumphs at Petrograd and London.

Although the threat of war was now suspended like a sword over the East, war did not immediately follow. The tsar himself professed that, though he wanted satisfaction, he did not desire war, while the British cabinet was so divided on the issue as to be unable to adopt a definite policy. Moreover, the other powers, notably Austria, busied themselves to throw water on the smouldering embers. Prolonged feverish negotiations in the interests of peace in the end, however, led to nothing, chiefly because the two principals refused to recede from their original position. In a formal sense the principals were the tsar and the sultan, but in reality they were Nicholas and Lord Stratford, with the question for a time in abeyance whether Lord Stratford was, as he claimed to be, the genuine and indubitable voice of the English government. For a long time divided over the support of its bellicose ambassador, the London cabinet was gradually won over to his policy by its most energetic and influential member, Lord

Palmerston. Before the autumn came the war party in the British government was definitely in the ascendancy. Under the circumstances the spirit of concession lost ground, the public respectively behind London and Petrograd was invaded with the hypnotic excitement of conflict, and, helplessly tossed about on the sea of circumstance, Britain and Russia drifted into war. The main events following Menshikoff's departure from Constantinople indicate that there was no rush to measure arms. Not till July did the tsar order his army to cross the Pruth and seize the Danubian principalities; and not till October did the Porte answer the Russian challenge with the demand for an immediate evacuation under penalty of war. With Russia and Turkey already at grips the issue at London was still trembling in the balance, when, on the last day of November, the Russian admiral in the Black sea fell upon the Turkish fleet, anchored in Sinope bay, and utterly destroyed it. At the news the angered British lion at last crouched to spring upon his foe. For with the Ottoman seapower shattered the Russians were already potentially on the Bosporus and the time for debate was over.

In the clear light of history the war which followed was a struggle between Great Britain and Russia over the issue of the preservation or destruction of the Ottoman empire. In such a conflict Great Britain, while commanding of course the support of its protegés, the Turks, ardently hoped to obtain, in addition, the aid of the other three powers, Austria, Prussia, and France, since these powers too had an apparent interest in saving the Porte from the Russian clutches. Austria and Prussia, however, insisted on proclaiming their neutrality, and in the end only France was won to the British side, largely because Emperor Napoleon, still smarting under the studied insults heaped upon him by Tsar Nicholas, eagerly seized the proffered opportunity for revenge. Besides, an alliance with his powerful neighbor across the channel would put an end to his isolation in Europe, thereby perceptibly strengthening the foundations of his improvised throne. In consequence, France and Great Britain succeeded in bringing their eastern policy into complete harmony and, after concluding alliances with each other and their common partner, the Ottoman empire, in March, 1854, they flung defiance at the tsar by serving him a declaration of war.

[margin note: Great Britain and France ally themselves with the Ottoman empire and declare war, March, 1854.]

[handwritten margin note: until they saw who was winning the war]

The
Crimean
War.

The struggle thus inaugurated is known as the Crimean War because its one memorable and absorbing episode is associated with an attack by the allies on the peninsula of the Crimea, jutting from the southern shore of Russia into the Black sea. The reason for this attack is not far to seek. By seizing, at the beginning of the controversy, the Danubian principalities, Russia had acquired the advantage of the offensive, to which it was expected she would resolutely cling. Consequently the original plan of the western allies was to join the Turks in a Danubian campaign to the end of defeating the Russians and driving them home. But this program was thwarted, largely by the action of Austria. Although anxious to keep out of the war, the Viennese cabinet was most uneasy over the presence of the Russians in Moldavia and Wallachia, directly adjoining the Hapsburg dominion on the east, and notified Russia in no uncertain terms that it would join forces with the western powers unless the principalities were evacuated. In order not to increase the number of his foes the tsar reluctantly yielded, and before the end of the summer of 1854 the last Russian troops had recrossed the Pruth. With the collapse of the Russian invasion the offensive passed into the hands of the allies. Casting about for something to do, they hit, in view of their own overwhelming sea-power, on the sea-power of Russia as a suitable point of attack. The heart of Russian maritime strength unquestionably was the great naval base on the southern extremity of the Crimea, Sebastopol. In September Great Britain and France forced a landing to the north of Sebastopol, at the bay of Eupatoria, and began the siege of the fortress.

The siege of
Sebastopol,
1854–55.

The siege lasted a whole year. It was an extremely difficult operation largely because, though the attacking party completely commanded the eastern waters, it had to bring its soldiers, equipment, and supplies in relatively small and slow vessels by the long journey over the Mediterranean sea. Nor was that all. The improvised Anglo-French camps were insufficient to protect the troops against the rigors of the Crimean winter and the ravages of disease, while the Russians, shut up in Sebastopol, put up a magnificent defense with other Russians, outside the fortress, ceaselessly battering the lines of the besiegers in the hope of effecting relief. By grimly sticking to their purpose the allies, however, gradually mastered the many difficulties in their way, and in September, 1855, they captured Sebastopol or rather the charred ruins to which it had been reduced. Though the immense territory of Russia had been no more than scratched by this triumph, the tsar's government showed that it had lost heart for the war. For one thing it had made the discovery that the administrative machinery of Russia was hopelessly inadequate for a struggle with the more perfect types of organization represented by the West; and, for another, the death in March, 1855, while the siege of Sebastopol was at its height, of the indomitable Nicholas, who was largely responsible for the war, threw the Russian ministry into confusion and lamed its will. Moreover, Alexander II, who succeeded his father, was a man of gentle temper and did not conceal his desire to end a struggle which was not of his making. For their part the allies, having obtained the satisfaction of a victory, gladly accepted the proffered hand. As a result a congress of the victors and vanquished, in which the two neutrals, Austria and Prussia, were invited to share, took place in Paris, and in March, 1856, terminated the war with a general pacification.

The treaty of Paris records the purpose of Europe, under the leadership of Great Britain, first, to make Russia pay for the loss of the war by the surrender of all the special advantages gained at the expense of the Ottoman empire since Kutchuk-Kainardji (1774), and second, to strengthen the Ottoman empire as far as possible in order to enable it to offer better resistance to future Russian aggression. The treaty therefore, first of all, obliged the tsar to renounce any and every claim to act as protector of the Greek Christians within the dominions of the sultan. As to the rights acquired at various times to protect Serbia and the Rumanian principalities of Moldavia and Wallachia, these too he was made to relinquish. Further, with a view to depriving Russia of that control of the shipping on the Danube which she had been recently exercising, the tsar was required to restore southern Bessarabia, Russian since 1812, to Moldavia and the Danube delta to the Ottoman empire.

Freed from Russian control, the navigation of the lower Danube, far from being reëntrusted to the incompetent hands

The Peace of Paris (1856): the Russian renunciations.

An international experiment: the navigation on the lower Danube put under international control.

of Turkey, was put under an international régime, which has proved one of the most enlightened and constructive measures ever embodied in a general treaty. An international commission was set up to exercise authority from the mouth of the Sulina channel to an inland point, which, by supplementary agreements, was finally extended as far upstream as Braila. Not only was the navigation of this stretch declared to be open to the ships of all nations, but the commission received the right to remove shoals, build lighthouses, levy tolls, and perform all other services required by the common good. As a successful example of how commercial impediments, due to friction among a number of competing states, may be removed, the international commission of the lower Danube deserves much more attention than it has generally been conceded.[1]

The Black sea neutralized.

If the freedom of the Danube represented more particularly a demand of Austria, the hobby of Great Britain was the freedom of the Black sea. While this, already secured to the merchantmen of all nations by virtue of earlier treaties, was solemnly reaffirmed, Great Britain insisted on going farther by depriving her enemy, Russia, of the means of exercising even potential control over the Black sea and the adjoining straits. Accordingly, the treaty neutralized the Black sea, specifically obligating Russia to refrain from having ships of war, arsenals, or naval bases within the compass of its waters.

The Ottoman empire put under the guarantee of the powers; the Christians put under the protection of the sultan.

In the matter of the Ottoman empire, which, as the ally of the victors, was treated with distinction, the treaty guaranteed the independence of the sultan and the territorial integrity of his state. In sign of the era of good will inaugurated by the alliance with France and England, the sultan, just before the convening of the congress of Paris, in February, 1856, had issued a new charter of liberties to his peoples. As this document, by reiterating in even more solemn form the promises

[1] In distinction from *the international commission,* which by the periodic renewal of its authority and the extension of its powers was in successful operation to the outbreak of the Great War (1914), *the commission of riverain states,* appointed by the treaty of 1856 to regulate the commerce on the Danube for the remainder of its course, has, owing to incurable national jealousies, proved a conspicuous failure. The lesson of these contrasting commissions leaps to view.

of the tanzimat of 1839, proclaimed the abolition of the rayah régime and the equality of Moslems and Christians before the law, the powers, gulled so often, asserted their willingness to be gulled again and wrote into the treaty the amazing statement that the protection of the Christians should henceforth be in the hands of none other than their legal lord, the sultan himself.

Such were the main provisions of the treaty which ended the Crimean war. Of this war, fought to preserve the Ottoman empire, it has often been remarked that it was a useless war, and of the peace of Paris, concluded in the Ottoman interest, that it was a futile peace. There is much to be said for this disparaging judgment. If the Ottoman empire was slowly perishing from dry-rot, as we have excellent reason to think was the case, it was diplomatic hocus-pocus, nothing less, to declare that, by reason of the paper promises of 1856, the state had been reborn and that it might properly take rank henceforward with the other European powers. As a matter of plain fact and entirely contrary to the assumption of the treaty, the Turkish decay continued without interruption. In consequence the Christians continued to be oppressed, the agitation in their favor persisted among their European sympathizers, and the powers, far from respecting their own pledge to honor the sovereignty of the padishah and the integrity of his territory, interfered in his affairs whenever they dared and, in substance, treated him not as an equal but as a ward. However, to be the ward of all Europe often made it possible for the sultan to play off one group of powers against another and assured him, on the whole, a much more independent position than in the days when he had been the ward of Russia only and had, willynilly, to dance to his guardian's piping.

With equal confidence it may be declared that the group of articles regulating the relation of Russia to the Black sea furnished abundant evidence of the familiar myopia of diplomats. The purpose of these articles was to deprive Russia of sea-power on the one front where sea-power was vital to her, and therewith to put her permanently at a disadvantage as compared with every other power in the world, including Turkey. Since no self-respecting state, fully conscious of its vigor, could

Futility of the provisions in favor of the Ottoman empire.

Futility of the neutralization of the Black sea.

possibly remain for long content with such insulting arrangements, it was to be foreseen that Russia would seize the first favorable opportunity to render the Black sea restrictions null and void. That opportunity came in 1870 with the Franco-German war. As soon as the world had fixed its attention on this struggle the government of the tsar quietly notified the signatories of the treaty of Paris that it no longer considered itself bound by the provisions regarding the Black sea. Of course the act was a rank breach of international law, but as no state, not even England, was willing to defend the treaty by the use of force, Russia reacquired the freedom of action, of which she should never have been deprived so long as equal rights in peace and war continue to constitute the basis of association among European states. The disability laid on Russia in this case was defendable neither in the theory nor practice of international justice.

Historical significance of the treaty of Paris to be found in the check administered to Russian imperialist ambitions.
But, granting that in trying to render Turkey strong and Russia weak the treaty attempted to invert the order of nature and necessarily failed, the fact remains that there were elements of this treaty which proved so tremendously important that they can hardly be exaggerated. That Russia, the losing power, paid the price of defeat by surrendering the whole sum of special prerogatives, which she had been engaged in assembling for about one hundred years, indubitably constituted a milestone in the history of Balkania and the whole Near East. Up to the Crimean war the tsar's government, in spite of occasional setbacks, had made such headway in getting its octopus arms wound round the sultan that the process would have had to continue but a little longer to render the victim completely impotent. By the treaty of Paris these suffocating members were hacked away, and not only was Turkey liberated, but her independence and territory were placed under the collective guarantee of Europe. True, Turkey in her feebleness was unable to take more than casual advantage of the favor of which she was the recipient, but Russia henceforth was like a man tied to a post, or rather she was like the mythical Sisyphus who, after laboriously rolling his stone up the hill, saw it slip from his grasp just as he was on the point of heaving it to the summit. If, following the peace of 1856, Russia should per-

chance take it into her head to revive the old dreams respecting the Ottoman empire and particularly Constantinople, there would be no alternative for her but, like Sisyphus, to begin once more at the bottom of the incline. That indeed is exactly what she did, but with the powers aligned against her and prompt to use the treaty of Paris as a club the moment she moved, she made as good as no progress toward her goal during the succeeding decades. The war of 1877–78 and the treaty of Berlin which followed it lend impressive weight to this contention, for, though Russia won the war, she was at Berlin deliberately deprived of all she strove for by the action of her rivals. Even as late as 1914 she stood, in regard to the Ottoman empire, precisely where the treaty of Paris had placed her, that is, on a level with all the powers who still declared it to be a cardinal point of their policy to maintain intact the sultan's empire. Moreover, in the matter of the Great War, it is as clear as day that it represented, as far as Russia was concerned, a last frenzied attempt to undo the effect of the treaty of Paris of more than half a hundred years before. In this war, as will be shown in due course, the patent purpose of the tsar was to regain a special position in the Ottoman empire, more particularly, by acquiring the unchallenged control of Constantinople and the straits. But we are anticipating, though but to clinch our argument. For, if we accept the contention that by virtue of her defeat in the war of 1856 Russia was checked, not for ten or twenty years but down to the present day, in what she conceived to be her march of destiny to the Mediterranean sea, we must be prepared to admit that the Crimean war was one of the most significant imperialist struggles among the European powers of the whole nineteenth century.

CHAPTER XXIII

THE AFFAIRS OF MOLDAVIA AND WALLACHIA AND THE FOUNDING OF THE RUMANIAN STATE

Europe, in the treaty of Paris, assumes responsibility for the Danubian principalities.

AMONG the many matters embraced in the treaty of Paris was a series of important stipulations, touching the principalities of Moldavia and Wallachia, which inaugurated a new epoch in their history. We are aware that, ever since the peace of Kutchuk-Kainardji (1774), Russia had been extending her control over the Danubian provinces until, at the outbreak of the Crimean war, she counted for more at Jassy and Bucharest than the legal sovereign, the sultan. To this situation the victors in the Crimean war firmly put an end by cancelling the Russian protectorate and substituting therefor the collective guarantee of Europe. At the same time the treaty, while recognizing the continued suzerainty of the sultan, decreed that the principalities should have " an independent and national administration " and that a commission of the powers should look into the question of their future organization with particular regard to the fusion of the hitherto separate governments into one. Implied in the political inquiry was the larger, and historically decisive, issue whether the Rumanian people had matured to the point of being able to exercise the rights and duties of an independent nation. That issue, if the reader is to arrive at an independent judgment, obliges us to assemble a few data bearing on the state of Rumanian society.

Rumania never subjected to direct Ottoman rule.

The familiar fact that the Ottomans, on bringing Moldavia and Wallachia within the sphere of their influence, permitted the native governments to be perpetuated, thus failing to replace them with a direct Ottoman administration, had considerable advantages for the Rumanian people. Although, under the heavy pressure of Constantinople, the fiscal tyranny of the native princes (hospodars) as well as of the Phanariotes, who in the eighteenth century succeeded them, was great, an incalculable benefit was conferred by the circumstance that the Moslems, by failing to establish either themselves or their religion in the region north of the Danube, introduced no such social cleavage as threatened to impair the harmony of many of the provinces south of the river. Granting that during the centuries of subjection to the Ottomans the Rumanian people led a miserable existence and that their civilization was at a very low ebb, they were at least not threatened with being supplanted on their own soil. It could even be contended that if the mass of the people, the overtaxed peasants, led the life of veritable beasts of the field, the landholding nobles, the boyars, were, in respect of the income derived from their estates and of their traditional local authority, in much the same position as before the Turkish conquest.

In spite of the alleviations experienced by Rumania as compared with other Christian sections of the Ottoman empire, it admits of no dispute that as regards those mental and spiritual activities constituting the basis of any civilization worthy of the name, the boyars, together with their peasant-serfs, were throughout the Ottoman period sunk in a gloom hardly broken by a single ray. The fact is the Rumans were not the inheritors of a rich and idiomatic culture which they were free to cherish. In sharp distinction from the Serbs and Bulgars they had not, in the course of the Middle Age, developed their own mental and spiritual forms, while the institutions of the Romans, from whom they claimed a somewhat dubious descent, had receded to such a distance as to be, for practical purposes, unavailable. All signs indicate that the Rumans of the medieval period were a very backward people who dwelt culturally in the shadow of the Slavs. Receiving from them their ecclesiastical institutions and learning, they were pleased to use the Slav liturgy in their churches, utterly incomprehensible though it must have been to the people. Further, the political terminology of the medieval Rumanians makes it clear that they borrowed also much of their state from their Slav neighbors. Then, in the eighteenth century, during the Phanariote period, Greek ideas and speech prevailed at Jassy and Bucharest to such a degree that all purely native expression was frowned on and stifled. Plainly it would require a powerful

Absence of a strong national culture among the Rumans.

combination of forces, active through several generations, to produce the miracle of a national rebirth among a people smothered under so many deposits of foreign influence.

The
Rumanian
awakening
due to
contact with
the West.

The national Rumanian awakening dates from the end of the eighteenth and the beginning of the nineteenth century and was due to the same general agencies as, at about the same time, blew the Serb and Greek embers into flame. These influences need not be here again rehearsed further than to recall that the decay of the Ottoman empire synchronized with the imperialist consolidation of its European neighbors, and that these in their progressive penetration of the Moslem world automatically served as carriers of western civilization. Among the great powers, it was Russia which first established direct contact with the Rumanians and which from 1774 (Kutchuk-Kainardji) exercised a species of protectorate over Moldavia and Wallachia. To be sure, Russia herself had only lately opened the doors to western culture and still constituted a backward, half-oriental society, but her upper and administrative circles were passionate occidentalists, capable and ready to mediate European ideas. In any case contact with Russia promoted a roundabout contact with the West. No wonder therefore that, just before the close of the eighteenth century, a small national party should have appeared on Rumanian soil, reflecting with more zeal than accuracy the idealism of the French revolution. The usual phenomena followed. The national language, which had fallen on evil days, was drawn into the light and became the object of reverent study. Literary expression multiplied and led to the foundation of schools. The awakened interest in current affairs inspired a few enterprising spirits to publish a newspaper. In short, Rumania experienced such a literary and educational movement as has, in the case of all the southeastern peoples, preceded their full political awakening.

The
Russian protectorate.

Inevitably the growing nationalism affected the relation of the provinces to their neighbor, protecting and benevolent Russia. Though they had, in the first place, welcomed the interference of the Slav giant and had rejoiced at the increased restraints put by the tsar, with each new decade, on the sultan, they were not asleep to the dangers lurking in the situation. As early as 1777 the Tsarina Catherine, in spite of the protectorate she exercised, had failed to protest when Austria appropriated the Bukovina, the northern district of Moldavia; and worse followed when, in 1812, by the treaty of Bucharest, Russia herself incorporated Bessarabia, Moldavia's eastern segment. Here manifestly was a protectorate exercised less in the interest of the protected than in that of the protector! Even so, it is undeniable that the provinces continued to receive important benefits at Russia's hands. In 1802, for instance, Russia obliged the sultan to appoint the hospodars for a term of seven years, instead of removing them at will and subjecting the helpless population to a rapid succession of appointees obliged to practice an unscrupulous extortion in order to repay the purchase price demanded by the Porte. Again, by the treaty of Adrianople (1829), Russia succeeded in having the hospodars appointed for life and narrowly reduced the connection of the sultan with the provinces to the claim of an annual fixed tribute. Furthermore, having occupied the provinces during the late war (1828–29), she prolonged her stay for a number of years and did not retire until she had endowed her wards with a modern and business-like, though aristocratic, administrative system based on a written code, the *règlement organique*. For these benefits the Rumanian patriots expressed their thanks but, for the rest, clung to their own ideas. They suspected, rightly enough, that Russia was acting primarily in her own interest, and that their best guarantee against the foreshadowed substitution of a Muscovite for a Turkish overlordship would be political independence.

With such ideas gaining currency, it was not long before the tsar became the object of the same animosity as had formerly been aimed at the sultan; and when the revolution of 1848 made the rounds of Europe, everywhere blowing the national movement into flame, the Rumanians rose in revolution, nominally against their own oligarchic government in order to effect its democratization, but really against Tsar Nicholas. That unbending autocrat quickly took up the challenge, occupied Moldavia and Wallachia with troops, and did not depart till he had crushed the nationalist rebels and once more securely tied the provinces as a tail to the Russian kite. In the Crimean war there took place the successive occupations of the Danubian states by Russia

The nationalist sentiment turns against Russia.

and Austria, which, by bringing home to the Rumans that they were mere counters in the game of the great powers, made them more in love with liberty than ever. In their own eyes they were, when the treaty of Paris was signed, emphatically ripe for the responsibilities of self-government.

The powers tardily prepare a constitution for the principalities and forbid their union. In the light of the Parisian settlement the troubled Rumanian prospects took on a sudden brilliance. Though affirming the formal suzerainty of the sultan, the treaty not only terminated the Russian hegemony, the firm hold of which the unaided Rumanian strength could never have loosened, but it established an European commission charged with the reorganization of the provinces. To a majority of the natives a reorganization, of which they were ready to approve, meant simply the creation of national unity under a modern constitution; but they were destined to discover that they could not have what they wanted merely for the asking. Though the powers, contrary to their usual, deep-seated conservatism, had, in the treaty, registered a very liberal attitude toward the Rumanian problem, they were by no means agreed as to the precise course to be pursued. Apart from Napoleon III, who whole-heartedly championed Rumanian nationalism, there was little enthusiasm for the Rumanian cause. In particular Austria, owing as much to her traditional conservatism as to her fear of the attraction likely to be exercised by a Rumanian state upon the Rumans within her own boundaries, set her face against authorizing the union of the two provinces. In consequence there was discussion, chicanery, and delay. The most the European powers could be moved to do, and that tardily (August, 1858), was, after endowing each province with its own separate constitution, to create a national committee empowered to treat certain affairs as common to both. While publicly accepting the Olympian verdict for the sake of the undoubted benefits which it conferred, the wily Rumanians privately resolved to adhere to their own nationalist plan.

The two assemblies elect the same prince, Alexander John Cuza. Early in 1859 the elected assemblies of Moldavia and Wallachia came together, each in its own capital, in order, according to the decision of the powers, to complete their organization by the election of a prince. Each was expected to pick a separate candidate, but when the vote was taken it was found that both the assemblies had chosen the same man, a native boyar, Alexander John Cuza. Besides being a gross affront to the powers, the proceeding was manifestly the result of a patriotic plot. What were the wise and omnipotent mentors to do? They might of course have levied war on their disobedient ward but war was too serious to be entertained. It was not the first time — nor the last — that a small Balkan state obliged the great governments to eat their words by confronting them with an accomplished fact. To cover their retreat they continued, like wrathful Jupiters, to thunder from on high until, gradually, one after another accepted the inevitable. The longed-for union had become a fact.

The new state was christened Rumania and its capital, in recognition of the greater importance of Wallachia, was fixed at Bucharest. Jassy, the seat of the former Moldavian government, was depressed to a provincial town. It was 1861 before the new prince was recognized by the sultan and the powers, and 1862 before he met his first united legislature. Awaiting the new government was a colossal task, involving nothing less than the bringing of an aspiring but long submerged nation into harmony with the age. In connection with this task peculiar elements in the structure of Rumanian society were bound to weigh heavily. The national wealth lay in the extremely fertile soil which, owned preponderantly by a relatively small group of great landlords, was worked by the peasant masses, whose status was substantially that of medieval serfs. There were few towns, little commerce, no industry, and of course no more than the nucleus of a middle class. The peasants constituted over eighty per cent of the population and were so ignorant and rested so abjectly under the thumb of their masters that, even in case they should be given the franchise, they could, on election day, be herded like cattle to vote as they were ordered. Political activity was the exclusive prerogative of the landlords aided by a small but active middle class of merchants and intellectuals. To be in the western fashion, these leading groups divided into a conservative and a liberal party, and although the liberal party was in a general way in favor of reform, neither party, in view of the character of its constituents, was deeply concerned about the peasants.

The structure of Rumanian society.

Nationalization of the Rumanian church.

Under these circumstances Cuza, as head of the state and director of its policies, was obliged to move cautiously. Certain reforms were adopted amidst general enthusiasm, above all, those involving the church. From a religious viewpoint the Rumanians had always been more or less under foreign influence, in the Middle Age under that of the Slavs, in the eighteenth century more particularly under that of the Phanariote Greeks. In consequence they had come to look upon the Orthodox church, although it embraced the whole people, as a tool of foreign oppressors, and the plan gradually gained support to weaken its hold on the nation. Turning upon the monasteries, which were credited with owning about one-fifth of the country's soil and which were exclusively in the hands of Greek abbots, the parliament at Bucharest confiscated this ecclesiastical property for the benefit of the nation and simply turned the monastic occupants adrift. Next, the legislature severed the connection of the church with the Constantinopolitan patriarch. Declared to be entirely independent, the national Rumanian church was put under the government of a Holy Synod, composed of the two metropolitans of Bucharest and Jassy together with their bishops.

Adoption of a make-believe system of popular education.

When, at Cuza's instigation, the legislature took up the problem of national education, acts were passed providing for universities at Bucharest and Jassy as well as for a number of secondary schools and special institutes. Nor was popular education forgotten, for a measure was carried establishing a general system of primary schools. In view of the backwardness and misery of the agricultural population, a vigorous school policy was, within a limited circle of forward-looking men, felt to be a leading public necessity, but the parliament, due to its landlord bias, was content with half-measures. Presenting a handsome front on paper, declared even to be free and compulsory for both sexes, the primary school system never became effective because of the government's failure to support it with grants of money. Here and there though the country-side schools struggled into existence, but as late as the beginning of the twentieth century, owing to a persistent lack of schools and teachers, sixty per cent of the Rumanian population above seven years of age was still illiterate.

That Cuza was animated with the lively zeal of a reformer became manifest when he attacked the agricultural problem, by far the gravest evil of Rumanian society. As he saw the task of the government it was, on the one hand, to put an end to all the legal implications of serfdom, and, on the other, to establish the peasants as small proprietors on the soil. That the neighboring Russian government was just then wrestling with the same problem must have encouraged him to persist in his purpose. In the form in which it was finally adopted, Cuza's rural law, while abolishing the dues and services which the peasant owed his lord, enabled him to become the owner of a small holding. Far from a resort to confiscation, the measure had a solid conservative character, since it compensated the landlords out of state funds for whatever property rights they surrendered and obligated the peasant-freeholders to make a fixed number of annual payments to the government to reimburse it for its outlay. Long before the bill became a law Cuza was made aware that he stood face to face with a nobiliary society, entirely out of sympathy with radical agricultural changes. His project met with such severe opposition that, in order to save it, he felt obliged to execute a *coup d'état*. Accordingly, he dissolved parliament (1864) with the aid of the military, and then promulgated a new constitution, so shaped that he could operate it to suit his pleasure. Only in this irregular way, by assuming the rôle of benevolent despot, did the prince succeed in spreading his rural law upon the statute book.

By his courageous championship of the peasants Cuza had broken with the most powerful group of Rumanian society. Henceforth it was war between him and the landlords. Opening a campaign of vilification against him at home and abroad, they repeatedly petitioned both the sultan and the powers for his removal. Certain unfortunate circumstances of a personal nature played into their hands. Himself a noble, Cuza was inevitably involved in the intrigues and jealousies of the ruling caste, while his private life was so conspicuously irregular as to leave him fairly open to attack on moral grounds. Furthermore, since he had violated the constitution, his opponents could with a certain propriety assume the mask of embattled friends of law and order. Gradually his position was undermined; and when a group of

Marginal notes:

Cuza's rural law aims to create a free peasantry.

Cuza's overthrow, 1866.

conspirators entered his palace at midnight and, at the point of the pistol, forced him to resign (February, 1866), not a hand was raised in his defense.

Prince Charles of Hohenzollern called to the Rumanian throne, May, 1866.

Cuza fell as a result of a combination against him of both political parties, of conservatives and liberals. Resolved not to repeat the experiment of a native prince, the victors now looked about for a suitable foreigner, and finally offered the throne to Charles of Hohenzollern. Charles belonged to the South German (Sigmaringen) branch of the ruling dynasty of Prussia, was twenty-seven years old, moderate, tactful, and intelligent. He accepted the tender, made his way in disguise through Austria, which was hostile to him, and on his arrival in Rumania was heartily acclaimed by the people (May, 1866). Not long afterwards he was formally recognized by his suzerain, the sultan, and the powers.

Charles's successful rule of almost half a century, 1866–1914.

Of course Charles's position in his new principality was insecure, not only because the country was in turmoil, but also owing to his complete ignorance of its affairs. His wife, the well-known writer and poet, Carmen Sylva, long afterwards reported that, on being invited to mount the throne of Rumania, he reached for an atlas to make sure where Rumania was. For a while he could take advantage of the unusual truce among the parties to which he owed his summons to the country. A new constitution was adopted which provided for an upper and a lower house, ministerial responsibility, and an executive veto upon all legislation. As might have been expected, the franchise was restricted in such a complicated way as practically to exclude the peasants from representation. No sooner were these foundations laid, however, than the bitter party strife was resumed, and, as between the Scylla of the conservatives and the Charybdis of the liberals, almost wrecked the fortunes of the prince. To cap the climax of his woes came the Franco-German war of 1870. The sympathies of the prince, as a German and a Hohenzollern, were enlisted on the side of Germany, but the Rumanians, as a Latin people, stood unanimously behind France. Somehow this and the other difficult corners were turned by the ruler and by the beginning of the seventies his situation was distinctly on the mend. It continued to improve, though not without an occasional setback, till the end of his reign. The long rule

(1866–1914) of the second sovereign of united Rumania proved, on the whole, a conspicuous success.

To this success the exceptional personal qualities of Charles contributed quite as much as the policy which he mapped out for himself and steadily pursued. In view of his training, which had been strictly military, his policy was peculiarly enlightened, since he acted on the principle that Rumania could most speedily be brought into the family of European nations by being endowed with the ideas and institutions of western economic life. Let us remember that hitherto agriculture had been conducted with the most primitive tools and methods imaginable, that the towns were no better than markets untouched by modern improvements, and that not only were there no railroads but even good wagon-roads were practically unknown. It is clear that the economic modernization of Rumania had yet to be effected, and with this in mind, we shall readily persuade ourselves that Charles was happily inspired in formulating and holding fast through life to a program of constructive, national labor. If successful, it would, besides sidetracking the unprofitable party strife, automatically raise the whole level of existence in Rumania. In fact a sound economic expansion would prove directly and generally educational.

Charles pursues a policy of economic development.

Of this economic development, which the persistent ruler witnessed and in which he may fairly claim a share, a few statements may serve to give a picture. If, in 1866, Rumania was without other than the most rudimentary means of transportation, before the end of Charles's reign she boasted over six thousand miles of metalled roads and over two thousand miles of railway. The growth of traffic on the Danube, Rumania's great natural artery, was particularly marked, and the towns on its lower course, like Braila, Galatz, and Sulina, developed into maritime ports provided with modern equipment and showing a steadily waxing import and export business. The capital, Bucharest, grew from an unsightly frontier town into a splendid metropolis of almost 400,000 inhabitants, serving as the focus of the intellectual and artistic, as well as of the economic life, of the nation. No one item, however, reflects the increasing agricultural prosperity of the country so convincingly as the large export of wheat and corn (maize); only the greatest grain-

Data illustrating Rumania's prosperity.

producing countries of the world, such as Russia, the United States, and Argentina, surpass Rumania in the amount of these staples delivered on the world market. When petroleum was discovered in the foothills of the Carpathians and its exploitation brought, before the end of the century, to a considerable development, a new and vast source of wealth was set to flowing. Since the Rumanian oil-fields are probably among the richest in the world, it is safe to predict the coming of a great industry based on this most economical of fuels.

Persistence of the related problems of the peasant and the public school.

Against these items in the credit column should be set a considerable debit. Partly because of his naturally conservative temper, and partly because he did not wish to stir up the hornet's nest which had routed his predecessor, the prince did not press the question of the peasants. That means that he took his stand with the political oligarchy in control of the country, composed of landholders and the growing urban group of merchants and men of the professions. To these circles Cuza's rural law signified the limit of concession, beyond which they were bitterly opposed to going. But Cuza, when all was said, had only grappled with the problem and had brought nothing to a settlement. The most hopeful consequence of his legislation was that several hundred thousand small freeholders now dotted the countryside. Nonetheless, the bulk of the arable land continued to be held in large estates, while many freeholds were found to be so small as to be impracticable. The liberated peasants, slothful and improvident owing to centuries of subjection, fell into debt, and in order to eke out a livelihood for themselves and their families, took to working for wages on the great estates. Before long, in spite of their ownership of a small property, they were indistinguishable from the mass of the agricultural laborers, regularly employed on the estates and constituting the rural equivalent of the modern city proletariat. In the hearts of these children of toil, still essentially serfs, unrest rocked eternally like a summer sea, to be lashed from time to time, under some special provocation, into a tremendous storm. In Charles's long reign as many as five peasant risings occurred, for the suppression of which the troops had to be called out; the last, which was also the most severe, took place in 1907. As soon as an outbreak was reported the government attempted to calm the storm with promises, only to forget promptly all about them on the restoration of order. Closely related to the economic unrest among the peasants is the problem of elevating them morally by making the public school something more than a paper promise. Both of these problems, or rather both these aspects of the same problem, the state of Rumania had, up to 1914, failed to look squarely in the face. Owing to promises made during the Great War legislative measures aiming an apparently serious blow at the great estates have recently (1921) been put into effect, but it is yet too early to say what permanent good the peasantry will extract therefrom.

Another issue, which has been a breeder of trouble, touches the Jews. There is, especially in Moldavia, a considerable Jewish population which plays the part of middlemen and money-lenders among the peasants. Owing to their greater mobility and intelligence, these aliens tend to become wealthy and often, by making loans to the needy and incautious peasants, succeed in getting a strangle-hold on them. By reason, on the one hand, of their economic power in the countryside and, on the other, of their stubborn resistance to absorption into the body of the nation, the Jews have been and remain decidedly unpopular with the ruling oligarchy, which succeeded in inserting an article in the constitution of 1866 excluding them from citizenship. In this illiberal action the Rumanians failed to reckon with the Jews of western Europe, who through their power in finance and in the press were able to persuade their home governments to interpose at Bucharest in favor of the persecuted Semites. Several powers therefore launched a protest against the Rumanian exclusion act and, after much angry discussion, the parliament at Bucharest saw fit somewhat to modify its attitude. By a new law the naturalization of Jews was made possible by the passing of a special legislative act for each individual who applies for citizenship. At the same time the measure was carefully tied up with so much red tape as to make certain that it would be resorted to but sparingly. In point of fact very few Jews have been naturalized in the thirty and more years which have elapsed since the adoption of the so-called measure of relief. Some three hundred thousand Jews dwelling on Rumanian soil were, up to 1914, aliens in the eyes of the law and, in addition, were

[margin note:] Illiberal and hostile attitude toward the Jews.

[handwritten margin note:] Jews were in Rumania long before Romanians

[handwritten margin note:] the author is defensive of antisemi-

obliged to put up with a special body of legislative restrictions regarding residence, the ownership of property, and the choice of an occupation or profession. The change in their outlook brought about by the Great War we shall treat later on. Familiar and, one might be tempted to say, usual as the phenomenon of Rumania's narrow and jealous nationalism is, by making victims of the Jews it has drawn on itself the condemnation of all the countries where the Jews are a powerful element, and in this way has subtly but effectively undermined the reputation of Rumania abroad.

Prince Charles accepted as the ally of Russia in the war of 1877.

It remains to point out that it was in the field of foreign politics that Prince Charles won the laurels which constitute the most important single contribution to the consolidation of his power. On coming to Rumania he was committed to accept a position of vassalage to the sultan, and although the obligations toward his suzerain were few and unimportant, he was resolved to get rid of them at the first opportunity. That came his way when the crisis of the seventies overtook the Ottoman empire and ended, as a Turkish crisis usually did, in a war with Russia. In order to clear the track for his advancing armies, the tsar arrogantly opened negotiations with Prince Charles and found, to his surprise, that the Rumanian ruler insisted on being treated as something better than a doormat. In the end, in order to gain an unobstructed passage through the Danubian principality, the northern autocrat was obliged to sign a solemn convention to respect the territorial integrity of his erstwhile protectorate (April, 1877). But the proffered military aid of Rumania the tsar haughtily refused until his defeat, under the walls of Plevna, moved him to send a hurry call to Prince Charles, who, on rushing up with the Rumanian army, held in readiness for this precise eventuality, was enabled to render conspicuous services to the Russians toward the winning of the war. (Bull)

Rumania issues a declaration of independence and wins her freedom on the battlefield.

This is not the place to treat of the Turco-Russian war of 1877. However, engaged in evaluating Prince Charles's conduct of foreign affairs, we may properly point out that he showed excellent judgment in joining with Russia in her war against the sultan. By his bold and virile action he struck a sympathetic chord among his people, who roused themselves to owe the final step in the long process of their liberation to their own efforts rather than to the favor of a foreign potentate. Just as among the Italian nationalists the proud word had once gone the rounds: *Italia farà da se* (Italy needs no help), so the Rumanians were minded to win their freedom, not in an European conclave but on the battlefield. They adopted their first measure toward this end when, as a prelude to the war, they issued a solemn declaration of independence (May, 1877). By following this act with the resounding blows which signally contributed to the Russian victory, they put their claim to independence beyond all cavil. In the treaty of Berlin (1878) Rumanian sovereignty received the unqualified recognition of both the sultan and the powers. A few years later (1881), on invitation of his parliament, Charles adopted the title king. As king, Charles added greatly to his reputation among his people, making a place for himself which grew visibly stronger to the end of his days.

The war, or rather the peace which followed the war, brought a severe disappointment to the Rumanian people on account of the exchange forced on them by Russia of fertile southern Bessarabia, won back in 1856, for the barren Dobrudja. We shall return to this transfer, which turned out much better than the boldest Rumanian patriot would have dreamed and for which a later generation had many reasons to be thankful. Summing up Charles's foreign policy down to and through the period of the congress of Berlin, we may repeat that it was conducted with as much firmness as good fortune: its fruits for his country were a successful war of liberation from the ancient Turkish yoke together with the achievement of the status of a sovereign kingdom.

The fruits of Charles's foreign policy.

CHAPTER XXIV

BETWEEN TWO WARS: BALKAN DEVELOPMENTS FROM THE TREATY OF PARIS TO THE TURCO-RUSSIAN WAR OF 1877

The treaty of Paris guarantees the independence of the sultan in return for a pledge of Europeanization.

IF, in pledging the powers to respect the independence and integrity of the Ottoman empire, the treaty of Paris expressed the collective will of Europe to save the "Sick Man" from the Russian ogre, it did not fail to introduce a provision, which proved that the much abused diplomats were not blind to the fact that the recovery of the invalid depended, after all, chiefly on himself. They obliged the sultan to publish the charter of 1856, a reiteration in a more detailed and binding form of the promises of the tanzimat of 1839. Its provisions, summarized, signified that the sultan gave his word that the traditional Ottoman system, by which the population of the empire was sharply divided, along religious lines, into oppressors and oppressed, into masters and rayahs, was forthwith to end and be replaced by the legal and administrative principles current in the West. In sum, Turkey pledged herself to a policy not of gradual and deliberate, but of immediate and precipitate Europeanization.

The fiction of the sultan's independence versus the fact of his subjection.

When Europe offered its broad guarantees to Turkey, it did not, it is true, limit them as to time, but no reasonable man, aware of the dependence of modern governments on public favor, may doubt that the pledges would be ignored if the promised Ottoman transformation should fail to be carried out swiftly and in entire good faith. In other words, the powers, though ostentatiously receiving the sultan into their exclusive circle on the basis of equality, by putting him under the obligation of a radical reform assumed a responsibility for him, by virtue of which he necessarily became their ward. The Ottoman reform would only have to be delayed at some conspicuous point, or the continued persecution of the Christians would only have to be manifested by an outbreak or a massacre, and an agitation would seize upon European opinion which the governments would be wholly impotent to resist. The ambiguity of the treaty touching the sultan's status would then stand revealed before the world, but would inevitably and in quick order be cleared up by the abandonment of the diplomatic fiction of the sultan's sovereignty for the view, in harmony with the unadmitted truth, of his subjection to the collective supervision of the powers.

In these circumstances the development of the relations between the Porte on the one hand, and the powers on the other, depended on the successful application of the famous charter of 1856. Many diplomats, especially in the British camp, which in its over-zealous defense of British interests had practically identified itself with Turkey, may ingenuously have believed that a miracle, such as had never yet been seen on land or sea, would now be staged at Constantinople; but, closely pressed for reasons for their faith, they would have been at a loss to answer. On last considering Ottoman reform,[1] we affirmed its absolute inevitability if the empire was to be saved from dissolution, but at the same time we took careful note of the immense obstacles piled across its path. Sultan Mahmud, we found, was an energetic if not an enlightened reformer, and his son, Abdul Medjid, was enlightened if not energetic; they received support from a small and moderately capable band of men, of whom Reshid Pasha was the vaunted oracle; and finally, we admitted that they must in justice be credited with certain limited achievements, the most effective no doubt being the substitution for the worthless Janissaries of a modernized army responsive to the sultan's will. For the rest, the endless decrees reorganizing the administration, the taxes, justice, education, and the other services of the state, registered substantially nothing more than good intentions. In each case the attempted reform broke down because there were no trained, active, and trustworthy officials to carry it through and, more important still, because it ran into the ever present opposition of the Moslem population. This population, endowed with a mentality solidified by centuries of unchallenged practice, saw no reason for supporting a reform which deprived it of its ancient superiority over the Christians and merged the two religious groups in a common citizenry based on strict equality. Not only was such a program contrary to long established custom,

Europeanization and the Moslem mind.

[1] Ch. XXII.

but it was distinctly irreligious inasmuch as it signified a denial of the Koran and the sheri, which in unmistakable terms designated the body of Mohammedan believers as masters privileged to lord it over the infidels whom the sword had tamed. In the thought of his Moslem subjects the sultan was acting under the compulsion of the hated giaours or, what was worse, he was secretly a giaour himself. By no possible twist of sophistry could the padishah, entrusted with the administration of the Sacred Law, have the power to annul it; and the instinctive attitude of all faithful Moslems to the blasphemous innovations of the ruler was to resist them with every means at their disposal.

The whole Ottoman reform issue came to this: its success would depend, not on the diligence with which the ministers of the sultan, under pressure from Europe, scattered rosy promises and issued paper decrees, but on the willingness and ability of the Moslems themselves to acquire a new mentality. Some hundreds of years before, in the Middle Age, the Europeans had been in much the same frame of mind as the Mohammedans of the nineteenth century, for they too had organized their life on earth according to religious concepts formulated by the church and deriving their final authority from divine revelation. It required the concentrated labor of many generations to replace the transcendental medieval outlook with the secular and scientific viewpoint which constitutes the basis of present-day thought. Was it reasonable for the Europeans, who had needed several centuries to free themselves from the medieval implications and build up the civilized system to which, because of its amazing success, they have ever since given an unstinted support and a glowing devotion, to expect the still essentially medieval Mohammedans to become modern over night? No equitable person will so declare, but, on the other hand, the self-assurance of the western nations being boundless and, let us add, their imperialist appetite being keen, it was not likely that in this Ottoman issue reason would prevail or a conspicuous patience be exercised. The West, people and governments alike, would demand a miracle, and when it failed to materialize, when in its room there appeared merely multiplied evidence of the dissolution of the Ottoman state and society, the cry would mount and swell till it became a storm that this putrid organism was an offense, which it was a moral obligation to sweep from the pathway of civilization.

Abandoning these general considerations, we can not but agree that Abdul Medjid, the signer of the charter of 1856, found himself in a cruel predicament. Whenever he promulgated a reform desired by himself and sternly demanded by Europe, he discovered that it was effectively sabotaged by the sullen opposition of his Moslem subjects; if, on the other hand, alarmed at his unpopularity he made concessions to his people's prejudices, he was denounced by the voice of a thousand western newspapers as a hypocrite and a deceiver. Observers on the ground noted that his reforms had just vitality enough to destroy the old inheritance without putting anything in its place. Doubtless their leading effect was a waxing domestic distrust and an increasing civic anarchy. With time, abundant time, at his disposal, Abdul Medjid might have overcome at least some of these disastrous consequences, but time was what was denied him, and, working under pressure, he faced as the only certain result of his labors the growing disorder in his dominions. Afflicted with a sense of his helplessness, he drank himself, according to common report, to death (1861), and was succeeded by his brother, Abdul Aziz (1861–76), who, a frivolous, half-insane spendthrift, was certainly much less well fitted than his predecessor to pluck order out of chaos.

Of this chaos the symptoms accumulated with alarming haste. The diplomats were still engaged in popularizing their myth of a rejuvenated Turkey when a bloody outbreak occurred (1860) in Syria, on Mount Lebanon, which was not suppressed until France, with the consent of Great Britain, had dispatched a military expedition to the troubled area. Four years after the publication of the treaty of Paris with its solemn pledge to respect the independence of Turkey, the leading authors of the treaty broke their own guarantee! And while the Syrian fires were still smouldering, a ferment began in that ancient hearth of troubles, in Crete, which, after vain attempts at suppression, led to a ferocious civil war lasting two years (1866–68). On its termination the sultan's government, naturally not of its own accord but on the "advice" of its European backers, conceded an extensive local autonomy (Organic Statute of 1868), by which the gap legally separating Christians and Moslems was somewhat reduced. In this connection it should be understood that Crete pos-

Neither Abdul Medjid (1839–61) nor Abdul Aziz (1861–76) able to improve the situation.

Disturbances on Mount Lebanon (1860–61) and in Crete (1866–68).

sessed a population solidly Greek in speech, of about 300,000 souls. Of these fifteen per cent at most, in the main landlords, had, by adopting Islam, acquired the privileged position of a ruling class. Although their privileges were impaired by the Organic Statute, the core of the Cretan question was hardly touched by this concession, for what the Christians, as intemperate Greek nationalists, wanted above all else was union with Greece. Until this was conceded, it would be necessary to reckon with the periodic insurrection of what throughout the Hellenic world was proudly called "the great Greek island."

Mysterious disappearance of the Bulgars during the Ottoman ascendancy.

Graver, if not in itself, at least in its probable consequences, was a movement in the heart of Balkania among a rayah group, which hitherto had not been the source of much anxiety to its Ottoman overlords. The Bulgars, the mass of whom dwelt on either side of the Balkan mountains between the Danube and the Rhodope range, had made submission to the Ottomans in the days of Murad, the victor of Kossovo; shortly after Kossovo, to punish them for a new uprising, they had been deprived of their national autonomy and been incorporated directly in the Ottoman system (1393). For over four centuries they had thereupon as completely disappeared from view under a thin layer of Turkish officials as if they had been buried alive. During all that time they slaved for their conquerors, were taxed at discretion, stripped naked in time of war, and, as a slight return for an inhuman patience, were grudgingly conceded an uncertain security of person and a limited religious toleration. No rayah people was drawn so completely under the wheels of the Turkish chariot as were the Bulgars and none sank so low in the scale of civilization. The explanation of the tragic intensity of their destiny is not far to seek. The proximity of the Ottoman capital exposed them to a much stricter supervision than the more remote Christian groups, while the disappearance during the conquest of their natural leaders, the nobles, gave them the character of a purely peasant people. The Serbs, reduced to the same social formula, had yet been able to preserve a certain racial idealism through the inspired leadership of their clergy. This clerical guidance was denied the Bulgars in consequence of the very early subjection of their national church to the Greek patriarch and by his policy of a stern and systematic

Hellenization. The Bulgar language was replaced by Greek in the service and Greek bishops, sent from Constantinople, took care to surround themselves with a clergy disposed and anxious to suppress in their parishioners every memory of a national past. Since the Ottomans classified the various peoples of their state not by race but by religion, they unwittingly lent their support to the policy of the patriarch by carrying the Bulgars on their official records as Greeks. In consequence of these many repressive influences the Bulgars actually became that weird thing, a lost nation, and with such dim consciousness as survived their barbarization thought of themselves as Greeks. Impressive evidence of this state of affairs was supplied by occasional European travelers as late as the first half of the nineteenth century. On the ground that a native of what was geographically called Bulgaria, when asked regarding his nationality, habitually responded that he was a Greek, they naïvely reported that the Greek race extended as far north as the Danube!

No wonder that in the days of the Serb and Greek quickening the stagnant waters of Bulgar nationalism for a long time showed not the slightest animation. These stolid Slav peasants were sunk in a swoon deeper than that of the Seven Sleepers of Ephesus. But gradually the glad tidings of a changing world penetrated even unto them. They heard whispers of the defeats of the Ottoman armies, of the victorious advance of the Christian nations of Europe, of the Serb and Greek rebellions, and slowly something occurred among them that was like the first stirring of the sap in an ice-bound forest. In 1835 a successful Bulgar merchant founded at his own expense a school at Gabrovo — the first purely Bulgar school in modern times. Other schools so rapidly followed that by the middle of the century there were already several score. Shortly after, books, newspapers, and periodicals made their appearance, printed mostly abroad to escape the Argus-eyed Turkish officials. Within a generation an educated class, so long lacking among these heavy glebemen, made its appearance and boldly essayed the rôle of leadership. And, intelligibly enough, its first concerted effort was directed at the ousting of the Greek interlopers in order to give the Bulgar church back to the Bulgar people.

The Bulgar awakening.

Reëstablish-
ment of a
Bulgar
national
church,
1870.

As soon as the patriarch and his Greek followers became aware that a Bulgar national agitation was on foot, they looked to their defenses. Some slight concession to native sentiment the patriarch was willing to make, but not enough by much to satisfy his opponents. In their waxing indignation the Bulgar leaders began to play with the idea of completely abandoning the Orthodox fellowship for that of the Roman Catholic church; and in point of fact they opened negotiations with the pope with the view to putting themselves under his protection. But at this point Russia interfered. Russia did not wish to see eastern Slavdom lose its solidly Orthodox character and promised the Bulgar leaders diplomatic support in an attempt to wring from the sultan what had been denied by the patriarch. Since the much buffeted padishah had no reason to love the ever rebellious Greeks better than the hitherto submissive Bulgars, he yielded after the usual wearisome procrastinations, and in 1870 published the firman which established an independent Bulgar church. Not only did this act recognize a Bulgar primate, to be called *exarch*, and assign to him as his ecclesiastical dominion the whole *vilayet* of the Danube, but, what was more, it provided for the future expansion of this dominion by conceding to the Christian parishes of Macedonia the right to join the exarchate whenever two thirds of the population expressed a wish to that effect.

Reëndowed after the lapse of centuries with a national church, the Bulgars were jubilant over their victory, while the patriarch and the Greek nationalists behind him gnashed their teeth in rage. The head of the Greek church did not even hesitate to issue a declaration of war in the form of a solemn excommunication of the new Bulgar church, called into being, it is curious to reflect, by an act of grace of the Moslem calif. The conflict that followed, far from confining itself to an exchange of verbal pistol-shots, soon became actual and devastating. By indicating Macedonia as debatable ground the firman gave rise, among the unconsulted and certainly at first passive Macedonians, to a fierce propaganda on the part of both patriarchists and exarchists which, ostensibly religious, was really political, since its ultimate purpose was to win Macedonia to the allegiance either of the Greek or the Bulgar nation. Macedonia, as a battlefield, after 1870, of Bulgar and Greek propaganda, gradually became a human inferno, from which, as we shall see, blinding clouds of smoke and fire spread over Balkania with unhappy consequences for all Europe.

While this conflict raged in the bosom of the Orthodox church, the Bulgar leaders, who, for the sake of a greater freedom of action, had mostly established themselves on foreign soil, took up the question also of political emancipation. However, as the Bulgar people were in the main averse to starting a rebellion against the sultan, while at the same time soliciting ecclesiastical favors at his hands, they hesitated to beat their plowshares into swords. The Hotspurs, of whom there was no lack, did indeed bring about a number of slight risings both before and after the Crimean war, but these movements were easily suppressed by the Turks and are notable merely as a prophecy of more serious outbreaks in the coming time. For that, sooner or later, the Bulgars would rebel against Ottoman misrule was a foregone conclusion. It should therefore cause no surprise to learn that when, in 1875, the Serb peasants of Herzegovina rose in behalf of freedom, the Bulgars were stirred to institute the first rebellion of a fairly national scope. We shall see that this movement of theirs was a factor in the tremendous Balkan upheaval to be recorded in the next chapter.

The political rebellions among the Bulgars few and slight.

As we approach the Ottoman crisis of the seventies precipitated by the Herzegovinian action, it is proper that we extend our view beyond the affairs of the provinces which composed the Ottoman empire, to those states which phoenix-wise had risen from the Ottoman ruins and had in varying measure advanced toward their goal of independence. I refer to Greece, Montenegro, Serbia, and Rumania. Having treated of Rumania in the previous chapter, we are free to attend to the other three states in order to take account of the recent developments in their midst, especially in so far as these developments bear upon the general situation of the Ottoman empire.

Need, in considering the Ottoman empire, to take account of the peripheral states.

When we took our last view of Greece the country had entered on a revolution (1843), the chief fruit of which was that King Otto I consented to become a constitutional sovereign. Wellmeaning, if deliberate and pedantic, he gave his attention thenceforth to satisfying, as far as lay in his power, the passionate nationalism of his people. However, neither his power nor that

Greece entirely dependent on the good-will of the powers.

of his small state went very far. Greek nationalism, aiming at
the redemption of Crete, Thessaly, Epirus, and other territories
groaning under the Moslem yoke, could be satisfied only by a
successful war against the sultan; but, apart from the probability
that the tiny kingdom was no match for the Ottoman empire,
the western powers, especially Great Britain, were just then
pursuing, as we know, the policy of bolstering up the sultan and
would suffer no attack on him from any quarter. This attitude
reached the height of its expression in the Crimean war. When
tsar and sultan squared off at each other, Greece in great excitement made ready to enter the fray on the side of Russia, that
is, it was rash enough to throw itself across the path of France and
Great Britain. Such presumption was met by a peremptory command from London and Paris to cease all preparations for war
forthwith; and when the Athenian government paused to argue the
point, it was cut short by a military occupation of the Piraeus.
Not till after the treaty of Paris had pacified the Near East did
the allied forces deign to leave the Hellenic soil (1857). Greece
had received its lesson and learned what it should have known
beforehand, that the success of its foreign policy would always
depend on the ability of the government to subordinate its
national program to the designs of the great powers.

Otto I
succeeded by
George I
(1863–
1913).

Though King Otto was as passionately national as any native-
born Hellene and only yielded to the allied threats under compulsion, the checkmating of his people's wishes counted against
him in the long run. Under the conviction that he was unable
to help them realize " the Great Idea," they grew restless and,
in 1862, rose again, this time to demand his abdication. Deserted
by all, he was, after a reign of almost thirty years, obliged
to return to his native Bavaria. A national assembly, summoned
to give the country a new government, sat for the next two
years in Athens and succeeded in solving the crisis. The vacant
throne was offered, with the consent of the three protecting
powers, to a prince of the royal line of Denmark, who in 1863
took up the reins as King George I. The new constitution, which
was completed in the following year, was given a sweeping democratic character by means of a provision calling for a single
chamber elected by universal manhood suffrage. In order to
create a true honeymoon sentiment between the new sovereign

and his people, Great Britain relinquished her title to the Ionian islands and permitted them to be incorporated in the kingdom. Greeks to the very core, the islanders had never ceased to agitate for union with the mother-country during the half century of the British occupation, and the withdrawal of Great Britain from their shores was hailed by them as the fruition of their highest hopes. For the Greeks of the kingdom, on the other hand, the new territory signified the first concession to their nationalist hunger since they had won their independence. Far from glutting their appetite, however, it mainly served to give it a keener edge.

When, shortly after King George's accession, the troubles of Crete led (1866) to the rebellion against the sultan which has already been mentioned, a fresh agitation seized upon the Athenian public. But again her stern mentors forbade Greece to act, and people and government, though straining at the leash, were obliged to play the part of spectators of the Cretan conflagration. No more bedded on roses than his predecessor, King George showed much more skill than Otto in steering his craft among the dangerous rocks of party politics. Besides, in the course of his long reign (1863-1913), he was decidedly favored by fortune. Than political skill and fortune no more desirable attendant genii could be imagined for the sovereign of a restless people like the Hellenes, of whom it is as true in our age as it was in the distant days of St. Paul that they seem to be engaged in perpetually seeking something new.

Explanation of the relative success of George I.

Of the two Serb states, the smaller, Montenegro, owing to its heroic resistance to the Ottomans, has received attention from the world entirely out of proportion to its size. When we examined it last, it was functioning as an hereditary theocracy under a prince-bishop or vladika in complete independence of the sultan. However, independence did not mean that the historic struggle with the Ottomans had come to an end, and the nineteenth century, exactly like its five predecessors, continued to resound with this irrepressible conflict. A Turco–Montenegrin war was so recurrent an event that it had acquired an almost stereotyped form. Friction at the border would lead to an invasion of Montenegrin territory by the Turks, or vice versa, until negotiations patched up what was called a peace but was, in point of

Montenegro continues to make war upon the Turks.

fact, only a truce. For the vladika the usual result of such an adventure was the extension of his authority over a new village or valley. Though a large-scale map would be necessary to illustrate this inch-wise progress, the fact remains that the mountaineers were able to indulge the proud boast that theirs was a growing commonwealth.

Seculariza-
tion of the
government
by Danilo
II, 1851.

More important than these primitive, Homeric combats were the signs of a gradual inner transformation. By degrees the Montenegrin institutions were accommodated to the system of the West, while, at the same time, many venerable customs of the people lost the edge of their savagery. By traveling abroad an occasional member of the ruling Petrovich family acquired an European outlook, which he was at pains to popularize on his return. Of these subtle influences an important effect was seen when, with the advent to power of Danilo II, the old theocracy was abandoned as no longer suited to the advancing times. Divesting himself of his religious functions as bishop, Danilo (1851–60) became a purely secular prince with the scepter hereditary in his family according to the principle of primogeniture. Not only did the enterprising young ruler now take unto himself a wife, who, a very cultured Serb lady hailing from Trieste, strengthened the small party of innovators, but he introduced judicial and other reforms with such precipitation that he made himself decidedly unpopular. He was in consequence assassinated (1860), to be succeeded, in default of male heirs, by his nephew, Nicholas I. This sturdy young man, but nineteen years old at the time of his accession, was still sovereign of Montenegro at the outbreak of the World War, fifty-four years later. In his long career Prince Nicholas, while witnessing the later phases of the age-old struggle of his people with the Turks, was destined, above all, to be involved in a new enmity of grave importance, the enmity with his Christian neighbor, Austria.

Serbia
dependent
on the
good-will of
the powers.

In spite of a certain growing adjustment to the standards of western life, by the middle of the nineteenth century the principality of Serbia had not yet brought either its domestic or foreign situation to any considerable clarification. In the Crimean war the sympathies of the people had been with Slav and Orthodox Russia, but the proximity of Austria and the influence of France and Great Britain had persuaded Prince Alexander to remain neutral. If he was overthrown in 1859, his misfortune may in the main be ascribed to the unpopularity of his unenterprising foreign policy. It can not, however, be maintained that he won no advantage for his country from his subservient attitude, for the treaty of Paris freed Serbia from the Russian protectorate in exchange for a collective guarantee of all the powers. The recall of Milosh, on Alexander's removal, was in so far important as it was brought about by popular sentiment and augured that the people would henceforth play a less passive rôle in national politics. The aged Milosh, however, died too soon (1860) to give Serb affairs a new orientation, which task accordingly devolved on his son and successor, Michael.

Prince Michael (1860–68), who had improved a natural intelligence by serious study and prolonged travel, clearly demonstrated in his short reign the value of a leadership combining energy with self-control. In his eyes the immediately pressing matter was to terminate the right of the sultan to occupy certain Serb fortresses; and he desired to win his point without a war through the diplomatic support of the great powers. A bloody conflict between Serbs and Turks which, in 1862, occurred in the streets of Belgrad served him as the basis of urgent representations at Constantinople as well as in the chancelleries of the European states. It was of course a tedious undertaking to persuade the sultan to surrender an acknowledged treaty right, but Michael, seconded by the diplomats who had been won by his pleading, clung to his purpose until, against every argument of probability, he gained his point. In 1867 the Ottoman garrisons were withdrawn and therewith ceased to give offense by occupying a land which, except for its nominal subjection to the sultan's suzerainty, was free and independent.

Michael (1860–68) gains an important point.

strife in the streets of Belgrad between Turk & Serb (1862)

With creditable forethought Michael concerned himself with establishing friendly relations with all the scattered members of the South Slav race in preparation for an irresistible national movement against the Ottoman empire. The South Slav and Christian fortunes of Balkania generally experienced a sharp upward turn under the care of his fostering hand. But he had only just made a beginning when, like many another Balkan ruler,

The succession of Milan, 1868.

he fell a victim to the animosities of party life and was assassinated. Rumor connected with the murder the rival house of Karageorge, but the matter was never cleared up. Since Michael had no legitimate offspring, the national assembly offered the throne to a relative, Milan Obrenovich. As Milan was but fourteen years of age, a regency was empowered to take over the government. There can be no doubt that the momentum gained under Michael was soon lost and that it was not recaptured when the young prince was declared of age (1872), for he was a frivolous spirit, averse to all hard work and supremely concerned with nothing beyond the unhindered pursuit of his pleasures. For the Serb people it was a grave misfortune that when, on the Herzegovinian outbreak of 1875, the whole question of the Ottoman empire was reopened, the decisions to be taken at Belgrad rested with an individual so little representative of the best Serb qualities and traditions.

CHAPTER XXV

THE TURCO-RUSSIAN WAR (1877) AND THE CONGRESS OF BERLIN (1878)

WE have thus far had little to do with the province of Bosnia and the smaller province of Herzegovina to the south of Bosnia and historically inseparable from it. Situated at the extreme northwest corner of the Ottoman empire, their distance from Constantinople might have proved a favorable factor in any movement of liberation if this remoteness had not been offset by a number of circumstances highly unfavorable to anything resembling a successful Christian uprising. Bosnia and Herzegovina constituted a mountain area so difficult of access that, shut off not only from the empire to which they belonged, but also from Europe, influences making for change long failed to penetrate at any point, thereby perpetuating political ideas and social forms which reached back to the Ottoman conquest. The tone of this conservative society was set by the ruling class, the medieval nobles of Serb race, who, in order to save their property and preserve their power, had gone over to Islam. The Serb peasants, on the other hand, constituting the majority of the inhabitants, had remained loyal to Christianity, which, generally speaking, took the Orthodox form, though Catholicism was represented in the western section adjoining Catholic Croatia.

Much as in the Middle Age, the peasants of the nineteenth century still cultivated the fields for a bare livelihood, while the lords (begs), who owned the fields, exacted certain personal services as well as a fraction of the crops, fixed in theory but disconcertingly variable in practice. If there had always been a social chasm between the two classes, it became an impassable gulf when the ruling class went over to an alien and abominated faith. From that day onward the life of the peasant took on a more tragic hue; for the nobles, on the other hand, the only considerable difference in the situation before and after the

Inevitable conservatism of remote provinces like Bosnia and Herzegovina.

The social situation: peasants and begs.

393

coming of the Turks lay in the circumstance that the sovereign of the country, instead of residing in their midst, dwelt in distant Constantinople. And that was wholly to their advantage. Especially since the decay of the Ottoman empire had palpably set in, the landlords had arrogated to themselves more and more power until the pasha sent to govern them played a largely ornamental rôle. In sign of their ascendancy the Bosniaks did not even permit him to stay in Sarajevo, the capital city, but obliged him to take up his residence in provincial Travnik. Loyal to the traditional system, to things as they were, they felt no personal loyalty toward their suzerain. If the chance which rules the affairs of men should ever give to the empire a sultan with an itch to introduce political and social novelties, he would soon discover that the Bosnian begs stood, a solid wall, across his path. For, than these Islamized Serbs there were no more fanatic Moslems within the whole compass of the padishah's dominion.

The Bosnian nobles resist the reforms of the sultans.

In view of this attitude of mind we can form a lively picture of how Mahmud's and Abdul Medjid's gestures of reform affected the feudal warriors of the western mountains. They refused at the first news of Mahmud's innovations to believe their ears, and, forced at last to believe, they raised a mighty outcry against the attack on the inherited system. Even the abolition of the Janissaries was received unfavorably, for were the Janissaries not an integral part of a sacred tradition? An ominous uprising took place, mild precursor of the veritable frenzy that swept over these stalwarts of the old régime when the tanzimat of 1839 impertinently abolished the inferior, the rayah status of the Christian peasants. The sultan had to dispatch his best general, Omar Pasha, with a large-sized army, to Bosnia before the rebels consented to return to their allegiance. Following his victory (1849), Omar defiantly established himself as pasha at Sarajevo and gave the administration of these outlying territories a more centralized character than it had recently boasted; however, apart from a few alterations at the top, he changed nothing in the organization of Bosnian society. Much as before his coming the courts discriminated against Christians in favor of Moslems, all public offices were reserved to men of the privileged faith, the taxes were collected from the peasants by corrupt and tyrannical tax-farmers, and the Moslem landlords relentlessly exacted the payments due them from their Christian tenants to the last fowl or sheaf of wheat.

Should the oppressed peasants ever revolt, it would be as much against their local lords as against the financial agents of the sultan, and in all probability the revolt would be due, on the one hand, to some fresh aggravation of the familiar evils, and on the other, to a new hope aroused by an increasing acquaintance with the stimulating ideals and improving conditions of the outside world. From Montenegro, from Serbia, from Austria, all of which states bordered on Bosnia and Herzegovina, streams of modern influence, communicating to the peasants a spirit of resistance, had for some time been making their way up the narrow valleys. When therefore in the spring of 1875, in spite of an almost complete failure of the crops, the tax-farmers went from house to house coolly practicing the usual extortions, the indignation knew no bounds. On July 1, the inhabitants of the village of Nevesinje, on a stony plateau not far from the Herzegovinian city of Mostar, raised the banner of rebellion. Immediately other villages fell into line until the conflagration embraced a considerable area. Then the fire leaped north to Bosnia and, appearing erratically here and there, threatened to envelop the whole land. The small garrisons maintained by the sultan were completely inadequate to cope with the insurgents, especially as the rebel bands were strengthened by volunteers from neighboring Serb areas and were equipped with rifles and ammunition which filtered across the border. Evidently the Serbs outside Bosnia, seized with a tremendous excitement at this rebellion of their kinsmen, were resolved to sustain them at every cost. Here lay the real peril of the situation. If the sultan did not soon succeed in crushing the uprising, public opinion in Montenegro and Serbia would oblige the rulers of these states to make common cause with the down-trodden peasants of Bosnia and a Balkan war would result, which, like all Balkan wars, might easily develop into a general conflict.

The cabinets of the great powers did not fail to see the dangerous implications of the Bosnian rising. They negotiated busily among themselves to the end of agreeing on a program of reforms, which, forced on the sultan and offered by him as a concession

The uprising of the peasants in the summer of 1875.

Serbia and Montenegro declare war on the sultan.

to the rebels, might serve as the basis of a truce. But, as usual, they harmonized none too well among themselves, and the Porte, aware of the secret divisions, managed to wriggle out of the acceptance of even such moderate suggestions as those of the (Andrassy note) (Dec., 1875) and the Berlin memorandum (May, 1876). Up to this point Nicholas of Montenegro and Milan of Serbia had managed to restrain their respective peoples. But in the face of the inextinguishable insurrection, which, even when suppressed at one point, straightway flared up at another, and of the stupid obstinacy of the sultan, their resistance broke down, and on July 1, 1876, Milan, and on the following day, Nicholas, to the delighted plaudits of their subjects, declared war on their hereditary foe. In their own minds they were about to strike a blow not only in behalf of their Serb countrymen still in Turkish bondage, but also for that ultimate goal of extreme Serb nationalism, the restoration by conquest of the wide empire of Tsar Stephen Dushan.

Meanwhile the prolonged Bosnian rebellion had quickened the hopes of Christian races other than the Serbs. The Bulgar leaders, operating largely from centers outside the Ottoman empire but maintaining underground connection with numerous agents on the spot, were convinced that no better opportunity to strike for freedom would ever arise and vigorously began preparations for a general insurrection. However, as their efforts were not well coördinated, the Turks managed without great difficulty to keep the movement under control. Then in May, 1876, on the northern slope of the Rhodope mountains, occurred one of those terrible incidents only too common when two peoples, long associated as masters and slaves, engage in civil conflict. In default of regular troops, wanted on the theater of war, Turkish militiamen, known as Bashi-Bazuks, a name sufficient in itself to strike terror to the heart, were dispatched into the disaffected area and, falling on a group of Christian villages, harried them with fire and sword. No less than ten thousand men, women, and children lost their lives as a result of these horrors perpetrated by the Turkish soldiers. When the news reached Europe an immense wave of indignation swept the public press. Even in Turcophil England the popular sentiment, lashed to fury by a famous pamphlet from the hand of the Liberal

statesman, Gladstone, loudly demanded the punishment of the
malefactors, while the conservative government of Disraeli (Lord
Beaconsfield) did not scruple to use very undiplomatic language
in warning the Porte of the consequences of its acts. Undeniably,
however, an immediate political advantage resulted for the Porte
from the bloody orgies celebrated on the slopes of the Rhodope.
The Bulgars, cowed, permitted the insurrection to collapse. It
was the Serbs only with whom the sultan had to deal in the
summer of 1876.

Even so, the combined crisis of domestic rebellion and peripheral
war with which the Ottoman empire was afflicted was so severe
that once again the question was raised whether the empire could
survive the strain. Seized with sudden alarm, a small group of
high-placed officials at Constantinople, constituting a party of
reform, resolutely took matters in hand. As a preliminary step
toward the execution of their program, they deposed (May 30,
1876) Abdul Aziz, who, a light-hearted wastrel, was wholly
unequal to the gravity of his task and of the hour. A few days
after his disgrace the erratic man graciously saved his country
further trouble by committing suicide. His nephew, Murad V,
whom the reformers placed on the throne, proved even less
capable than his predecessor, and, after three feverish months,
was in his turn deposed in favor of his younger brother, Abdul
Hamid II. In choosing him, the conspirators, all men of a
liberal disposition, unwittingly dug their own graves, for Abdul
Hamid turned out to be as reactionary as he was cunning and
able. For a while indeed he permitted the political group, to
which he owed his elevation to the throne, to lord it over him
and the empire. Then quietly he laid his plans to recover the
reins and, having once again got them in hand, he clung to them
with so set and autocratic a will that he gradually became the
single center of authority throughout his dominions.

A series of palace revolutions at Constantinople ends with the elevation of Abdul Hamid II.

While these breathless events were engaging the attention of
the capital, the war with Serbia and Montenegro was running
its course. Under the anything but fortunate leadership of a
Russian general the Serbs adopted a plan of invasion for which
they lacked the necessary means. After a few trivial successes
they were badly beaten and fell back in such confusion that the
Turks had only to move upon Belgrad and the war would be

The defeat and elimination of Serbia.

over. However, before the Ottoman army had gone far on its
journey, it was met by an ultimatum from Russia. On November
1, it agreed to sign an armistice with its opponents. Four months
later negotiations at Constantinople led to a peace by which
Serbia retired unscathed from the war.

The
successes of
Monte-
negro.

The smaller Serb state, Montenegro, conducted its war far
more creditably than its larger neighbor. After winning several
minor combats the Montenegrins penetrated into Turkish territory and did not sign a truce till they were well entrenched
within the Ottoman border. The diplomatic negotiations which
followed failed to reach a conclusion because Prince Nicholas
boldly asked for more territory than the Porte was ready to
grant. Accordingly, the prince made ready for a new campaign
in the spring of 1877. Without doubt his decision to continue
the war was aided by the conviction that he would be relieved of
all further anxiety by the appearance of a champion prepared
to draw the Ottoman fire. For by the time the March winds
blew, events on the European stage had taken a turn which made
it safe to predict that another Turco-Russian war was unavoidable.

The
European
powers
continue to
press reforms
on the
sultan in the
hope of
maintaining
peace.

The stirring events of the year which we have just reviewed,
involving rebellion, massacre, war, and an almost melodramatic
crisis in the sultanate, greatly flustered the chancelleries of
Europe. In spite of a general desire to maintain peace, it was
clearly recognized that peace was imperiled unless the sultan
promptly and sincerely adopted a program of reforms embracing
the disaffected areas of Bosnia, Herzegovina, and Bulgaria. It
was because of the unwillingness of the Porte to accept such
modest suggestions as were contained in the Berlin memorandum
that Serbia and Montenegro had declared war. When the struggle
went against Serbia, the sultan became even less disposed than
before to listen to reason, but the European governments, pushed
by the ardent sympathy of their respective publics for the hard-
used Christians, resolved to make one more effort to open his
eyes to the situation. The western states, and Great Britain in
particular, were aware that unless some alleviation of the lot of
the Christian subjects of the sultan was secured by diplomatic
action, Russia, identified with Orthodoxy and Slavdom and
burning to champion them with the sword, would take the field

against the obdurate padishah. In a war fought for a purpose of which the opinion of the civilized world approved, Russia would have to be given a free rein and might therefore recover the informal protectorate over the Ottoman empire so disastrously lost in the Crimean war. This perilous possibility sufficed to give all the rivals of Russia a strong interest in a peaceful settlement. They were resolved that the sultan should give a pledge to remove the most crying abuses, for only in this way could they placate the excitement of the press and people at home and at the same time block the design of Russia to resume her interrupted march to the Dardanelles. In a supreme effort to force their collective will on the Porte they gave one another a rendezvous with the sultan's ministers at the Ottoman capital.

The conference of Constantinople, thus forced on the unwilling Porte, had hardly opened its doors (Dec. 23, 1876), when the loud booming of cannon caused the delegates to exchange astonished glances. In great excitement their Turkish colleagues explained that the joyous salvos of artillery commemorated the issuance by the sultan of a constitution, which terminated once and for all the traditional absolutism of their country and gave all the subjects of the Porte, Moslems and Christians alike, a share in the government. In the face of this happy democratization, they argued, the conference of ambassadors had lost its point, for all the heaped abuses of the state, not merely those minor ones of which the diplomats complained, would disappear almost at once as the result of the voluntary action of an enfranchised people. Naturally the conferees, familiar with oriental subtleties, suspected a trick and refused to be turned from their purpose. Constitution or no constitution, they asked that the Porte subscribe to a program involving administrative reforms in the disputed area to be carried out under European control; and when the obdurate sultan accepted the reforms but refused to compromise his independence by giving Europe authority in his dominions, the conference broke up in despair (Jan. 21, 1877). An armed conflict was now certain, for Russia was at the end of her patience. On April 24 she took the decisive step of issuing a declaration of war.

Since the tsar's armies were obliged to cross Rumania in order to reach the Danube, the Russian government negotiated a

The conference of Constantinople balked by the reform party in power which issues a constitution, Dec. 1876.

Russia
declares war
and wins
a decisive
victory,
1877-78.

treaty with Rumania securing the necessary permission in return for a promise to respect the integrity of the small state. An offer of active military assistance made by Prince Charles was haughtily refused. Thereupon, on having filtered through Rumania, the ·Russians proceeded to cross the Danube in the systematic pursuit of an offensive which aimed at the Ottoman capital as its ultimate goal. As the Turkish forces, instead of being concentrated to meet the brunt of the Russian attack, were indefensibly scattered over a wide area, the Russian advance was proceeding with remarkable speed when it was unexpectedly checked at the fortress of Plevna. Acting on his own initiative, Osman Pasha, the only Turkish general who won any laurels in this war, flung his army into this stronghold and there stood at bay across the Russian path. In the course of the summer the Russians suffered a series of heavy defeats in an attempt to take Plevna by storm, and, considerably humbled by their experience, consented to accept the aid of Rumania, for which, a few weeks before, they had expressed so frank a contempt. Prince Charles was even promoted to the command of the Russo-Rumanian army which was ordered to reduce Plevna by means of a regular siege and which, after many months of heroic attack and desperate resistance, obliged it to capitulate. On December 10 Osman Pasha and his starved and decimated troops succumbed to their captors. The Turks offered no further resistance. Pouring over the Balkan passes, the Russians reached Adrianople in January, and before the end of the same month arrived at the sea of Marmora, whence they could view the delicate minarets of Stambul outlined against the sky. If they had not fully realized their ancient dream of capturing the city on the Golden Horn, they were at least nearer their goal than at any time in their history. Wholly incapable of continuing the struggle, the sultan agreed to open negotiations for peace at the little village of San Stefano.

Jealous
agitation of
the powers,
especially of
Great
Britain and
Austria.

No sooner was the overwhelming victory of the Slav titan reported in Europe than the ill-contained jealousy of the other powers burst through every restraint. More particularly Austria and Great Britain, with undeniably enormous interests at stake, grew feverishly restive. Russia, on entering the war, had not failed to give assurances to Vienna about the adjoining province of Bosnia, to London about the straits, but the question now agitating the diplomatic bosom was whether, flushed by victory, the tsar would honor his engagements. Manifestly Turkey no longer counted, for she lay, bound and gagged, at Russia's feet and would have to meet any terms the victor exacted. In hot agitation Great Britain and Austria bombarded the Russian foreign office with dispatches, asking for enlightenment as to its purposes; and in their effort to make it plain that they would under no circumstances permit themselves to be ignored, Austria stationed an army of observation in the Carpathians and Great Britain dispatched her fleet to Besika Bay at the mouth of the Dardanelles. In February the British war-ships even entered the straits, and to bring home the full significance of this movement the British cabinet let it be known that, should Russia enter Constantinople, the *casus belli* would be at hand. Black, ominous war-clouds gathered along the European horizon and, though Russia discreetly refrained from entering the Ottoman capital, nevertheless when, early in March, she completed her secret deliberations with the Turkish plenipotentiaries and published the result to the world, it seemed almost certain that the storm would break.

Through a mass of minor provisions in the treaty of San Stefano the sharp scrutiny of the European diplomats quickly penetrated to the point of central significance, which was that the rule of the sultan in Europe had, to all intents, been abolished. This result was mainly achieved by means of a Big Bulgaria which reconstituted the medieval empire of Tsar Simeon. To the sultan was left the area of the straits with its Thracian hinterland and, in addition, a detached Albania, with which it would be impossible to keep in direct and effective touch. Even over Big Bulgaria, the padishah was to retain a general suzerainty, but manifestly Russia planned to reserve the real authority to herself. Seen through the spectacles of Great Britain and Austria, Bulgaria was simply the instrument through which Russia hoped to realize her control, primarily of the sultan, secondarily of the whole peninsula. Their policy through the nineteenth century having been steadily directed to thwarting just such plans, they were not going to knuckle under to them now, at least not without a struggle.

The Big Bulgaria of the treaty of San Stefano.

Great
Britain,
supported
by Austria,
insists on
revising the
treaty of
San Stefano
in a general
congress.

The strain to which the European peace was put in the months following the treaty of San Stefano was as severe as any recorded in the long and agitated history of the eastern question. The argument advanced by Great Britain and Austria, to which Germany, France, and Italy gave at least tacit assent, was that Russia had undertaken to revise the treaty of Paris, an international settlement, by her single action, and that such a procedure was inadmissible. The London and Vienna cabinets tried therefore to force the tsar to submit the San Stefano document to revision in a general congress. Russia struggled with all her might against this termination of her adventure, and if she had met with the slightest encouragement from any quarter would have risked war rather than surrender. It appeared at the time and was made even clearer afterwards that she entertained the hope that Germany would do her the favor to — to use a diplomatic term — "contain" Austria. She would in that case apparently have braved England in the hope that England would not fight alone. But when Bismarck, in charge of German foreign affairs, refused to meet the Russian wishes, the tsar's isolation became manifest. Unwilling to stage a new version of the Crimean war, he reluctantly gave way to Austro-British pressure. Immediately the political tension relaxed, and when, in June, 1878, the congress of Berlin came together it was under a blue and peaceful sky.

What
happened to
Big Bulgaria
at the
congress of
Berlin.

The congress of Berlin completed its revision of the treaty of San Stefano in the course of a single month. Held under the presidency of Prince Bismarck, it was attended by Lord Beaconsfield as representative of Great Britain, by Prince Gortchakoff as representative of Russia, and by other well-known statesmen in representation of the other powers. In their overwhelming anti-Russian sentiment, the delegates went as far as they dared in undoing the settlement which Russia had dictated. Their deliberations were guided in the main by two considerations, the identical two which had dominated all the conferences of the century: Turkey must be strengthened, Russia must be hampered and set back. In consequence, Big Bulgaria, the cornerstone of Russia's plan, was broken into three parts. Between the Danube and the Balkan mountains a self-governing *principality of Bulgaria* was set up with no obligation to the sultan save the payment of an annual tribute; between the Balkan and the Rhodope mountains a province, to be called *Eastern Rumelia,* was left in the military occupation of the Turks but was conceded administrative autonomy under a Christian governor; and finally, the strategically invaluable province of *Macedonia* was handed back to the sultan in order to fit him out with sufficient territory to enable him to play an effective Balkan rôle. In this way was the weapon forged by Russia in her own and Bulgaria's interest struck from her hand. In order somewhat to soothe the tsar's ruffled feelings, the congress made no

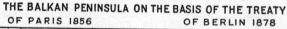

THE BALKAN PENINSULA ON THE BASIS OF THE TREATY OF PARIS 1856   OF BERLIN 1878

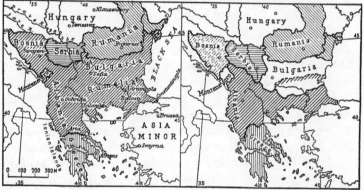

difficulties about meeting his wishes in certain minor respects. Thus he was permitted to retake from Rumania southern Bessarabia, lost in 1856, and to present to his late ally, in its stead, the Bulgarian Dobrudja. In Asia Minor he was authorized to advance into the Armenian borderland by the incorporation of a strip of territory including the important cities of Kars and Batum.

Even for these rather scanty concessions Austria and Great Britain were careful to secure adequate compensation. Bosnia and Herzegovina, where the grave crisis, which the congress of Berlin attempted to legislate out of existence, had had its origin, were entrusted to Austria to " occupy and administer." Though the sultan's sovereignty was specifically reserved and the occupation was declared to be provisional, no one doubted that Austria

Austria receives Bosnia and Great Britain gets Cyprus.

had become the unqualified master of these Serb lands.   In addition, Austria was given the right to garrison, but not to administer, the funnel-like sandjak of Novibazar which separated Serbia from Montenegro.   No less than Austria, Great Britain, under the vigorous imperialist guidance of Lord Beaconsfield, clamored for her reward and received it in the form of the island of Cyprus, which, by a special convention, the sultan ceded — saving his suzerainty — in return for a British undertaking to come to his aid in the event of another Russian attack on his Asiatic dominions.   For Russia these advantages reaped by her rivals filled her cup of sorrow to overflowing.   She had made another bid for the control of the Ottoman empire in the ultimate hope of getting a foothold on the straits, and though, at San Stefano, she had enjoyed a nearer view of her longed-for prize than ever before, she had once more encountered the ancient and persistent hostility of the other powers, who obliged her to abandon her hopes and fall back to her starting-point.

Complete independence of Rumania, Serbia, and Montenegro.

It remains to consider in what shape and condition the small Balkan states emerged from the congress of Berlin.   Rumania, which had done yeoman's service at the side of Russia, received, as we have seen, very cavalier treatment in the San Stefano pact.   In spite of the protests of Prince Charles, the powers at Berlin made no change in these arrangements.   For southern Bessarabia, which she surrendered to Russia, Rumania received the dry and barren plateau of the Dobrudja, which, in the long run, proved a much better bargain than any contemporary dreamt. To the two Serb states of Serbia and Montenegro much more respectful treatment was meted out by their big Slav brother. Montenegro had played the part of a belligerent from the start, while Serbia, which, after its defeat in 1876, made peace with Turkey, had reëntered the war when, on the Ottoman breakdown, it was entirely safe to do so.   Though both states were, in the San Stefano document, conceded a considerable increase of territory, and though both, but especially Serbia, asked for still more at Berlin, they met with little sympathy from the powers.   In fact their San Stefano allotments were somewhat cut down.   In partial mitigation of this frigid paternalism, Serbia, and Rumania likewise, received one memorable present from the congress in that they were declared free and independent and quit of the last vestige of dependence on the Ottoman empire. To emphasize their arrival at full-blown sovereignty Serbia and Rumania, shortly after the Berlin declaration, transformed themselves from principalities to kingdoms, while their respective rulers took the title king. In the case of Montenegro a declaration of independence was unnecessary since Montenegro was no longer subject to Turkey; but such a declaration was none-the-less written into the treaty in order to give Montenegro the advantage of an international guarantee.

In an attempt to distribute their favors evenly the statesmen did not fail to consider the pleas of Greece. As Greece had been independent since the founding of the kingdom, her representatives were content to ask not for a higher status but for territorial increase at the expense of Turkey. This the treaty of Berlin duly promised, leaving the details to negotiations between Athens and the Porte. When, after the usual procrastinations, these were brought to a conclusion (1881), Greece was authorized to move her boundary northward so as to take in Thessaly and a small fraction of Epirus.

Greece wins Thessaly and a part of Epirus.

Lifting ourselves, in conclusion, to a contemplative plane above the events, we cannot but agree that, considerable as were the shortcomings of the treaty of Berlin in its accommodation to the true situation of the Ottoman empire, it represented an enormous improvement in this respect over the treaty of Paris drawn up twenty-two years before. Admittedly the later treaty, exactly like its predecessor, represented an effort to save the state of the sultan, but the gross delusions of the Paris document concerning the nature of that state were not perpetuated. In place of hollow professions about the integrity of the Ottoman empire, there was not only a frank recognition of its necessary subjection to the collective will of Europe, but also an unqualified acknowledgment that the sultan, left to himself, was not likely to carry out any administrative improvement worthy the name. This pessimism explains, at least in part, why Bosnia was entrusted to Austria and Bulgaria made autonomous. Of Christian territories remaining under the sultan's scepter the most important were Eastern Rumelia, Macedonia, Crete, and Armenia, and instead of recommending them, in the manner of the diplomats of Paris, to their sovereign's loving care, the statesmen of Berlin, in sterner mood,

The treaty of Berlin free of offensive delusions about the Ottoman empire.

bound the Porte to promise these regions more or less definite reforms. To be sure, the indicated ameliorations were not likely to be carried out if the powers, falling apart, failed to exercise a persistent pressure on the sultan; but it was refreshing evidence of a return to common sense that Europe ceased to expect anything at all from Ottoman initiative.

The treaty of Berlin sanctions the policy of gradually replacing Turkey-in-Europe with the new Christian states.

Furthermore, if Europe was still firmly resolved to bar Russia, as far as possible, from the Balkan peninsula, it showed by the treaty of Berlin that its policy was no longer a pure negation and that it was working out, though with fumbling insecurity, a constructive plan. The decline of Turkey had in the past produced and was in the present continuing to produce a vacuum which had imperatively to be filled. That, in a nutshell, was the political problem of Balkania. For some decades the view had been gaining adherents among European intellectuals that a most satisfactory replacement of the Ottoman empire could be effected through the Christian states struggling into existence on Balkan soil. In the Berlin document this sensible view received its first formal recognition. Hence Serbia, Montenegro, Rumania and Greece were enlarged territorially and were besides relieved of the last surviving taint of dependence on the sultan. For good measure the congress called into being a new Christian state, the principality of Bulgaria, and gave it an unmistakable, though somewhat grudging, encouragement. The European public, however, greatly pleased that another Christian people had been rescued from Moslem tyranny, went much farther than the diplomats and gave the new arrival a most hearty welcome. It is probable that the reappearance of none of the submerged peoples was attended by so general an outpouring of good-will.

CHAPTER XXVI

THE MAKING OF BULGARIA

THOUGH the principality of Bulgaria was born under the aegis of the powers and was received with marked sympathy by the European public, it was not bedded on roses. Far from it. Within the narrow territorial limits drawn at Berlin the liberated Bulgar people were invited to provide themselves with a government essentially independent, though tributary to the sultan; and difficult as this might prove, they were saddled with a still harder task in that they had to raise their social and economic organization to the west European level or else reckon with the breakdown of their political structure for lack of a proper foundation. If we are to comprehend the troubles and agitations that now ensued, we must have a clear picture of Bulgar society. Since 1393, that is, for about five hundred years, there had been no Bulgar state and the Bulgar people, compressed to a uniform mass of Christian peasants, had undergone the terrible exploitation of a Moslem régime which viewed them as appointed, under a divine dispensation, to play the part of helots. Very slowly, as we have seen, and only with the beginning of the nineteenth century did scattered rays of hope penetrate the profound dark in which they lived and make it possible for a group of self-appointed champions to spread a message calculated to lead the people out of bondage.

Starting with the historic school at Gabrovo (1835), a handful of leaders succeeded in providing a widely distributed system of primary instruction which gradually diminished the shameful national illiteracy.[1] Presently the mounting self-respect of these laborious plowmen led to the demand for a Bulgar church and the issuance by the sultan of the firman of 1870. Additional evidence of awakened energy was supplied by the political

The problem before the liberated Bulgar people.

A peasant people with a small group of intellectuals at the top.

[1] For details of this development see p. 385

407

societies at home and abroad, which aimed at a general insurrection and which, without achieving a single notable success, contributed none-the-less to the great crisis of the seventies terminating in the gift of autonomy. Movement, then, there had been, and important changes had been effected; but it would be a mistake to exaggerate the Bulgar development, for, in the mass, the Bulgar people still was a backward peasant group unable to grasp the immensity of the task before it, while the leaders, peasants by birth who had risen above their fellows, had picked up a superficial European culture which, as a source of excessive self-esteem, might easily prove more pernicious than helpful. All competent observers admitted that the Bulgar peasants were extraordinarily industrious and persevering, though rather dour and unsympathetic. They were a race of plodders who must not be hurried. Undeniably, however, the circumstances called for hurry, and the over-confident leaders, masters, as they thought, of the elements of civilization, were ready, so far as they were concerned, to move at a break-neck speed.

The policy of Russia. Grave as was the problem of Bulgarian organization, it was made extremely grave by the presence of another factor, by Russia. The Russians had come to Bulgaria as liberators and their victory had broken the secular yoke of the Turks. They were received everywhere with the enthusiasm which benefactors habitually elicit—at least at first. Before long, however, the Bulgars discovered that the tsar, like every other ruler, was pursuing not primarily a Bulgar policy, but one conformable to the Russian interest as he conceived it. When his chosen instrument, the Big Bulgaria of San Stefano, was struck from his hand, he resolved to do the best he could with the Bulgarian nucleus provided at Berlin. That was the principality, which, under the treaty, was to be administered by a Russian commissar until a popular assembly had met and formulated a constitution. Russia, therefore, was granted a directive position in Bulgaria, and though it was only provisional, the temptation was strong to make the most of the opportunity and build up something in the nature of an informal protectorate. By this procedure the northern bear would be enabled to plant a firm paw on Balkan soil and would regain, in spite of the rude interference of Lord Beaconsfield, the position of power and prestige which had been sacrificed at Berlin.

In the execution of this plan the Russians counted with confidence on the support of their Bulgar brothers, who owed their young liberty to the intervention of the tsar. The Russian bureaucrats, however, who came to Bulgaria charged with the organization of the new government, relied less on gratitude than on the principle of authority and made no attempt to conceal their disdain for the ignorant peasants, among whom they moved. Before long the national spirit had been subtly irritated by these haughty interlopers. To the Bulgars, awakened from a sleep of centuries, liberation meant liberation and not the exchange of a Turkish for a Russian bondage. In a surprisingly short time the sentiment of gratitude, which a diplomatic wit once defined as a lively sense of favors to come, showed, on the cessation of favors, significant signs of giving way to suspicion. But it will be best to turn to the events themselves and learn from them how the Bulgar nationalism, which the Russians had fosetered to play as a trumpcard against the Ottoman empire, became a most disconcerting boomerang.

The Russian commissar who provisionally ruled Bulgaria, in February, 1879, duly summoned an assembly of notables to provide the new state with a constitution. The draft which he submitted was swiftly transformed into a very democratic instrument by the young, self-confident doctrinaires who dominated the debates. The completed constitution was characterized by a single chamber, elected by universal male suffrage, and by a prince, as executive, entrusted with the power to appoint the ministers; these were, however, to be responsible not to the prince but to the chamber. This last provision, dividing the control of the ministry, was most unfortunate, since it was certain to precipitate a conflict for supremacy between ruler and parliament. Next in order came the election of a prince. As soon as it was taken up, it was seen at once that the general favorite was Alexander of Battenberg. German by birth, he was twenty-two years of age, intelligent and upright, but without any save the most cursory knowledge of the local situation and with no political experience whatever. The decisive point with the assembly was that he was a nephew of Tsar Alexander II and favored by him for the post. It did not of course make him less popular that he had volunteered in the Russian army during the late war and was no stranger to the country. In April, 1879, the young man was unanimously elected and shortly after arrived in Bulgaria to take the oath of office.

Although Prince Alexander was resolved, with laudable conscientiousness, to do his level best for his people, he came to Sofia, his capital, with the idea firmly implanted in his mind that he was an agent of Russia. He embarked therefore on the difficult task of serving two masters, while the youthful parliamentarians of the Sobranye, as the Bulgar parliament was called, were chiefly concerned with exercising the authority themselves. They were ambitious; they coveted the offices, which, though numerous, were not numerous enough to go around; and they had no aversion whatever to cantankerous quarrels of a purely personal nature. Before long the situation was passionately embittered and ministry succeeded ministry to the grave detriment of the affairs of state and for no other reason than in response to the capricious tides of sentiment rocking the parliamentary waters. In a surprisingly short time the prince and his Russian backers as well had become convinced that the constitution was a failure. Accordingly, in 1881, he sprang a *coup d'état* and suppressed it. For the following two years he conducted a veiled absolutism, for the maintenance of which, with his subjects almost unanimously against him, he had to lean heavily on Russia. During those two years two Russian generals, Soboleff and Kaulbars, sent from Petrograd, dominated the ministry, and more or less delicately conveyed to the prince that his position was titular. Overshadowed in this way, he began to see the error of his ways. To escape from Russian tutelage only one choice was possible. That was to be reconciled to his people.

In 1883 Prince Alexander restored the constitution and immediately won back popular favor. The Russian tools, Soboleff and Kaulbars, left the country in a huff, and the new tsar, Alexander III, who, in distinction from his late father, had no natural liking for his relative, gave unmistakable signs of his displeasure. True, the Bulgar ruler made desperate efforts to avoid a breach with Russia, but, committed henceforth to his people, he drifted, in the very nature of things, farther and farther away from Petrograd. For a complete reconciliation with his subjects it was necessary, above all, that he share their national passions and promote a plan which had filled all minds ever since the birth of the principality. That was the union with East Rumelia. By the treaty of Berlin, it will be recalled, East Rumelia, though returned to the sultan, was accorded self-governing rights only a little less complete than those of the sister-state to the north. Since 1879 an administrative system, created by a commission of the powers, was functioning, under which East Rumelia presented the appearance of an imperfect copy of Bulgaria. If not the only, the most striking difference between the two states was that while one had a prince of its own choice, the other was ruled by a Christian governor, appointed by the sultan for a term of five years.

From the first it was the natural wish of the Bulgars on either side of the Balkan mountains that the two states should be merged as soon as possible. By 1885 the wish had become imperious, and in September of that year a revolution took place in Philippopolis, the capital of East Rumelia, which, to the wild applause of the people, proclaimed union with the principality. When a Rumeliote delegation waited on Alexander to invite him into their midst, his momentary hesitation to make the dangerous plunge was overcome by Stambuloff, a Bulgar patriot destined to achieve fame, who told him sternly that either he would go to Philippopolis or — to Darmstadt, his German home. He chose the ancient city on the Maritsa, where he was hailed amid ringing cheers as the first ruler of a united Bulgaria.

Revolution in East Rumelia and union with Bulgaria, 1885.

Promoted to his enlarged position by the will of the people, Alexander had still to reckon with the powers whom he had openly flouted by countenancing a breach of the treaty of Berlin. While the sultan was the person chiefly aggrieved, all the powers, signatories of that document, had the legal obligation to protest against Alexander's usurpation and to uphold the international law they themselves had sanctioned. In their wonted manner they began to feel one another out but were still exchanging dispatches when the attention of the world was drawn elsewhither. Among the other Balkan states, but chiefly in Serbia and Greece, the Bulgar union had staged a veritable witch's sabbath. These small polities, whose infant years had been fed on violent and exclusive hatred of the Turk, were now in their confident adolescence beginning to show active signs of jealousy

Jealousy of the other Balkan states and the emergence of the doctrine of a Balkan balance of power.

of one another. Excited by the sudden expansion of Bulgaria, Greece and Serbia stepped forth as champions of the theory of a Balkan balance of power and urged the need of an immediate increase of territory on their part in order to keep abreast of their youngest Christian rival. Serbia went the length of mobilizing its army, apparently against Turkey; but when, on reflection, an attack on Turkey seemed unlikely to yield results, the Serbs turned suddenly on their Slav neighbor in the hope of acquiring a section of his border. On November 14, 1885, the Serb army under King Milan wantonly invaded Bulgaria.

The Serb-Bulgar war of 1885.

The ensuing Serb-Bulgar war furnished Europe with a great surprise inasmuch as it was generally expected that Serbia, as the older and better consolidated state, would administer a sound beating to its neighbor. However, Bulgar patriotism responded electrically to the situation by welding the people into a single mass. Besides, the Bulgar army, thanks to Russian training and Russian equipment, proved a far from despicable weapon. Just before the war broke out, the tsar, to further indicate his displeasure with his too independent cousin, had withdrawn the Russian officers in the Bulgarian employ. Their importance is indicated by the statement that they filled all the military posts above the rank of captain. Though this act had seriously disorganized the service, the inconvenience which it caused was somehow overcome and, animated by a do-or-die spirit, the Bulgar army flung itself into the fight. On November 17, the opposed forces met at Slivnitza and a battle was engaged in which, after three tumultuous days, ended in a Serb rout. The victorious Bulgars pursued the enemy across the border but had only just reached Pirot when they were met by an Austrian ultimatum. For reasons intelligible only to the devious diplomatic mind the Austrians undertook to save Serbia. Under pressure from Vienna Prince Alexander was obliged to agree to a truce, followed shortly by a treaty which permitted Serbia to escape from the consequences of its folly without loss of territory or the payment of an indemnity. That was a wholly desirable ending if the two neighbors were to mend their ways and live thereafter in peace and amity. To justify such hopefulness, however, the records of the past supplied but little evidence. The two Slav states, which had just celebrated their national rebirth by flying at each other's throat, had in the Middle Age fought together desperately and continuously until suppressed by the irresistible power of the Ottomans. Unquestionably the war of 1885 boded ill for the future relations of the young commonwealths.

One undoubted benefit, however, the Bulgars did obtain from their victory and that was the suspension of all action against them on the part of the powers. Not only was their victory, won against an unmistakable aggressor, popular in Europe, but the diplomatic circles were impressed with the Bulgar strength and, as usual, trimmed their sails accordingly. A tendency to accept the accomplished fact made itself felt in all quarters except— in Russia. Russia, the former paternal friend, was now extremely bitter against its thankless child, and in its resentment even went the length of suggesting to the " unspeakable Turk " to charge himself with its punishment. But Russia was not the only power which changed sides in the new phase of the Bulgar question. Great Britain, Bulgaria's chief enemy at Berlin, now covered it with its wing and succeeded in persuading Abdul Hamid to accept the situation. By April, 1886, the union of the two Bulgarias had received the sanction of sultan and powers.

Recognition of the union of the two Bulgarias by sultan and powers.

Only with the greatest reluctance did Tsar Alexander acquiesce in the aggrandizement of his cousin, who, by throwing in his lot with the Bulgar nationalists had, in the Russian view, betrayed his benefactor. Revolving plans of revenge, the Russian government discovered that the virulent party divisions of Bulgaria, only temporarily hushed by the war with Serbia, might be discreetly manipulated in the Russian interest. With a little prompting by the secret agents of Petrograd, certain disgruntled elements, chiefly officers who had failed to obtain the advancement they considered their due formed a conspiracy directed at the overthrow of the prince. The plot, as conceived and executed, fully confirmed the preëminence of Balkania as the world's main source for the raw materials of comic opera. Entering the palace of the prince at Sofia in the dead of night, the conspirators roused him from sleep, forced him, at the point of the pistol, to sign his abdication, and then, hustling him into a carriage, whisked off with him into the darkness. When the morning of August 21, 1886, dawned, the news was flashed around the world that the prince had been kidnapped.

Abduction of Prince Alexander.

The next step of the plotters was to seize the government and overawe the adherents of the prince. Momentarily successful in the face of a dazed public opinion, they soon encountered an opposition, which in the course of a few days became an irresistible tide. The upshot was that they were either imprisoned or scattered to the winds, while the country with a hearty unanimity gathered around a group of nationalist defenders, of whom the vigorous Stambuloff was the dominant figure. Meanwhile it became known that the abducted prince had been taken down the Danube to the nearest Russian point and there released with the order to keep moving in any direction he pleased so long as it was away from Sofia. On arriving on Austrian soil, he was met by a telegram from Stambuloff urgently pressing him to return to Bulgaria. A little over a week after his abduction Prince Alexander reëntered his capital amidst unrestrained demonstrations of loyalty. But his stay was brief. On his way back he had, in an unguarded moment, sent a message to Tsar Alexander wherein he declared that he did not wish to reassume his scepter without the imperial blessing. Quick to see his opportunity, the tsar sent an ungracious answer, and the prince, partly because he was bound by his word, partly because he hoped to turn the wrath of Russia from his adopted country by the sacrifice of his person, renewed his abdication and, in spite of the protests of his people, rigorously carried it out. On September 8, after appointing a regency of three men, he left Bulgaria forever.

In this situation the main question before the regency continued to be the issue of Russian preponderance. Once more Petrograd made a bid for renewal of control through an energetic agent who toured the country to unite the Russian sympathizers, but once more the country showed that it had no desire to take rank as a Russian satrapy. When a special assembly, called to elect a new prince, refused to listen to Russian dictation or to name a Russian candidate, the aggrieved tsar again withdrew the light of his countenance from Bulgaria and sternly hid himself from view within his northern fogs. As unconcernedly as possible Bulgaria, under the direction of the regents, went about its business of picking a new ruler. So difficult was it to find a sovereign even approximately answering to the fancied requirements of the case that almost a year passed before the assembly offered the crown to Prince Ferdinand of Saxe-Coburg, whom a committee, scouring the drawing-rooms of Europe, encountered in Vienna. Ferdinand was the antipodes of his handsome predecessor, being physically unprepossessing, a poor horseman, and boasting neither the bearing nor the training of a soldier. However, he was not without merits; he was young, intelligent, an amateur botanist of note, and, under the prompting of an ambitious mother, sufficiently self-reliant not to be frightened by the prospects of a precarious throne. In the summer of 1887 he took the oath of office, but as Russia refused to recognize him, the other powers, not to offend Russia, followed suit. That meant that Prince Ferdinand, though visibly acting as head of the state, enjoyed the sanction neither of Europe nor of his suzerain, the sultan.

For the next seven years Ferdinand contented himself to acquire, as it were, a Bulgarian education and left the government to Stambuloff, whom he made prime minister. During this long tenure Stambuloff won an enormous reputation by virtue of his remarkable energy and almost uniform success. He was a coarse peasant, lit by a spark of genius and troubled by no scruples in the pursuit of his one great purpose, the security and independence of his country. For this cause he was ready to persecute and imprison his enemies, to manipulate the elections, to bribe and intrigue. Since his experience had made him Russophobe and prompted him to pursue an anti-Russian policy, his political enemies naturally played themselves up as friends of the great Slav power. Obliged to look about for some counterweight to the enmity of Russia, acrimoniously manifested both at home and abroad, he drew near to his former foe, the sultan, and with characteristic audacity resolved to extract an advantage for his beloved Bulgaria from this enforced association.

The long ministry of Stambuloff, 1887–94.

Ever since the creation of the principality, popular opinion had been agitated over Macedonia. Included in the Big Bulgaria of San Stefano, it had been clipped from that paper sketch by the diplomats at Berlin and coolly handed back to the Ottoman empire. To the average Bulgar patriot it represented *Bulgaria irredenta*, an unredeemed Bulgaria, which must at some not too distant date be absorbed by the Sofian nucleus. Touching

The goal of Bulgar patriotism — unredeemed Macedonia.

Macedonia there were in Bulgaria two opposed schools of thought, one of which maintained that the correct procedure was conspiracy and insurrection, leading ultimately to a war of conquest, while the other preached political patience in order to gain time thoroughly to honeycomb Macedonia with Bulgar educational propaganda. The former tactics must have had a strong appeal for Stambuloff, who was a born man of action and who in his callow youth, before Bulgaria saw the light of day, had pursued this identical program. However, while gaining in years, he had gained also in astuteness and foresight, and, obliged to remain on good terms with Turkey, he recognized the wisdom of giving up, at least temporarily, an activist policy. To the immense disgust of the agitators, with whom he had once been hand and glove, he ostentatiously discouraged conspiracies and concentratetd on a policy of peaceful penetration. At the same time he was restrained by no false modesty from bringing his noble conduct to the sultan's attention and on two occasions (1890, 1894) was rejoiced by receiving a reward in the form of imperial decrees establishing four Bulgarian bishoprics in Macedonia. In this manner the exarchate largely pushed the rival establishment of the patriarchate out of a territory where it had hitherto reigned supreme. The Bulgar bishops of course installed a Bulgar clergy and set up Bulgar schools, and priest and schoolmaster together made it their business firmly to anchor the Macedonian consciousness in Bulgar nationalism. If it was afterwards found very difficult to cure the Macedonians of their Bulgar leanings, this stubborn preference may in no small part be ascribed to Stambuloff's success in planting a virgin soil with the organized propaganda of church and school.

Fall and murder of Stambuloff. Meanwhile Prince Ferdinand had finished his royal apprenticeship and began to show signs of impatience over the leading strings in which he was kept by his imperious minister. He had recently married and naturally hoped to perpetuate his dynasty. As a step in that direction he desired to be recognized by Europe and he was clever enough to see that he would, by way of preliminary, have to knock at the portals of the tsar and be admitted to his favor. Such considerations made Stambuloff, the Russophobe statesman, seem a much less desirable pilot of the ship of state than he once had been. Under these altered circumstances a quarrel developed between prince and minister which in 1894 caused the latter to hand in his resignation. Perhaps he thought he was indispensable and would quickly be called back to power. Instead his foes, whose name was legion and who raised a chorus of thanksgiving over his dismissal, banded themselves together to hinder his return. Like other men fallen from high estate, he found himself deserted even by his former henchmen, and, left naked to his enemies, in little more than a year after leaving office, he perished by the hand of an assassin.

Ferdinand, at last master in his own house, gradually effected a radical change in Stambuloff's policy. Taking advantage of the death of the implacable Alexander III (1894), he made timid advances to the new tsar, Nicholas II, and after some hesitation was admitted to the imperial presence to recite his *pater peccavi*. As a supreme pledge of his Russophil atitude, he, a Roman Catholic, agreed to have the heir to the throne baptized in the Orthodox church. Then, at a sign from Petrograd, the taboo was lifted and official recognition poured in on him from all sides.

Prince Ferdinand reconciled to the new tsar, Nicholas II.

The legalization of his position was a proud achievement for Ferdinand but fraught with undeniable risks, since friendly relations with Russia implied a frigid behavior toward the Porte and the entry on a new era of ill-will. Gradually the Macedonian conspirators came back into favor, while Stambuloff's policy of pacific penetration was replaced by a growing preference for direct action. In the long run this was sure to lead to war with Turkey, perhaps to a general Balkan war, especially if Russia resumed her Constantinopolitan plans and felt encouraged to realize them by another thrust at the "Sick Man." It happened however that, in the decade following Stambuloff's removal from office, Russian policy unexpectedly carried out a dramatic shift by concentrating its energy and attention on the Far East. While this deflection of interest offered a partial guarantee that, with the Balkan equilibrium undisturbed by its most usual disturber, the peace of the Near East would be maintained, it did not hinder a tremendous and feverish underground activity in the disputed area of Macedonia. Thither, as to a land of plenty, not only Bulgaria turned its gaze, but Serbia and Greece, regretting their past neglect, did the same and hurriedly invaded

Bulgaria passes to an activist policy in Macedonia and arouses Serb and Greek activism.

the desirable province with all the approved paraphernalia of propaganda and conspiracy. For the remainder of Ferdinand's reign the Macedonian question stood out as the burning issue of Balkan politics, though it did not lead to war until Russia, balked in her far eastern ambitions by Japan, once more swung round to face the eternal question of the straits. But that is matter for a later chapter.

Economic, administrative, and educational progress of Bulgaria.

In conclusion, it is proper to point out the notable progress made by Bulgaria in the period following its liberation. A remarkable zeal was manifested for highways and railroads in order to facilitate internal communication, while the improvements carried out at Varna on the Black Sea and at Rustchuk and other ports on the Danube made these points important centers of export. For its wheat and cattle Bulgaria received manufactured goods from the West, the statistics indicating a steady growth of these exchanges with Europe as well as a rising level of national well-being. As befitted a country with a foreign policy which envisaged the possibility of new wars, the army was organized on a professional basis and its preparedness brought to a high pitch by the feature of universal military service. In spite of the heavy army expenditures, the government did not stint the public school system which was put on the obligatory basis for both boys and girls. The love of education was widespread among these simple agriculturists with the result that the illiteracy averages have regularly declined with each new census. Through Robert College at Constantinople and the industrial school at Samakov the United States has made a valuable and highly appreciated contribution to the intellectual ferment in Bulgaria. It is an interesting fact that these two foundations, maintained for over half a century by the munificence and broad humanity of American citizens, have graduated a notable fraction of the men who have distinguished themselves in the professions and in the public life of the young state.

The peasant the backbone of Bulgar society.

Every consideration of Bulgar society must begin and end with the small freehold peasant who is the backbone of the country. His steadiness and industry are at the bottom of the economic advance, which continued uninterruptedly in spite of the political disturbances at the center of government. As the peasants did not concern themselves overmuch with affairs of

state, these unhappily showed a tendency to become the prerogative of a relatively small group of intellectuals making a
business of politics. A political awakening among the peasants,
noticeable since the beginning of the twentieth century, may serve
to correct this undue importance of the lawyers, journalists,
and other professional politicians, thereby bringing Bulgar politics into quickening touch with the realities of Bulgar existence.

CHAPTER XXVII

SULTAN ABDUL HAMID II. — NEW PHASES OF OTTOMAN DECAY: ARMENIA, CRETE, MACEDONIA

The sultan's calculation in accepting Midhat's constitution

WHEN the small group of Ottoman reformers, gathered around Midhat Pasha, raised Abdul Hamid II to the throne, it was, as we have seen, with the intention of establishing in office an intelligent promoter of their plans. For a short time following his elevation the new sultan accepted the direction of the men to whom he owed his dignity. Above all, he permitted Midhat to issue (Dec. 23, 1876) an Ottoman constitution, persuaded thereto by Midhat's assurance that it would so flatter the liberal professions of the European powers that, affirming their satisfaction with the new turn of affairs, they would instantly dissolve the obnoxious conference of Constantinople, called to draw up a program of reforms to be forced upon the Porte.

Midhat dismissed, the constitution withdrawn.

However, the Ottoman chaos had gone too far and the suspicions of Europe were too aroused for Midhat's melodramatic *coup* to produce the least effect. The conference obstinately insisted on reforms under such binding guarantees that all Turks, liberals and conservatives alike, looked upon them as constituting an impairment of Ottoman sovereignty. In consequence they joined in urging the government to reject them, in spite of the solemn warning that the decision would unavoidably precipitate war with Russia. To the objective student the crisis of 1876 in Ottoman affairs may seem to have had a fateful, necessary character, against which it was useless to struggle; but to the sultan, who was not objective and who, moreover, had been won to Midhat's program by the argument that the breach with Europe might be avoided by the proclamation of a constitution, the outcome was a terrible disappointment. Early in February, even before the Russains had gone the length of declaring war, he punished Midhat for his failure to influence Europe by dismissing him from office. Then he took the government into

420

his own hands. As it was too late to block the elections to the promised Ottoman parliament, in the month of March this body duly came together in the capital. To the sober spectator there was something suggestive of a solemn farce about a free representative assembly in this most backward state of Europe, but to many hopeful-minded people the world over it had the persuasive significance of a symbol. Was Turkey about to be democratized? To an age enamored of democracy it seemed an amazing triumph, but the hope held out was of short duration. As soon as the Ottoman parliament, getting down to business, undertook to give orders to the government, it was abruptly sent home. As, at the same time, the constitution was suspended, the first Ottoman experiment with the parliamentary system came to a close before it was well under way, with the sultan once more exercising absolute control.

As we have already followed the Turco-Russian war of 1877 to its conclusion in the treaty of Berlin, we are aware that, though the Ottoman empire was once again saved from Russia by the intervention of the powers, it was at the same time almost wrecked, at least in Europe, by a series of acts, including the raising to full sovereignty of Rumania, Serbia, and Montenegro, the surrender of Bosnia and Herzegovina to Austria, the creation of the principality of Bulgaria, the formation of an autonomous East Rumelia, and finally, by the exasperating stipulations regarding administrative improvements to be carried out in Crete, Macedonia, and Armenia. Abdul Hamid never forgot the crushing defeat and the almost equally crushing peace with which he had inaugurated his reign. The terrible experience convinced him that while Russia might be his chief foe, all Europe was against him, in exact proportion to the intensity with which each state nursed expectations of sharing in the Ottoman inheritance. In the face of this general covetousness he concluded that his best chance would lie, on the one hand, in cunningly utilizing the inevitable disharmonies of the European concert and, on the other, in tenaciously holding fast to every hereditary right identified with the sultanate. This stark conservatism gives the measure of his personality. Dry, unimaginative, and pedantically devoted to labor of a purely clerical sort, he was at the same time an old-fashioned Turk with a mentality bounded by the Koran and

Abdul Hamid an enemy of reform and a champion of conservatism.

with a fierce, instinctive aversion to this terrible and enigmatic Europe apparently descending on him with the inevitableness of an avalanche. His father, Abdul Medjid, had attempted to exorcise the occidental peril by " liberal " magic: he had issued the tanzimat of 1839 and the charter of 1856 with disappointing results. While the imperial edicts, unrelated to the realities of Moslem life and society, had been evaded and set at naught, they exhibited just enough force to discredit and undermine the institutions of the past. The upshot of half a century of " reform " had been, on the one hand, to accelerate decay and, on the other, to multiply the interference of the powers and to stimulate their territorial appetite. To the alarmed Abdul Hamid it was reasonably clear that his European neighbors would partition his state as soon as they had reached an agreement on their respective shares. Since, at the congress of Berlin, agreement was so unattainable as to be not even discussed, the powers had done the next best thing and set themselves up as receivers-general of the empire.

Abdul Hamid's conservatism involves an absolute régime.

Abdul Hamid, convinced that the path trod by his father, the path of reform, led straight to annihilation, instinctively resolved to stand still, to keep things as they were. Above all, he would rely on the ancient principle of the Ottoman state, in accordance with which all power and influence emanated from the sultan's person. In respect to this immobile plan certain improvements in the army and administration, though indubitably associated with the despised reforms, came decidedly to his support, for they put into his hands a centralized machine which, however poor an imitation it might be of the European article, facilitated a personal domination of the state. Seated in the heart of power, he resolved, if confronted with new popular ferments, not to nurse and coddle but to suppress them without ado; and if the powers, following their usual course, rushed in to interfere, he would cleverly play one against the other, until, the resources of the diplomatic game exhausted, he would win another respite by drawing up a reform-program on paper, the execution of which he would treat dilatorily and end by adjourning to the Greek calends.

While this was conservatism and absolutism at the same time, it had, on close inspection, very little resemblance to the system of the great sultans of the past. Their absolutism was built on strength, and for its successful exercise, called for a warrior steeled in the furnace of adventure. Compared with the forceful system of his ancestors, Abdul Hamid's absolutism was a low, contemptible growth, of which the main elements were deceit and fear, and which to operate with even temporary success required a tireless, subterranean plotter, a creature half fox, half rat. If, identified with a government of this type, Abdul Hamid became, with the passing of the years, one of the most base and degraded tyrants revealed in the whole history of the orient, it is at least remarkable with what completeness he shaped his practice to his principles. Since acts of government were emanations of his will and embodied his good pleasure, he had no need of conferences with his ministers. Ministers were but department heads acting on orders, which it was convenient to transmit to them through the imperial secretaries. By this device the government was completely focussed in the sultan's residence, for which, abandoning the city proper, he selected the summit of a near-by hill. Called *Yildiz* (starry) in the romantic language affected by the East, it commanded a magnificent prospect of the domed and minareted capital under its brow, the blue channel of the Bosporus, and the green hills of the Asiatic shore. To this paradise Abdul Hamid retired, shutting himself up within a walled enclosure which gradually came to embrace many kiosks for the use of himself and his harem, a theater, a stable, a banqueting-hall, a garden, in short, all the appurtenances of a royal city of some two thousand souls dedicated to the service of a single master. Only within this fortress-like residence did he feel safe and only on stated occasions, as, for instance, for the obligatory Friday prayers, did he abandon it. Within its walls, patrolled by companies of troops chosen with an eye to their fidelity, the fears which haunted him like a specter somewhat abated as he went through his tedious daily routine, which, besides the dictation to slavish secretaries of orders for his ministers, consisted of the perusal of the endless, detailed reports sent in by the spies scattered throughout the empire. These hateful communications were his meat and drink, for by supplying secret information of what his enemies were doing, they enabled him to strike before they struck, to imprison, to banish,

Practical aspects of an absolutism built on fear and deceit.

to execute, in short, to serve Lord Allah and the Ottoman nation by the fixed and glorious policy of resisting change, regardless of every consideration of honor and decency.

There can be no doubt that his experiences in the period following the congress of 1878 did much to confirm Abdul Hamid in his anti-European bent. Let us recall that in addition to the many Ottoman losses which were exactly specified, the treaty of Berlin contained articles which, as it were, issued promissory notes to certain claimants, whose case, for one reason or .another, was not brought to an immediate decision. One such promissory note had been issued to Greece and, in spite of the sultan's cleverest turns and dodges, he was, in 1881, obliged to surrender Thessaly to the Hellenic kingdom. East Rumelia, already considered by us,[1] produced a similar disappointment. Under the Berlin treaty the padishah continued to enjoy important privileges in this Bulgar province, but when its union with the principality took place (1885), they were found to amount to nothing at all. Against all such encroachments, involving the liberation of oppressed Christians, there was no redress since European opinion heartily approved of them. But Abdul Hamid, the tenacious heir of a decaying state, saw in them, for his part, nothing but a conspiracy to rob him piecemeal of his empire. With a similarly impotent hate the feeble Byzantine emperors must, some centuries before, have regarded the relentless descent on them of Abdul Hamid's ancestors. Had the sultan been a philosopher, he might have met the situation with a shrug: *hodie mihi, cras tibi.* Being, instead of a Socrates, a greedy autocrat, he defended every foot of ground with the futile cunning, once proclaimed as peculiarly Byzantine, but, in recent years, declared by every ready-writer to be just Ottoman, pure Ottoman.

To assemble material illustrative of the sultan's attitude we cannot do better than follow his relations to three important territories which in the treaty of Berlin the powers designated as objects of their paternal interest. By Article XXIII they insisted that Crete and Macedonia receive an improved administration suited to the local wants, and by Article LXI they made a similar reservation for Armenia. These three, Armenia, Crete,

---

[1] See pp. 410–411.

and Macedonia, represented very nearly all that was left to the Ottoman ruler of preponderantly Christian areas, and the cautious interest in them displayed by the powers signified the entering wedge which in the past had regularly served to pry a territory loose from the Ottoman grasp.

Many authors preface their account of the painful story of these three regions under Abdul Hamid by declaring that the sultan might have saved them for the Ottoman empire if he had at once conceded the reforms demanded by the treaty. It is far more likely that he would thereby have merely expedited their achievement of complete independence. While such a solution would, from an abstract and idealist point of view, have been wholly unobjectionable, it was not what the powers alleged as the goal of their endeavors nor what Abdul Hamid considered desirable. Clinging obdurately to power, he sensed, and not without reason, in the grant of local autonomy the hateful first step toward complete surrender of authority. He was therefore resolved to resist to the utmost even the smallest concession. To oblige him to act the powers would have had to employ force, and of force they were exceedingly chary because its exercise was almost certain to precipitate a general war. Under these circumstances the disputed areas became the occasion for an endless exchange of diplomatic notes; from time to time one power or another, becoming impatient, voiced a threat; and rarely, very rarely, they all agreed on a course of timid action which, however, being action, never failed to produce a result. We may fairly summarize the long conflict over Armenia, Crete, and Macedonia by saying that, as long as the sultan succeeded in keeping these issues on a purely discussional plane, he remained the unquestioned master of the situation. Each issue has, however, its own physiognomy, which it is thoroughly worth while to examine.

Abdul Hamid's aversion to autonomy and his resolve to balk the powers.

The Armenians are a people who from ancient times have dwelt in the difficult mountain regions of northeastern Asia Minor. Converted to Christianity at an early date, they welcomed the creation in their midst of the Gregorian church, which, named after its founder, St. Gregory (d. 332), proudly boasts to be the oldest Christian church in existence. Although resembling in many respects the Greek Orthodox church, the church of the Armenians has been and remains an absolutely separate organiza-

The Armenians a Christian people amenable to modern ideas.

tion under a chief official called catholicus. In the course of the Ottoman advance the Armenians fell under the Moslem yoke and were, as Christians, reduced to the status of rayahs. Largely given to trade and possessed of a keen intelligence, enterprising members of the race penetrated to all the cities of the empire, including Constantinople, until the Armenian merchant communities disputed with the Greeks and the Jews the position of leading commercial people of the Near East. Thus matters stood when, with the dawn of the nineteenth century, western civilization forced admission into the Ottoman empire. Without delay the wide-awake Armenians began to appropriate the new ideas and methods. They were aided and abetted by Catholic and Protestant missionaries — the latter from the United States — who found their way into the distant uplands and stimulated much intellectual curiosity without, however, weaning more than a handful from devotion to their ancient church. The climax in this development was reached when the Armenians were moved to establish a system of modern schools which quickly raised their efficiency index far above that of the various peoples about them.

The racial situation in Armenia.

To such a people, consciously marching under the banner of modernism, the ideas of freedom and nationality were bound, sooner or later, to become a cherished possession. Unfortunately there were special difficulties which militated against the early realization of a liberal political program. For one thing not all the Armenians were under the sultan, since some dwelt on territory conquered in the course of the nineteenth century by Russia. The majority, however, amounting perhaps to 1,200,000 souls, were Ottoman subjects distributed through the six vilayets of Sivas, Bitlis, Erzerum, Harput, Diabekir, and Van. These provinces, together with the Russian border-strip, constituted, ideally speaking, Armenia; but the fact was — and it has had and still has tragic consequences — that, owing to changes wrought by chance and time, the Armenians failed to represent a clear majority in any district with which they were historically associated. Of the three peoples who dwelt with the Armenians on Armenian soil, to wit, Turks, Greeks, and Kurds, not one, it is true, could claim a majority either. However, the Turks, as Moslems and conquerors, comported themselves as lords of the land,

and if, as commonly happened, the Armenians made up for their inferior status by their superior intelligence and amassed considerable wealth, the indolent Ottomans could always redress the balance by calling on their brothers in Islam, the roving Kurds, to reduce the pride of the Armenians by relieving them of their goods. To an invitation to plunder mere dogs of infidels, the Kurds, a semi-savage mountain people, were only too happy to respond. Unmistakably the Turks and Kurds were in control.

By reason of these difficult elements in the local situation there had been no considerable movement in behalf of Armenian independence before Abdul Hamid's time, and, in effect, there had been no Armenian political problem. But the treaty of Berlin with its stipulation in favor of Armenia wrought an immediate change. While the prospect of European intervention in the interior of Asia Minor struck terror into the sultan's heart, it encouraged the Armenians to agitate in behalf of an early realization of the autonomy already decreed by the Berlin areopagus. Either the powers should have proceeded straightway to enforce the Armenian provision by military means or they should have withdrawn it. Short-sightedly and cruelly they preferred to toss Article LXI as an apple of discord in the midst of Turks and Armenians and with folded arms to await developments.

Article LXI an apple of discord.

When these developments duly matured, assuming the form of a harrowing national tragedy, the European governments gave vent to their surprise and indignation, although, in view of the Bulgarian massacres of 1876 and of other similar incidents, they might have fully known what to expect. Perpetually nagged about Armenia by the powers, Abdul Hamid, being what he was, was sure to excogitate a plan to put the troublesome issue out of the world. Might not what had failed in Bulgaria succeed in Armenia, a region of Asia, not of Europe, and effectively concealed from the scrutiny of the curious behind a screen of lofty mountains? Might not a systematic butchery, organized by the authorities instead of being left to the unregulated bloodlust of Bashi-Bazuks, sufficiently reduce the Armenian numbers to stifle forever the cry of independence? On this plan the sultan resolved to act and, beginning in 1894, for three years kept the world in excitement with the news of the periodic

The Armenian massacres, 1894–96.

slaughter of the Armenian sheep by the bloody Mohammedan wolves, Turks and Kurds, in their midst. Probably 100,000 men, women, and children were ruthlessly dispatched in the towns and villages of their historic home-land, while other tens of thousands, who fled to the mountains, died of starvation and disease. Horrified Europe did not fail to protest to the Sublime Porte, but not till the massacres were extended to the capital, to Constantinople, where on two occasions (1895, 1896), the streets ran red with Armenian blood, did the protest assume a sufficiently severe form to effect a halt. A point to be always kept in mind is that, although the sultan availed himself of the fanaticism of the Moslem populace in order to achieve his purpose, there was nothing spontaneous about the movement. It was an organized butchery utilizing religious passion for a political end. And the end was not even gained. The Armenian nation was not destroyed and, though decimated and exhausted, with intenser fervor than ever looked forward to the day of freedom.

We have already glanced at the grave troubles of Crete which, under pressure from the powers, the Porte attempted to remedy by means of the Organic Statute of 1868. That this did not solve the problems of the island should not surprise us. The concessions of the sultan, involving the sacrifice of some of the traditional preëminence of the local Moslems in administrative, financial, and judicial matters, were yielded with ill-will and executed as imperfectly as possible, while the Christians, though glad to pocket any favor which might be offered them, were disinclined to put an end to agitation until they had achieved their one absorbing purpose, which was union with the mother-land of Greece. In the circumstances a truce was possible between the two island factions but no peace. When the crisis of 1876 overtook the Ottoman empire, the Cretan Christians immediately grew restive and were only dissuaded from an outbreak by the promise of Great Britain to undertake a new diplomatic action in their favor. In consequence there was written into the treaty of Berlin an international guarantee for Crete and in the same year (1878) the Organic Statute was expanded into the pact of Halepa. As this, among other benefits, established a local assembly with a Christian majority, it opened the prospect of a genuine

Continued
agitation
in Crete.

amelioration of the lot of the harassed Greeks. However, if the amelioration occurred, it was only temporary by reason of the recurrent breach of contract either by the Porte itself or by its local spokesman, the governor ruling in the sultan's name. It would be as tedious as unprofitable to follow the see-saw of charges and counter-charges between rulers and ruled or the periodical outbreaks by which the Christians vented their displeasure at each new irregularity.

From a troubled picture of more or less chronic revolt the insurrection of February, 1897, stands out because, comet-wise, it carried in its wake a long trail of consequences. The new rebellion was caused, as usual, by continued Moslem misgovernment; its end, also as usual, was union with the Greek kingdom. The fighting immediately became fierce, the Christian rebels taking possession of the country-side and the Moslem minority crowding into the towns where they enjoyed the advantage of protection by the Turkish troops of occupation. An ominous attendant circumstance was from the first the wild demonstrations of sympathy manifested throughout the neighboring Greek monarchy. On previous occasions too, the free Greeks had grown restive the moment their brothers of Crete rose against the sultan, but they had regularly yielded to the admonitions of their government and kept themselves in check. The government in its turn had, unwillingly of course, been held to the rôle of spectator by order of the powers, which from fear of a general conflagration, positively forbade interference in the island. Owing to a nationalist society which had recently been founded and which reached every town and village of the kingdom, the pan-Hellenic movement possessed just then the most effective organization of its history. It therefore happened that when the pan-Hellenic leaders gave the sign to support the new insurrection, Greece rose practically as one man in order to throw its weight on the side of the Cretans. Helpless before the tidal wave of national sentiment, the Athenian government consented to send gunboats and troops in aid of the insurgents. As this was an act of war against Turkey, the alarmed powers, with the view to separating the combatants, interfered. Quickly ordering battleships to the scene and landing troops of their own, they obliged both sides to agree to an armistice.

The insurrection of February, 1897, and the sympathetic action of the free Greeks.

The Turco-
Greek war
of 1897.

However, on this occasion neither the prompt action nor the
rather unusual unanimity of the powers served to stave off a
Turco-Greek war. Greek sentiment, stirred to the depths, refused
to be quieted, and yielding perforce to the riotous demonstrations of the Athenian populace, the government continued
its preparations for war. Personally, it is true, King George,
fully aware of the glaring deficiencies of his country's military
establishment, was strongly averse to fighting, but what was he
to do? Volunteer bands, without waiting for orders, had
already marched north into Thessaly and if the monarch had
not begun a general mobilization, he would, like his predecessor,
have been simply dethroned. In April, 1897, the undisciplined
Greek bands engaged in a series of raids across the border which
the Turks answered by a declaration of war.

Quick
defeat of
the Greeks.

If the Greek army was in a state of sad neglect, the army
of the Turks was at a relatively high level of efficiency since
it had recently been reorganized under the direction of a group
of German officers. The reorganization is memorable as marking the entering wedge of German influence in Turkey. Of this
more anon. Under the first impact of the Turks the Greek
army ignominiously collapsed. Seized with panic the Greeks
scattered in wild flight, while the elated Moslems, penetrating
into Thessaly, made ready to march on Athens. But at this
point the powers spoke up. They forced (May) an armistice
agreement on the combatants, which before the year was out
had been converted into a definitive peace. Greece was saved
from the consequences of her folly, but she had to submit to
slight rectifications of the Thessalian border in Turkey's favor
and to agree to pay a money indemnity.

Crete,
freed from
the Turks,
becomes self-
governing.

If the war brought no increase of either territory or honor
to the Greeks, it did indubitably effect the emancipation of
the Cretans from the Ottoman yoke. Carried to the island
by their desire to pacify it, the powers had induced the
Christian rebels to lay down arms on the solemn promise
of a genuine autonomy. Not without the usual delays they
now proceeded to redeem their pledge. By the end of 1898
they had obliged the sultan to withdraw his troops and
civil officials from the island and to be content with a merely
nominal authority. True, Austria and Germany, unwilling, for

reasons of their own, to put constraint upon the Porte, withdrew from the European concert, but as they made no attempt to cross the decisions of the remaining powers, the fate of Crete rested henceforth in the hands of the well-disposed chancelleries of London, Rome, Petrograd, and Paris. Hardly had the Turks departed when the four powers installed Prince George, second son of the king of Greece, as governor, thereby making open acknowledgment that the island was essentially Greek and Christian. Under a constitution, which, besides granting broad popular powers, attempted to put the rights of the Moslem minority on a secure basis, Prince George ruled for almost eight years. Toward the end of his governorship he met with difficulties, owing in part to his autocratic temper. He was relieved (1906) by a Greek commoner, Zaimes by name, who, with the consent of the powers, received his appointment from the king of Greece, and under whom the pacification of the island made such progress that the international troops of occupation were entirely withdrawn. None-the-less, and in spite of all improvements, political and economic, one issue remained which caused active discontent. The " Great Greek Island " continued to long for unrestricted union with the mother-country and until it had achieved its purpose there would be a Cretan problem in the world.

If Armenia and Crete attracted considerable attention in the post-Berlin period, it is understandable that when, toward the end of the century, disturbances broke out in Macedonia, they should have completely overshadowed the Cretan and Armenian troubles for the simple reason that Macedonia, owing to its central location, was the natural focus of the whole Balkan world. Of indeterminate boundaries Macedonia may be defined as the territory of the Vardar valley together with the dependent coastal strip dominated by the city of Saloniki. We are aware of the important rôle played by this area in the past, in that every power which had aspired to hold the peninsula in subjection had found itself obliged to dominate the great north–south thoroughfare. This control position explains, on the one hand, why the return of Macedonia to the Porte at the congress of Berlin effectively reconstituted the Ottoman empire and, on the other, why Abdul Hamid resolved at all costs to thwart the article in the treaty —

Macedonia the heart of Balkania.

Article XXIII — which promised Macedonia an autonomous régime. Occupied with other matters, the powers failed to oblige the sultan to execute his Macedonian engagement, but this indifference did not hinder the small neighboring states from concerning themselves with the province in their own interest. Prompted by both racial and political reasons, they directed their gaze to Macedonia and made preparations to take over such parts as lay convenient to their hand whenever the progressive collapse of the Porte should oblige it to retire from the Vardar.

The racial situation in Macedonia: Greeks and Slavs.

At this point it becomes indispensable to familiarize ourselves with the racial situation in this crucial area. If it was the most complicated to be found anywhere within the whole compass of the peninsula, this was due to the fact that all the successive Balkan migrations had passed through the Vardar corridor and that each had left a deposit behind. In this way Macedonia became a veritable museum of all the Balkan peoples. Although in some areas the various groups were all inextricably intermingled, it is pertinent to point out that in other sections a given race decidedly predominated. In the southern districts, for instance, and more particularly along the coast, the Greeks, a city people given to trade, had the upper hand, while to the north of them the Slavs, peasants for the most part working the soil, held sway. These Slavs may properly be considered as a special Macedonian group, but since they were closely related to both Bulgars and Serbs and had, moreover, in the past been usually incorporated in either the Bulgar or Serb state, they inevitably became the object of both Bulgar and Serb aspirations and an apple of bitter discord between these rival nationalities. As an oppressed people on an exceedingly primitive level, the Macedonian Slavs had as late as the congress of Berlin exhibited no perceptible national consciousness of their own. It was therefore impossible to foretell in what direction they would lean when their awakening came; in fact, so indeterminate was the situation that under favorable circumstances they might even develop their own particular Macedonian consciousness. With conditions thus unclarified, an enormous advantage accrued to the Bulgars in that they were the first to seize the opportunity of gaining the sympathy of the Vardar Slavs. In the seventies, even before

DISTRIBUTION
OF
BALKAN PEOPLES

Scale in miles

25   0   25   50   75   100

Slavs   Rumanians   Greeks

Magyars · 25 · · 30

Galatz

Romania · 45

Crajova

Bucharest

Danube R.

A a r i a n s

fia · BULGARIA · Turks

Philippopolis

S r k s · Adrianople

Turks · Scutari

Constantinople

40

Turks

Smyrna

Athens · 25

Turks · Albanians · Magyars · Germans

the Bulgar state had seen the light of day, they undertook to win the Macedonians to their cause by an amazingly competent propaganda conducted chiefly through church and school.

This Bulgar propaganda became so weighty a factor in Balkan affairs that it deserves to be examined, especially as it was presently copied by all the other Balkan peoples, thus producing a war of rival propagandas, which has not ceased to this day and which, incidentally, has developed terrors hardly second to those of a war conducted with shot and shell. The Bulgar point of departure was the sultan's famous firman of 1870 which constituted a national Bulgar church under its own primate called exarch. While in this edict only Bulgaria proper was staked off as the religious province of the new church, a clause provided that a petition of two-thirds of the Christian residents of any other district inhabited by Bulgars might secure its transfer from the patriarch to the exarch. On the strength of this provision Bulgar churchmen began an agitation in Macedonia which, before long, met with startling success. Long humiliated by the religious exploitation of the Greeks, the Macedonian Slavs lent a willing ear to the siren voices lisping their own speech and in increasing numbers looked to Bulgaria for deliverance from religious bondage. In the course of the seventies the struggle between patriarchists and exarchists was carried into every village of the Vardar valley and everywhere the patriarchists lost ground, owing to the popular aversion to the foreign, that is, the Hellenic priests. Not till early in the nineties, however, did the sultan act on the petitions with which he was bombarded and accord four Bulgar bishops to Macedonia, who, with their dependent priests, greatly extended the authority of the exarchate. A splendid ecclesiastical victory — but it did not persuade the Bulgars to rest on their oars. They followed it up with a system of popular schools, usually as adjuncts to the churches, and taught the rising generation the Bulgar language and history, with the result that it grew up imbued with a thorough-going Bulgar consciousness.

Not till the Bulgarization of a large section of the Macedonian Slavs was well under way did the Serbs take alarm and organize a propaganda in their turn. The area immediately across their southern boundary, known in Serb history as Old Serbia,

Method and success of the Bulgar propaganda.

Organization of the Serb and Greek propagandas.

possessed an unmistakable Serb element, which stood in no need of being converted to Serb nationalism; but when the Serb agents continued their southern march, penetrating into the upper Vardar valley, they encountered the Bulgar influence and were effectively halted. They did not for this reason give up but vigorously continued to struggle, often, for tactical reasons, allying themselves with the Greeks, whom the Bulgar aggressiveness had of course forced to organize their own national propaganda. Thus, before the close of the nineteenth century, Macedonia was the scene of a triangular struggle conducted chiefly with the tools of church and school for the conquest of the *mind* of the inhabitants; and if by that time the bulk of the Vardar Slavs had gone over to the Bulgar camp, the Serbs had at least managed to gain a foothold to the north of the Shar Dagh mountains, while the Greeks solidly maintained their traditional grip on the southern district contiguous to Thessaly.

Kutzo-Vlachs and Spanioles.

With the enumeration of Bulgars, Serbs, and Greeks we have not, however, exhausted the Macedonian racial situation. Most often perched in scattered highland villages were to be found a people of nomad habits known as Kutzo-Vlachs (Lame Vlachs). They belonged to the Orthodox church, spoke a Latin dialect, and were plainly related to the Rumanians. A propaganda, fostered from Bucharest, succeeded in creating a demand among them for a national church of their own, but, apart from this ecclesiastical agitation, had little effect, since the Kutzo-Vlachs were too few and too dispersed to figure in the general situation. Even less numerous and less important were the Jews. They were the descendants of members of their race exiled from Spain in the sixteenth century and welcomed by Solyman the Magnificent to Turkey, where they became known under the name of Spanioles. The Spanioles were to be found in the Macedonian towns as merchants, but were outstandingly important only in the single city of Saloniki, in which they constituted an indisputable majority of the population.

Albanians and Turks.

Of far greater significance than the two last-named groups were the Albanians. In the course of recent generations they had been slowly drifting from their highlands into western Macedonia and Old Serbia, in both of which regions they had come to constitute, toward the year 1900, a considerable element, perhaps a majority. As an illiterate and ill-organized mountain people, they neither possessed nor developed a propaganda, except that of the pistol and rifle. In the use of this form of moral suasion they were, however, remarkably expert, encouraged rather than hindered therein by the Turks, who were pleased to play into their hands on the ground of a common faith. As for the Turks themselves, aside from a handful of landlords called beys or begs, there were few to be found except in the army and civil service.

In these chaotic circumstances it was plain that, when the Ottoman régime broke down, as, before long, it was bound to do, Macedonia would fall not to its disunited inhabitants but to such neighboring states as were prepared to advance some sort of a moral claim to the land and would, at the same time, prove themselves strong enough to make the claim respected. As of neighbors of this type only Greece, Serbia, and Bulgaria entered into consideration, we are supplied with the reason why they were so feverishly engaged in applying the entering wedge of their respective propagandas. And now, toward the end of the nineties, as if to celebrate the approach of a new century, the triangular rivalry, which, if acrid, had been relatively peaceful, took on a new form. Tortured in spirit by the cry that rose from their oppressed nationals in Macedonia and disgusted with the indifference of the European powers, the men charged with the Bulgar propaganda and known as the Macedonian committee, determined to pass from words to action. They secretly organized armed bands, which, descending into the Vardar valley, waged private war on the Turk garrisons and officials, while at the same time overawing the patriarchist villages. When the Greeks heard of these outrages, they promptly followed the Bulgar example. Before long the whole countryside was in an uproar. To put an end to the destructive raids of the Greek and Bulgar brigands, fresh Turkish troops were loosed on the province, but, in spite of the ferocious punishment they meted out, they were wholly unable to ride the storm.

In deliberately plunging Macedonia into anarchy the Bulgar propaganda was chiefly moved by the desire to produce a strong reverberation in European public opinion. Since the powers were so criminally remiss, they were to be forced to concern

The Bulgar propaganda passes from words to deeds.

Interference by the powers and the Mürzsteg program, 1903.

themselves with the neglected province. And, strange to relate, the plan actually succeeded, for the wanton murders, the smoking villages, the epic misery of Macedonia which went ringing through the newspapers, were too gross to be ignored by even the most callous diplomats. Shufflingly, as usual, they took counsel, and in 1903 accepted the so-called Mürzsteg program elaborated by Austria and Russia in the name of all the powers. This program, which, because it had a unanimous Europe behind it, the sultan was obliged to accept, attempted to restore peace in the disturbed area by means of an internationally organized mounted police. Macedonia, which, as we have seen, was only a geographical term, corresponded approximately to the three Turkish vilayets of Kossovo, Monastir, and Saloniki. These vilayets were so apportioned among five of the powers — the sixth power, Germany, though giving tacit support, refused to participate — that each assumed responsibility for the public peace in its allotted sector, while coördinated action was secured by the creation of a central command.

The sultan
practically
displaced
but order
is not
achieved.
Although not long after this first interference the powers also imposed on the sultan an international commission for the control of Macedonian finances, it took some years for all the difficulties piled in the way of the new institutions to be removed. However, even after they had begun to operate they achieved only a comparative success, since the pestilential Greek and Bulgar bands stubbornly persisted. The best that can be said for the international organization is that it enforced peace within the immediate radius of the towns in which it set up its machinery. If it was a gain that the Turks were largely superseded as rulers of the country, the fact stands out that the animosities among the component ethnic groups, principally, it is true, among Bulgars and Greeks, but, to a lesser degree, also among Serbs, Kutzo-Vlachs, and Albanians, had become so unbridled that reason and common sense were set at naught, while the whole population indulged in an orgy of self-destruction. In this novel manner the Macedonians, vigorously abetted by the ring of neighboring governments, attempted to settle the vexed question as to who should succeed the sultan as ruler of the country. Small wonder that in the face of such fanaticism the international

organizations of police and finance were helpless to produce a comprehensive peace. Then suddenly, in 1908, the news was flashed from Constantinople of the Turkish revolution and the Macedonian situation underwent an immediate and dramatic change.

CHAPTER XXVIII

NEW PHASES OF EUROPEAN POLICY. — THE BAGDAD RAIL-WAY. — THE TURKISH REVOLUTION OF 1908

The official policy of Europe is "the integrity of the Ottoman empire."

THE Turkish revolution of 1908 was less the result of local conditions than of the powerful reverberation in Turkey of certain threatening developments of international politics. For a proper understanding of the upheaval it is therefore desirable to examine the later phases of European policy toward the Ottoman empire. Internationally, we are aware, the Moslem state, so far as the nineteenth century is concerned, reached its most favorable position in 1856 when the congress of Paris underwrote the sovereignty of the sultan and guaranteed his territory. But, as we have also learned, the diplomats took their pledges with familiar professional levity and, twenty-two years after the Paris conference, at the congress of Berlin, authorized the grave amputations which reduced the sultan to a very precarious state. None-the-less the action at Berlin, considered in all its bearings, was unmistakably inspired by the desire to save Turkey from its greatest enemy, Russia; and for many years following 1878, in fact down to the eve of the Great War, the foreign ministers of the powers never wearied of reiterating that their guiding star in all the affairs of the Near East was that curious will o' the wisp, the integrity of the Ottoman empire. Even the sultan's arch-enemy, Russia, frequently made the same profession and not necessarily in conscious and reprehensible bad faith. For the fact was that unless all the powers officially subscribed to a mutual engagement to uphold the Ottoman empire, they would be obliged to open a discussion regarding its partition, which would unescapably lead to diversity of opinion and, in the end, to a general war. From this dangerous prospect, however, they all shied away in instant alarm.

Under these circumstances the policy of hands off, imposed by the formula of the integrity of the Ottoman empire, appeared to be the only feasible official platform from which the concert of Europe might hope to discourse its harmonies. But, unfortunately, it was an insecure and dishonest platform, first, because whatever the diplomats stated or believed, the Ottoman empire was, in point of fact, in hopeless dissolution, and second, because the powers, all and severally, never hesitated to make mock of their vows whenever the general situation was such that an invasion of Turkish rights could be compassed without fear of spilling the apple-cart and precipitating the much-dreaded general conflict. Of this last consequence, in view of its catastrophic implications, they all had, as already said, a wholesome terror. But, short of war, each and all were ready for any move calculated to promote their particular interest.

The integrity convenient diplomatic fiction.

Examining the international situation from the height of the congress of Berlin, we can entertain no doubt that the central Ottoman issue was the Anglo-Russian rivalry and that the Russian offensive, directed at Constantinople and the straits, had been squarely defeated by Great Britain, largely because she enjoyed the support of the other powers, equally, or almost equally, interested with her in keeping the Russian bear from planting himself across one of the most commanding crossroads in the world. But the Anglo-Russian chapter is not the whole story of the European impact on the decaying Ottoman mass. There remain for consideration Austria and France with their more limited objectives. Ever since the days of Prince Eugene, Austria had persisted in her effort of southeastern penetration, to be blocked in her turn by Russia and, in the nineteenth century, by the ring of Balkan states, which Russia had helped call into being, in no small measure for the very purpose of creating an anti-Austrian barrier. Bosnia, conceded to the Hapsburgs in 1878, represented their most considerable advance into Balkania. As for France, she had in the nineteenth century directed her attention chiefly to two areas convenient to her hand. By means of a well-planned educational and religious propaganda she had acquired a strong moral influence in Syria, while in Algeria, lying directly across the Mediterranean from her own southern coast, she had applied not moral but straight military means to the end of effecting an unequivocal conquest. To be sure, the exhausted Porte had, as far back as the seventeenth

The Ottoman aims of Great Britain, Russia, France, and Austria.

century, been obliged to withdraw its hand from so remote a province as Algeria, but in 1830, when France launched her attack, the technical inclusion in the Ottoman empire of the whole north-African coast as far west as the border of Morocco was beyond legal challenge. The Algerian conquest undertaken by France turned out to be very difficult, owing to the independent spirit and the fighting qualities of the native tribes, but in the course of more than a generation it was accomplished with the result that France undertook to build up, around Algeria as a center, a vast African colonial empire.

Somewhat past the middle of the nineteenth century the whole near eastern question, owing to its transfusion with new elements, began gradually to take on a new aspect. In the first place the unification of Italy and Germany brought two new powers on the scene, which, as soon as they had become oriented with reference to the disturbing problem of the Porte, began to formulate their own Ottoman policies. As late as the congress of Berlin, however, these were still ill-defined, Italy fixing an uncertain eye on the African littoral and Germany being content to take her cue from Austria. More important, in fact far more important in lending a new face to European relations than even the advent of two new powers, was the vigorous and complicated movement conveniently summarized as the industrial revolution. Although this book is not the place for an analysis of this, the most transforming agency of our time, it is both proper and necessary to trace its effect on foreign policy. Up to the early nineteenth century commercial ambitions, coupled with conceptions of military and naval security, largely determined the near eastern attitude of the European powers. The proportion in which the elements of commerce and security were mixed differed in each case, but both elements were invariably present, producing a ferment sufficient to account for the very vigorous rivalry recorded in these pages. What the industrial revolution, with its release of new economic energy, brought about, can in substance be described as an intensification. The need for markets capable of absorbing the surplus home manufactures became more imperative than ever; with restless energy and a keen scent for a usurious profit capital sought promising investments in backward areas; and exploitation, in disguises ever

Intensification of European rivalry produced by the industrial revolution.

more Protean, seized upon the neglected resources of the whole globe in the hope of private wealth and power. Of this ever-waxing enterprise of an enormously stimulated individualist age the several governments became the natural champions, the more willingly as political control in each country was rapidly passing into the hands of the very group identified with manufacture, banking, and the other occupations brought to the front by the economic upheaval. The upshot was that the pace of European rivalry was greatly quickened and that the coveteousness, of which the Ottoman empire together with every other retarded area was the object, was stimulated almost to the point of frenzy. For this accelerated pace of European expansion the accepted name has come to be imperialism.

As a convenient date for uncovering the effects on the Ottoman situation of a full-fledged imperialism, the year 1878 with its great event of the congress of Berlin is fairly serviceable. Undeniably the congress was officially at pains to conceal the imperialist designs of its members; to this end it blew the breath of new life into the invalid sultan and appointed itself his protector. But did it not at the same time authorize his spoliation for the benefit, on the one hand, of Austria and Russia, and, on the other, of the small Christian states? Did it not accept without protest the extremely subtle arrangement by which England laid hands on the island of Cyprus? These departures from the line of action officially laid down may have been as inevitable as they were justified in a purely idealist sense, but they brought into relief the contradiction existing between profession and performance and gave a tremendous stimulus to the imperialist appetite. In any case, dating from Berlin, we have to deal with a period of fresh invasions of the sultan's rights, chiefly, owing to their accessibility by sea, in his Mediterranean provinces. In 1881, France, engaged in rounding off her African possessions, occupied Tunis, which, as had been the case with Algeria, was nominally, if no longer in strict fact, a Turkish province. In the very next year England occupied Egypt. This was a much more serious matter since Egypt was a colonial prize of the first order and an indubitable dependency of the sultan. Indeed, so great is the importance of the English seizure that we are obliged to scan it more narrowly.

New inroads on Turkish territory after 1878: the encroachments of France and Great Britain.

De Lesseps
with the
support of
Khedive
Ismail builds
the Suez
Canal, 1869.

When we last dealt with the land of the pharaohs, it was under the rule of the successful adventurer, Mehemet Ali, who, but for the interference of the powers, would have substituted his empire for that of the house of Osman. He had, in the end, to be content with the minor success of securing the pashalik of Egypt as an hereditary possession. One of his descendants, Ismail, who came to the throne in 1863, a generation after Mehemet's death, inherited some of the more showy talents of the founder. In place of pasha he adopted the more exalted title of khedive, and in the time he was able to spare from his absorbing pleasures he occupied himself with various projects for the development of Egypt. Or, it would be perhaps more correct to say, he was induced to lend his protection to projects which wide-visioned advisers from Europe brought to his notice. More particularly a Frenchman, de Lesseps by name, urged the building of a canal through the isthmus of Suez, and, with the khedive's approval, set about his monumental task. In 1869, the project planned as a private enterprise and carried through chiefly with French capital, was brought to a successful conclusion and inaugurated amidst elaborate ceremonies, in which the whole world participated. By reason of its considerably shortening (and cheapening) the journey to the Far East, the new waterway proved an immense boon to commerce and established itself at once in the public opinion of the world as an unqualified success. Besides, it conferred specific benefits, hardly to be exaggerated, on Egypt itself, for the ancient land of the pyramids, so long a country of the dead, suddenly found itself planted on one of the great lines of world communication and confronted with a brilliant future.

Great
Britain
acquires the
the canal
shares of
the khedive
and, to-
gether with
France,
takes over
financial
control of
Egypt.

The very brilliance of its prospects, however, became the country's political undoing. Through the Suez canal, essentially a private French enterprise, France seemed likely to become the chief European beneficiary of the Egyptian revival. Of course such a development was not at all to the taste of the sea-faring neighbors of the French, the English. Owing to her immense Asiatic interests, the Suez route was of paramount interest to England, though her statesmen, blind to their own advantage, had from the start and to their best ability discouraged the de Lesseps project. Now that the canal was built and in successful operation, they quickly changed their tune and, in 1875, succeeded in acquiring a belated foothold on the great east–west route. Through secret agents Disraeli, the then premier, quietly bought the total holdings in canal shares of Khedive Ismail, thereby at a stroke acquiring for the British government a weighty voice in the directorate. Only because of his terrible financial straits did Ismail agree to a transaction so injurious to his country. But, an incurable spendthrift, he had soon squandered the British gold and was obliged to continue to struggle in an ocean of debt which threatened to submerge him. In 1878 the French and British governments, yielding to the loud clamor of Ismail's creditors, bankers for the most part of London and Paris, interfered in his affairs by forcing him to accept their financial advice; and in the following year they brought pressure to bear upon the sultan resulting in Ismail's deposition and the proclamation of his son and successor, Tewfik.

No sooner had France and Great Britain established their dual financial control at Cairo than they were obliged to face a new difficulty in the form of a strong nationalist movement of protest. In 1882 this culminated in an irresistible revolt to the cry of "Egypt for the Egyptians." A native government was swept into office swayed by a strong animus against the two powers. After studying the altered situation for some time the London cabinet came to a decision and proposed to Paris a combined military intervention; and when France, unwilling to assume the risk, declined the offer, the British government went in alone. In 1882 the British fleet bombarded and captured Alexandria, and when a British army, forcing a landing, penetrated to Cairo, the nationalist movement collapsed like a punctured balloon. Though British statesmen repeatedly and solemnly pledged their word that the occupation was temporary and would come to an end as soon as order was restored, the plain fact was that a vigorous imperialist nation had come into possession of one of the most important nerve-centers of the world and that it would be breaking all known rules of political conduct if it surrendered such an advantage except under duress. From 1882 on Egypt was to all intents a British province.

The French and British successes, in Tunis and Egypt respectively, must have been highly calculated to stimulate the

The Egyptian revolt and the British occupation, 1882.

The
Russian
attention
concen-
trated for a
time on the
Far East.

ambition of Russia, since in all cases of rivalry the triumph of
one competitor invariably acts as a potent incentive to all the
others. It was the period after the treaty of Berlin when the
tsar, in spite of the limitations imposed on him by that document,
attempted to work out a system of Balkan control through a
submissive Bulgaria. We are aware of how all his plans in this
regard came to naught, chiefly because Bulgaria elected to be
that affliction, more bitter than a serpent's tooth, a thankless
child. In sullen irritation Russia temporarily withdrew her hand
from Bulgaria and all her other Balkan protégés, and, facing
eastward, gave her attention to a field which seemed to promise
less ambiguous rewards. There followed a hesitating commitment
to Chinese and Pacific projects, which became irrevocable when
Japan advanced into the arena as an imperialist rival and in
1895 assumed the leadership of the native East by a war which
laid China in the dust. From now on Russia and Japan stood
face to face, becoming ever more involved over the control of the
Pacific, until, in 1904, they resolved to put the issue to the arbitrament of arms. Russia's defeat followed and so seriously
checked her progress in the Far East that she was persuaded to
give her attention once more to interests nearer home. Exclusively
absorbed by her prospects in China, she had for over a decade
played a passive rôle in Balkania, not, however, without first
acquiring a certain security against her leading rival, Austria.
In 1898 Vienna and Petrograd signed an agreement pledging
themselves to undertake nothing against each other in Balkania
or against the *status quo*. Accordingly, when the Macedonian
troubles broke out, the two cabinets adopted a disinterested and
coöperative attitude and elaborated the plan of pacification already familiar to us as the Mürzsteg program (1903). But it was
a question how long this unusual team-work would continue. Immediately after her check in Manchuria Russia gave signs of a
revived interest in the Near East, and Austria, as if stimulated
by the Russian activity, began at the same time jealously to
quicken her diplomatic pace.

The temporary self-elimination of Russia supplied a splendid
opportunity to effect a lodgment in the Balkan world to a power,
which, since its achievement of unity in 1871, had, politically
and economically, been advancing with gigantic strides. I refer

of course to Germany. Almost immediately after her victory over France the prevailing imperialist point of view began to exercise an irresistible charm on her people and slowly to push the government into colonial projects and world politics. Conspicuous among the various openings of an imperialist nature which beckoned over the face of the globe was the Near East, where the Ottoman carcass was being attacked, on the one hand, by the great powers, and on the other, by the small Balkan nationalities, lately risen from the dead. On fastening her attention on this area, Germany could not fail to take note that the western stretch of African coast had been preëmpted by France, while England had ensconced herself in Egypt and along the all-important waterway of Suez. Between French Tunis and British Egypt intervened the wide and unprofitable desert of Tripoli. Subject to the sultan but really belonging only to the Arab tribes which moved across its sun-scorched wastes, it was known to be ear-marked by Italy, which would take it over in its own good season. As for Austria, she was engaged in digesting the Bosnian dish prepared for her at the congress of Berlin, while Russia by a hundred years of effort had indicated that the goal of all her Balkan strivings was the key position of the straits.

Under these circumstances Germany, last come among the powers, resolved to stake out an Ottoman claim as little likely as possible to conflict with older claims, validated by proximity and custom: she chose Asia Minor. There had by that time, through the experience of the older colonizing powers, been worked out a successful technic by which a great state with military and naval power and with a flourishing capitalist régime might acquire a foothold in a backward country to be transformed, by slow accumulations, into a more or less veiled control. That technic, involving a gradual multiplication of contacts with Asia Minor and its government, Germany now began to set in motion. The moment, as already said, was auspicious, for Russia was occupied with the Far East, while Great Britain, having fortified her position in the Mediterranean beyond her boldest dreams through the occupation of Egypt, showed a declining interest in Turkey and withdrew from the close association with the sultan maintained through the nineteenth cen-

German military and economic penetration.

tury. A vacuum, as it were, had been created at Constantinople which Germany rushed in to fill. As was to be expected, the movement was gradual and unobserved, though
it had its dramatic moments. Early in the eighties a door
was opened to German military influence through the invitation extended by the Porte to a German military mission
to reorganize the Ottoman army. Its head, the very capable
General von der Goltz, soon became a conspicuous figure at
Stambul. At the same time German commercial travelers invaded
the Ottoman markets and German banks opened branches in the
leading cities. Then, in 1890, Emperor William II, recently come
to the throne, paid his respects to the sultan in a much heralded
visit, which clearly revealed that he regarded the Ottoman empire
as an object of special interest. Sultan Abdul Hamid, flattered
by the unusual honor of entertaining a western sovereign,
responded to William's advances by extending to Germany and
German enterprises his particular favor. The first step had been
taken toward a Turco-German understanding.

German railway enterprise culminates in the Bagdad line. In the course of the decade following the Kaiser's visit, German
enterprise, while expanding in all directions, concentrated more
and more on the building of railroads in Asia Minor. That
vast and potentially wealthy province was practically inaccessible
from any quarter, owing to the total absence of modern means of
communication. True, an English company had received and
exercised a concession to build a short railroad out of Smyrna,
but the capital, Constantinople, was wholly without an avenue
of penetration eastward other than a very decrepit highway. In
the early nineties a German company, starting at Haidar Pasha,
opposite Stambul, built a line to Angora and followed this up
(1896) with a southeastern extension reaching as far as the old
Seljuk capital of Konia. Delighted with these results, the sultan
was very desirous to extend the system beyond Asia Minor to
Mesopotamia, and the German capitalists, now well entrenched
in his favor, were the more ready to comply with his wish as
they were assured of a contract yielding an exceedingly handsome
profit. The outcome was the line to Bagdad, for which the
first charter was granted in 1899, probably as the direct
consequence of a second and even more theatrical appearance of
Emperor William at Constantinople in the previous year.

Frequently revised, the Bagdad concession did not receive its final form till 1903, when, with all obstacles removed from the path, construction began in earnest. It proceeded rapidly from Konia southeastward until it struck the Taurus mountains, where the engineering difficulties encountered were of such an order that the last tunnel had not yet been pierced at the outbreak of the Great War.

The excitement and uproar manifested in France and England by press and parliament, when the full significance of the Bagdad project reached the bankers and business men, can hardly be exaggerated. If it had been just the question of a backward province to be opened up by the enterprise of a single national group, seeing that such a game was familiar to all the powers and a recognized mode of imperialism, a manifestation of jealousy might have been reasonably expected but hardly a prolonged and violent agitation. The fact was that in its ulterior implications the German railway scheme was much more than the economic subjugation of just Asia Minor: it looked far beyond that peninsula to Mesopotamia and the Persian gulf. In short, it opened up the highway between Europe and Asia traveled ever since the dawn of civilization by a steady procession of peoples and empires. Fallen into neglect and abandonment under somnolent Turkey, this route, traversed by a modern railway, would offer an unexampled opportunity to an enterprising people like the Germans not only for dominating the markets of the Near East but also for reaching the teeming populations of southern and eastern Asia. Even the water-route *via* the Suez canal seemed in the eyes of the English business men suddenly to lose some of its splendor on being set against an overland project which, when complete, would with an enormous saving of time carry passengers and goods from Hamburg and Berlin to the very door of India. And if, as was by no means excluded, the German government should at some future time replace the German railway company, thereby converting an economic into a political agency, not only the Indian markets but India itself would be imperilled.

It was this unmeasured prospect, promising Germany an enormous advantage in the frenzied imperialist race, which threw such consternation into the ranks, primarily of the

Real significance of the Bagdad project.

Instead of
being inter-
nationalized
the
Bagdadbahn
is carried
through as
a German
enterprise.

English, and, to a less degree, of the French commercial groups.
And without doubt their instinct was justified, for the Bagdad
line was probably the most valuable single prize still unappropriated in our day in the colonial world. For this reason it
should from the first have been internationalized, that is, have
been made available on equal terms to all. But — one of the
grave defects of the intense nineteenth century movement of
civilization — a generally acceptable form for international
enterprises had not yet been elaborated, and when the German
Bagdad syndicate, alarmed at the outcry in France and England, invited French and English capital to participate in the
enterprise, the London and Paris cabinets, under pressure
from an excited public opinion and against their own better
judgment, forbade their national banking houses to accept
the offer. It was not the first time — nor the last — that
popular emotions proved a poor guide for responsible statesmen, for the project, now abandoned to the Germans, became
an object of German glorification and tended irresistibly to
assume the character of a German monopoly. There were many
conflicts of rival national ambitions in the generation before
the war, but not one of them contributed to the poisoning of
the political atmosphere in anything approaching the same degree
as the *Bagdadbahn*. Certain, on its purely economic side, to
prove an immeasurable boon in waking the slumbering peoples
of the East to new life, it was turned into a curse for East and
West alike by becoming an object of political contention among
governments and peoples crazed by imperialist ambition.

Russia
takes alarm
and seeks
touch with
Great
Britain
and France.

From the diplomatic quarrel over the Bagdad railway, Russia,
fully occupied with her far eastern plans, stood at first somewhat aloof. But when, after her defeat at the hands of Japan
(1905), she once more took up the threads of her Balkan policy,
she immediately assumed an unfriendly attitude to German
penetration of Asia Minor. What particularly wounded the
susceptibilities of the tsar was the conviction that, in measure
as the Bagdad railway became a great east-west artery, the
German influence must continue to grow at Constantinople, and
that in consequence he would wake up some morning to find as
formidable an enemy as ever England had proved to be, blocking
the Black sea outlet at the straits. In grave alarm Petrograd

instinctively sought touch with Paris and London, and as Paris and London were agitated by similar suspicions in their own behalf, the diplomatic atmosphere was prepared which served to bring about the famous Triple entente.

The formation of the Triple and Dual alliances.

Although, as students of Balkan affairs, we are solely concerned with the imperialist impact on the Ottoman empire, arrived at this juncture, we must none-the-less take a wider view of the world situation and note that the powers were simultaneously embroiled at numerous other points. Some of these issues, as for instance, over China, Persia, and Morocco, belong to exactly the same category as Turkey, that is, they were quarrels over the control of backward areas in the colonial field outside Europe. But there were also older disputes, lying nearer at home and considerably antedating the rise of modern imperialism, as for instance, the Alsace-Lorraine question between France and Germany, the *Italia Irredenta* question between Italy and Austria, and the Polish independence question particularly interesting to Russia. Both these groups of issues played a part in the diplomatic thrust and counter-thrust of the powers and had, even before the Bagdad conflict became acute, produced an alignment which is essential to our story. Between 1879 and 1883 the three central European states, Germany, Austria, and Italy, had, largely under Prince Bismarck's direction, formed the Triple alliance, by virtue of which each member pledged itself to come to the other's support in case of attack. About a decade later — in 1892, to be exact — France and Russia, the remaining continental powers, resolved to balance the Triple alliance by means of a dual partnership. That left Great Britain, unwilling to commit herself to either group, in "splendid isolation."

Great Britain inaugurates a policy of alliances, first with Japan, then with France.

At the beginning of the twentieth century, however, Great Britain's leading public men made up their minds that the long-standing isolation of their country, ceasing to be splendid, had become directly dangerous. Great Britain had interests all around the globe over which diplomatic clashes with rival powers were both severe and frequent. Cases in point are the conflicts with France on the upper Nile (Fashoda incident, 1898) and with Russia in central Asia and northern China (both before and after 1900). With Germany, too, her relations had become strained, owing to the increasing flood of German goods, in-undating the markets of the world, coupled with the German determination to build a formidable navy. In the hope of achieving a greater security the London cabinet gradually came to the conclusion that it would be the part of wisdom to re-place the policy of isolation for one of alliances, and turned, first of all, to Japan. But the Anglo-Japanese treaty (1902) was limited in its action to the Pacific and left broad British interests unprotected. To safeguard these the support of an European state was necessary, and for some time Great Britain hesitated to come to a decision as between France and Germany. At last, in 1904, the choice fell in favor of France and an Anglo-French treaty inaugurated an understanding or entente by boldly disposing of two imperialist issues which had in the past caused much bad blood between the contracting parties. In return for a free hand in Morocco, France agreed to withdraw all claims from Egypt, thus conceding to England the unchallenged mastery of that eminently strategical position.

The Anglo-Russian agreement over Persia, 1907.

From the moment of this happy reconciliation France had a lively interest to bring about a similar understanding between England and her ally, Russia. Accordingly she was delighted when, in 1907, Great Britain and Russia ended a vicious, long-standing feud over Persia by substantially dividing the realm of the shah between them. Manifestly Great Britain, France, and Russia were forming a lucrative imperialist partnership, which, while disposing of certain colonial areas on the principle of *do ut des,* had, however, no apparent reference to Turkey and the Bagdad railway. But, apart from the dates, which in them-selves speak volumes, from the coming of the new century the Asia Minor venture of Germany so completely dominated the diplomatic situation in Europe and produced such a turmoil of opposition in London, Paris, and Petrograd that it may safely be accepted as the, of course, not sole, but certainly leading cause of the Franco-Anglo-Russian engagements of 1904-7, which gradually expanded into the Triple entente.

The Young Turks.

In the spring of 1908 the members of the Triple entente were known to be giving their attention to the Ottoman empire, more particularly to Macedonia, whose stubborn anarchy had long been a bloody stain on Europe. There was therefore reason to expect a more vigorous intervention in the Vardar area, and if the prospect alarmed the sultan, it also filled with misgiving the group of the Young Turks. The Young Turks were his majesty's opposition party, which was made up chiefly of young men with a varnish of European culture and a set aversion for the immobile ways of the older Ottoman generation, derisively called the Old Turks. In fact the Young Turks were native reformers who had arrived at the conclusion that their country could only be saved by a policy of deliberate Europeanization. Ever since the days of the Sultan Mahmud there had been, we are aware, a party of reform in the empire, though it had usually been weak and its triumphs ephemeral. Under the reactionary Abdul Hamid the reformers had been systematically persecuted, but most of the leaders, making their escape from the country, foregathered in foreign parts and continued their agitation. By newspapers, pamphlets, and secret agents they gradually won over to their side many elements of the rising generation, not difficult to convince, in view of Turkey's manifest decline, that the old régime was hopelessly out of fashion.

The greatest success achieved by the agitators was their conversion of many army officers, for precisely from these the blow fell which brought down the rotten throne of the sultan. Made bold by reports of the rapid progress of their propaganda among the more enlightened elements of the population, the conspirators, in 1906, transferred their headquarters from Paris to Saloniki. They were still discussing various plans for a rising when the prospect of a new Macedonian intervention, championed by the Triple entente, coupled with a number of incidents of a purely local character, moved them to strike without further delay. Military uprisings, begun among the regiments stationed in Macedonia, spread like wild-fire, the Young Turk officers setting the pace and raising everywhere the cry for a constitution. So large was the section of the army infected with the revolutionary virus that Sultan Abdul Hamid at once gave up all idea of resistance. On July 24, 1908, bewildered by the rapid march of events, he issued a decree reinvigorating the constitution, the suppression of which had been one of the earliest acts of his reign; at the same time he published a writ summoning a national parliament. Without resistance and without

The Turkish revolution of 1908.

bloodshed the vicious absolutism of the sultan, because its time was ripe, crashed to the ground, to be replaced by a constitutional régime of an occidental pattern which it fell to the lot of the successful rebels, the Young Turks, to put into working order.

Unfounded expectations aroused by the event.

It is almost impossible to exaggerate the rejoicing with which the news of the Turkish revolution was received within and without the empire. Even in that human inferno of Macedonia all strife ceased at once, while Christians and Mohammedans, Bulgars and Greeks, Albanians and Serbs passionately embraced in church, mosque, and public square, comporting themselves as if they verily believed that all men had become brothers. It was a delirium, which it was necessary to have seen to accept as a fact, and which, like all emotional extravagances, involved a colossal self-deception. For, the day or the week following the festival of fraternization, the people would be sure to awaken from their intoxication and, suddenly sobered, to make the discovery that the world was not materially changed by reason of an ecstasy. Bulgars would be found to be Bulgars, Turks would still be Turks, while Greeks, Armenians, and Serbs would think and feel exactly as they did before a millennial prospect disclosed itself at the sound of a magic word, the word constitution. But far more strange and unaccountable than the excited aberration of the backward peoples of Turkey, was the fact that large and important circles of Europe were seized with the same folly. Serious political journals spoke gravely of a democratic miracle, and Sir Edward Grey, foreign minister of Great Britain, ventured the amazing prophecy that "the Macedonian question and others of a similar character will entirely disappear." The Turkish revolution was not the only incident supplying evidence that a considerable section of the peoples of Europe dwelt before 1914 in a complete fools' paradise.

The Young Turks, above all, passionate nationalists.

To us, fully acquainted with the desperate Ottoman conditions, it must be clear that, far from being curable by political sleight of hand, they could be remedied only by the most devoted and persistent labor extending over generations. Even if the Young Turks, who took over the wreck of the old régime, had been much more intelligent and experienced than they were, they would have been confronted by a task beyond their strength. For in substance they were called upon to shatter and recast in a western mold a bankrupt oriental state and society, and that, in the nature of the case, could not be done by a body of legislators operating with paper decrees. It would have to be achieved, if at all, through the slow action of time. It throws no discredit on the Young Turks to say of them that they were average products of their environment — human, all too human. If they enthusiastically mouthed the current phrases about liberty and democracy, they were not on this account minded to set free the divers peoples of the realm and thus effectively to break up the empire. Together with western constitutionalism they had absorbed western nationalism in its most uncompromising form. A constitution there should be, according to them, and full civil rights for all the former subject peoples, but in return for these gifts, the Christians would be expected to become loyal citizens of the empire, accepting with their new rights the common duties of Ottomans. As soon as the Greeks, Bulgars, and other oppressed groups discovered that this was the Young Turk interpretation of the revolution, they fell away from it in dismay. One thing they were quite sure about in all the vague and ecstatic talk about freedom, and that was that freedom meant freedom from the Turks. In their eyes it was nothing less than an insult for the Young Turks to attempt to reduce all the antagonistic racial elements to a dead level of Ottomanism. The early revival of Christian opposition was therefore inevitable.

The irrepressible domestic conflict was delayed for some months by the uncertainty of the Young Turk tenure and the persistence under the surface of reactionary tendencies. Abdul Hamid had been scotched but not killed. True to his nature he continued to plot for power and in April, 1909, with the aid of certain regiments in Constantinople sympathetic to his cause, he suddenly emerged from the obscurity into which the revolution had plunged him. However, the sentiment of both nation and army was in its vast majority now emphatically arrayed against him. The revolutionary troops dispersed the sultan's satellites and Abdul himself, taken prisoner, was unceremoniously deposed. Thereupon the victors proclaimed his younger brother sultan under the title Mohammed V. As the new sovereign was a harmless imbecile, broken by years, the Young Turks, or rather the Com-

Last resistance followed by the abdication of Abdul Hamid, 1909.

mittee of Union and Progress, as the party organization of the reformers was called, became the undisputed master of the situation.   Henceforth, with nothing more to fear from the Old Turks, the Young Turk policy could be energetically applied.   As soon, however, as the Young Turks undertook to show their hand, the era of inter-racial good-will, with which the revolution had been inaugurated, was certain to terminate abruptly.

CHAPTER XXIX

THE ANNEXATION OF BOSNIA AND THE EUROPEAN CRISIS OF 1908.— DOMESTIC POLICY OF THE YOUNG TURKS.— REVOLT OF ALBANIA.

BEFORE pursuing further the domestic developments in the Ottoman empire, we must give our attention to the European crisis, which followed on the heel of the Turkish revolution and which shook the continent to its foundation. The naïve but general expectation in Europe was that the reform about to be taken in hand by the Young Turks would rejuvenate the state and again make the Ottoman empire a power to be reckoned with. To this delusion the Committee of Union and Progress itself helped give force by talking glibly and confidently about an early resumption of Ottoman authority over Crete, Bulgaria, and Bosnia. These were all areas which since 1878 had been detached from the Porte, though the sultan still exercised a shadowy sovereignty over them. The boastful rhetoric of the successful reformers created alarm and led to three significant acts calculated to clip the wings of Turkish ambition. On October 5, 1908, in the ancient capital of Tirnovo, Prince Ferdinand of Bulgaria declared his country free of the last vestige of dependence on the sultan and, in sign of his new status, took the title of tsar; on October 7 the Austrian emperor finally and fully annexed Bosnia and Herzegovina; and on October 12 the Cretan assembly voted its union with the kingdom of Greece.

The Cretan act, being merely the reaffirmation of a position to which the Christian population had long ago unanimously subscribed, produced no particular commotion. The Greeks of the island and those of the kingdom were willing to be joined in holy matrimony, but the sea yawned between them and until the powers, which dominated the Mediterranean, gave their blessing to the union, it could not be consummated. As, instead of blessing the match, Europe continued to frown upon it, the

455

resolution of the Cretan assembly had no effect except once more to inform the world of the passionate Greek sentiment of the islanders.

Bulgarian independence secured by a Turk-Bulgar treaty.

The Bulgar action created a more serious situation, but even the Young Turks did not in their heart of hearts believe that they stood the smallest chance to recover their lost position in the principality. They therefore contented themselves with raising the question of an indemnity, asking of course more for the surrender of their faint prerogatives than the Bulgars were willing to pay. When the situation became deadlocked, Russia, which had returned to its earlier rôle of Bulgar champion, stepped in as mediator and by magnanimously paying, out of her own claims on Turkey, the difference between the Ottoman demand and the Bulgar offer, perfected an accommodation. In April, 1909, the treaty was signed by which the sultan recognized the full sovereign status of Bulgaria.

Austria and Bosnia, 1878–1908.

It was chiefly Austria-Hungary's annexation of Bosnia which made Europe rock with a crisis, which afterwards was correctly recognized to have been in effect a rehearsal for the fateful drama of July and August, 1914. Considered by itself the Austrian act was not particularly important. Thirty years before, at the congress of Berlin, Austria had been authorized to " occupy and administer " Bosnia and had in the interval performed a fairly satisfactory piece of civilizing work. The country had been pacified, an orderly system of finance and justice had been introduced, roads, even railroads, had been built, and the standard of living had been carried to a higher level. In short, the worst of the age-old abuses had been swept away. On the other hand, self-government had been denied the people on the ground that they were not yet ripe for it especially in view of the serious religious divisions among them. In this connection it will be remembered that although the members of the Orthodox church constituted the strongest single group and, with the Catholics added to their number, secured to the Christians a majority of the population, the Moslems made up a minority, which had distinctly to be reckoned with both because of its size and of its ancient prestige as a ruling class. While by the terms of the treaty of Berlin the Austrian occupation was only provisional, no responsible person in Europe dreamed that it was other than permanent. When therefore, after thirty years of secure possession, Austria declared that she would henceforth disregard the slight bond of Turkish suzerainty, she would have caused no more than a diplomatic ripple if the Bosnian question had not possessed highly explosive implications.

Destiny, pursuing as ever its deliberate march, had brought it about that at the very moment when Austria thought to perfect her hold on Bosnia, this territory assumed a position of crucial significance in connection with two issues, to which the age was peculiarly responsive. Seen from one angle Bosnia was a nationalist, from another an imperialist issue. Both angles call for a detailed discussion. Taking the nationalist angle first, we may remind ourselves that Bosnia was an element of the general Serb problem, and that this had emphatically been brought home to Europe in 1876, when, on the occasion of the rising of the peasants in Bosnia and Herzegovina, Serbia, moved by racial sympathy, had declared war against the Ottoman empire. Having suffered defeat, she was given little consideration in connection with the peace negotiations; and when, at the congress of Berlin, the two provinces came up for discussion, they were without more ado assigned to Austria, the power which had long aspired to possess them. It was a decision typical of diplomatic mentality, since it frankly set aside the claims of nationalism in favor of the expansion policy of a great power. Serbia, finding no friends among the Berlin conferees, had to submit, though wounded in her deepest sentiments.

The decades immediately following the congress of Berlin constitute a very depressing chapter of Serb history. True, Serbia had not been wholly neglected at Berlin, for, in addition to a slight territorial increase, she had been relieved of the last bonds tying her to Turkey. In consequence she felt encouraged to assume a higher status and had transformed herself from a principality to a kingdom. But her guidance, under Milan I, was peculiarly unfortunate. Not only did the king, pushed, it must be admitted, by the clamor of the people, engage (1885) in a very discreditable war with Bulgaria, but the looseness of his private morals and his open quarrels with his Russian wife became one of the chief and most succulent subjects of contemporary European scandal. Unable further to confront the

Bosnia, becomes 1) a nationalist, 2) an imperialist issue.

Serbia under the last Obrenovichs.

opprobrium visited upon him, Milan resigned in 1889 in favor of his son Alexander, a minor. It may be doubted if the change denoted an improvement. In 1893, at the age of sixteen, Alexander seized the power by ousting the regents set over him, and forthwith began a career which revealed a violent and autocratic temper. His people were already as sick of him as they had been of his father, when, in 1900, he insulted them past forgiveness by marrying a very questionable woman, the widow of an engineer, whom he officially installed in the palace as Queen Draga. The general disgust went so far that when, to put an end at last to his vagaries, a band of conspirators murdered him and his consort under circumstances of revolting brutality, the vile deed was hailed in Belgrad with demonstrations of public joy.

The accession of Peter I.

As King Alexander was the last of the line of the Obrenovichs, the representative of the rival Karageorgevich line was called to the throne as Peter I (1903-21). The new sovereign was a reputable man, who helped gradually to disperse the cloud of dishonor which had settled over the country during the reigns of Milan and Alexander; but far more important in rehabilitating Serbia in the eyes of Europe than any question of personalities was its sudden accidental elevation to a central area of conflict between the two rival groups of the Triple alliance and Triple entente. And therewith we touch upon the imperialist aspect of the Bosnian crisis of 1908 and the association with it of Serbia and the whole race of the Serbs.

Serbia and the Bagdad railway.

It was in the very year in which Peter I ascended the throne that the Ottoman government granted a private German company the concession to build the Bagdad railway. While we are aware of the brilliant prospects unfolded by this enterprise and of the loud reverberation caused by the Turco-German friendship in the countries competing with Germany for imperialist prizes, we have not yet examined the specifically European implications of the Bagdad scheme. The actual mileage to be built by the German company had, to be sure, to do only with Asia, but if the Asiatic line was to achieve its maximum utility and become a vast intercontinental thoroughfare, it would have to be tied up with various European systems all the way to Berlin and Hamburg. Such a program involved a friendly coöperation not only between

Turkey and Germany, but also among the intermediate states of Austria-Hungary, Serbia, and Bulgaria. As Austria-Hungary was Germany's ally and Bulgaria not unfriendly to Berlin, the outlook for a far-reaching coöperative railway enterprise was promising indeed except for the single link of Serbia. This little kingdom would naturally scent in the increased Austro-German influence, which a flourishing east–west route was sure to bring about, a threat addressed to its independence.

The uncompromising attitude of Serbia obliges us to give our attention to the development of her relationship with her immediate neighbor, Austria. At no time in their history had their association been really intimate and trustful for the simple reason that no small state dwells comfortably in the shadow of a great military power. If Serbia in her frequent helplessness needed a protector, she usually preferred to apply to Russia, first, because Russia was remote, and second, because the heart of Russia, as a Slav and Orthodox power, might be supposed to nurse a fraternal feeling for the Serbs. Undoubtedly Austria, in order to curry favor with the Serbs, did her neighbor an occasional good turn. As late as 1885 she interposed in the Serb-Bulgar war and saved King Milan from the worst consequences of his defeat. As a matter of fact King Milan throughout his reign consistently leaned on Austria in the conviction that the friendship of the great Hapsburg monarchy was the best guarantee of Serb security. But the policy, pursued, though in a modified form, also by Alexander, always had numerous native opponents and, in the end, was submerged under the flood of opprobrious rancor which buried from sight everything carrying the taint of the hated house of Obrenovich.

So far as the Serb people is concerned the issue between them and the Hapsburg monarchy was decided once and for all when, in 1878, Austria occupied Bosnia and Herzegovina. This was an invasion of Serb territory which threatened to render impossible the realization of the nationalist ideal of a union of all the Serbs. In this plan the existing kingdom of Serbia figured as no more than a nucleus, to which, in the course of time, should be attached not only the Serbs of Montenegro, Macedonia, and Bosnia, but even those lying across the Danube and subject historically to the house of Hapsburg. When we reflect that in

The relations of Austria and Serbia.

Bosnia an apple of discord between Serbia and Austria.

these speculations the house of Hapsburg was to be ultimately deprived of its Serb sections, we can measure the indignation of the patriots, who saw their cherished dream shattered by the initiation of an inverted process of absorption, of which the first step was the assimilation of Bosnia to the Austro-Hungarian monarchy. By the time the Obrenovichs fell, the patriots had succeeded in massing the whole population of the kingdom solidly under the banner of nationalism, and Peter I, on assuming office, was left in no doubt that the only popular foreign policy was an unflinching anti-Austrianism. Enraged by the new official tone, the Viennese government met it with bungling ineptitude. It raised a customs barrier against Serb exports, and as these were chiefly pigs, there followed the grotesquely amusing but cantankerous pig-war (1905-7), in which the last remnant of decent neighborly feeling received its death-blow. Henceforth the fires of Serb nationalism burned without check.

Serbia a meeting-point of imperialist cross-currents.

If we now recall that the pig-war synchronized with the German Bagdad concession and the formation of the Triple entente, we shall fully understand how this narrowly circumscribed economic conflict came to be raised to the level of an international issue. Russia, with her revived interests in Balkan affairs and her newly aroused alarm at the growth of Austro-German influence at Constantinople, put herself in the matter of the pig-war behind Serbia and encouraged her resistance to Austrian demands, while Russia's associates, France and Great Britain, stood by as silent aiders and abettors. Only this powerful backing explains the bold and courageous front with which Serbia faced her great opponent. Little Belgrad had, with bewildering suddenness, become a leading diplomatic center of contentious Europe. Since the city was the natural gateway from Europe to Balkania, Austro-German plans, looking to ascendancy in the Near East, would, if blocked at this point, become paralyzed. Not only Berlin and Vienna were aware of this, but in no less degree Petrograd, London, and Paris. Hence at this vital crossroads the great counter-currents of European ambition came together and, amidst a loud roar, flung out a cloud of spray, in which Serbia, a pigmy among giants, was practically buried from sight.

Into a situation already strained to the breaking-point Austria in October, 1908, flung the annexation of Bosnia and immediately released a commotion which shook Europe like an earthquake. On the surface the act signified an injury of Turkey, and the irritated Young Turks were prompt to enter a protest. But as between Austria and the Ottoman empire the issue was not serious, for the Young Turks were intelligent enough to recognize that Bosnia was lost to them in any event; and, after a vigorous cannonade of official declarations to cover their retreat, they agreed to come to terms with Vienna on the basis of a money indemnity and the evacuation by Austria of the sanjak of Novibazar. This narrow district, it will be remembered, Austria, since 1878, had held in military occupation.

The perilous crisis of 1908. The Austro-Turk agreement.

But Serbia and its friendly protectors of the Triple entente were by no means minded to permit the Bosnian incident to be closed with an Austro-Turk accommodation. As one man and in entire independence of what Turkey might see fit to do or not to do, the Serbs rose to protest against hated Austria fortifying her position in a land which, although technically lost to them, they still claimed on the score of nationality. At the same time they appealed to the entente and the entente gave them an interested and vigorous support. Moreover, as Austria had committed an undeniable breach of the treaty of Berlin, the cabinets of Petrograd, Paris, and London could take excellent legal ground in frowning on Austria's annexation. But as Austria, in her turn, had the backing of her ally, Germany, she felt encouraged unflinchingly to maintain her stand. The result was that an immense agitation seized alike upon governments and peoples in Europe threatening from moment to moment to precipitate that general war, of which everybody had for years been talking and which everybody professed to abhor. It was a bitterly tense season, the winter of 1908-9, but in the end war was avoided. Great Britain, not yet firmly wedded to the entente and doubtful of the wisdom of involving herself in an issue so far from her shores, gradually withdrew her support from Serbia. When France followed Great Britain's lead Russia, left alone, continued for some time to hesitate in view of the loss of Balkan prestige that her abandonment of Serbia would be sure to occasion. In March, 1909, a German note delivered at Petrograd, announcing German support of Austria in every eventuality, decided the issue, and reluctantly the Russian

The Bosnian crisis becomes general and rocks Europe.

foreign office advised Serbia to accept the accomplished fact. Troubled Europe heaved a sigh of relief: the crisis had passed. But as the contending forces and issues which centered at Belgrad remained absolutely the same, as nothing even approaching a cure of an evil situation had been effected, it was as certain as fate that the Bosnian crisis would make an early reappearance.

Disastrous consequences of the policy of Ottomanization. We may profitably utilize the breathing-spell which Europe was afforded by returning to a consideration of the domestic affairs of Turkey. In the Liberal opinion of the world the task before the Young Turks was to reorganize their empire along western lines by endowing it with a parliament, constitutional liberties, a public school system, and the other characteristic institutions of civilization. To this program, in so far as their limited intelligence was able to grasp it, the Young Turks themselves subscribed, but with the significant addition of Ottomanization. By this they meant the voluntary assumption by all the subjects of the empire, Moslems and Christians alike, of the full duties of citizenship coupled with a loyal support of the government. Furthermore, on its purely administrative side Ottomanization involved an intense centralization, that is, substantially the continuation of the old, familiar despotism under another name. To this policy the Young Turks were prompted by their fiery nationalism, and failed to reflect that, instead of appeasing the insidious racial rancor, they were choosing the course most certain to lash it to renewed fury. As soon, therefore, as the first enthusiasm for the revolution had effervesced, except the Turks themselves, no people could be found which was willing to lend a hand to rebuild the empire. Before long events occurred in widely separated districts which proved that nothing had been essentially changed under the new régime. As early as April, 1909, an abominable massacre of several thousand Armenians took place in Cilicia, which, like the Armenian massacres of the preceding decade, was systematically provoked by the Moslem authorities. At the same time in Syria, preponderantly Mohammedan though it was, a home rule movement gained ground, while in Arabia, the Holy Land of Islam, a rebellion occurred which aimed at nothing less than complete Arab independence.

Grave as were these incidents in the Asiatic provinces, they were completely put in the shade by what happened in Europe. As we have already noted, in that racial hotbed of the peninsula, in Macedonia, the revolution had, on its first appearance, precipitated a mania for fraternization. Even the abundantly cynical statesmen of Europe were so convinced of the coming of the millennium that they dissolved the international commissions, their own Macedonian handiwork, on the ground that European supervision was no longer needed in a land ruled by the most perfect harmony. But no sooner had the Young Turks come out with their program of Ottomanization than the Christian groups in Macedonia recognized that they had been deceived. Exactly what they had expected by way of concrete benefit it would be hard to say, but in any case it was not the perpetuation of the hated Ottoman rule under a Liberal disguise. In consequence the festivals ceased, the lanterns and festoons were removed from the streets, and slowly the Bulgar and Greek patriots slunk back to the hills to resume, to the glory of their respective nations, the honorable occupation of highwaymen and assassins. Following its short truce of God Macedonia replunged with gusto into its familiar anarchy.

Return of the Macedonian anarchy.

But the fiercest hornet's nest stirred up by the Young Turks proved, to every one's surprise, to be Albania. In the course of the nineteenth century the Serbs, the Greeks, the Rumans, and the Bulgars, that is, all the subject nationalities of the Ottomans in Balkania, had in turn revolted against the sultan, but not the Albanians. That was partly due to the fact that they were not to the same degree ground under the heel of the Turk, who, unable to exercise effective rule in the difficult western mountains, had, generally speaking, agreed to leave the Albanians to themselves in exchange for formal submission. As a result their ancient organization into tribes or clans and their cherished customs were hardly affected by the centuries of Turkish overlordship, and in the midst of a progressive Europe they presented the picture of an unchanging primitive society. In this petrified condition lay a further explanation of their failure to rise against their masters. In order to join the modern procession the Albanians would indispensably have first to acquire something of the modern mentality. However, shut off from the

The strange case of Albania.

world by the barrier of their mountains and prompted to an edu-
cative intercourse, even among themselves, by neither commerce
nor highways nor railroads, they were not subjected to influences
calculated to introduce them to a new outlook on life.

In spite of their almost unbelievable isolation the Albanian
shepherds and peasants were animated by a strong love for their
mountain home. In fact their country, together with the family
and clan, largely filled their lives. So strong was the patriotic
sentiment among them that it was impaired neither by the absence
of political unity nor by the presence of ecclesiastical division.
These religious differences were not the least curious feature in a
highly idiomatic situation. Originally wholly Christian, though
the north Albanians belonged to the Catholic and the south
Albanians to the Orthodox fold, so many tribes, both north and
south, had gradually gone over to Islam that by the time the
nineteenth century made its appearance a considerable majority
of the nation professed adherence to the Koran. Travelers, however, never failed to notice that the Albanian Moslems were no
fanatics and that, Albanians first and Moslems afterwards, they
vied with their Christian fellow-countrymen of both the Greek
and Latin rite in devotion to the rugged country of their birth.
Wild, untamed, and not averse to a life of brigandage, the Albanians were excellent fighters of the guerrilla type and proved
themselves in all personal relations to be singularly honest and
reliable. No greater disgrace could befall a tribesman than to
be guilty of breaking his word. Learning, on the other hand,
enjoyed no following, and not only were the people universally
illiterate, but they were without schools and books and did not
till the end of the nineteenth century develop that prerequisite
of even the simplest mental culture, an alphabet and a written
language.

Secluded and self-secure as the clans long were in their inaccessible mountains, nineteenth century Europe began to pound at
their doors, informing them in no uncertain voice that they were
no longer to be permitted to live unto themselves alone. Perhaps
the first time the powers as a whole became aware of the existence of such a people as the Albanians was when, on the occasion of the congress of Berlin, they met with resistance in
connection with the award to neighboring Montenegro of a small
Albanian district. This cavalier disposal of their land aroused

lively resentment and an Albanian League was formed (1878) to lodge a concerted protest against any transfer of soil, indubitably Albanian, to neighboring states. The sultan himself originally favored the League as a convenient device for influencing the European powers against the cession of Ottoman lands; but when he discovered that the League was the nucleus of a new national movement, he became alarmed and dissolved it by force. Abdul Hamid had had enough of national movements and entertained no doubt as to their final goal. A perfectly correct instinct told him that the Albanians would be lost to the empire as soon as they attained to self-consciousness through an association expressly formed for political action. No less dangerous would be an Albanian school system and he gave precise orders to his local agents that all educational movements among his " faithful " highlanders should be rigorously suppressed.

The revolution of 1908 blew the lid off this policy of repression with startling effect. The Albanians interpreted the loudly proclaimed liberty to mean freedom to agitate for their nationality and set busily about organizing schools, circulating newspapers, and making preparations for an autonomous state. As early as 1909 this frankly separatist policy got on the nerves of the Young Turks, who attempted to interpose with their nostrum of Ottomanization. Troops were ordered into the country and scattered clashes occurred between natives and invaders. Suppressed at one point, the national movement quickly flared up at another with the result that, following at a long distance the example set by the other Balkan peoples, Albania found herself involved in a war of liberation. By 1912 the Turks had shot their bolt and, perplexed by the growing disturbances elsewhere, more particularly by a war with Italy, which had broken out in 1911, and by the almost certain prospect of a war with their Christian neighbors in Balkania, they resolved to come to terms with the insuppressible Albanians. By a peace concluded in the summer (1912) the brave mountaineers received practically all they asked. In return for accepting the sultan as suzerain, they were accorded a broad home-rule, which, while leaving them independent as of yore, conceded them in addition the right to establish native schools and to circulate native books and newspapers.

The revolution of 1908 produces an Albanian war of liberation.

Albania as
defined in
the treaty
with Turkey,
1912.

Far and away the most considerable concession which they obtained, however, was a territorial definition of Albania. The country had hitherto been a mere geographical expression without precise limits. If it was now to start on a political career, it would have to be endowed with boundaries and, naturally enough, the victorious Albanians insisted that these be drawn as liberally as possible. Accordingly the Turkish government recognized that Albania was comprised of the four vilayets of Scutari, Janina, Monastir, and Kossovo. It was, to say the least, doubtful if the Albanian nationality could justly claim all this territory; in any case, the older neighboring states, which had long pressed claims of their own to these districts or to parts thereof, were not likely to sit quietly by while the Balkan people which was the last to open the fight for freedom, satisfied its national aspirations in their most extreme form. These neighbor states, as we know, made no merit of a retiring modesty. The Greeks, for instance, passionately coveted the vilayet of Janina and the Montenegrins that of Scutari, while Monastir and Kossovo were Macedonian areas which had for years been the meeting-place of the bitter rival activities of Bulgar, Greek, and Serb bands.

The neighbor
states
resolved to
resist the
creation of
a large
Albania.

As soon as it became apparent that an autonomous Albania was about to come into existence which would encroach heavily on the expectations of its neighbors, these were of one mind regarding the experiment. They would fight it tooth and nail, and as the projected Albania would be a part of the Ottoman empire, with which they had a multitude of other scores to clear, they began to gird their loins for a life-and-death struggle with their ancient foe. Moreover, it was manifest that the Young Turks, once aptly described by an observer on the scene as "young men in a hurry," and fatally disorganized the empire and made it vulnerable. The time to strike was therefore now, while the Ottoman state was weak and the Albania of the four vilayets no more than a paper sketch.

CHAPTER XXX

NEW OTTOMAN WARS: (1) THE WAR WITH ITALY (1911); (2) THE FIRST BALKAN WAR (1912); (3) THE SECOND BALKAN WAR (1913)

SINCE the growing feebleness of the Ottoman empire made itself felt, first of all, at sea, it was the north African dependencies, capable of being held to their allegiance only by sea-power, which were the first to assert their independent authority. As soon as the radical economic changes of the nineteenth century, familiarly summarized as the industrial revolution, accelerated the pace of European expansion, those detached shorelands were sure to become objects of interest to the powers in whose path they lay, and consequently the development occurred, of which we have already taken account, whereby France effected a lodgment in Algeria and Tunis and England in the basin of the Nile. The next step in this appropriation of the African littoral took place when, in 1904, France and Great Britain formed an entente based substantially on an adjustment of their Mediterranean interests. In return for being left in undisturbed possession of Egypt, Great Britain agreed to promote the absorption by France of the as yet independent sultanate of Morocco. That left as the only unappropriated African shore-district the long barren stretch of Tripoli. *Great Britain and France appropriate the African shore.*

If Tripoli had possessed any particular value, very probably either France or Great Britain would have put forth a claim to it in the course of their various north-African ventures. But Tripoli, besides being a burning desert-hell dotted with occasional oases, did not even boast a harbor, suitable as a naval base, and offered to the prospective owner hardly more than the prospect of considerable expense without an adequate return. Having dined off the fat of Africa, the governments of Paris and London discreetly declined to touch the bleached Tripolitan *Italy casts her eye on Tripoli.*

467

bone, but Italy, which had not yet dined at all, gradually drew near to it. The young kingdom had been mortally offended when, in 1881, France seized Tunis, thereby planting herself at the point of the African coast where it thrust out a threatening spear-head in the direction of Sicily. The Roman government's disgust went the length of driving it into the arms of France's enemy, of Germany, and in 1883 it came to terms with the governments of Vienna and Berlin, thus completing the Triple alliance. As a youthful power, but recently arrived at statehood, Italy was extremely desirous of entering the colonial and imperialist game, preferably within the basin of the Mediterranean. Gradually a popular sentiment began to make itself felt in press and parliament in favor of seizing the last remaining African foothold before it was too late. That Tripoli, considered purely as an investment, had little or no power of attraction, induced a certain amount of hesitation. But, while delaying action, the Roman foreign office discreetly initiated negotiations with the other powers directed at the effort of getting from them a formal acknowledgment of Italy's reversionary rights, that is, of her position as heir-at-law of the Ottoman empire. In the course of a generation the Italian claim had been duly buttressed by a series of diplomatic agreements with the general result that by the time the Turkish revolution of 1908 took place, it was well understood in all the capitals of Europe that, at the auspicious moment and without encountering objection from any European power, Italy would cross the sea and unfurl her banner on the Tripolitan coast.

Italy pounces on her prey, September, 1911.

At the beginning of the twentieth century Tripoli was still a part of the Ottoman empire, but in reality it was ruled by the spirited Arab tribes, which for countless generations had made their home among its desolate sands. In this traditional situation the busy Young Turks, following their victory of 1908, produced a change in so far as they manifested a desire to draw Tripoli into closer dependence on the home government. We are already aware that their much vaunted reform meant essentially a more effective centralization. They therefore began to interfere with the measures of economic penetration, which the Italians had for some time been pursuing and which constituted the usual preliminary phase of every well-regulated imperialist venture. Italian merchant companies, already on the ground, discovered that they were meeting with underground resistance, while all requests for new concessions, including one for a purely scientific expedition to be conducted by Italian archaeologists, were curtly rejected. Strained relations followed, which certain personal influences such as always enter into diplomatic situations, but are really unimportant since they are symptoms rather than causes, did nothing to improve. Suddenly, on September 27, 1911, and, so far as the world of bystanders was concerned, with no adequate provocation, Italy hurled an ultimatum at Turkey and without waiting for an answer dispatched an armament to Tripoli.

After successfully occupying the insignificant and widely scattered coast towns, the Italian army proceeded to penetrate to the interior and straightway encountered enormous difficulties. Not only did the Arabs, abetted to the best of their ability by the Turks, contest every foot of ground, but, more effectively than any human enemies, the heat, sand, and utter desolation of the country conspired to thwart the Italian advance. Irritated by the loss of men and treasure, the Italian government, in the hope of bringing the Turks to terms, ordered its navy to attack them nearer home. Accordingly, in May, 1912, Rhodes and the group of small islands to the north of Rhodes, known as the Dodekanese, were occupied without opposition. Still the obdurate Turks refused to treat, and might have continued indefinitely to refuse, if the development of the Albanian insurrection and the prospect of even worse storms ahead on the Balkan peninsula had not suggested the need of caution. Tardily and with great reluctance negotiations with Rome were opened at Lausanne and, on October 18, 1912, led to the signing of a peace. Italy received the coveted but dubious treasure, to which she gave the name of Libya, and promised on the retirement of the Ottoman forces from the ceded territory to evacuate the Aegean islands. *The Turco-Italian war.*

But even before the Italian war had been brought to its official close, another and far more serious war had broken out in the Balkan peninsula. It took the form of an attack on Turkey by the four contiguous Christian states, Bulgaria, Greece, Serbia, and Montenegro. The alliance of the liberated *The Young Turk policy causes the Balkan states to draw together.*

Christians, former rayahs of the Ottoman empire, to the end of solving the remaining problems of the peninsula, had often been suggested, but the idea had regularly suffered shipwreck on the fierce competitive nationalism of the youthful states. The feelings harbored toward each other by the Serbs and Bulgars were amply divulged by the war of 1885, while the desolating, unofficial conflict in Macedonia among Bulgars, Greeks, Serbs, and Albanians, left no doubt as to the jealousy rampant among these four groups. But what no statesmanship in or outside Balkania working over time had been able to accomplish, the mistaken zeal of the Young Turks brought about in a few months. Their purpose, reduced to its simplest terms, was a resuscitated Ottoman empire. But this, the patriotic hope of the Young Turks, was to the Christian communities only recently rescued from Turkish bondage, nothing less than a nightmare filling them with fear and horror.

The alliance of Bulgaria, Greece, Serbia, and Montenegro.

Instinctively the Christian groups drew together to take common counsel, and no sooner had diplomatic conversations been initiated among them than they reached the not surprising conclusion that their best defensive course would be to take the offensive. However, they agreed patiently to await the favorable hour; but when the hour struck, they proposed of one accord and without the least delay to leap at their foe. Gradually the discussions crystallized in formal treaties. By March, 1912, a treaty of alliance had been signed between Bulgaria and Serbia; and in the months immediately following, other treaties, drawing Greece and Montenegro into the circle, perfected a fighting union of the four Balkan neighbors. Unfortunately the crucial question of the division of the spoils was left unsolved. In the eyes of all the main purpose of the common drive was the conquest of Macedonia, but instead of agreeing beforehand upon each ally's share in the disputed borderland, as between Bulgaria and Greece a division was not even mentioned, and as between Bulgaria and Serbia a half-hearted arrangement was sketched which, after apportioning certain sections to the contracting parties, left the core of Macedonia as a no man's land to be referred, if necessary, to the arbitrament of the Russian tsar. This fatal evasion of the territorial issue involved in the war made, in case of victory, a struggle among the allies absolutely certain. Did not the governments, one asks in blank astonishment, foresee this peril? Likely enough they did, but no less likely they recognized that complete agreement on the point at issue was impossible and that, should it have been insisted on, the alliance would never have been concluded.

Although no precise time had been set for the attack on Turkey as the summer of 1912 wore on the allies began to exhibit signs of restiveness. They felt strong in their union, they wished to take advantage of the embarrassment caused at Constantinople by the Italian war, and, last but not least, they resented the Albanian victory, just won, by virtue of which Albania was to be constituted as an autonomous state composed of the four vilayets of Scutari, Janina, Monastir, and Kossovo. Should this Albanian proposal be carried out, each of the four allies would find the door shut on a district which he particularly coveted. Alarmed lest they be too late for the feast, new hurried deliberations among the respective foreign ministers fixed the unleashing of the dogs of war for early autumn. The tiniest of the Balkan states, Montenegro, having agreed to take the lead, on October 8 King Nicholas once more formally challenged the Turk to combat. A few days later the sovereigns of the other three states sent an ultimatum to Constantinople and the war became general.

Outbreak of the war, October, 1912.

The Balkan war of 1912 caused great and universal surprise because the world was not prepared for the quick and resounding victory won by the four allies. But the victory was natural enough, being due in the main to the significant moral, economic, and military progress made by the Christian states since their liberation. By patient labor they had succeeded in taking over much of the European mentality and institutions, and, thus equipped, they engaged in a struggle with an Asiatic people which had steadily resisted Europeanization or had yielded to it reluctantly and just enough to destroy the effectiveness of its own inherited system. Many bystanders, who falsely prophesied an Ottoman victory, did so on the strength of their belief in the Ottoman rank and file, " the invincible Turkish soldier." In other words they paid their respect to the simple peasant from Anatolia, who, drafted into the service, had never failed to distinguish himself for his frugality, discipline, and bravery. But the Young Turks, who dilettanti-wise tampered with everything,

Explanation of the resounding victory of the allies.

had tampered also with the army, that last bulwark of the state, and acting on their catchword of Ottomanization, had inserted into the willing Moslem mass the recalcitrant Christian and Jewish elements under their dominion. As might have been foreseen, at the first contact with the enemy these conscripts wavered and ran away, promptly communicating their demoralization to the Moslems with whom they were brigaded. This unsound military situation should be kept in mind in connection with the unexpected cataclysm of the Turkish armies; but while it helps account for the campaign, it does not in the least detract from the military, administrative, and other types of western efficiency displayed by the victorious allies.

The Bulgar victories.

The story of the war is soon told. Each ally operated in the section of Ottoman territory most accessible to him, Bulgaria in the Maritsa valley, Serbia in the Morava and upper Vardar valleys, Greece in the lower Vardar valley and in Epirus, and Montenegro in northern Albania. In these circumstances the brunt of the fighting fell of necessity on the Bulgars, whose operations aimed at the heart of the Ottoman power and threatened Constantinople itself. They acquitted themselves with distinction, beating the Turks in severe battles, first at Kirk Kilisse, and afterwards at Lule Burgas. From the field of Lule Burgas the Ottoman army fled in a wild rout which was not stayed till the girdle of fortresses had been reached, known as the Chataldja lines and only some twenty miles distant from the capital. Early in November the Bulgars, in triumphant possession of all Thrace except the fortified city of Adrianople, began the siege of the Chataldja lines in the hope of penetrating to the Golden Horn.

The Serb, Montenegrin, and Greek victories.

Meanwhile the other allies had scored a number of hardly less brilliant successes. Pouring across their border into Old Serbia, the Serbs had encountered the Turkish army at Kumanovo (October 22–25) and won a complete victory. They then occupied Uskub (Skoplje), the capital of their short-lived medieval empire, and penetrated southward into Macedonia as far as Monastir. At the same time their brothers of Montenegro surrounded the great fortress of Scutari on the lake of that name, while the Greeks pushed, on the one hand, into Epirus, where they laid siege to the city of Janina, and, on the other, toward

Saloniki, which they successfully entered early in November.
More important, however, than the action of the Greeks on land
were their achievements at sea. The inferior Ottoman navy was
bottled up in the Dardenelles and practically all the Ottoman
islands, with the exception of Cyprus, held by Great Britain, and
Rhodes and the Dodekanese, held by Italy, passed without resistance into Greek hands.

Confronted by these overwhelming disasters, the panic-stricken
Porte applied for mediation to the powers, which, on December 3,
procured a cessation of hostilities. There followed a conference
of the belligerents in London for the discussion of the terms of
peace. On the day the conference opened the beaten Turks still
held in Europe Constantinople with its immediate environs, the
three invested fortresses of Adrianople, Janina, and Scutari, and
not a foot of land besides!

Armistice
followed by
the London
conference.

But already fresh clouds were gathering on the horizon, blown
up by two incidents of ominous import. The first has to do with
Saloniki. Hardly had the Greeks in early November entered the
city, when a detachment of Bulgars made its appearance at the
gates. Although it was admitted, the Greeks made it clear to
their Slav allies that they were unwelcome guests and that
Saloniki was and must remain Greek. If the respective main
armies had not still had work to do against the common enemy,
war might have broken out then and there, for the issue was not
a small one — the ownership of the most important harbor of
the Aegean sea. The second incident was no less disturbing.
Blocked from the lower Vardar by Greece and Bulgaria, the
Serbs, intoxicated by the completeness of their victory, resolved
to push for open water by the only remaining avenue, that is,
through Albania. Consequently, toward the end of November,
Serb detachments occupied the Albanian coast at Alessio and
Durazzo. But the Serbs had hardly launched their daring coup
when a vigorous protest made itself heard in two widely separated
camps. No sooner did the European powers get wind of the Serb
intention to strike for the Adriatic than, at the prompting of
Austria and Italy, the two states which claimed the Adriatic as
their private domain, they interposed a firm veto. If in its despite the Serbs persisted in their course, it was because they hoped
that the concert of the powers would not be maintained and that

Two ominous
incidents.

particularly Russia would end by swinging to their side. At the same time the Albanians protested for themselves against the Serb measure. In wild alarm at the sudden rising to their upland country of the tide of war, they called a meeting at Valona (Avlona) and proclaimed their complete independence from the Ottoman empire. By this belated act they hoped to save themselves from being distributed as spoils of war among the victors.

The powers declare for an independent Albania.
It was admittedly an immensely complicated situation which faced the London conference. The Albanian question, however, which by the Serb invasion had leaped into sudden prominence, proved no obstacle to agreement. Not only did the powers stand by their original veto against a Serb occupation of the Adriatic coast and by their irresistible might force the Serbs to evacuate the Albanian ports, but they satisfied the wishes of the Albanian nationalists and officially committed themselves to the creation of a free Albania. In a preliminary statement they declared that the Albania of the future was to have a prince selected by the powers, that it was to enjoy, while getting on its feet, the help of an international committee of control, and that it should receive reasonable boundaries to be determined by a special commission of inquiry. With the Albanian problem removed by this dictum from the realm of discussion, the London deliberations among the plenipotentiaries of the combatants might have made rapid progress if it had not been for the obstinacy of the Ottoman commissioners. Reluctant to give up Adrianople, Scutari, and Janina, on which the four allies, having them in the grip of their armies, naturally insisted, they spun out the negotiations till January, when a *coup d'état* at Constantinople drove them from power. The *coup d'état* was sprung by Enver Bey, who stood at the head of a Young Turk party of action. Enver's access to power was correctly interpreted as a stiffening of the Ottoman position, the conference broke up, and the war was resumed.

The treaty of London, May, 30, 1913.
Although Enver was a man of resolute daring, the Ottoman situation was already past help and all further struggle proved futile. On the resumption of hostilities Janina, Adrianople, and Scutari fell into the hands of their respective besiegers, the Greeks, the Bulgars, and the Montenegrins, and in April Enver's government had humbly to apply for a reopening of the peace conference. This time the negotiations proceeded smoothly, and on May 30,

1913, the treaty of London was signed, by virtue of which Turkey
was almost, if not quite, ejected from the continent of Europe.
Save Constantinople and the narrow strip of land behind a line
drawn from Enos on the Aegean to Midia on the Black sea all
Ottoman territory was surrendered to the victorious allies. Of
course Albania, too, was excluded from the cession, since, though
detached from the Ottoman empire, it had already received a
charter of independence from the powers.

What now to do with the spoils, which in simple truth were
tremendous, embracing as they did Crete, the Aegean islands,
Epirus, Thrace, and Macedonia in the most liberal interpretation
of that geographical expression? Late, too late, the triumphant
four had begun negotiations with one another looking toward a
peaceful accommodation of their conflicting claims. Unfortunately their mood was the dangerous mood of victors and, full
each one of his own importance, they refused to listen to reason.
Bulgaria was in a particularly truculent frame of mind due to
an unhappy combination of circumstances. While pursuing the
plan of campaign, which, from a purely military point of view,
was impeccable, of driving southeastward into Thrace, she had
abandoned Macedonia, undoubtedly her true political objective,
to Greece and Serbia. These two states were consequently in
secure possession of the Vardar area and very reluctant to surrender it or any part thereof. Their contention was that Bulgaria
should glut her appetite on conquered Thrace and leave Macedonia to her allies. Though this sounded fair and reasonable in
the light of a purely quantitative standard, it failed to appeal to
Bulgaria, which claimed Macedonia on nationalist grounds and
had for decades been engaged in working up a hot Bulgar sentiment among the natives.

To this thwarting of Bulgaria's desires in Macedonia was added
a second source of irritation. The war had hardly begun when
Rumania, which was not contiguous with the Ottoman empire
and which had therefore not joined in the assault upon it, projected herself into the Balkan negotiations. The government of
Bucharest could not reasonably demand a share in the Turkish
spoils, but it could and did defend the position that if the other
Balkan states, and particularly Bulgaria, were to experience an
increase of might, some territorial compensation would have to

The question of the Turkish spoils.

Rumania demands Silistria and a strip of the Dobrudja.

(handwritten marginal note:) Rumanian always no fighters but grabbers.

be offered to Rumania in order to maintain the existing balance of power. Acting on this view, the Rumanian ministry promptly indicated the Bulgarian fortress of Silistria, together with a strip of the Bulgarian Dobrudja, as objects of desire and firmly requested their surrender. Committed with all its strength to the struggle with the Ottoman empire, Bulgaria, on being exposed by the Rumanian threat to a flank attack, voiced an angry protest, but in May, 1913, yielded to necessity and signed a treaty embodying the required cession.

Outbreak of the war among the allies, June 29, 1913.

Perhaps the very pliancy of the Bulgar leaders in the Dobrudja matter produced, by a natural and usual reaction, a stiffening of their backbone in regard to Macedonia. Negotiations touching the disputed area, which had been begun with Greece, were broken off, and those with Serbia, though continued, made no headway. Dark intrigues on the part of the great powers, which, it goes without saying, were, as usual, only superficially harmonious, contributed to the muddying of the waters. That the situation on the Macedonian front, where the allied forces faced one another in full battle strength, was becoming strained to the breaking-point was indicated by spontaneous clashes among the excited soldiery. All hope of an amicable settlement had already been reduced to a mere taper, when, on June 29, it was rudely extinguished by an order of the Bulgar military authorities to attack the Serb positions. The first shot did the rest and the fated war among the allies had begun. In certain anticipation of the event Greece and Serbia had some weeks before signed an alliance, to which Rumania, in spite of the concession wrung from Bulgaria, now eagerly applied for admission. The war among the allies therefore took the form of Bulgaria *versus* Greece and Serbia supported by the fresh and unexhausted strength of Rumania.

Defeat of Bulgaria followed by the treaty of Bucharest.

The new war lasted less than a month, for Bulgaria, caught between the Serb and Greek armies advancing from the west and south, and the Rumanian army striking from the north, was so badly mauled as to be speedily put at the mercy of its foes. When the Bulgar cause was already lost, Turkey, under the alert direction of Enver Bey, took up arms on its own account and marched an army up the Maritsa valley for the reconquest of Adrianople. In the face of this fourth invasion Tsar Ferdinand threw up the sponge and asked for peace. At a conference of

the combatants which, early in August, came together in the
Rumanian capital, a treaty was agreed on, called the treaty of
Bucharest, which, as was to be expected, brought the war to a
close at the expense of the loser. Macedonia, the main object
of dispute, was divided between Serbia and Greece, while Rumania
received an increased strip of the Dobrudja. Bulgaria was, however, not wholly excluded from participation in the Turkish spoils,

THE BALKAN PENINSULA AFTER THE PEACE OF BUCHAREST (1913)

for she received a part of Thrace with access to the Aegean sea-
board at the small and miserable harbor of Dedeagatch. Of the
remaining territory surrendered by the Ottoman empire Greece
acquired Epirus with its capital Janina, and Serbia took over the
province of Old Serbia (Kossovo) and the eastern half of Novibazar. The western half of Novibazar was awarded to
Montenegro.

Turkey recovers Adrianople.

As the Porte was not admitted to the conference of Bucharest, Bulgaria was obliged to come to terms with it through separate negotiations. These led in September to a treaty, by which the Slav kingdom receded Adrianople and a small part of Thrace to their former owner. The new Turk-Bulgar boundary was drawn in a manner so unfortunate for Bulgaria that she even lost control of the railway running to her one meager Aegean port. Disastrous for the Bulgars, the treaty was a personal triumph for the Young Turk leader, Enver Bey, who thereby greatly strengthened his hold on the government. Nor was that all. The conflict among the victors had given Turkey an opportunity not only to recover a slice of her lost territory but also to reassert her claim as a factor in the general Balkan situation. The year 1913 closed with Turkey in a position of much greater authority than any one would have dreamed possible a short six months before.

Disposition of the Aegean islands.

There still remained to be settled two territorial issues which the European powers had removed from the competency of the Balkan states and reserved to themselves. One of them concerned the disposal of the Aegean islands. Though Crete was without more ado transferred to Greece and was thus at last enabled to fulfill its heart's desire of union with the mother-land, Europe treated the question of the islands along the Asia Minor coast more dilatorily. On the basis of nationality Greece could fairly demand them all, but there were other claims to be considered beside those of race and language. If the Ottoman empire was to retain the Dardanelles, it was reasonable that the two islands of Imbros and Tenedos, which commanded the entrance to the strait, should be left under its control. This reservation made, the powers took up next the Italian tenancy of Rhodes and the Dodekanese. According to the treaty of Lausanne (1912) the Italians were to withdraw from these positions as soon as the Turks had evacuated Libya. Though the Turks had lived up to their end of the bargain, the Italians absent-mindedly staid on, and as they could be ejected only by armed force, the powers discreetly connived at the continued occupation. With these two exceptions the Aegean islands were handed over to Greece, thereby making the young kingdom dominant in the waters which were the historic home of the Hellenic race.

Touching the other territorial issue, which they had reserved to themselves, that of Albania, the powers were thrown into a considerable quandary. They had taken the Albanians under their protection, but, on closer inspection, they discovered that the backward tribesmen were indeed brave and indomitable individuals but not a united people in the modern sense. It was therefore decidedly questionable whether they were prepared for the responsibilities of statehood. Nevertheless, having assumed obligations toward them, the powers resolved to proceed with the creation of a government and, after much deliberation, named a small German prince, William of Wied, ruler of the country. At the same time they took up the difficult question of the Albanian boundaries. Montenegro and Serbia laid claim to certain Albanian border areas of the north and east, while the Greeks coveted the whole of southern Albania, regarding it as nothing but the continuation of Epirus, acquired by them as a result of the war. The Albanian boundary issue was a sea dotted with dangerous reefs, but port was at last made and the country officially delimited. As usual, the result was a compromise, satisfying neither the Albanians nor their neighbors, but at least permitting the new state to get under way. In March, 1914, Prince William arrived at Durazzo, where without taxes or officials, without even the simplest elements of a modern government, he attempted to set up his authority. Many of the tribes, unused to restraint in any form, soon defied him. Civil commotions followed which threw the country into turmoil. When, some four months after his arrival, the Great War broke out, his position became untenable and, resigning his crown of thorns, he abandoned the country. The first government of independent Albania had proved an unqualified failure, but that did not convince the world, and certainly not the Albanians, that they were now ripe for absorption by their more civilized neighbors. Nothing daunted, the handful of nationalist enthusiasts continued to travel up and down the land preaching the doctrine of unity, and more and more the seed of their sowing fell upon fertile soil.

Pausing for a moment to bring the changes produced in Balkania by the wars of 1912 and 1913 into a general historical perspective, we are forced to admit that the picture before us

Prince William of Albania.

Credit and debit of the year 1913.

has both encouraging and alarming elements. Once more the Ottoman empire has receded, this time to the straits, and its paralyzing hand has been lifted from lands which it had systematically brought to ruin. The Christian states, on the other hand, have reached a new milestone of their steady and hopeful development. To Greece, Serbia, and Montenegro it was particularly gratifying that they had almost doubled their area. Even Bulgaria, despite the disastrous ending of the second war, came out of the struggle with an increase of territory in Thrace. Rumania gained least and the little she did gain was Bulgarian soil, which she could not by any stretch of the imagination claim on nationalist grounds. And therewith we touch the aspect of the new Balkan boundaries particularly inviting reflection. Drawn or at least largely drawn on the basis of might, they frequently cut with ruthless unconcern across established ethnic lines. It was, however, axiomatic that these would have to be treated tenderly and with respect if a genuine pacification of the peninsula was ever to be realized.

Tragic defeat of the idea of federation.   Long before the partners of 1912 undertook their war of liberation, it was clearly indicated by the progress of events that the days of the Ottoman empire in Europe were counted and that something would have to be found to replace it. That something was prepared in the womb of Time in the shape of the Christian states, which in the course of the nineteenth century had bravely struggled through adolescence into manhood. By the beginning of the twentieth century it was clear that, after taking over the remainder of the Ottoman heritage, they would either have to combine on some formula of neighborliness and coöperation or else run the risk of a ferocious enmity, certain ultimately to thrust them back into a chaos as bad as the Turkish oppression from which they had been delivered. Out of fear of this sinister development the well-wishers of the Christian states the world over had greeted the quadruple alliance with delight, and when within a few weeks it fell so tragically to pieces, they viewed the catastrophe with angry consternation. Let us be in no doubt about the new and terrible hatreds bred by the war of 1913 and the treaty which concluded it. That Macedonia had been divided between Greece and Serbia would never be forgotten in Bulgaria; and if it should be argued that Macedonia was an ulcer of long standing which had already poisoned the relations of its Christian neighbors for the past generation, such was not the case with the Dobrudja, which did not become an area of conflict till Rumania saw fit to add the Bulgarian slice to what she already possessed. Neither Bulgaria, nursing an untamed rancor in her heart, nor her three Christian neighbors, gloating over her discomfiture, were fit partners in a genuine Balkan federation. The predatory attitude of Serbia and Greece toward nursling Albania points to the same conclusion. The federative idea, the only earnest of a Balkan settlement bringing peace and healing in its wings, would have to be abandoned for many a day, perhaps forever. Therefore from the satisfaction which a sympathetic observer might reasonably draw from the increasing strength and civilization of the expanding Christian states, a serious deduction would have to be made in view of the prospect of the perpetuation of those agitations and conflicts which had made the Balkan chaos a byword in Europe. More visibly than ever there floated over that chaos not peace but a sword.

CHAPTER XXXI

THE GREAT WAR AND THE BALKAN PENINSULA

The concert of the powers maintained during the Balkan wars.

ALTHOUGH the European powers were greatly perturbed by the Balkan wars, they showed a laudable disposition to keep in touch with one another by means of ambassadorial conferences and, throughout the long crisis, managed, to the surprise of many observers, to hold fast to a line of concerted action. Undoubtedly their harmony was due to the fact that the Balkan conflict revolved about issues largely of a circumscribed and local character with little or no immediate bearing on the imperialist policies of the great states. Whenever it happened that the struggle momentarily extended its circles so as in any way to affect a direct interest of the Triple alliance or Triple entente, an interference followed which was as swift as it was unflinching and Olympian. Thus the attempt of Serbia to get a footing on the Albanian coast was resented as an incursion into an area reserved by Austria and Italy to themselves and produced an immediate veto, which there was no gainsaying. Again when Bulgaria seemed likely to break through the Chataldja lines to the end of advancing on Constantinople, Russia was quick to let Sofia know that this would under no circumstances be permitted. Constantinople was of course sacred to the ambitions of Russia. In short, the powers formed, as it were, a close ring around the Balkan combatants with the set purpose of keeping the war localized, and it was because their effort succeeded that the peninsular disturbance did not expand into a world struggle among the two groups of the Triple alliance and the Triple entente, both armed to the teeth and long nervously apprehensive of an impending clash.

Unsolvable character of the Austro-Serb controversy.

But in spite of the determination of Europe not to be drawn into the Balkan imbroglio, an issue, which some years before had come painfully near to throwing the spark into the powder barrel, made a grim and ghost-like reappearance in the wake of the

Balkan wars. We have seen how, after a vast and dangerous
agitation, the Bosnian crisis of 1908 had been brought to rest.[1]
The final act had taken place in March, 1909, when, on the withdrawal of the support of the Triple entente, Serbia had been
obliged, in a note delivered at Vienna, to accept without reservation the Hapsburg sovereignty over Bosnia and to take the
express pledge " to live in future on terms of good neighborliness " with Austria-Hungary. If this promise meant that the
Serbs undertook henceforth to repress their nationalist passions,
it neither would nor could be kept, for, regardless of what the
government officially declared, the various patriotic societies,
whose precise purpose was to spread the propaganda of a Greater
Serbia, would obstinately continue their underground labors in
Bosnia as well as in the other Hapsburg provinces inhabited by
people of Serb stock. When, in 1912, the call to war sounded
like a trumpet through the land, all Serbia was electrified, and
when presently there followed in swift succession the decisive
victories over Turks and Bulgars, a veritable intoxication seized
upon all ranks of society. That the Serbs, largely under Austrian
pressure, were obliged to relax their grip on the Albanian sea-
coast did not improve the tone between Belgrad and Vienna,
which, in the course of 1913, became so exacerbated that, in
August, Austria seriously considered the advisability of attacking
Serbia without further delay. Only the unwillingness of her
allies, Germany and Italy, to give her their support moved her
to abandon the project. It was clear to any intelligent observer
that the relations of the two neighbors would speedily have to
improve or lead to a catastrophe. And yet how could the relations improve in any essential sense with the Serb people dedicated to a national hope, which, now that the Ottoman empire
had gone down to defeat, was kept from realization by the single
obstacle of the Hapsburg monarchy? And as for Austria-Hungary, patchwork of many races, how could it, with its integrity
already threatened by the many national movements in its midst,
put up with the secret Serb propaganda without inviting an early
dissolution? To all appearances the friendly coexistence of
the two states had become impossible.

[1] See pp. 460–461.

Not only for Serbia and Austria-Hungary, but for all the powers of Europe as well, the brief period intervening between the Balkan wars and the cataclysm of the summer of 1914 was a season of feverish agitation. However, among the black and threatening signs pointing to the coming storm, there were some favorable portents which held out the hope that the tempest might, after all, pass by. To a diplomatic weather-prophet, anxiously surveying the political heavens, it was, to begin with, an occasion for congratulation that the Balkan disturbances, just passed, had not set the powers by the ears; and in this connection it was particularly gratifying that the main reason for the maintenance of the European concert during the recent crisis was to be found in the unexpected coöperation of Great Britain and Germany. This curious drawing together, on the eve of the Great War, on the part of the two most formidable powers of Europe is one of the strangest and, in view of the subsequent catastrophe, one of the most tragic episodes of pre-war diplomacy. Nor need we be in doubt as to its explanation. For years both governments had been blindly and heedlessly approaching an abyss, and on having suddenly revealed to them the black depth beneath their feet, they experienced a frightened change of heart and made belated, frantic efforts to arrive at a better understanding. In an agreement, drawn up in June, 1914, and lacking only the official signatures to be complete and binding, they came, incredible though it may sound, to an understanding about several disputatious issues, including even the Bagdad railway! After all, the central feature in the imperialist conflicts of Europe, the nub of the whole business, was the Anglo-German rivalry, and could this have been genuinely appeased, the probability of a general war would have been vastly diminished.

But against this welcome relaxation of tension between London and Berlin there were almost countless signs of waxing strain and exasperation in the situation taken as a whole. Since we are concerned merely with the history of Balkania, it will suffice to mass the evidence rather than elaborately to detail the particular facts bearing on this point. Moreover, the evidence of facts promotes our inner understanding of Europe, on the eve of its agony, less effectively than does a realization of the spiritual atmosphere, the fear and suspicion, which, like silent, ghostly hunters in pursuit of game, never ceased stalking the troubled governments and peoples. For, in last analysis, it was *the European state of mind* which chiefly accounts for the terrible explosion of the war. That is not to say that a close student of the tragic phenomenon may dispense with the obligation of considering all the threads of the colored web of circumstance, but rather that we, with our more narrowly defined task, may excusably concentrate upon the subjective implications of the intense economic rivalry of the last decades and upon the almost unbearable state of nervous tension which resulted therefrom. The rivalry, we are aware, had centered upon markets, raw products, backward areas, and was in its turn the result of such relatively recent forces of our civilization as are broadly indicated by convenient general concepts like nationalism, capitalism, and colonialism. Each power, swept along in the rushing current of these forces, had formulated a policy of aggrandizement commonly called imperialism, and had, in its support, provided a powerful army and navy. In other words it had supplied itself with means, nominally of defense but really of offense, to realize its ends. It is this instant preparedness for conflict which constitutes the essence of what is so frequently condemned as militarism. The heavy military increases, registered annually by the budgets of all the powers, furnish a very accurate measure of the waxing nervousness experienced by the cabinets and peoples. Only when the popular mind was at rest and secure — an Arcadian condition practically unknown in the imperialist age — was the usual increase in armament temporarily abandoned. Generally speaking, European armaments had grown uninterruptedly, especially since the Franco-German war of 1871.

Now it was highly ominous that the months which immediately preceded the outbreak of the Great War witnessed, as a direct consequence of the vague alarm aroused by the Balkan wars, a perfect frenzy of increased preparedness in every corner of Europe. England and France drew closer together by means of a secret naval agreement. Germany made vast military appropriations and increased her standing army to over 800,000 men; France, in order to bring her forces to the same figure, raised the obligatory service with the colors from two to three

Hectic military and naval preparations in the period 1912–14.

years; Russia swelled her peace establishment to the enormous
total of 1,500,000 men; Turkey, resolved to reorganize her beaten
army, gave a German commission broad powers toward this end;
Austria and Italy enlarged their forces in proportion to their
strength, while even small states, like Belgium, caught the in-
fection and made notable additions to their armament. Admitting that the ordinary politico-economic rivalry of the powers
contained poison enough to produce a rancorous and diseased
psychology, we can not but see that in the face of these open
preparations for every eventuality, these threatening gestures
across each other's boundaries, a state of mind became endemic
which, fed by a stridently patriotic press, may without the least
exaggeration be described as national hysteria. Under these circumstances it might easily come about that a relatively unimportant provocation would suffice to throw governments and
peoples into a panic and move them to leap at each other's
throats on the prompting of the moment and regardless of consequences.

The murder
of the
Archduke,
Francis
Ferdinand,
followed by
the Austrian
ultimatum.

The provocation which produced the European cataclysm was
the murder, on June 28, 1914, of the Archduke Francis Ferdinand and his wife in the streets of Sarajevo, the capital of
Bosnia. Francis Ferdinand was the nephew and heir of Francis
Joseph, the reigning emperor of Austria-Hungary, and his murder was the result of a conspiracy on the part of a number of
Serbs, youthful victims of the intense anti-Austrian propaganda
conducted by various patriotic societies. While the horror caused
by the foul deed was general, in the official circles of Austria-
Hungary it released a wild and vindictive desire for revenge.
As, in the Viennese view, the murder furnished indisputable evidence of the subtle war conducted by Serb opinion against the
integrity of the Hapsburg monarchy, it gave to that monarchy an
invaluable opportunity to humble the Serb pride. Accordingly, on
July 23, the Austrian ambassador presented at Belgrad an ultimatum, couched in exceedingly harsh terms and requiring that
within forty-eight hours Serbia give solemn assurance that she
would put an end, once and for all, to all agitation against her
neighbor. When Serbia, while accepting most of the demands,
demurred against certain extreme proposals for inquiring into the
origin of the Sarajevo plot, some of which threatened to impair

Serb sovereignty, Austria rejected the reply as insufficient, and three days after the expiration of the ultimatum declared war on Serbia (July 28).

There is no doubt that Austria planned a signal punishment of the Serbs and that, before formulating her demands, she carefully secured the adhesion of Germany to her policy. Emperor William and his chancellor, Bethmann-Hollweg, nursed the idea that, owing to the European indignation at the Sarajevo outrage, the punishment of Serbia, provided it remained within bounds and did not compromise the integrity of Serb territory, would not be violently opposed in any quarter, and that consequently the Austro-Serb conflict could be successfully localized.

This German plan was based on a complete and almost naïve delusion, in view of the attitude of Russia. The great Slav monarchy, which looked upon Serbia as the main tool of its Balkan policy and which, moreover, owed a certain moral obligation to its little Slav brother, was not in the least minded to deliver Serbia into Austrian hands without express guarantees securing Serbia against conquest, either whole or in part. These guarantees Austria indeed supplied, but only tardily and after she had permitted the impression to go abroad that she was unwilling to bind herself beforehand to any line of action. In any case Russia, prompt to yield to suspicion where Austria was concerned and unable to restrain her impatience, on the day following the expiration of the ultimatum (July 26), began a partial mobilization of her army to keep pace with the Austrian mobilization against Serbia. This feverish movement, once begun, rapidly passed beyond the control of Tsar Nicholas and the civil functionaries and ended, on July 30, with the general mobilization order which turned the whole vast empire, from the borders of Germany to the Pacific ocean, into an armed camp. It is now known that this sweeping and fatal order was wrung from the reluctant tsar by means of the flagrant misrepresentations of two military leaders, the chief of staff and minister of war, whose set purpose was precisely to create a situation which would render diplomatic intervention impotent. On the same day and practically at the same hour the mobilization of Austria, which had at first been only partial and directed against Serbia, became general also. Apparently the Austrian militarists were no less

The German plan of a localized Austro-Serb conflict.

The story of the Russian and Austrian general mobilizations.

eager than their Russian brethren to create an accomplished fact, against which no belated negotiations on the part of the diplomats could prevail. The sword, somewhat discredited of late, was once again to prove itself mightier than the pen. Before the last day of July had dawned the two Balkan rivals faced each other in full panoply of war.

Germany abandons "localization" for "direct negotiations," but too late.

Every one at all familiar with the precarious European situation will agree that only by a successful localization of the Austro-Serb conflict could the long-threatened general war have been avoided. On the assumption that localization was possible the German authorities had given their support to Austria and urged her to go ahead. Not till the Russian protest against the high-handed Austrian procedure, accompanied by the first step in the Russian mobilization process, was reported in Berlin, did the Kaiser and his chancellor awaken to the fact that their policy was based on an erroneous reading of Russian and European opinion. They then made frantic efforts to induce their Austrian ally to resolve the crisis which had arisen by means of "direct negotiations" with Russia, but without avail. The evil which had been done by giving Austria *carte blanche* could not again be undone. The Austrian foreign minister, Count Berchtold, wrapped himself in sphinx-like silence until it was too late, and the militarists at Vienna and Petrograd, by snatching the reins from the hands of the civil authorities, had achieved the decisive double mobilization. If direct negotiations between Vienna and Petrograd had been well under way by July 30, the militarists of either capital might not have succeeded in unmuzzling the dogs of war.

The German declaration of war against Russia and France.

At once on the announcement at Berlin of the Russian general mobilization the whole German situation suffered a complete change. By European tradition general mobilization was tantamount to war and was so understood by the general staffs of all the powers. Furthermore, since Russia was allied with France, it was by these same militarist criteria to be expected that French mobilization would follow the Russian lead without delay. In fact the Franco-Russian treaty was precise on this head and stipulated that general mobilization was to be interpreted as the exact equivalent of a declaration of war. In the face of this critical situation the German military authorities, which

had thus far failed to dominate the situation at Berlin, gained
the upper hand over the civilian chancellor at a single stroke.
They persuaded the emperor to dispatch an ultimatum to Russia,
requiring her to rescind her general mobilization order within
twelve hours.   On Russia's refusal to comply, Germany
on August 1 mobilized in her turn and at the same time
launched a declaration of war against Russia.   When an ultimatum dispatched to Paris and requesting an immediate statement of the intentions of France, had elicited an evasive answer,
Germany, on August 3, declared war also on France.

All eyes were now turned to Great Britain, which though
greatly agitated and secretly bound to France by a military-
naval convention, hesitated to come to a decision.   The fact
was that war, according to English constitutional procedure,
could only be declared by parliament, and that parliament was
ignorant of the engagement entered into by the cabinet.   But
when on August 3, Germany, in her advance on France, broke
the neutrality of Belgium, to which she, as well as all the other
powers, were solemnly pledged, the British government hesitated no longer, and on August 5, with the enthusiastic support
of people and parliament, declared war on Germany.   The only
remaining power, Italy, affirmed her neutrality on the ground
that her obligations to Germany and Austria did not cover an
offensive war.   Before a year had passed, however, Italy had
revised her decision and, facing completely about, entered the war
on the side of the entente.   In contrast to Italy, Japan never
wavered and plunged into the maelstrom at once at the bidding
of her ally, England.   Thus it came about that, when the fearful
general struggle, so long prognosticated by political Cassandras,
had, with the suddenness of a tornado, been unloosed over an
awed and frightened earth, Austria and Germany, the two central
European powers, faced Russia, France, Great Britain, and
Japan, in addition to the three small states of Serbia, where the
conflict had originated, of Montenegro, which, prompted by its
Serb consciousness, came unhesitatingly to Serbia's aid, and of
Belgium, which had been dragged into the whirlpool by Germany's
unwarranted and criminal assault.

The history of the Great War does not fall within the scope
of this book.   But while it is, of course, necessary to define the

*The
alignment of
the powers.*

*Enumera-
tion of the
fighting
fronts.*

rôle of Balkania in the monumental struggle, it will not be easy
to do so without keeping, for purposes of reference, an eye
on all the other theaters of war. The first fact to master is
that, as soon as the great powers faced one another, Balkania,
in spite of the war having originated on its soil, became a subsidiary area. The western front, which ran across France and
Belgium and which absorbed the main fighting energy of Germany, on the one hand, and France and Great Britain, on the
other, easily took first place in the order of importance. Of
hardly less weight in the scales, however, was the eastern front,
where Germany and Austria confronted Russia; while what one
may call the sea front, which Great Britain's superior navy
established in the North sea and by which it maintained an
economic blockade of Germany, yielded little, if anything, in the
significance of the pressure which it brought to bear upon the central empires to either of the more active fighting fronts. But
to concede the preëminence of the three fronts named is not to
say that the large group of subsidiary fronts was negligible. No
person in his senses would pass such a slighting judgment on, for
instance, the Italian front, where Austria and Italy locked horns,
and even less would he be justified in an attitude of conscious
depreciation toward the Balkan segment of the world struggle.
All the fighting fronts hung intimately together and the action
at any one subtly and powerfully influenced the development
at every other. That is the reason why the student of the Great
War, taken as a whole, must lift himself to an attitude above the
battle, from which he is enabled to keep the changing phases of
the immense and complex struggle under his eye; and that is
also the reason why the presentation, to which we are committed,
of the events of a limited area, will necessarily have the character
of a rather painful incompleteness.

The Ottoman empire takes sides with Germany and Austria-Hungary, Oct. 1914.   Although the war began with an Austrian attack on Serbia, a
vigorous struggle on this front failed for some time to develop,
because the main Austrian effort, as soon as the war became
general, was necessarily directed against Russia. However, the
storm had hardly broken when all Balkania became gravely agitated. Every Balkan government anxiously scanned the situation
in the hope of discovering whether its particular interest lay with
the entente or with the central powers; and at the same time

diplomatic agents of the rival sides at Sofia, Bucharest, Athens, and Constantinople busily plied their trade to the end of persuading the governments, to which they were accredited, to adopt and become identified with their cause. The first state to fall in with these persuasions was Turkey. The Young Turks, among whom Enver Bey possessed an unquestionable ascendancy, had entered into relations of such intimacy with Germany that it is doubtful if they could have kept out of the struggle if they had wished. But, as their burning desire was to recover as much of their lost prestige as possible by the traditional Ottoman method of war, and as war at the side of the central powers seemed to promise success, toward the end of October, 1914, they ended their hesitation and ranged themselves with Germany and Austria.

The entrance of the Ottoman empire into the struggle plunged the entente into serious embarrassment, not so much because of the armies which Turkey could muster, although these, led by German officers and equipped with German material, were by no means to be regarded lightly, but chiefly owing to the closing of the Bosporus and Dardanelles, avenues necessary to the western powers if they were to remain in close and fruitful touch with Russia. Moreover, Russia, a backward non-industrial state, soon gave evidence that she could not sustain a prolonged struggle of the modern type without frequent replenishment of her war stores from the factories of her allies. In the course of the winter it therefore became clear that the western powers would have to break down the Turkish barrier at the straits or run the risk of having the Slav colossus fall by the wayside. Accordingly, in February, 1915, an attempt was made by the Franco-British fleet to force the entrance to the Dardanelles. Renewed in March, the attack brought the loss of so many battleships, chiefly through floating mines, that it had to be abandoned. The straits could not be penetrated by a frontal attack from the sea. Thereupon the Franco-British strategists evolved a new and different plan, which relied on the army as the chief weapon of assault. Forcing a landing on the western and southern shores of the Gallipoli peninsula, the allies resolved to take the forts along the Dardanelles by an attack from the rear; and throughout the summer they clung stubbornly

Allied attack on the Dardanelles, 1915.

to this program, although it occasioned extraordinarily heavy sacrifices. Some progress was undoubtedly made, but not enough to silence the Turkish forts. Before the end of the year the whole enterprise had to be given up as a failure.

German-Austrian attack on Serbia, October, 1915.

What finally decided the Gallipoli issue was an important development in the Serb sector. While it is true, as already said, that the main effort of Austria was necessarily diverted to Russia, the Hapsburg monarchy, in the months following the declaration of war, had thrice attempted to invade its little neighbor and had been thrice repelled. Following its last effort, which occurred in December, 1914, it stood on the defensive, and Serbia, gravely exhausted by the wearing, if triumphant, struggle, was content to do the same. However, about a year later, on October 7, 1915, a sudden storm burst over Belgrad with overwhelming force. Under the capable German general, Mackensen, an Austro-German army had been secretly assembled in southern Hungary in order to subdue Serbia and open a path to Constantinople. So long as Turkey and Germany were separated by a hostile Serbia, they could not effectively coöperate, nor was Germany in a position to lend the full weight of her backing to her ally. To establish an uninterrupted connection between Berlin and Constantinople was the fundamental purpose of the October drive on the South Slav kingdom.

Bulgaria joins the central powers and helps to conquer Serbia.

Hardly had the Serbs, overcome by a tremendous bombardment, abandoned their capital, and hardly had the Austro-Germans crossed the Danube to begin their invasion, when, on October 14, the Bulgars declared war on Serbia and fell upon her exposed eastern flank. For over two years, ever since their defeat at the hands of the Serbs in the second Balkan war, the sullen subjects of Tsar Ferdinand had been waiting for just this opportunity. Aware of their vengeful mood, the central powers had promised them, in return for their joining in an attack on Serbia, the lost province of Macedonia, for which they had never ceased to grieve. The bargain, clinched in the late summer, supplies the clue for the combined attack of the autumn, to which Serbia speedily succumbed. Before winter had laid the green earth to sleep, the whole of Serbia had been occupied by the central powers and their Balkan ally, while the worn and shattered remnant of the Serb army made its way, amidst terrifying hardships, across the snowbound Albanian mountains to the Adriatic shore, where it was met by allied transports and carried in safety to the island of Corfu. Following up their success against Serbia, the Austrians broke down the resistance of the remaining Serb state, tiny and heroic Montenegro, and in January, 1916, occupied its capital, Cettinje.

France and Great Britain, which had failed to foresee the attack on Serbia, made a belated and inadequate attempt to come to their ally's aid. They landed a small force at Saloniki and exercised pressure on Greece to the end that Greece, by declaring war on Tsar Ferdinand, might paralyze the Bulgar action against Serbia. A Greco-Serb alliance, in existence since 1912, obliged Greece to support Serbia in case of a Bulgar attack, and Venizelos, the authoritative prime minister of Greece and tried friend of the entente, publicly declared that he intended to live up to his treaty pledges. He reckoned without King Constantine, who since the death of his father, George I, in 1913, occupied the Greek throne. The Greek sovereign, either because of personal ties — he was married to the sister of the Kaiser — or because of genuine alarm at the irresistible military power of Germany, refused to succor Serbia, curtly dismissed Venizelos, and contented himself with proclaiming " armed neutrality," to be characterized, he graciously elucidated, by " sincere benevolence " toward the entente. Deprived of the expected Greek aid, the small Franco-British force at Saloniki could do nothing, and even after it was strengthened by the army from Gallipoli, when, in December, that disastrous venture was at last given up, it was far from having the requisite vigor for an offensive campaign in Macedonia. The most that can be said for the allied action in favor of imperilled Serbia was that, though it started late and was poorly coördinated, it secured a foothold at the head of the Aegean, which might at some future date be turned to account for an attack upon the communications of the central powers with the Near East.

The relations with Greece, in spite of her " benevolent neutrality," remained strained and obscure and long hindered the Saloniki front from becoming active. In fact not till the allies, their patience at an end, had by open threats brought Greece to their side and forced the resignation of their subtle enemy,

The allies create a new front at Saloniki.

The allies oblige Greece to fight on their side.

King Constantine, did they feel fully secure on the Greek shorés. That abdication, however, resulting from direct military pressure by the Franco-British forces, did not take place till June, 1917. With the king's departure from the country his second son, Alexander, became sovereign, and Venizelos, resuming control, immediately plunged the country into war on the entente's side. The Greek army together with the Serb forces, refreshed in spirit and brought with entirely renewed equipment from their haven in Corfu, swelled the Franco-British contingent at the Saloniki base until the motley elements, consolidated under the command of a French general, were at last in a position to take an effective hand in the Balkan game.

Germany, by means of a federated Mitteleuropa, dominates the Near East.

The entrance of Bulgaria into the war on the side of the central powers, followed by the successful conquest of Serbia, tremendously raised Teutonic prestige throughout Balkania and the Near East. With Serbia eliminated, the four allies, Germany, Austria-Hungary, Bulgaria, and Turkey, formed an unbroken chain stretching from the North sea to the Persian gulf. For Germany, the directing head of the combination, her boldest imperialist dream had suddenly come true. Uninterruptedly the railway ran from Berlin through Viennna, Budapest, Belgrad, Sofia, and Constantinople to Bagdad, magic city of the Arabian nights on the far-off Tigris. Friend and foe alike realized — but with what different feelings! — that the quadruple alliance signified a novel and incalculable political entity, a federated *Mitteleuropa*, dominated by imperial Germany and spreading the net of its influence over the whole Near East as far as the isthmus of Suez and the Mesopotamian basin. At the end of the second year of the war not only did Germany appear victorious, but such a dazzling prospect lay before her that neither leaders nor people perceived the dark perils lurking in the situation.

The war, by becoming a war of attrition, spells the doom of the central powers.

On close scrutiny the German difficulties reveal themselves in their full extent and furnish the explanation why the entente, even when passing through the valley of humiliation, did not lose confidence in ultimate victory. Germany was joined with three relatively weak and brittle states, which would inevitably go to pieces if the war became a test of endurance. Obliged to supply not only its own war material but that of its friends as well, and required to lend numerous divisions of its troops to strengthen their wavering lines, the Teuton empire ran a lively risk of itself becoming exhausted, should the struggle prove to be unduly prolonged. When Germany failed in 1914 to settle the war with a hoped-for, smashing victory, it became reasonably clear to the initiated that the struggle would be one of mutual attrition, and in such a conflict the powers of the entente, with their vast population, their unmeasured wealth of raw and finished products, and with their access, by reason of their command of the sea, to every clime and harbor of the world, possessed an overwhelming advantage. For some time after 1914 the scales still seemed to tip in favor of Germany, owing to the efficiency of her military and industrial organization. Possibly the end of 1915 saw her at the zenith of her fortunes. With the year 1916 an impalpable decline set in. It was as if the ocean tide, having reached its acme, paused an appreciable period before deciding to retire. Such recession as there was in 1916 signified that the attention of the limited German resources was beginning to tell. Taken as a whole, the campaign of this year presents the picture of locked battle lines in substantial equilibrium.

To be sure, in the spring of 1916 Germany lost heavily at Verdun in an attempt to break through the French lines; but in the summer months the allies, on essaying to smash the German defenses along the river Somme, were equally unsuccessful. Timing their action with the Somme drive, the Russians under General Brussilov made a concentrated assault on the Austrian sectors of the eastern battle front, and pushing victoriously into Bukovina, threatened Hungary itself. This vigorous double pressure on the central powers, east and west, encouraged the only Balkan state still at peace, Rumania, to take the leap which it had long been contemplating. During the larger part of the long reign of King Charles the Latin kingdom had been an outpost of the Triple alliance, and hanging, as it did, on the Russian flank, was a valuable link in the central European system. But the Balkan crisis of 1912 put an end to this flirtation with Germany and Austria, since Rumania found it advantageous to align herself with Serbia and Greece and to court the goodwill of Russia. Charles, the Hohenzollern monarch, remained personally attached to the central powers, but he died in October

Rumania joins the allies, August, 1916.

1914, and his nephew, Ferdinand, who succeeded him, was a man without political color and with no strong preferences of any sort. Under these circumstances the government cautiously met the outbreak of the world war with a declaration of neutrality, but, with an eye to the main chance, sharpened its sword in order to use it for the national program if the opportunity should come. In the summer of 1916 the leaders of Rumanian opinion came to the conclusion that the Austrians were so badly broken by the Russian advance into Bukovina that a thrust through the Carpathian mountains into Transylvania would probably finish them. Transylvania and Bukovina were largely populated by Rumanians and constituted, as a *terra irredenta*, the goal of Rumanian national hopes. The entente, entirely willing to purchase Rumanian aid by the proffer of Austrian territory, solemnly promised the irredentist areas to the Bucharest government, which, thus encouraged, on August 27, 1916, declared war.

Defeat of Rumania.

But Rumania made its reckoning without the host. The Austrians received immediate and efficient help from Germany, which took the whole perilous situation into its own masterful hands. A double attack on Rumania, the one directed from the west at the Carpathian passes, the other from the south at the Dobrudja, was entirely successful, the Rumanians were outflanked, defeated in repeated battles, and finally driven out of Bucharest and the whole province of Wallachia. With a shattered remnant of their army they found themselves reduced, when winter set in, to a last stand along the Sereth river in Moldavia. The campaign of 1916 disposed of Rumania almost as completely as the campaign of the year before had disposed of Serbia, and to a discouraged Frenchman or Britisher the imperial eagle of Germany may have seemed to be soaring higher and to be surveying a more splendid prospect than ever.

Turning of the tide in 1917.

But all the while the exhaustion of the central powers was proceeding apace, though by scarcely perceptible stages. When in April, 1917, the United States of America entered the struggle and put its tremendous resources of men and material at the service of the entente, the war was as good as decided. With uplifted spirits the allies resumed their task and, although they met with obdurate resistance, they scored in the new campaign a number of important successes, especially in the Near East. In February,

1917, a British expedition under General Maude began a march from the Persian gulf up the Tigris and in March captured Bagdad. Although halted for the moment, it henceforth threatened the hold of Turkey on its eastern provinces. Later in the year another British expedition under General Allenby undertook an even more promising invasion from the isthmus of Suez in the direction of Syria, and in December entered in triumph the sacred city of Jerusalem.

In connection with the advance into Palestine highly important services were rendered the British by their Arab allies. And therewith we touch upon a significant feature of the beginning Ottoman disintegration. The nationalist movement, enormously stimulated the world over by the propaganda of the war, had at last penetrated even to the remote children of the desert, and, though they were Moslems like the Turks, they took advantage of the British offer of help against the sultan and struck for political independence. Easily the most eminent Arab tribal chieftain was Hussein, the sherif of Mecca, the Moslem holy city. Taken in 1916 under the British wing, he no longer hesitated to act and proclaimed himself (November) king of the Hedjaz, that is, king of the territory which appears on the map as a long and narrow strip of west Arabian coast. King Hussein's wild horsemen, equipped by the British with modern implements of war, proved effective allies in the desert fighting in southern Palestine. But quite apart from the question of their military worth, their mere defection from the standard of the Ottoman calif delivered a staggering blow to the prestige of Turkey in the Near East. It was not likely that the battered fabric of the Ottoman state could long withstand the vise-like pressure applied at Bagdad and Jerusalem.

The end not only for Turkey, but for Bulgaria, Austria-Hungary, and Germany as well, came with dramatic and breathless suddenness in the campaign of 1918. Concerned only with a small segment of the war, we are obliged to pass over the many contributory factors in Europe and throughout the world which produced the allied victory at that particular point of time. Though the triumph came late, precisely because it came late and only after the central powers had been drained of the last ounce of strength, it was unqualified and complete. The first

Ottoman disintegration: the revolt of Arabia.

Breakdown and surrender of Bulgaria, September, 1918.

break occurred in Bulgaria. This state, facing the allies on the
Saloniki front, was condemned to military inaction during the
long period when the Saloniki army was being assembled and
whipped into shape for a powerful, future offensive. We have
seen how the refusal by King Constantine of Greece to enter the
war on the side of the allies effectively paralyzed the Saloniki
army till 1917. From then on its numbers, as well as its offensive
power, grew rapidly until on September 14, 1918, it received
orders to begin a general attack. By that time the fighting spirit
of the Bulgars, chiefly peasants longing for their fields and families and unable to understand the policy which divorced them
from their normal existence, had been reduced to zero, and they
broke disastrously all along the line. That subtle spiritual
energy, called morale, had disappeared and, over night almost,
the Bulgar defeat became a rout. Pushing their advantage, the
allied forces streamed up the Vardar valley, crossed the water-
shed, and threatened Sofia itself. In utter panic the government
offered to treat, and on September 30 signed an armistice on the
basis of unconditional surrender. To mark the passing of the
old order the discredited Tsar Ferdinand abdicated in favor of
his son, Boris.

**Break-
down and
surrender of
Turkey.** An equally formidable blow, so timed as to fall upon the Turks
at the moment when the Bulgars were already reeling, brought
about the Ottoman collapse. On September 19 the Palestine
drive of General Allenby and his Arab friends was resumed with
such power and daring that the opposing Turkish army was, in
the course of a few weeks, practically annihilated. The capture
of Aleppo on October 26 enabled the British to cut the Bagdad
railway. The consternation at Constantinople over these
lightning-like blows was so great that Enver Bey and his Young
Turk associates resigned office and the chastened sultan hurried
to come to terms with the victors. An armistice, signed October
30, ended the war in the Near East.

**Break-
down of
Austria-
Hungary and
Germany.** The turn of Austria-Hungary came next, and when, in early
November, the ramshackle structure crashed to the ground, it fell
hopelessly and finally apart. The various racial groups deposed
the house of Hapsburg and proclaimed their independence. Last
came the fall of Germany. On November 11 agents of the
German government signed an armistice, which put Germany at

the mercy of the victors, save for such protection as might be derived from the pledge of the allies to be governed — with certain specific reservations — by the famous peace program of President Wilson, known as the Fourteen Points. Even before the armistice was signed, the last hour of the imperial government had struck. A revolution at Berlin led to the proclamation of a republic and on November 9, William II, spurned by his people and even by his once devoted army, fled ingloriously to Holland.

The terrible struggle which had stretched the world upon the rack for over four years, and had ended by bringing down, like a house of cards, not only the four defeated powers but also the vast empire of Russia, was at an end. The victors were masters of the situation. It remained to be seen what they would make of their unparalleled triumph.

Unparalleled triumph of the allies.

CHAPTER XXXII

THE PEACE — AND AFTER

The Paris conference of 1919. THE Peace conference of the victorious allies, which, in January, 1919, assembled at Paris, does not concern us for its own sake any more than did the Great War. We are interested only in the arrangements which it made affecting the Balkan peninsula and the Ottoman empire. However, as these arrangements resulted from the same general conditions and the same state of mind as determined the other decisions arrived at in Paris and laid down in a succession of international treaties, it is necessary that we turn our attention briefly to the main influences struggling for ascendancy among the diplomats who came together in the French capital to act as spokesmen and representatives of the victorious nations.

Composition of the victor group. The war, we are aware, was an imperialist struggle, the inevitable upshot of the frantic competition inaugurated by the commercial and industrial development of Europe and by the determination of the great powers to draw such backward continents as Africa and Asia within the sphere of their influence. To still further embitter the situation the spirit of nationalism had increasingly asserted itself, prompting the small and submerged groups everywhere to aim at independent statehood and moving all groups, large and small alike, to win a fuller scope for their language, their customs, and their culture. On the termination of the war the victorious allies embraced, besides the four great powers, Great Britain, France, Italy, and Japan, almost a score of minor states, among which Belgium and Serbia stood out most conspicuously. Russia, so to speak a charter member of the entente, had in 1917, in consequence of the Bolshevist revolution, dropped from the allied ranks. Its place had been taken and more than filled by the United States of America which, though only informally bound to the allies, had proved a leading factor in the overthrow of the central monarchies.

Save the United States, which had entered the war late and for reasons of its own, the victors were, when the surrender of Germany ended the struggle, filled with unrestrained rejoicing, primarily on the ground that they might now satisfy their imperialist and nationalist aims at the expense of their defeated enemies. In anticipation of such an ending they had, even while the struggle was at its height, entered into negotiations with one another to obtain a general acknowledgment of the advantages which each one envisaged as his stake in the war. A whole series of secret treaties had resulted, which, laid on the peace table at Paris, to a large extent determined the course of the negotiations before they were begun. The president of the United States, who had signed no secret treaties and who entertained no imperialist aims, would doubtless have been gratified if the atmosphere could have been cleared by a sweeping renunciation of all private understandings; but as there was a universal unwillingness to even consider this step, Woodrow Wilson, who had gone to Paris to act in person for his country, bowed to the inevitable. The secret treaties were validated and every victor got his pound of flesh.

The secret treaties.

At the same time the president resolved to mitigate the effect of the secret treaties and to weaken the selfish spirit which was behind them by championing a pacifist program of world organization. In liberal circles generally, throughout Europe and America, the ugly hatreds and mad destructiveness of the war had produced a powerful sentiment in favor of finishing once and for all with the vicious system of imperialist rivalry. Another such orgy, it was deeply felt, and our boasted civilization would go down like a scuttled ship. Of all such forward-looking groups President Wilson had made himself the admired mouthpiece by virtue of a number of official pronouncements, among which the Fourteen Points, being fourteen principles conceived as the basis of a new democratic and anti-imperialist world order, particularly caught the popular fancy. To flatter the powerful representative of the United States the diplomats at Paris gave eloquent lip-worship to his idealism, but as they simultaneously and stubbornly held fast to the concrete advantages secured to them by the

President Wilson, champion of the League of Nations.

secret treaties, the most that the president could obtain was the adoption of a new international code — for future use. This was laid down in the Covenant of the League of Nations and incorporated as an integral part in the treaty of Versailles. It certainly did not augur well for the furtherance of that international justice, in the name of which the League of Nations was founded, that it was tied up with the treaty of Versailles, probably as harsh a product of the ruthless spirit of victory as is recorded in history; but as President Wilson could get his world organization on no other terms, he reluctantly put his name to the compromise. Though he had won a very dubious victory, he might justly claim not only that he was the prophet of a new world but that he had set up, and for the first time in history, international machinery, which, if men would only muster the necessary good will, might effect a cure of the worst evils threatening the security and happiness of the world. In default of an informing spirit of candor and brotherhood the League of Nations would of course prove to be a lifeless institution, an unhandsome piece of useless junk; but that would not be President Wilson's fault, since all that one man might reasonably be expected to do would be to lead the way out of bondage, putting it up to his generation to follow him or not.

The treaties with the vanquished the exclusive work of the great victor powers. Apart, then, from the vaguely radiant promise held out by the League of Nations, the peace treaties which the victors dictated to the vanquished were highly characteristic expressions of a world moved by imperialist and nationalist passions. When, on June 28, 1919, the treaty of Versailles had been disposed of by receiving the signature of the new German republic, the negotiations were taken up in turn with the defeated associates of the former German empire, with Austria, Hungary, Bulgaria, and Turkey. In September, 1919, the treaty of St. Germain received the signature of Austria, while two months later Bulgaria humbly submitted to the treaty of Neuilly. Owing to revolutionary trouble in Hungary, that state did not have the treaty of Trianon presented to it for signature till January, 1920; and, owing to still graver difficulties in Asia Minor, the treaty with the Ottoman empire, called the treaty of Sèvres, was not ready till August, 1920. All these treaties were drawn up by the Supreme Council of the great powers, that is, of Great Britain, France,

Italy, Japan, and the United States, and were almost as completely dictated to the small Balkan governments, members of the entente, as to the vanquished states. It goes without saying though, that the Supreme Council favored its friends, Serbia, Greece, and Rumania, at the expense of its enemies, Austria, Hungary, Bulgaria, and Turkey, which paid the price of defeat with the loss of territory, a huge indemnity, and in countless other ways. Doubtless the dictatorship of the magnates conferred one inestimable benefit in that it tended to eliminate disputes among the smaller powers. For let no one doubt that if Rumania, Serbia, and Greece had been left free to draw their boundaries according to their own taste, they would have preferred demands, even against each other, which would have led to interminable debates and, in the end, to a new explosion. As it was, the authority of the Paris dictators, though great, was not great enough to avoid some very dangerous outbreaks.

Let us now examine in turn the Balkan states as they emerged from the Paris conferences; and since Serbia was such a considerable factor in the Great War let us begin our round with the little Slav kingdom. Not only had the already excessive nationalism of the Serbs been still further stimulated by the war, but the closely related Slav groups to the west, the Croats and Slovenes, had been drawn into the whirlpool. Proclaiming the need of founding a Jugoslav or South Slav state on the ruins of the Hapsburg monarchy, representatives of the three peoples had met in 1917 on the island of Corfu and outlined as their goal a kingdom of the Serbs, Croats, and Slovenes united under the Serb dynasty of Karageorgevich. To this program the Peace conference gave unqualified support and set about drawing the boundaries of the new state. Of course the South Slav statesmen, admitted to consultation, suggested boundaries representing extreme national demands. As against Austria, Hungary, and Bulgaria, defeated neighbors of the South Slavs, these wishes were granted readily enough, but in the case of Italy, Rumania, and Albania, which also bordered on the South Slavs and which could raise a voice in their own behalf in the circle of the mighty, an accommodation became necessary. In each instance it proved exceedingly difficult. With Rumania the trouble arose over the former Hungarian banat of Temesvar. Both Bucharest and

Recognition by the Peace conference of Jugoslavia.

Belgrad claimed this rich agricultural district, which by a Solomonic verdict the Supreme Council finally divided between the two disputants. In the case of the young and extraordinarily weak state of Albania the quarrel was joined over the valley of the Drin with its outlet *via* Scutari to the Adriatic sea. Though the Paris conferees took the side of Albania, the Belgrad government can hardly be said to have fully acquiesced in the decision, since as late as the autumn of 1921 it attempted to seize the Drin valley by an armed *coup*.

Boundary conflict with Italy. But graver than either of these difficulties of the young South Slav state was the conflict with Italy. In order to persuade Rome to enter the war on their side, the allies had been obliged to make the numerous territorial concessions embodied in the secret treaty of London of April, 1915. This document handed over to Italy considerable territory under Hapsburg rule, but racially South Slav, in Dalmatia, in Istria, and in the hinterland of the great Adriatic port of Trieste. Intoxicated by the total collapse of Austria-Hungary, the Italian delegation at Paris claimed, in addition to the above concessions, the only other outlet of central Europe on the Adriatic, the city of Fiume. This excellent port was demanded by the Italians on nationalist grounds. As a matter of fact, although Fiume, like Trieste, possessed an Italian majority, the countryside all round was so completely Croat that Fiume was by the most favorable interpretation an Italian island in a South Slav sea.

The Fiume controversy. Over Fiume a tremendous storm broke when a band of Italian super-patriots, led by the fiery nationalist poet, Gabriele d'Annunzio, marched in and seized it (September, 1919). The ensuing strain was terrible and more than once war threatened between Italy and her South Slav neighbor. In the end, however, owing to the moderating influence of the other allies, saner counsels prevailed and in the agreement of Rapallo (November, 1920) Italy wisely receded from her extreme demands, consenting even to modify the terms of the treaty of London. Although she retained her dominant position at the head of the Adriatic (Trieste, Istria), she gave up her claim to the Dalmatian coast excepting only to the city of Zara, with a limited hinterland, and to a few small, but strategically important islands. Dalmatia is almost solidly South Slav and very properly goes to the South

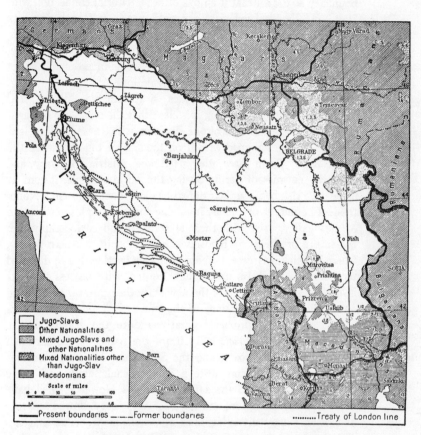

THE BOUNDARIES OF JUGO-SLAVIA (1919)

Key to numerals: 1, Jugo-Slavs; 2, Italians; 3, Germans; 4, Czecho-Slovaks; 5, Magyars; 6, Rumanians; 7, Bulgarians; 8, Albanians; 9, Macedonians; 10, Greeks; 11, Vlachs; 12, Turks. From Isaiah Bowman's *The New World.* Copyright, 1921, by World Book Company, Yonkers-on-Hudson, New York.

Slav kingdom. Further, Fiume was declared a free city and its boundary so drawn that it enjoys direct territorial connection with Italy. If the decision does not spell peace, it is calculated to bring about the adjournment of strife. The Adriatic remains, as planned by the treaty of London, under the control of Italy, but Jugoslavia is by a free Fiume afforded an economic outlet and need not fear commercial strangulation.

Jugo-slavia's border difficulties with six neighbors. Settled as these boundary issues with Rumania, Albania, and Italy seem temporarily to be, it is clear that the new state of Jugo-slavia is involved in dangerous disputes with these three neighbors, all of them aligned with it on the side of the entente in the Great War. From three other neighbors, Austria, Hungary, and Bulgaria, enemies of Serbia during the world struggle, it runs at present no risk because their defeat has left them impotent. None-the-less boundary problems, involving the ever explosive question of nationality, exist with these states also and considerably dim the future prospects of Jugoslavia. Only on its southern border, where it touches Greece, is there no active friction due to disputed territorial claims. Its unfortunate contact with no less than six ill-disposed neighbors gives the new state the appearance of being one of the weakest creations of the war.

Centraliza-tion *versus* provincial autonomy. Serious internal problems greatly add to the gravity of the situation. Offically Jugoslavia bears the name of the kingdom of the Serbs, the Croats, and the Slovenes. The three member groups indubitably constitute a single racial family, all using dialectic variations of the same language. However, they have never been united before and have for ages past followed separate and often widely diverging lines of development. The Slovenes and Croats, as Roman Catholics, have had a western orientation, whereas the Serbs, as adherents of the Greek Orthodox church, have taken their civilization largely from the east. This spiritual gulf explains why the centralized monarchy, desired by the Serbs, is not to the taste of the Slovenes and Croats, who would much prefer a federal system giving the non-Serb elements a liberal measure of home-rule. Some extremists among the Croats and Slovenes even go so far as to champion the abolition of the royal house of Karageorgevich and the establishment of a loosely joined republic. In the hope that time would allay the domestic controversy the making of the constitution of the new state was discreetly adjourned for three years. Finally, in 1921, there met at Belgrad a constitutional assembly, in which a majority declared for a centralized monarchy modified by a certain measure of self-government for the administrative districts, into which the country is to be divided. Apparently Bosnia, Dalmatia, Croatia and the other historical entities composing the new state are earmarked for disappearance. The kingdom of the Serbs, Croats, and Slovenes is to be a unitarian rather than a federative government.

Nor are we at the end of Jugoslavia's troubles, present and prospective. In Bosnia some 600,000 Moslemized Serbs, many of them begs, that is, great landholders, represent an unassimilated and perhaps unassimilable element, while the Slavs of annexed Macedonia constitute a no less serious problem. Racially as close indubitably to the Serbs as to the Bulgars, they were in their majority drawn to the Bulgar side by the intensive exarchist propaganda, of which we have taken note, and may not prove easy to de-Bulgarize. Finally, Montenegro should not be forgotten. A mountain eyrie, never conquered by the Turks, it early raised a clarion voice for freedom which was heard around the world. Throughout the Great War it fought shoulder to shoulder with its brother-state of Serbia against the Hapsburg monarchy. On the creation of the Jugoslav union the reason for Montenegro's separate existence passed away and it was, without more ado but with the consent of at least a portion of its people, incorporated in the new state. However, a conservative element, proud of the great traditions of the Black Mountain, vigorously protested against political extinction. Rallying around the dynasty, which, although exiled, was not forgotten in the homeland, a band of Montenegrin stalwarts continued to hold out for the perpetutation of the little Serb state which by its heroic past had deserved well of the nation. Doubtless before long the Juggernaut Time, indifferent to historic merit and concerned only with the needs of the passing hour, will ruthlessly drive its iron chariot over the Montenegrin opposition. Ancient Montenegro, absorbed by Jugoslavia, will then be nothing but a cherished memory.

Difficulties caused by the Bosnian Moslems, the Macedonian Slavs, and the Montenegrins.

In conclusion, a word may be devoted to statistics. Of the approximately 13,000,000 inhabitants of Jugoslavia less than

Jugoslav statistics.

one half are Serbs, less than one fourth are Croats, and less than one twelfth are Slovenes. If not an absolute majority, the Serbs are thus at least the preponderant element. In order to carry through the centralized government at which they aim, they must more or less completely assimilate not only the Croats and Slovenes but the Moslemized Serbs and Macedonian Slavs already mentioned and, in addition, the not inconsiderable minorities of Germans and Magyars along the northern and northwestern frontier. Such is the present problem; how or if it will be solved, only the future can tell.

Rumanian territorial increases authorized at Paris. For its share in the war Rumania was rewarded at Paris by receiving from Hungary the mountainous Transylvania together with a part of the rich lowland to the west of it, from Austria the province of Bukovina, and from Russia Bessarabia. These territories were preponderantly occupied by people of Rumanian speech and swelled the total population of the kingdom to 16,000,000. As less than four million of this number were non-Rumanians, the relatively compact racial character of the enlarged state is not subject to challenge. None-the-less, the borders, as in Jugoslavia, though not to the same extent, augur trouble in the days to come.

Rumanian border troubles with Bulgaria, Hungary, and Russia. In the Dobrudja the boundary with Bulgaria stands as established in 1913. But as it was then drawn at the expense of Bulgaria and in clear defiance of the principle of nationality, it will probably long remain a source of ill-will between the two neighbors. More serious is the friction with Hungary, for although the Hungarian lands conceded to the Latin kingdom were mainly Rumanian, it proved impossible to draw practicable boundaries for Rumania without including within them about two million Magyars and Germans, whom it will not be easy to reconcile to their lot. Bessarabia, taken over from Russia, is another difficulty. Its lowlands, north of the mouth of the Danube, are inhabited chiefly by Ukrainians, who may gravitate toward the Ukrainian state, provided such an entity ever emerges from the existing Russian chaos. Besides, Russia itself may recover its strength in the not too distant future and may then raise the question as to the rights of the Rumanians to a province which they have seized but which Russia has never formally relinquished.

One of the greatest difficulties experienced by the Rumanian state ever since its founding in 1859 bears the name of the Jews. Unquestionably the acquisition of Bessarabia dangerously strengthens the numbers of this people. The point to note about the Jews both in Rumania and Russia is that they have remained a persistently alien element subjected to rigorous exceptional legislation.[1] Before permitting Rumania to enter into complete enjoyment of her enlarged boundaries, the Paris conferees obliged her to sign the so-called minorities treaty. It was not an isolated action on their part, since similar treaties were imposed on the other Balkan states to the same end of securing to the racial minorities of each country a guarantee against conspicuous inequality of treatment. Under this pact the Jews and every other minority group enjoy not only full citizen rights but the free cultivation of their language, religion, and customs. While the safeguards provided for the racial minorities look ample on paper, it remains to be seen if Rumania, and for that matter any other Balkan state, means to be bound by them. The problem is peculiarly thorny and not to be disposed of with a sweeping *a priori* judgment. For, as even a political novice can see, if the provisions of the minority treaties are scrupulously carried out, each state will be nursing irredentist centers in its bosom; if, on the other hand, the provisions should be disregarded, the minorities are sure to raise the cry of persecution, than which there is no more effective means of national propaganda in the world.

The question of the Jews and of minorities generally.

The conspicuous agricultural and mineral riches of Rumania hold out a promise of great future prosperity. If the people are backward in the arts and are educationally behind the times, they have the habit of work and, ethnologically, are uncommonly homogeneous. Therefore, in spite of serious border and minority troubles, Rumania may be considered to be one of the strongest states developed on the widely scattered ruins of the Ottoman, the Hapsburg, and the Russian empires.

The basis of Rumanian hopes.

Bulgaria came out of the war heavily damaged not only in prestige and wealth, but also in territory. That she lost Macedonia, which she had held from 1915 to 1918 and for the sake of which she had joined the central powers, goes without saying.

The territorial losses of Bulgaria.

[1] See p. 377.

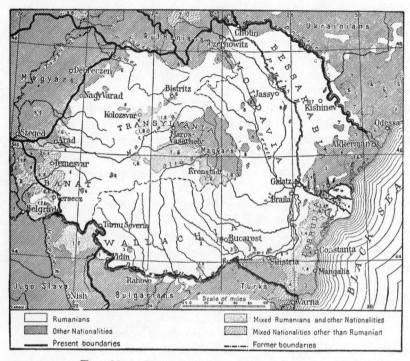

THE NEW BOUNDARIES OF RUMANIA (1919)

Key to numerals: 1, Rumanians; 2, Jugo-Slavs; 3, Bulgarians; 4, Turks; 5, Greeks; 6, Germans; 7, Ukrainians (Ruthenians); 8, Magyars; 9, Czecho-Slovaks; 10, Poles. From Isaiah Bowman's *The New World.* Copyright, 1921, by World Book Company, Yonkers-on-Hudson, New York.

In addition, Serbia insisted on certain boundary rectifications on strategical grounds, while Greece was content with nothing less than the whole Aegean littoral and Thrace. This Greek action was a body-blow since it deprived southern Bulgaria of access to the sea by its natural route following the Maritsa river. President Wilson long hesitated to yield to the extreme Greek demands, but the Greeks had powerful friends among the statesmen at Paris and carried the day. Bulgaria at present has three neighbors, Greece on the south, Jugoslavia on the west, and Rumania on the north. Against all three she nurses a territorial grievance, a circumstance which makes her future look dark and which does not promise well for the peace of the peninsula.

Defeated and diminished Bulgaria has about 4,000,000 inhabitants, no more than a fraction of the population of the victorious and enlarged states of Jugoslavia and Rumania. On the other hand, Bulgaria is not weakened by the presence, in numbers, of racial minorities and boasts an industrious peasant population eager to be educated and generally progressive. On the elimination, through the war, of Tsar Ferdinand, his young son, Boris, succeeded him, but the real power passed into the hands of the organized peasants. Under their leader, Stambolisky, they have established what looks like an agrarian republic with strong anti-urban and anti-capitalist tendencies. Of course the relatively small group of professional men and merchants has indicated its distaste for this turn of affairs and may presently effect a compromise, since Bulgaria, stripped and bankrupted by the war, cannot get along without a capable productive organization of a modern type. Involved in a radical economic experiment and confronted, although herself disarmed under the treaty of Neuilly, with three neighbors who remain armed to the teeth, Bulgaria is undisguisedly in a sorry plight. Only peace and hard work through generations can put her on the road to recovery. *Internal difficulties of Bulgaria.*

During the stress of the Great War the feeble state of Albania went wholly to pieces. That it would ever be reconstituted seemed very doubtful in view of the fact that Greece and Jugoslavia coveted large southern and northern slices while Italy claimed very nearly all the remainder. Only the fortitude and *Albania comes to terms with Italy.*

resolution of the Albanians themselves saved the situation. During the peace negotiations at Paris they organized sufficiently to drive the Italians to the sea and finally even out of the commanding position of Valona. Thereupon the government of Rome, discreetly drawing in its horns, recognized the independence of Albania in return for the right to occupy the spit of land that guards the approaches to the coveted Valona. In this manner, while gaining the good will of a small neighbor, Italy secured herself against the utilization by any rival power, for purposes of its own, of the Gibraltar of the Adriatic. That name, currently given to Valona, conveys an idea of its remarkable stragetic importance.

Albania admitted to the League of Nations as an independent state.
The Italian treaty greatly raised the prestige of the provisional government which had undertaken the task of creating an Albanian state. In December, 1920, the provisional government further strengthened its hand by persuading the League of Nations to admit Albania to membership. As the boundaries were not finally drawn by the omnipotent powers till a year later, the difficulties of the fledgling state remained great and were utilized by envious Jugoslavia to press an attack in the direction of the Drin outlet. The South Slavs, as we have seen, aim to control the Scutari region. Fortunately the rude invasion was defeated by the stern veto of the council of the League of Nations — one of the rare occasions on which the new international authority has proved that it is not wholly without teeth.

The uncertain Albanian outlook.
The future of the new state is as doubtful as that of a young lamb stalked by hungry wolves and protected by the vague benevolence of a distant assembly of patriarchs. Albania has but 1,000,000 inhabitants, economically and intellectually the most backward in the peninsula. Moreover, they are hindered from forming an effective union by the clan organization of the northern districts, by the persistence of the blood feud, and by religious differences. Even in the face of the almost innumerable perils confronting the state, the existing government has not succeeded in winning the allegiance of all the sections of the country. Domestic explosions continue unabated. Doubtless a stable Albanian state would contribute to the peace and security of Balkania; but should it be achieved within the decade following the world war, it would have to be accounted a political miracle.

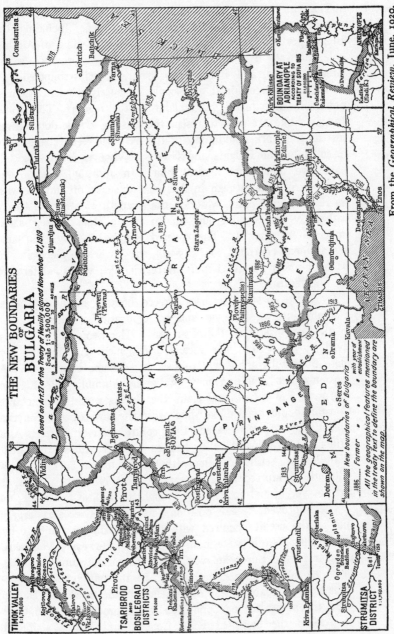

THE NEW BOUNDARIES
OF
BULGARIA

Based on Art.27 of the Treaty of Neuilly signed November 27,1919

Scale 1:3,500,000

From the *Geographical Review*, June, 1920.

Greece
acquires
Thrace,
Smyrna, and
the Dode-
kanese.

The chief territorial increase accorded to the kingdom of Greece by the Peace conference was Thrace, including the Bulgar port of Dedeagatch and the important mart of Adrianople, hitherto a Turkish city. Thrace is a province where Greeks, Turks, and Bulgars are inextricably intermingled. So far as can be ascertained, each could, on purely ethnical grounds, put forth an equally valid claim to the region. Turks and Bulgars alike are sure to resent the existing Greek domination, just as the Turk domination of the past had been clamorously resented by the Bulgars and Greeks. Whoever is top-dog will have two under-dogs against him. In addition, Greece was given, across the Aegean in Anatolia, the city of Smyrna with its rich outlying plain, while on the strength of a special treaty with Italy the island group, known as the Dodekanese, passed under Greek control. The coveted Rhodes was by this same arrangement conceded to Italy till 1925, when a plebiscite, to be held under certain important restrictions, was to determine its final status.

Greek
ambition.

By these coastal increases Greece became more than ever a dominating Aegean power and, by implication, a weighty factor in all the concerns of the Near East. Her people have always lived by trade and her recent development has pushed her more powerfully than ever to seek her fortune on the sea. A too unbridled ambition may prove her stumbling-block. On the pretext of a historical claim the Greeks would fain acquire Constantinople and, dissatisfied with the size of the Smyrna salient, they aspire to extend their control over all western Asia Minor. This forward policy has, as an aftermath of the Great War, led to serious conflict with the Anatolian Turks. Intermittently conducted since the armistice of November, 1918, it has not yet (June, 1922) been brought to a close.

The rivalry
between
Venizelos
and King
Constan-
tine.

The improved Aegean position accorded to Greece is largely due to the credit acquired with the allies during the war by the leading Greek statesman, Venizelos. However, Venizelos, popular in the European west, is by no means universally beloved among his own countrymen. In the parliamentary elections held in 1920 he was overwhelmingly defeated and had to yield the power to the opposition which promptly called back to Athens the banished King Constantine. Party strife in

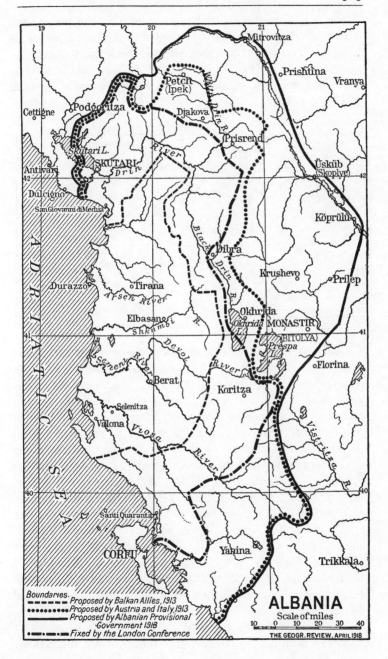

ALBANIA
Scale of miles

Boundaries.
––– ––– Proposed by Balkan Allies, 1913
•••••••• Proposed by Austria and Italy, 1913
––––––– Proposed by Albanian Provisional
·Government 1918
•–•–•–• Fixed by the London Conference

THE GEOGR. REVIEW, APRIL 1918

Greece, owing to the political passions of a mobile people, has a frenzied character which interferes with a gradual and well-balanced development and intermittently lands the ship of state upon the rocks. The Greeks have yet to learn that a successful policy depends on more than a strong patriotic emotion, recklessly indulged.

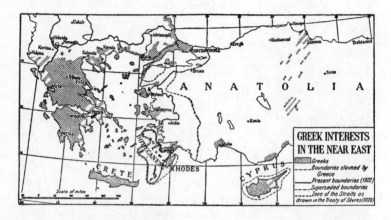

GREEK INTERESTS IN THE NEAR EAST
Greeks
Boundaries claimed by Greece
Present boundaries (1922)
Superseded boundaries
Zone of the Straits as drawn in the Treaty of Sèvres(1920)

Internationalization of Constantinople and the straits.

Doubtless the hardest nut which the Peace conference had to crack was the age-old question of Constantinople. A secret treaty, drawn up in 1915 by the leading allies, conceded this key position to Russia, but Russia, having gone Bolshevik, was adjudged to have forfeited the prize. After prolonged debates it was resolved (treaty of Sèvres) to try one of the most original experiments of our time by declaring Constantinople and the straits area an international zone. Territorially the Zone of the Straits is insignificant, for it includes only a narrow strip of land on either side of the Bosporus, the sea of Marmora, and the Dardanelles. As a concession to Mohammedan sentiment the sultan was left in nominal possession of his ancient capital. Under the terms of the treaty the famous metropolis together with the Asiatic shoreland is to be administered by the Turks, while the Greeks receive similar administrative rights on the European side. This means that, though the actual shores have a neutral status, the government is divided between the two peoples on the ground, that is, Greeks and Turks. However, the all-important waterway is directly put under the control of an international commission which performs all the functions necessary to keep the channel open on equal terms to the ships of all the nations of the world. That the neutral character of the straits is emphatically affirmed in the Sèvres document will appear from the statement that they must remain open in peace and war alike to every kind of craft of every country, and that they must not be fortified or blockaded or subjected to any kind of hostile act. Should these regulations eliminate Constantinople as an apple of discord among the powers and turn the straits into an avenue of intercourse free to all the world, a step will have been taken hardly inferior in importance to the League of Nations as a cure for the evils afflicting a contentious and anarchic world.

Against the Ottoman empire the Peace conference rendered, to put it simply and succinctly, a verdict of death. The sentence is laid down, with all the details of the contemplated execution, in the treaty of Sèvres of August, 1920. By that instrument the vast areas of Arabia, Syria, and Mesopotamia were completely freed from Turkish control. Inhabited chiefly by Arabs, they had in part revolted during the war and were conceded a variable treatment according to the interests of the powers. The Hedjaz (Arabia) was declared independent under Hussein, the sherif of Mecca, who since 1917 has borne the title king of Arabia. Palestine, proclaimed a Jewish homeland, was given to Great Britain acting as mandatory of the League of Nations; and Mesopotamia was treated the same way. Syria was handed over to France, also on the mandate basis. The tragic case of the Armenians sufficiently appealed to the conferees to induce them to sketch an independent Armenian state in northeastern Asia Minor, without, however, moving them to assume any responsibility for its creation. The Armenia of the treaty of Sèvres still awaits realization and will, unless all signs deceive, wait long. What happened to Constantinople we have already seen and also how Greece had a slice of western Asia Minor carved out for her at Smyrna. These vigorous surgical operations left of the once extensive empire nothing but Anatolia, since the eleventh century the home of the Turk race and practically the only section of the empire in which it constituted a compact mass and an indisputable majority.

Dispersion of the Ottoman empire.

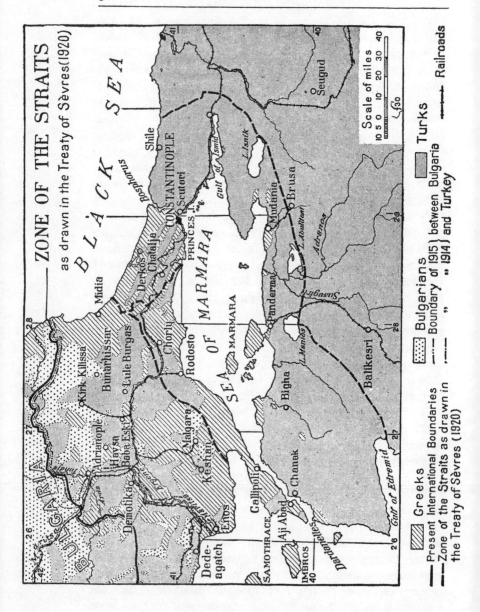

ZONE OF THE STRAITS
as drawn in the Treaty of Sèvres (1920)

BLACK SEA

SEA OF MARMARA

BULGARIA

Scale of miles
10 5 0 10 20 30 40

Greeks
Bulgarians
Turks

Present International Boundaries
Boundary of (1915) between Bulgaria and Turkey
        "   " 1914"
Zone of the Straits as drawn in the Treaty of Sèvres (1920)
Railroads

But even this reduced Anatolian Turkey was by the treaty of Sèvres by no means left in the hands of its owners. To begin with, Great Britain, France, and Italy, the makers of the treaty, asserted their right to all the privileges and monopolies, financial and economic, conceded to them prior to 1914. Next they took over, by means of various commissions, many of the essential functions of government. A further step was to carve out large spheres of influence in Anatolia, where each gained acknowledgement of " exclusive interests " — the familiar phrase indicative of a policy of economic penetration. Finally, they agreed to share the title to the once German-owned Bagdad railroad. Ottoman rule, reduced to a shadow, was apparently to continue, even as a shadow, only until the three victors, acting as receivers of a bankrupt estate, should be ready for the final distribution of its. assets.

Turkish rule reduced to a shadow even in Anatolia.

Unconsulted about these arrangements, the Anatolian Turks haughtily refused to accept them. Under the vigorous Mustapha Kemal Pasha they organized for resistance and set up a provisional government at Angora. The Greeks, already established at Smyrna and rendered confident by their recent successes, offered to act as a sheriff's posse and, in the name of an outraged Europe, to bring the malefactors to a wholesome sense of their impotence. They have made several attacks on the Angora government but so far (June, 1922) without striking success. The Turkish nationalists are masters of most of Anatolia and laugh at the treaty of Sèvres. The unrest produced by this contumacious conduct has spread to the whole Near East, keeping it simmering with discontent and revolt at a dozen points. Over this conspicuous failure of their authority the allies, and, more particularly, France and Great Britain have fallen violently apart. In November, 1921, France went so far as to pass over to the Kemalist side and to sign a private treaty with the Turks, which, should it be ratified, would practically abrogate the peace of Sèvres. How the Near East chaos will resolve itself no one can say, but three things are by now reasonably clear: (1) The treaty of Sèvres as drawn up in 1920 will never be executed; (2) the Anatolian Turks are a nationalist entity which may not be treated as negligible; (3) the imperialist rivalry of the powers over the Ottoman remains is as keen as ever with the difference that, owing

The successful resistance of the Anatolian Turks.

to the eliminations effected by the war, the rivalry has entered upon a new, a Franco-British phase.

Looking backward.

Our long journey, affording a view of three thousand years of Balkan development, is at an end. It would be yielding to a natural impulse to take a sweeping backward look over our trail and to comment on what we have heard and seen in the spirit of a traveler eager to extract from his experience observations and conclusions serviceable for his and his contemporaries' guidance. Surely we have encountered abundant matter relating to religion, education, social classes, methods of production, and forms of government. With these varied data numerous students of the Social Sciences have made and will continue to make it their business to concern themselves. Their task it is to sift, classify, and interpret until the troubled experiences of a limited section of mankind have been given scientific formulation available for the present and future development of our race.

Imperialism and nationalism the master-keys to the recent history of Balkania.

For one who, like the writer of this book, has consistently aimed at a straightforward record of occurrences, comment and deduction on this huge scale would be highly inappropriate. Yet one form of reflection is fairly within his range. In this last section he has shown how all recent events point to the dominance in Balkan politics of two great forces or rather force complexes. We have called them imperialism and nationalism and have dealt with them, without praise or blame, in the calm spirit of inquiry, as leading impulses or urges determining the main line of Balkan development. What we have encountered during the last century as movements of organization and disorganization, or what has appeared to us in the guise of revolt, war, reform, economic penetration, and international bargains, was mainly their work. They are the two master-keys to that Balkan mystery, which our busy generation, impatient of difficulties beyond the horizon of its immediate interests, has preferred to call the Balkan chaos and impatiently to dismiss from its presence.

Ideals are substantially programs of human adventure.

Now the interesting and notable thing regarding these two forces of imperialism and nationalism is that in all the European countries wherein they have dominated there has lately arisen a certain skepticism, a desire to reassess them from the point of view of the future of mankind. For, sooner or later, men will always ask if the spiritual agencies which they themselves have created and to which they have entrusted themselves as to a river sweeping onward to the open sea, are likely to conduct them to their goal. Regularly the hopefulness with which they have been hailed on their first appearance will be found to yield by slow degrees to doubt. The social psychologist, whose business it is to concern himself with these recurrences, should be able to formulate them in terms of law. Certainly a law is suggested by the rhythmic rise and fall in the valuation of all the concepts which have served to carry mankind from stage to stage in the long journey of its evolution. Christianity, humanism, democracy, rationalism, and science, to enumerate a few of these directive ideals of more recent date, will serve to illustrate the point. Greeted at their invasion of the human consciousness with vast enthusiasm as new and creative means of coming to grips with life, they soon developed drawbacks, declined from the level of sweeping panaceas to that of useful but limited devices, in short, underwent sea-changes by virtue of which they gradually assumed an entirely different form and hue.

That is what in recent years has almost imperceptibly been happening to the purposes and programs summarized as imperialism and nationalism. Belonging to nineteenth century Europe, they released an endless satisfaction in their day. The age now departed regarded them with a full and naïve faith as the best hope of the future. Only with the twentieth century did the suspicion begin to dawn that they had been overdone and that, carried further without check or correction, they would lead to a catastrophe. And in point of fact, because faiths firmly established are but slowly undermined, the prophesied catastrophe, indubitably the logical outcome of the whole trend of nineteenth century thought and effort, overtook the world in the Great War. But even before the war, and certainly since, a sentiment began to spread and solidify which has sought to supplant the national-imperialist faith with its feature of extreme and reckless struggle with the associative idea represented by a world union. No one alive today can any longer be ignorant that this idea has been gathering momentum and that its First Fruits are already here in the League of Nations of 1919 and the Washington Conference

Recent skepticism regarding the national-imperialist faith.

called in November, 1921, to consider the limitation of armaments
and the problem of peace in the Pacific. Imperfect creations
both, they are yet in their infancy but may, under favorable
nursing, reach an auspicious manhood.

Present
misery and
anarchy of
the Near
East curable
only by
modifica-
tion of the
national-
imperialist
faith.

How does all this bear upon the situation in our particular
field? Nationalism raised from the grave the buried Balkan
nationalities and together with the imperialism of the great powers
wrecked the Ottoman empire. By destroying what had ceased
to be useful and by encouraging what was vital and full of
promise nationalism and imperialism unquestionably served the
collective purpose of mankind. But by their excess they
threaten, like Father Chronos, whom the suggestive myth presents as devouring his own offspring, to end by destroying their
best handiwork. It admits of no question in view of the present
distressing and intolerable situation throughout the Near East
that if the nineteenth century achievements are to be saved, the
living generation must reformulate the national-imperialist
faith in terms of international coöperation. Coöperation in
place of selfish struggle — that is what, often dimly enough
it is true, we have in mind when we talk of leagues and
associations and world-wide agreements as the imperative
need of our time. If the new idea does not conquer the
thought of our hitherto imperialist societies, instead of recovery, there will be throughout the vast area once constituting the Ottoman empire, a rapid decline preliminary to
an unmitigated chaos. A Syrian poet recently expressed this
apprehension in striking terms: "Once" — he was glancing
mentally at the vanished Ottoman era — "I wept all day long;
now I weep for that day!" No one can look at the misery daily
increasing throughout the Near East without agreeing that unless
the program signified by the League of Nations makes headway
and that swiftly, we may live to see the time when the vanished
Ottoman empire, which at least maintained a certain semblance
of peace within its boundaries, will be mourned like a lost Eden.

League of
Nations and
Balkan
Federation
as comple-
mentary
programs.

In the narrower field of Balkania the situation is different and
yet the same. To a certain limited extent the League of Nations
is already operative there and makes for peace. Had it not
directly or indirectly imposed its authority, Jugoslavia and
Albania, Greece and Bulgaria, would already have taken each

other by the throat. To a degree, too, the imperialist greed of the powers is less active, partly because of their exhaustion through the war, and partly because of the temporary settlement of the problem of the straits. For the moment therefore the Balkan outlook is more hopeful. But the imposition of an irresistible external authority on the rival states is not enough. Unless the various peoples, that is, the individual men and women composing them, develop a certain sense of fellowship together with the will to live for a common human end, there will be no security and no spiritual development worthy of the name. For the realization of this more perfect local coöperation the only feasible device which has ever been suggested is a Balkan Federation. While there has been no lack of talk of a Balkan Federation, and while sometimes the talk has even been quite active talk, on the whole the project has made little, if any, headway. Yet as every one can see it is the necessary Balkan complement to an effective League of Nations. If peace is the supreme desideratum, and such seems to be the common opinion of our day, the microcosm of Balkania must learn to adjust its national passions to a common program, exactly as, with a similar end in view, the macrocosm of this our earth must effect its unity and organize its efforts in accordance with a plan embracing all humanity and realizable only through some form of international association.

CONCLUSION

THE BALKAN PENINSULA AND THE NEAR EAST: THE NEWEST PHASE OF AN ANCIENT PROBLEM.

ALTHOUGH this book has treated the history of man on the limited area of the Balkan peninsula, it will be found that, without an express effort on the part of the author and merely by reason of the entanglement of the peninsula with its associated Mediterranean areas, the completed work has something of the character of a history of the whole Near East. Hardly a page will fail to testify to the necessity of viewing the Balkan peninsula less as a circumscribed, self-dependent territory than as a vital link in the chain of lands around the bend of the eastern Mediterranean and, therefore, as no more than a single factor in the story of their long and inter-related evolution. Especially whenever in the ages past a movement was under way directed to the end of bringing all the east-Mediterranean countries under a single rule has the Balkan peninsula been wont to leap to the front and to assert what looks like a predestined primacy. The empire of Alexander the Great, the Roman empire, the Byzantine empire, and the Ottoman empire, all dedicated to the purpose of effecting the unification of the Near East, alike utilized the Balkan peninsula as their administrative center; and the last three, under a geographical pressure which could not be resisted, set up their capital at Constantinople. If history may be said to warrant any confident deduction from the successsive political phases of the Near East, it is that Constantinople and the straits area constitute the natural center of gravity of the whole east-Mediterranean basin.

In the long succession of imperial ventures which illustrate the commanding position held in the Near East by the Balkan peninsula the Ottoman empire is the last. About two-thirds of the present book is taken up with telling the story, on the one hand, of how the Ottoman empire came into being and, on the other, how by exasperatingly slow stages it went to pieces and became the prey of its domestic and foreign foes. Finally, in 1918, as a result of the Great War, came the end. With a reversion to its fighting tradition, which is fairly amazing in the light of an unbroken recent record of cowardice and chicane, the Ottoman empire perished, sword in hand. We, the living, for the most part viewed the passing with a deep-drawn sigh of satisfaction and relief, but also, it may well be, in measure as we are responsive to the touch of human tragedy, not without a sense of awe.

The Ottoman phase of near eastern history may now be regarded as closed. But the newest phase, which opens with the Paris treaties of 1919 and 1920, is wrapped in such deep obscurity that it is by no means easy to present even in outline and harder still to grasp in its full historical significance. And yet a book which has set itself the task to guide the reader through the maze of Balkan occurrences from the beginning cannot be excused from lighting at least a taper to illuminate, as well as may be, the prevailing gloom. Unavoidably the difficult attempt must be made to tabulate the troublesome and contentious elements which compose the present picture of the Near East. Never was there a situation more amazingly fluid and uncertain. Even the trained observer may well be filled with despair at being projected into such a wilderness. Only on rare occasions in Mediterranean history, as when the empire of Alexander or the Byzantine empire went to pieces, was there a remotely similar atomization and confusion. Will, as regularly happened in the past, a new conquest follow from this recurrent chaos or will something result of which the ancient peoples did not dream, something new, democratic, free?

In order to gauge properly the existing east-Mediterranean world we must keep our attention riveted on the whole crescent of territories extending from the Macedonian highlands through Asia Minor and Syria to the lower Nile. At every point at which our glance lingers we encounter a more or less troubled and critical condition of affairs. This is our first and all-important discovery. It permits, nay, obliges us to conclude that in the year 1922, that is, more than three years after the armistice, nothing whatever has yet been realized of those fine promises of a better political order so freely extended to the stricken peoples of the Near East during the recent hurly-burly. For clear and unmistakable signs of a rebirth under the generous tutelage of a maternal Europe the most hopeful searcher will look in vain. On the contrary, in place of evidences of renewal, the troubled eye falls on a sheer innumerable multitude of rancorous conflicts, open or concealed, and offering so little prospect of an early settlement that we are obliged to confess that hardly anywhere on this torn, post-bellum globe may there be found a more authentic piece of primitive chaos.

For this discouraging result it has become fashionable to blame the victors in the war who met at Paris to lay the foundations of a new world. Let us concede at once and without argument that, far from laying such foundations, the victors showed neither a clear understanding of the forces dominating our present-day society nor — with the notable exception of the representative of the United States — the most meager vision of a new type of political organization adequate to the stage of evolution at which the world has apparently arrived. Freely granting these deficiencies of the human instruments, we may yet insist that the Near East or, for that matter, any other area which in the winter of 1918–19 was tossed into the political debate at Paris, should, if we aim at genuine, scientific understanding, be primarily viewed in the deep perspective of its evolution; wherefore it serves no useful purpose to represent Lloyd George, Clemenceau, Wilson, and the host of lesser satellites who revolved around these central luminaries, as having enjoyed at Paris the unique opportunity of making over all or any part of the world according to a formula of abstract righteousness. We are much nearer the truth if we think of the Paris diplomats less as powerful Olympians than as a breed of rather busy and self-important manikins in the grip of forces which are as old as history and which to recognize at their real value would have been the best service the council leaders could have rendered themselves and the world. So little did they command and ride these historical forces that we are much nearer the truth when we insist on their own uttter subjection to them. Certainly the pretensions advanced by the conference, in connection with the treaty of Sèvres, of categorically laying down the law to the Near East were with almost diabolical promptness turned to open mockery. If one thing is at this moment clearer than another it is that the Near East has gone its own way, urged onward by a ferment of tremendous forces. Unquestionably that way is perilous and may lead to destruction, but for all their air of omnipotence the cabinets of London and Paris have ceased exercising any but a nominal control over occurrences in those Ottoman areas which they have parceled out with such gay self-assurance.

To adopt a profitable view-point toward the events in the Near East since the armistice, it is necessary to bear in mind the long, losing struggle of the Ottoman empire during the nineteenth century and to be aware that when the empire finally collapsed there were on hand two groups of claimants who could not be denied, first, because they had studiously helped prepare the catastrophe, and second, because, checked by no false modesty, they at once stepped forward to insist on their reward. While the Christian states of the Balkan peninsula constituted one of these groups, the other and far more important one was made up of the great victor powers. For these latter the war had been fought with a set of rival powers for the very purpose of deciding to whom the Ottoman spoils should belong. After giving its verdict against the central powers, destiny in its unaccountable way turned also on a member of the victor group, on Russia, involving it in the same hard sentence as the conquered. That left the wreath of victory in the hands of Great Britain, France, and Italy, which, swept along by the triumphant tide of imperialism, elatedly resolved to appropriate all the lands of the Near East which they were strong enough to seize. The division of the spoils was not easy since each power felt abundantly suspicious and envious of the other. However, it was managed at last, largely because the cooler heads among the negotiators perceived that a rupture was dangerous and that, besides, there was booty enough for all. On this basis the Paris treaties were drawn up, that of Neuilly with Bulgaria and that of Sèvres with Turkey being particularly relevant to this discussion. By virtue of these two documents Great Britain, France, and Italy apportioned the near eastern lands among themselves saving only the Balkan peninsula, from which, because it already was in the firm possession of the lesser group of Ottoman heirs, reluctantly and with a studied gesture of magnanimity they graciously withheld their hand.

The political aspect which the Near East took on as a direct result of the peace treaties is as interesting as it is confusing. Three main areas need to be distinguished. Of these the Balkan area has already been treated with a certain fullness. We took note that in drawing the new Balkan frontiers the three disposing powers favored their friends, Greece, Serbia, and Rumania, at the expense of their enemies, Turkey and Bulgaria, but otherwise kept their fingers out of the Balkan mess. Balkania, it was implied, was to belong to the Balkan peoples. True, the rancors released by the, in many instances, inequitable settlement made it exceedingly doubtful whether a better day had dawned among the former Christian subjects of the sultan, though it was, after all, something of an achievement that henceforth the new nations would in some measure enjoy the control of their own destinies.

Constantinople and the straits constitute a second area, which also we have already glanced at. For centuries the apple of discord among the ambitious peoples of the earth, and without question the chief prize of the war, the fair city on the Golden Horn was esteemed an invaluable treasure by all the three victors. Simply because there was no other way out, they at last agreed to set off the city itself, the waters of the straits, and a narrow strip of shore on either side the channel, as an international zone under their combined control. Both in peace and war the water-passage was to remain open to the merchantmen and war-ships of every nation of the earth. While these pronouncements set forth the great principle of a united world and have an equitable ring, it is plain that the international régime must, in the event of war, redound to the advantage of Great Britain, since by reason of its naval superiority Great Britain can in any crisis always drive its rivals from the sea. In the light of past experience there is no room for doubt that, when the next war comes, Great Britain will be found using the straits and that, besides herself, no power not on her side and not enjoying her patronage will share this decisive advantage. For this reason the international zone of the straits is a British solution of the Constantinopolitan problem and neither France nor Italy would have accepted it if they could have discovered any other way out of the tangle. More particularly France has so little stomach for the settlement that it was no sooner agreed on than the Paris government, first by secret intrigues and latterly by open negotiations, has attempted to supersede and nullify it by restoring the power of the sultan. Rather than have the British at Constantinople the French are prepared to scrap the whole treaty of Sèvres.

All the remaining provinces, formerly Ottoman, constitute a third and particularly troubled area, embracing Egypt, Arabia, Syria, Mesopotamia, and Asia Minor. It was the undoubted plan of the victors to distribute these territories among themselves and, as far as they could, to rule and exploit them as colonial dependencies. But, exhausted as the victorious nations had been by the long and terrible war, they were, on the one hand, checked in their action by their reduced strength, and, on the other, they had in some instances contracted obligations during the struggle with the central powers which they were unable to evade. There, for instance, was the sherif of Mecca. In 1915, in order to divide the Mohammedan world, the British had prompted him to rebel against the sultan, and to reward him for his considerable services they had finally permitted him to proclaim himself independent king of the Hedjaz (Arabia). Again, to the Jews throughout the world, Great Britain, in order to secure their invaluable financial support, had at the height of the war issued a promise to set up Palestine as a Jewish home-land. Accordingly, at Paris, Palestine was organized as a British protectorate in the form of a mandated area. Though Great Britain stands in a different relation toward these two improvisations of hers, no one may doubt that, alike created to serve her imperial ends, they will fall under her complete control as soon as ever she is restored to her pre-war vigor.

In regard to Egypt, Great Britain at the outbreak of the Great War acted with such dispatch that no legitimate doubt may be entertained touching the frankly acquisitive character of her policy. In a formal proclamation the last bond joining Egypt to the sultan was deliberately broken and Egypt declared a British protectorate (November, 1914). If the Egyptian people had now remained quiescent, this bold action would have settled the issue. But the war was no sooner over than a nationalist fervor seized upon the natives which gravely disconcerted their British masters. In the face of their serious post-war exhaustion they were obliged, instead of riding rough-shod over the opposition, to open negotiations which in March, 1922, have been brought to a provisional conclusion. The British permitted the khedive — a khedive of their own appointment — to proclaim himself independent king of Egypt on the understanding that certain imperially vital matters, as for instance, the Suez communications, remain reserved to their control. While some Egyptian elements may be satisfied with this solution, the ultra-nationalists will unquestionably continue to agitate in the hope of achieving a complete and unqualified sovereignty.

As for Syria and Mesopotamia, France and Great Britain respectively have taken them over as mandated areas, but their hold on them remains precarious owing either to the active or passive resistance of the natives. Though the inhabitants of both regions are mainly Arabs, they have little in common beyond their Mohammedan faith, since the Syrians are a people laborious, sedentary, and relatively advanced in the arts, while the war-like tribes of Mesopotamia are thieving, tent-dwelling nomads. The novel and disconcerting attitude of these and all other near eastern peoples was in part due to the very powers whose predatory plans have since miscarried. In the course of the war Great Britain and France had raised the cry of freedom for the oppressed and self-determination for all, and in no section of the globe had these alluring watchwords produced a more powerful reverberation than in the Near East. Syria, Mesopotamia, and Egypt are therefore far from being the source of any very deep satisfaction to their would-be French and British masters. If we further take into account the disorder of the French and British finances as well as the irritated refusal of the common people of the two countries to engage in fresh military adventures, we are able to understand to what an extent the cabinets of London and Paris find themselves hampered in the execution of their imperialist plans. In view of their multiplied difficulties it is not inconceivable that they may be obliged to withdraw, at least temporarily, from all their near eastern outposts.

Asia Minor presents another and by no means the least interesting phase of the stalemate to which the game of near eastern imperialism has for the moment been reduced. The treaty of Sèvres recognized a Turkish Anatolian state, but under such ignominious conditions of tutelage to France, Great Britain, and Italy that the Turks indignantly refused to accept it. Under a nationalist leader, Mustapha Kemal Pasha, they have successfully defied the treaty and its sponsors. As for the Armenia sketched at Paris, it has never got beyond the paper stage, since the allies, unable to shake the grip of Mustapha Kemal on Anatolia, are of course impotent to give effect to their Armenian resolutions. If the three victor powers may be said to have at least edged their way into the other Ottoman lands which they have allotted to themselves as prizes, in unconquered Anatolia not only does their law not run, but from Anatolia, as a center, incitement to rebellion pours in an uninterrupted stream into all the adjoining lands.

Such, hurriedly summarized, is the disastrous situation in the Near East three years after the conclusion of the war. Where, we may ask, are the fruits of victory? For the moment at least, imperialism, which animated the counsels of all the powers and which during the last hundred years has moved from triumph to triumph, has suffered a sensible check. Can it be that it has passed its meridian and that, at least in the Near East, if as yet nowhere else, its days are counted?

What in this crisis of imperialism stands out as far and away the most significant feature in near eastern lands is the new temper of the people. No longer minded to be exploited by the more efficiently organized peoples of the West, averse to continue further as mere hewers of wood and drawers of water, they have resolved to put an end to foreign domination. Whether they can realize so audacious a dream lies primarily with themselves and will depend chiefly on their ability to reshape their minds and, incidentally, their economic conditions in such a manner as to put themselves on approximately even terms with their western exploiters. At a disadvantage in a score of ways, they suffer most conspicuously from a backward civilization and from that phenomenon which invariably goes along with a settled immobility of customs, a backward mentality. For such heavy disabilities the only conceivable cure is constructive labor in state and society courageously continued for many generations

The extreme gravity of the problem is well illustrated by the predicament of the Turks throughout the nineteenth century. Although the only effective defense of the subjects of the sultan against the aggression to which they were exposed lay in themselves becoming European, they were unable to carry through so radical a transformation in time to save themselves from disaster. And just as the chief barrier to a successful Europeanization of the Ottomans proved to be the Mohammedan religion, so this Asiatic faith is today the leading obstacle in the path of all the near eastern peoples. Signs are not lacking that Mohammedanism is passing through a crisis, that it is being honeycombed and presently may be transfused and vitalized by western science and education, but until this is done and the doors of the oriental mind are thrown open to the ideas and methodological procedures which are the source of western power, nothing will have taken place capable of securing to the near eastern peoples that free and independent participation in the affairs of the modern world which they so passionately crave.

An invaluable boon to them during the long period of their necessary apprenticeship to western civilization would be a League of Nations or some similar world association honorably mindful of its obligation to promote the interests of all the peoples of the earth. In fact without an effective protection of the backward groups which, though as yet unprovided, is at least sketched in the already existent League of Nations, it is hardly credible that they can survive the trials and crises to which they already are and must in the years ahead be increasingly exposed. An ornamental and non-operative League of Nations, unable to offer counsel and, if necessary, to utter a solemn warning accompanied by decisive action, will oblige the numerous near eastern peoples and their ambitious European mentors already on the ground to work out their own haphazard system of political balance. That can only mean Franco-British rivalry and interminable local war until, exactly as through all the centuries of the past, a period of mutually destructive conflict will be followed by a new unity established by the sword. In that event the Ottoman empire, having traveled its appointed round from youth to old age, would have broken up only to mark the beginning of a new cycle of conquest. Nor would that be all, for in that event crushing new evidence would have been accumulated in support of the pessimistic faith that men are incapable of summoning the wisdom necessary to restrain their passions and to overcome the many evils inseparable from their earthly lot.

BIBLIOGRAPHY

Bibliographical Aids

For the Slavs we have the excellent and highly serviceable work of R. J. KERNER, Slavic Europe, A Select Bibliography in the Western European Languages, comprising History, Language, and Literature. Section VI, entitled The Southern Slavs, is of particular interest for the Balkan student. It is to be regretted that there exists no bibliographical work of equal merit for the Ottoman Empire and the non-Slav peoples, the Greeks, the Rumans, and the Albanians. Under the circumstances the most convenient bibliographical approach to the general Balkan field is through the two general histories, the Histoire Générale (Lavisse et Rambaud) and the Cambridge Modern History. In Histoire Générale see the bibliographies attached to Vol. X, Chapters V, XXVI; Vol. XI, Chapters VI, XV; Vol. XII, Chapters XII, XIII, XIV, XV. In Cambridge Modern History see the bibliographies belonging to Vol. X, Chapters VI, XVII; Vol. XI, Chapters IX, XI, XXII; Vol. XII, Chapter XIV.

A convenient, select bibliography is attached to W. MILLER, The Ottoman Empire, 1801–1913.

Manuals and General Works

(Covering more or less completely the whole Balkan field since 1800)

W. MILLER, The Ottoman Empire, 1801–1913.
J. A. R. MARRIOT, The Eastern Question: An Historical Study in European Diplomacy.
LORD EVERSLEY, The Turkish Empire: Its Growth and Decay.
S. LANE POOLE, The Story of Turkey.
W. MILLER, The Balkans.
N. FORBES (and others), The Balkans.
E. DRIAULT, La Question d'Orient depuis ses origines jusqu'à nos jours.
L. DOMINIAN, The Frontiers of Language and Nationality in Europe.
L. W. LYDE AND MOCKLER–FERRYMAN, A Military Geography of the Balkan Peninsula,
SIR CHARLES E. ELIOT, Turkey in Europe.
E. DE LAVELAYE, The Balkan Peninsula.
LADY BLUNT, The People of Turkey. 2 vols.
E. PEARS, Turkey and its People.

W. Miller, Travels and Politics in the Near East.

Zur Kunde der Balkanhalbinsel (17 Hefte, Geographical and Political Studies issued by the Institut fuer Balkanforschung, Sarajevo).

Sir E. Hertslet, The Map of Europe by Treaty (1814–91). 4 vols.

T. E. Holland, The European Concert in the Eastern Question: A Collection of Treaties and Other Public Acts.

The Cambridge Modern History. Vol. X, Chapters VI, XVII; Vol. XI, Chapters IX, XI, XXII; Vol. XII, Chapter XIV.   Histoire Générale, (Lavisse et Rambaud), Vol. X, Chapters VI, XXVI; Vol. XI, Chapters VI, XV; Vol. XII, Chapters XII, XIII, XIV, XV.

The Ottoman Empire

Sir E. Creasy, History of the Ottoman Turks.

W. E. D. Allen, The Turks in Europe.

W. S. Monroe, Turkey and the Turks.

L. von Sax, Geschichte des Machtverfalls der Tuerkei.

N. Jorga, Geschichte des Osmanischen Reiches. Vol. V.

A. de la Jonquière, Histoire de l'Empire Ottoman.

P. H. Mischeff, La Mer Noire et les Détroits de Constantinople.

S. Goriainow, Le Bosphore et les Dardanelles.

C. de Freycinet, La Question d'Egypte.

S. Lane Poole, Life of Lord Stratford de Redcliffe.

Duke of Argyll, The Eastern Question.

A. W. Kinglake, The Invasion of the Crimea. 8 vols.

Peace Handbook (issued by the Hist. Section of the British Foreign Office, 1920), Vol. III, The Eastern Question; Turkey in Europe.

L. M. J. Garnett, Turkish Life in Town and Country.

L. M. J. Garnett, The Women of Turkey.

E. Pears, Forty Years in Constantinople.

W. M. Ramsay, Impressions of Turkey during Twelve Years Wanderings.

D. G. Hogarth, A Wandering Scholar in the Levant.

C. Hamlin, Among the Turks.

Sir Mark Sykes, The Caliphs' Last Heritage. (Part II, a valuable record of travels.)

Syed Ameer Ali, Life and Teaching of Mohammed or the Spirit of Islam

E. Engelhardt, La Turquie et le Tanzimat ou Histoire des Réformes dans l'Empire Ottoman depuis 1826 jusqu'à nos jours.

E. Banse, Die Türkei: eine Moderne Geographie.

W. H. Hutton, Constantinople.

H. G. Wright, Constantinople Old and New.

A. H. Lyber, Constantinople as Capital of the Ottoman Empire. (Am. Hist. Association. Annual Report for 1916).

L. S. Woolf, The Future of Constantinople.

M. Jastrow, The War and the Bagdad Railway.

P. Rohrbach, Die wirtschafthiche Bedeutung Westasiens.

G. W. Prothero, German Policy before the War.

A. Chéradame, Le Plan Pan-Germaniste Démasqué.

H. Grothe, Die Bagdadbahn und das Schwäbische Bauernelement in Transkaukasien und Palästina.

C. R. Buxton, Turkey in Revolution.

E. F. Knight, The Awakening of Turkey.

V. Bérard, La Révolution Turque.

R. Pinon, L'Europe et la Jeune Turquie.

Ahmed Emin, The Development of Turkey as Measured by its Press.

J. Bryce, Transcaucasia (with Supplement on the Armenian Question).

H. F. B. Lynch, Armenia: Travels and Studies. 2 vols.

K. Aslan, Armenia and the Armenians from the Earliest Times until the Great War.

N. E. Buxton, Travel and Politics in Armenia.

M. Ormanian, The Church of Armenia.

J. J. M. de Morgan, Histoire du peuple Arménien depuis les temps les plus reculés jusqu'à nos jours.

Greece, Crete.

G. Finlay, History of Greece. 7 vols. (ed. Tozer).

K. Mendelsohn-Bartholdy, Geschichte Griechenlands (from 1453 to 1835).

W. A. Phillips, The War of Greek Independence (1821–33).

L. Sargeant, Greece in the Nineteenth Century.

V. Bérard, Les Affaires de Crète.

H. A. Gibbons, Venizelos.

S. B. Chester, Life of Venizelos.

Peace Handbooks (Issued by the Hist. Section of the British Foreign Office, 1920). Vol. III, Greece.

E. M. Church, Sir Richard Church in Italy and Greece.

Lord Byron, The Works of Lord Byron. Letters and Journals (ed. Prothero). Vol. VI.

W. Miller, Greek Life in Town and Country.

L. M. J. Garnett, Greece of the Hellenes.

H. F. Tozer, Islands of the Aegean.

P. F. Martin, Greece of the Twentieth Century.

G. F. Abbott (editor), Greece in Evolution (Studies prepared under the auspices of the French League for the Defense of Hellenism).

H. P. Fairchild, Greek Immigration to the United States.

E. About, La Grèce Contemporaine.

V. Bérard, La Turquie et l'Hellenisme contemporain.

Serbia, Montenegro, Bosnia

H. W. V. Temperley, The History of Serbia.

L. Ranke, The History of Servia.

S. Novakovic, Die Wiedergeburt des Serbischen Staates (1804–13).

Prince and Princess Lazarovich-Hrebelianovich, The Servian People· their past glory and their destiny.

R. W. Seton Watson, The Southern Slav Question and the Habsburg Monarchy.

P. Coquelle, Le Royaume de Serbie.

B. von Kallay, Geschichte der Serben.

B. von Kallay, Geschichte des Serbischen Aufstandes.

F. Cuniberti, La Serbia e la dinastia degli Obrenovich (1804-93).

Peace Handbooks (issued by the Hist. Section of the British Foreign Office, 1920), Vol. IV, Montenegro; Serbia.

W. Denton, Montenegro: Its People and Their History.

R. Wyon, and G. Prance, The Land of the Black Mountain.

P. Coquelle, Histoire du Monténégro et de la Bosnie depuis les origines.

S. Gopcevic, Montenegro und die Montenegriner.

G. M. Mackenzie and A. P. Irby, Travels in the Slavonic Provinces of Turkey in Europe. 2 vols.

A. J. Evans, Through Bosnia and Herzegovina on Foot.

M. E. Durham, Through the Land of the Serb.

S. Gopcevic, Serbien und die Serben.

F. Kanitz, Das Koenigreich Serbien und das Serbenvolk.

C. Mijatovich, Servia and the Servians.

A. Stead, (editor), Servia by the Servians.

H. Vivian, Servia: the Poor Man's Paradise.

J. Mallot, La Serbie Contemporaine.

G. V. Devas, La Nouvelle Serbie.

A. Strauss, Bosnien, Land und Leute.

F. Krauss, Sitte und Brauch der Suedslaven.

F. Scherer, Bilder aus dem Serbischen Volks und Familienleben.

Mayer, Die bäuerliche Hauskommunion in den Königreichen Kroatien und Slawonien (Heidelberg Dissertation).

G. Prezzoloni, La Dalmazia.

L. Voinovich, Dalmazia, Italia, ed Unità Jugo-slava.

Bulgaria, Macedonia

J. Samuelson, Bulgaria Past and Present.

E. Dicey, The Peasant State.

W. Monroe, Bulgaria and her People.

A. von Huhn, The Struggle of the Bulgarians for National Independence under Prince Alexander.

A. von Huhn, The Kidnapping of Prince Alexander.

R. von Mach, The Bulgarian Exarchate.

L. Leger, La Bulgarie.

A. H. Beaman, Life of Stambuloff.

R. P. Guérin Songeon, Histoire de la Bulgarie.

N. Staneff, Geschichte der Bulgaren (1393-1912).

Peace Handbooks (issued by the Hist. Section of the British Foreign Office, 1920), Vol. IV, Macedonia; Bulgaria.

C. Jirecek, Das Fuerstenthum Bulgarien.

F. Kanitz, Donau-Bulgarien und der Balkan.

M. E. Durham, The Burden of the Balkans.

H. N. Brailsford, Macedonia: its Races and their Future.

A. Upward, The East End of Europe: Macedonia during the Bulgar-Greek Folk War of 1906-7.
V. Bérard, Pro Macedonia.
V. Bérard, La Macedoine.
F. Moore, The Balkan Trail.

Rumania

J. Samuelson, Roumania Past and Present.
N. Jorga, Geschichte des Rumänischen Volkes. 2 vols.
A. D. Xénopol, Histoire des Roumains.
F. Damé, Histoire de la Roumainie Contemporaine.
A. G. B. Wace and M. S. Thompson, The Nomads of the Balkans.
Peace Handbooks (issued by the Hist. Section of the Brit. Foreign Office, 1920). Vol. IV, Rumania.
King Carol I (Charles I), Reminiscences (S. Whitman, editor).
G. Benger, Roumania in 1900.
E. Pittard, La Roumanie.
L. Colescu, Progrès economiques de la Roumanie réalisés sous la règne de S. M. le roi Carol I.
P. Eliade, Histoire de l'esprit public en Roumaine au XIX^m siècle.
L. D. Creanga, Grundbesitzverteilung und Bauernfrage in Rumaenien (In Schmoller's Staats und Sozialwissenschaftliche Forschungen).
C. V. Clark, Greater Roumania.

Albania

E. Legrand, Bibliographie Albanaise (from the fifteenth century to 1900).
W. Peacock, Albania: The Foundling State of Europe.
C. A. Chekrezi, Albania, Past and Present.
C. A. Dako, Albania: the Master Key to the Near East.
M. E. Durham, High Albania.
S. Story (editor), The Memoirs of Ismail Kemal Bey.
P. Siebertz, Albanien und die Albanesen.
A. Baldacci, Der Neue Albanesische Staat und seine Graenzen (with map). In Petermann's Mitteilungen, Vol. 59, Pt. 1.
Peace Handbooks (issued by the Hist. Section of the British Foreign Office, 1920). Vol. III, Albania.

The Turco-Italian and the Balkan Wars

W. H. Beehler, The History of the Italian-Turkish War.
T. Barclay, The Turco-Italian War.
F. McCullagh, Italy's War for a Desert.
Lord Courtney of Penwith (editor), Nationalism and War in the Near East (by a Diplomatist).
H. A. Gibbons, The New Map of Europe, Chapter XIII.
J. G. Schurman, The Balkan Wars, 1912-13.

I. E. GUESHOFF, The Balkan League (with many documents).
N. BUXTON, With the Bulgarian Staff.
W. H. C. PRICE, The Balkan Cockpit.
D. J. CASSAVETTI, Hellas and the Balkan Wars.
H. WAGNER, With the Victorious Bulgarians.
R. RANKIN, The Inner Story of the Balkan War.
A. H. TRAPMANN, The Greeks Triumphant.
E. ASHMEAD-BARTLETT, With the Turks in Thrace.
Carnegie Endowment for International Peace: Report of International Commission to Inquire into the Causes and Conduct of the Balkan Wars.

The Great War

The enormous mass of material bearing on the Great War remains to be organized. Beginnings have been made as, for instance, by
C. J. H. HAYES, A Brief History of the Great War, pp. 431–6.
The following selected references may prove serviceable:

C. J. H. HAYES (as above).
M. NEWBIGIN, Geographical Aspects of Balkan Problems in their Relation to the European War.
A. J. TOYNBEE, Turkey, a Past and a Future.
R. W. SETON WATSON, German, Slav, and Magyar. A Study in the Origin of the Great War.
R. W. SETON WATSON, Roumania and the Great War.
M. E. DURHAM, Twenty Years of Balkan Tangle.
M. JASTROW, The War and the Bagdad Railway.
M. JASTROW, The War and the Coming Peace.
M. JASTROW, The Eastern Question and its Solution.
A. H. E. TAYLOR, The Future of the Southern Slavs.
E. JAECKH, Der Aufsteigende Halbmond.
P. HIBBEN, Constantine I and the Greek People.
A. MANDELSTAM, Le Sort de l'Empire Ottoman.
The Balkan Review (ed. Crawfurd Price), 1919+.
A. F. PRIBRAM, Secret Treaties of Austria-Hungary, 1879–1914. 2 vols.
L. STODDARD, The New World of Islam.
I. BOWMAN, The New World: Problems in Political Geography.

APPENDIX

A. LIST OF EAST-ROMAN OR BYZANTINE EMPERORS
(*Beginning with the Founder of Constantinople*)

Constantine I, called the Great 306–337
Constantius 337–361
Julian, the Apostate 361–363
Jovian 363–364
Valens 364–378
Theodosius I, called the Great 379–395
Arcadius 395–408
Theodosius II 408–450
Marcian 450–457
Leo I 457–474
Zeno 474–491
Anastasius 491–518

THE JUSTINIAN DYNASTY

Justin I 518–527
Justinian I 527–565
Justin II 565–578

Tiberius II, Constantine 578–582
Maurice 582–602
Phocas 602–610

THE HERACLIAN DYNASTY

Heraclius 610–641
Constantine III and Heracleonas 641–642
Constans II 642–668
Constantine IV 668–685
Justinian II 685–695
    Restored 705–711

Leontius 695–697
Tiberius III 697–705
Philippicus 711–713
Anastasius II 713–715
Theodosius III 715–717

THE ANGELI

Isaac II 1185–95
    Restored and associated with his son, Alexius IV 1203–1204
Alexius III 1195–1203

Alexius V, Ducas 1204

THE NICEAN EMPERORS

Theodore I, Lascaris 1204–22
John III, Vatatzes 1222–54
Theodore II, Lascaris 1254–58
John IV, Lascaris 1258–59

THE LATIN EMPERORS

Baldwin I (of Flanders) 1204–5
Henry I 1205–16
Peter I 1217
Robert I...1221–28
Baldwin II 1228–61

THE PALEOLOGI

Michael VIII 1259–82
Andronicus II 1282–1328
Andronicus III 1328–41
John V 1341–91
    Co-regent: John VI, Cantacuzenus 1341–55
Manuel II 1391–1425
John VII 1425–48
Constantine XI 1448–53

B. GENEALOGICAL TABLE OF THE HOUSE OF OSMAN

   1. Osman (1288–1326)
     |
   2. Orkhan (1326–1359)
     |
   3. Murad I (1359–1389)
     |
   4. Bayezid I, the Thunderbolt (1389–1402)
     |
   5. Mohammed I (1413–1421; from 1402 to 1413 civil war
     | among sons of Bayezid)
   6. Murad II (1421–51)
     |
   7. Mohammed II, the Conqueror (1451–81)
     |
   8. Bayezid II (1481–1512)

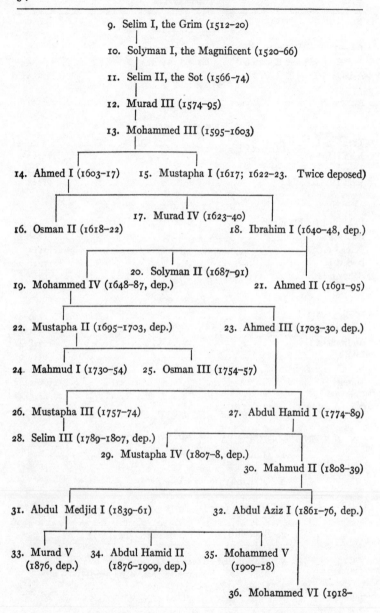

9. Selim I, the Grim (1512-20)

10. Solyman I, the Magnificent (1520-66)

11. Selim II, the Sot (1566-74)

12. Murad III (1574-95)

13. Mohammed III (1595-1603)

14. Ahmed I (1603-17)　　15. Mustapha I (1617; 1622-23.　Twice deposed)

17. Murad IV (1623-40)

16. Osman II (1618-22)　　18. Ibrahim I (1640-48, dep.)

20. Solyman II (1687-91)

19. Mohammed IV (1648-87, dep.)　　21. Ahmed II (1691-95)

22. Mustapha II (1695-1703, dep.)　　23. Ahmed III (1703-30, dep.)

24. Mahmud I (1730-54)　25. Osman III (1754-57)

26. Mustapha III (1757-74)　　27. Abdul Hamid I (1774-89)

28. Selim III (1789-1807, dep.)

29. Mustapha IV (1807-8, dep.)

30. Mahmud II (1808-39)

31. Abdul Medjid I (1839-61)　　32. Abdul Aziz I (1861-76, dep.)

33. Murad V　34. Abdul Hamid II　35. Mohammed V
(1876, dep.)　(1876-1909, dep.)　(1909-18)

36. Mohammed VI (1918-

C. SOVEREIGNS OF GREECE

Otto I (of Bavaria) ....1833–62 (deposed)
George I (of Denmark) ....1863–1913 (assassinated)
Constantine I (son of George I)..................... .. 1913–17 (deposed)
Aiexander I (son of Constantine I)...........................1917–20
Constantine I (restored)..1920-

D. SOVEREIGNS OF SERBIA

Milosh (Obrenovich), 1817–39, deposed; restored 1859–60
Michael (Obrenovich), 1839–42, deposed; restored 1860–68 (murdered)
Alexander (Karageorgevich), 1842–59 (deposed)
Milan I (Obrenovich), 1868–89 (proclaimed first king of Serbia, 1882; abdicated 1889)
Alexander I (Obrenovich), 1889–1903 (murdered)
Peter I (Karageorgevich), 1903–21
Alexander II (Karageorgevich), 1921–

E. SOVEREIGNS OF MONTENEGRO

(The rule of prince-bishops, called vladikas, continued for several centuries
till Danilo I secularized the sovereignty)
Danilo I (Petrovich) ....1852–60 (murdered)
Nicholas I (Petrovich) ....1860–1917 (obliged to flee)
Nicholas proclaimed king in 1910; died in exile 1920.
Montenegro absorbed into Jugoslavia as result of Great War.

F. SOVEREIGNS OF RUMANIA

Alexander (Cuza)......................................1859–66 (deposed)
Charles I (of Hohenzollern-Sigmaringen)........... 1866–1914
(Elected prince, 1866; proclaimed king 1881)
Ferdinand I (nephew of the above)..............................1914–

G. SOVEREIGNS OF BULGARIA

Alexander (of Battenberg)..........................1879–86 (abdicated)
Ferdinand I (of Saxe-Coburg) 1887–1918
(Elected prince of Bulgaria, 1887; proclaimed tsar 1908; abdicated 1918)
Boris I (son of the above)......................................1918–

INDEX

Abbassids, Arab dynasty, 84, 105
Abdul Aziz, 383, 397
Abdul Hamid II, accession, 397;
grants and withdraws constitution,
420-21; enemy of reform, 421;
absolutism, 422-24; and the Armenian massacres, 427-28; and the
Young Turk revolution, 451, 453
Abdul Medjid, succeeds to throne,
351; champions reform, 354, 383;
issues Charter of 1856, 362, 363
Aboukir Bay, Battle of, 279
Absolutism, Byzantine, 115, 116
Achaia, Principality of, 166, 206
Acciajuoli, in Athens, 167
Adana, 350
Adrianople, captured by Murad I,
184; Ottoman capital, 184; captured by Russians, 340; besieged
by Bulgars, 472; captured by Bulgars, 474; recaptured by Turks,
476, 478; granted to Greece, 514
Adrianople, Peace of, 323, 340, 369
Ahmed I, 250
Akindjis, 229
Alaric, 39, 40
Albania, led by Scanderbeg, 203,
204; partial conversion to Islam,
306, 464; tribal government, 307,
463; general situation in twentieth
century, 463-64; wins autonomy,
465; territorially defined, 466; proclaims independence, 474; recognized by powers, 474; under William of Wied, 479; as constituted
by Peace conference, 511
Albanians, in Macedonia, 434-5; see
Illyrians
Alexander the Great, 5, 27
Alexander VI (Pope), and Prince
Jem, 211
Alexander I (Tsar), ally of Napoleon, 282; makes war on Ottoman
empire, 282-84; and Greek independence, 331, 332
Alexander II (Tsar), succeeds to
throne, 361; patron of Bulgaria,
409
Alexander III (Tsar), 417

Alexander Karageorge (of Serbia),
accession, 325; deposition, 390-91
Alexander (of Battenberg), 409; co-
operates with Russians, 410; acquires East Rumelia, 411; wins
Serb war, 412; abduction, 413;
abdication, 414
Alexius I (Comnenus), situation at
accession, 124, 125; defeats Nor-
mans, 128; and the First Crusade,
128, 129, 130; partial reconquest
of Asia Minor, 129-30; conces-
sions to Venetians, 130
Alexius III (Angelus), 133, 134
Alexius IV (Angelus), 133, 134, 135
Algeria, 221, 252, 293; French con-
quest, 430
Ali of Janina, 296, 331, 333, 347
Allenby (British General), 497
Anastasius (Emperor), 48, 49
Anatolia, see Asia Minor
Angora, Battle of, 190, 213
Anne (Tsarina), 266, 267
Anthemius of Tralles, 56
Apostles to the Slavs, see Method
and Constantine
Arabia, home of Mohammed, 79; in
revolt against Ottoman empire,
295, 462, 497; as constituted by
Peace conference, 517
Arabs, union effected by Mohammed,
79; their triumphant advance, 80,
81; first assault on Constanti-
nople, 81; second assault on Con-
stantinople, 83; plan to conquer
Europe, 83, 84; decline of power,
84, 85, 105, 106; superseded at
Bagdad by the Turks, 126
Archipelago, Duchy of, 166, 167, 168
Armatoles, 328
Armenia, and congress of Berlin, 424-
25; history, 425-26; racial situation, 426; massacres of 1894-95,
427-28; massacres of 1900, 462; at
the Peace conference, 517; after
the Peace conference, 531
Asen, John and Peter, first tsars of
restored Bulgaria, 147-48
Asia Minor, conquered by Seljuk

545

548 INDEX